IRISH MONASTICISM

JOHN RYAN SJ

IRISH MONASTICISM

Origins and Early Development

*New Introduction
and bibliography*

CORNELL UNIVERSITY PRESS

ITHACA, NEW YORK

© 1972 by John Ryan

First edition Dublin 1931

This reprint is a photolithographic facsimile of the first edition and is unabridged, retaining the original printer's imprint.

International Standard Book Number 0–8014–0613–7
Library of Congress Catalog Card Number 70–137677

PRINTED IN THE REPUBLIC OF IRELAND AT SHANNON
BY ROBERT HOGG PRINTER TO IRISH UNIVERSITY PRESS

INTRODUCTION

The fundamental purpose of *Irish Monasticism* was to show the relationship between monasticism as it was known in Ireland and monasticism as it was known elsewhere in the world, in all the churches of the East and West. During the many years that have elapsed since publication the book has been much reviewed and widely discussed. It is a pleasure to note that nothing which I have read or heard calls for any fundamental revision. There are, however, points that would be given greater precision were the book being published today for the first time.

To begin with, there is the matter of organization. St Patrick and his helpers, Roman citizens drawn from lands of urban civilization, were of necessity at a loss in a country where the civilization was entirely rural. They met the situation as best they could by placing bishops and sees near important political centres—at Armagh, near Emain Macha; at Dunshaughlin, near Tara; at Killossy, near Naas, a stronghold of the Uí Dúnlainge, Kings of North Leinster; at Aghade, near Rathvilly in Carlow, a stronghold of the Uí Cennselaig, dynasts of South Leinster; at Elphin, near Rathcroghan; and so on. It is obvious that this method left room for improvement. The Church in Ireland was searching for a mould within which it could grow and prosper. This is found in the sixth century, surprisingly enough, perhaps, in the great monastery. The very name *civitas,* applied to so many of these, suggested that the monastery was felt to be the substitute for the Latin *city;* and the very name *princeps,* applied to the abbot, suggests that his authority, in the ecclesiastical world, was felt in Irish minds to correspond with that of the local *flaith* or prince in the secular sphere.

What then of episcopal jurisdiction, when the abbot was not a bishop? Dealing with Lindisfarne, the Venerable Bede (HE. III, 14) states that 'by unusual arrangement' the three bishops who came from Iona to Northumberland remained subject as monks to the abbots in the mother monastery. Not only has this statement been accepted at its face value but it has been given universal application—quite wrongly, in my judgment. It is true that in the course of time, thanks to the generosity of the faithful (especially of the wealthy, not too happy about their prospects in eternity) the successful monasteries had acquired great possessions and the title 'abbot' had come to connote high authority. It is, however, equally true that the abbot in Ireland was always inferior to the bishop in dignity. This is manifest not merely from the *Collection of Canons* and from the *Lives of the Saints* but quite unequivocally from

(v)

the native secular law. Every Irish noble had his 'honour price'. The 'honour price' of a bishop was equivalent to that of a king, a distinction which no abbot, however wide his lands and however outstanding his personal and professional qualities, could claim. In all references to clerics (in the Old Irish Litanies, for example) the bishops come first and are treated with special honour. They are often invoked in groups of seven and even in groups of greater number. It is not extravagant to suggest that the multiplication of bishops in Ireland was in itself an effort to keep abbots, however mighty because of their possessions, in their proper subordinate place.

We may go further still. There is a remarkable document in the Irish language called after St Patrick: Riagail Pátraic. In date it may belong to the eighth century. According to this 'Rule' every *tuath* or state should have a chief bishop (prím-epscop), to ordain clergy, act as confessor and spiritual father to princes and nobles, see to it that the *tuath* has worthy priests, to celebrate Mass, administer the sacraments, bury the dead with due rite and ceremony. The care of all priests rests with the bishop, it is his duty to see that they give conscientious service to the faithful. It is clear that the bishop here is by far the most important ecclesiastic in the state. He may live within a monastery but even if he does he is certainly not subject to its abbot. The general conclusion is justified that a monk, once raised to the episcopate, ceased to owe obedience to any abbot. The proper comparison of these Irish monastic bishops is with the bishops of regular Orders and Congregations today in the pagan mission fields. Such a bishop, before consecration, was a member of his Order. All his clergy belong to the Order and are ruled immediately by a Superior nominated by the Order. Yet the bishop is not subject to the General or any other person of the Order; nor would he become subject to any priest superior of his Order were he to retire and return to a house of the Order in his own country. The monk-Bishop, owing obedience to his abbot, is an illusion.

A peculiarity of the Irish monastery was its close connection with education. The school and library were taken for granted as an essential section of the institution. A reason for this I take to be the prominence of the old druidic schools, in the centuries before the introduction of Christianity. People expected that a proportion of the children should be educated. If Christian schools were not available the children would be sent, by habit, to the pagan schools. The problem was faced and the need was met; as we learn from the Convention of Druim Ceat (AD 575) where the King of Ireland, Aed son of Ainmire, claimed that the druidic schools themselves were by then an anomaly and a nuisance and thus ripe for suppression.

The austerity of Irish monastic tradition caused some severe shocks abroad. At home it was well understood and appreciated. The principle was recognized that the Christian, to be worthy of the Christian name and Christian dignity, should live in God's grace. Should he have the misfortune to fall into sin he should free himself from it at once, through the sacrament of Penance. To the Irish monk, a Christian whose soul was not in sanctifying grace was something of a contradiction in terms.

Hence the growth in the practice of private Confession and the prominence of Penitential discipline in the Irish Church. The tradition persisted. Charges of Jansenism and Puritanism, levelled against Irish missionaries in the nineteenth century, have little or nothing to do with the heresies named; they touch on a hatred of moral evil embedded in the Irish conscience for fifteen hundred years.

Monasticism in Ireland, as in all other countries, had its moments of weakness and of failure. The growth in worldly wealth led inevitably to worldly greed and ambition. A martial age was tempted to solve its problems by martial means. Battles between Cork and Clonfert, over disputed lands in Tipperary; between Durrow and Clonmacnois, on issues probably of mere prestige, were tangible proofs of decline. Captains and Colonels, instead of Saints and Scholars, were dangerous products of monastic life. It is true that the monks did add to the disgrace by taking themselves to the use of arms. The miniature armies were drawn from the tenants on the monastic lands. What is surprising is the title *manaig* 'monks' applied quite commonly in time to these tenants; and the correlative obligation to find a new term *firmanach* 'true monk', for the religious under vows, for whom the simple title *manach* should be the proper and sufficient description. Holy men in many parts of Ireland grew alarmed and a reform movement of great promise was inaugurated. Its purpose was to restore the old inspiration and the old discipline. Tallaght was its best-known centre and its chief representatives were known as *Céli Dé*. The coming of the Northmen brought the movement to an abrupt end. Ireland was a small island, with many and wide rivers, and the Vikings, experts in arson, robbery and murder, could penetrate with ease into every part. Not one monastery in the land escaped, certainly not one of any prominence. Some ceased to exist. Others became wraiths or phantoms of what they once had been. The holding of two or more abbatial titles showed that the day had come when the abbot was not a monk at all. A number of monasteries survived rather as schools than as places of worship and prayer, with the abbot as headmaster. By the year AD 900 Irish literature, in its many forms, had succeeded Latin and Latin literature as the subject of main interest to scholars.

Clontarf saw a great effort of renewal, but the process of secularization had gone too far to allow of real remedy. Local families everywhere were in possession of the monastic properties. Even in the seventeenth century there were lay heads of families bearing monastic titles, *comarbada* and *airchinning*. St Malachy, himself a perfect representative and indeed a glory of traditional monastic Ireland, came, no doubt sadly, to the conclusion that the old order was fated to go, to be replaced by the new mediaeval Orders, Canons Regular and Cistercians. By AD 1200 Irish Monasticism was in its death-throes. Here and there an old foundation continued under a new rule, Inisfallen, for instance, under the rule of St Augustine, and Inis Cathaig, Scattery Island, as a College of Secular Canons, with lands in Clare, Limerick and Kerry. In general, monastic property was absorbed by the new bishoprics, Termonféichin by Armagh, Swords and Tallaght by Dublin; and so on.

What could not be destroyed was the memory of the past; above all, the memory of those Irish men and women, whose lives of heroic sanctity won for them a place in the Martyrologies, in the Félire of Oengus, the Félire of Tallaght, the Félire of Gorman. Their number is about seventeen hundred, a goodly company, whose virtues Catholic Ireland of the centuries since has sought but rarely to emulate and has never been able to surpass.

John Ryan

IRISH MONASTICISM

ORIGINS AND EARLY
DEVELOPMENT

IRISH MONASTICISM

Origins and Early Development

BY

REV. JOHN RYAN, S.J., M.A.

THE TALBOT PRESS LIMITED
DUBLIN AND CORK

DE LICENTIA SUP. ORD.:

JOHANNES FAHY, S.J.

Praep. Prov. Hib.

DUBLINI, *die* 3 *Januarii*, 1931.

NIHIL OBSTAT:

J. B. O'CONNELL

Censor Theol. Deput.

IMPRIMI POTEST:

✠EDUARDUS

Archiep. Dublinen.,

Hiberniæ Primas.

DUBLINI, *die* 14 *Januarii, anno* 1931.

Printed by CAHILL & CO., LTD. DUBLIN

DICATUR

HOC · QUALECUNQUE · OPUSCULUM

HONORI · ET · MEMORIAE

OPERIS · QUOD · SEDULO · NAVARUNT

IOANNES COLGAN · STEPHANUS WHITE · MICHAEL O'CLERY

CETERIQUE HAGIOGRAPHI · HIBERNI

DUM · SECULO · A · CHR · XVII

RELIGIONIS · PATRIAEQUE · ASSERTORES

S. PATRITIUM · ROMAE · IN · FIDE · PROBATUM

PATRITIIQUE · SUCCESSORES

EGREGIIS · EDITIS · SCRIPTIONIBUS

VEL · IN · MEDIO · RERUM · TURBINE

ILLUSTRARUNT · LAUDARUNT · VINDICARUNT

PREFACE

THAT the Irish Church for six centuries was markedly
" monastic " in character is a commonplace of ecclesiastical
history. Now monasticism, as an organised institution, was
not a phenomenon peculiar to Ireland, for it was found all
over the Christian world. The date and place of its birth,
the stages in its propagation, the different forms which it
assumed in different countries, can be determined with
considerable precision. In Ireland the line of monastic development was obviously very distinct from the line of development
elsewhere. In what, then, we ask ourselves, did the points
of difference consist ? What, in other words, was the relation
of monasticism as it existed in our island, to monastic
institutions as known in the leading Christian lands ? Was
Irish Monasticism Western in its characteristics, or did it
derive directly from the Orient ? Had it features that were
entirely its own, and, if so, how many ? When, again, was it
introduced into Ireland ? Had it a place in the Church which
St. Patrick founded ? If it had, was that place predominant,
as in the later centuries ? If not, when did the change take
place, under what auspices, due to what causes ? Certain it
is from our historical records that about A.D. 600 Ireland was
well-supplied with monasteries. What external appearance
did these present ? How were the monks recruited, how
governed ? What were their occupations ? Were all the
monks clerics, or were some only in holy orders ? Did the
country possess a clergy with no monastic connections ?
What was the position with regard to episcopal sees and to
the ecclesiastical hierarchy ?

When I looked for answers to these and cognate questions,
I learned, to my surprise, that they were nowhere to be found ;
so I decided to seek them out for myself from the original
sources. Thanks to the scholarship of the last century and
of our own time, to Lanigan, Todd, O'Donovan, Reeves,
McCarthy, Gwynn, Plummer, Bury and other honoured names
among the living and the dead, the task was not impossible
of fulfilment. The work was planned in 1921–3, when I was
studying under Prof. Monsignor Albert Ehrhard, Prof. Levison,
and Prof. Thurneysen, at the University of Bonn, but it was

not completed until two years ago. Its progress through the press has been retarded by various accidents. The literature which has since appeared has thrown new light on points of interest, but as these in every case were matters of detail only, they were not deemed important enough to justify the expense of revision and further delay in publication.

My regret is keen that Dr. James F. Kenney's fine bibliographical work (*The Sources for the Early History of Ireland*. Vol. I. Ecclesiastical) did not issue from the press until my book was written. Readers who desire complete bibliographies, rather than the select bibliographies prefixed to many of my paragraphs, will find their needs catered for in Dr. Kenney's monumental volume.

In dealing with so difficult a subject, with problems so many and so thorny, I cannot be sure that I have always found the right solution ; but I shall be delighted to accept a better, whenever it can be found. The purpose of the book is not, indeed, so much to supply conclusions as to stimulate the interest of scholars in our early ecclesiastical history. An enormous amount of pioneer work awaits enterprising students in that field.

It is hoped to pursue the history of Irish Monasticism into the later centuries and to publish, in due course, some sections that, for reasons of space, have had to be omitted from the present volume.

My thanks are due to Père Delehaye and his associates of the *Société des Bollandistes* for special facilities in the use of their admirable library. My debt is also very great to the Faculty of Celtic Studies, University College, Dublin ; above all to Prof. Eóin Mac Neill, who read through the work in manuscript, and made valuable suggestions and emendations. The frequency with which his name recurs in the notes gives some idea of what the various chapters owe to his kindly and untiring help. With him I must couple my learned friend, Père Paul Grosjean, S.J., who was likewise good enough to peruse the manuscript and to give every page the benefit of his critical pen. I am also under weighty obligations to Dom Louis Gougaud, O.S.B., D.Litt., from whose scholarly treatises much could always be learned, to Prof. Thurneysen, whose classes were always an inspiration, and to my colleague, Fr. Daniel O'Connell, S.J., M.Sc., on whose assistance I could always rely.

My gratitude is finally due to the Librarians and staffs of University College, Dublin ; Trinity College, Dublin ; the University of Bonn ; the British Museum ; the Biblioteca Nacional, Madrid ; and very particularly to Dr. Best and the staff of the National Library, Dublin, on whom the heaviest demands were made and whose patience proved superior to every test.

J. R.

Feast of St. Brigid, *February* 1st, 1931.

CONTENTS

SECTION I

SECTION II.

LIST OF ABBREVIATIONS

A. Clon=*The Annals of Clonmacnoise.* Ed. D. Murphy.

A.F.M.=*The Annals of the Kingdom of Ireland by the Four Masters.* Ed. O'Donovan.

A.U.=*The Annals of Ulster.* Ed. Hennessey and McCarthy.

AA. SS. Boll.=*Acta Sanctorum quotquot orbe coluntur.* . . . Ed. Bollandus, etc.

AA. SS. Hib.=*Acta Sanctorum veteris et maioris Scotiæ seu Hiberniae, insulae Sanctorum.* Ed. Colgan.

Adam.=*The Life of St. Columba, by Adamnan.* Ed. W. Reeves.

Alb.=*S. Pachomii abbatis Tabennensis regulae monasticæ.* Ed. B. Albers.

Anal. Boll.=*Analecta Bollandiana,* Brussels.

An. Tig.=*The Annals of Tigernach.* Ed. Stokes in the Revue Celtique XVI–XVIII.

B. Arm.=*The Book of Armagh.* Ed. Gwynn.

B.N.E.=*Bethada Naem n-Erenn.* Ed. Plummer.

c. or *cc.*=*column or columns where reference is to P.L. or P.G.*

C.B.S.=*Lives of the Cambro-British Saints.* Ed. W. J. Rees.

Conf.=*The " Confession" of St. Patrick.* Ed. N. J. D. White.

C.S.E.L.=*Corpus Scriptorum ecclesiasticorum latinorum.* Ed. by the Wiener Akademie der Wissenschaften.

Codex Salm.=*Acta Sanctorum Hiberniae ex codice Salmanticensi.* Ed. De Smedt and De Backer.

Coll. Sacra=*Collectanea sacra, seu S. Columbani hiberni abbatis . . . necnon aliorum . . . Sanctorum acta et opuscula.* Ed. Fleming.

E.H.R.=*English Historical Review.*

Gesch. des d.K.R.=*Geschichte des deutschen Kirchenrechts by E. Löning.*

H.B.S.=*Henry Bradshaw Society, for the Publication of Liturgical Texts.*

H.E.=*Historia Ecclesiastica (of Sozomen, Eusebius, Bede).*

H.L.=*Historia Lausiaca.* Ed. Dom C. Butler, " The Lausiac History of Palladius."

H.M.=*Historia Monachorum in Aegypto.* Ed. Preussen in "Palladius und Rufinus."

H. and S. Councils.=*Councils and Ecclesiastical Documents relating to Great Britain and Ireland.* Ed. Haddan and Stubbs.

I.E.R.=*The Irish Ecclesiastical Record.*

I.K.=*Die irische Kanonensammlung.* Ed. Wasserschleben.

J.R.S.A.I.=*The Journal of the Royal Society of Antiquaries of Ireland.*

K.G.D.=*Kirchengeschichte Deutschlands, by Albert Hauck.*

Laws=*The Ancient Laws of Ireland.* Ed. in the Rolls Series.

Lism. L.=*Lives of Saints from the Book of Lismore.* Ed. W. Stokes.

L.L.=*Lebor Laigen,* or *The Book of Leinster.*   *L.U.*=*Lebor na h-Uidre.*

Mansi=*Sacrorum Conciliorum nova et amplissima collectio.* Ed. Mansi.

M.G.H.=*Monumenta Germaniae Historica. I. Scriptores. II. Auctores Antiquissimi III. Epistolae. V. Scriptores Rerum Merovingicarum.*

M.P. and M.N.P.—See p. 193.

Mon. of Tall=*The Monastery of Tallaght.* Ed. Gwynn (E.J.) and Purton

Onom. Goid.=*Onomasticon Goedelicum locorum et tribuum Hiberniae et Scotiae* by E. Hogan.

P.G.=*Patrologiae cursus completus. Series graeca.* Ed. J. P. Migne.

P.L.= ,, ,, ,, ,, *latina.* ,, ,,

P.R.I.A.=*Proceedings of the Royal Irish Academy.*

Rev. Bén.=*Revue Bénédictine.*

Rev. Celt.=*Revue celtique.*

Rule of Tall.=*The Rule of Tallaght.* Ed. E. Gwynn.

S.P.C.K.=*Society for Promoting Christian Knowledge.*

Thes. Pal.=*Thesaurus Paleohibernicus.* Ed. Stokes and Strachan.

Tr. Thau.=*Triadis Thaumaturgae, seu divorum Patricii, Columbae et Brigidae . . . acta.* Ed. Colgan.

V. Col.=*Vita Sancti Columbani* by *Jonas of Bobbio.* Ed. Krusch.

V.S.H.=*Vitae Sanctorum Hiberniae.* Ed. Plummer.

V. Trip.=*The Tripartite Life of St. Patrick.* Ed. W. Stokes.

Z.C.P.=*Zeitschrift für keltische Philologie.*

Z.K.G.=*Zeitschrift für Kirchengeschichte.*

IRISH MONASTICISM

SECTION I

CHRISTIAN MONASTICISM IN GENERAL

CHAPTER I

PROGRESS TOWARDS MONASTICISM

Möhler : *Geschichte des Mönchtums in der Zeit seiner Entstehung und ersten Ausbreitung. (Gesammelte Schriften und Aufsätze.* Bd. II. Regensburg, 1840.)

Zöckler : *Askese und Mönchtum.* Frankfurt a. M., 1897.

Harnack : *Das Mönchtum.* Giessen, 1881. Eng. trans. London, 1901.

Heimbucher: *Die Orden u. Kongregationen der kath. Kirche.* 2nd ed. Paderborn, 1907–8.

Leclercq : " *Cénobitisme,"* in *Dict. d'archéologie chrétienne et de liturgie,* T. II, col. 3047–3248. Paris, 1910.

Dom C. Butler : " *Monasticism,"* in *Cambridge Med. History.* Vol. I., ch. xviii. Cambridge, 1911 ; and in *Encyl. Britannica,* 11th ed. under same title.

J. O. Hannay : *Spirit and Origin of Christian Monasticism.* London, 1903.

H. B. Workman : *The Evolution of the Monastic Ideal from the Earliest Times to the Coming of the Friars.* London, 1913.

F. Martinez : *L'Ascétisme Chrétien pendant les trois premiers Siècles de l'Église.* Paris, 1913.

Dom G. Morin : *L'Idéal Monastique et la Vie Chrétienne des Premiers Jours.* Maredsous, 1912. English translation. London, 1914.

J. Lebreton : *La Vie Chrétienne au Premier Siècle de l'Église.* Paris, 1927.

§1—Its Foundation in Christian Teaching

THE model of Christian life is no other than the Founder of the Christian Faith—Christ Our Lord Himself. " If any man will come after Me," He said, " let him deny himself, take up his cross daily, and follow Me."[1] He who wishes to be a Christian, then, in very truth as well as in outward seeming, must renounce his selfish inclinations, and strive with all his might to imitate his Divine Master. The two duties are correlative, renunciation having for its only purpose the following of Christ, and marking again by the generous or churlish spirit with which it is practised the degree of that imitation.

For in the Kingdom of God, established by Christ on earth,

---

[1] Luke, ix, 23.

detachment from self and creatures may be more or less
perfect, since it is not demanded of all in equal measure.
The rich young man who asked in holy sincerity about life
everlasting was told that he could secure it by keeping the
Commandments.   There is thus a minimum of Christian
observance necessary at once and sufficient for salvation.
But in the Father's house there are many mansions, and he
who would enter into the finest among these must travel
along higher and more arduous paths.   "If thou wilt be
perfect," said Christ to the excellent and eager young man,
"go, sell what thou hast, and give to the poor . . . and come
follow Me."[1] Were this invitation accepted, further sacrifices
would in due course be demanded, for "every one of you
that doth not renounce all that he possesseth cannot be My
disciple."[2]   Elsewhere the Master expressly mentions as
objects of detachment the love for father and mother, wife
and children ; even the love for life itself.[3] Included in this,
according to the interpretation generally accepted since the
earliest times, is the recommendation to continence and
perfect chastity. Detachment again for those who aspire to
the closest following of Christ, must be in deed, not in desire
or inclination only, just as the poverty, hunger, thirst,
sufferings, passion and death of Christ were actual.   Those
not called to this final form of detachment (and of necessity
they are the great majority) may reach a high and heroic
degree of sanctity by renouncing in spirit the things of earth,
and overcoming the endless obstacles by which they remain
surrounded to advance with ever-increasing strides in charity.

As the purpose of renunciation is the securing of ampler
freedom to follow Christ, so the zealous disciple will imitate
his Master by a more intense love of God and his neighbour,
for it is in this that Christian perfection consists.   "Thou
shalt love the Lord thy God with thy whole heart and with
thy whole soul and with thy whole mind, and with thy whole
strength. This is the first and greatest Commandment. And
the second is like to this : Thou shalt love thy neighbour as
thyself. On these two Commandments dependeth the whole
law and the prophets."[4] Love of God finds expression in praise,
reverence and adoration, and in absolute conformity with

[1] Matt. xix, 16–21.   Mark x, 17–31.   Luke xviii, 13–30.
[2] Luke xiv, 33.
[3] Luke xiv, 25 ff.   Matt. x, 37 f.
[4] Matt. xxii, 36–40.

the Divine Will.[1] Love for one's neighbour (and neighbour is a term in which all men, even enemies, are included) is shown especially by humility, then by the practice of the other virtues set forth as fountains of particular blessings by our Saviour on the Mount.[2]

A problem here presents itself, for a life so filled with love for God and man is utterly beyond the resources of unaided nature. St. John, more fully than the other Evangelists, shows how this difficulty is overcome. The Christian, he teaches, is not left in the helplessness of his unregenerate state, but is born again of water and the Holy Ghost, to a new, supernatural[3] life, in which he depends vitally upon Christ as the branch depends upon the vine.[4] Begun in faith[5] and in the quickening grace of baptism[6] this intimate union of Christ with the faithful soul is intensified by the Eucharist, that miraculous Food of His own Body and Blood[7] by which the Good Shepherd feeds His flock. United thus closely with Christ, the true believer cannot but love God ; and loving God, he cannot but love his neighbour, for " he that loveth not his brother whom he seeth, how can he love God, Whom he seeth not ? "[8]

§2—The Idea of Combat in the Spiritual Life Emphasised by St. Paul. Asceticism thus a Necessity[9]

The Apostle, like St. John, dwells on the amazing fact that the Christian, born anew through the saving waters of baptism, becomes one body with Christ. Before the transformation has been achieved, and therefore while the influences of sin are still predominant, the future Christian is referred to by the Saint as *the old man*. Once the call to grace has been heard and answered he becomes, in St. Paul's terminology, *the new man*.[10] Under the former aspect (man unmade by sin), he is spoken of again in figure as *the flesh ;* under the latter

[1] Luke, xi, 2.
[2] Matt. v, 3–10.
[3] John iii, 3–6.
[4] Ib. xv, 5.
[5] John iii, 36.
[6] Ib. iii, 5.
[7] Ib. vi, 54–8.
[8] 1 John iv, 20.
[9] Prat : *La Théologie de St. Paul.* Eng. transl. London, 1926.
[10] Col. iii, 9. Eph. iv, 22. Cf. Prat op. cit. ii, 73.

aspect (man remade by grace) he is referred to in a more flattering figure as *the spirit*.[1] To grasp the full significance of the last-mentioned term, we must remember that St. Paul conceived the Church as the mystical body of Christ ; a body of which Christ is the Head, the Faithful are the members, and the Holy Spirit is the soul.[2] A connection so intimate with the Holy Ghost, the sanctifier, results for the Christian in an inward renewal—the creation within himself of a higher nature endowed with new qualities and new activities.[3] It is to the predominance of this nature in *the new man* that St. Paul refers when he speaks of him as *the spirit*.

As conversion, according to the Apostle, is death to *the old man* and to the flesh, whilst baptism is a mystical resurrection with Christ, the believer must endeavour to shape his conduct in harmony with the life of the risen Saviour. Relapse into sin brings with it an added horror, inasmuch as it is a crime against his newly acquired nature. The true Christian will not dream of incurring such guilt, but will " put on " rather, more and more absolutely, " the new man who, according to God, is created in justice and holiness and truth "[4]

Owing, however, to that concupiscence or tendency to evil, which is a deplorable consequence of original sin, *the old man*, destroyed in principle by our incorporation into Christ crucified through baptism, is destroyed in practice only with extreme difficulty. St. Paul himself bears witness to this phenomenon when he confesses that " to will is present with me, but to accomplish that which is good I find not. For the good which I will I do not ; but the evil which I will not that I do . . . For I am delighted with the law of God according to the inward man ; but I see another law of my mind and captivating me in the law of sin that is in my members."[5] The flesh is thus in rebellion against the spirit, and can be brought to submission only by constant mortification. " I chastise my body," says St. Paul, " and bring it into subjection."[6] Allies of the flesh in this rude conflict are the world, or the multitude of men whose ways are opposed to the

---

[1] Prat, op. cit., p. 72 ff.
[2] Prat, op. cit., p. 300–8, D'Herbigny, *Theologica de Ecclesia*, Paris, 1921, II, p. 234 ff.
[3] 2 Cor. v, 17. Gal. vi, 15. Eph. ii, 15. Prat., op. cit., p. 72.
[4] Eph. iv, 24. Col. iii, 10.
[5] Rom. vii, 18–23.
[6] 1 Cor. ix, 27.

wishes of God ; and the spirits of wickedness, all the more powerful because immaterial and invisible.[1] The Christian is thus compelled to fight the good fight, constantly and courageously, if he is to reach the end for which he was created. For this reason St. Paul, in the first Epistle to the Corinthians, compares him to an athlete in the public games, who subjects his body to a strict regime of exercise and privations, that he may gain the prize. If, urges the Apostle, the desire for worldly renown impels the athlete to reject so resolutely the cravings of his lower nature, how sternly ought not the follower of Christ discipline his body that he may gain a crown that is imperishable ?[2] Temptation, indeed, is the lot of all, but " God is faithful, Who will not suffer you to be tempted above that which you are able, but will make with the temptation issue, that you may be able to bear it."[3] It is thus clear that God's grace will never be wanting to overcome all obstacles and to make us conformable to the image of His Son ; but it is also clear that our own co-operation with divine grace is needed, if that image is to be reproduced within us. He who believes in Christ must imitate Christ in love of God and his neighbour.[4] As the imitation is hard, he must school himself to practise it : a labour which implies (given the evil tendencies of his nature) severe self-repression, penitential exercises and, in short, the austere regulation of life comprised in the term *asceticism.*

We have already pointed out that activity in this direction, at least to the extent of renouncing what is forbidden under pain of grievous sin, must be shown by every Christian determined to save his soul. But renunciation will increase in proportion to the ardour with which Christ is loved. Those who follow Him with generosity will not content themselves with abandoning what is unlawful, but will add those ascetical practices, counselled, though not ordered, by Holy Writ. Amongst these are : voluntary poverty,[5] perpetual virginity,[6] separation from family and friends,[7] disciplinary inflictions, like abstinence and fasts.[8] Thus they prepare themselves

---

[1] Cf. 1 Thess. iii, 5. Eph. vi, 11, and Prat, op. cit. ii, p. 423.
[2] Cor. xx, 25.
[3] 1 Cor. x, 13.
[4] Phil. ii, 5.
[5] Matt. xix, 21 ; viii, 20. Luke ix, 57–62.
[6] 1 Cor. vii, 25–6 ; 32–4.
[7] Matt. xix, 28–9.
[8] Matt. vi, 16–8 ; xxx, 12. Luke v, 33–5.

for that more intimate union with Christ, the Redeemer, which is the ideal of Christian perfection.

§3—Private Asceticism within the Christian Communities of the First Three Centuries

In the Acts of the Apostles it is related that four daughters of St. Philip, the Deacon, were virgins and prophetesses at Caesarea.[1]   St. Paul himself practised perfect continence, and no doubt recommended it as an observance of supererogation to the more heroically inclined among his converts at Corinth.   He forwarded later to the Community of that city a detailed statement of his teaching on the whole question of marriage and virginity.   " I would," he says, " that all men were even as myself; but everyone hath his proper gift from God, one after this manner, and another after that."[2] Marriage, then, is good ; virginity better.[3] For the latter he has no commandment from the Lord, but he counsels those who, by the aid of God's special grace, can abide in it, to do so.[4] The time, he explains, is short. " The fashion of this world passeth away." Now, " he that is without a wife is solicitous for the things that belong to the Lord : how he may please God " ; whilst " he that is with a wife is solicitous for the things of the world : how he may please his wife,"[5] and his attention is thus divided. St. John, in the same way, speaks with particular respect of virgins " purchased from among men, the first fruits to God and the lamb." " These follow the lamb whithersoever he goeth."[6]

Hegesippus, writing about A.D. 160, tells of the Apostle James, Bishop of Jerusalem, that " he was holy from his mother's womb, drank no wine nor strong drink, nor ate anything in which was life. No razor came upon his head; he anointed himself not with oil, and used no bath . . . Alone he entered into the sanctuary, and was found on his knees asking forgiveness on behalf of the people, so that his knees became hard like a camel's, for he was continually bending

---

[1] Acts xxi, 8–9.
[2] 1 Cor. vii, 7.
[3] 1 Cor. vii, 1, 38, 40.
[4] 1 Cor. vii, 25.
[5] 1 Cor. vii, 31–4.
[6] Apoc. xiv, 4.

the knee in worship to God, and asking forgiveness for the people. In fact, on account of his exceeding great justice, he was called " the Just."[1]

Renunciation of goods was practised by the first Christian Community at Jerusalem. " And all they that believed were together and had all things common. Their possessions and goods they sold and divided them to all according as every one hath need."[2]

In the generation succeeding the Apostles the form of asceticism most generally observed was continence. Those who made a profession of virginity were drawn from both sexes ; they lived in their own homes, and participated in the common life of Christian society ; but in the churches they formed somewhat of a group apart. So great was the esteem in which they were held by the other members of their congregations that the weaker amongst them were in danger of falling victims to presumption. " If anyone," writes St. Ignatius of Antioch to St. Polycarp (about A.D. 107), " is able to honour the flesh of the Lord by remaining in virginity, let him do so without ostentation and self-conceit. If he prides himself thereon, he is lost ; if he places himself above the Bishop, he is deceiving himself."[3] The same writer, in his letter to the Church at Smyrna, mentions the group of virgins as an important section of the Christian community.[4]

Further on in the second century the Christian apologists bear witness to the fact that the ascetical movement continues. Horrible rumours of Christian immorality were then current among the heathen. St. Justin, rebutting these charges about A.D. 150, gives a brief statement of Christ's teaching on adultery. Having shown that the very desire to commit this crime is an appalling sin, and as such abhorrent to Christian ideas, he goes on to point out, to the greater confusion of the accusers and to attract their admiration, that " many of the male as well as of the female sex brought up from childhood in the law of Christ, and now sixty to seventy years of age, have preserved their bodies unspotted during all that period. These I can show you in all classes of society."[5] Some

---

[1] Preserved in Eusebius H. E. ii, 23.
[2] Acts ii, 44–5. Cf. v, 1–4.
[3] Ad Poly. c. 5. Cf. 1 Clem. ad Corinth, c. 38.
[4] Ad Smyr., c. 13.
[5] Apol. xv, 6.

two decades later Tatian[1] and Athenagoras[2] give evidence to the same effect.

As with the second, so with the third century. Clement of Alexandria, shortly before its opening, speaks of those among the Faithful who strive by perpetual continence to secure closer union with Christ.[3] About ten years later he mentions ascetics who have renounced not only marriage, but also flesh meat and wine.[4] Origen praises those admirable members of the Christian fold who practise asceticism[5]; of this he specifies four forms—virginity, poverty, abstinence from meat and wine, fasting.[6] Tertullian glories in the number of noble-minded men and women who preserve their bodies immaculate to the grave, white-haired with age, but children in their innocence.[7] St. Cyprian composed a special tract in honour of virgins: "the flower of the Church's garden, the pride and ornament of heavenly grace . . . the image of God, stamped with the sanctity of the Lord, the most illustrious portion of Christ's flock."[8] St. Methodius, Bishop of Philippi (died A.D. 311), wrote a panegyric of virginity in the form of a symposium. According to him virginity is a flower of celestial growth, brought to earth for the first time by Christ, the Prince and Teacher of virgins.[9] He likewise emphasises the value of the practice in giving virility to the Christian soul: "for those vowed to chastity are pledged to undergo a kind of perpetual martyrdom. Not only for a few brief moments do they endure the burden of the body, but during their whole life long. They fear not to engage in the truceless and truly Olympian labour of chastity, and to resist the cruel transports of the passions."[10]

§4—Privileged Position of Ascetics in Christian Society.

That ascetics enjoyed the highest esteem within the Church is clear from what has already been said. Clement of Alex-

---

[1] *Oratio ad Graecos.*
[2] *Legatio pro Christianis*, c. 33.
[3] *Paed.* i, 7.
[4] *Stromata* vii, 12.
[5] *Contra Cels.* i, 26 ; v, 49.
[6] *In Jerem.* xix, 4, 7.
[7] *De Virg. vel.*, c. 10.   *Apol.*, c. 9.
[8] *De Habitu Virg.*, c. 3.   P.L. iv, col. 455.
[9] Symposium (*Convivium decem Virginum*) Or. i, 2. P.G. xviii, col. 40. Cf. iii, 7. Ib., cc. 70–1.
[10] Symposium vii, 3. Ib., cc. 128–9. Cf. St. Ambrose, *De Virgin.* 5. P.L. xvi, col. 194.

andria, representing more or less the general Christian view, did not hesitate to describe them as "the elect among the elect."[1] In the gatherings for public worship they were advanced to places of honour immediately next to the clergy.[2] The two letters "to the Virgins" falsely attributed to St. Clement of Rome, but belonging to the third century, show them as a class apart among the Faithful[3]; whilst Hippolytus of Porto reckons them with the Apostles, Martyrs, bishops and priests among the seven columns that sustain the Church.[4] We may be certain that their position was not quite identical in the various congregations, but we may be certain, too, that they were nowhere confused with the other members of the Community. The distinction became more marked when the ascetics bound themselves solemnly before God by vow to persevere in virginity, as the first and most necessary condition for a life of exceptional self-denial. That this took place in the third century we know from Clement of Alexandria, who speaks of continence as repression of the body in consequence of a promise made to God.[5] Origen testifies to the solemnity of the obligation: "Now when we come to God and vow our permanence in chastity, we express with our lips and swear that we will punish or ill-treat our flesh and bring it into subjection, that we may be able to give life to the spirit."[6] St. Cyprian speaks of virgins who have pledged themselves to Christ, and devoted themselves, both body and soul, for ever, to the service of God.[7] Such a vow, when made by a member of the female sex, was regarded as a form of nuptials with Christ[8]; and its violation was spoken of as adultery.[9] Marriage, however, contracted in despite of the vow, was valid,[10] though scandalous, and the culprit had to make reparation by penance[11] which, in places at least (as we learn from the 13th canon of the Council of Elvira, celebrated about A.D. 300), was extremely severe.[12]

---

[1] τῶν ἐκλεκτῶν ἐκλεκτότεροι—*Quis dives salvetur*, c. xxxvi. P.G., ix, col. 641.
[2] Tertullian, *De exhortat. cast.* xi.
[3] P.G., i, col. 330–452.
[4] *Fragmenta in Proverbia* P.G., x, col. 627.
[5] *Strom.* iii, 1. P.G., viii, col. 1103.
[6] *In Levit. Hom.* 3, n. 4. P.G. xii, col. 428.
[7] *De Habitu Virg.*, c. 4. P.L. iv, col. 455–6. Ep. 60. P.L. iv, col. 371.
[8] Tertull. *De Virgin. vel.* c. 16. P.L. ii, col. 911.
[9] Cyprian. Ep. 62. P.L. iv, col. 381.
[10] Cyprian, op. cit., col. 377–8.
[11] Cyprian, op. cit., col. 381.
[12] Hefele-Leclercq. *Hist. des Conciles*, T. 1, p. 229.

Elaborate precautions were taken by the ecclesiastical authorities to ensure that ascetics should remain worthy of the high honour in which they were held by the remainder of the Faithful. Great importance was attached to gravity in outward behaviour and modesty in dress as necessary bulwarks of defence against temptation. Virgins were thus warned against unbecomingly rich apparel, against ornaments and jewels, lipstick and powder-puff,[1] wedding feasts and dances.[2] Tertullian recommends that at all public gatherings they should wear a veil which is " a helmet against the tempter, a shield against the suspicions and the slanderous small talk of the ill-disposed."[3] But the most vehement denunciation was reserved for the irregularity by which ascetics of opposite sex went on journeys, or lived together under the same roof. However intense the piety of these and however excellent their intentions, the practice was exposed to such dangers that it called for and received rigorous suppression.[4]

§5—Manner of Life Led by the Ascetics

Except for the general watchfulness employed by the Church to ensure that the ascetics lived true to their professions, and especially to their vow, where such an obligation had been undertaken, there is no evidence that she interfered beyond measure with their liberty. As the choice of this more disciplined state of life had been voluntary and the vow private, so, too, the practices adopted depended very much on the personal initiative of each. The Evangelical Counsels being, however, at basis the general form for all, a certain uniformity became inevitable.

Thus the profession of asceticism was inconceivable without celibacy or virginity, and this again brought with it, as a natural consequence, much reserve and retirement from the world.[5]

In what concerns renunciation of property, Origen lays

---

[1] Cyprian. *De Habitu Virg.*, 9.
[2] Methodius, *Symposium*, v, 6.
[3] *De Virg. velandis*, c. 15.
[4] *Ep. Clem. ad Virg.* i, 10. St. Cyp. : *Ep.* iv, 4. Council of Ancyra (A.D. 314), can. xix. Hefele-Leclercq, i, p. 321.
[5] Cf. Clem. Alex. : *Quis dives salvetur*, c. xxxvi. P.G. ix, col. 641. Origen *In Levit. Hom.*, xi. P.G. xii, c. 529. Tertull. *De Virg. velandis*, c. 3. P.L. ii, col. 891.

down as of strict necessity that those who wish to be perfect must act on Christ's recommendation : " Go, sell what thou hast, and give to the poor."[1] The Alexandrian scholar practised what he preached, for he stripped himself of all that he possessed, including his library, only reserving from the price a few obols per day for his support.[2] His distinguished pupil, St. Gregory Thaumaturgus, imitated his example.[3] Clement of Alexandria, too, speaks with high praise of the heroic souls who abandon the riches of earth for the sake of eternal life.[4] Likewise St. Cyprian, who proved the sincerity of his words by bestowing his whole possessions upon the poor.[5] It may be taken for granted that the ascetics, as a body, were not behind these in the exercise of voluntary poverty ; but as they lived for the most part in their homes, and had to reckon with an intimate and legitimate family interest in the disposal of family property, it is probable that the alienation of wealth in notable quantity was the exception rather than the rule.

Fasting and abstinence held a prominent place in the ascetical life. " We meet frequently with Christians," writes Origen, " who might enter into wedlock and thus spare themselves the hard struggle between the flesh and the spirit. But they refrain by preference from exercising this right, and lay upon themselves instead hard penances, keeping their bodies in subjection by fasting and bringing them under obedience by abstinence from certain foods ; and thus in every way mortifying by the spirit the works of the flesh."[6] From the early days of the Church the faithful had been accustomed to fast two days a week, after the manner of the Jews, who set Monday and Thursday apart for that work of penitence. To separate themselves more fully from the Jews the primitive Christian congregations changed the fasting days to Wednesday and Friday.[7] The ascetics, like all the faithful, were expected to observe these and such other fast days (Easter Saturday, stations, etc.) as were common to the

---

[1] *In Matt.* c. 15, n. 15. P.G. Vol. xiv, c. 1295, ff
[2] Euseb. H.E. vi, 3.
[3] Greg Nyss. : *Vita Greg.*, c. 28.
[4] *Quis dives salvetur*, c. 11.
[5] *Vita S. Cypr.* P.L. ii, col. 394.
[6] *In Jerem. Hom.* xix, 7. P.G. xiii, col. 517.
[7] *Didache*, viii, 1. *Apostolic Frs.* Ed. Lightfoot-Harmer, 1898, p. 221. *Hermas, Sim.* v, 7. Ed. Lightfoot, op. cit. p. 347. Tertull. *De Ieiunio*, 14. *Ad Uxor*, ii, 4.

Church, but they were at liberty to go beyond this minimum
and choose further days or periods on their own account.
This they zealously did. In addition, they abstained from
flesh meat and wine[1] and doubtless, too, from various dishes
that would prove more than ordinarily gratifying to the taste.

Since efforts to obtain unusual purity of life and to advance
more rapidly in imitation of the Saviour were foredoomed
to failure without frequent and fervent prayer, the ascetics
devoted much time to this exercise. The *Didache* (written c.
A.D. 80-90) recommended the repetition of the *Pater Noster*
three times a day.[2] This and other prayers were recited by
the ascetics at the third, sixth and ninth hours,[3] in commemoration respectively of Christ's condemnation, crucifixion
and death. There were likewise prayers before meals,[4] and
long liturgical prayers in church before the celebration of
the Eucharist, not to speak of the weekly vigils, in the night
between Saturday and Sunday, when the Christian Community as a body hurried to the House of God and remained
till daybreak chanting hymns and psalms, listening to readings
from the Old and New Testaments and to homilies from
the presiding Bishop or his representative.[5] Before long these
vigils were celebrated, too, on the anniversaries of martyrs
and on days of solemn intercession or penitence. The more
prayer was accompanied by good works, such as acts of
charity and almsgiving, the more likely it was to prove acceptable to God ; for, as St. Cyprian pointed out, the sterile is by
definition unproductive, wherefore barren prayer must remain
unfruitful and unheard.[6] Hence the ascetics, in a degree
beyond their fellow-Christians, spent themselves in charitable
services. Christ's suffering members—the poor, the sick,
and the orphaned—were the special objects of their care.[7]

A serious difficulty for the ascetics at this period must
have been the manifold distractions inseparable from a life
in the midst of family and friends and within their own homes.
Before the end of the third century we find many of them,
at least in Syria and Palestine, seeking to overcome this by

---

[1] Origen, l.c.
[2] Lightfoot-Harmer, op. cit., p. 221.
[3] Cf. Acts iii, 1 : x, 9. Clem. of Alex. : *Strom.* vii. P.G. ix, c. 456.
[4] Tertull. *De Orat.*, 25.
[5] Tertull. *De Orat.*, 28.
[6] *Ep. Clem. ad Virg.* i, 12-3. *Symp*; xi, 1. *Canons of Hippol.*, 157. Cypr.
De Opere et eleem, 26.
[7] Cypr. *De Opere et eleemos.* 5. *De dom. orat.*, 32.

gathering together in groups.[1] It need hardly be said that the virgins or female ascetics lived absolutely by themselves, and that the celibates, or male ascetics (much fewer in numbers), lived in places far apart. About this period, too, *Parthenons*, or Communities of virgins, began to arise in Egypt, and the institution became general in the next century. For those who continued to live in their own homes stricter rules of conduct were drawn up by St. Athanasius,[2] St. Ambrose[3] and St. Jerome.[4] They should dress in black ; wear a veil of the same colour, placed on their heads solemnly by the Bishop at their consecration to God ; cover their arms to the fingers, and keep their hair cropped close to the head.[5] They should have but one meal a day, and that of bread and vegetables after the hour of none ; this, too, they were to have in common if possible, and to share with some poor women.[6] They were to study the Holy Scriptures, rise during the night to pray, and gather together in the churches to chant psalms at the traditional hours.[7] Thus, from the beginning of the fourth century onwards, free lance asceticism among virgins tended to disappear absolutely and to be replaced by communities where all lived under the same roof and were subject to the same rule. Where virgins still remained isolated in the world they were likewise urged to live as far as possible a common life, and to obey a common rule. As we shall see presently, the advance in this direction did not take place quite as early among ascetics of the other sex.

§6—ASCETICISM IN THE DESERT. ST. ANTHONY. THE ANCHORITES.

If the allurements of the world made it an uphill task for the ordinary Christian to concentrate his thoughts on God and on eternal salvation, and if participation in the religious exercises of the community, coupled with an unavoidable minimum of human converse, proved distracting

---

[1] *Ep. Clem. ad Virg.* i & ii. P.G. 1, col. 379 ff.
[2] *De Virginitate* (Λόγος σωτηρίας πρὸς τὴν παρθένον) defended as genuine by Von. der Goltz. Texte und Unters., N.F. 14. 2a. P.G. xxviii, c. 251 ff.
[3] *De Virginibus.* Lib. iii. P.L. xvi, c. 221 ff.
[4] *Ep.* cxxx *ad Demetr. Ep.* xxii *ad Eustochium.*
[5] *De Virginitate* 16, 12. *De Virginibus* iii, 18, 20.
[6] *De Virginitate* 16, 12. *De Virginibus* ii, & iii & St. Jer, l.c.
[7] *De Virginitate,* 20.

to the ascetics, why should not the lover of a perfect life
abandon this world and its dangers altogether, and seek
safety for his soul in solitude ?   The thought must have
occurred to many ascetics, especially among those who, to
save their lives, had made longer or shorter sojourns in the
desert during the Decian persecution of A.D. 250.[1]   It is not
unreasonable to suppose that some of these never returned
to the haunts of men, and that one among them, named Paul,
lived in eremitical retirement in a cave near the Red Sea,
where he died about A.D. 340.   St. Jerome wrote the life[2] of
this " First Hermit," but in a style so rhetorical that the
very existence of this hero was questioned, even in the author's
own day.[3]   Scepticism on the last mentioned point seems to
be unjustified, though the detailed description of Paul's
career certainly belongs to the region of romance.[4]

The influence of Paul of Thebes on the development of the
anachoretical life was, however, negligible.   Not he, but
St. Anthony is rightly regarded as the father and founder
of the eremitical institution.   Anthony[5] was born of well-to-do
parents in A.D. 251 at Coma, a village near Heracleopolis,
in middle Egypt.   His childhood was marked by great shyness
and reserve, amounting almost to a dislike for human company.
He never went to school, and never learned to read his native
Coptic language, not to speak of Greek.   When his parents
died, about A.D. 270, he sold off his property and gave the

---

[1] Dionysius Alex., in *Euseb.* H.E. vi, 42.

[2] *Vita S. Pauli.* P.L. xxiii, col. 17 ff.

[3] Hier. *Vita. Hilarionis.* Introd. P.L. xxiii, c. 29.

[4] Bidez : *Deux versions inédites de la vie de Paul de Thèbes,* Ghent, 1900.
Nau : *Le texte original de la vie de S. Paul de Thèbes. Anal. Boll.* T. xx, p.
121 ff. Kugener : *S. Jerôme et la vie de Paul de Thèbes. Byzantinische
Zeitschrift.* T. xi, p. 513 ff. De Decker : *Contribution à l'étude des vies de
Paul de Thèbes,* Ghent, 1905. Schwietz : *Das morgenländische Mönchtum,*
Mainz, 1904 Bd. i, p. 50. Dom Butler : *Lausiac History of Palladius,*
vol. i, p. 231. Vol. ii, p. 261.

[5] *Vita Antonii* by St. Athanasius. P.G. xxvi, c. 837 seq. The work was
made known to the West in a contemporary Latin version by Evagrius of
Antioch. P.L. lxxiii. Attempts of recent critics, more particularly Weingarten :
Der Ursprung des Mönchtums. Zeitschrift für Kirchengeschichte i, p. 6 ff.,
and 454 ff ; and Reitzenstein : *Des Athanasius Werk über das Leben des
Antonius* (Sitzungsbericht der Heidelberger Akademie der Wissenschaften.
Phil. hist. Klasse, 1914) to deny the authorship of St. Athanasius and to
discredit the life must be pronounced unsuccessful. Cf. Mayer : *Die Echtheit
der dem hl. Athanasius d. Gr. zugeschriebenen Vita Antonii. Katholik,*
Bd. lv., 495 ff, 619 ff and lvi, 173 ff. Berlière : *Les origines du monachisme
et la critique moderne.* Rev. Bénéd. T. viii, p. 1–19, 49–69. Grützmacher :
Theol. Literaturzeitung, 1897. No. 9. Dom. Butler : *Lausiac Hist.* i, p. 226–8.
Amélineau : *S. Antoine et les commencements du monachisme en Égypte*
(*Revue de l'histoire des religions.* T. lxv, jan.-févr. 1912.). Mackean : *Christian
Monasticism in Egypt.* London, 1920, p. 68.

proceeds to the poor ; next he placed a younger sister who remained under his care, in a *Parthenon* or house of virgins ; after which he began to live as an ascetic near his home.[1] Hearing, however, of an aged holy man who led a rigorous life on the outskirts of the village, he took up his abode in his neighbourhood. The day was spent in prayer and manual work. By means of the latter he earned money enough to provide for his meagre wants, and had a little over to alleviate the sufferings of the poor. In church he listened attentively to the reading of the Holy Scriptures, and retained what he heard in memory, so that he could repeat afterwards whole passages by heart. From time to time he visited distinguished ascetics, and noted their characteristic virtues : " he observed the graciousness of one ; the unceasing prayer of another ; he took knowledge of another's freedom from anger ; of another's loving kindness ; he fixed his attention on one as he watched, on another as he studied ; one he admired for his endurance, another for his fasting and sleeping on the ground ; the meekness of one, and the long-suffering of another he noted with care, whilst he took heed of the piety towards Christ and the mutual love which animated all."[2] Everywhere he was esteemed as a true friend of God.[3] To keep the flesh in submission to the spirit he subjected it to many privations, eating but once a day, after sundown, and confining himself then to bread, water and salt ; sleeping on a mat of rushes or on the bare ground, and often spending the night in vigils. Later he changed his abode to an empty tomb some miles away, without, however, severing relations with the ascetics and the villagers.

When this form of life had lasted for fifteen years he experienced within himself an irresistible impulse to withdraw to greater solitude. Accordingly, in A.D. 285, he crossed the Nile and directed his steps towards the mountains on its right bank. Here, at a place called Pispir, in a region appallingly wild and lonely, he discovered the ruins of an old fort, and by building up the entrance transformed it into an abode.[4] A spring nearby supplied water to slake his thirst, and friends (doubtless from among the ascetics) re-

---

[1] *Vita Antonii*, c. 3. Cf. Duchesne : *Histoire ancienne de l'Eglise.* T. ii, p. 488 ff. Schiwietz : l.c., p. 69:
[2] *Vita Antonii*, c. 14.
[3] θεοφιλής.
[4] *Vita Ant.*, c. 10.

newed his supply of bread every six months. For twenty
years he lived thus in complete isolation, never leaving his
habitation and rarely seen by visitors; occupied in prayer
and in weaving mats; wrestling, too, with demons, who
plagued him incessantly with sinful suggestions, and at
times, it would appear, sought to drive him from communion
with God by physical violence.[1]

Meanwhile the fame of his virtues had been noised abroad,
and one day, about A.D. 305, Anthony saw his fort besieged
and stormed.[2] The newcomers, who had forced themselves
thus rudely on his notice, were ascetics determined on becoming
his disciples. There was no gainsaying their demand. So
in a moment of high importance for the future of the Church,
the venerable anchorite sallied forth from his long solitude
to teach, advise and direct a group of enthusiastic followers.
Strange indeed was the spectacle when the inhospitable waste
round Pispir was thronged like a busy city, and the barren
peaks re-echoed sounds certainly never heard in their midst
since the creation of the world. The multitude of anchorites
dwelt in separate cells and spent their days in pious reading,
prayer, the chanting of psalms, and work. Fasts were many
and strict. Charity unfeigned ruled in their midst. From time
to time Anthony called them all together and expounded in
brief addresses the principles by which their lives should
be governed. It was the dawn of Christian Monasticism.[3]

When persecution reigned under Maximin, in A.D. 311,
and the anchorites discovered that distance saved them from
its dangers, Anthony, with some chosen disciples, travelled
north to Alexandria, in the hope of gaining a martyr's crown.
In this he was disappointed, but he was able at least to encourage the heroic confessors of the Faith, and to serve them
with devotion in the prisons and in the mines.[4]

His appearance under such circumstances added to his
fame, and when he returned to Pispir it was to find the
number of hermits increasing so rapidly that it was quite
impossible to direct them properly. Added to this was the
trouble from visitors, who came in a multitude to seek for
interviews. Did he attend to all as they desired—and even

---

[1] *Vita Ant.*, c. 12–3.
[2] *Vita Ant.*, c. 14–5.
[3] *Vita Ant.*, c. 44.
[4] *Vita Ant.*, c. 46.

demanded—the Father of Anchorites must himself have ceased to be an Anchorite. Anthony solved the problem with the simplicity of the desert : he fled.[1] Joining a caravan of Bedouins, he journeyed for some days in the direction of the Red Sea, until he reached a mountain region blessed with a spring, some palm-trees, and a patch of fertile land. Here he could rest in comparative peace for the remainder of his life. He returned on occasion for a few days to Pispir to bestow guidance and encouragement on his old disciples[2] ; whilst in A.D. 338, at the age of 87, he dragged himself once more from his beloved solitude, and travelled to Alexandria to proclaim in person his attachment to St. Athanasius, and his detestation of the Arian heresy.[3] He died in A.D. 356, at the age of 105, leaving to his friend, St. Athanasius, his sheepskin tunic and the worn cloak which for many years had served him as a bed. At his express command he was buried by two faithful followers in a place unknown to others, lest honour beyond the common should be shown to his remains.[4]

In physical appearance Anthony is described as commonplace : " neither in height nor breadth was he conspicuous above others, but in the serenity of his manner and the purity of his soul."[5] Again, " his manners were not rough, as though he had been reared on the mountain and there grown old, but graceful and polite, and his speech was seasoned with the divine salt."[6] Newman praises his doctrine, " pure and unimpeachable, and his temper high and heavenly—without cowardice, without gloom, without formality, without self-complacency."[7] Truly a remarkable man, for without eloquence or learning, by the sheer force of an overwhelming love for God he rose to a position of extraordinary prominence in the history of the early Church. To the attractiveness of his saintly personality the eremitical and the semi-eremitical life owes its origin. When disciples flocked to him in numbers, he directed them with astonishing practical wisdom, grouping their cells in such wise that they could succour and support without needlessly disturbing one

---

[1] *Vita Ant.*, c. 49.
[2] *Vita.* c. 54, 61, 63, 89.
[3] *Vita Ant.*, c. 69–71.
[4] *Vita Ant.*, c. 91–2.
[5] *Vita Ant.*, c. 67.
[6] *Vita Ant.*, c. 73.
[7] Church of the Fathers. *Anthony in Conflict*, p. 166.

another. Realising keenly that a solitude too prolonged
tends to reduce the human being to savagery by making him
forget the most elementary notions of social conduct, he
secured that the hermits should re-unite at intervals to
benefit by spiritual conferences ; doubtless, too, for worship
and the celebration of the Holy Mysteries.[1] In this way he
paved the way for common life, which is the basis for monastic
order in its fully developed form. Thus the monks of a later
period rivalled the anchorites in their veneration for Anthony,
and extolled him in their traditions as the inaugurator of the
whole monastic system.

§7—Development of the Semi-Eremitical Life in Egypt

Palladius : *Historia Lausiaca.* Ed. Dom C. Butler, *The Lausiac
    History of Palladius,* 2 vols., Cambridge, 1898–1904 (Eng. Transl.
    of Greek text, W. K. L. Clarke, S.P.C.K., 1918). *Historia
    Monachorum in Aegypto.* Ed. Preussen in *Palladius und Rufinus,*
    Giessen, 1897. Cf. Butler, op. c., p. 198 ff. Cassian : *De Institutis
    Coenobiorum. Conlationes. C.S.E.L.,* XIII, XIV. Ed. Petschenig,
    1886–8 (Cf. Butler, op. c. p. 23 ff,).
Vita Pachomii. Acta SS. T. iii, Maii.
Sozomen : *Historia Eccles.* P.G. LXVII.
Sulpicius Severus : *Dialogus I. C.S.E.L.,* I. Ed. Halm, 1866.
R. Reitzenstein : *Historia Monachorum u. Historia Lausiaca,* Göt-
    tingen, 1916.
Apophthegmata Patrum P.G. LXV. *Verba Seniorum* P.L. LXXIII. Cf.
    Butler : *Lausiac History,* i, p. 208 ff. Wilmart : *Revue bénéd.*
    T. XXXIV, 1922, p. 185 ff. Bousset : *Apophthegmata. Studien
    zur Gesch. des ältesten Mönchtums.* Tübingen, 1923.
W. Bousset : *Komposition u. Charakter der Historia Lausiaca (Nachr.
    der Gesell. der Wiss. zu Göttingen,* 1917), p. 173 ff.
Dom C. Butler : *The Lausiac History. Journal of Theol. Studies,*
    1921, p. 222 ff.
W. Bousset : *Zur Komposition der Hist. Lausiaca. Zeitschr. für
    neutest. Wiss.* Bd. XXI, 1921, p. 81 ff.

The purely eremitical life, as led by St. Anthony before
disciples flocked to his solitude, continued to attract many
in Egypt during the fourth century. Noted among these was
John of Lycopolis, who immured himself upon a lofty
mountain and received the necessaries of life through a window
from a faithful visitor.[2] Another prominent anchorite was
Elias, who spent seventy years alone in the desolate waste
of Antinoë.[3] In the desert of Calamus, near the Red Sea,
some eight days' journey from human habitation, a number

---

[1] *Vita Ant.,* c. 16 ff.
[2] H.L., 35. H.M., 1. *Inst.,* iv, 23–6. *Conl.,* i, 21.
[3] H.M., 7.

of anchorites had their cells. Posidonius the Theban dwelt for a year in this region, and bore witness to the eerie loneliness of his existence. " The whole year I met no man, heard no talk, touched no bread. I subsisted merely on a few dates and any wild herbs I found."[1]

Hermits, however, were few compared with those who led a semi-eremitical life of the type that prevailed at Pispir during the latter stage of St. Anthony's career. Here each lived in solitude, and more or less according to his own ideas, but the cells were placed within reasonable distance of one another, and there was a guide and a teacher, voluntarily chosen, whose influence was felt over the entire colony. Various settlements of the Pispir pattern may be distinguished.

(a)—Chenoboskion.

Near Chenoboskion, some three hundred miles up the Nile from Pispir, a little group of anchorites flourished at the beginning of the fourth century. Their leader was Palaemon, a man of few words and of austere life. His days were spent in work ; his nights in meditation and prayer—all this on a diet of bread and salt. The importance of this hermit arises from the fact that the founder of monasticism, in the strict sense, Pachomius (whose history we shall have to consider presently), was for a time his disciple.[2]

(b)—Nitria.

Towards the end of the fourth century the most celebrated of the semi-eremitical settlements was that of Nitria, a dreary valley, thirty miles by six in extent, about sixty miles south of Alexandria.[3] The district owes its name, still preserved as Wadi-Natroun, to certain salt lakes, in which natron or sodium carbonate was produced. The founder of the colony here was Ammon, the scion of a rich and aristocratic family.[4] He had been compelled to marry when a young man, but had lived with his wife eighteen years in virginity. They then decided to live separately, she becoming the leader of a group of virgins, and he retiring to the desert of Nitria (c. A.D. 320–330). Ammon died twenty-two years later, but

---

[1] H.L., 36.
[2] *Vita Pachomii*, 3–8.
[3] Cf. Butler. *Lausiac Hist.*, ii, p. 188 ff.
[4] *Vita Ant.*, 60. H.L., 8. H.M., 29. Sozomen. H.E., iv, 32.

left disciples in plenty to carry on his mode of life.[1] Before the century closed their number was estimated at five thousand.[2] Each lived according to his own inclinations, for there was no rule ; and those who lost the desire for such heroic self-renunciation might retire without further ado. The cells were at no great distance from one another, whilst two or more of the anchorites often dwelt together. Work lasted from daybreak till the ninth hour (about 3 p.m.) ; then all gathered in their cells, and in clear loud voices chanted psalms and hymns in praise of Christ the Lord. In the centre of the valley stood a church where the monks gathered for common worship on Saturdays and Sundays. For the service of the altar eight priests were placed at their disposal by the Bishop of Hermopolis Minor. Seven bakeries supplied the various groups with bread. Discipline had to be maintained, even in the desert, and so we find, beside the church, three palm-trees, " each with a whip suspended from it. One is intended for the solitaries who transgress ; one for robbers, if any pass that way ; and one for chance comers." Near the church was a guest house " where they receive the stranger who has arrived, until he goes away of his own accord, without limit of time, even if he remains two or three years. Having allowed him to spend one week in idleness, the rest of his stay they occupy with work, either in the garden, or bakery, or kitchen. If he should be an important person they give him a book, not allowing him to talk to anyone before the (appointed) hour."[3] Doctors, confectioners, and wine sellers were to be found in the colony. One of the monks who knew no handicraft served the association by travelling to Alexandria and carrying back eggs, cakes, raisins, drugs, and other articles needed for the sick, " and one might see him from every morn till the ninth hour going the round of the cells and entering in at each door in case any should be ill in bed."[4] Great importance was attached to the learning of the Scriptures by heart, and we hear of a monk who had actually committed the whole Bible to memory.[5] Linen making was the chief form of manual labour,[6] but writing is

---

[1] *H.L.*, 8.
[2] *H.L.*, 7 ; 13.
[3] *H.L.*, 7.
[4] *H.L.*, 13.
[5] *H.L.*, 11.
[6] *H.L.*, 7.

already recognised as an ascetical exercise.[1] The value of work was likewise emphasised, not only as a necessary means of support, but also as a powerful defence against the solitaries' formidablē enemy, *accidia*, which we may translate familiarly as " the dumps." It is described more in detail as " that weariness of heart which the monk knew so well, when at times he was filled with dislike for the place, disgust for his cell, contempt for his brethren, and weariness of his work."[2] It was already an old saying that " the monk who works is plagued by one, but the idle monk by a thousand, devils."[3]

(c)—Cellia.

Some five miles from Nitria lay a waste of still more awful solitude, called Cellia or Cells. It was peopled by six hundred hermits, who lived in single huts, so placed that their inmates could neither see nor hear one another.[4] The settlement had a church, where the hermits met on Saturdays and Sundays, but rarely otherwise, save for spiritual conferences.[5] Macarius, " the city man,"[6] or the Alexandrian, as he was called, to distinguish him from Macarius the Egyptian, and various other bearers of the name, resided at intervals in this region. He was noted for the spirit of emulation in his ascetical practices. " If ever he heard of any feat, he did the same thing, but more perfectly. For instance, having heard from some that the monks of Tabennisi all through Lent eat only food that had not been near the fire he decided for seven years to eat nothing that had been cooked ; and except for raw vegetables, when such he found, or moistened pulse, he tasted nothing."[7] Then he heard of another ascetic, whose food was only a pound of bread a day, so he took his own hard-baked cake, put it into a jug with a narrow neck, and contented himself for his daily ration with the few ounces his hand could extract in one draw.[8] He tried also to do without sleep, and remained in the open for twenty days, but nature then overcame his body, if it could not overcome his will. Afterwards he admitted that this was a happy

---

[1] *H.L.*, 13.
[2] Mackean. *Christ. Monas. in Egypt*, p. 83.
[3] Cass. *Inst.*, x, 23.
[4] Sozom., *H.E.*, vi, 31.
[5] Sozom., l.c.
[6] ὁ πολιτικός.
[7] *H.L.*, 18. Cf. *H.M.*, 30.
[8] *H.L.*, 18.

deliverance, for the result would otherwise have been perpetual insanity.[1] Despite the rigour of his habits, he lived to be almost a centenarian.

(d)—Scete.

Probably in the north or north-west of Nitria, and separated from the latter by a pathless desert, lay the barren land of Scete, seat of an eremitical colony, founded about A D. 330 by Macarius the Egyptian.[2] Of him it is related that he was a priest and lived sixty years in the desert, before his death at the age of ninety. " He was said to be in a continual ecstasy and to spend a far longer time with God than with things sublunary."[3] Owing in large measure to his gift of healing, he was harassed by numerous visitors, to escape from whom he excavated a tunnel from his cell to a cave half a mile away. " And if ever a crowd of people troubled him, he would leave his cell secretly and go away to the cave, and no one would find him."[4] Two disciples remained ever by his side, one occupied almost wholly with the unfortunates who came to the saint to be cured.

There were four churches in the colony, each with its own priest.[5] Among the celebrated monks was the priest, Paphnutius, renowned for his patience and for his punctuality at the Saturday and Sunday gatherings, though his cell lay five miles away.[6] Very remarkable was the monk Moses, " an Ethiopian by race, and black,"[7] who had been house servant to a Government official, but who had been dismissed for immorality and violence. He then took to the highways as leader of a robber band. So appalling was his conduct that it finally shocked himself, and led him to think seriously of breaking with the past. This he did with the assistance of divine grace. In the long and bitter struggle with his evil habits he showed a resolution altogether exceptional, eating twelve ounces only of dry bread a day, praying much and working hard. Yet this regime did not save him from temptations, which were particularly trying during the night. As a radical remedy against these, he sought to deprive himself

---

[1] Ib.
[2] *H.L.*, 17.
[3] *H.L.*, 17.
[4] Ib. Cf. *H.M.*, 28.
[5] Cass., *Conl.*, x, 2.
[6] Cass., *Conl.*, xviii, 15 ; iii, 1.
[7] *H.L.*, 19.

completely of sleep. " So he remained in his cell for six years
and every night he stood in the middle of the cell praying
and not closing his eyes." But the remedy proved ineffectual.
" So he suggested to himself yet another plan and going
out by night, he would visit the cells of the older and more
ascetic monks, and taking their jugs secretly would fill them
with water. For they fetch their water from a distance, some
from two miles off, others half a mile." Only once did Moses's
early training turn to his advantage, and that was when he
was attacked by four robbers in his cell. The sequel is briefly
told : " He tied them all together, and putting them on his
back like a truss of straw, brought them to the church of the
brethren saying ' Since I am not allowed to hurt anyone,
what on earth am I to do with these ? ' "[1]

(e)—Other Colonies.

There were various other large colonies near Alexandria
and along the lower Nile. At Arsinoe a thousand hermits
were settled under the guidance of the priest, Serapion, who
" taught all to earn provisions by their labours, and to provide
for others who were poor. During harvest time, they busied
themselves reaping for pay ; they set aside sufficient corn
for their own use, and shared it with the rest of the monks."[2]
In the Thebaid the distinguished ascetic Or held the leadership of another large group. When a newcomer arrived,
the older ascetics helped him to build his cell, some cutting
wood, others carrying bricks or spreading the mud.[3]

The life in all these colonies was exceedingly simple. There
was one meal at the sixth or ninth hour,[4] never before, except
when visitors arrived on days free from fast.[5] Some took
no food till sundown ; others only once in several days,[6]
but excess in fasting was not held to favour virtue.[7] The
customary allowance of bread was two hard-baked biscuits,
weighing between them about a pound, for every day.[8]
Cassian describes a "most sumptuous" Sunday repast—

[1] *H.L.*, 19.
[2] Soz., *H.E.*, vi, 28.
[3] *H.M.*, 2.
[4] *Conl.* ii, 25 ff ; xxi, 11.
[5] *Inst.* v, 24.
[6] *Conl.* ii, 17.
[7] *Inst.* v, 19.
[8] *Conl.* ii, 16.

the height of luxury in the desert—where each received a vegetable mess with a liberal amount of oil and salt, three olives, five grains of parched vetches, two prunes, and a fig.[1] Sleep was restricted to a couple of hours before dawn. The older and more experienced brethren guided the younger with kindness and sympathy,[2] whilst all worked with their hands, and spent long hours in prayer.

In general it may be said that according to the semi-eremitical system, every ascetic was left very much to his own devices. There was no authoritative government, though many of the elders enjoyed widespread influence, owing to their acknowledged sanctity and greater spiritual wisdom. Ill-balanced enthusiasts could fall easily into extravagances, and just as easily abandon the ascetical life altogether when extreme fervour was followed by extreme desolation. Private conferences of two or more, on Holy Scripture and progress in spirit, were frequently held; and there were greater conferences on occasion. A broad hint or a stern rebuke from an elderly ascetic was the usual corrective for abuses. Thus the organisation was loose, and the union between the parts so haphazard that intense individualism was very largely the rule.

[1] *Conl.* viii, 1.
[2] *Conl.* ii, 13.

CHAPTER II

CENOBITISM; OR MONASTICISM IN THE STRICT SENSE

Historia Lausiaca ; Historia Monachorum ; Cassian : *Instituta* and
Conlationes ; Sozomen : *H.E. ;* Sulpicius Severus : *Dialogues I ;*
Vita Pachomii and *Apophthegmata* as in Chap. i, § 7.
Amélineau : *Etude historique sur S. Pakhôme et le cénobitisme primitif.*
Cairo, 1887. *Histoire de S. Pakhôme.* Paris, 1889.
Grützmacher : *Pachomius u. das älteste Klosterleben.* Freiburg i. Br.
1896.
Ladeuze : *Etude sur le eénobitisme pakhomien pendant le IVe siècle.*
Louvain, 1898.
Schiwietz : *Das morgenländische Mönchtum I.* Mainz, 1904.
W. E. Crum : *Theological Texts from Coptic Papyri. Anec. Oxon. XII.*
Oxford, 1913.
Th. Lefort : *La règle de S. Pachôme. Le Muséon XXXIV*, p. 60 ff.
B. Albers : *S. Pachomii abbatis Tabennensis regulae monasticae.*
Bonn, 1922.
Hengstenberg : *Pachomiana* Festgabe Alb. Ehrhard. Bonn, 1922.

§1—PACHOMIUS

IN the heart of Upper Egypt, more than three hundred
miles south of Pispir, and five hundred miles south of
the Nitrian desert, the monastic system reached complete
development under St. Pachomius. The future patriarch
was born of pagan parents near Latopolis,[1] and was pressed
into service in Constantine's army when still in early manhood.
Whilst marching through the town just mentioned, he was
befriended by the local Christians, who practised the second
great commandment of their Faith by bestowing food and
drink on the weary soldiers.[2] Pachomius was struck by their
example, and resolved at once to imitate it. Constantine's
victories enabled him to obtain a speedy release from the
army. He hurried back to Chenoboskion in the upper Thebaid,
and after some elementary instruction, was baptized in the
village church. Hearing soon of Palaemon, who guided a
group of anchorites in the neighbourhood, he set forth to

---

[1] *Vita Pach.*, 77.
[2] *Vita Pach.*, 1–3.

join him.   Soon, however, Pachomius felt himself called—
report said, by a voice from Heaven—to build a cell of his
own some distance off, in a deserted village called Tabennisi
on the east bank of the Nile.[1]   Palaemon assisted his disciple
in carrying this proposal into effect, and the two parted—
Palaemon to return to his hermitage, Pachomius to embark
on his providential mission.

Unlike all former directors of ascetical groups (save one,
Aotas, whose effort was a failure)[2] Pachomius determined that
those who placed themselves under his guidance should be
subject to his authority, live, as far as possible, under one
roof, and observe one and the same rule.   It was the beginning
of common life and of monasticism in the strict sense.[3]

The innovation was criticised, but its success was immediate
and lasting. Pachomius had soon more than a hundred monks
under his command.[4]   When the space available at Tabennisi
became congested, a new monastery was built at Peboou,[5]
three or four miles to the north, and likewise on the right
bank of the Nile.   One of the hermit groups at Chenoboskion
embraced, in a body, the Pachomian Rule, and transformed
their settlement into a monastery, with the aid of monks
from Tabennisi and Peboou.[6]   Communities were likewise
formed at Temouschous,[7] on the western bank of the Nile,
and at Thebeu,[8] where the superior, Petroniu‑, enriched the
association by bestowing upon it all the possessions of his
family.   By A.D. 328 the fame of the new Order had reached
the ears of St. Athanasius at Alexandria.   Before the death
of Pachomius, in May, 346, four other communities had been
formed, three at or near Akhmin,[9] some sixty miles north of
Tabennisi, and the fourth at Latopolis,[10] about an equal
distance south of the same monastery.

A part only of the Rule was committed to writing, nor was
the Rule static from the beginning, but changed from time

[1] *Vita Pach.*, 7.
[2] *Vita Pach.*, 77.
[3] Μοναστήριον (Monastery) means, properly speaking, a place where
one lives alone, not a place where many live together ; though the latter
is the sense which it traditionally bears. The correct word for a place of this
kind would be Κοινόβιον.
[4] *Vita Pach.*, 18.
[5] Ibid., 52.
[6] Ibid., 35.
[7] Ibid.
[8] Ibid., 50.
[9] Ibid., 51.
[10] Ibid., 52, 78.

to time, according as experience showed that this or the other
prescription could be improved upon.[1] Many detailed letters
on points of discipline or administration were sent by Pachomius
to the heads of monasteries.[2] Hence it is easy to understand
that numerous divergences should appear in the Rule, as
later transmitted.[3] Study of the diverse editions has not
advanced far enough as yet to allow of a decision as to what
exactly was the practice in the founder's day, and what was
added under his early successors. What purported to be the
original Rule, written in Coptic, and rendered into Greek
for brethren acquainted with that language only, was translated into Latin by St. Jerome in A.D. 404. This is the most
complete and faithful record we possess of the Pachomian
observance, such as it existed in the latter part of the fourth
century. As it agrees perfectly with what we know from other
sources of Pachomian institutions, there can be little doubt
but that it represents very substantially the teaching and
legislation of Pachomius himself.[4]

§2—The Pachomian Constitution in Detail

Each monastery, according to this Rule, was surrounded by
a wall[5] ; within this were a church,[6] a general meeting place,[7]
a refectory,[8] a library,[9] a store-room for clothes,[10] kitchen
and larder,[11] bakery,[12] infirmary,[13] blacksmith's, tanner's,
carpenter's, fuller's and shoemaker's shops.[14] One monastery
might contain as many as thirty or forty houses,[15] with from
twenty-two to forty monks in each.[16] In the houses every
monk had his own small cell,[17] and there was a large room

---

[1] Ibid., 10, 16, 17, etc.
[2] Ibid., 63.
[3] Cf. Dom Bruno Albers, op.c., p. 1–7.
[4] Ladeuze, op. c., p. 272.
[5] *Regulae*, P.L., xxiii, 84. Albers, l.c., 50.
[6] *Reg. Praef.*, Alb. 3,
[7] *Reg.*, 1. Alb., 6.
[8] *Reg.*, 28. Alb., 14.
[9] *Reg.*, 82, 100.. Alb. 59.
[10] *Reg.*, 49, etc. Alb., 29.
[11] *Reg.*, 41. Alb., 23.
[12] Cf. *H.L.*, 32.,
[13] *Reg.* 42, 43. Alb., 24.
[14] *Reg.*, 111, 112. Alb., 63. Cf. *H.L.*, 32.
[15] *Reg. Praef.*, 2. Alb., p. 10
[16] *Ep. Ammon.*, 4, 11. *Reg. Praef.*
[17] *Reg.*, 88, 89, 112, 114. Alb., 64–5.

where the brethren could assemble on occasion.[1] Near the
door of the monastery stood a guesthouse, where visitors,
particularly clerics and monks, were to be received with
kindliness and honour.[2] For women a special place was
reserved, far removed from the habitations of the other sex.[3]
The monastery, too, had its vegetable garden, from which
nobody was allowed to abstract anything without leave.[4]

Over all the monasteries stood the Archimandrite or
Superior-General ($\pi\alpha\tau\eta\rho$, $\check{\alpha}\beta\beta\alpha\varsigma$),[5] who appointed the provosts
(praepositi), or local Superiors, transferred them or their
subjects from one house to another when he thought fit,
and visited their communities at intervals for purposes of
supervision.[6] On his deathbed or earlier he nominated
his successor.[7] Local Superiors as well of monasteries as
of houses, were helped by seconds, who took command when
they happened to be absent.[8] Three or four houses formed
a tribe,[9] over which one of the house superiors presided.[10]
The monks were divided into houses, as far as possible
according to their work.[11] Twice a year, at Easter and on August
13th, there was a general re-union of all the brethren at
Peboou; at Easter to celebrate the grandest of Christian
festivals together like one great family; in August to discuss
questions of temporal interest.[12] Local administrators here
rendered an account to the Economus Generalis ($\mu\acute{\epsilon}\gamma\alpha\varsigma$ $o\acute{\iota}\kappa o\nu\acute{o}\mu o\varsigma$),
the chief steward or business manager of the brotherhood.
Those who had any complaints to make could voice them to
the Superior-General; the Rule and the manner of applying
it could be discussed; changes made, if necessary, in the
personnel of the various houses; instructions delivered on
points of doctrine and of discipline.[13] The proceedings ended
with a striking scene of mutual reconciliation, when the offences,
great and small, that had marred the harmony of community
life during the year were repented of anew, and the monks

---

[1] *Reg.*, 181. Alb., 100.
[2] *Reg.*, 50. Alb., 30. *Vita.*, 19.
[3] *Reg.*, 51. Alb., 31.
[4] *Reg.*, 73. Alb., 41. Cf. *H.L.*, 32.
[5] *Reg. Praef.*, 7. Alb., 4.
[6] *Vita. Pach.*, 52, etc.
[7] *Vita Pach.*, 74, 75 ff.
[8] *Reg.*, 8, 152-4. Alb., 5, 121-7. *Vita Pach.*, 19. *Doctr. Orsisii*, 18.
[9] *Reg. Praef.*, 2. Alb., p. 10. *Reg.*, 16.
[10] *Reg.*, 115. *Vita Pach.*, 19.
[11] *Reg. Praef.*, 6. Alb., p. 10.
[12] *Reg. Praef.*, 7, 8. *Reg.*, 27. Alb., 4. *Vita Pach.*, 52.
[13] Ibid.

placed under solemn obligation to forgive and forget.[1] Thus every effort was made to preserve peace, good-will, and unity within the congregation.

Novices were received at all ages and from every rank and condition of life ; slaves, however, only with the consent of their masters[2] ; and priests only on the understanding that they were to submit absolutely to monastic discipline, despite the respect which had, of necessity, to be shown them because of their high order.[3] Those alone were excluded who had contracted habits of crime, and were therefore incapable of observing the Rule ; or at least required special surveillance. Candidates were kept some days outside the door of the monastery, under the care of the porters, who taught them prayers, psalms, and the elementary duties of the monastic profession. At the end of some days the candidate, if judged suitable, was relieved of his secular dress and clothed in the monastic costume ; after which he was conducted by a porter to join the brethren at prayer.[4] There was no noviceship, properly so called, but the newcomer was placed under the care of a senior monk, who watched over his conduct and gave him various select exercises to perform. If he failed in these, and if his behaviour on the whole was unsatisfactory, he was dismissed by the Superior.[5] Otherwise he became in time an ordinary member of the monastic community, without, it would seem, binding himself by vow to observe the primary obligations of his state. Two of these obligations, poverty and chastity, remained as for the anchorites ; a third, obedience, was peculiar to the new institute.

All Pachomian monks were dressed alike, each in a sleeveless linen tunic that descended a little below the knees, and was secured by a girdle of linen or leather. Over the tunic was worn a kind of cloak (μηλωτή) made of tanned sheepskin or goatskin. Round the neck was a cape (κουκούλλιον) to which was attached a hood, that could be drawn over the head.[6] On the back of this was a sign (e.g., a red cross), indicating the monastery and house to which the wearer belonged.[7] Ordinarily the monks went barefoot, but they were provided

---

[1] Ibid. Alb., 4. *Ep. Pachomii*, vii.
[2] *Reg.*, 49. Alb., 29.
[3] *Vita Pach.*, 18.
[4] *Reg.*, 49. Alb., 29. Cassian : *Inst.* iv, 5.
[5] Cf. Ladeuze, op. cit., p. 281–2.
[6] *Reg. Praef.*, 4. *Reg.*, 2. Alb., 1.
[7] *Reg.*, 99.

with sandals when they travelled.[1] Then also they carried a stick or staff.[2] Two outfits were allowed to each, but that which was not in actual use had to be kept in the common clothes-room, under the charge of one of the brethren.[3] He who lost an article of clothing received a severe penance, and had to wait more than three weeks before the garment was replaced.[4]

Prayers were held in common every morning at dawn,[5] possibly also at midday, and certainly at sundown, when the members of each house gathered once more for " six prayers and psalms "[6] before they retired to rest. After a few hours' sleep the whole monastery was roused for the midnight service.[7] The Superior of the settlement presided at these gatherings,[8] and the monks assisted in cape and mantle,[9] but not in sandals.[10] Those working far away in the fields and those on journeys observed the hours of prayer as if they were present in the monastery.[11] On Saturdays and Sundays, Mass was celebrated with much solemnity, and Holy Communion was distributed to the brethren.[12] Private prayer and meditation on things divine was expected never to cease.[13]

Spiritual instruction was given by each " house " Superior to his subjects twice a week, on the two fast days[14] ; and by the head of the monastery to his whole flock once on Saturday, and twice on Sunday.[15] It was obligatory for the monks to be present at these instructions, and to hear them out to the end.[16] There was a general regulation that anyone who fell asleep while they were being delivered should be waked at once and compelled to stand until the speaker made a sign to him to sit.[17] Pachomius was accustomed to address his monks on such subjects as prayer, meditation, passages from

---

[1] *Reg.*, 61, 81, 101.
[2] *Reg.* 81. Alb., 1.
[3] *Reg.*, 66, 72. *Vita Pach.*, 38.
[4] *Reg.*, 131. Alb., 75.
[5] *Reg.*, 20. Alb., 11.
[6] *Reg.*, 24, 121, 155. Alb., 105. *Vita. Pach.*, 39.
[7] *Reg.*, 10. Alb., 6.
[8] *Reg.*, 8. Alb., 5.
[9] *Reg.*, 91.
[10] *Reg.*, 101.
[11] *Reg.*, 142. Alb., 77.
[12] *Reg.*,14–9. Alb., 9. Cf. *H.L.*, 32.
[13] *Reg.*, 3, 28, 36, etc. Alb., 14, 19, etc.
[14] *Reg.*, 115, 138.
[15] *Vita Pach.*, 19.
[16] *Reg.*, 21, 23. Alb., 11, 13.
[17] *Reg.*, 22. Alb., 12.

Holy Writ, the Incarnation, the Passion and the Resurrection of Christ.[1] Ammon, who entered Peboou as a novice a few years after the death of Pachomius, gives a detailed account of such a gathering. The Superior-General Theodore presided, and the assembly was held under a palm-tree. First came a long confession of faults, each of the monks in turn rising and accusing himself of offences against the Rule. Penalties proportionate to the faults confessed were inflicted by the President. Then Theodore gave an instruction, taking as his theme the persecution then being suffered by the Church at the hands of Arians. When this had ended, a number of the brethren exposed to him their difficulties about certain aspects of the spiritual life, and certain points of the Rule. Theodore answered to their satisfaction, and his words were translated into Greek for the monks who knew no Coptic. Finally the Superior-General gave all his blessing, and the brethren separated,[2] to discuss in groups, as was their custom, the doctrine they had just heard, and afterwards to meditate upon it.[3] Great importance was attached to the study of the Scriptures, and all were expected to know goodly portions of them by heart.[4] Twenty psalms or two epistles of St. Paul are mentioned as a beginner's lesson.[5] Those who entered the monastery illiterate had to learn to read. They received lessons at the first, third, and sixth hours,[6] also the necessary books or rolls, which they had to put back in a special place each evening,[7] that poverty might be duly observed.

Work, too, was part of the general observance for all. It began in the early morning after prayer[8] and proceeded with vigour and despatch, for it was magnificently organised.[9] The most common occupation was the weaving of Nile rushes into mats and baskets, but numbers were set aside for special work in the kitchen, refectory, infirmary, and workshops.[10] The general service for the Community was performed for a week by each house in turn ; with assistance from another

---

[1] Vita Pach., 37.
[2] Ep. Ammon., 2–4.
[3] Cf. Vita Pach., 79. Reg., 20, 122, 138. Alb., 11, 71.
[4] Reg., 13, 49. Alb., 29. Cf. H.L., 32.
[5] Reg., 139. Alb., 77.
[6] Ib.
[7] Reg.,100. Alb., 59.
[8] Reg., 5, 25.
[9] Reg., 58–66. Vita Pach., 50, 68, 81.
[10] Reg., 33, 40, 49, 51, etc. Alb., 17, 22, 29, 30, etc. Cf. H.L., 32. Vita Pach., 19.

D

house of the same tribe, if the number available in the first was insufficient.[1] As time went on, and more and more of the land belonging to the monasteries was reclaimed for tillage, the annual produce of the monks' labours became enormous. What remained over after the needs of the numerous houses had been provided for was carried to neighbouring towns or to Alexandria[2] by specially selected brethren and sold in the open markets. Within the life-time of the founder, the congregation had two ships on the Nile for transport purposes.[3] When a monk made use of exceptional business talent to drive a particularly hard bargain, Pachomius was profoundly shocked ; he penalised the culprit and dismissed him from his office, after having ordered him to refund his ill-gotten gains. On another occasion, however, when a monk sold too cheaply to an intimate merchant friend, he compelled him to return and receive current market value for his wares. As the congregations hoarded nothing, their earnings were given to the poor, and, above all, to the famine stricken.[4] Pachomius esteemed work, not only as a necessary means of self-support, but also as the most natural and the most healthy of ascetical exercises. When properly carried out it could be a very meritorious form of divine service. Talk and laughter during work were therefore strictly forbidden ; rather should the monks pray, meditate, or chant psalms while they laboured. When communication with one another was for any reason necessary, it should be carried on by signs and briefly, that the mind might not cease to busy itself with higher thoughts.[5] Despite all precautions, however, the advance in wealth grew in time to be excessive, and the consequences were soon felt in a threatened schism within the congregation.

At Tabennisi and the other Pachomian monasteries there were two meals daily, the first about noon,[6] the second in the evening.[7] Many of the monks came to one meal only. Others found even this too sumptuous and remained in their cells, where a repast consisting of bread, water and salt, was carried to them.[8] There was no reading in the refectory during meals, but silence was observed,[9] and each had to keep the hood

---

[1] *Reg.*, 15. *Vita Pach.*, 19.
[2] *Vita Pach.*, 73.
[3] *Vita Pach.*, 73. *Reg.*, 118, 119. Alb., 68.
[4] *Vita Pach.*, 9, 27.
[5] *Reg.*, 59, 60, 68. Alb., 37. *Vita Pach.*, 57.
[6] *Reg. Praef.*, 5. Alb., 2. *Vita Pach.*, 43.
[7] *Reg. Praef.*, 5. Alb., 2. *Vita Pach.*, 49.
[8] *Reg. Praef.*, 5. *Reg.*, 80. Alb., 2, 47.
[9] *Reg.*, 31. Alb., 15. *Inst.*, IV. 17. H.M. 3

drawn well forward over his head so that he might not see what his neighbour was eating.[1] The tendency to reduce the amount of food consumed to the minimum was very marked[2] ; yet excessive asceticism in this respect was discouraged, as experience showed that it made monks unfit for devotions and still more unfit for work.[3] Bread, cheese, herbs, charlock, preserved olives and fruit were the chief articles of food.[4] Meat and wine[5] were expressly forbidden. Every three days sweetmeats of some kind (τραγήματα; dulciamina) were distributed to the monks as they left the refectory[6] ; otherwise they might retain nothing in the nature of food in their cells.[7] On fast days, such as Wednesday and Friday outside of the Paschal season,[8] the mid-day meal was dropped[9] ; and during Lent the use of uncooked food seems to have been common, whilst some ate only at intervals of two or more days.[10]

The monks slept, each in his own cell,[11] on the bare ground or on a mat[12] or sitting on a bench with back leaning against the wall.[13] Profound silence was prescribed during the period (from " the six prayers " to midnight : some five or six hours) set aside for rest.[14] Those who wished might spend all or part of his time in vigils[15] but the doors of the cells had to be left open, that Superiors, should they care to go the rounds, might see for themselves how their subjects were behaving.[16] During the intolerable summer heat, the monks might sleep on the roofs.[17]

For the sick a special house or infirmary was provided,[18] with clothing, food and service to suit the invalids' needs.[19] As most cases of illness were due to excessive physical labour and excessive concentration at prayer[20], they were cured easily by short spells of warmth and good food. Wine and meat[21] were thus used freely in the infirmary kitchen. Promiscuous visits

[1] *Reg.*, 29, 30. Alb., 15.   [2] *H.M.*, 3.
[3] *Ep. Ammon.*, 13.   [4] *Vita Pach.*, 35. Cf. *H.L.*. 32.
[5] *Vita Pach.*, 34. *Reg.*, 45. Alb., 25.   [6] *Reg.*, 39. Alb., 19.
[7] *Reg.*, 114. Alb., 65.
[8] *Reg. Praef.*, 5. Alb., 2. *Vita Pach.*. 19.
[9] *Ep. Ammon.*, 13.   [10] *H.L.*, 18.
[11] *Reg.*, 126.
[12] *Reg.*, 88. Cf. *Arabic Life of Pach. Annales du Musée Guimet.* xvii, p 605, and Alb., p. 33.
[13] *Heraclidis Parad.*, 3. Alb., p. 65. *H.L.*, 32.
[14] *Reg.*, 126.   [15] *Vita Pach.*, 67.
[16] *Reg.*, 107.   [17] *Reg.* 87.
[18] *Reg.*, 42. Alb., 24   [19] *Reg. Praef.*, 5. Alb., 2.
[2] *Reg.*, 45. Alb., 25.   [21] *Vita Pach.*, 34.

to the sick were not allowed, but leave was readily granted
where the patient was in a condition to receive company.[1]
Should a monk die of illness a requiem service was held beside
the remains.[2]   On the following day the body was wrapped
in linen, and, when Mass had been offered for the soul of the
deceased,[3] borne to the graveyard with chant of psalms and
hymns.   From this procession nobody might absent himself,
without express permission[4] ; even the sick were encouraged
to be present, special helpers being appointed to accompany
them on the way.[5]

Human nature remains human, and therefore peccable,
even within the monastery, and Pachomius was compelled
to encourage the observance of his rule by inflicting penalties
on transgressors.   Those guilty of a breach of silence, of
unseemly laughter or of unpunctuality at the gatherings for
prayer, were condemned to stand with lowered head before
the altar and to receive a reprimand from the presiding
Superior.[6]   The latter punishment was repeated afterwards
in the refectory.   He who came late to meals had not only
to endure humiliation, but to return foodless to his cell.[7]
More serious cases were dealt with by the Superior of the
monastery.[8]   He who constantly gave way to anger was
degraded to the lowest place in the assemblies[9] ; murmurers
were sent to join the sick in the infirmary[10] ; detractors
received seven days on bread and water[11] ; whilst thieves[12]
and perverters of souls[13] were helped to repentance by the
vigorous application of the whip.   All other means failing,
the offender was expelled.[14]

Pachomius not only inaugurated monasteries, properly
so called, for men, but also monasteries for women.   The first
of these settlements, near Tabennisi, was placed under the
direction of his sister, Mary[15] ; later a community was formed
in the neighbourhood of Tismenae, and another near Peboou.[16]
The rule observed in these was similar to that of the Pachomian
monasteries for men.   An aged and discreet monk was appoint-

[1] Reg., 42, 47. Alb., 24, 27.   [2] Vita Pach., 75, 95.
[3] Vita Pach., 65.   [4] Reg., 127.
[5] Reg., 129.   [6] Reg., 8. Alb., 5.
[7] Reg., 31 Alb., 16.   [8] Reg., 151. Alb., 118.
[9] Reg., 161. Alb., 82.   [10] Reg., 164. Alb., 85.
[11] Reg., 160. Alb., 81.   [12] Reg., 149. Alb., 120.
[13] Reg., 163. Alb., 84. Inst., iv, 16.
[14] Ep. Ammon., 12, 16. Inst., iv, 16.
[15] Vita Pach., 22.   [16] Vita Pach., 86.

ed to instruct the nuns, especially in Holy Scripture.[1] Building work required by the women was performed by the monks, but under conditions of separation so strict that the monks had to return for meals. Palladius describes one of the monasteries for women seen by him as situated on the far bank of the Nile opposite the monastery for men. " So when a virgin dies the other virgins, having prepared her body for burial, act as bearers and lay it on the river bank. But the brethren, having crossed in a ferry boat, with palm leaves and olive branches, take the body across, singing psalms the while, and bury it in their own cemetery. But apart from the priest and deacon, and they only on Sunday, no man goes across to the women's monastery."[2]

Not only Copts, or native Egyptians, but Latins, Greeks, and other foreigners were found in the Pachomian monasteries.[3] So numerous were these at Peboou that a special house was assigned to them with an Alexandrian at its head.[4] The monks of the Thebaid, all told, numbered five or seven thousand[5] at the beginning of the fifth century. Palladius, who dwelt in this region from A.D. 406 to A.D. 412, is responsible for the latter estimate.[6] According to his account the normal monastery contained from 200 to 300 monks,[7] but Peboou was of abnormal size, with 1,300 or 1,400 brethren.[8] In his time, too, a three years' probation seems to have been a preliminary to admission ; the numbers had so grown that two or three had to live in one cell ; bedsteads had been introduced ; and stranger monks were not allowed to associate with the community.[9] Experience may have proved the last named regulation to be desirable, but it marked a departure from the founder's practice.[10] His relations with other monks were remarkably friendly and cordial.[11] They were welcomed to the guest house, comforted with various small services, like the washing of the feet, and invited to join the brethren in the offices of common prayer.[12] For Anthony Pachomius

[1] *Vita Pach.*, 22.
[2] *H.L.*, 33.
[3] *Reg. Praef.*, 1, 2. Alb., p. 9, 10..
[4] *Ep. Ammon.*, 4.
[5] 5,000, Cass., *Inst.*, iv, 1.
[6] *H.L.*, 32.
[7] Ibid.
[8] 1,300 *H.L.*, 32 ; 1,400, *H.L*. 18.
[9] *H.L.*, 32.
[10] *Vita Pach.*, 28.
[11] Ibid.
[12] *Reg.*, 50. Alb., 30

had unbounded esteem[1] and the feeling was reciprocated by the great anchorite.[2] With the monks of Nitria,
too, the Tabennesiots had sympathetic intercourse.[3]

Thus the leading idea of the Pachomian rule was to establish
a fixed minimum of observance which would be obligatory
upon all.   Physical discomfort was not greater than the
average child of Adam could bear, given goodwill and a reasonable degree of bodily health.   In cold weather permission
to light a fire might be conceded.[4] Nor were visits to and
from relations entirely discountenanced, provided precautions
were taken to preserve both vocation and recollection.[5]
Greater austerity of life was permitted, and even recommended,
to those who had strength and zeal enough to undertake
it ; always, however, without prejudice to obedience.[6] The
last named virtue acquired, indeed, in monasticism an
importance that had never before been attached to it in the
ascetical life.   Remarkable in the Pachomian institute is
the highly centralized system of government characteristic
of a fully organised congregation or order.   Though general
chapters were regularly held, their function seems to have
been merely advisory ; supreme power remained, in fact
as well as in theory, in the hands of a single Superior. Remarkable, too, is the prominence given to work.   Amongst the
anchorites this was of a sedentary kind (mostly the weaving
of osiers into baskets, or of thread into linen) and its purpose
was to supply the necessaries of life, or to fill in time not
occupied with contemplation or spiritual reading.   In the
Pachomian monasteries it was undertaken for its own sake
as an ascetical exercise ; it was strenuous in form (tillage
and various laborious trades), and it alternated with prayer
and psalmody in the busy routine of the lengthy day. Not,
however, in such wise as to hinder devotion, for in profound
realisation of divine truth and in unbroken communion with
God, often high and mystical in its intimacy, the monks of
Egypt set an example from which the faithful since have
never ceased to profit.

---

[1] *Vita Pach.*, 87.
[2] *Vita Pach.*, 77.
[3] *Ep. Ammon.*, 22.
[4] *Reg.*, 5, 23, 120. Alb., 13, 69. *Vita Pach.*, 39.
[5] *Reg.*, 53, 55, etc. Alb., 33, 35, etc.
[6] *Reg.*, 3, 11, 23, 30, etc. Alb., 7, 13, 15, etc.

§3—THE "WHITE MONASTERY" AT ATRIPE. SCHENOUDI.

Amélineau : *Mémoires publiés par les membres de la mission archéolo-*
    gique française au Caire. T. IV, pp. 1–91, 229–46, 277–87, 633–49.
Zoega : *Catalogus Codicum Copt.,* 212, 230.
Leipoldt : *Sinathii archimandritae vita et opera. Corp. Script. orient.*
    Zweite Reihe. Bd. II. Leipzig, 1906–13.
Amélineau : *Vie de Schnoudi.* Paris, 1889.
Ladeuze : *Etude sur le cénobitisme pakhômien.* Louvain, 1898. P. 209, ff.
Leipoldt : Schenute von Atripe. Leipzig, 1903.
Leclercq : *Dict d'arch. chrêt.* T. II, col. 3104–8.
Workman : *The Evolution of the Monastic Ideal.* London, 1913.
    P. 353, ff.
Mackean : *Christian Monasticism in Egypt.* London, 1920. P. 110, ff.

West of the Nile, on a ridge of the Libyan chain, hard by
the ruined village of Atripe near Akhmin, an imposing building like a fortress may still be seen.[1] The edifice was, however,
erected for purposes of spiritual rather than of temporal
warfare, since it is no other than the *Deir-el-Abiad,* or " White
Monastery" of Schenoudi. An anchorite named Bgoul had
settled on this spot towards the middle of the fourth century,
and when disciples gathered round him had transformed
them into a monastic community after the example of
Pachomius. After his death about A.D 385, he was succeeded
by his nephew Schenoudi, a man of great zeal, iron will and
exceptional capacity for affairs. The community counted
then some thirty members, but under Schenoudi's rule the
numbers grew into hundreds ; new buildings had to be erected
to shelter them, and a large church wherein they could pray ;
a convent also in the neighbourhood, for women desirous of
living under the abbot's direction.[2]

Though the manner of life in the White Monastery was
essentially Pachomian, there were a number of peculiar
features due to the irrepressibly strong personality of the ruler.
In the first place the observance was much more rigorous
than among the Tabennesiots.[3] One meal a day was deemed
sufficient for all,[4] but the dining hour—noon or eventide
—was left to individual choice.[5] Pachomius was content
with a tacit undertaking on the part of his monks to observe
the rule ; Schenoudi, on the contrary, required a solemn

[1] *Mém.,* 5, ff.
[2] *Mém.,* 230, ff, 331.
[3] *Ibid.*
[4] *Mém.,* 8, etc.
[5] *Mém.,* 267, 281.

declaration in writing and before witnesses.[1]   Above all,
Schenoudi, unlike Pachomius, did not consider common
life in the monastery as the highest form of asceticism, but
allowed fervent monks of approved virtue to retire to the
desert, where they might practise unhindered the austerities
traditional among anchorites.[2] The gardener of the monastery
was deputed to provide vegetables for their sustenance.[3]
Four times a year—at least at a later date—they returned
to the company of the brethren for a short period. Schenoudi
himself made a prolonged retreat in a desert grotto at frequent
intervals.[4] His absence, it is to be feared, was not regretted
overmuch in the monastery, for his government was of the
sternest kind ; when reprimand or imprisonment did not
produce the desired amendment, he had recourse readily
to the scourge, and plied it with merciless vigour.[5] In fact
a letter is still extant, directed to the Superioress of his nuns,
in which he commands her to inflict with her own hand blows
with a rod, varying from ten to thirty in number, on twelve
of her erring nuns.[6]

Administration so harsh defeated its own end, for it provoked
disaffection.   Insubordination was a common failing among
Schenoudi's subjects.   We hear, too, of monks who left the
monastery, without leave, some to converse with old
companions who had been expelled for misconduct ; of others
who feigned illness in order to receive the comforts of the
infirmary ; of others still, whose fastidiousness in dress would
have been ridiculous, even in worldlings ; and finally, of
jealousy and tale-bearing among the brethren.[7] But the great
majority seem to have been men of virtue who, beneath the
ruthlessness of their abbot, could discern his real gifts—his
eloquence, zeal for souls, sympathy with the poor,[8] and his
energy in the overthrow of paganism [9] It is noteworthy,
that in his congregation, the names of the dead were preserved
on a special tablet, and their memory was held in special
honour.[10] This distinguished Archimandrite (as he was called)

[1] Mém., 234.
[2] Mém., 20, 65, 75, 637.
[3] Ladeuze, op. cit., p. 212.
[4] Leipoldt, Schen. von A., p. 68.
[5] Leipoldt, op. cit., 140–45.
[6] Leipoldt, op. cit., 147–53.
[7] Leclercq, op. cit., col. 3107.
[8] Mém., 18, 42, 242, etc.
[9] Mém., 45, 66, 238, etc.
[10] Mém., 278.

ruled his monastery for some sixty years, since his death did not occur until about A.D. 451,[1] when, if the account given in his *Life* be true, he had attained the age of 118 years. A certain violence of character and passion in the application of his rule marred the effectiveness of his work during life and left his system bereft of attractiveness when his commanding personality had been removed by death.[2]

§4—OTHER EGYPTIAN MONASTERIES

Historia Monachorum. Cassian : *Instituta* and *Conlationes*, as in
    Chap. i, § 7.
St Jerome : Epis. 22. *C.S.E.L.*, vol. LIV, p. 146, ff.
Leclercq : Op. cit., col. 3129–3136.
Workman and Mackean as in § 3.

Formed on the Pachomian model, though independent, like Atripe, of the Pachomian congregation, was a large monastery near Hermopolis, founded by an ascetic named Apollo, who had lived for many years as a solitary in a cave.[3] His monks in time numbered five hundred. They had a common table, and but one refection a day after the hour of noon. Following the earlier custom of the Church, they celebrated Mass and partook of the Holy Eucharist just before this meal, but they advanced beyond the practice of the Christian past by offering up the Holy Sacrifice every day. They treated visitors with unusual honour, for they went out in a body to meet them, singing psalms and greeting them with obeisance and embrace. Then some of the monks formed up in front, others behind, the singing recommenced and the visitors were led in procession to the abbot. When he, too, had given proofs of welcome, the visitors' feet were washed and they were invited to refresh their wearied bodies with food and repose. Here, as elsewhere, the brethren were keen students of Holy Scripture. Their manner of life was austere, but joy was a characteristic of their community.[4]

Monasteries, Pachomian in form but more loose in their organisation, are also found in the neighbourhood of the Delta.[5] The trial of candidates for admission was here unusually

---

[1] Leipoldt, op. cit., 41, ff. Ladeuze, op. cit., 241 ff.
[2] Leclercq, op. cit., col. 3108.
[3] *H.M.*, 8.
[4] *H.M.*, 8.
[5] *Inst.*, v, 36 ; iv, 1 ; iv, 30, *Conl.*, xiv, 4 ; xix, 1 ; xx, 1. Soz. *H.E.*, vi, 29.

strict. They were deprived of all money on arrival and then kept for ten days outside the monastery door, where they fell on their knees before each monk who passed, and asked his leave to enter.[1] If their constancy withstood this test, they were given the monastic habit by the abbot[2]; they were then deputed to aid the *senior* or elderly brother who had charge of strangers and chance callers. When a year had been spent in humble services under his orders they were transferred in groups of ten to other *seniors* whose duty it was to form them specifically for their new profession.[3] This they did chiefly by systematic exercises, designed to curb and crush the disorderly passions of youth—above all the passions of sensuality and self-will.[4] Once the period of training was complete they were received into the ranks of the brethren, who were arranged, too, in groups of ten under leaders called *decani*, and in groups of a hundred under a higher officer.[5] Over the whole community was the abbot, who was selected from the most holy, humble and experienced *seniores*, and who was expected to have prepared himself for government in the hard school of obedience.[6] During the extreme heat of summer or the extreme cold of winter and during infirmity the monks wore sandals, which, however, they removed when approaching the altar to receive Holy Communion.[7] On journeys they carried a staff, like the just men of the Old Testament; but symbolically as a weapon against the dogs and invisible wild beasts of vice.[8] There were two, and only two,[9] gatherings for prayer daily, one in the early morning, the other towards nightfall. At each gathering twelve psalms and twelve prayers were recited, with two readings from Holy Writ.[10] As the monks were weary from fasts and vigils, they were allowed to sit on low stools made of reeds during these offices.[11] Mass was celebrated on Saturday and Sunday about 9 a.m.[12]; on the former day there was no fast,[13] whilst

[1] *Inst.*, iv, 3.
[2] *Inst.*, iv., 5.
[3] *Inst.*, iv, 7.
[4] *Inst.*, iv, 8. Cf. *Conl.*, xiv., 9.
[5] *St. Jer. Ep.*, 22, 35.
[6] *Inst.*, ii, 3.
[7] *Inst.*, i, 9.
[8] *Inst.*, i, 8.
[9] *Inst.*, iii, 2.
[10] *Inst.*, ii, 4, 6, ff iii, 2   *St. Jer. Ep.*, 22, 35.
[11] *Inst.*, ii, 12.
[12] *Inst.*, iii, 2.
[13] *Inst.*, iii, 9.

on the latter day work was discountenanced, meals were improved, and the time was spent wholly in prayer, meditation, and spiritual reading.[1]   On the other days of the week manual work was incessant.[2]   Whatever goods remained over after the needs of the community had been satisfied, were distributed among the poor and afflicted.[3]   A permanent cook was appointed in these monasteries,[4] though everywhere else in the Orient it was customary that this office should be filled by the brethren week by week in turn—with results which the epicure would shudder to contemplate.   It was part of the duty of the *oeconomus* or steward to taste the dishes when they had been cooked.[5]   Public penance was exacted for serious offences, especially for such as even remotely endangered chastity.[6]   Night vigils were practised ; and a monk on occasion went around putting his ear to the cell doors to discover what the occupants were doing.[7]   If they were negligent and slothful they were visited more frequently.

On the whole it must be said that the regime in these Egyptian monasteries was marked by moderation and that the government was considerate and mild.

---

[1] *Inst.*, iii, 11. Cf. *Conl.*, ii, 21.   *St. Jer. Ep.*, 22, 35.
[2] *Inst.*, ii, 12, 14, etc.
[3] *Conl.*, xviii, 7.
[4] *Inst.*, iv, 22.
[5] *St. Jer. Ep.*, 22, 35.
[6] *Inst.*, ii, 15.
[7] *St. Jer. Ep.*, 22, 35.

CHAPTER III

THE SPREAD OF MONASTICISM THROUGHOUT THE CHRISTIAN WORLD

St. Jerome : *Vita S. Hilarionis P.L. XXIII.* This life is semi-historical in character. Cf.
Winter : *Der literarische Charakter der Vita beati Hilarionis des Hieronymus.* Zittau, 1904.
Pesch: *Die Originalität und literarische Form der Mönchsbiographien des hl. Hieronymus.* München, 1910.
Zöckler : *Hilarion von Gaza. Neue Jahrbücher für deutsche Theol., III.* P. 146–78.
Sozomen : *Hist. Eccl.* Cf. Chap. 1, § 7. *Peregrinatio Sylviae C.S.E.L., XXXIX,* p. 35 ff. Eng. Transl. McClure and Feltoe : *The Pilgrimage of Etheria.* London, 1919.
Cassian : especially *Inst. II & III.* Cf. Chap. 1, § 7.
Cavallera : *S. Jérôme, sa vie et son oeuvre.* Louvain, 1922.
Card. Rampolla : *Santa Melania giuniore, Senatrice romana,* Rome, 1905.
Goyau : *Sainte Mélanie.* Paris, 1908.
Génier : *Vie de S. Euthyme le Grand* (377–473). Paris, 1909.
Schiwietz : *Das morgenländische Mönchtum.* Bd. II. Mainz, 1913.

§1—Its Progress in the East.

(a)—Palestine.

THE introduction of monasticism into Palestine is connected with the name of St. Hilarion, who was born of heathen parents, near Gaza, became a Christian during his student days at Alexandria, and retired for a while to the desert to live as an anchorite under St. Anthony. When he returned to his native district early in the fourth century, it was to continue his eremitical mode of life. After many years his place of retreat was discovered by admirers who insisted on becoming his disciples. These he directed as he had been directed himself by St. Anthony. In addition to the usual anachoretical austerities, which he zealously practised, he never washed his dress, on the plea that it was unreasonable to look for too great cleanliness in haircloth.[1] His settlements, despite their eremitical character, were missionary centres for the conversion of the pagan countryside.[2]

---

[1] *Vita Hil.,* 3–31.
[2] Soz. *H.E.,* v. 15.

In the " desert " or sterile lands about Jerusalem a number of lauras (λαῦραι) were established early in the fourth century. The direction in these was so systematic that it resembled cenobitical government, and the element of common life was greater than in the Antonian hermitages. There was, for example, a steward who assigned weekly tasks to each of the brethren, and saw that the tasks were fulfilled. In substance, however, the life was eremitical, for each lived in his own cell, and general re-unions were unknown, save on Saturdays and Sundays. The most famous of these settlements was that founded by the Armenian, St. Euthymius (died A.D. 473).[1] Noteworthy about this saint was his determination that only men tried in virtue should be allowed to attempt the semi-eremitical or laura life ; candidates not yet schooled in asceticism were sent for training to a neighbouring cenobium ruled by his friend, St. Theoctistus.[2]

The Holy City itself was at this time peopled by ascetics of all kinds.[3] Famous among its anchorites was Adolius of Tarsus, whose manner of life was superhuman, " so that the very demons, trembling at his austerity, dare not approach him."[4] By reason of his excessive abstinence and his vigils his physical appearance had become such that he was suspected by some of being a phantom.[5] Attracted by the fame of the Egyptian monks, Rufinus of Aquileia journeyed from Italy to visit them, and spent some years in company with the anchorites of Nitria and Cellia.[6] There, in A.D. 373, he met Melania the Elder, grand-daughter of a Consul, and representative of the very highest aristocracy in Rome, who had come to study Egyptian monasticism at first hand.[7] She later founded a monastery of the Pachomian type at Jerusalem, and ruled a community of fifty virgins till her death.[8] Rufinus established a monastery for men, mostly Latins like himself, on the Mount of Olives.[9] The copying of books seems to have been their chief work.[10] Meanwhile Rufinus was of the greatest assistance to Melania as spiritual

---

[1] *Vie de S. Euthyme*, p. 10, ff.
[2] Ib., p. 11, 244–5.
[3] *Peregr. Syl. passim.*
[4] *H.L.*, 43.
[5] Ibid.
[6] *Apol. ad Anast.*, 2. *Apol. in Hieron.*, ii, 12. *Hist. Eccl*, ii, 4, 8
[7] St. Jer. *Ep.*, iii *ad Ruf.*, iv *ad Flor. P.L.*, xxii, cc. 352–6.
[8] *H.L.*, 46.
[9] *Rufini Apol.* ii, 8. *P.L.*, xxi, cc. 591–2.
[10] Ibid.

director and counsellor, until his return to Europe in A.D.
397. They planned and erected a hospice for the benefit of
poor pilgrims of all nations, for the attraction of the Holy
City, as the most sacred place on earth, had begun to be felt
already throughout Christendom. As much of her great riches
as she could spare for the purpose was employed by Melania
in other works of mercy, especially in rendering aid to the
sick and the imprisoned.[1]

St. Jerome, whose furtherance of the ascetical life among
the patrician ladies of Rome had brought him into great
disfavour with the nobility, shook the dust of that city from
his feet in the fall of A.D. 385, and betook himself to Bethlehem.
Paula, the most distinguished among the ascetics, and her
daughter, Eustochium, also journeyed thither, and so many
gathered round them that a large monastery had soon to be
built to give them shelter.[2]   St. Jerome himself ruled a
monastery of men a short distance south of the city.[3]   Here,
again, the chief work done by the monks was the copying of
books.[4] Prayer was held daily in the monastery, but on
Sundays the monks (as also the nuns from their convent)
attended Mass and the liturgical Offices in the church of the
Nativity, where also they received Holy Communion.[5]

(b)—Syria and Mesopotamia.

Palladius : *Historia Lausiaca.* Cf. Chap. i, § 7.
Sozomen : *Hist. Eccles. VI.*
Cassian : *Instituta. Conlationes.*
Theodoret : *Philotheus or Historia Religiosa P.G.* LXXXII. col. 17,
  29 ff.
Aphraates : *Demonstratio VI & VII. Patrol. Syr. I.* Paris, 1894.
  Cf. F. C. Burkitt : *Early Eastern Christianity.* London, 1904. Dom
  Connolly : *Jour. Theol. Studies.* July, 1905.
Thomas of Marga : *Book of the Governors.* Ed. and transl. E. W. Budge.
  London, 1893.
Vita Simeonis Stylitae. Ed. Lietzmann. Leipzig, 1908. Cf. H. Delehaye :
  Les Saints Stylites. Brussels, 1923.
Life of Mar Awgin. Bedjan. *Acta Martyrum.* Vol. III, p. 376 ff.
Labourt : *Le Christianisme dans l'empire perse sous la dynastie sas-
  sanide.* Paris, 1904.

Monasticism made its way at an early date to Syria.   In
the great city of Antioch there might be found ascetics living

---

[1] *H.L.*, 54. Cf. Paulinus of Nola *Ep.*, 29. *P.L.*, lxi, cc. 312-21.
[2] St. Jer. *Ep.*, 108 and 66.
[3] St. Jer. *Ep.*, 108. *Sulp. Sev. Dial.*, i, 4.
[4] St. Jer. *Ep.*, 125.
[5] *Anec. Maredsol.*, iii, 3.

a life of voluntary austerity in their homes[1], and monks living a life of ordered activity in monasteries. But the majority of those desirous of devoting themselves completely to God dwelt as hermits on the neighbouring mountains. St. John Chrysostom spent some six years in their midst, until ill-health caused by indiscreet austerities compelled him to withdraw. He speaks with enthusiasm of his companions as angels in human form.[2] In the desert of Chalcis, east of Antioch[3], in the town of Cyrus,[4] in Coele-Syria,[5] and Osrhoene[6] there were likewise settlements. High repute was gained for Edessa by St. Julian Sabbas, who was first a solitary, then director of an anchoretical group near its walls.[7] The reputation of the city was later enhanced by the eloquent and gentle St. Ephraim[3]. St. Aphraates, speaking of Mesopotamia, about the middle of the fourth century, refers to " Sons of the Covenant," or ascetics of both sexes living in their own homes[9] ; but if we may believe an early tradition, monasticism in the strict sense, or cenobitism, was carried to these regions by Mar Awgin, a disciple of St. Pachomius.[10]

Noteworthy in Syria and Mesopotamia was the preference shown for the purely eremitical as distinct from the semi-eremitical or cenobitical life.[11] In Egypt the opposite tendency had by this time begun to gain ground.[12] In austerities, too, the Orientals surpassed all that the ascetics of the Nile country had ever dreamed of. Fast days were multiplied, even within the Paschal season ; the canonical offices became more numerous and more protracted ; bodily torture was intensified by means of scourgings, spikes, chains, weights, and other artificial instruments of penance.[13] Some of the Syrian monks made their repast off freshly-cut grass, as though they were cattle. These ascetics were called by contemporaries " Shepherds," but, as Monsignor Duchesne tartly remarks, they might more appropriately be called " sheep," so closely akin

---

[1] Cf. *St. Chrys. On the Priesthood*, i, 4 ff.
[2] *Hom.*, i in *Matt. P.G.*, lvii, c. 20.
[3] *St. Jer. Ep., ad Eusthoc.*, 7. *P.L.*, xxii, c. 393. Cf *Vita*, Ib , c. 39.
[4] Theod. *Hist. Relig.*, iii, l.c., col. 323 ff.
[5] Soz. *H.E.*, vi, 39.
[6] Soz. *H.E.*, iii, 14.
[7] Theod. op. cit. ii, col. 1306. Soz., op cit. iii. 14.
[8] Cf. *Pereg. Syl.*, 64.
[9] *Dem.* vi. *Patr. Syr.*, ii. 8.
[10] Bedjan, op. cit., p. 376.
[11] Theod. *Hist. Relig., passim*.
[12] Cass., *Conl.*, xviii, 4.
[13] Theod. *Hist. Relig.*, 23, op. cit.. col 1343, 1350. 394. 1415 etc.

to the practice of animals was their manner of taking food.[1]
Most amazing of all the Syrian monks was St. Simeon Stylites,
who, when troubled by visitors in his hermitage near Antioch,
mounted on a pillar (στύλος), at first about ten feet high,
but afterwards of three times that elevation. His austerities
in food and sleep are well-nigh incredible ; thus he was
accustomed to spend the whole period of Lent without
nourishment of any description. From his lofty perch he
addressed words of spiritual exhortation to the curious who
came to gaze at him, and he worked many conversions.[2]

(c)—Lands of Greek Speech.

The ascetical works of St. Basil, especially *Regulae fusius tractatae*
and *Regulae brevius tractatae*. P.G. XXIX-XXXII. (Transl.
W. K. L. Clarke, London, 1925.)
Epistolae 2, 14, 22, 23, 42–6, 173 of St. Basil ; and *Epistolae* 1, 2,
4, 5, 6 of St. Greg. Naz. to St. Basil.
Kranich : *Die Ascetik in ihrer dogmatischen Grundlage bei Basilius
dem grossen*. Paderborn, 1891.
Holl : *Enthusiasmus u. Bussgewalt beim griechischen Mönchtum*.
Leipzig, 1898.
Allard : *Saint Basile*. Paris, 1903.
Petrakakos : Οἱ μοναχικοὶ θεσμοί, Leipzig, 1907.
Pargoire : " *Basile* " *Dict. d'archéol. chrét*. T. III, col. 501 ff.
Morison : *St. Basil and his Rule*. London, 1912.
Clarke : *St. Basil the Great*. Cambridge, 1913.
Loofs : *Eustathius von Sebaste*. Halle, 1898.

Monasticism, probably of the strict or Pachomian form,
was introduced into Asia Minor (that part of the Greek-
speaking world where Christianity was most firmly established)
early in the fourth century. Its first sponsor seems to have
been Eustathius, later Bishop of Sebaste, who " founded a
society of monks in Armenia, Paphlagonia and Pontus," and
became the author of a zealous discipline " both as to what
meats were to be partaken of or to be avoided, what garments
to be worn, what customs and precise mode of conduct to be
adopted."[3]
The work begun by Eustathius was perfected by St. Basil,
whose influence as a monastic patriarch was paramount in
the East and of high importance in the West. He was born
about A.D. 329 of pious, rich and honoured parents in

---

[1] *Hist. Ancienne*, T. ii, p. 516.
[2] Theod. *Hist. Relig.*, 26.
[3] Soz. *H.E.*, iii, 14. Cf. viii, 27.

Cappadocia.[1] Having received an excellent religious training from his grandmother, Macrina, he was sent to Cæsarea, in Cappadocia,[2] and then to Athens, where he studied with great success under the most distinguished teachers of the age. He returned to Cæsarea in A.D. 356, to find the world lying at his feet, but he soon determined to renounce his brilliant prospects and devote all his energy to the cultivation of his soul. Possibly at the suggestion of Eustathius,[3] he journeyed to Egypt, Palestine, Coele-Syria, and Mesopotamia to study at first hand the ascetical institutes of these countries. What he saw of the monks filled him with amazement. " I admired," he writes, " their continence in living, and their endurance in toil ; I wondered at their persistence in prayer and their triumph over sleep ; subdued by no natural necessity ; ever keeping their soul's purpose high and free, in hunger, in thirst, in cold, in nakedness, they never yielded to the body ; always, as though living in a flesh that was not theirs, they showed in very deed what it is to sojourn for a while in this life and what it is to have one's citizenship and home in heaven."[4]

Basil soon became the recognised leader of the monastic movement in Cappadocia and Pontus. The framework of his system was Pachomian, but he introduced some important modifications.[5] Thus he emphasised much more strongly than the Egyptian Patriarch the value of common life. In Tabennisi and its sister settlements the monks lived under the same or under neighbouring roofs, obeyed the same head, performed the same or similar tasks, used the same church and refectory, but anyone who thought this minimum of observance insufficient might add to it such other ascetical exercises as his fancy suggested. Should he feel strength enough to live by himself in solitude there would be no protest on the score that this was a less desirable way. Basil, however, held strongly that the cenobitical was in itself superior to the anachoretical form of life : to leave the monastery for the hermit's cell should be considered a retrogression.[6] That a kindly family spirit might prevail

---

[1] Greg. Naz. *Or.* 43.
[2] *Ep.*, 204.
[3] Duchesne, *Hist. anc.*, ii, 384.
[4] *Ep.* 223.
[5] Clarke, *St. Basil the Great*, p. 123.
[6] *Reg. fus. tract.*, 7, 36. *Reg. brev. tract.*, 74. *Ep.* 42.

E

among his monks, he decreed that no monastery should contain more than thirty or forty brethren,[1] experience having proved in Egypt that the more peopled monasteries tended to develop into barracks rather than homes. The Superior's power, too, was held in check, since the *seniores* or elder brethren were allowed to test his commands by the standard of the divine law.[2] In each monastery a school was set up where boys were trained "in all godliness," as well for life in the world as for life in the cloister, should they choose to devote themselves to the service of God when their studies were ended.[3] Finally St. Basil desired that the traditional charity of the Church towards the sick and suffering might be exercised through the agency of his monasteries[4], and with this end in view he erected hospitals and hospices at Cæsarea and other centres.[5]

In A.D. 384 Constantinople possessed but one monastery[6] ; within twenty-five years, however, the movement of expansion had set in, and progress was such that in the sixth century monasteries within or beside the city were counted in hundreds. The rules of St. Basil formed more or less the basis of their observance ; but there were other practices prescribed by Councils or derived from the earlier monastic tradition. Hospices for strangers, the poor, the aged, the sick, were likewise founded and administered by the monks.[7]

§2—Progress of Monasticism in the West.

(a)—Italy.

Epistolae Sancti Hieronymi. C.S.E.L. Vol. LIV–LVI. Tracts against Helvidius, Juvinian, Vigilantius. P.L. XXIII. *Epistolae Sancti Paulini.* C.S.E.L. XXIX–XXX.

Spreitzenhofer : *Die Entwicklung des ältesten Mönchtums in Italien.* Vienna, 1894.

Grützmacher : *Hieronymus.* Berlin, 1901–8.

Card. Rampolla : *Santa Melania giuniore.* Rome, 1906.

Albers : *Rev. Stor benedettina,* IX. 1914. P. 174 ff.

Cavallera : *St. Jérôme.* Louvain, 1922.

In Italy, as elsewhere in Christendom, asceticism had been

---

[1] *Reg. fus. tract.,* 35. Cf. Clarke, op. cit., p. 117

[2] *Reg. fus. tract.,* 27, 48, 49. *Reg. brev. tract.,* 103.

[3] *Reg. fus. tract.,* 15. *Reg. brev. tract,* 292.

[4] *Reg. brev. tract.,* 145.

[5] *Ep.,* 94, 142, 143. Soz. *H.E.,* vi, 34.

[6] Callinicus, *Vita S. Hypatii.* Leipzig edit., 1895, p. 8.

[7] Leclercq, l.c., col. 3156.

practised from an early date, but in no very organised manner.[1] Progress to monasticism proper was due to the influence of St. Athanasius, who, a fugitive from his See in A.D. 339 owing to his heroic advocacy of the Catholic faith against Arianism, spent three years in Rome and an equal period in other Italian cities. Through him the story of Anthony's life and the doings of the Egyptian monks were brought to the notice of the West, where they made an extremely deep impression.[2] Two monks, Isidore and Ammonius the Tall, accompanied him on his journey. The latter, during his stay in the Eternal City, devoted himself entirely to contemplation, refusing to visit any even of the holy places, save the tomb of the Apostles.[3] Isidore, on the other hand, " became known to all the Senate at Rome and to the wives of the nobles ;"[4] chief among the ladies influenced was Marcella, who soon began to live a life of monastic seclusion at her home on the Aventine.[5] Marcella in turn converted the celebrated lady Paula to the same manner of life.[6]

The ground was thus prepared for St. Jerome when he came to Rome with the Bishops Paulinus and Epiphanius in A.D. 382 to assist at a Council convoked by Pope Damasus.[7] For some time the saint contented himself with giving brilliant lectures on Holy Writ to the aristocratic ascetical group on the Aventine ; but he later became their spiritual director and helped them with his robust good sense and wide experience. After he had retired to Bethlehem and founded in that city religious houses for both monks and nuns, Marcella likewise abandoned her home in the heart of Rome, and betook herself to a suburban villa, which she transformed into a monastery. It was the first of its kind in the city of the Cæsars, but it soon found imitators, for under Pope Siricius (384–398) Manichaeans who renounced their heresy were ordered to do penance for a period in monasteries.[8]

Eusebius, who became Bishop of Vercelli in Northern Italy about A.D. 340, prescribed some form of cenobitical rule for his cathedral clergy, thus uniting the clerical and the monastic

---

[1] Cf. Spreitzenhofer, op. cit., p. 8.
[2] St. Jer. *Ep.*, 127.
[3] Soz. *H.E.*, iv, 23.
[4] *H.L.*, I.
[5] St. Jer. *Ep.*, 47, 3.
[6] St. Jer. *Ep.*, 46, 1.
[7] Soz. *H.E.*, vi, 32.
[8] *Liber pontificalis*, i, 216. Spreitzenhofer, op. cit., p. 11.

states in a manner unknown to Egypt and the Orient.[1] His ascetical training stood him later in good stead, for when driven from his See in A.D. 355 by the Arian Emperor Constantius, he bore grievous sufferings with endurance, whilst the Bishop of Milan, his companion, reared in a less exacting school, succumbed to the hardships of exile.[2]

St. Ambrose likewise furthered the monastic institute during his episcopate at Milan, for St. Augustine speaks with admiration of a monastery founded by him beside that city.[3] Aquileia, too, had a settlement of the same kind before A.D. 370. Here Rufinus and his friend St. Jerome spent their first years as monks before departing for the Orient.[4] Amidst the innumerable Italian monasteries of the fifth century, the most distinguished was certainly that of St. Paulinus at Nola. Paulinus was a native of Gaul, who had abandoned family, honours and rich possessions to live as a simple monk in the above-named Campanian town. An accomplished theologian, he became later a bishop, but the cares of that office did not prevent his attachment to monastic observances. He died in A.D. 431.[5]

(b)—Africa.

St. Augustine : *De Opere Monachorum*, P.L. XL. *Sermons*, 355, 356,
    P.L. XXXVIII. *Ep.* 211. P.L. XXIII.
Besse : *Le Monachisme Africain*. Ligugé, 1900.
Leclercq : *L'Afrique Chrétienne*. Paris, 1904. *Dict. d'archéol. chrét*, ii,
    Col. 3225-32.
Albers : *Riv. Stor. benedettina*, IX, 1914, p. 321 ff.

Though the profession of virginity was held in high esteem in Africa since the days of St. Cyprian, monasticism seems to have been unknown in that country when St. Augustine left Carthage for Rome in A.D. 383. The great saint relates how a couple of years later at Milan he and his friend Alypius were visited by a countryman, Pontitianus, a devout Christian. " A conversation arose (suggested by what Pontitianus related) on Anthony the Egyptian monk whose name was in high repute among Thy servants, though till that hour unknown to us. Which when he discovered he

---

[1] Spreitzenhofer, op. cit., p. 13.
[2] *Ambrosii Ep.*, 63.
[3] *Confess.*, viii, 15.
[4] *Vita Rufini*, P.L. xxi, col. 80.
[5] Spreitzenhofer, op. cit., p. 21.

dwelt the more upon that subject, informing us and wondering at our ignorance of one so eminent. But we stood amazed, hearing Thy wonderful works so fully attested, in times so recent and almost in our own, wrought in the true Faith and in the Catholic Church. . . . Then his discourse turned to the flocks in the monasteries and their holy ways, a sweet smelling odour unto Thee ; and the fruitful deserts of the wilderness, whereof we knew nothing."[1]

When ordained priest at Hippo in A.D. 391, Augustine founded a monastery which he continued to direct as Bishop (A.D. 395–430).[2] In his episcopal residence, as at Vercelli, the clerical and the cenobitical states of life were united, for the clergy vowed poverty, and lived together under a common religious rule.[3] Many of these priest-monks were given the care of parishes ; others were consecrated bishops and propagated the monastic mode of life in their new homes.[4] At the same time monasteries of the earlier type were not unknown in Africa, with monks without orders and governed by an abbot who was like themselves a layman.[5]

(c)—Gaul.

Sulpicii Severi Vita S. Martini. Dialogus I and II. C.S.E.L., vol. I. Cf. :
    Babut : *S. Martin et Sulpice Sévère.* Brussels, 1920.
Hilarii Arelat. Sermo de Vita S. Honorati. P.L., L, col. 1249 ff. *Eucherii
    De laude eremi..* P.L. L, col. 701. *Cassiani Conl.* xi. *Praef. ad
    Instituta.* Cf. Chap. 1, §7. *Sidonii Apollinarii Epistolae.* P.L. LXI.
Besse : *Les Moines de l'ancienne France.* Paris, 1906.
Besse : *Les premiers monastères de la Gaule méridionale. Rev. des
    quest. hist.* 1902, p. 394 ff.
Arnold : *Caesarius von Arelate.* Leipzig, 1894.
Malnory : *S. Césaire, évèque d'Arles.* Paris, 1894.
Hauck : *Kirchengeschichte Deutschlands. Erster Teil.* Leipzig, 1904.
Leclercq : *Dict. d'archéol. chrét.* ii, col. 3192–3205.
Albers : *Riv. stor. benedettina.* T. X, 1915, p. 5 ff.

St. Athanasius, Patriarch of Alexandria, had brought the practices of the Egyptian monks to the notice of the Gauls during his period of exile at Trier. His accounts were no doubt listened to with wonder and delight, as in Italy, but imitation of the Egyptian Fathers was neglected until the enthusiastic St. Martin appeared on the scene. That great

---

[1] *Conf.*, viii, 6.
[2] Possid. *Vita Aug.*, c. 5. *Aug. Serm.*, 355. P.L. xxxix. col. 1570.
[3] Cf. *Serm.* 355 and 356.
[4] Poss. *Vita Aug.*, c. 22.
[5] Cf. *Serm.*, 355 and *Vita Aug.*, cc. 10, 11, 14.

saint, a Pannonian by birth, was but a boy of twelve when he conceived the idea of withdrawing to a hermitage.[1] But he was compelled by his father, a veteran of the imperial army, to serve as a soldier, and secured his discharge only at the age of twenty-two.[2] He was soon a recluse in one of the islands of the Mediterranean.[3] Later, about A.D. 360, he established at Ligugé, near Poitiers, what was probably the first monastery on Gallic soil. Its organisation was of the semi-eremitical kind, and Martin, like Anthony, ruled more by example than by precept. In A.D. 371 the saint was induced by stratagem to leave Ligugé—to find himself ambushed and carried by force to Tours, where he was proclaimed bishop of the city.[4] Instead, however, of abandoning his old way of life, he tried to perpetuate it, and founded, some two miles from Tours, in a place so remote that it might well be compared to a desert solitude, the large monastery of Marmoutier, whither he retired as often as the duties of office would allow.[5] From Ligugé and Marmoutier, as from parent hives, so many swarms went forth that the monks present at the saint's funeral (probably in A.D. 397) numbered two thousand.[6] His " Life," written in a most engaging manner by Sulpicius Severus, penetrated to Rome, Africa, Egypt and the East soon after St. Martin's death and rivalled the " Life of St. Anthony " in popularity.[7] It is noteworthy that though the Saint's dearest wish was to spend his days in seclusion, he had in practice to forego this pleasure, and labour strenuously for a quarter of a century as a bishop and missionary.[8] A number of disciples accompanied him always on his journeys[9]; others took charge of parishes or of dioceses.[10] In a word, Ligugé and Marmoutier were semi-eremitical or Antonian settlements, but with a character of their own, for it was regarded as a matter of course that a number should consider these monasteries as schools of ascetical training only, and abandon them at will to engage in pursuits of a more active kind elsewhere.

---

[1] *Vita Mart.*, 2.
[2] *Vita Mart.*, 4, 5.
[3] *Vita Mart.*, 6.
[4] *Vita Mart.*, 9.
[5] *Vita Mart.*, 10. Greg. Tur *De Virt. Mart.* iv, 30.
[6] *Ep.*, 3 18.
[7] *Dial.* i, 23.
[8] *Vita Mart.*, 10.
[9] *Ep.*, iii 7.
[10] *Vita Mart.* 10. *Dial.* ii 15, 2.

At the beginning of the fifth century, the famous monastery of St. Victor at Marseilles was founded by John Cassian, who had embraced the monastic profession in early youth at Bethlehem,[1] and had later spent the greater part of the years A.D. 390–400 with the Antonian monks of Lower Egypt.[2] He was ordained deacon at Constantinople by St. John Chrysostom, and priest at Marseilles about A.D. 412.[3] At this time he established the monastery of St. Victor for men, and another of the same kind for women,[4] with the avowed purpose of propagating the primitive Egyptian ideal.[5] Closely, however, as he wished to adhere to the practices of the Nile country, he had to admit that certain mitigations were desirable, first because of different climatic conditions, and then because of the diverse customs of the Occident.[6] Under his influence the monastic institute, favoured by various Bishops, spread throughout South-Eastern Gaul. Of the importance of Cassian's writings we shall have more to say in the course of the present volume.

Just at this time, too, there was established on the tiny island of Lérins, near Cannes, a monastery whose predominance in Gaul was to be unquestioned during the fifth century. The founder was St. Honoratus, scion of a noble Gallic family of the North. While still a youth he had renounced fortune and friends to follow Christ.[7] After a journey eastwards as far as Greece, he returned to Gaul and chose this solitary isle, then infested by snakes and scorpions, as the place of his retreat.[8] A number of disciples soon placed themselves under his direction, and the monastic life commenced. Here, once again, the Antonian institutions of Egypt were the model.[9] Each monk had his own cell, where he lived and slept ; but all met together for the Mass and the hours of the Divine Office ; possibly also for meals. At some distance from the main group of cells, but within the islet (or in the neighbouring island of Léro) some of the more elderly and virtuous brethren lived as hermits. There was no written

---

[1] *Inst.*, iii, 4 ; iv, 31. *Conl.*, xi, 1 ; xix, 1.
[2] *Conl.*, vii, 26 ; xi 1–3. *Inst.*, v, 36.
[3] Gennadius *de viris inlus.*, c. 61
[4] Ibid.
[5] *Inst.*, *Praef.*, 8.
[6] Ibid.
[7] Hil. *Sermo.*, l.c., col. 1251.
[8] Ibid., col. 1257.
[9] Euch. *de laude eremi*, 42. Faustus of Reiz *Hom.* 13. Cf. Tillemont, *Mémoires*, xii, 475.

rule ; there was, however, the prescription of custom which seems to have obliged as sternly as any written rule could do.[1] Lérins, indeed, owed much of its success to the strict manner in which its abbots maintained discipline. Among the distinguished monks who left the island to govern churches must be mentioned St. Honoratus himself, founder of the monastery, who died bishop of Arles in A.D. 429 ; St. Hilary and St. Cæsarius, who ruled the same see ; St. Lupus of Troyes, Maximus and Faustus, Bishops of Riez, and St. Eucherius, Bishop of Lyons.[2]

[1] Arnold, op. cit. Appendix vj, p. 520-1.
[2] Ib., p. 41, note 116.

SECTION II

THE INTRODUCTION OF MONASTICISM INTO IRELAND

CHAPTER I

ST. PATRICK

*The " Confession " of St. Patrick and his " Letter Denouncing Coro-
ticus,"* ed. by N. J. D. White. P.R.I.A. Vol. xxv, Sect. C. No. 7.
Dublin, 1905.
Hymn of Secundinus. Liber Hymnorum. Ed. by Bernard and Atkinson.
London, 1898.
Life of St. Patrick, by Muirchu Moccu Machtheni in four groups of
chapters, of which the second deals with Patrick's years of prepar-
ation in Gaul, the facts of this period being " known probably
through the traditions of Churches founded by those who came
with him from that country as fellow-workers."
Memoir of St. Patrick by Tírechán.
Additions to Tírechán and Notulae. All the above published in the
Book of Armagh. Ed. Gwynn. Dublin, 1913.
Hymn " *Génair Patraicc." Thesaurus Paleohibernicus,* ii, p. 307 ff.
Ed. Stokes and Strachan. Cambridge, 1903.
Tripartite Life of St. Patrick. Ed. Stokes. London, 1887.
Todd : *Life of St. Patrick.* Dublin, 1864.
Bury : *Life of St. Patrick.* London, 1905.
Healy : *Life of St. Patrick.* Dublin, 1905.
Gougaud : *Les chrétientés celtiques.* Paris, 1911.

§1—His Monastic Training.

THAT there were Christians in Ireland before the coming
of St. Patrick is certain ; but beyond the fact of their
existence nothing whatever is known about them. Such
indirect evidence as is available points to the conclusion
that they were few in number and unorganised.[1] They cannot,
at any rate, be connected with the origins of Irish monasticism.

The traditional importance of St. Patrick as the Apostle
of the Irish Nation has been challenged[2] and vindicated[3]

---

[1] Zimmer's contention to the contrary (article " Keltische Kirche " in
the *Realencyclopaedie für prot. Theologie u Kirche.* Bd. x, p. 204 ff—English
transl. " The Celtic Church," by Miss A. Meyer, London, 1902) is refuted
by MacCaffrey : *Irish Theolg. Quarterly,* vol. i. p. 47 ff ; and Gougaud, op.
cit., p. 37–8.
[2] By Zimmer, op. cit., who distinguished between a " historical " and a
" legendary " St. Patrick. The former ended his days as a missionary in
abject failure, and was soon forgotten everywhere save in a small region of
Leinster where he was active. The latter, a grotesque exaggeration of the rea
Patrick, was invented by the " Roman party " of the South in the seventh
century, and adopted by the North, whose representatives exploited his
imaginary achievements.
[3] Especially by Bury, op. cit., p. 384, ff., and (in a final manner) by Gwynn,
op. cit., p. xcvii, c.

by modern scholars. To him then belongs the credit of having established the first organised Christian Church among our people. What part did the monastic institute play in this organisation ? As the question is fundamental and the reply admittedly difficult, it will be well to approach it with the query : Was St. Patrick himself a monk ? And if he was, what particular form of monasticism did he profess ?

In the twenty odd years which intervene between the Saint's departure from Ireland (about A.D. 407) and his return (in A.D. 432) two faint glimmers of light relieve the general obscurity. The first is a tradition, recorded by Tírechán,[1] that Patrick journeyed in Gaul, Italy and the islands of the Tyrrhenian Sea ; the second a tradition of intimate connection with the church of Auxerre, and especially with St. Germanus.[2]

Tírechán quotes as his authority for this statement an account left by Patrick himself[3] and preserved in the *Book of Armagh* (compiled a century or more after Tírechán's memoir) as a "*dictum Patricii.*"[4] He adds that the Saint's sojourn in these regions occupied seven years, and that one of the islands visited was Lérins.[5] The last-mentioned detail he had heard from the lips of Ultan, Bishop of Ard Breacain, in Meath, who died in A.D. 657.

Turning now to the *Confession*, we find nothing in any way out of harmony with Tírechán's record ; on the contrary, Patrick seems to imply that a few years[6] elapsed between his escape—first from Ireland, then from the barbarian invaders of Gaul, who had taken him and his sailor acquaintances captive—and his return to home and friends in his native Britain. There is no need to question the equation between Patrick's " few " and Tírechán's more precise " seven." His career then during this period may be outlined broadly thus. After six years as a slave in Ireland he had fled from his master, and walked two hundred miles to find a ship that

---

[1] *B. Arm.*, 17 b. Cf. *Génair Pátraicc*, line 11. *Thes. Hib.*, ii, p. 312.

[2] *B. Arm.*, 3a, 39a. *Gén. Pátr.*, l.c., ll. 10, 13.

[3] " *Ut ipse dixit in commemoratione laborum,*" *B. Arm.*, 17b.

[4] " Timorem Dei habui ducem itineris mei per Gallias atque Italiam etiam in insulis quae sunt in mari Tyrrheno." l.c., 17a.

[5] Reading *Aralanensis* as *Lerinensis*, according to the emendation suggested by the Bollandists (AA. SS. T. ii *Mart.*, 528), and generally accepted. Dr. Gwynn's alternative suggestion *Arelatensis* is unconvincing, for the island referred to is almost certainly in the Tyrrhenian Sea. A difficulty, too, would remain, even if *insula* were interpreted correctly as *monastery*, since there was no monastic settlement until the pontificate of St. Honoratus (A.D. 426–9). Cf. Malnor : *Césaire, évêque d'Arles*, p. 24.

[6] *Conf.*, § 23 ; *et iterum post paucos annos Britannis eram cum parentibus meis.*

would take him on board for charity, since he had neither goods nor money.[1] The boat brought him, no doubt to his sore disgust—not to Britain, but to a port of western Gaul, Nantes or Bordeaux. There the crew disembarked, and started off with their merchandise to some inland mart, carrying Patrick along with them. After 28 days of cautious travelling the whole party fell into the hands of barbarian marauders and suffered much as prisoners for two months, until at last the " Lord delivered Patrick and his companions out of their hands."[2] His plight at the moment of release must certainly have been pitiable. He was alone in the midst of a strange population, probably in the south-east of Gaul, or in the neighbouring province of Italy,[3] without resources and without friends. The problem of making himself understood must likewise have been serious, for the Latin of his boyhood—bad and provincial perhaps at best—cannot but have still further suffered during his isolation on the Antrim hills.

Help, however, noble in motive and generous in kind, would soon be forthcoming in the Christian land where Patrick now found himself. Neglect of strangers was an offence, according to Gospel teaching, which the Just Judge might punish without mercy on the day of final reckoning.[4] For them then, as for the poor and the infirm, some portion of revenue was set aside in every Christian Community[5] ; and it was a function of the deacon to inform himself of their arrival, and to bring notice of it to the bishop.[6] Patrick would thus be brought, for the first time since boyhood, into intimate contact with the Christian faithful and their clergy, and would hear inspiring tales—all the more wonderful because falling on ears accustomed to pagan accents—of the life and miracles of St. Martin. The tales would often be retold and would lose nothing in the telling, for there were Gauls very proud indeed of the great saint of Tours, whose virtues they lauded with an emphasis that included a note

---

[1] *Conf.* § 17, 18 and 338 *ff.*
[2] *Conf.* § 19–22. I owe this very satisfactory explanation of the passage in the *Confession* to Dr. MacNeill.
[3] Bury, op. cit., p. 36.
[4] Matt. xxv, 43.
[5] Lallemand : *Histoire de la charité.* Paris, 1900–12. Benigni : *Storia sociale de la Chiesa.* Milan, 1907–15. Marx : *Zur Gesch. der Barmherzigkeit im Abendl.,* 1917.
[6] Leclercq : *Art " charité " Dict. d'archéol. chrétienne,* col. 614.

of challenge to the Orient.[1] On a soul so passionate in its love for higher things,[2] the story of St. Martin's life must have made a deep impression. Here was self-renunciation radical enough to satisfy the most exacting of human hearts.

The desire to imitate would grow strong within him, and he would ask, with a strange eagerness in his eyes, whether there still existed men who had imposed upon themselves the hard, ascetical way of life for which the saint of Tours had become famous. We can imagine Patrick, once he had received welcome information on this point, starting off to Milan[3] to make acquaintance at close quarters with the community founded by St. Ambrose. Here the only drawback was the geographical situation of the monastery, for it might seem a little incongruous that men who had fled from the world should have halted, as it were, at the threshold, almost within earshot of the noisy city. Were there any whose withdrawal from the world might be considered yet more complete than the withdrawal of the monks of Milan ? Some there certainly were ; and to them Patrick would now direct his footsteps.

In the blue waters of the Mediterranean, yet not far from the Gallic and Italic coasts, lay a number of islets and small archipelagos—Gallinaria, Capraria, Gorgon, the Hyères— that had already become popular places of retirement for hermits or ascetical groups. Thus, St. Martin, when expelled from his monastic settlement at Milan by the Arian bishop of the city, had journeyed to Capraria, and lived for a while on that island with a priest-friend in prayerful solitude. Herbs and roots were his only food. Not being an experienced botanist, he innocently included hemlock among the herbs consumed, and was probably saved from death only by the meagreness with which he had partaken.[4] Of Capraria and

---

[1] *Sulp. Severii Dial.* i, 25, 26.

[2] Cf. *Conf.*, § 16. " Now, after I had arrived in Ireland tending flocks was my daily occupation ; and constantly I used to pray in the day-time. Love of God and the fear of Him increased more and more, and faith grew and the spirit was roused, so that in one day I would say as many as a hundred prayers, and at night nearly as many, even while I was out in the woods, and on the mountain-side. Before daybreak I used to be roused to prayer, and I felt no hurt, whether there were snow, frost, or rain, nor was there any sluggishness in me . . ."

[3] For the close connection between S. Gaul and Milan at this period (with consequences felt in Spain, Britain and Ireland) see Duchesne : *Fastes épiscopaux de l'ancienne Gaule*, i, 92–3 ; *Origines du culte chrétien*, 32 ff ; and Williams : *Christianity in Early Britain*, p. 187.

[4] *Vita S. Martini*, c. 6.

Gorgon we learn from the pagan poet, Rutilius Claudius Namatianus, in an elegiac description of a journey from Rome to Gaul, published about A.D. 416. The life of the hermits on these islands filled the cultured heathen with disgust. It was bad enough, he thought, to have to contend with misery when it came, but to seek out misery as a blessing by embracing a life of poverty, servile work and suffering —that was surely lunacy, not philosophy, too silly in truth to merit the poisoned shafts of a poet's disdain.[1] But the bitterness of the pagan plaint shows that the new order of things had taken firm root in the soil of the dying Empire. The foolishness of the Cross inspired anger, but the power of the Cross inspired impatience and fear. Cassian, a few years later, testifies to the presence of monks on the Hyère isles, near Marseilles, where the establishment does not seem to be of recent date.[2]

Which of these islands St. Patrick visited it would be useless to conjecture, though it may be noted that a journey from Milan to Pisa (or some coastal town further south) before embarking for Capraria or Gorgon would afford a moderate amount of substance to Tírechán's claim that he journeyed through *all* Italy.[3] Like St Basil and Cassian among the Monks of Egypt, St John Chrysostom among the hermits near Antioch, and many others, St Patrick is thus to be pictured learning from the holy men with whom he sojourned the principles of Christian self-renunciation, and imitating their devout practices. Like the former, too, he would have had no hesitation in moving from one teacher or settlement to another. Each place had advantages peculiar to itself from which a fervent soul might draw profit. Owing to constant arrivals and departures, intercourse was maintained between the various colonies of ascetics and the news would in time reach Patrick's ears, that on the isle of Lérins there ruled an abbot whose method of guidance was more systematic than any yet known in the Occident. The abbot's

---

[1] *De Reditu suo*, i, 439 ff. :—
"Processu pelagi iam se Capraria tollit.
Squalet lucifuga insula plena viris . . .
Munera fortunae metuunt, dum damna verentur.
Quisquam sponte miser, ne miser esse queat.
Quaenam perversa rabies tam stulta cerebri.
Dum mala formides, nec bona posse pati ? "
[2] *Conl.*, pars ii. *Praef.*, § 3. C.S.E.L., xiii, p. 312.
[3] *B. Arm.*, 17b " per *totam* Italiam."

name was Honoratus. So favourable an opportunity of acquiring spiritual training of unusual value Patrick could not lose,[1] and he would soon resume his travels with the island monastery as his objective.

His life under the care of Honoratus would be just like that of the other monks,[2] " waifs from the shipwreck of the storm-tossed world," many of whom, like himself, had come from distant parts.[3] Prayer, especially the singing of psalms in common at the canonical hours ; and labour, manual or mental, occupied the day and a considerable portion of the night. Prolonged fasts and the more severe exercises of exterior self-discipline were permitted only to the older, well-tried monks, who dwelt in cells apart, as semi-anchorites. The younger members of the Community were formed rather by the interior discipline of the will, and thus mortified themselves chiefly by exact observance of the order of time, and unquestioning obedience to Superiors. Patrick, during his stay on the island, would belong to this class. Of him, no doubt, as of the distinguished Saint Hilary of Arles, who may have been his colleague at Lérins, it could be said that his later career as a bishop manifested the excellence of his early training. He came amongst the brethren with a contrite spirit and with an ardour that no desolation could damp. He set himself to study the lives of the most perfect, and to copy, as far as the rule allowed, their vigils, their abstinence, their humility, and, above all, the fervour of their prayer.[4] In faith, in hope, in charity, in the modesty of his gait, the serenity of his countenance, the alacrity of his obedience, the heroism of his silence, he would be one of that " angelic host " of Lérins whose sight filled Eucherius with heavenly joy.[5] Patrick's stay with Honoratus can hardly have been prolonged, yet it left upon his memory an impression so vivid that four decades later, when the evening shades were gathering and the night was at hand that would end his work, he tells

---

[1] " Honoratum expetiit quisquis Christum desideravit." *Hil. Sermo de vita S. Honor.* P.L. l., col. 1258.

[2] That details in this period in Patrick's life are not forthcoming need cause no surprise. Almost nothing, for instance, is known of St. Caesarius of Arles during his stay (c. 493–502) at Lérins. This, too, though a rich account has been preserved of all other periods in Caesarius's life. Cf. Arnold : *Caesarius von Arelate,* p. 47.

[3] *Hil. Sermo..* l.c., c. 1258. " Quae adhuc terra, quae natio, in monasterio illius cives suos non habet ? "

[4] *Vita S. Hil.,* c. 5. P.L. l., col. 1226.

[5] *De laude eremi.* P.L. l., col. 711-2.

of the desire that had often filled his breast to return to Gaul and re-visit the saintly brethren.[1] For him as for so many others, Lérins was in truth a " terrestrial paradise," the one spot in a very imperfect world where man could imitate in some degree the life of the elect and participate in celestial privileges.[2]

But the mystic voice that had consoled Patrick's wearied slumbers on the Antrim hills with news of impending release had promised return to his British homeland, not monastic quiet with saintly friends under a cloudless Mediterranean sky,[3] and the fervent monk, whose only desire was to do exactly what God wanted, could thus regard the island only as a temporary resting-place. Superiors would respect his scruples ; all the more easily because the principle of stability was not yet recognised as essential in the Lérins rule.[4] With the blessing, therefore, of Honoratus and the kiss of peace from everyone of the sorrowing community Patrick left the monastery and journeyed back to Britain to his kinsfolk and friends. Their joy at his unexpected appearance was inexpressibly great, for they had long lost hope of ever seeing him again in this world. Now that he had been providentially restored to them, they argued, he must make up his mind to stay with them for the remainder of his days.[5] Whatever his own plans for the future may have been, he soon discovered that the Almighty Himself had designed him for a special and a mighty work : " And there indeed, I saw in the night visions a man whose name was Victoricus coming as it were from Ireland with countless letters. And he gave me one of them, and I read the beginning of the letter, which was entitled ' the Voice of the Irish ' ; and while I was reading aloud the beginning of the letter I thought that at that very moment I heard the voice of them who lived beside the wood of Foclut, which is nigh unto the Western Sea. And thus they cried as with one mouth, ' We beseech thee, holy youth,

---

[1] *Conf.*, § 43 : " Non id solum, sed etiam usque ad Gallias, visitare fratres, et ut viderem faciem sanctorum Domini mei : scit Deus quod valde optabam " —where the terms " fratres " and " sancti " imply that those whom he wished to visit were monks. The reference is most probably to Lérins.

[2] " Terrestrem ingreditur Lirinensis insulae paradisum." *Vita Hil.*, op. cit. col. 1226. Cf. *De laude eremi*, l.c., col. 711.

[3] *Conf.*, § 17 : " et ibi scilicet quadam nocte in somno audivi vocem discentem mihi : Bene ieiunas, cito iturus ad patriam tuam."

[4] Leclercq, op. cit., col. 3197.

[5] *Conf.*, § 23.

to come hither and walk once more among us.' "[1]   Patrick
accepted the invitation, though he knew that acceptance
meant separation from his kinsfolk and his people as well
as suffering and tribulation without end.

Having made up his mind to undertake the evangelisation
of Ireland, Patrick would set about preparing himself for the
task. Indispensable were his ordination to one of the higher
ecclesiastical orders and a commission from the authorities
of the Church. He seems to have resolved to proceed directly
to the Apostolic See, but to have changed his mind when he
reached Auxerre, and to have attached himself to the clergy
of that city, thus abandoning or postponing indefinitely his
visit to Rome.[2]

It is not improbable that he was ordained deacon shortly
after his arrival by the ruling bishop, St. Amator,[3] for the
diaconate was then a ministry that did not require deep
theological knowledge in him who exercised it, and Patrick's
training at Lérins, combined with the maturity of his age
(thirty years or over) would make him a suitable candidate
for the order. If the tradition recorded by Muirchu is correct[4]
(and there is certainly no better to replace it) Patrick made
his home at Auxerre until he set out to begin missionary work
in Ireland. We are told that he studied the " Canon," that
is to say the text of the Old and the New Testament, under
the illustrious St. Germanus, who succeeded Amator as bishop
about A.D. 418. During this period he must, therefore, have
acquired that profound intimacy with Holy Writ which his
writings reflect,[5] though we may be sure that the foundations
had been laid long before at Lérins. Other studies than
Scripture he seems never to have attempted, in striking
contrast with the leading church men of his age in Gaul—
Honoratus, Hilary, Eucherius, Lupus, Vincentius, Faustus,
Germanus—all of whom had received the education of their
class in eloquence and polite literature.[6]

[1] Conf., l.c.
[2] So much may be deduced from the introduction to Muirchu's narrative,
tituli 5 and 6, B. Arm., 39 a : " De aetate eius quando iens videre sedem
apostolicam voluit discere sapientiam. De inventione Sancti Ger(mani)
in Gallis, et ideo non exivit ultra." Muirchu's text of these chapters, missing in
the Dublin MS., is reproduced from a Brussels MS., in ed. of B. Arm., p. 444.
[3] Cf. Bury, op. cit., p. 338.
[4] B. Arm., p. 444.
[5] Cf. the long list of scriptural quotations in White's edition of his writings,
pp. 300–16.
[6] Tillemont, Mémoires xii, p. 464. Cf. xv. p. 36 ; the works of Hilary,
Euch., Vincent, Faustus ; and infra, p. 371 fi.

As Germanus had established a monastery on the other side of the Yonne, not far from his episcopal city, whither he retired as to a solitude when the pressure of affairs permitted,[1] the question may be asked whether Patrick belonged to that Community or rather to the clergy who served the city churches. The latter alternative is the more probable. He was preparing now for a trying apostolate as priest and preacher, and would thus be anxious for a training that fitted him directly for an active calling. His return to the well-ordered routine of daily life in religious brotherhood would imply the opposite choice of seclusion from the world and perseverance until death in a career of retirement and contemplation.[2] But there are good grounds for believing that his ascetical habits remained, as well as his esteem and love for the monastic system, and that he was a frequent and honoured visitor in the holy enclosure beyond the Yonne. It is possible, too, that the " barbarian " monks who are mentioned among his followers when at last he came to Ireland[3] were members of that institution. St. Patrick was thus trained as a monk and loved the monastic order, but it was as a cleric, not as a monk, that he began his work among our people.

§2—IMMEDIATE PREPARATION FOR HIS MISSION

In due course Patrick would discuss his plans for the mission to Ireland, the " votum animae suae,"[4] with his colleagues among the clergy, and finally with his ecclesiastical superiors. There was one in particular among his friends who gave him

---

[1] *Vita Germ. by Constantius.* Ed. Levison in *M.G.H. Script. RR. Merovin.*, vii, c. 6, p. 254 and c. 9, p. 256.

[2] The concept of a monastery as a missionary centre was at this time unknown in the West. Thus the many brethren (about 80) who followed St. Martin to Marmoutier rarely left their cells, save to betake themselves to prayer in the common oratory (*Vita S. Martini*, c. 10), and this at a time when the help of active workers was sorely needed by St. Martin in the Gallic countrysides. For this reason, among others, the view put forward by Dr. Healy (*Life of St. Patrick*, p. 81) and by Williams (*Christianity in Early Britain*, p. 307) that Patrick's stay at Lérins came after his stay with kinsfolk and friends in Britain is less convincing than that adopted by Bury (*Life*, p. 337–8) that the sojourn at Lérins preceded his first return to the homeland. The chronological difficulty urged by Williams has little weight, for Lérins must have come into existence about A.D. 410, if its foundation does not go back to an earlier date.

[3] *B. Arm.*, 22a : " in illa reliquit ii barbaros Conleng et Ercleng, monachos sibi."

[4] *Conf.*, § 6.

much encouragement,[1] but many others regarded the idea
as presumptuous,[2] and years went by before any practical
step was taken. Not until A.D. 429, when St. Germanus and
St. Lupus of Troyes came to Britain as representatives of
the Holy See and of the Gallic Church to quell the storms
that followers of Pelagius had aroused, does the question
of sending a missioner to Ireland seem to have been seriously
considered. Perhaps because of information provided by the
British prelates the religious wants of the neighbouring island
were discussed. Germanus evidently became convinced that
an organised effort should be made to assist the struggling
little Christian communities that already existed, and to
convert the pagan population. It would appear that Patrick's
dearest friend, who knew the inmost wishes of his heart,
and treated them with the fullest sympathy, had accompanied
Germanus from Auxerre, and was present at these deliberations,
when he availed himself of the opportunity to recommend
Patrick as leader of the proposed expedition.[3] He went further
indeed than Patrick had ever hoped, and pressed his claims
with vigour.[4] When Germanus returned to Auxerre in A.D. 430,
but before he had presented his report to the Roman See,
a further step was taken in the matter of the proposed Irish
Mission. It was agreed that it should be led by a bishop,
and as Patrick was known to be a candidate (not because
he considered himself worthy, but because be believed that
he had received a call from God to undertake the task) his
qualifications for episcopal office were discussed in what
was evidently a large clerical gathering at Auxerre. The
opposition to his person was here so marked that the event
became the saddest memory of his life. Gallic tradition required
that none should be raised to the episcopal dignity save men
distinguished for scholarship and address, worthy representatives in the popular estimate of a Church that was now
the most important society within the body politic.[5] In the
case of St. Martin this rule had not been observed, but his
election was carried through despite the protests of the
neighbouring bishops,[6] and his isolation in the Gallic hierarchy

---

[1] *Conf.*, § 27 : " amicissimus meus."
[2] *Conf.*, § 46 : " multi hanc legationem prohibebant."
[3] *Conf.*, § 32., insinuates strongly that this incident took place in Britain.
[4] *Conf.*, § 32 : " nec a me orietur (oriebatur-Bury, *Life P.*, p. 298) ut et
ille in mea absentia pro me pulsaret."
[5] Hauck : *Kirchengesch. Deutschlands*, i, p. 61.
[6] *Vita Mart.*, c. 9.

was so complete that for many years he attended no synods.[1]
At his death, moreover, his bitterest opponent, Brictius,[2]
was chosen as his successor ; whilst one of his disciples,
who in religious character resembled his master but too closely,
was driven from the bishopric in A.D. 412.[3] Thus, however
necessary holiness of life and zeal for the divine honour might
be, other qualities were considered desirable in him who
should be consecrated to the pastoral care of souls. Now
Patrick's " rusticity " was so notorious that it was of itself
sufficient to secure his rejection.[4] But there was a further
element, and that of a peculiarly painful kind, to turn the
scales in his disfavour. The " dearest friend " already spoken
of, he to whom Patrick had entrusted his very soul,[5] he to
whom, in a moment of scruple, before his diaconate, he had
confided a sin of his irresponsible boyhood, committed before
he was fifteen, turned suddenly against him and basely disclosed
his secret.[6] Why his friend had acted thus, Patrick was at
a loss to know.[7] But the consequence was that public
dishonour[8] was added to the rejection of his candidature.[9]
Palladius, who had secured the sending of St. Germanus to
Britain[10] and who may have been himself a native of that
country,[11] was probably recommended in his stead ; it was
he, at any rate, whom Pope Celestine despatched the following
year, A.D. 431, as their first Bishop[12] to the Irish who believed
in Christ. Patrick was so affected by the treachery of his
friend and by the shattering of his missionary hopes that
he began to doubt the genuineness of his vocation ; to use his
own words : " On that day I was thrust at and sorely shaken
that I might fall now and forever,"[13] but in a vision of the
night the action of his friend was condemned and the sufferer
comforted. " We have seen with displeasure," said a divine

---

[1] *Sulp. Sev. Dial.* iii, 13.
[2] Ibid. iii, 15.
[3] *Prosper, Chron.*, s.a. 412, p. 466.
[4] *Conf.*, § 46 : " Non ut causa malititae, sed non sapiebat illis, sicut et ego ipse testor intellegi propter rusticitatem meam."
[5] *Conf.*, § 32 : " cui ego credidi etiam animam."
[6] *Conf.*, § 27.
[7] *Conf.*, § 32.
[8] Ib. : " ut coram cunctis, bonis et malis, et me publice dehonestaret."
[9] *Conf.* § 29 : " in illo die quo reprobatus sum a memoratis supradictis."
[10] *Prosper, Chron.* s.a. 429.
[11] Caspari : *Briefe, Abhandlungen u. Predigten aus den zwei letzten Jahrh. des kirchl. Altertums*, p. 385. Cf. Williams, op. cit., p. 211.
[12] *Prosper, Chron.*, s a. 431.
[13] *Conf.*, § 26.

voice, " the face of such-and-such (the false friend), mentioning his name," and there was a note of special graciousness in the words, for as Patrick takes care to remark, " He said not ' *thou hast* seen,' but ' *We have* seen,' as though He joined me with Himself."[1] The decision against him was in fact already annulled in Heaven. Within a year Palladius was dead. Patrick was consecrated his successor and sent, at long last, as a missionary to our island.

. . . .

In the foregoing reconstruction it has been assumed that the " reprobation " of Patrick by his *seniores* has reference to his promotion to the episcopal order, not to an impeachment of his conduct after he had been many years active as a bishop in Ireland. White (op. cit., p. 227), Bury (op. cit., p. 332–4) and Gwynn (op. cit., p. lxxxiv.), against Todd (op. cit., p. 392) and earlier writers, adopt the latter alternative. They argue chiefly from Patrick's words (Conf. § 26) : et quando temptatus sum ab aliquantis senioribus meis, qui venerunt et peccata mea contra laboriosum episcopatum meum—sed Dominus pepercit proselito et peregrino propter nomen suum. Bury comments : " It is quite clear that the occasion when the fault was urged against him by *aliquanti seniores* was not the occasion of his consecration, but later, probably much later. The writer's language so obviously implies this that I find it difficult to conceive how it could have been otherwise interpreted." And again, " The word *laboriosum* shows conclusively that the intervention of the *seniores* did not occur till Patrick had been working long enough in Ireland to describe his bishopric as ' laborious ' ; and the words ' *proselito et peregrino*', describing his position in Ireland manifestly confirm this interpretation."

Does the evidence offered justify so confident a conclusion ? The grounds for a negative answer are many. In the first place Patrick is writing in the evening of his days.[2] Twenty-five years or more of life in Ireland, years rich in effort, toil and danger, lie behind him—truly a " laborious episcopate," and this is the career ("laborious " and painful as it could have been foreseen to prove, and as it certainly was in the retrospect) which the authorities in Gaul would at one time have prevented him from entering on !

---

[1] *Conf.*, § 29.
[2] *Conf.*, § 10 : " in senectute mea." *Conf.*, § 62 : " this is my Confession before I die."

That this is his thought seems to be clear from the following paragraph.[1] In candidates for holy orders a virtuous manner of life was the first quality sought for, and superiors were bound to investigate the past conduct of those who presented themselves, lest any should be received into the sacred ministry who were not likely to do it honour. Now Patrick when a youth of some fifteen years had the misfortune to commit a serious fault that, objectively at least, must have been a grievous sin. As the day approached for his ordination to the diaconate, this youthful misdeed troubled his conscience sorely, and he sought advice about it from his dearest friend. The latter was able to allay his fears ; whence we may conclude that the offence was not of the heinous kind commonly regarded as an impediment to orders.

Where there was question of promotion to the episcopal office a particularly rigorous examination of the candidate's character was necessary, since prelates, by the very nature of their office, were expected to be conspicuous for high virtue. In Gaul these investigations could hardly fail to be thorough, for the custom then was that the clergy and people combined should select their new bishop, their choice, however, being subject to confirmation by the metropolitan.[2] In Patrick's case the procedure would be somewhat different, since he was destined for a distant mission, but an inquiry into his fitness for the episcopal dignity could not be omitted. It is to the happenings at this enquiry that sorrowful reference is made in his " Confession." The proceedings were public in character.[3] Depositions were taken by some of the more venerable clergy of the city, Patrick's *seniores,*[4] under whom he had served in a minor capacity for years. Here his lack of learning and his lack of culture (rusticitas) were emphasised, but Patrick took this objection as a matter of course, knowing that it was justified.[5] What he could not understand, and what stirred him to the very depths of his soul, was the base action of his friend, who before had encouraged Patrick in his aspirations, but who now came forward as his accuser, and disclosed his boyish misdemeanour. Possibly the circumstance of youth

---

[1] *Conf.,* § 27.
[2] Martène : *De Antiquis Ecclesiae Ritibus, Rotomagi,* 1700. Lib. i, pars. 2, p. 323-33. Thomassin : *Dict. de discipline ecclés.* Migne, *Encyclop. Theol.,* T. 25, col. 981 ff.
[3] *Conf.,* § 32 : " ut coram cunctis, bonis et malis, et me publice dehonestaret.
[4] *Conf.,* § 26.
[5] *Conf.,* § 46 : " propter rusticitatem meam."

was not properly stressed. At any rate, the *seniores* conceived a poor notion of Patrick's moral character[1] and drew up a report[2] in unfavourable terms.[3]　The poor stranger and sojourner for God's sake[4] (words perfectly applicable to one who had lived long years in exile in the hope of realising a missionary ideal) felt that he was trampled on,[5] and might have sunk spiritless into the grave, did not the Lord Himself deign to come to his aid.[6] Obstacles were, therefore, removed and he was able to set about the work which Christ the Lord had commissioned him to undertake.[7]

Viewed from the canonical standpoint, the alternative view involves very serious difficulties.　Patrick, according to this theory, is a bishop and has already been active for many years in Ireland.　But the only *seniores* who could call a bishop to account would be fellow-bishops acting as judges in a properly constituted synod.[8]　Was Patrick called to Gaul to defend himself before such a gathering ?　Did a number of Gallic Bishops travel to Ireland to impeach him ?　Would some of his episcopal colleagues in the mission-field have formed themselves into a conventicle to judge him ?

The last-mentioned suggestion may be dismissed at once, for almost all these bishops were consecrated by Patrick himself, and all performed their functions in complete subjection to his authority, as we shall see presently.　His " Confession," too, does not convey the slightest hint that the *seniores* in question were men who ought to have acted as his subordinates.

Nor does the idea of a synod, whether at home or abroad, harmonize with the context.　According to his own testimony, the ground on which he was rejected was his boyish misdeed, a matter surely so trivial that no synod could have discussed it without ridicule.　If greater complaints had been raised against him it is incredible that this alone should be mentioned as the cause of all his humiliation.

---

[1] *Conf.*, § 26.
[2] *Conf.*, § 29 : " Scriptum."
[3] Ibid. : " Reprobatus sum a memoratis supradictis."
[4] Ibid. : " Proselyto et peregrino propter nomen suum."
[5] Ibid. : " in hac conculcatione."
[6] Ibid. : " benigne et valde mihi subvenit."
[7] *Conf.*, § 30 : " a profectione quam statueram et de mea quoque opera quod a Christo meo didiceram."
[8] This ancient custom was made a law of the Empire by Constantius and Constans, and adopted later (A.D. 438) into the Theodosian Code. Cf. Mommsen's edit. i, 838.

An unofficial admonition by a group of bishops is again
no adequate explanation, both because this could hardly
have rankled so bitterly in his memory, and because it is
contrary to his own statement that he was publicly
dishonoured.[1] Moreover, the standard of conduct in the
Gallic bishops of the fifth century was by no means so angelic
that stones could be thrown at an episcopal colleague for a
fault committed before he was fifteen.[2]

This terrible crisis in Patrick's life is, therefore, to be
understood of the investigation that preceded his consecration
as bishop. Disagreement must also be expressed with Bury's
view[3] that in the statement, " after the lapse of thirty years
they found occasion, and that against a word that I had
confessed before I was a deacon,"[4] the thirty years are to be
understood from the confession, not from the commission,
of the fault. " The truth is that the length of time which
elapsed since the wrong-doing is not pertinent," but rather
its unaccountable disclosure by the " dearest friend " after
a lapse of thirty years. The Latin is admittedly ambiguous,
and must be interpreted in accordance with the general sense
of § § 26-32. If, as has been contended in the foregoing pages,
the point at issue was Patrick's fitness for episcopal office,
then the length of time that had elapsed since the fault was
committed is distinctly pertinent. A certain weakness had
been alleged against his moral character. The allegation he
thought unjust, for of the weakness in question there was
but one instance, and thirty years had passed without a
recurrence. After such an interval it might surely be conceded
that the defect had been overcome. How did his friend come
to know of it at all ? Because Patrick had disclosed it to him
in strictest confidence before his ordination as deacon. His
complaint is then that his trust had been betrayed, and that
a solitary blemish, which thirty years of virtuous living had
effaced, was urged against his integrity. This would have been
hard to bear in any case, but it was almost impossible to bear
in the actual circumstances, when the betrayer was a dear
friend, whose mean motive was to thwart a purpose which
he had often, of his own accord, praised and supported.

---

[1] *Conf.*, § 32.
[2] For examples of episcopal weakness cf. Arnold : *Caesarius von Arelate*,
p. 115, n. 339a.
[3] *Life*, p. 333.
[4] *Conf.*, § 27.

Compared with these expressions of friendship and good-will, the length of time during which he knew of Patrick's secret may well be regarded as of secondary importance.

There seems, therefore, to be no convincing reason why this passage in the " Confession " should not be understood (as it was understood by Todd, Neander and Zimmer) to mean thirty years after the commission of the fault. Since he was then about fifteen and since he was consecrated bishop in A.D. 432, his birth would have to be placed in A.D. 385-6, a date that agrees well with the facts of his life as otherwise known.

§3—GENERAL CHARACTER OF ST. PATRICK'S WORK IN IRELAND

The chief sources are the descriptions of his life and work found in the *Book of Armagh* (Ed. Gwynn. Dublin, 1913.) In particular :
(*a*) *The Life of St. Patrick* by Muirchu Moccu Machtheni, a native of Leinster. who wrote the First Book of his narrative at the request of Aedh, Bishop of Sletty, about A.D. 690 (MacNeill, *J.R.S.A.I.* lviii, p. 18). In this book the third group of chapters, distinguished by the fulness and accuracy of the topography, is drawn from the traditions of the churches of Down and Saul. In the following group the triumph of Patrick's mission at Tara is recorded. One of the four supplementary chapters gives a legendary account of the foundation of Armagh, whilst a Second Book gives an account (derived in part, at least, from the tradition of Down) of Patrick's religious life and of his death. There is not much in Muirchu's narrative which bears on the points here under discussion, but so much as there is leaves the impression that it can be accepted as historical.
(*b*) The memoir by Tírechán. This author was a native of Mayo, but a disciple of Ultan, Bishop of Ard Breccain, in Meath (who died in A.D. 657). He wrote for readers of Ultan's territory about A.D. 701. His work is divided into two books, of which the first deals with Patrick's labour in Central Ireland, and the second with his missionary journeys through Connacht, western and northern Ulster, back to Selca, near Cruachu, in Roscommon), thence (in a very succinct survey) to Leinster and Cashel. Tírechán's account of Patrick's activity in Meath agrees in substance with the account given by Muirchu, and both accounts go back to a common, but distant, source, which can hardly be placed later than the middle of the sixth century, and may be many years earlier. Such is the conclusion of Gwynn, *Introduction*, p. lii. As Tírechán's record is very largely a summary of places visited and of churches founded, it is of particular interest in the present study. Its value is, however, limited by the fact that Tírechán, as a zealous partisan of Armagh's *parochia*, embellishes his story with statements that can hardly have a basis in genuine tradition. But on the main point at issue in the present chapter (the character of the early foundations) his testimony is incidental, and we see no reason why it should be rejected as unhistorical.

(*c*) Documents added from the archives of the Primates at Armagh, narrating the foundation of the Church of Trim, and of other churches in Connacht and Leinster.

(*d*) The *Liber Angeli*, drawn up at Armagh in the eighth century from an original that must have been in existence before A.D. 700, and setting forth the prerogatives and supremacy claimed for the See and its Primate at that time.

Evidence, meagre but very important, is also found in the *Confession* (ed. White ; cf. Section i) ; in the *Catalogus Sanctorum Hiberniae* (Composed about A.D. 700–50) ; a sound historical record in outline, though accuracy in detail has been sacrificed to symmetry. Ed. Haddan and Stubbs. *Councils and Eccles. Documents.* London, 1869–78. Vol. ii, p. 292–4, and in the *Annals of Ulster* (Ed. Hennessy. Dublin, 1887), which incorporate an old Irish Chronicle reaching from A.D. 437 to A.D. 661. This fact was discovered by Dr. MacNeill in his study of the *Annals of Innisfallen*, which have incorporated the same Chronicle. Cf. also his paper in *Ériu*, viii, p. 166, ff.

Obscure as is the chronology of St. Patrick's career, two dates emerge from it with certainty—A.D. 432 as the opening year of his Irish mission, and A.D. 461 as the final year of his life. The case for the first rests on clear and unvarying tradition, and has never been seriously challenged. That for the second is derived from Tírechán's testimony, supported independently by the earliest and best of the annals, but it has had to struggle against a myth, popular, picturesque, and century-old, which claimed for Patrick at his death the six score years vouchsafed to the patriarch Moses. To Dr. Bury belongs the credit of having unearthed, restated and vindicated the genuine historical record.[1] Patrick's labours in Ireland thus extended over a period of twenty-nine years.

His main work as an apostle lay in the North, the Midlands, and the West. In Leinster the Bishop' Iserninus seems to have filled the leading role, but he got into difficulties with the secular ruler and was expelled. During the following reign Patrick paid a visit to that region and secured leave for Iserninus to return.[2] We hear, too, of a journey made by Patrick further south along the Barrow, for the purpose, it would seem, of organising the Christian communities in that territory. To undertake the leadership and higher spiritual care of these he chose the poet Fiacc, the first of the men of Leinster to receive episcopal consecration.[3] Of Munster we

---

[1] *Eng. Hist. Review*, xvii, p. 239 ff ; and *Life*, Append. 3, p. 331 ff ; and Append. 20, p. 382, ff.
[2] *B. Arm.* Add. 35 a and b.
[3] Ib., 35b.

know from Tírechán nothing beyond the bare fact that Patrick visited Cashel,[1] but the *notulae* added further on in the *Book of Armagh*[2] commemorate an apostolic journey that reached North-Eastern Cork and took in most of the present County of Limerick.

Such Christian congregations as existed before Patrick's arrival must have had their home in the far south, or in the south-east, nor can they have been imposing, either in numbers or in influence, for Patrick everywhere speaks of himself as a worker in an utterly heathen country.[3] Many were the trials and dangers through which he passed,[4] but God had brought him safely through them all, and given such success to his labours that he found himself exalted beyond measure in this world.[5] Why he should be the recipient of such favours he failed to understand, for he expected nought save poverty and disaster—fit reward for his demerits—and he hoped for nothing but servitude and martyrdom.[6] Yet his converts could be reckoned by thousands,[7] if indeed they were not beyond reckoning, since he speaks of them again as countless numbers.[8] That the Irish should be won from paganism and born anew in Christ was thus due, under God, to his preaching.[9] To the kings or princes, as the leading personages in the various states, he made a special appeal, which now and then was successful. In such cases the new faith was likely to be more easily accepted by the population over whom the converted king or prince held sway. But it must be pointed out that the sources lend no support whatever to the view that the conversion of the people was entirely from above—through the greater princes[10]—or that the

---

[1] Ib., Tir., 30b.

[2] Ib., 37 b. These, too, were probably compiled by Tirechán (MacNeill, *Journ. R.S.A.I.*, lviii, p. 98).

[3] *Conf.*, § 41 : " nunquam notitiam Dei habuerunt nisi idola et immunda usque nunc semper coluerunt."

[4] *Conf.*, §§ 52, 35. Cf. *B. Arm.*, Tír, 19b.

[5] *Conf.*, § 35.

[6] Ib. and § 59.

[7] *Conf.*, § 14 : " Quos in Domino ego baptizavi, tot milia hominum." Cf. §§ 38, 50.

[8] § 42 : " et de genere nostro qui ibi nati sunt nescimus numerum eorum." *Ep. Contra Cor.* Cf. § 12.

[9] *Ep. contra Cor.*, §§ 5, 9, 12.

[10] Loiguire, the High King, refused to become a Christian. *B. Arm.*, Tir., 19b. Likewise Enda Cennsalech, King of Leinster. Ib., § 35b ; Fiachu, son of Niall, who slew two foreign members of Patrick's household (Ib. 19b) ; Enda son of Amolngad and grand-nephew of Niall (Ib. 20b). True it is that Conall, son of the last-mentioned, was converted (20b), also Crimthann,

adoption of the new religion by one of these meant its adoption (almost as a matter of course) by his followers.[1]

§4—PATRICIAN FOUNDATIONS.

Next to the purely spiritual side of his ministry—baptizing, confirming and ordaining clergy[2]—Patrick's most important work would be the foundation of churches. Judged by modern

---

son of Enda Cennsalech, King of Leinster (35b) ; Conall, too, son of Niall (19b) ; and Feidlimid, son of Loigure, who granted the site for Trim.

But Patrick's chief benefactors, and evidently the mainstay of the Church in its earliest years, were minor lords like Dichu (4b), Daire (12b), Cairthin and Caichán (33b) and Féth Fio (33) of the Calraige. The poets Dubthach moccu Lugair (8b) and Fiacc of Sléibte (35b) ; two sons of a " faber aereus " (a well-to-do professional man—25a), and three propertied ladies who became nuns (34b) are among these particularly mentioned as his supporters. Grants of land made by these needed the consent of the tenants who were settled on the soil (33b : " atropert flaith ocus aithech inso huile i tosuch iar tabuirt baithis duaib—Lord and client granted all this immediately after baptism had been conferred on them " ; and cf. MacNeill, *Celtic Ireland*, p. 150), as well as of the King (MacNeill. l.c.). It is hardly likely that the clients would allow themselves to be so transferred until they had been won over by preaching to accept the new religion. Kings, however, when not converted themselves, were ready to allow Patrick a free hand for a consideration ; so much, at least, is to be gathered from the *Confession* (§ 52 : " interim praemia dabam regibus praeter quod dabam mercedem filiis ipsorum, qui mecum ambulant." Cf. *B. Arm.*, Tir., 19b : " Patrick had struck a bargain with Loiguire that he should not be slain in his kingdom). As the Apostle himself refused to take the smallest reward or gift from his converts (§ 49 and § 50 : " vel dimidio scriptulae—not even half a farthing ") the question arises where he procured the means to make these and similar (§ 53) payments. Was he helped by friends in Gaul ? This is the likeliest hypothesis. St. Hilary relates in his sketch of St. Honoratus that the alms entrusted to the latter saint for distribution were so enormous that he had to appoint trusty representatives in various places to dispose of them (P.L. l, col. 1261 : " plurimos multis locis probatissimos viros habuit, quorum semper manibus, quod sibi deferebatur, expenderet "). Honoratus received not only goods, but gold, and that in generous quantity (l.c. : " unum iam ex *multis miñbus* nummum aureum . . . arca retineret). Perhaps Lérins itself was the source of Patrick's affluence ; but a great church like Auxerre would likewise be able to aid his enterprise from its abundance.

[1] *B. Arm.* Tir., 20 a and b. Enda, son of Amolngad, of Mag Domnann, says of Patrick : " ego autem et fratres mei non possimus tibi credere usque dum ad nostram plebem pervenerimus, ne inrideant nos." Instead then of the conversion of the people following automatically on that of their rulers, the latter were afraid to accept the new faith without the consent of the former. This suggests that the whole question would be discussed, first, no doubt, by the ruler with his *airecht*, and then by the whole people at an oenach, or general gathering of the State. So, too, Enda Cennsalech (*B. Arm*, 35b) banishes the sons of Cathub, not so much because they become converts as because they became converts *ria cách* " before the rest " ; that is to say, without popular concurrence, which would normally be expressed in an assembly.

[2] *Conf.*, § 51 : " usque ad exteras partes ubi nemo ultra erat, et ubi nunquam aliquis pervenerat qui *baptizaret*, aut clericos *ordinaret*, aut populum *consummaret* (*consummatio*, whence Old Irish cosmait=confirmation). Cf § 38, § 50 and *B. Arm*. Tir. 18a.

standards these buildings were small, for the " great church "
of Patrick on the lands of Conall Gulban in Meath measured
but sixty feet in length.[1] The material, as a rule, was wood,
but where this was not forthcoming, the walls were constructed
more simply of clay or mud.[2] To whose care were these
churches entrusted ? In fifty and more cases where foundation
by Patrick is recorded, no details are given. But the instances
are likewise many where the narrative directly or indirectly
indicates the person or group of persons to whose care the
church was handed over. Tírechán maintains that bishops
were placed in charge of Argetbor (Meath),[3] Collumbus
(Meath),[4] Domhnach Mór (Donaghmore, Mayo),[5] Achad Fobuir
(Aghagower, Mayo),[6] Cellola Tog (Mayo),[7] Baslic (Roscommon),[8]
Dall Bronig (Meath),[9] Ardagh (Longford),[10] Bile (Longford),[11]
Raithen (Longford),[12] Forgnaide (Forgney, Longford),[13] Ail
Find (Elphin, Roscommon),[14] Saeoli,[15] Árd Sratho (Ardstraw,
Tyrone),[16] Cúil Raithin (Coleraine, Derry),[17] Dún Sebuirgi
(Dunseverick, Antrim),[18] Telach Ceneóil Oingusa (Drum-
tullagh, Antrim),[19] Domnach Maigen (Donaghmoyne,

---

[1] *B. Com.*, Tír, 19b.

[2] Ib., 28b : " fecit ecclesiam terrenam de humo quadratam, quia non
prope erat silva." Cf. Ib. 24a.

[3] *B. Arm.*, Tir., 19a : " in qua Kannanus episcopus, quem ordinavit
Patricius."

[4] Ib. : " in qua ordinavit Eugenium sanctum episcopum."

[5] Ib. 20b : " Mucneus, frater Cethiaci episcopi, cuius sunt reliquiae in
silva magna Fochlithi." 28b : " in qua sunt ossa sancta Mucnoi episcopi."

[6] Ib. 26a : " du Achud Fobuir, in quo fiunt episcopi. . . . et ordinavit
filium patris illius Senachus, . . . et episcopum fecit illum."

[7] Ib. 27a : " Cellola Tog in regionibus Corcu Teimne Patricii fuit. Cainnechus episcopus, monachus Patricii, fundavit eam."

[8] Ib. 25a : " frater episcopi Basilicae." Cf. *V. Trip.* i, 110. Tír,. 18b :
" Sachellus episcopus."

[9] *B. Arm.*, Tír., 21a : " et altera super fossam Dall Bronig quam tenuit
episcopus filius Cairtin, avunculus Brigtae."

[10] Ib. : " et venit in ii Tethbias et ordinavit Melum episcopum." Cf.
Vita Trip i, p. 82, 84, 86.

[11] Ib. : " et ecclesiam Bile fundavit et ordinavit Gosachtum filium Milcon
maccu Booin." Ib. : " 18 Gosacht episcopus."

[12] Ib. : " et mittens Camulacum . . . digito illi indicavit locum, ecclesiam
Raithin." Ib. 18b : " Camulacus episcopus."

[13] *B. Arm.*, Add. 32a : " Episcopus Manis hi Forgnidiu la Cuircniu."

[14] Ib. 22a : " et posuit ibi Assicum et Betheum filium fratris Assici et
Cipiam matrem Bethei episcopi." Ib. 18b : "Assicus episcopus." Cf. 22b.

[15] Ib. 22b : " et tertium in ecclesia magna Saeoli, super altare Felarti
episcopi." Cf. Healy, *Life*, p. 211.

[16] Ib. 29b : " et venit in Ard Sratho et Mac Ercae episcopum ordinavit."

[17] Ib. : " locum in quo est cellola Cuile Raithin in Eilniu, in quo fuit
episcopus."

[18] Ib. : " et in Dún Sebuirgi . . . ; ordinavit ibi Olcanum sanctum episcopum, quem nutrivit Patricius. . . ."

[19] Ib. Not. 36b : " epscop Ném i Telich Ceniuil Oingosa."

Monaghan),[1] Ath Truim (Trim, Meath),[2] Cell Usaile (Killishee, Kildare),[3] Cell Cuilinn (Kilcullen, Kildare),[4] Sléibte (Sletty, Carlow),[5] also of Caisel Irae (Cell-easpuig-Bróin : Killaspugbrone, Sligo),[6] and probably of Cell Alaid (Killala, Mayo),[7] and of Imgoe Már Cerrigi (barony of Costello, Mayo).[8] Tírechán in a catalogue of Patrician Bishops enumerates forty-two, but adds that there were many others.[9] A dozen or more not included in Tírechán's list are mentioned in the *Book of Armagh*, amongst them Tassach, Patrick's artisan, who brought Holy Viaticum to the dying Saint.[10] Tassach in later documents is styled Bishop of Ráth Colpa (Raholp) in Down.[11]

To priests were entrusted Cell Mór (Kilmore, Mayo),[12] Senchua (Shancoe, Sligo),[13] Cluain Caín i n-Achud (possibly Achonry, Sligo),[14] Mag Echnach (Meath),[15] Mag Réin (South Leitrim or West Longford),[16] a church beside Bile Torten (Meath)[17] others in Mag Foimsen (Mayo),[18] Ráth Muadain (Ramoan, Antrim)[19]; and at some place that cannot easily

---

[1] Ib. 30a : "et ordinavit Victoricum Machinensem episcopum, et ecclesiam magnam fundavit."

[2] *B. Arm*, Add. 32a : "et mansit Lomman cum Foirtcherno in Vado Truimm, usque dum pervenit Patricius ad illos et aedificavit ecclesiam." 32b : "Foirtchernus etc. Hi omnes episcopi fuerunt et principes." . . .

[3] *B. Arm*., Not. 37a. Cf. 18b : "Auxilius episcopus."

[4] *B. Arm*. Tír., 30b : "et ordinavit Mac Taleum in Cellola Cuilinn." 18b : "Mac Taleus episcopus."

[5] Ib. : "ordinavit Feccum Album i Sléibti." Cf. 35b : "Dubbert grád n-epscoip. fair." 18b : "Feccus episcopus."

[6] Cf. *B. Arm*. Tír., 29a.

[7] *V. Trip*., 134.

[8] *B. Arm*., Tír., 25b. Cf. 454b : "et diaconus fuit Patricio . . . episcopus, presbyter bonus, et fundavit ecclesiam in Imgoe Mair Cerrigi liberam."

[9] Ib. 18b.

[10] Ib. Muir, 15b : "sacrificum ab episcopo Tassach . . . ad viaticum beatae vitae acceperat."

[11] Gloss. on Fiacc's Hymn. *Thes. Paleoh*. ii, 319. Also note in *L.B*. on Calendar of Oingus, April 24th.

[12] *B. Arm*., Tír., 18b : "Olcanus monachus qui fuit in Cellola Magna Muaide presbyter."

[13] Ib., Not. 36b : "Ailbe in Senchui." Tír. 29a : "ordinavit Ailbeum sanctum presbyterum."

[14] Ib. Add. 33a : "et ipse Patricius eam (ecclesiam) commendavit sanctis viris, id est, presbytero Medb et presbytero Sadb."

[15] *B. Arm*. Tír. 21a : "alteram in Campo Echnach in qua fuit Cassanus presbyter." Cf. ib. 24b and *V. Trip*. i, 74 : "Cruimtir Cassan i nDomnach mór Maigi Echnach."

[16] Ib. : "et venit in Campum Rein, et ordinavit Bruscum presbyterum et ecclesiam illi fundavit."

[17] Ib. 30a : "exiit et fecit ecclesiam Justano presbytero iuxta Bile Torten."

[18] Ib. 26a : "et exinde exiit ad Campum Foimsen . . . et reliquit in illo loco Conanum presbyterum."

[19] Ib., Not. 36b : "et presbyter Erclach in Raith Muadain." Cf. *V. Trip*., i, p. 146.

be identified.[1] Of Cell Airthir and Cluain Ernáin, two further churches over which priests presided,[2] we do not know whether they owe their establishment to Patrick or not.

A foundation at Ard Licce (Kilkeevan, Roscommon) was given in charge to a deacon[3]; another at Ard Senlis (Roscommon?) to one of his followers who apparently was a consecrated virgin.[4] Two nuns were likewise established in the wood of Fochlud, in the West,[5] and another, Adrochta, daughter of Talan, in a church which still gives its name (Cell Adrochta, Killaraght) to a parish in Sligo.[6] Only in one instance, Airne (in barony of Costello, Mayo) is it said that a church was handed over to an abbot.[7] The community here seems to have included bishops (Sachell and Loarn) and priests (Broccaid and Medb)[8] but these were probably active evangelists, but loosely attached to any residence, whilst two of them appear elsewhere in independent positions with other Patrician churches under their rule.[9] Communities were likewise established at Ath Broon (Meath), where three brethren and a sister are referred to by name,[10] and at Senella Cella Dumiche (Sligo), to which three brethren (one of them

---

[1] Ib. *Add.* 33b : " Binean filius Lugni, scriba atque sacerdos . . . et benedixit (Patricius) illum et reliquit illum in suo loco." P. Grosjean (*AA. SS. Boll.*, T. iv Nov. p. 178, n. 8) identifies the place as Kilbannon, the church which gave its name to a parish situated, for the most part, in the Barony of Dunmore, Co. Galway. On the genealogy and date of Binean filius Lugni there is a learned note by the same scholar in *Anal. Boll.*, xliii, p. 255 ff.
[2] Ib., Not. 36b : " Presbyter Lugach in Cell Airthir. Presbyter Colomb in Cluain Ernain." Cf. *V. Trip.* i, 74.
[3] *B. Arm.*, Tír., 24a : " et fundaverunt (Patricius et socii eius) ecclesiam in Ard Licce . . . et posuit in illa Coimanum diaconum." Cf. *Concil. Eliber.* (c. A.D. 300). Can. 77 : " diaconus regens plebem."
[4] Ib. : " et tenuit Patricius Ard Senlis, et posuit filiam in ea sanctam Lalocam."
[5] Ib. 28b : " duae filiae venerunt ad Patricium et acceperunt pallium de manu eius, et benedixit illis locum super silvam Fochlithi."
[6] Ib. 25a : " Adrochta filia Talain, et ipsa accepit pallium de manu Patricii."
[7] Ib. 25b : " et invenit Iarnascum sanctum sub ulmo . . . et plantavit ibi ecclesiam, et tenuit illum abbatem."
[8] Ib. *Add.* 33a : " S. Patricius familiam suam in regione Ciarrichi . . . id est episcopum Sachellum et Brocidium et Loarnum et presbyterum Medb."
[9] Sachell—*B. Arm.* Tír., 25a. Cf. *V. Trip.* i, 110. Loarn—bishop in Brechtan (Bright). *Trip.* i, 38. Medb. Ib. *Add.* 33a : " et ipse (Patricius) eam ecclesiam commendavit sanctis viris, id est, presbytero Medb et presbytero Sadb."
[10] Ib. 19b : " et ibi ecclesiam fundavit in qua reliquit tres fratres cum una sorore ; et haec sunt nomina illorum Cathaceus, Cathurus, Catneus et soror eorum Catnea."

a priest) and a sister were again assigned.[1] Furthermore,
fifteen foreign monks (of whom but two, who had received
episcopal consecration,[2] are specified), and a foreign sister,
were provided for in various places.[3] Different from these
seem to have been the two "barbarian" monks, Conleng
and Ercleng, left by Patrick in Mag Glais (Moyglass, Roscommon).[4] It is likely, but not certain, that the "family"
to whose care Patrick confided a church "in the bosom of
the sea," near Killala, was monastic.[5] Cainnech, bishop and
monk,[6] Olcán, priest and monk,[7] and Coimán, deacon and
monk,[8] have already been mentioned. Assicus the bishop,
Patrick's goldsmith, who had been placed over the community
of Elphin, deserted his post and fled to a hermitage in Tír
Chonaill, where he dwelt in retirement for seven years. He
was then discovered by his monks and prevailed upon to
return, but he died at Ráth Cungai (Racoon, Donegal) on the
way.[9] A nun named Comgella rendered special aid to Bishop
Cethiacus, who himself may have had monastic vows[10];
whilst Cipia, mother of Bishop Betheus,[11] two sisters of Bishop
Felartus,[12] and a sister to an anonymous bishop of the race
of Corcu Teimne, [13] are among the other pious women who
assisted in the work of conversion.

---

[1] Ib. 22b : " et fundavit in illo loco ecclesiam quae sic vocatur Senella
Cella Dumiche, in quo reliquit viros sanctos Macet et Cetgen et Rodanum
presbyterum. Mathona quae tenuit pallium apud Patricium et Rodanum
monacha fuit illis." Cf. Ib. 13b : " a familia Dumiche." Not. 36b and 458 (1).
[2] *B. Arm.* 18b—2.
[3] *B. Arm.*, Tír., 24b : " Franci vero Patricii exierunt a Patricio viri fratres
XV cum sorore una . . . et multi loci illis dati sunt."
[4] Ib. 22a : " posuit cellolam magnam . . . et in illa reliquit duos barbaros
Conleng et Ercleng, monachos sibi." Why are these called *barbari ?* Dr.
MacNeill notes that both names are Gaelic, and suggests that they may belong
to Irish settlers in Britain, who, from the standpoint of a Roman citizen,
would be barbarians. It is likely enough that such, if Christians, would help
in the conversion of their own people. A Latinised form of the name Ercleng
occurs in a Cornish inscription : " tres filii *Ercilinci*"—Hübner, Inscript.
Brit. Christ. No. 10. Holder, Altkeltischer Sprachschatz, s.v.
[5] Ib. 28b : " et aedificavit ecclesiam quandam apud familiam in sinu
maris, id est, Ros filiorum Catni."
[6] Ib. 27a.
[7] Ib. 18b.
[8] Ib. 24a
[9] *B. Arm.*, 22b, Not. 36b;
[10] Ib. 24a. Cf. 454a : " quia Cethiaci monachi dicunt monacham esse
Comgella Cethiaco."
[11] Ib. 22b.
[12] Ib. 24b, cf. 454b.
[13] Ib. 29b.

§5—The Church Founded by St. Patrick primarily
Episcopal and Clerical.   Monasticism had in it
an Important but a Secondary Place.

In his letter denouncing Coroticus, St. Patrick speaks of
himself as a bishop,[1] proclaiming thereby his ecclesiastical
authority over his Irish neophytes. As their superior he has
the fullest right to protest. Again in the "Confession" he
laments in moving terms the opposition offered by many to
the "laborious episcopate" which he was anxious to undertake.[2] In the passage it is implied that he is sole bishop in
the island, but this may reasonably be interpreted to mean
that all others—including bishops—owed allegiance to him
as their superior. His supreme jurisdiction over the Church
in Ireland is indeed assumed as a matter of course in his own
writings, and is confirmed by Irish tradition. The *Annals
of Ulster* record that in A.D. 439 three bishops came from
abroad to Patrick's aid.[3] One of these, Secundinus, before
his death in A.D. 447, wrote in his master's honour a laudatory
poem which is still extant.[4] From this fact alone it is evident
that Patrick was the great outstanding figure of the mission.
The two remaining Bishops, Auxilius and Iserninus, are found
closely associated with their leader in a joint letter to the
Irish clergy, in which various rules of ecclesiastical conduct
(with penalties for violation) are determined. As Secundinus
is not mentioned with the others we must conclude that the
letter was not published until after his death in A.D. 447.
From the superscription of the letter it is likely that even
then, more than sixteen years since the beginning of the

---

[1] *Ep.*, § 1.: "Hiberione constitutum episcopum me esse fateor."
[2] *Conf.*, § 26.
[3] A.U. 439: "Secundus, Auxilius et Serninus mittuntur—et episcopi
ipsi—in Hiberniam in auxilium Patricii."
[4] Ussher, *Works* vi, 383f. Todd, *Liber Hymn.*, 7-42. Atkinson and Bernard,
Liber Hymn,. i, p. 3-13. Manitius, *Geschichte der christlich—lateinischen
Poesie*, p. 238, identifies the writer of this hymn with a Secundinus to whom
Sidonius Apollinaris sent a letter, but this identification is chronologically
impossible. That the hymn is a genuine work of St. Patrick's helper is
generally admitted. The Saint is spoken of as still living and working with
immense success. Though addressed in a vague phrase to "omnes amantes
Deum," it seems to be intended chiefly for the learned clerics in Gaul and
Britain who opposed Patrick's undertaking. Its purpose is, therefore, that
of the later *Confession*—to exonerate the Apostle of Ireland from the charge
of presumption in applying himself to a task for which he was utterly unfitted.
In the lines "perfectamque propter vitam aequatur apostolis" and "cum
apostolis regnabit sanctus super Israhel," may perhaps be sought the origin
of the legend that Patrick will judge his Irish children on the day of doom.

mission, Auxilius and Iserninus were Patrick's sole episcopal helpers.[1] But there is never any suggestion that their position was other than subordinate.[2] Of our native-born bishops the most prominent, Benén or Benignus,[3] is represented as a disciple of the Saint from boyhood and subject absolutely to Patrick's authority until his death.[4]

Patrick thus appears as chief bishop of the Irish Church and its supreme local ruler. His jurisdiction extended over the whole island,[5] which for ecclesiastical purposes was regarded as a single province.[6] Over the more important churches which he founded Patrick, as his work progressed, placed bishops, many of them drawn from the group of clerics by whom, like St. Martin,[7] he was habitually accompanied.[8]

---

[1] Haddan and Stubbs, *Councils*, ii, 328 : " Presbyteris et diaconibus et omni clero Patricius, Auxilius, Iserninus episcopi salutem." Dr. MacNeill was the first to draw attention to the implication stated in the text.

Haddan and Stubbs, following Todd and Wasserschleben, regard this document as spurious. For an able defence of its genuineness see Bury, *Life*, 233–45. Todd rejected the early date of the Canons and assigned them to the ninth or tenth century, chiefly because of the injunction in Canon 6 that the clergy should wear the Roman tonsure, and the implications in Canons 30 and 34 of " a more near approach to diocesan jurisdiction as well as a more settled state of Christianity in the country than was possible in the days of St. Patrick." Bury's answer to both objections is satisfactory. With regard to the second, it may be added that to speak of " a near approach to diocesan jurisdiction " as an indication of lateness is to make a singularly weak appeal. For no century is the proof of diocesan jurisdiction easier than for that in which St. Patrick lived.

[2] Cf. *Chron. Scot.* s.a. 438, and *Annals of Inisfallen*, s.a. 440 : " nec tamen tenuerunt apostolatum, nisi Patricius solus."

[3] Rejecting Bury's theory (*Life*, 164 and 310) that Iserninus was an Irishman. The Irish called him Fith, but this alone is insufficient as a proof of his Irish birth. Again the statement (*B. Arm. Add.* 35a) that he came to his " district " or " territory " (cennadach) can be understood of the district entrusted to his missionary care. For Dr. MacNeill's theory of how the name Fith arose see *J.R.S.A.I.*, vol. lviii, p. 7–8. The form Iserninus is British, not Irish (cf. Pedersen, *Vergleich. Gram.* i, 73).

[4] *B. Arm.* Tír., 18a, 19a, 24b, 33.

[5] Implied in the *Epistle*, § 1. The tradition to this effect was strong at Armagh (*B. Arm.* 21b. Cf. *Liber Angeli* 40b), nor is there any reason to reject it. Cf. Bury, *Life*, 162 f.

[6] Cf. *A.U.* 443 : " Patricius episcopus ardore fidei et doctrina Christi florens in *provincia nostra*." Todd, *Life*, 470 note, understands the word *provincia* of the district round Armagh ; adding the strange comment : " From the pen of Maguire (compiler of the *Annals*) in the fifteenth century the word would scarcely have meant anything than the district round Armagh." As if Maguire invented this annal, and did not transcribe it, as he transcribed the rest, from old (and admittedly excellent) sources. For " provincia " in the sense of all Ireland see the letter of Pope-Elect John IV to Irish ecclesiastics in A.D. 640 (Bede, *H.E.*, ii, 19) : " repperimus quosdam provinciae vestrae . . . novam ex veteri haeresim renovare conantes. . . ."

[7] *Sulp. Sev. Ep.* iii. *C.S.E.L.* i, p. 147 : " ita profectus cum suo illo, ut semper, frequentissimo discipulorum sanctissimoque comitatu."

[8] *B. An. Muir.* 6a : " Patricius cum suis." Ib. 8b : " benedictis in nomine Jesu Christi sociis suis octo viris." Ib. 15a : " cum comitibus suis." *Tír.* 20b : " cum exercitu laicorum (et) episcoporum sanctorum 22a, etc."

Where the church was of less significance, he placed it under
the care of a priest or deacon. What the particular qualifications were which gave a church its distinction and made
it the site of an episcopal see, we cannot now determine, but
the evidence goes to show that they were not very exacting.
Armagh was originally but the foremost church in the territory
of Dáire, a petty chieftain. Its proper *parochia*[1], or diocese,
governed directly by the Bishop of Armagh, was probably
confined at first to Dáire's diminutive principality ; though
even then the see had a pre-eminence of its own, because of
the special position of its ruler, who was not merely Bishop of
Armagh, but chief bishop of the country. Trim, in the same
way, was the episcopal church in the territory of Féidlimid,
son of Loiguire, and all other churches in that territory would
be subject to its bishop.[2] Munis had his episcopal see at
Forgney in Longford, with jurisdiction evidently over the
small state called Cuircne, now represented in the greater part
by the Westmeath barony of Kilkenny West, bordering on
Loch Ree.[3] Iserninus seems to have been placed over " the
tiny people (or small state) of Catrige, in Cliu," to the west of
the Barrow, from Sléibte northwards.[4] Fiacc Find, " the
first bishop to be consecrated amongst the Leinstermen,"[5]
was intimately connected with Crimthann, son of Enda
Cennsalach, and it is not improbable that the sphere of his
authority coincided with the territory afterwards known as
Uí Cennselaig.[6] As this Leinster state was comparatively
extensive, Fiacc's see of Sléibte was of some importance amid
the early Christian settlements of the country.[7] Bishop

---

[1] *Parochia* is the common Latin word for diocese until the ninth century.
Hinschius : *Kirchenrecht* ii, 38. Cf. Eusebius, *H.E.*, l. 5, c. 23. Du Cange,
Gloss, s.v. Παροικίαι in Eusebius, l.c., is applied to groups of Christians
scattered in various regions but attached to one ecclesiastical centre and
under one bishop.
[2] *B. Arm. Add.* 31b–32a : " Statimque credidit Fedelimidius, cum omni
familia sua et immolavit illi et Sancto Patricio regionem suam." Trim was
the principal church of this region. 32b gives a list of its first eight bishops.
[3] Ib. 32a : " Episcopus Manis hi Forgnidiu la Cuircniu."
[4] Ib. *Add.* 35a : " dutét dia chennadich, aicme becc i Cliu, Cotrige (or
Catrige) a ainm. MacNeill, *J.R.S.A.I.*, lviii, p. 8–9, gives the correct form
of the name, *Cuthraige*, and shows where the sept was located.
[5] Ib. 35b : " Conide epscop insin citaruoirtned la Laigniu."
[6] *B. Arm.*, Tír., 30b : " Ordinavit (Patricius) Album i Sleibti." Cf. *Add.*
35b. 36a : " Dulluid iarsuidiu Patricc co Fiacc ocus durind a locc les . . .
ocus adopart Crimthann in port sin du Patricc."
[7] Dr. Gwynn : *Introd.* to *B. Arm.* p. lxxi, calls Sletty " the metropolis
of Leinster," but " metropolis " is perhaps a too pregnant term. Ireland
as a single province had but one metropolis—Armagh. The Preface to
Fiacc's Hymn, to which Dr. Gwynn refers (*Lib. Hymn*, i, 96), says that Fiacc
was " the chief Bishop of Leinster thenceforth, and his successor after him."

Cainnech, of the people called Corcu Teimne or Temenrige, in Mayo, had his church in their midst, and may have exercised episcopal jurisdiction over the whole of their diminutive state.[1] With regard to the other sees established by St. Patrick,[2] it is more difficult to tell the exact territories of which they were meant to be the centres. This may be due to our ignorance of Fifth Century civil divisions, but it is more probably due to St. Patrick's policy of not committing himself from the beginning to a hard-and-fast scheme of ecclesiastical boundaries. The country had still to be converted, so that when sees had been established in more or less central positions, the need of the moment was satisfied. The exact limits of their jurisdiction might be left undecided until time had shown how the sees would develop. Patrick could appeal to tradition in leaving matters thus indeterminate, for *even in Southern Gaul*, where Christianity had been planted at such an early period, *the frontiers of dioceses were not absolutely fixed in the middle of the fifth century*.[3] Yet the Church in Gaul was then excellently organised, for the *Notitia Galliarum* (A.D. 390–413) shows the country provided with 113 cities, of which 110 were dioceses, grouped in 17 provinces.[4] If the organisation, however elaborate, was not yet complete in that country, what was to be expected of Ireland, where Christianity was barely beginning to make its first great conquests? In Southern Germany a similar condition of affairs prevailed as late as A.D. 750.[5]

One point at least which emerges clear from the story of St. Patrick as recorded by Tírechán is the conviction that the Apostle was prepared to place prelates over quite small districts. Tírechán relates that the saint consecrated for the Irish Church no less than 450 bishops,[6] a figure manifestly

---

[1] Ib. 27a : " Cellola Tog in regionibus Corcu Teimne Patricii fuit. Cainnechus episcopus monachus Patricii fundavit eam." Cf. 29b.

[2] See supra, p. 78 f.

[3] Hauck : *Kirchengeschichte Deutschlands*, i, 41 : " Immerhin zeigen die südgallischen Verfügungen dass die Bistümer um das Jahr 450 *weder innerhalb der eigenen Grenzen konsolidiert noch klar gegen einander abgegrenzt waren*. Vollends ihre Verbindung zu grösseren Kirchenkörpen, wie sie sich im Morgenlande entwickelt hatte, war noch in den Anfängen."

[4] M.G.H. *Auct. Ant.* ix, 584 ff.

[5] Noch immer gab es weder feste Bischofssitze noch bestimmt abgegrenzte Diözesen (Hauck, op. cit., p. 383).

[6] *B. Arm.* 18a : " de episcoporum numero quos ordinavit in Hibernia, CCCCL." Cf. *Catal. SS. Hib.* Ussher, *Works*, vi, p. 477, where the number given is 350. It may be noted that the baronies, which in most cases represent ancient *tuatha* or civil divisions, numbered (including half-baronies) 325. O'Curry, *Manners and Customs* I, xcviii.

extravagant, though it may perhaps be true that an exceedingly high number would have been reached had the whole island been parcelled out into episcopal districts, no larger than those over which bishops had actually been placed.[1] It is significant, however, that Tírechán's list[2] of bishops (already mentioned) contains but forty-two names ; nor will additions from other sources bring the total number beyond sixty. Even this figure is exceedingly large for St. Patrick's lifetime, and the suspicion is justified that some of the prelates in Tírechán's collection never had any existence outside of that author's imagination. Such bishops as were appointed by St. Patrick in the first period of his apostolate were drawn, no doubt, from the foreign helpers referred to in the Catalogue.[3] That he experienced much difficulty (at least in the, early years of his mission) in finding suitable native candidates for the episcopal office is only what we should expect, recent converts from paganism being unfit, as a rule, for such high responsibilities. There were, of course, exceptions, like Fiacc Find, a distinguished man of letters, and the first to be raised to episcopal office among the Leinstermen, but the story of Fiacc's selection betrays the fact that the field of choice was then extremely limited. Patrick asked his friend Dubthach to point out " a man of good birth, without defect or blemish, and of moderate wealth " ; preferably (since the possibility of discovering a celibate of parts among adult converts was too remote to be worth considering),[4] " a man of one wife into

---

[1] The practice of multiplying sees became widespread in the fourth century. Thus Peter, Patriarch of Alexandria, consecrated fifty-five bishops within a period of eleven years (A.D. 300–11), P.G. xviii, col. 455). This can be explained only by assuming that he created many new dioceses. In Africa the number grew from about 75 at the beginning of the third century to 150 at the death of St. Cyprian (A.D. 257). By A.D. 411 Catholic and Donatist bishops combined reached a total of about 750, and the Donatist prelates, when converted, were allowed to retain their sees in all places where Catholic bishops had not already been established. Sees were thus to be found in the most insignificant localities. Yet it was not Africa but Asia Minor that ranked as the classic land of bishops. Thomassin : Vetus et nova Eccl. Disciplina i, ch. 54, p. 108 f ; Bingham : Antiquities, ii, 51 f. Cf. Dict. de Theol. cath. T.v., part ii, col. 1692–3.

[2] B. Arm., Tir. 18b.

[3] Haddan and S., Councils ii, p. 292.

[4] St. Paul's desire (1 Cor. vii, 7–8) that all men should be like himself — unmarried—would hold especially for ministers of the Gospel, but the burden was one which few could then bear. Elsewhere, then (1 Tim. iii, 2 ; Titus i, 6), we find the Apostle demanding of candidates for bishop's and deacon's orders only a measure of moral stability of character, displayed, in an age of frequent divorce, by faithfulness to one wife. This remained the common custom of the Church, both East and West, down to the fourth century. Marriage, unless contracted more than once, did not exclude from

whom hath been born but one child," and Dubthach replied that only one man possessing such qualities was known to him.[1] That Patrick had no wish to multiply sees unnecessarily is clear from the fact that he entrusted many churches to clerics in lower orders, and perhaps[2] from his treatment of Sachell and Cethech, who had consecrated bishops (and ordained clergy) in Roscommon without his consent.[3] The two made reparation for this offence by a period of severe penance at Armagh.[4]

---

the higher orders ; but it was forbidden to those who had not entered into it before ordination. At the Council of Nicaea (A.D. 325) it was proposed that married bishops, priests and deacons should be compelled to renounce their conjugal rights, but the assembled Fathers judged it more prudent to leave renunciation to the free choice of those concerned. In the West celibacy was made a matter of precept by the local Council of Elvira, in Spain (c. A.D. 300) ; then by a Roman Council under Pope Siricius in A.D. 386. The decision of the latter Council was communicated by the Pope to the bishops of Africa and Spain (to those of the latter Church through Himerius, Bishop of Tarragona). Neglect of the ordinance was to be punished with excommunication. Pope Innocent I (A.D. 402–17) addressed letters to Victricius, Bishop of Rouen, and Euperius, Bishop of Toulouse, on the same subject ; whilst Pope Leo the Great (died A.D. 461) extended the application of the law to sub-deacons. The great western writers of the fourth and fifth centuries—St. Ambrose, St. Jerome, St. Augustine, St. Hilary and others— gave strong support to the law by their teaching. Fiacc of Sletty, once consecrated, would thus be obliged to separate from his wife or to live with her as a sister. His selection for a bishopric, despite the conjugal bond, is to be explained only by the dearth of suitable celibate candidates. But fifth century Gaul provides illustrious examples in the persons of St. Paulinus of Nola, Sidonius Apollinaris of Clermont and others. On the general question of ecclesiastical celibacy see Thomassin : *Nova et vetus Eccl. Disciplina* ii, chaps. lx–lxiii, p. 238 ff ; Funk : *Kirchengesch. Abhandlungen*, Paderborn, 1897, Bd. i, p. 121 ff ; Vacandard : *Études de critique et d'histoire religieuse*, Paris, 1905, p. 71 ff ; Hefele-Leclercq : article " célibat " in *Dict. d'archéol. chrét.* ; Böhmer : *Die Entstehung des Zölibats* in *Geschichtl. Studien A. Hauck dargebracht*, 1916.

[1] *B. Arm. Add.* 35b : " Áliss Patricc Dubthach im damnae n-epscuip dia desciplib di Laignib, idón, fer sóer, socheniúil cen on cen ainim nadip ru-becc nadip ro-mar bed a sommae. *Toisc limm fer oínsétche dunarruchtae act oentuistiu.* Frisgart Dubtach : nifetorsa dim muintir act Fiacc Find di Laignib."

[2] Patrick's objection in this case may not have been to the creation of new bishops and clergy, but to their creation by his subordinates, without permission from himself. In Gaul and in the Western Church generally, at this period, the bishop of a widowed see was selected by the clergy and people over whom he was to rule, but the document attesting their choice (decretum electionis) had to be presented to the metropolitan for approval. If this were granted, the metropolitan, assisted by two or more bishops of the province, proceeded to consecrate the new prelate. Such a system would naturally need to be modified in a missionary country, and we can well understand that St. Patrick reserved the appointment of all bishops to himself—or at least insisted on his right to confirm selections made by others. Bingham : *Antiquities*, ii, ch. 16, sect. 12, p. 63 f. Leclercq : Article " Consécration épiscopale," in *Dict. d'archéol. chrét.* T. iii, pt. 2, col. 2183.

[3] *B. Arm.*, Tír., 17a : " Caetiacus itaque et Sachellus ordinabant episcopos, presbyteros, diaconos, clericos sine consilio Patricii in Campo Aii."

[4] *B. Arm.* Tír., 17a : " et accusavit illos Patricius et mittens epistolas illis exierunt ad poenitentiam ducti ad Ard Mache ad Patricium, et fecerunt poenitentiam monachorum."

Had Ireland possessed cities after the Continental model, St. Patrick would undoubtedly have made them centres of ecclesiastical government, following the invariable practice since the first days of the Church. But cities were not forthcoming ; the dún of the ruling prince could not be used, since it was his private dwelling-place ; and points of vantage like the hills of assembly could not be occupied because of the traditional purposes which they served. The see had thus to be fixed in a locality apart ; but the position, we may be sure, was selected with a special eye to its suitability as an administrative centre. As the bishop everywhere else in Christendom ruled in a *civitas*, so conversely the seats of ecclesiastical rule in Ireland, though not civitates in the Latin sense, came to be known by that term. In the Patrician documents the word is used of Armagh,[1] Slane[2] and Sléibte[3] ; and is in general connected with bishops and with the National Apostle.[4] At a later period the word (like its Irish equivalent *cathair*) was applied in a wider sense to any important monastery[5] ; and again by a further extension to places of assembly like Tara[6] and Tailtiu[7].

These primitive ecclesiastical " cities " were probably diminutive in size. Some details of Sléibte are preserved in the Book of Armagh, where it is related that an angel came to Fiacc with orders to transfer his establishment to the West

---

[1] *B. Arm. Muir.* 13a : " et illa est *civitas* quae nunc Ardd Machae nominatur."

[2] *B. Arm. Muir.* 13a : " in illa *civitate* quae vocatur Slane." That this see was founded by St. Patrick is likely, for the death of its bishop is recorded A.D. 512.

[3] Ib. 40a : " dictante Aiduo Slebtiensis *civitatis* episcopo."

[4] *B. Arm. Lib. Angeli* 41b : " item omnis ecclesia libera et *civitas* ab episcopali gradu videtur esse fundata in tota Scotorum insula." If we accept this reading it is clear that when the *Liber Angeli* was written (before A.D. 700) there was a tradition (grown by that time somewhat indistinct) that each *civitas* was originally founded as a bishop's see. If, on the other hand, we read with Bury (*Life*, p. 378, note 2) : " omnis ecclesia libera et civitas (quae) ab episcopali gradu videtur esse fundata " (a reading which agrees better with the context), the phrase becomes the subject of what follows : " in speciali societate Patricii Pontificis et Heredis cathedrae eius Aird Machae esse debuerat." Here the *civitas* founded by a bishop is distinguished implicitly from that founded by a presbyter (see next note), and the former is declared to depend in a particularly intimate way upon Armagh. The ultimate reason for this is again the fact that the *civitas* was originally a bishop's see founded by St. Patrick.

[5] *A.U.* 715 : " Pascha commutatur in Eoa *civitate*." Ib. 781 : " Cormac mac Breasail, abbas Airdd Breccain et aliarum *civitatum*." Cf. Ib. s.a. 807, 824, 834, 837, 839, etc. ; and *Trip. Life.* Index s.v. *city* ; and Bury l.c., p. 378.

[6] *B. Arm.* 19b : " ad civitatem Temro."

[7] *A.U.* 783 : " ad civitatem Tailten."

side of the river. " On the spot where they would find the
wild boar, there they should place their refectory, and on the
spot where they would find the doe, there they should place
their church. But Fiacc said to the angel that he would not
go until Patrick should come to mark out his settlement for
him, and to consecrate it, and that it was from Patrick (alone)
that he would receive it. Patrick in fact did come to Fiacc
and marked out his settlement for him, and placed his
measuring-rod on it."[1] From this we infer that the site for an
ecclesiastical settlement was measured out by the founder,
and that the church and refectory were the chief buildings.
A record in the Tripartite Life, certainly ancient and credible,
gives a fuller account of the first foundation at Armagh.[2]
Patrick, according to this record, allowed seven score feet to
the enclosure, twenty-seven feet to the large house, seventeen
feet to the kitchen, and seven feet to the oratory. " And it
was thus that the houses of the ecclesiastical establishment
(congbála) were built always." The normal settlement was
thus a *less* or enclosure, 140 feet in diameter, surrounded by a
high wall of earth. Within this enclosure were three buildings
—a " large house " wherein the clerics dwelt, a church or
oratory where Mass was celebrated, and a kitchen, which
probably served also as a refectory. Distinct from these
" cities," peopled by the bishop and his helpers, were the
isolated churches, served by one or two clerics. It seems likely
that the bishop and his clergy, according to Patrick's scheme
of organisation, should form in every case a relatively large
establishment—such in fact as might be termed a " *civitas* "—
but if these foundations were at all as numerous as Tírechán
states the majority of them did not fulfil their promise, and
sank later into obscurity

What is to be said of the view that most, if not all, of St.
Patrick's helpers were bound by monastic vows ?[3] Let us
examine the evidence. Muirchu is silent about monks or
monasteries. So, too, is Tírechán to the end of his First Book,
save in the Catalogue of Patrick's missionaries,[4] where in a
total that exceeds seventy he designates three as monks.
Similarly in the account of churches entrusted by St. Patrick

---

[1] *B. Arm. Add.* 35b ; 36a.
[2] *Trip. L.* i, p. 236.
[3] Bury, *Life*, 378 : " Hence Patrick's bishops were probably in most cases
monks." He quotes, however, but one instance in support of this statement.
[4] *B. Arm.* 18b.

to various followers some twenty bishops are mentioned, but one only among these is described as a monk.[1] Of another bishop, *Assicus*, we learn incidentally that he held the government of a monastery, but the story which preserves the record portrays him as an utter failure in his abbatial as well as in his episcopal capacity, for he fled secretly from Elphin to a hermitage in Donegal, and lived there in retirement as a contemplative. When discovered by his monks after a search of seven years, and led homewards in a kind of honourable captivity, he escaped the responsibilities which awaited him by dying upon the way.[2] Monks are likewise mentioned in connection with the Patrician bishops, Cethiacus,[3] and Iserninus[4] and the monastic character of a fifth is possibly suggested.[5] Elsewhere a priest[6] is described as a monk ; also a deacon,[7] two " barbarians "[8], and one of the Saint's disciples in Armagh.[9] Finally there is reference to an abbot,[10] placed by St. Patrick over a newly-founded church, and to fifteen " Frankish brethren,"[11] some of whom may have been monks, for the ecclesiastical status of only two amongst them is specified.[12]

To these must be added the consecrated virgins, one of whom was appointed to aid three brethren in the care of the church[13] ; another served the Frankish brethren just mentioned[14] ; a third, Mathona, took the veil from Patrick and

---

[1] *B. Arm*, Tír., 27a : " Cainnechus episcopus, monachus Patricii."
[2] *B. Arm*, Tír., 22b. Cf. 29b.
[3] Ib. 24a ; 45a : " quia Cethiaci monachi dicunt monacham esse Comgella Cethiaco." Ib. *Add* 33b.
[4] Ib. *Add*. 35b.
[5] *B. Arm*., Tír., 29b : " episcopus cum sorore una monachi Patricii."
[6] Ib. 18b : " Olcanus monachus, presbyter."
[7] Ib. 24a : " Coimanus."
[8] Ib. 22a : " Conleng et Ercleng."
[9] Ib. 25b.
[10] Ib. 25b: " Iarnasc. Et tenuit illum abbatem."
[11] Ib. 24b.　　　　　　　　　[12] Ib. 24b. Cf. 18b.
[13] Ib. 19b ; Cf. 29b : " episcopus cum sorore una, monachi Patricii."
[14] Ib. 24b. Could there have been *Frankish* brethren among Patrick's helpers ? It is well known that the conversion of the Franks to Christianity followed the baptism of their king, Chlodovech, at Rheims, probably on December 25th, 496. Auxiliary troops of Franks are found in the Roman army from the third century onwards. A small colony of the same nation received lands in imperial Gaul in the fourth century, whilst individual Franks occupied high positions in the army and the State under the Emperors. But all these, with negligible exceptions, seem to have remained pagans (Hauck : *Kirchengeschichte Deutschlands*, i, 102-7). The Burgundians, on the other hand, had gone over in a body to Christianity at latest in A.D. 416 (op. cit., p. 100). Dr. MacNeill suggests that the name *Franci* is " perhaps only an anachronism of nomenclature. From later usage it appears that *Galli, Gaill*, came to mean Continentals generally, not Scots, nor Picts nor Britons. This would necessitate a special name for the inhabitants of Gallia, and Franks would carry that meaning even for the earlier time."

Rodanus, " et monacha fuit illis[1]." Of two others it is recorded that they took the veil from the Saint's hand, and that he blessed for them a settlement in the Western wood of Fochlad[2]; of another, Adrochta, merely that she took the veil,[3] but as she gave her name to a church—Cell Adrochta, Killaraght—it is evident that she had her permanent abode in that place. Of two more nuns it is said simply that they took the veil from Patrick's hand at Naas.[4] Nor must we omit Cipia, presumably a widow consecrated to the service of God, for she was deputed by the Apostle to assist Bishop Assicus, and later her son, Bishop Bitheus, in Elphin.[5]

These monks, nuns and religious matrons were certainly regarded by St. Patrick as the fairest fruits of his missionary labours. However much he might rejoice at the general success of his ministry, at the thousands whom he raised from the saving waters of baptism,[6] and whom he confirmed in Christ,[7] at the multitude of clergy whom he was able to ordain out of the ranks of his neophytes,[8] there was a favour still greater for which he returned thanks to God with special fervour. This was the vocation of so many to the stricter way of life represented by the monastic institute. For Patrick, then, it was much that a nation like the Irish, ignorant of the Almighty and addicted to the worship of idols, should become a people of the Lord and be called children of God, but it was a veritable triumph when he could point out that " sons of the Scots and daughters of chieftains are seen to become monks and virgins of Christ."[9] He goes on to speak with enthusiasm of a particular instance : " a blessed lady of Irish birth and noble rank, most beautiful, grown to womanhood, whom I baptized ; and after a few days she came for a certain cause. She disclosed to us that she had received an answer by the good pleasure of God, and He warned her to become a virgin of Christ, and live closer to God. Thank God, six days after, most admirably and eagerly " she fulfilled her purpose, and took the veil as a nun. This, he continues, is a typical case. " All

---

[1] Ib. 22b.
[2] Ib. 28b.
[3] Ib. 25a.
[4] *B. Arm.*, p. 462 (44). Cf. *Trip.*, p. 184.
[5] Ib. Tir. 22b. Cf. Bury, *Life*, p. 377.
[6] *Conf.*, § 50, § 38.
[7] *Conf.*, § 38. *Ep.*, § 2 : " quos ego innumeros Deo genui et in Christo confirmavi."
[8] *Conf.*, § 38 : " clerici ubique illis ordinarentur." Cf. §§ 40, 50.
[9] *Conf* 41.

virgins of God do in like manner ; not with the consent of
their fathers, but they endure persecution and lying reproaches
from their parents. Nevertheless their number increases more
and more, and we know not the number of our race who are
there born again ; in addition to widows and continent persons."
He has a special word of praise for the slave-girls. Their
sufferings, he tells us, were exceptionally heavy ; they constantly endure even terror and threats. But the Lord gave
grace to many of my handmaids, for they eagerly follow the
ideal of virginity, though forbidden to do so.[1] " Albeit
unskilled in all things," he says again, " I have done my little
best to keep myself in good, as also the Christian brethren,
the virgins of Christ and the religious women, who insisted on
bringing me gifts, and even left their jewellery upon the altar ;
but I insisted on returning all they gave."[2] The number of
these elect souls was very considerable, for the Saint himself
exclaims that they were beyond his power to reckon ! " The
sons of the Irish and the daughters of chieftains who were
monks and virgins of Christ I am unable to enumerate."[3]
Compared with these striking expressions of enthusiasm the
references to monasticism in the other Patrician documents
look few and meagre indeed. The more these documents are
studied the more the conclusion imposes itself that the
tradition they enshrine is strongly clerical and episcopal, as
distinct from monastic. In one case only is it said that St.
Patrick appointed an abbot[4] ; in every other instance the
appointment or ordination is of a bishop or cleric.[5] At his
arrival, according to Tírechán, he is accompanied by a multitude of bishops and clerics, not of abbots or monks.[6] Many
of those baptized by him were raised to the priesthood or to the
episcopate (not placed in monasteries)—so many to the priesthood that it would be impossible to give an account of them
all.[7] The daughters of Loiguire found Patrick (beside the
fountain at Rathcroghan) surrounded by " a synod of holy

---

[1] Conf., § 42. That the slave girl belonged, body and soul, to her master.
is clear from a story in Cogitosus, Vita S. Brigidae, Trias Thau. p. 519.
[2] Conf., § 49.
[3] Epis., § 12.
[4] B. Arm. Tir. 25b.
[5] Cf. appointments to churches, supra.
[6] 17b : " et secum fuit multitudo episcoporum sanctorum et presbyterorum
et diaconorum ac exorcistarum, hostiariorum lectorumque."
[7] Ib. 18b : " de presbyteris non possimus ordinare, quia baptizabat quotidie homines et de aliis episcopos et presbyteros faciebat."

bishops,"[1] and these are mentioned as his companions elsewhere, too, in the West.[2] Of the numerous bishops and priests to whom churches were entrusted we have already spoken.[3] The saint foretells (or possibly predetermines) the destiny of a youth by conferring on him a priestly[4] or an episcopal[5] blessing, but there is no trace of a similar action on his part with regard to future monks. When a man of kindly disposition saved Patrick from a plot against his life, he was rewarded with the prophecy : " There shall be bishops and priests of thy race."[6] And the good people of Achad Fobair were encouraged with a similar promise : " There shall be good bishops here."[7] In a word, bishops and priests are encountered on every page ; references to monks are few and casual ; and the word monastery is not mentioned until we come to the later records, which describe the honours claimed by Patrick through his successors at the time when the Book of Armagh was written.[8]

Combining these data, Patrick's distinct predilection for the monastic order and the still more distinct clerical and episcopal character of the organisation which he founded,[9] the conclusion lies ready to hand. Patrick entrusted the spiritual care of the country which he had evangelised to bishops, priests and inferior clergy, not to monks as such, but he approved enthusiastically of the stricter mode of life which the monks professed, and encouraged his clergy to undertake it. A number (especially, it would seem, of the neophytes whom he had trained up from their youth)[10] responded to his desires ; there is no ground for supposing that the majority of his clergy did. Amid the womenfolk the proportion desirous of consecrating their lives to God was so great that it surprised himself.[11] These were placed in small groups to assist the clergy in the service of churches, rather than in monasteries proper.[12]

---

[1] Ib. 23a.
[2] Ib. 24..
[3] Supra, p.
[4] Ib. 28b.
[5] Ib. 29b.
[6] Ib. 26a.
[7] Ib. 26a.
[8] *B. Arm. Add.* 31a.
[9] The tradition to this effect is all the more credible because contained in the *Book of Armagh*, a work compiled in the ninth century, when monasticism had been supreme for generations.
[10] Cf. supra.
[11] Supra.
[12] Cf. *Catalogus.* Ussher, *Works* vi, p. 474, where it is said of the *primus ordo* of Irish saints : " mulierum administrationem et societatem non respuebant."

Between the practice of St. Patrick in Ireland and the practice of St. Martin in Gaul there is sufficient resemblance to justify the suspicion of direct dependence. St. Martin, when chosen to govern the church of Tours, retained all his love for the monastic system, and maintained, as well as possible in his new circumstances, the regular habits of the monastic life.[1] He established a settlement at Marmoutier, two leagues from the city, whither he could retire when free, but his visits here can hardly have been frequent, seeing how occupied his life was with episcopal and missionary cares. Whilst first and foremost a bishop, he continued to be at heart a monk.[2] Similarly with St. Patrick, who was probably never happier than during the forty days of his prayer and fast on Cruach Aigle.[3] Both had monks among their disciples (some of these later charged with the government of churches), both founded monasteries, both recommended regular ascetical exercises to their clergy, but it is in no wise certain that the majority of these, whether in Tours or in Ireland, bound themselves formally by vow to the observance of a monastic rule.

That Patrick should be well acquainted with St. Martin's life and deeply impressed by his heroism is only what we should expect, for in the early fifth century the biography of the Bishop of Tours from the pen of Sulpicius Severus was popular, not merely in Gaul, but throughout the Christian world.[4] There exists, in addition, evidence of a positive character to the same effect. Appended to the other documents in the Book of Armagh is a copy of the Gallic writer's works, chiefly the *Vita* and the *Dialogi*. When this Armagh text was examined for Dr. Gwynn by M. Ch. Babut, an expert in Martinian literature, it was found to be of a rare and archaic type.[5] Some passages in the *Dialogi* gave rise to dissensions in Gaul during the course of the fifth century and were expunged from the MSS. In later centuries the suppressed passages were restored, but even then the disturbance left effects which can still be easily traced. " The Book of Armagh is the only one of the MSS. hitherto examined which bears no trace of the suppression. . . This is a very strong ground for believing that

---

[1] *Vita*, ch. 10, p. 119–20.
[2] *Vita*, ch. 10 : "inplebat episcopi dignitatem ut non tamen propositum monachi virtutemque desereret."
[3] *B. Arm.*, Tír., 26b.
[4] Cf. supra. p. 54.
[5] Introd. to *B. Arm.*, p. cclxviii.

the Irish branch of the Sulpician tradition diverged from the stem before 460."[1] After a discussion of other remarkable features, M. Babut draws the general conclusion that "the Sulpicius Severus of the *Liber Ardm.* is to be regarded as Sulpicius Severus of the early years of the fifth century—a reproduction (so to speak) of the *Editio princeps* which has disappeared elsewhere."[2] To the question who brought this excellent copy of the original *Vita* and *Dialogi* to Ireland sometime between their first appearance and A.D. 460, there can hardly be two answers. Thanks to the conspicuous literary gifts of Sulpicius, St. Patrick had an intimate knowledge of the great Saint of Tours—his mercy, his humility, his union with God, his austerities and his miracles. And Martin, too, was a missioner. Patrick could thus find in his life not only much to admire, but much that he could directly imitate. This is the substratum of historical truth underlying the contention that the Irish apostle owed his formation to the illustrious apostle of the neglected Gallic countrysides : personal contact there was none, except in legend, but the younger saint had in very truth imbibed the spirit of the older.

Whether the majority of bishops, priests and clerics who aided St. Patrick in his missionary work were monks or not (and, as we have seen, there is no satisfactory ground for believing that they were) the greater settlements were organised from the beginning after a fashion that must have made them closely resemble monasteries. In prominent foundations, like Armagh, Trim and Sletty, the clergy lived under their bishop within the narrow confines of a *lios*. They thus became, almost by force of circumstances, a religious family, of which the bishop was *princeps* or head. Patrick himself, and after him Benignus, governed such a family at Armagh. Again when the Apostle consecrated Fiacc in Leinster, he gave him seven of his " family " to form the nucleus of a community. Abundant increase could soon be chronicled, for sixty of Fiacc's family had died before the poet-bishop was warned by an angelic visitor to seek a new site west of the Barrow at Sletty. The manner of life inside these enclosures was severe and regular, and the discipline, no doubt, strict, all the more so because of the younger candidates for orders who received their religious and intellectual training within the settlements.

---

[1] Ib, p. cclxix.
[2] Ib., p. cclxx.

Such communities, though they did not profess monasticism, would differ little in externals from monasteries, just as a modern seminary, where there is no question of a religious rule, differs little in externals from the house of studies of a religious Order or Congregation. Still, if the vow or vows of religion be accepted as an essential part of the monastic profession, it is not quite certain that they were monasteries. It may, however, be admitted as extremely likely that they had bound themselves by vow to lead a regular life and submit to a strict code of religious discipline, just as had the clergy of St. Eusebius at Vercelli and the household of St. Augustine at Hippo. This would leave them in essence communities of clerics rather than communities of monks. From the documents in the Book of Armagh, which imply that monks were an important group in Patrick's following, yet a distinct minority; from the *Catalogus*, which describes the saints of the First Order simply as bishops; and from the Annals which have no record of monks until a later period, it is difficult to see how any other conclusion can be drawn.

Assuming that the conditions in Armagh, Trim and Sletty were such as we have described, the transition to a more formal type of monasticism would be very easy, but we have no proof that an advance of the kind took place until after Patrick's death. Few of the smaller settlements—churches served by one or at most by a few clerics—can have had a monastic character; and in a missionary country the great majority of settlements had perforce to be small.

In a word, the place of monasticism in the church founded by St. Patrick was important, but secondary. The great apostle, like all preachers of the Gospel elsewhere, relied on bishops and clergy, not on monks as such, to carry on his work, and to bring it, in due course, to completion.

CHAPTER II

MONASTICISM IN THE IRISH CHURCH BETWEEN THE DEATH OF ST. PATRICK, A.D. 461, AND A.D. 520

The Annals of Ulster (A.U.), Vol. i. Ed. Hennessy, Dublin, 1887.
The Annals of the Four Masters (A.F.M.). Ed. O'Donovan, Dublin, 1851.
Catalogus SS. Hib., in Haddan and Stubbs, Councils and Ecclesiastical Documents relating to Great Britain and Ireland. (Vol. ii, p. 292 f). Oxford, 1869-78.
The Book of Armagh. Ed. Gwynn, Dublin, 1913.
The Martyrology of Oengus. Ed. Stokes for Henry Bradshaw Society. London, 1905.
The Martyrology of Gorman. Ed. Stokes for Henry Bradshaw Society. London, 1895.

FOR the period between the death of St. Patrick and the rise of the great monasteries, the only general account that has survived of the development of the Irish Church is that contained in the *Catalogus*. According to this document the First Order of Irish saints continued to the death of the High-King, Tuathal Moelgarb, in A.D. 544. "The first order of Catholic saints," it relates, "was in the time of Patrick ; and then they were all bishops, distinguished and holy, and full of the Holy Ghost, 350 in number, founders of churches. They had one head, Christ, and one chief, Patrick. They had one mass, one liturgy, one tonsure from ear to ear. They celebrated one Easter, on the fourteenth moon after the vernal equinox, and what was excommunicated by one church all excommunicated. They did not reject the service and society of women because founded on the rock, Christ, they feared not the blast of temptation. This order of saints lasted for four reigns, those namely of Loiguire, of Ailill Molt, of Lugaid son of Loiguire, and of Tuathal.[1] All these bishops were sprung from the Romans and Franks and Britons and Scots."[2]

Thus the characteristics of the Irish Church at this epoch, according to the tradition recorded by the writer of the *Catalogus* were four :—1. The prominent ecclesiastics were all bishops,

---

[1] The reign of Muirchertach mac Erca, A.D. 513-33, is here ignored.
[2] Haddan and Stubbs, *Councils*, ii, p. 292. The translation (with some slight changes) is adopted from Todd, *Life*, p. 88 n.

which is equivalent to stating that the episcopal constitution
of the Church was observed as a matter of course ; 2. a great
number of these were foreigners ; 3. all obeyed St. Patrick
during his lifetime as the highest ecclesiastical authority within
the country ; and retained after his death the customs which
he had introduced respecting liturgy, tonsure and the mode of
observing Easter ; 4. consecrated virgins and pious women
co-operated freely with the clergy in the service of the churches.

To check this statement the material at our disposal is but
meagre. As far, however, as it goes, it bears witness to the
substantial accuracy of the eighth-century writer's account.
In the *Book of Armagh*[1] we have a description of the foundation
of Trim, included among the old traditions which the heirs of
St. Patrick had exerted themselves to collect.[2] Whatever
may be said of the details, which have a decidedly legendary
flavour, there is no reason to doubt the main argument of this
story—that Trim was founded by St. Patrick or under his
auspices, and that it was governed in the manner recorded.
According to ancient tradition, then, Lommán, a Briton,[3]
and Patrick's disciple, came to the Ford of Trim, where he met
Foirtchernn, son of Féidlimid, lord of that district, himself a
son of the High-King Loiguire. Lommán preached to
Foirtchernn, who believed and was baptised. His mother, too,
who was a Briton, rejoiced to find in the cleric a man of her
own race. Nor was Féidlimid less enthusiastic than his wife
and son in offering Lommán welcome, for his mother had
likewise been a British princess. "And Féidlimid saluted
Lommán in the British tongue, asking him in order concerning
his faith and family. He answered : "I am a Briton, a
Christian, the disciple of Patrick,who is sent by the Lord to
baptise the peoples of Ireland, and to convert them to the faith
of Christ : who hath sent me hither, according to the will
of God." And forthwith Féidlimid believed with all his family
and he offered up to Lommán and to holy Patrick his territory.
with all his goods, and with all his race. All these he offered
to Patrick and Lommán and to Foirtchernn, his son, unto the
day of Judgment."[4]

---

[1] *B. Arm. Add.* 31b.
[2] Ib. : "alia pauca serotinis temporibus inventa . . . curiositate heredum
diligentiaque sanctitatis."
[3] Likely from his name to have been an Irish Briton. The Britons proper
affected Latin names.
[4] Ib. 31ᵇ, 32a.

The writer goes on to relate how Patrick came to Lommán and Foirtchernn at Trim, and established a church there for them, long before the foundation of Armagh. When Lommán felt his death approaching he committed his church to holy Patrick and to Foirtchernn. " But Foirtchernn refused to hold the heritage of his father, which he had offered to God and to Patrick, until Lommán said : ' Thou shalt not have my blessing unless thou accept the government (principatum) of my church.' He retained the government, however, for three days only after the death of his master, until he arrived at the church of Trim, when he handed over his church at once to Cathlaid, the pilgrim."[1]

But the church and its possessions returned before long to Féidlimid's descendants who had governed the place for eight generations when this account was written.[2] " Now these were all bishops and rulers venerating holy Patrick and his successors."[3] As the corresponding lay princes descended from Féidlimid are enumerated and reach to nine generations,[4] the last-mentioned of them (tenth in descent from Loiguire, who died in A.D. 463) must have been alive about A.D. 750. We are thus justified in concluding that not merely during the period ascribed to the First Order of Irish saints, but thereafter until the eighth century the rulers of the church at Trim, as well as of the ecclesiastical principality of which

---

[1] Ib. 32a : Todd (Life, p. 152) teaches that Foirtchernn's objection was because " if he became bishop the ecclesiastical and civil chieftainship would be combined in his person, and he feared lest it should seem as if he was taking back to himself the gift which his father had given to the Church." The second part of this statement is adequate as an explanation of Foirtchernn's scruple. Féidlimid, his father, had dedicated his possession at Trim to God. That the gift might be complete, he had abandoned his own home beside the ford and gone to settle on another part of his territory called Clóin Lagen. To let the lands which he had bestowed upon Patrick now return to his son as bishop would look like a withdrawal of the gift from God.

[2] Ib. 32b : " Haec est ecclesiastica progenies Fedelmtheo, Fortchernus, Aed Magnus, Aed Parvus, Conall, Baitan, Ossan, Cummene, Saran." Cathlaid, not being a descendant of Feidlimid, is omitted.

[3] Ib. : " Hi omnes episcopi fuerunt et principes, venerantes sanctum Patricium et successores eius." Todd (Life, p. 153) comments on this as follows : " In other words they belong to the First Order of saints and gave allegiance to Armagh ; and we may infer incidentally that this was not then universally done, or else it would not have been here so particularly mentioned in especial praise of these bishops." But the inference is rather that allegiance was rendered universally to Armagh by saints of the First Order, whilst some churches in a later age ignored, if they did not reject, its primacy. This is what the writer has in mind. Cf. Tírechán, B. Arm. 21b.

[4] Ib. : " Plebilis autem progenies eius haec est : Fergus filius Fedelmitheo," etc. If, as the parallelism with the ecclesiastical rulers seems to imply, the government was held by these descendants of Féidlimid, the mode of succession would be exceptional. Cf. MacNeill, Celtic Ireland, p. 123 ff.

Trim was centre, were all bishops. In this church, then, the manner of government established by St. Patrick was maintained with relative fidelity.

Noteworthy also in the original grant is the stipulation of Féidlimid (implied in the story, if not definitely expressed) that the ecclesiastical rulers should be of his own race. His son, in objecting to succession as bishop under such conditions, might be regarded as reflecting St. Patrick's own views on the subject, were it not for the statement that Lommán, St. Patrick's elder disciple, insisted on acceptance. Of another church establishment made by Patrick at Druimm Lias, in Leitrim, it is recorded also that a certain Féth Fio[1] acted as patron on a similar understanding. "This is Féth Fio's confession and his testament (made) two years before his death, to the monks of Druimm Lias, and to the nobles of Calrige, between the chancel and the altar of Druimm Lias, that the family right of inheritance to Druimm Lias is reserved to the race of Féth Fio, if there be any of that family at once well born, devout and conscientious. If none such is forthcoming, a suitable candidate is to be sought from among the community of Druimm Lias or from the monks dependent on that monastery. If among these again there is none, the position is to go to an outside candidate from Patrick's community."[2] But this appears to have been an addition to the original grant and to have taken place, more likely than not, long after St. Patrick's death. We are consequently left with the single record of a disagreement between the Saint's disciples as to the proper attitude to adopt in face of this problem. The disagreement, perhaps, is in itself significant, indicating, as it does, that the conferring of such a privilege on the family and descendants of him who made the endowment was left an open question in St. Patrick's day. Restrictions of this kind, if we may judge from general accounts of church foundations, were rare in the fifth century, but they developed later into a grave abuse.

Turning to the *Annals of Ulster*, we find that all St. Patrick's successors at Armagh, during the time allotted to the First Order of Irish saints, are described as bishops.[3] Lists of the

---

[1] Dr. MacNeill takes Féth Fio to be a bye-name of Bineanus filius Lugni (*B. Arm.* 33b.).

[2] *B. Arm.* 33a and b : " Issí inso coibse Fetho Fio ocus a edocht," etc.

[3] *A.U.*, s.a. 467 : " Quies Benigni secundi *episcopi*, successoris Patricii."
481 : Rest of Iarlaithe, 4th *bishop* of Armagh. 496 (*recte* 497) : Cormac, *bishop* of Armagh and successor of St. Patrick died. 512 (*recte* 513) : Dubthach, *bishop* of Armagh, died. 525 (*recte* 526) : Ailill (I) *bishop* of Armagh,

Armagh prelates have likewise been preserved in a fragment of the Psalter of Cashel transcribed for Mac Richard Butler by one of the O'Clerys (MS. Laud 610 of the Bodleian Library), in the *Leabhar Breac*, the *Yellow Book of Lecan* and the *Book of Leinster*, but none of these make mention of the ecclesiastical order possessed by the holders of the office.   In the *Book of Leinster*, however, is another tract entitled " *Do Flaithesaib ocus amseraib h-Erenn iar cretim*"[1] " Of reigns and dates in Ireland since the introduction of Christianity," and in this, Benignus and Iarlaithe are given as bishops.[2]   But Cormac, who succeeded Iarlaithe, is referred to, not as bishop, but as abbot,[3] indeed as first abbot, and all Cormac's successors bear the monastic, not the hierarchic title.   In the list of Patrick's successors, too, given in the *Book of Leinster*, it is stated that Cormac was the first abbot, and that he was sprung from the Clann Chernaig.[4]   Seeing that in the tract just mentioned this Cormac and his three successors Dubthach, Ailill I and Ailill II, are designated abbots, whilst in the *Annals of Ulster* they are referred to simply as bishops, the conclusion is likely that during the pontificate of Cormac as bishop, the clerical community at Armagh was re-organised and reconstituted on a formally monastic basis. As already pointed out, the settlement had been from the beginning a semi-monastic seminary, where the details of daily life had probably been minutely regulated and the discipline had been strict, so that the change would not be severely felt.   But the

---

died.   535 (*recte* 536) Ailill (II) *bishop* of Armagh, died. The next successo of St. Patrick, Dubthach (in other lists *Duach*) whose obit occurs under 547 (*recte* 548) is called *abbot* of Armagh. It will be noted that in the annal above quoted Iarlaithe is called *fourth* bishop of Armagh. Cf. next note but one.

[1] All four lists, as well as the ecclesiastical data included in the tract, are published by Todd from the MSS. mentioned (*Life*, p. 174–88). Dr. MacNeill dates the Laud 610 list A.D. 742. An accurate copy of the *Book of Leinster* list is published by Drs. Lawlor and Best. *P.R.I.A.*, xxxv., p. 359–60. The whole question of the succession at Armagh is discussed by the same scholars, ib., pp. 316 ff.

[2] " Quies Benigni secundi *episcopi*." (On the reading *secundi* see Grosjean, *AA. SS.* T. iv, Nov., p. 167–9.) " Quies Iarlathi tertii *episcopi*." Iarlaithe is here placed in proper order as *third* bishop of Armagh, a fact which suggests reliable tradition of very high antiquity as the basis of the tract. In the *Leabhar Breac* list, Secundinus, and in the remaining three lists Secundinus and the fictitious Sen-Pátraic are intruded as bishops. A disturbance of the genuine Armagh tradition on this point arose when the popular legend of Patrick's patriarchal age (120 years) at death found universal acceptance. Cf. Bury, *Life*, 343–4. Lawlor and Best, op. cit., p. 339.

[3] Cormac primus abbas.

[4] Cormac XII (years as ruler). " Primus abbas de Chlainn Chernaigh." First Abbot.   Of the Clann Chernaig.

clergy and students would now acquire a new and more intimate relation towards one another as brethren ; whilst the bishop would rule them henceforth, not merely by virtue of his episcopal authority, but also by virtue of his position as head of the community or abbot. Why this change was made we cannot tell. It may have been in response to the well-known desire of St. Patrick, realised in but a fragmentary manner during his lifetime, that the land should abound in monks. It may be connected with the dying off of Patrick's Continental helpers (many of whom, like their colleagues in Gaul, were no doubt averse to the monastic ideal), and the predilection of the native Irish for that form of life, a predilection manifested so strikingly during the sixth and following centuries. From this time forward until the middle of the eighth century (as we hope to show in a later chapter) the offices of bishop and abbot were combined in the same person at Armagh. In theory, as the *Book of Armagh* makes abundantly clear,[1] the episcopal office predominated, nor is there any reason to believe that theory and practice were in conflict whilst the First Order of Irish saints survived.

Granted that Armagh, the chief church in Ireland, had adopted a monastic constitution (though its abbot retained his old and primary position as bishop of the metropolitan see) it is easy to understand why no opposition was offered to the great sixth century founders like St. Finnian of Clonard. The primatial city had itself set the fashion, and, if not perhaps as thorough-going as enthusiasts of a later date, had at least general sympathy with their aspirations. Armagh esteemed and practised the monastic virtues, whilst seeking to remain faithful to the episcopal constitution which St. Patrick had imposed upon it. So high, in fact, was the honour in which it held the monastic system that when the movement for the propagation of that system began to sweep the country in the second or third decade of the sixth century Armagh allowed

---

[1] Note especially the evidence from the *Liber Angeli*, composed towards the end of the seventh century, at a time when the monastic, as distinct from the episcopal, scheme of organisation was overwhelmingly strong in Ireland. Yet the ruler (*rector*, 41b) of Armagh is to receive from any monastery he visits " *receptio archiepiscopi heredis cathedrae meae urbis, cum comitibus suis numero quinquaginta* " (41a). In an alternative account (42a) we read : " de honore *praesulis* Airdd Machae *episcopi* praesedentis cathedram pastoris perfecti." Here, it is said, that if the *pontifex* arrives at eventide and seeks hospitality, such is to be offered him in worthy measure, as also to his suite, which may number one hundred. The heritage of St. Patrick is thus in Irish tradition emphatically episcopal.

it to develop unchecked.   It did not even insist that the
dominant episcopal character of its own ruler should be imitated
in the new.foundations.   As a result of this neglect, Church
organisation in Ireland developed along lines which St.
Patrick had certainly not intended, and which threatened to affect
unfavourably Armagh's own place as the primatial see.

Of Sléibte no account has been preserved from the time of
Fiacc, its first bishop, to the time of Aed, who died A.D. 700.[1]
The large community there assembled, even in Fiacc's day,
had no doubt advanced from a less strict to a more strict
constitution, probably in the 6th century ; but Aed is referred
to specifically twice as bishop,[2] never as abbot ; and as with
him so with his predecessors it is likely that the episcopal was
much more strongly marked than the abbatial character.
While it would be absurd to claim that the *Annals of Ulster*
contain an exhaustive list of the prominent churchmen who
went to their reward within the sixty years following St.
Patrick's death,[3] it is at least significant that the obits recorded
are exclusively of bishops.[4]   It is true that the episcopal rank
of Ciannán of Daimliag[5] and Mochaoi of Noendrom is not
expressly stated, but there is evidence from other sources
which makes it fairly likely.[6]

---

[1] *A.U.*, s.a. 699.

[2] *B. Arm. Supp.* 36a : " *Epscop* Aed bof i Sléibti." Ib. 40a : " Dictante
Aiduo Slebtiensis civitatis *episcopi*."

[3] Not one for instance of the early rulers of Trim (*B. Arm. Suppl.* 32b)
or of the rulers of Sléibte between Fiacc and Aed (died A.D. 700) is mentioned
in *A.U.*.

[4] *A.U.* 467 (Benignus), 468 (Iserninus), 487 (Mel of Ardagh), 489 (MacCaille),
494 (MacCuilinn of Lusk), 496 (Cormac of Armagh), 499 (Ibar), 503 (Cerpan,
near Tara), A.F.M. 505 (MacCairthinn of Clochar), 511 (Bron), 512 (Dubthach
of Armagh), 513 Aliter 506 (Aengus MacNissi of Connor), 519 (Conlaed of
Kildare), 523 (Beoaid of Ard Carna), 525 (Ailill of Armagh), 526 (Ailbe of
Emly).

[5] For Ciannan Cf. *Book of Leinster, R.I.A. Facs.*, p. 365, col. d. : " Nomina
episcoporum Hibernensium incipiunt," where he is included in the list.
Also *Martyr. Oeng.* (H.B.S. ed. ; gloss on Nov. 24th, p. 244) where it is said
that a noble bishop used to cut Ciannan's hair every Maundy Thursday.
The *Martyr. Gorm.* gl. on Nov. 24th reads : " epscop Doimhliag i mBregaib."
From what source the glossator derived his information we cannot tell, but
his statement may be accepted as a genuine tradition as long as nothing
to the contrary can be urged against it. Cf. *Marytr. Donegal*, ed. O'Donovan,
p. 314.

[6] According to the *Tripartite Life* i, p. 40 ; ii, p. 452, Mochaoi received
a crozier from Patrick. In all the *Annals* he is referred to simply as " Mochoe
of Noendrom." Similarly in the *Martyr. of Oengus* (June 23rd) ; but the
Martyr. of Gorman has the gloss : " Abbot of Noendrom : Coelan was his
first name." This was copied by O'Clery into the *Martyr. of Donegal* and
accepted by Colgan (*Tr. Thaum.*, p. 110, col. 1.) and Reeves (*Eccl. Antiq.*,
p. 144). Mr. H. C. Lawlor (*The Monastery of St. Mochai of Nendrum*, Belfast,
1925, p. 50 ff) subjects Reeves's identification of Mochaoi and Coelan (the
second part of Gorman's gloss) to sharp criticism ; but, like Reeves and

If some lost *Acta* of St. Coelan and the *Lives* of St. Finnian of MagBile[2] and St. Colman of Dromore[3] may be trusted, the first mentioned ruled at Noendrom as abbot about A.D. 520.[4] Colman was there his disciple, whilst Finnian was sent thither for instruction, but soon, according to the story, handed over to Nennius, founder of the *Candida Casa* in Galloway. So much is legendary in these lives that it is hard to accept as true any statement made by them, unless the statement is confirmed from other sources ; but there is nothing improbable in the tradition that, as at Armagh, so in Noendrom, monasticism stood high in favour about this period.

Summing up, then, from the meagre data at our disposal, we conclude that the esteem which St. Patrick showed for the monastic institute was inherited by his successors, and led to important changes at Armagh before the end of the fifth century. Similar changes probably took place in other ecclesiastical centres, but of these we know nothing. There is no formal mention of any monastery and no suggestion that abbots as such, held a position of eminence. Bishops, on the contrary, are frequently commemorated as the leading ecclesiastics of the nation. Characteristic, therefore, of the period between St. Patrick's death and A.D. 520 is the growing popularity of the monastic ideal, but without serious interference, as yet, with the episcopal constitution which the Apostle had established within the country.

Lanigan (*Eccl. Hist.* i, p. 422) he offers no objection to the first part of the gloss, and considers Mochaoi to have been abbot as well as bishop. If the monastic institute was known at Noendrom under Mochaoi, its place there was no doubt secondary, as at Armagh under Cormac, the rulers of both establishments being, in the first place, bishops.

[1] Utilised by Ussher : *Britt Eccl. Antiq.* (*Works*, vi, p. 529) and Ware (*Bishops*, ed. Harris, p. 194). Cf. Grosjean, *Anal. Boll.*, xlvii, p. 40-1
[2] Colgan, *AA. SS. Hib*, p. 438.
[3] *AA. SS.*, vol. ii, *Jun.*, p. 26.
[4] Cf. H. C. Lawlor, *Saint Mochai of Nendrum*, p. 48.

CHAPTER III

PERIOD OF THE GREAT MONASTIC FOUNDERS

Bede : *Hist. Eccles.* (ed. Plummer), iii, 4, gives, in a short paragraph, all that is known with any certainty of Ninnian, founder of the *Candida Casa.* A *Vita Niniani,* written by Ailred, abbot of Rievaulx, in the twelfth century is extant. Criticism by Mackinnon in a thesis entitled : " Ninian und sein Einfluss auf die Ausbreitung des Christenthums in Nord-Biitannien, Heidelberg, 1891." A *Life,* in Irish, quoted by Ussher (*Works,* vi, 209, 565) but now lost. Its historical value does not seem to have been great.
Tillemont : *Mémoires* x, p. 340.
Forbes *;* *Lives of St. Ninian and St. Kentigern.* Edinburgh, 1874.
Pinkerton : *Lives of the Scottish Saints.* Revised edit., 1889.
Metcalf : *Legends of St. Ninian and Machor.* Paisley, 1904.
Colgan : *AA. SS. Hib.* i, 438 records the traditional connection of the Irish saints with Ninian's foundation.

§1. The Impulse from Outside.

(a)—From the Candida Casa, *Whitern in Galloway.*

FOR the trend towards monasticism which manifests itself at Armagh before the end of the fifth century no external cause can be assigned, and it is likely that it developed naturally from St. Patrick's teaching. As yet, however, the conversion of the country cannot have been complete, and the need for continued missionary effort must have made a life of rigid monastic seclusion well-nigh impossible. Many of the brethren at Armagh had no doubt to serve as priests among the converted and as preachers among those not yet won from paganism. Complete enclosure, an essential part of a strict monastic rule, cannot thus have been observed.

Similar conditions seem to have prevailed in the first missionary centre of North Britain, established by St. Ninian in Galloway a generation or so before St. Patrick came to Ireland. Ninian, according to Bede's account,[1] was a Briton by birth, and made a pilgrimage to Rome, where he was trained " in faith and in the mysteries of truth." Consecrated a bishop,

---

[1] *H.E.,* iii, 4.

he established his see at Whitern, on the northern shore of the Solway. Here he built a church of stone, not of wood (the material used universally among the Britons) and dedicated it to St. Martin. The settlement was called "*Ad Candidam Casam*," from the unusually bright appearance of the building. This event took place probably after St. Martin's death, perhaps within the first decade of the fifth century. Ninian laboured among the Southern Picts, many of whom he converted to the faith ; and he found a resting-place at Whitern when the days of his earthly pilgrimage ended.

Some loose form of monasticism may have existed at the *Candida Casa* from the beginning, but of this we cannot speak with certainty, since evidence is completely lacking. After Ninian's death the place disappears from history, to reappear about a century later, celebrated now as a school of training for the monastic life. In the Irish traditions, dating from the early sixth century, it bears the name *Rosnat*, or *Magnum Monasterium*, and enjoys high repute as a novitiate for the spiritual life. St. Enda of Aran, St. Tigernach of Cluain Eois, St. Eogan of Ard Sratha, St. Finnian of Mag Bile, and St. Coirpre of Cúil Raithin are reputed to have made their early studies within its walls.[1]

The first in order of time and the most important of these saints is Enda of Aran, whose death, of which no mention is made in the *Annals*, probably took place about A.D. 530.[2] The salient features in the tradition of his life are these : he had priest's orders only, he founded a settlement on the greatest of the Aran islands, and followed, with many disciples, a rule of astonishing severity. With him, as far as can be ascertained, monasticism in the strict sense (embracing vows, complete seclusion from the world and a stern system of discipline) began in Ireland. How much he adopted without change from his teachers at the *Candida Casa* is not quite clear, but there is reason to believe that he did not rest content with slavish imitation. The organisation at Aran had a character very much its own. It is significant, for example,

---

. [1] Colgan, *AA. SS. Hib.*, i, 704, ss.

[2] Cf. Ussher, *Index Chron.*, s.a., 529. *Works* vi, p. 589. This date harmonises with what is said of those who are reputed to have been his disciples. The accounts, on the other hand, which would make him a contemporary of St. Patrick, and prolong his life to A.D. 540 or later (cf. Colgan, op. cit., p. 714 ; Ware, *Antiq.*, p. 249) are based on fantastic legends in the lives of Brendan and other saints.

that Enda was but a priest whereas Tigernach of Cluain Eois (died A.D. 549 ; *A.U.* 548), trained in the same monastery, was a bishop. The later saints Eogan of Ard Sratha, Finnian of Mag Bile and Coirpre of Cúil Raithin had also received the higher order,[1] whence it is safe to conclude that the *Candida Casa* fathers regarded it as a matter of course that some of their followers should be burthened with episcopal cares.

The most famous among the disciples of Enda is Ciarán of Clonmacnois (died A.D. 549). Others commemorated in tradition are Finnian of Mag Bile (died 579), Iarlaithe of Tuam (fl. c. 540), Colmcille (died 597), Coemgen of Glenn dá locha (died 618) and Mochuda of Rathain (died 637)[2] ; but of these the three last mentioned must certainly be excluded ; whilst Finnian's stay in the West is extremely doubtful. Elsewhere[3] he is said simply to have received his early training at the *Candida Casa*.

(b)—The Impulse from Britain.

Catalogus of Irish Saints. Ed. Haddan and Stubbs, *Councils* ii, 292 f. Also in Ussher, *Works*, vi, p. 477 ; in Fleming, *Collectanea Sacra*, p. 420–1, and in *Acta SS. Hib. ex Cod. Salm.*, cc. 161 ff. A MS. copy in *Brit. Mus. Add.*, 30, 512, examined and transcribed by P. Grosjean, still awaits publication.
Colgan : *Acta Sanctorum Hiberniae.* Louvain, 1645.
Acta Sanctorum Hiberniae ex Codice Salmanticensi. Ed. de Smedt and De Backer. Edinburgh and Bruges, 1888.
Lives of the Saints from Book of Lismore. Ed. Stokes. Oxford, 1890.
Vitae SS. Hiberniae. Ed. Plummer. Oxford, 1910.
Bethada Naem n-Erenn. Ed. Plummer. Oxford, 1922.
Lives of the Cambro-British Saints. Ed. Rees, 1853.
Gougaud : *Les Chrétientés celtiques.* Paris, 1911.
Hugh Williams : *Christianity in Early Britain.* Oxford, 1912.
Life of St. David. Ed. A. W. Wade Evans. (*S.P.C.K.*, 1923.) The notes to this edition are of great value.
Cecile O'Rahilly : *Ireland and Wales.* London, 1924.
C. H. Slover : Early Literary Channels between Britain and Ireland. (University of Texas *Studies in English*, Nos. 6 and 7), 1926.

Intercourse of the most intimate kind existed between the Irish and British churches of the sixth century, as we learn from the tradition of both countries, preserved in various *Vitae*.[4] However much legends and anachronisms may abound

---

[1] Colgan, op. cit., p. 438.
[2] Colgan, *AA. SS. Hib.*, i, 714.
[3] Capgrave, *Nova Legenda Angl.* Ed. Horstmann, 1901, i, 415.
[4] The intercourse must have been strengthened by the presence of a large Irish element in Wales, especially South Wales. MacNeill, *Birthplace of St. Patrick*, P.R.I.A., xxxvii. Sect. C. No. 6, p. 120 f., 128 ff.

in these *Lives*, the broad fact of active communion between the " saints " of the two races cannot be called in doubt. We may regard it, too, as certain that in the opening half of the sixth century the relation between the churches was largely that of master and disciple. Britain, the elder sister, taught, whilst Ireland, the younger sister, gladly learnt. The teaching of these British Fathers, much more than the lessons given by Ninian's successors at the *Candida Casa*, directed and encouraged native enthusiasm for the monastic life. Helped forward by mighty religious leaders, the movement gathered momentum with the years, and by A.D. 550 had begun to modify profoundly the organisation of the Church within the country. It is important at this point to examine somewhat closely the extent to which the influence of the British teachers contributed towards this result.

Of monachism in Britain during the fifth century we know merely that it existed and that it maintained some connection with Lérins. Faustus, a Briton by birth and a monk at that monastery, succeeded Maximus as abbot in A.D. 433.[1] How long he held that office is uncertain, but he was bishop of Riez before A.D. 462. In the theological struggles of his day, especially in the campaign against Pelagianism, he took an active part, but his own teaching on the question of grace and free will was defective, and he has been classed by later ages with Cassian as the ablest of the Semipelagian leaders. But the unorthodox tendency of his theology was hardly suspected by contemporaries, for it was at the request of Gallican synods at Arles (A.D. 473) and Lyons (A.D. 474) that he wrote his two books *De gratia*. Ten letters from his pen and a large number of sermons are likewise preserved.[2] Faustus was popular, not merely with his diocesans, who thought the asceticism of his life a sure mark of heroic virtue, and who revered him as a saint after his death, but also with men of·learning and culture, of whom Sidonius Apollinaris is an ideal representative.[3]

From a chance reference by Sidonius[4] we learn that a

---

[1] Monographs by Englebrecht : *Studien zu den Schriften des Bischofs von Reji*. Prague, 1889. Koch : *Der hl. Faustus, Bischof von Riez*. Stuttgart, 1895. Krusch, in introd. to edition of letters.
[2] Published by Engelbrecht, *C.S.E.L.*, xxi. Vienna, 1891. Incompletely in Migne, P.L. 58. Letters in *M.G.H. Auct. Ant.* viii. Ed. Krusch.
[3] Cf. the *Eucharisticum to Faustus*. Carmen xvi of Sidonius *M.G.H. Auct. Ant.* viii. Ed. Lütjohann.
[4] *Ep.* ix, 9, op. cit., p. 157 : *Riochatus, antistes et monachus*.

certain British bishop and monk, named Riocatus, made two journeys to Gaul, probably to visit Faustus, for on the second occasion works of that writer are found in his possession as he wended his way homewards. Riocatus called on Sidonius at his villa in Auvergne (probably again on the recommendation of Faustus) and was detained there for a spell owing to the activities of the barbarians, so that Sidonius had time to read the books which he was carrying. This visit must have taken place between A.D. 470, about which date Sidonius returned to Gaul from Rome, and A.D. 475, when he was a prisoner in the hands of the Visigoths. Monachism, then, existed at this time in Britain ; but since he who professed it was a bishop as well as a monk, it was probably of the looser kind, such as that practised by St. Martin when bishop and missionary at Tours.

Of Riocatus, the first British monk to be mentioned by name, nothing further is known, and when monasticism next appears it is in the hazy atmosphere of the *Lives*. About the chronology, in particular, impenetrable clouds of conjecture, contradiction and legend tend to gather. Thus we are told of Cadoc, one of the outstanding saints of early Britain, that he was the teacher of Illtud,[1] but again that he was a contemporary of Saint Samson of Dol, St. Paul of Léon, St. David, St. Gildas and others who themselves were Illtud's disciples.[2] Cadoc, too, was said to have visited Ireland, led thither by his quest for knowledge (*discendi gratia*)[3] but we know that a teacher of Illtud, in the latter half of the fifth century, would find Ireland very little to his purpose if learning were his quest. The fact is that the account of Cadoc's relation to Illtud is a legend. His period is rather that of Gildas, with whose father, Caw, he was on friendly terms, and to whom he acted probably as spiritual director or " soul friend."[4] Cadoc enjoyed high distinction among the holy men of his age, who called him Cadoc " the Wise,"[5] and his monastery at Llangarvan (or Nantgarvan) must have been a place of consequence in the third decade of the sixth century.

---

[1] *Vita Cadoci*, C.B.S., p. 46. *Vita Iltuti*, ib., p. 160–1.
[2] *Vita Iltuti*, ib., p. 167. See Williams, op. cit., p. 317, 341, 356.
[3] *Vita C.B.S.*, p. 35. The value of this notice may be judged from the statement that Cadoc spent three years at Lismore with St. Mochuda, who did not settle in that place until A.D. 636.
[4] So Wade-Evans concludes, op. cit., p. 75.
[5] The " Wisdom of Cadoc," or " *Y Gwyddfardd Cyfarwydd a gant Catwg Ddoeth*," contained in the *Myvyrian Archaeology* cannot, however, have been composed by him. Williams, op. cit., p. 360–1.

The first noted teacher of British Christianity after the
Saxon invasions is Illtud, an Armorican or Breton by birth,
if the testimony offered by his *Vita* can be trusted.[1] It is
impossible to establish any connection between him and the
Riocatus already mentioned, though such a connection
probably existed, for Illtud's monachism bears distinct traces
of Southern Gaul.   His settlement was on the little island
called Ynys Pyr (later Caldey), and his influence had reached
its height about A.D. 520.   Illtud was a presbyter abbot,[2]
like the monastic ruler at Lérins.   Like the latter, he never
sought episcopal orders, and had no jurisdiction outside of
his own household.   His primary purpose in the handling
of his disciples was manifestly spiritual—to make them men
of prayer and solid virtue—but he also taught them something
of the liberal arts.   " In truth," says the *Life of Samson*,[3]
" Illtud was of all the Britons the most accomplished in all
the Scriptures, of the Old namely and the New Testament,
and in learning of every kind, to wit, geometry, rhetoric,
grammar, arithmetic and all the theories of philosophy."
Illtud was thus the first great *abbot* of the British Church,
the first to establish monasticism on a strong and permanent
footing, the first to organise a school and studies as a normal
complement to ascetical training, and the first to send forth
disciples who in their turn would propagate the way of life
that he had inaugurated.

The earliest of these disciples are St. Samson of Dol, Paulus
Aurelianus (St. Pol de Léon) and St. Cadoc ; slightly later,
but within the lifetime of Illtud, come Gildas and possibly

---

[1] *AA. SS. Boll.*   T. iii, Nov., p. 225, 234.   *C.B.S.*, p. 158–9.
[2] Priestly orders were said to have been conferred upon him by St. Germanus of Auxerre (*Life of Samson*, ch. 7), but as Germanus died in A.D. 448
this account must be regarded as legendary.
[3] *Vita*, ch. 7. The best edition of Samson's life is that published by Fawtier :
La vie de Saint Samson. Paris, 1912. Fawtier derives his text from a MS.
of the eleventh century, but he gives variants from nineteen other MSS.
The eleventh century text goes back in substance to an original of the early
seventh century.   Fawtier's evaluation of the historical content of the *Life*
is hypercritical, and its defects have been exposed by Loth : " La vie la
plus ancienne de Saint Samson de Dol (Extrait de la *Révue Celtique*), Paris,
1914 ; and Duine :   " Questions d'Hagiographie. Vie de S. Samson, Paris,
1914." The seventh century writer's weakness for miracles is paralleled by
the twentieth century writer's weakness for " légendes topographiques."
An English translation of the Fawtier text was published by the S.P.C.K.,
London, 1925.   The introduction to this by the translator, T. Taylor, is
valuable.   A useful paper on the Life of St. Samson, from the pen of F. C.
Burkitt, is found in the *Journal of Theol. Studies*, vol. xxvii, 1925, p. 42–57.
Bibliography in Duine :   *Memento des sources hagiographiques de l'histoire
de Bretagne* (p. 34–5).   Rennes, 1918.

St. David.[1] It is interesting to trace the influence of the master in the careers of these.

Samson left Llanilltud and soon became abbot of a neighbouring monastery. He visited Ireland, so the story runs, and lived after his return a rigorous and solitary life in a cave near the Severn, until summoned by a synod and consecrated bishop. Long before this he had persuaded his parents, brothers, uncle and aunt to embrace the religious life, and he now spent some time consecrating the churches which they had built. His uncle Umbraphel had at one time expressed the wish that he should live always in Samson's company, but the latter had replied somewhat sharply that flesh and blood should not be permitted to decide such questions. His uncle answered that his only desire was to follow Samson after a spiritual manner. " Then St. Samson, prudent in spirit, said to him ' Thou indeed, brother Umbraphel, oughtest to be a pilgrim.' " Umbraphel agreed, and after ordination to the priesthood was sent to preside over a monastery in Ireland.[2] Samson himself, soon after his consecration as bishop, followed the same counsel, and broke the ties that bound him to his native region by departure first to Devon and then to Brittany. There he founded the monastery of Dol, which he ruled as abbot, exercising likewise, in all probability, episcopal jurisdiction over as much of the surrounding territory as looked to the new institution for ecclesiastical leadership.[3]

Paulus Aurelianus,[4] born like Samson in Britain, and trained at Llanilltud, spent some time afterwards as a recluse. He was ordained to the priesthood, and, with others of the same order, was active as a preacher. But, again like Samson, he felt that he should add exile to his sacrifices, and therefore departed for Brittany, where he died bishop of Léon.

Cadoc,[5] as we have seen, was probably a contemporary of Samson and Pol de Léon. His settlement was noted as a school of monasticism, and he may have ruled it as abbot

---

[1] Cf. Williams, op. cit., p. 356, 367.
[2] *Life*, S.P.C.K. ed., ch. xl, p. 42.
[3] Taylor, op. cit. *Introd.*, p. xxix. Cf. Loth. op. cit., p. 113.
[4] *Vita* in *AA. SS.* T. ii, Mart., and *C.B.S.*, p. 22 ff. Another *Vita* in *Analecta Boll.*, vol. i, p. 234 and *Rev. Celt.* v, p. 417. Bibliography in Duine, *Memento*, p. 60-1.
[5] Account of *Vita* and Bibliography in Duine, op. cit., p. 116-8. Slover, op. cit., p. 18 f, discusses a possible descent of Cadoc from Irish ancestors of Dési stock settled in Britain ; but the evidence seems to call for a negative conclusion.

only, not as bishop, for the eleventh century writer of his
" Life " has him carried off in a cloud to Benevento before
he attains to the higher dignity. As his name fell soon enough
into comparative obscurity, the record of his intimacy with
Finnian of Clonard is unlikely to be a late invention. Though
the two were contemporaries, and Finnian, if anything, the
older, the relation between them seems to have been largely
that of master and disciple. But this is a question which we
shall consider at some length in the course of the present
chapter.

More interesting a personality than any of those already
mentioned is Gildas.[1]   He was born about A.D. 500[2] in
" Arecluta " (later Arglud), the district beside the Clyde,
now known as Lanarkshire and Renfrewshire.   His father
was named Caw, and had, as " soul-friend," St. Cadoc,
through whose influence, no doubt, it was that Gildas was
placed in the monastery of St. Illtud.[3] His subsequent career
is obscure. He is said to have corresponded with St. Brigid
of Kildare, but this statement must be ruled out of court,
for St. Brigid died about A.D. 524 (*A.U.* 523, with alternatives
524, 525) when Gildas must have been a junior cleric utterly
unknown to fame. He may have worked for a while in his
native district, converting the heathen Picts ; it is likely
that he visited Ireland in the reign of Ainmire (killed in 569),
son of Sétna, for the *Annales Cambriae* record such a visit
under the year 565 ; he is said finally to have migrated to
Brittany, like Samson and Pol de Léon, his colleagues at
Llanilltud, and to have founded the monastery of Ruys,
where about A.D. 570[4] he found a last resting-place.[5] Not
a single foundation in Britain bears witness to his religious
activity, yet his name survives as enduringly as if written
on the proudest monument of brass or stone. He was a critic

---

[1] *Vita* i, written by a monk of Ruys (a monastery in Brittany, said to have
been founded by Gildas) in the eleventh century, but from an older original.
Vita ii, written much later by Caradoc of Llancarvan   Both published by
H. Williams in his edit. of Gildas's works for Cymmordorion Society.
Parts I and II. London, 1899. These works are the tract " de excidio Britan-
niae " (published also by Mommsen, *M.G.H. Auct. Ant.* xiii, Pt. I, *Chron.
Min.* iii) a Lorica, some fragments, and a Penitential.

[2] The most satisfactory discussion of the date of Gildas's birth is by
Thurneysen, *Zeit. für Celt. Phil.* xiv, p. 15.

[3] Wade Evans, op. cit., p. 73.

[4] *A.U.* 569. *Annal. Cambr.*, s.a. 570 Gildas obiit.

[5] Loth : *Le nom de Gildas dans l'ile de Bretagne* (*Rev. Celt.* xlvi, p. 5) shows
that the legend to this effect is based on fraud, or at least on confusion with
a genuine Armorican saint.

of his age. He stood, like a prophet of old, upon the holy Mount of Sion and fixed his angry gaze upon the iniquities of the world. His patience grew less and less until one day in an ecstasy of righteous indignation he dipped his pen in fire and launched forth into a philippic against the leaders of his race and nation. Lay and clerical alike, they were castigated with a wild ferocity. The crime with which they were charged was indeed heinous, for it was nothing less than the destruction of the country ; whence the name *De Excidio Britanniæ* by which the indictment is known to history. The contrast which Gildas draws between Christian life as it was in Britain and Christian life as it ought to be reflects his own religious ideals. Thése were preached to his Irish friends as well as to his own countrymen, and were adopted (if in unequal measure and nowhere, probably, in their entirety) on both sides of the Irish Sea. There is every reason to believe that Gildas was the ablest and most venerated teacher of the Celtic peoples in the sixth century, and that it is to him, more than to any other, that the distinct monastic form assumed by the Church in Ireland is chiefly due. Proof of this assertion shall be offered in due course.[1]

St. David[2] (Dewi Sant, the national saint of Wales) seems likewise to have exerted considerable influence upon the Irish churchmen of his day. Like Gildas, he was a pupil of St. Illtud.[3] His principal foundation is the monastery of Mynyw (in Latin *Menevia*, later called Ty Ddewi, anglicised

---

[1] Infra, chapter iv.

[2] *Vita* by Rhygyfarch, ed. by Rees, *C.B.S.*, p. 117. Though the eleventh century writer pretends to draw upon earlier documents preserved at St. David's, the *Life* is in the main a tissue of fables. Eng. transl. by Wade-Evans, op. cit. See also Williams : *Christianity in Early Britain*, p. 380–91, La Borderie : *Histoire de Bretagne*, i, p. 512–22. Lloyd : *History of Wales*, i, p. 152–09.

[3] Rees, op. cit., p. 167 : " Very many scholars flowed to him (Illtud), of the number of whom these four, Samson, Paulinus, Gildas, and Dewi (David) studied with him." According to Wade-Evans, op. cit., p. 73 : " but little credence can be attached " to the statement that David belonged to this group. The objection is valid if the date of David's death given by the *Ann. Camb.* (A.D. 601) is correct, but there is not the slightest likelihood that it is. Rhygyfarch and Giraldus Cambrensis record that David's decease took place on the first of March, which that year fell upon a Tuesday, a detail that can hardly be an invention. Arguing from this, Ussher (*Antiq.*, c. xiv. *Works* vi, p. 44) calculates that the year was 544 ; but this is much too early, Lloyd (*Hist.* i, p. 158–163) proposes A.D. 589, a year in which the first of March would likewise fall on a Tuesday. This is probably the true date since it accords perfectly with what we know otherwise of St. David's history. It is furthermore supported by the Irish tradition preserved in the *Chron. Scottorum*, which places his death in 588. He could thus be a disciple of Illtud and a younger contemporary of Gildas and Finnian.

J

St. David's) where he ruled as abbot and bishop. Many
Irishmen were numbered among his disciples, among them
Aedán or Maedóg of Ferns[1] (died 626),[2] Scuithín or Scolán
of Slieve Margy, near Carlow,[3] Modomnóc of Tibragny in
Kilkenny,[4] whilst Finnian of Clonard,[5] Senán of Inis Cathaig,[6]
Barre or Findbarr (a native of Connacht, but active in Munster,
where he founded Cork)[7] and Brendan of Clonfert (died 577
or 583)[8] were said to have visited his monastery.[9] This
establishment, called in the Gaelic tongue, *Cell Muine*, was
indeed a household word on this side of the Irish Sea, and
the biographer of the Saint could claim that Menevia enjoyed
some kind of ecclesiastical supremacy over the southern
portion of our eastern province.[10] This certainly represents
Menevian ambitions, but it gives a false idea of the situation
as it really stood. The truth is suggested rather by the
Catalogus of Irish Saints,[11] which records that the churchmen
of the Second Order received a *missa* or liturgy from Bishop
David and Gildas and Docus,[12] the Britons. Nor was British
influence confined to matters of liturgy. It extended likewise
to ecclesiastical organisation, for it helped to accentuate
the strongly marked national leaning towards monasticism.
The tradition of both countries is at one in declaring that
in the sixth century the Irish were the borrowers.

(c)—The Impulse from Abroad in Summary.

It is well perhaps to pass in review what has been said
in the preceding paragraphs, and to give where possible a
more precise point to the conclusions. The monastic ideal,

---

[1] *Life*, § 35, etc.
[2] *A.U.* 624. Cf. Plummer, *V.S.H.* i, p. lxxviii. *Martyr. Oeng.* 41.
[3] *Life*, § 37. Cf. *V.S.H.* i, xxi.
[4] *Codex Salm.*, c. 191.
[5] *Life*, § 41. Cf. *V.S.H.* ii, 365.
[6] *Lism. Lives*, p. 62.
[7] *Life*, § 39. Cf. *V.S.H.* i, xxxi and 69.
[8] *A.U.* s.a., 576, 582.
[9] *Life*, § 39, § 40.
[10] *Life*, § 42. Cf. Wade-Evans, op. cit., p. 104.
[11] Haddan and Stubbs, *Councils*, p. 293. Ussher, *Works*, vi, p. 478.
[12] Not Cadoc, but Doche (Dochou, Docgwini), founder of Lann Doche,
beside Cardiff, according to Williams, op. cit., p. 372, note 1, and p. 324,
note 2 ; and Loth, *Rev. Celt.* xlvi, p. 13–4. This is possible if Doche is a
contemporary of Gildas and David, as Williams holds (ib. p. 356–7) ; and
Loth (l.c.), quoting *A.U.* 572 : " quies Docci episcopi sancti abbatis Britonum."
Cf. *Life of Cadoc, C.B.S.*, p. 48. But cf. Loth : *La vie la plus ancienne*, p. 24–5,
and Duine, *Memento*, p. 122. The *Life of St. Finnian* (*Lism.* l, p. 75) suggests
that Cadoc is meant, for it groups him with Gildas and David : " Fuair tri
suithe aracind annsin, .i. David ך Gillas ך Cathmael (Welsh Cadvael, which
became Catoc, Cadog) a n-anmanna."

then, lauded by St. Patrick, began to secure firm hold in Ireland, before the end of the fifth century. There is no trace whatever of influence from abroad at this period, though such influence may have been felt, for Whitern then existed and Riocatus the monk and bishop must have had colleagues and successors. Early in the sixth century a new era opens with St. Enda of Aran and St. Finnian of Clonard. The former of these was trained at the *Candida Casa* in Galloway, where a fairly rigid ascetical rule was at this time observed. The rule was transplanted to Aran whither the attraction it exercised drew the youthful Ciarán, son of the artificer, and many other religiously minded men. But Aran's fame as a school of asceticism and regular observance was soon eclipsed by the rival school of St. Finnian of Clonard. In the life of Cadoc[1] the saint of Clonard is numbered among Cadoc's disciples, but as Finnian died in A.D. 549[2] his establishment at Clonard was probably older than Llangarvan.[3] The fact is that Finnian, under the influence chiefly of Cadoc, transformed Clonard, founded originally (like Trim, the home of his early teacher, Foirtchernn) after the loose Patrician pattern, into a monastery strictly so called. It is not unlikely that he visited Britain, whilst it is certain that he corresponded with Gildas on matters of monastic discipline.[4] From Cadoc and his friends, too, the Second Order of Irish saints (of whom Finnian may be regarded as the patriarch) received a liturgy,[5] and the two churches remained on intimate terms throughout the century.[6] Llangarvan had indeed relations of confraternity with Clonard,[7] and had even an endowment of land upon the

---

[1] *C.B.S.*, p. 44, 79, 85.
[2] *A.U.* 548.
[3] See supra, p. 112
[4] *Ep. Columbani M.G.H. Ep.* iii, p. 158 : " Vennianus auctor Gildam de his interrogavit et elegantissime ille respondit." *Seebass Z.K.G.* xiv, 437, regards this Vennianus as Finnian of Mag Bile, but his arguments are not conclusive. Finnian of Clonard's connection with Britain is a commonplace of Irish tradition, and Gildas was a man of distinction, nearly fifty years old before Finnian died. On the other hand, Finnian of Mag Bile was trained at Whitern, and we do not hear that he had any special intimacy with Britain. For a full discussion of the evidence on this point cf. J. T. MacNeill, *The Celtic Penitentials.* (Paris, 1923). pp. 32–8. Cf. infra. pp. 120–1, note 6.
[5] *Catalogus.* H. and S., *Councils* ii, 293.
[6] Cf. Plummer, *V.S.H.* i, p. cxxiv–v.
[7] *C.B.S.*, p. 79. The testimony here given is striking : " Testificantur etiam periti Hibernensium qui apud Clunererd in monasterio discipuli sui beati Finiani degerunt, quod si quis ex clericis sancti Cadoci iverit ad illos honorifice eum suscipiunt et ipsum velut unum ex illis heredem faciunt." Relations seem thus to have been so intimate that a monk from Llangarvan could be eligible for election as Abbot of Clonard.

Liffey.[1] This connection must go back to the first half of the sixth century, for with the growth of St. David's in the second half of the same century the fame of Llangarvan waned and the foundation ceased to be a place of any significance. Finnian thus had probably established his monastery before he came in touch with Cadoc and Gildas on the other side of the Irish Sea, but he did establish contact with them,[2] and he profited by their teaching. British monasticism, with its background in Lérins, laid stress on study, particularly sacred study, as part of the daily round of duties. Finnian adopted this principle, and the monasteries founded by him and his disciples soon rivalled, if they did not surpass, the schools of secular learning. A similar early development in Whitern, Aran, or in the monasteries founded by Enda's disciples, is not recorded. During Finnian's time again there was among the monastic leaders in Britain a strong belief (to which Gildas gives violent expression) that the religious standing of the secular clergy, especially of the bishops, was lamentably low, and there was a tendency, in consequence, to emphasise unduly the advantages of the purely monastic as distinct from the clerical profession. To the influence of Gildas on St. Finnian may be due in part the amazing extension of the monastic institute in Ireland and the more rigorous concept of the monastery as a place of retirement from the world This led, ultimately, in a manner certainly never envisaged by its advocates, to a grave curtailment of episcopal powers in the ecclesiastical government of the country. To this question of jurisdiction we shall devote a special chapter at a later stage. For the moment it is sufficient to note that Finnian was influenced profoundly by Cadoc and Gildas, who were thus indirectly responsible for the progress and the character of the monastic movement in Ireland in the first half of the sixth century.

---

[1] Ib., p. 78.
[2] Probably through his half-British teacher, Foirtchernn, a disciple of St. Patrick, and Bishop of Trim. *Lism. L*, p. 74. Cf. *B. Arm.* 31b, 32b.

§2—IMPORTANT FOUNDATIONS.

(a)—Due to the Initiative of St. Finnian and His Disciples.

Colgan : *AA. SS. Hib.*, p. 293 ff, gives the *Vita S. Finniani* from
the *Salamanca Codex*, adding copious notes. Cf. edit. of same
Codex by De Smedt, De Backer, cols. 188–210. References to
St. Finnian in *Martyrologies* in Colgan, op. cit., p. 402. References
in lives of other saints, ib., p, 403–5. *Disciples of St. Finnian*
ib., p. 405–6. *Celebrated Monks of Clonard*, ib., p. 406–7.
Irish Life of Finnian in Lism. L., p. 75–83.
Various references to Finnian in lives of his disciples, *V.S.H., passim.*

The purpose of the *Lives* was to arouse admiration for their
subjects, and as this was achieved most easily by an imposing
description of their miraculous powers, the panegyrists
exaggerated, often to the point of ridicule, this side of their
heroes' activities. Like historical novelists of our own day,
their chief interest was the story, not the history,
but again like the novelists, the historical background
of their tales, in cases where control is possible, is often found
to be extremely accurate. In dealing with these *Lives*,
excessive scepticism and excessive credulity are equally to be
eschewed.[1]

If we may believe the hagiographers, the saints of early
Christian Ireland were directed in almost all perplexities by
angelic visitors. One of these, then, as a matter of course,
led St. Finnian to the peaceful pasture land of Erard (Cluain
Iraird—Clonard), in Meath, where was to be the place of his
resurrection.[2] Thence " like a sun in the high heavens, he
sent forth rays of virtue and holy teaching to enlighten the
world." We know with certainty from the testimony of
Adamnan[3] that he had received the episcopal order, but it
was as ruler of a monastery, not as ruler of a diocese, that he
won his extraordinary place in the Annals of the Irish Church.
To any high-souled youth of the early sixth century, the
attraction of Clonard seems to have been irresistible. Disciples
in vast numbers[4] grouped themselves round Finnian's cell
and found in him not only a great saint, but a great *teacher*.
To his name, as it has come down to us in tradition, the epithet

---

[1] The principles of sane criticism in this regard are stated admirably by
Dom Gougaud : *Chrét. celtiques*, p. 61 ff.
[2] *AA. SS. Hib.*, p. 395.
[3] *Adam,* i, c. i. Ib. ii, c. i.
[4] Three thousand became the accepted figure (Colgan, op. cit., p. 401)
possibly owing to the influence of Palladius, (*H.L.* 7) who gives this as the
number of monks subject to Pachomius.

Magister[1] is inseparably attached. In this quality we may see his peculiar strength, and the chief cause of his success, for the current of religious idealism then ran high and offered a magnificent opportunity to anyone capable of directing it into the right channels.

Writers of a later period fixed the number of Finnian's leading disciples at twelve, whom they styled, in a picturesque phrase, " the twelve apostles of Ireland."[2] The names of these " apostles " are Ciarán of Saigher, Ciarán of Clonmacnois, Colmcille of Iona and Derry, Brendán of Clonfert, Brendán of Birr, Colmán of Tír-dá-glas, Molaisse of Daiminis, Cainnech of Achad Bó, Ruadán of Lothra, Mobí of Glas Noiden, Senell of Cluain Inis, and Nannid of Inis Maige Sam.[3]

Ciarán of Saigher was a native of Ossory, and enjoyed great fame as the patron of that territory. Whilst his *Life*[4] makes him a contemporary of Oengus (killed A.D. 490 : *A.U.*) and of various sixth century saints, another line of tradition states that he, Ailbe of Emly, Ibar of Beg Ére in Wexford Harbour, and Declan of Ardmore, were known in Ireland as active missionary workers before St. Patrick's coming.[5] Whether this tradition has its origin in a fertile imagination, or whether it is wholly or partially true, cannot be settled with certainty, owing to the meagre (and oftentimes contradictory) nature of the evidence and the impossibility of satisfactory control. Ciarán and Declan are not mentioned in the Annals, but Ibar and Ailbe are, and it is significant that their obits belong to the sixth century.[6] Ossory again was a principality with a long tradition of political independence,[7] which it may have endeavoured to confirm by the claim of special antiquity and privilege for its patron. The

---

[1] " Magister sanctorum Hiberniae," *Mart. Gorm.*, Dec. 12th. *Mart. Oeng.*, p. 202 : " aite noem n-Érenn. Cf. Colgan, op. cit., 402.

[2] *AA. SS. Hib.*, p. 405-6. Cf. p. 113, 192, 395. *Mart. Oeng.*, p. 118. *Mart. Gor.*, Dec. 12th.

[3] *AA. SS. Hib.*, p. 405.

[4] *AA. SS. Hib.*, p. 458-76. *V.S.H.*, i, p. 217-34.

[5] Ussher, *Works*, vi, p. 332, 342-6. *Index Chron.* s.a. 360, 388, 397, 401, 412, 449. Ware ed. Harris, i, p. 490-2. Lanigan, *Eccl. Hist.* i, p. 23 f. Todd : *Life of St. Patrick*, p. 206, 220. Bury, *Life*, p. 351-2. Plummer, *V.S.H.* i, xxx, liii, lxi. Power : *Life of St. Declan*, 1914, p. 164.

[6] Ibar died A.D. 499, 500 or 503 *A.U.* ; 500 *A.F.M.Chron. Scot.* ; 501 *A. Cambr.* ; 504 *A. Clon.* Ailbe died A.D. 526 *A.U. Ann. Innis.* ; 531 *Chron. Scot.* ; 541 *A.F.M.* Laud 610, the oldest of the regnal lists, and written before A.D. 750, places the death of Ailbe during the reign of Eochu, son of the Oengus mentioned above. *Z.C.P.* ix, p. 471.

[7] Mac Neill, *Phases*, p. 109-10.

Déisi, among whom Declan enjoyed high honour as protector, likewise had a strong sense of their state rights as against the Eóganacht rulers of Munster. A possible explanation of the peculiar legends attaching to the names of these four saints is that they belong to the obscure period between the death of Patrick and the great advance under the monastic founders, and were the first to undertake missionary work in their respective districts. Local patriotism would then seek to add to their distinction by making them contemporaries and semi-independent colleagues of the national Apostle. Until further light is thrown—if it ever can be thrown—on this vexed question, the notice that Ciarán of Saigher sojourned at Clonard must be considered extremely doubtful. His place, however, in such company shows that Saigher was regarded as a monastery of some eminence from about the middle of the sixth century onwards.

Ciarán of Clonmacnoise differs from his older namesake in that the main features of his life are well known to history.[1] His father belonged to Meath, but had migrated to Connacht, where the burden of taxation was more tolerable than in the realm of Tara. He probably belonged to a tributary sept, and was of pre-Celtic blood,[2] whilst his profession was that of a worker in wood (soer). It is to be noted that according to the polity of ancient Ireland, craftsmanship of this kind entitled him who exercised it to a place in the *nemed* class. Full franchise as free men was conceded to these, and even equality in dignity with the *soernemid*, a class that comprised the clergy, the nobles, the learned, and the owners of landed property.[3] Ciarán's father is spoken of as " a rich man,"[4] and he certainly was well provided with cattle, the chief wealth of that time. The boy received his religious training from Enda of Aran,[5] but chiefly from St. Finnian in " the city of Cluain Iraird," in the territory of the Southern Uí Néill. In due course the disciple became a master, and founded beside the Shannon, " over against the province of the Connachta,"

---

[1] *Lives* in *V.S.H.* i, p. 200 ff : *Codex Salm.*, col. 155–60. *Irish Life in Lism. L.*, p. 117 ff. Translation of these three lives (and of a fourth in Latin) with interesting notes by Professor Macalister : *The Latin and Irish Lives of St. Ciaran. S.P.C.K.*, 1921.
[2] Macalister, op. cit., p. 104–6.
[3] MacNeill, *Celtic Ireland*, p. 106–7. *The Law of Status or Franchise, P.R.I.A.* Vol. xxxvi, Sec. l., n. 16, 1923, p. 280.
[4] *Vita*, § 1. *V.S.H.* i, p. 200.
[5] *Vita Endei*, §§ 25–6. *V.S.H.*, p. 71–2.

the great monastery of Cluain moccu Nóis. The establishment was yet in its infancy,[1] and the founder little more than
thirty years of age,[2] when in A.D. 549 he passed to his eternal
reward. Clonmacnois soon stood almost without a peer
amid the ecclesiastical " cities " of the country, and its pre-
eminence was later such that legend ascribed Ciarán's premature death to the prayers of his contemporaries. " His
influence had prevailed already over half of Ireland," so the
legend ran, " and if his life had been allowed to reach the
normal human limit, there would not have been the place of
two chariot horses in Ireland that would not have been his."[3]

If St. Ciarán was of moderately gentle birth, his contemporary and fellow-pupil,[4] St. Colmcille, belonged to the
noblest lineage of the land, for he was descended on the father's
side from Niall of the Nine Hostages (whose line was to provide
the country with High Kings for more than five centuries),
and from Loarn, first ruler of the organised Irish colony of
Dál Riada in Scotland ; whilst on the mother's side he could
claim descent from Cathaoir Mór, famed in story as the most
illustrious of Leinster Kings. When Colmcille was born,
his half-uncle, Muirchertach, son of Erc, sat on the throne of
Tara, and the saint lived through the reigns of six cousins.
He was eligible himself for the highest dignity in the country
had he not preferred to abandon the world and devote his
life to the service of God.[5] After a boyhood spent in piety,
Colmcille repaired to Clonard, where in due course he was
ordained deacon and prepared for the priesthood.[6]   If we

---

[1] In the first year of its foundation, *Vita*, § 32. *V.S.H.* i, p. 225 ; in the
seventh year, *An. Tig. Rev. Celt.* T. xvii, p. 138–9.
[2] Thirty-three years old, *Vita*, l.c.   Thirty-one years only, *An. Tig.* l.c
[3] *Lism. Life*, p. 133.   Cf. *Martyr. of Oengus, H.B.* ed. p. 204.
[4] Colgan : *AA. SS. Hib.*, p. 395.
[5] Reeves' *Adam.*, p. 8, note u.
[6] An earlier period of study under Finnian of Mag Bile, though it forms part
of the tradition recorded by the *Irish Lives* and was accepted by scholars
like Lanigan (*Eccles. Hist.* ii, 117) and Reeves (*Adam.* lxxii, 103, 195) is very
doubtful.   Colgan gives a summary account of this tradition (*AA. SS. Hib.*,
p. 644–6), but he did not quite overcome his scruples about its trustworthi-
ness (Cf. op. cit., p. 403.).   Reeves (op. cit., p. 195 n.a.) notes that in the two
cases mentioned by Adamnan, where Finnian of Mag Bile seems to be the
person designated, Finnian is referred to as *bishop*. " In support of this choice
it may be observed that Adamnan in both places calls Finnian *bishop* , and
that while Finnian of Mag Bile is generally acknowledged to have been of
this order, Finnian of Clonard is nowhere, either in his *Life* or the *Calendars*
so designated, and the only place where he is called a bishop is in the *Life
of St. Columba of Tír-dá-Glas* (Colgan *AA. SS. H.*, p. 404a)." But if Finnian
of Mag Bile is meant, the text itself makes an assertion which it is difficult
to reconcile with the known chronology of that saint's life. " Another time,"

accept the statement of the Irish memoirs that he tarried for a while in the monastery of St. Mobí at Glas Noiden (Glasnevin) with Comgall, Ciarán and Cainnech as companions, he must have left Clonard before A.D. 545, for Mobí died of the plague in that year. At any rate, Colmcille is found at home in his native territory and constructing a monastery at Derry in A.D. 546.[1] About ten years later he began the construction of a monastery at Dairmag (Durrow), in the principality of Fir Ceall, beside the lands of the Southern Uí Néill.[2] Kells, in north-western Meath, if its origin goes back to St. Colmcille's day, must have been a place of little importance, for no mention

---

it declares, " the holy man (Colmcille) came along to the venerable bishop, Finnian, his master ; he (Colmcille) being a youth, and Finnian being then an old man." (Alio in tempore vir sanctus venerandum episcopum Finnionem, suum videlicet magistrum, iuvenis senem, adiit, *Adam.*, p. 195). Now Finnian of Mag Bile died in A.D. 579 (*A.U.* and *An. Tig.* 578) and it is nowhere said that he had reached an extraordinary age. Colmcille died eighteen years later (A.D. 597), having reached the respectable age of seventy-six. There is thus no reason to believe that the difference in years between the two exceeded twenty. While Colmcille then could be described as a youth, Finnian could not seriously be described as an old man. Finnian of Clonard, on the other hand, died in A.D. 549, when Colmcille was twenty-eight years old ; and was thus elderly or even aged when Colmcille was receiving instruction at Clonard. To the objection that this Finnian is not spoken of generally as a bishop we may answer that in dealing with one who *par excellence* was the *abbot* of early Christian Ireland, silence on this point need cause no surprise. Reeves concedes (l.c.) " that there is no reference to St. Columba in the *Lives* of the former Finnian (of Mag Bile), with whom tradition regards him as being in serious dispute ; " and again (p. 103, note b), that if the *Bishop* Finnian mentioned is Finnian of Mag Bile " the legend of the quarrel between him and St. Columba, both as to cause and fact (is) extremely improbable." As to the story that Colmcille was sent to Bishop Etchen of Clonfad for ordination (whence it is inferred that Finnian himself lacked the episcopal order) it is wise to conclude that Reeves (op. cit., p. lxxii, note l) : " That the whole story seems a fiction of a later age." In the *Life of Laisrén* or Molaisse of Daiminis, it is stated definitely (*V.S.H.* ii, 137) that Laisrén brought Finnian to consecrate his monastery, and the chief monastic building was the church, which Finnian could not consecrate unless he were a bishop. This is also the tradition of the *Lives* in the *Salamanca Codex* (Col. 324 : " ad Finnianum episcopum Cluana h-Iraird," col 442 : " iuxta reliquias sancti Finniani episcopi," Cf. col. 446.) All things considered, it is almost certain that the Bishop Finnian, under whom as master Colmcille studied, is in every case Finnian of Clonard.

[1] *A.U.* 545 : " Daire Coluim Cille fundata est." But the site was then called Daire Calgaich. Daire Coluim Cille appears in *Annals of the Four Masters* for the first time, s.a. 950. Reeves, op. cit., 160, note r.

[2] Bede represents (*H.E.* iii, 4) Durrow as already founded before Colmcille left Ireland (A.D. 563). On the other hand Adamnan records (i, 3, p. 23) that Colmcille *was founding* Durrow while Ailithir was abbot of Clonmacnois and Ailithir did not succeed to the abbacy until A.D. 585. Both statements may be correct, since the establishment may have taken years to complete. If this solution seems forced, Adamnan's account must be preferred to Bede's, for the former remained throughout life in most intimate touch with the Columban tradition, whereas Bede's acquaintance with it was cursory and at second-hand. Cf. Reeves, op. cit. p. 23.

of it is found in the Annals until A.D. 804,[1] when Norse incursions caused the harassed community at Iona to think of it as a place of refuge.[2] The same must be said of the many other Columban monasteries, like Tory, Drumcliffe and Swords, whose foundation tradition ascribed to the activities of Colmcille himself.

Of the two Brendans who were numbered among St. Finnian's disciples, one founded the monastery of Birr, the other that of Clonfert. Little is known of Brendan of Birr, beyond the general fact that he held a high place among contemporaries,[3] and that St. Colmcille had a special Mass celebrated at Iona for his soul's repose on the morning following his death.[4] It is uncertain when Brendan settled at Birr, but the event probably took place about the middle of the century, when he was already celebrated.[5] His namesake of Clonfert, a native of the small state (Ciarraige) which gave its name to the modern county of Kerry, was famous as a navigator.[6] His exploits, in a duly exaggerated form, made an irresistible appeal to the vivid medieval imagination [7] We know that Brendan, with other saints, visited Colmcille at Himba, near Iona,[8] and that he founded churches in Perth and in the adjacent isles.[9] His seafaring deeds may, perhaps, have been genuinely remarkable, for he was on terms of friendship with Cormac Ua Liatháin, whose long and dangerous voyages in the storm-swept northern seas are recorded by Adamnan.[10] Brendan founded Clonfert in A.D. 559,[11] and he died in A.D. 577 or 583.[12]

---

[1] *A.U.*, s.a. 803. Dr. MacNeill thinks that Kells may have come into possession of the Columban congregation for the first time in this year. " Constructio *novae* civitatis Columbae Cille hi Ceninnus," is recorded under A.D. 807. When the building of the great church was complete (A.D. 813) Cellach, Abbot of Iona, resigned his position in that monastery and came to Kells to live.

[2] Reeves, op. cit., p. 278.

[3] Ussher, *Works* vi, p. 240. Colgan, *Trias Th.*, p. 462. Cf. *AA. SS. Hib.*, p. 395.

[4] Reeves, *Adam.* iii, n. p. 210. Brendan's death took place probably in 572. (*A.U.* and *A.F.M.* give 571. *A.U.* as an alternative 564. *An. Tig.* 573.).

[5] *An. Tig.*: " Ascensio Brenaind in curru suo in aerem." Cf. *A.F.M.* s.a. 553. *A. Clon.* s.a. 562.

[6] *AA. SS. Boll.* T. iii. *Maii.* p. 599. *AA. SS. Hib.*, p. 721–5. *Lism. L*, p. 99 ff. *V.S.H.*, p. 98 ff. Cf. p. xxxvi–xlvii. *Beth. Naem nE.*, p. xvi–xxv. *Z.C.P.* v. p. 124 ff.

[7] *Immram Brendain. Lism. L*, p. 106–15. Zimmer : *Zeitschr. f. deutsches Alterthum*, xxxiii, 129 ff., 257 ff. Schulze : *Zur Brendan-legende. Zeitschr f roman. Phil.* xxx, 257, ff. Plummer, *Z.C.P.* v., 124 ff.

[8] Reeves, *Adam.*, p. 220.

[9] Ib., p. lxxiv.   [10] Ib., p. 166, ff.

[11] *A.U.* 558. *Chron. Scot.*, 554.   [12] *A.U.* 576 and 582.

Another disciple of Finnian, Colum, son of Crimthann,[1] founded the monastery of Tír-dá-glas (Terryglass) before his death of the plague in A.D. 549.[2] This, too, was soon celebrated as a home of religion and learning, and it was visited by Colmcille—possibly because of his old friendship with the founder at Finnian's school—during one of his sojourns in Ireland after he had settled in Iona.[3]

Cainnech, on the other hand, visited Colmcille more than once in his island home.[4] He belonged by birth to the Ciannachta of Dún Geimin, in modern Derry ; but worked for a while in the western isles and on the mainland of what is now Scotland. Numerous dedications in these districts[5] confirm the accounts given in his life.[6] On his return to Ireland he journeyed southwards and founded his principal church and monastery at Achad Bó, in Upper Ossory, where he died in A.D. 600.[7]

Less well known than the saints above-mentioned are the remaining five of Finnian's twelve disciples. Laisrén, or Molaisse, established a monastery at Daminis on Lough Erne,[8] where he died in A.D. 564.[9] In the legend of St. Colmcille's departure to Iona, as an act of reparation for the slaughter at Cúl Dremne, Molaisse is mentioned as Colmcille's counsellor ; but another account attributes this role to his namesake of Inis Muiredaig.[10] Ruadán[11] settled at Lothra, in Ormond, near the northern end of Lough Derg, at what exact date within the sixth century we cannot tell. This saint has secured an unenviable notoriety in Irish hagiographical literature because of the leading part ascribed to him in a fantastic encounter with the civil authorities at Tara.[12] Diarmuid Mac Cerbaill (died 565 or 572) is given in this legend as the ruling High-King. Mobí Clárainech (" the flat-faced "), included among the pupils at Clonard, must have left that school before the time of Colmcille, for he is represented

---

[1] Vita. Cod. Salm. cc. 445 ff.
[2] A.U. 548.
[3] Adam. ii, 36, p. 153.
[4] Adam. i, 3., p. 28 ; ii, 14, p. 123 ; iii, 17, p. 220.
[5] Forbes : Calendar of Scot. Saints, p. 227. Adam., p. 417.
[6] Codex Salm., cc. 371 ff. V.S.H. i, p. 152 ff.
[7] A.U. 599.
[8] Vita in Silva Gad. i, 17-37 ; ii 18-34. V.S.H. ii 131 ff.
[9] A.U. 563.
[10] Adam., p. 252, 287. Rev. Celt. xx, 254, 434.
[11] Vita in Codex Salm. cc. 319 ff. V.S.H. ii, 240 ff.
[12] For the unhistorical nature of this record see MacNeill, Phases, p. 231.

as the latter's master,[1] and he died at his monastery of Glas Noiden (Glasnevin) as early as A.D. 545.[2] Nothing is known of Senell save that he was a disciple of Finnian, and that he founded a monastery at Cluain-inis on Loch Erne.[3] Ninnid, of whom likewise little is known, had a settlement at Inis Maige Sam, on the same lake.[4]

(b)—Due to the Initiative of Others.

The greatest, perhaps, of the sixth century monastic founders who did not receive their training under St. Finnian[5] is St. Comgall of Bennchor (Bangor),[6] a native of the Pictish state called Dál nAraide, and afterwards its patron saint. He was born in A.D. 517,[7] and settled at Bennchor " in the Ards of Ulster," on the southern shores of Belfast Loch, in A.D. 555 or 559.[8] He visited Scotland later, where he founded a monastery " in terra Heth (Tiree)."[9] With Colmcille he maintained the friendliest relations[10]; and he died in A.D. 603.[11] As a leading saint of the Irish Church, he is included in the Litany of those whose aid is invoked at the commencement of the Stowe Missal, and is commemorated among the priests in the diptychs of the same liturgy, whilst a hymn in his praise and a panegyric of his rule are found in the so-called Antiphonary of Bangor, written at that monastery within the eleven years A.D. 680–91.[12] Until the coming of the Danish marauders, Beannchor was to remain a religious-centre of the very highest repute. St. Bernard in the twelfth

---

[1] *Lism, L.* p. 26.
[2] *A.U.* 544.
[3] *Mart. Gorm.*, p. 216 : " Sinell mórmac Mianaig, glossed—ó Claoninis for Loch Eirne."
[4] *Mart. Oeng.*, p. 46. *Mart. Gorm.*, p. 16. *Mart. Tallaght,* p. 58.
[5] Colgan : *AA. SS. Hib.*, p. 405, following an Irish life of St. Ciarán of Clonmacnois, classes Comgall amongst St. Finnian's disciples, but the evidence available is against this statement. It is stated in his *Life (V.S.H.* ii, p. 4) that his early studies were made at Cluain Eidnech ; later at Clonmacnois (ib., p. 6). He must have been almost a contemporary of Fintan, founder of the former monastery, for both died the same year (A.D. 603). The connection with Cluain Eidnech is, however, probable, for Fintan was famous for the austerity of his rule, and the rule at Bangor seems to have partaken of his spirit.
[6] *Life* in *AA. SS. Boll.* T. ii, *Maii,* p. 582–8. Fleming : *Coll. Sacra,* p. 303 ff. *V.S.H.* ii, 3–21. *Codex Salm.* cc. 773–8.
[7] *A.U.* 516.
[8] *A.U.* 554 and 558.
[9] *V.S.H.* ii, p. 22.
[10] *Adam.* i, 49 (p. 92, 96) ; iii. 13 (p. 213) ; and iii. 17 (p. 220).
[11] *A.U.* 602.
[12] *Antiph. of Bangor.* Ed. Warren, ii, p. 16 and 28.

century, recapitulating its history, calls it "a place truly sacred, the nursery of saints which brought forth fruit most abundantly for the glory of God."[1] One member of that congregation, he goes on to say, is reputed to have founded a hundred monasteries, and from that we may judge how great was the total number of monasteries that looked to it as a mother. Saints poured forth from it, too, like an inundation into distant lands, and one of them, Columbanus, built the monastery of Luxeuil, and gathered round him a great multitude. Such was the glory which Comgall's establishment in the Ulster Ards was soon to achieve.

Scarcely less distinguished than Comgall was Finnian of Mag Bile,[2] sprung from the Dál Fiatach, the royal sept of the Ulaid or Ultonians, whose patron he was to become.[3] In addition to Mag Bile, situated at the northern end of Loch Cuan (Strangford Loch), but a few miles distant from Beannchor, he had a monastery at Druim-fionn (Dromin), in Louth.[4] Here it is that the alleged dispute between him and Colmcille took place, the point at issue being a transcript copy of Finnian's Gospels which Colmcille had made without the owner's leave. There is something about all this tale that smacks of the inventor's art, but there is at least one curious record about Finnian that is probably in substance genuine. This record is to the effect that Finnian was the first to bring the Mosaic Law to Ireland.[5] It is more likely that this was a copy of the Old Testament than that it was a complete copy of the Gospels, as the glossator of the Calendar suggests.[6] Finnian died in A.D. 579,[7] and his monastery long retained its place among the most flourishing in the land.

From the constant references to his name in the hagiography of the period we must conclude that Aedh, son of Breac,[8] was a saint of much prominence in the sixth century. He

---

[1] *Vita Malachiae* ed. *AA. SS. Boll.* T. ii, Nov.; Messingham, *Florilegium* p 356. Transl. Lawlor *S.P.C.K.*, p. 28.
[2] The data bearing on his life are collected and discussed by Todd in his edition of the *Liber Hymnorum*, Dublin, 1885, p. 98–105. Cf. Lanigan : *Eccles.Hist.* ii, p. 25 ff.
[3] *AA. SS. Hib.* i, p. 646 : "Ar cúl Fhinnéin Moighe Bile, Ulaid uile." Cf. Reeves : *Eccles. Antiq.*, p. 151.
[4] *Adam.*, p. 103.
[5] *Martyr. Oeng.*, p. 193.
[6] *Martyr. Oeng.*, p. 204 . "Nó is for soscéla doberait ainm rechta *hic,* ar is é Findia tuc *totum Evangelium ad Hiberniam prius.*"
[7] *A.U.* 578.
[8] *Vita* in *AA. SS. Hib.*, p. 418 ff. *Codex Salm.* cc. 333-60. *AA. SS. Boll.* Nov. 10th. *V.S.H.* i, p. 34 ff. *Martyr. Oeng.*, Nov. 10th.

belonged to the royal line of the Southern Uí Néill, and had his chief settlement at Cill-áir, near the hill of Uisneach (in Westmeath) ; but he was active, too, in Connacht, Munster and Leinster, and had even some connection with Tír Chonaill, possibly owing to his distant kinship with the rulers of that territory. He is everywhere referred to as a bishop, and his death is placed in A.D. 589.[1] Cill-áir, whether the site of a monastery or not, seems to have been a place of importance during Aedh's lifetime, but it soon sank into comparative insignificance, and the same fate befell the monasteries or churches in other parts of the country[2] which looked to Aedh as their founder.

To the early sixth century belongs, in all probability, the establishment of a monastery at Louth, in the small Pictish state called Conaille. Its foundation is attributed everywhere to St. Mochta,[3] said to have been a Briton, and a disciple of St. Patrick,[4] but this leads to a tangle in his chronology which it is not quite easy to unravel. His decease took place, according to the *Annals of Ulster*, in A.D. 535,[5] and there is added to the record the superscription of a letter purporting to be from his pen : " Mauchteus peccator, presbyter, sancti Patricii discipulus, in Domino salutem." He had previously been mentioned by the same Annals (quoting from the *Liber Cuanach* under the year A.D. 471),[6] but the notice there given does not require that he should have written (or even that he should have been alive) at that time. He may, however, have reached mature manhood by that date, for there is nothing impossible in the assumption that he was brought across from Britain in early boyhood and placed amid St. Patrick's followers. If still in his teens when the Apostle died in A.D. 461, he would have reached a fine, but by no means an incredible, old age in the third decade of the following century.[7] Much

---

[1] *A.U.* 588.
[2] Eanach Briúin in Muscraige Tíre (Ormond), and Rath Aedha, in Westmeath, are mentioned as the chief of these. Cf. *AA. SS. Hib.*, notes, p. 442–423.
[3] *Vita* in *AA. SS. Hib.*, p. 729–32. *Mart. Oeng.*, p. 100, 176. *Mart. Gorm.*, p. 60 and 160.
[4] *Adam. Pref.*, p. 6 : " Quidam proselytus Brito, homo sanctus, sancti Patricii episcopi discipulus." Cf. note 6.
[5] *A.U.* 534, but the date was uncertain, for 536 is given as an alternative.
[6] " Preda secunda Saxonum de Hibernia, ut alii dicunt, in isto anno deducta est, ut Maucteus dicit. Sic in libro Cuanach inveni."
[7] The medieval writers solved the chronological difficulty by making Mochta live 300 years. Colgan (op. cit., p. 734–5) reduces this period to 130 years ; but, as shown above, the records do not postulate an age of more than 90

more amazing than the statement made about his age is the statement about his household. This, according to the legend, was composed of eighty brethren, three hundred priests, and two hundred bishops. Despite the vast size of the community, it performed no manual labour, but devoted wholly to study what time remained over from prayer.[1] This account must be purely romantic, for the multiplication of priests and bishops on so reckless a scale is quite alien to the spirit of monasticism—Irish monasticism with the rest. In so far, however, as the legend implies that Louth was a monastery of distinction, it has a basis in fact, for the Annals refer to it with respect down through the centuries.[2] Mochta seems to have had priest's orders only; and the site of his monastery (if we may trust a curious but probably credible record) had till then been the property of the druids.[3]

To the second half of the century belongs St. Fintan of Cluain Eidnech[4] (Cloneenagh, in the barony of Maryborough West, part of the ancient principality of Loígis). He was a disciple of St. Colmán of Tír-dá-glas, but surpassed his master and all the other saints of his age in austerity of life. Yet large numbers were ready to submit to the rigour of his rule. From various parts of Ireland they flocked to him, says the writer of his " Life," and working with their hands, after the manner of hermits, tilled the earth with a hoe. They refused the use of any animal, and had not a single cow. If offered a little milk or butter they declined it with thanks. Should it happen perchance that somebody had brought milk into the place unknown to the stern abbot, the vessel upon discovery had to be broken at once.[5] Wild herbs or greens seem to have been the common food of the community,[6] as water

---

[1] *AA. SS. Hib.*, p. 734. *Martyr. Oeng.*, p. 188 : " Nírbo dochta do Mochta, Lughbaid liss. Trí cét sagart, dá cét espoc, maille fris. Ochtmoga saerchlann salmach, a theglach, aidhble réimenn, cen ár, cen buain, cen tíradh, cen gnimrad acht mad léighend." There was no niggardliness with Mochtae, of the enclosure at Lugmed ; he had 300 priests, 200 bishops along with him. Eighty psalm-singing (monks) of gentle birth formed his household . . . who ploughed not, reaped not, dried not, or worked at aught save study.
[2] List of references in Colgan, op. cit., p. 736–7.
[3] *Codex Salm.*, c. 905 : " magorum possessio."
[4] *Vita* in *AA. SS. Boll.* Tom. iii, Febr. *AA. SS. Hib.*, p. 349–53. *V.S.H.* ii, 96–106. *Cod. Salm.*, cc. 289–304. *Martyr. Oeng.*, p. 76 and 224. *Martyr. Gorm.*, p. 38.
[5] *Vita AA. SS. Hib.*, p. 350. *V.S.H.* ii, p. 98.
[6] *AA. SS. Hib.*, l.c. *V.S.H.*, p. 99 : " in illo scilicet die coquus nihil aliud habebat parare fratribus, nisi olera agrestia, sicut frequenter aliis diebus."

was their only drink.[1] Fintan himself was yet more mortified, according to a quatrain quoted by the glossator in the *Martyrology of Oengus*. " Generous Fintan," says this account, " never consumed during his time (aught) save bread of withered barley and clayey water of clay."[2] There is a story in the " Life " that some neighbouring ascetics, with Cainnech of Achad Bó at their head, thought the harshness of Fintan's rule excessive, and came to expostulate with him about it. Fintan, however, forewarned by an angel, received his admonitors with all kindness, conceded a square meal to his community in honour of their visit, regaled them with pious conversation while they stayed, but once they had departed put his community back on greens and clayey water of clay, exactly as before.[3] He died in A.D. 603.[4]

At the same time as Fintan lived Molua[5] or Lugaid, whose father belonged to the Uí Fidgente, the great Eóghanacht sept settled in modern Co. Limerick, whilst his mother was a native of Ossory. He was trained, according to the " Life," under Comgall of Beannchor[6] and Finnian of Clonard,[7] but the latter notice is untrustworthy, for Finnian must have been dead, if not before Molua's birth, at least long before Molua had reached the age to learn. In due course Molua founded the " great and famous " monastery which afterwards bore his name—Cluain Ferta Molua (Clonfertmulloe or Kyle).[8] The site, says the author of the " Life," lay on the confines of Leinster and Munster, between the states of Osraige, Éile and Laoigis, but it formed part of the last-named principality, whose king, Berach, is mentioned as donor of the site.[9] The saint had other churches in Sliab Bladma (Slievebloom), Druimsnechta in Fernmag (Drumsnatt, Co. Monaghan) and elsewhere.[10] Tenderness to men and animals is recorded with

---

[1] Litany in *LL*. 373, c. 39 : " Monaig Finntain meic hua Echach ní chaithitis acht lossa in talman ocus usci." Fintan's monks used to eat nothing but herbs of the earth with water.

[2] Op. cit., p. 76. : " Finntan fial, niro tomail re ré riam, acht arán eorna foeda, is usci creda criad."

[3] *Vita, AA. SS. Hib.*, l.c. *V.S.H.*, p. 98.

[4] *A.U.* 602.

[5] *Vita* in Fleming : *Collectanea*, p. 368–79. *Codex Salm.*, cc. 261–8, 879. *AA. SS. Boll.* T. i. Aug., 342–51. *V.S.H.* ii, 206–25. Molua is simply a hypocoristic form of Lugaid.

[6] *Vita*, c. 15. *V.S.H.*, p. 210.

[7] Ib. c. 25. *V.S.H.*, p. 214.

[8] *Vita*, c. 28. *V.S.H.* ii, p. 217.

[9] Ib.

[10] *Martyr. Oeng.*, p. 181.

admiration as the most noteworthy element in his character. " Now this is that Molua who never killed a bird or any living thing," and when he died in A.D. 608,[1] Mael-Anfaid, abbot of Lismore, " beheld a certain little bird bewailing and lamenting. ' O my God,' says Mael-Anfaid, ' what has happened yonder ? I will not partake of food until it is revealed to me.' Now, when he was there he saw an angel coming towards him. ' That is well, O cleric,' says the angel ; ' let not this put thee into grief any more. Molua mac Ocha has died, and therefore all living creatures bewail him, for never has he killed any animal, little or big ; so not more do human beings bewail him than the other animals, and the little bird which thou seest.' "[2]

About the same period lived Colmán[3], son of Beogna, who dwelt among the Southern Uí Néill. The events of his early youth cannot be traced, for the " Life " says vaguely that the holy senior Coemán (Colmán's first teacher), seeing the great grace with which the boy's soul was adorned and the striking miracle which he wrought, " sent him safe in body and mind to other holy abbots, that he might see their rules and their manner of life, and study the Scriptures with them."[4] These venerable Fathers, impressed by the learning and sanctity of the youth, ordained him priest, and gave him some disciples. He settled for a while at Connor in Antrim, where rests the holy Bishop MacNisse (died A.D. 514),[5] and he voyaged more than once in Scotland,[6] but returned finally to Meath, where in the district called Fir Ceall, but four miles from Durrow, he founded the famous monastery of Lann Elo (Lynally).[7] As Lann is the ordinary British word for monastery,[8] we should suspect that Colmán came in some way under British influence, but no hint of this appears in his " Life."[9] Colmán seems to have been a man of note as a

---

[1] A.U. 607.
[2] Martyr. Oeng., p. 56.
[3] Vita in V.S.H. i, 258 ff. B.N.E. i, 168–82. Codex Salm., cc. 415–44. Cf. Martyr. Oeng., p. 196 and 212, 214.
[4] V.S.H. i, p. 259.
[5] A.U. 513.
[6] Adam. i, 5 (p. 29) and ii, 15 (p. 124–5).
[7] V.S.H. l.c.
[8] The site was called Fid Elo at the time of Colmán's settlement. V.S.H. l.c.
[9] Land Abaich (Glenavy, Antrim), Land Mocholmóc and Land Rónáin Find (Magheralin, Co. Down), Land Beachair (Kilbarrick, Dublin), Land Luacháin (in Meath), Land Léri and Land Maelduib (in Brega) (Cf. Onom. Goid., p. 475–6) are all within easy reach of the Irish Sea, and may thus have had more intimate contact with Britain. The word lann in British passed

scholar, for to him is attributed the authorship of the tract called " Aibgitir in Chrábaid," the " Alphabet of Devotion "[1]; and there is a story that in punishment for his pride of intellect he was deprived of his memory, which, however. was restored through the good offices of St. Mochua.[2] Colmán died at Lann Elo in A.D. 611,[3] aged 56.

Seven years later there passed away a saint of still greater renown, Cóemgen[4] (Kevin) of Glenn-dá-locha (Glendalough). In our oldest calendar he is celebrated in a fine quatrain which reads " A soldier of Christ into the land of Ireland, a high name over the.sea's wave : Cóemgen the chaste, fair warrior, in the glen of the two broad lakes."[5] All that can be said with certainty of the youthful Cóemgen is that he was of Leinster stock, and reared in piety.[6] He loved the profound solitude of the lovely valley between the lakes, and there in time he founded his monastery " where two sparkling rivers meet."[7] Many disciples came to him until his monks were indeed a multitude, and numerous monasteries and cells besides Glendalough were subject to his rule. About a mile further up the lake, in a narrow spot between hill and lake, where the trees stood thick and the streams ran clear, he built a skeleton hut, and lived therein as a hermit for four years without fire or roof But the wild creatures of mountain and forest offered him companionship and drank tamely from his hand. At the end of the period stated he was induced to return to his monks.[8] The fame of Glendalough was already assured when Cóemgen died at a good old age in A.D. 618.[9]

Earliest among the important sixth century founders of

---

through three stages. Its earliest sense was "land enclosed for a special purpose." Then it came to mean "monastery" and, finally "church" (Williams : *Christ. in Early Britain*, p. 266–8). In Gaelic the word was common in the compound ith-lann, " corn enclosure," or haggard (*Mod. Irish iothlann*). It is cognate with *land* of the Teutonic languages. Pedersen, *Vergleichende Gram.*, ii, p. 3.

[1] Ed. Meyer, *Z.C.P.* iii, p. 447 ff.
[2] *V.S.H.* ii, p. 184–5.
[3] *A.U.* 610. *Ann. Tig. Rev. Celt.* xvii, p. 169.
[4] *AA. SS. Boll.* T. i, *Junii*, p. 312–22. *Cod. Salm.* cc. 835–44. *V.S.H.* i, 234–57. *B.N.E.*, p. 131–67.
[5] "Míl Crist i crích nÉrenn / ard n-ainm tar tuind trethan / Cóemgen cáid, cáin cathar / i nGlinn dá lind lethan." Cf. *Martyr. Oeng.*, June 3rd, p. 138 : *Mart. Gorm.*, June 3rd, p. 108.
[6] *Vita*, *V.S.H.* i, p. 234–40.
[7] Ib., p. 241.
[8] Ib., p. 241-2.
[9] *A.U.* 617.

whom little is known is Búithe,[1] founder of Mainistir Búithe
(Monasterboice) in the land of his own people, the Cianachta
of Brega. The statement in his " Life " that his parents
were worried when the child was born, " because priests were
then few, and such as existed lived far away from them,"[2]
probably contains a genuine tradition. The same may be said
of the record that his death synchronizes with the birth of
Colmcille,[3] in which case the date of his decease would be
A.D. 521. He would thus be a contemporary (and almost
certainly an older contemporary) of St. Finnian of Clonard.
As his establishment in Brega seems to have borne the name
" Mainistir " (monastery) from the beginning there is no
reason to doubt that its monastic character goes back to the
founder. Hence once again the conclusion that the movement
in favour of the strict cenobitic life had begun to make progress
before the end of the fifth century. Búithe had been raised
to the episcopal dignity.[4]

To a later period in the sixth century belong Iarlaithe,
founder of Cluain Fois (near Tuam), and Tuaim-dá-gualann
(Tuam)[5]; Colmán or Mocholmócc, founder of Druim Mór in
Uí Echach Ulad (Dromore, Co. Down)[6]; Senán, founder of
Inis Cathaig (Scattery Island)[7]; Fachtna, founder of Ross
Ailithir in Corcu Loegde (Rosscarbery, Cork)[8]; Nessan, founder
of Mungret, beside Limerick[9]; Commán, founder of Ros

---

[1] *Vita* in *V.S.H.* i, 87 ff. Cf. *Martyr. Oeng.*, p. 132 (Dec. 7th, p. 257). *Mart. Tall.*, May 16th.
[2] *V.S.H.*, p. 87.
[3] *A.U.* s.a. 518 and 522.
[4] *A.U.* s.a. 518 and 522. Cf. *Litany* in *LL.* 373. c. 49 : " Trí I fir ailithir dar muir la Buti n-*epscop.*" Also Reeves, *Adam.*, p. lxviii–ix.
[5] *Martyr. Oeng.*, Dec. 26th, p. 262. Cf. Poem attributed to Cuimmín of Connor, *Z.C.P.* i, p. 66. *Catalogus*, H. and S., p. 293.
[6] *Cod. Salm.* cc. 827–34. *Martyr. Oeng.*, p. 138, 144. *Martyr. Gorm.*, p 112. *Martyr. Doneg.*, p. 148. Reeves : *Eccles. Antiq.*, p. 104n.
[7] *Lism.* L, p. 54–74. (Substance in *AA. SS. Hib.*, p. 530–6.) *Martyr. Oeng.*, p. 80, 81, 86, 90. *Amra* in praise of Senan, publ. by Stokes in *Z.C.P.* iii, p. 220.
[8] Reference in *Vita S. Mochoemóg V.S.H.* ii, p. 165 : " Ipse sanctus (Fachtna) in australi Ybernie plaga iuxta mare, in suo monasterio, quod ipse fundavit (ibi crevit civitas, in qua semper manet magnum studium scholarium quae dicitur Ross Ailithry) habitabat." Cf. *Martyr. Oeng.* p. 176, 186. *Z.C.P.* i, 64.
[9] Reference in *Vita Albei V.S.H.* i, p. 61–2 : " egregius et sanctissimus diaconus Nessanus." Cf. Ussher, *Works* vi, p. 531. *Catalogus*, H. and S., *Councils* ii, p. 293, where Nessan is numbered among saints of the Second Order. His obit is given in *A.F.M.* under A.D. 551. *Martyr. Oeng.*, p. 164, 170. *Martyr. Gorm.*, p. 142. Cf. *Tr. Thaum.*, p. 157. That Mungret ranked among the great monasteries is proved by the letter of Cumméne to Segéne of Iona (Ussher, *Works* vi, p. 501), where the successor of Nessan is mentioned among the distinguished abbots present at the Synod of Magh Léne.

Commáin[1]; Colm of Inis Celtra (Holy Island in Lough Derg, near Killaloe)[2]; and Bairre, founder of Corcach (Cork)[3]. All these were bishops, save Nessan, who had remained content with the lower order of deacon.

§3—Less Important Foundations.

Foundations of smaller importance attributed to disciples of St. Finnian are those of Mogennóc at Cell Duma in the south of Brega (Kilglinn, Meath)[4]; Nathí at Achad Conaire (Achonry)[5]; Daig at Inis Caoin Dega in Conaille Muirthemne (Inishkeen in Louth, near Monaghan border)[6]; Eoghan of Ard Sratha (Ardstraw, Tyrone)[7]; and Coirpre of Cúil Raithin in the north of Dál n-Araide (Coleraine, Derry).[8] The two last-mentioned saints, however, like their companion in the north, Tigernach of Cluain Eois in Airgialla (Clones, Monaghan),[9] seem to have received their training rather at the *Candida Casa* than at Clonard.[10] To these may be added Laisrén or Molaisse of Inis Muiredaig (Inishmurray Island,

---

[1] *Martyr. Oeng.*, Dec. 26th, p. 254 and 263. *Martyr. Gorm.*, p. 246. Ussher, *Works* vi, p. 532. *AA. SS. Hib.*, p. 405. (Ib., p. 791, n. 12. This Commán is wrongly confused with a namesake who was abbot of Clonmacnois and who died A.D. 743, *A.F.M.*)

[2] *AA. SS. Hib.*, p. 150, n. 31. His death of the Buide Conaill is recorded in *A.U.* s.a. 548 (549). Nothing further is known of his history. In the *Vita* of Colmán of Tír-dá-Glas (*Codex Salm.*, c. 453 f) he is confused with that saint. Whether the monastery of Inis Celtra owes its foundation to Colm or to one or other of the saints Stellan (Ussher, *Works* iv, p. 427) or Caimin (flor. c. 640 *AA. SS. Hib.*, p. 746. Cf. p. 337) must remain uncertain. For all that is known of Inis Celtra see Prof. Macalister's monograph : *The Hist. and Antiquities of Inis Celtra*, *P.R.I.A.*, vol. xxxiii, p. 93–174.

[3] *Vita* in *V.S.H.* i, 65–74. *Martyr. Oeng.*, Sept. 25, p. 196, 211–2. *Martyr. Gorm.*, p. 184 : " Bairre cáid ó Corcaig, gloss. episcopus et confessor." He was of Connacht origin, but active in Munster and possibly in Scotland. For his cult in latter country see *V.S.H.* i, p. xxxi, note 3.

[4] *AA. SS. Hib.*, *Vita Finn*, ch. 19, p. 395. Cf. p. 405 and *Trias Thaum.*, p. 129 and *B. Arm. Add.* 32a, where Mogennóc is said to be a " germanus " of Lommán of Trim. *A.U.* s.a. 834 shows that the place was then a " civitas." Cf. Lanigan : *Eccles. Hist.* ii, p. 235.

[5] *AA. SS. Hib.*, *Vita Finn.*, p. 396. *Martyr. Oeng.*, Aug. 9th, p. 175, 185. *Martyr. Gorm.*, p. 153.

[6] *A.F.M.* s.a. 586 : " Dagaeus episcopus filius Carelli obiit die 18 Aug. Cf. *AA. SS. Hib.*, p. 193, 344, 731, 732, n. 20. *Martyr. Oeng.*, p. 177, 186. *Martyr. Gorm.*, p. 158.

[7] *AA. SS. Boll.* T. iv, Aug. *Codex Salm.* cc. 915–24. *Martyr. Oeng.*, p. 178, 189. *Martyr. Gorm.*, p. 162. Cf. *AA. SS. Hib.*, p. 406.

[8] *AA. SS. Hib.*, p. 406. Cf. *Martyr. Oeng.*, p. 234, 240. *Martyr. Gorm.*, p. 216. Reeves : *Antiq.*, p. 75n., 247.

[9] *AA. SS. Boll.* April 5. *Codex Salm.* cc. 212 ff. *Martyr. Oeng.*, April 4th, p. 104, 110. *Martyr. Gorm.*, p. 70.

[10] Cf. Supra p. 107. *V.S.H.* i, p. cxxvi.

off the Sligo coast)[1] ; Colmán, son of Leinin of Cluain Uama in Uí Liatháin of Munster (Cloyne, S. Cork), said to have been a disciple of St. Iarlaithe of Tuam[2] ; Sinchell, abbot of Cill Achaid Dromafota (Killeigh in Offaly) [3]; Abbán moccu Cormaic of Mag Arnaide (Moynarney, Wexford) and Ross-meic-Treóin (New Ross, Wexford)[4] ; Fínán Cam of Cenn-étig (Kinnity, barony of Ballybrit, Offaly)[5]. Leitrioch Odráin in Muscraige Tíre (Latteragh, barony of Upper Ormond, Tipperary), founded by St. Odrán[6] (who died in A.D. 549)[7] ; Cluain-fota-Baetháin in Feara Bile (Clonfad, parish of Killucan, Meath), founded by St. Etchen[8] ; Menadroichid in Uí Fairchelláin (Monadrehid near Borris-in-Ossory), founded by St. Laisrén[9] ; and Ros-ech in Caille Fallamain (Russagh near Killalon, in Meath), founded by St. Caemán Brec,[10] if places of note in their early years, did not maintain their position in the later centuries.

---

[1] *Martyr. Oeng.*, Aug. 12th, p. 176, 184. *Martyr. Gorm.*, p. 154 : " Molaissi ainm aile dhó ⁊ ab esidhe."

[2] *AA. SS. Hib.*, *Vita Iarl.*, ch 3, p. 309. Cf. p. 310, n. 14. *Martyr. Oeng.*, Nov. 14th, p. 236, 246. *Martyr. Gorm.*, p. 224.

[3] *AA. SS. Hib.*, p. 191. *Martyr. Oeng.*, March, 26th, p. 84, 100. *Martyr. Gorm.*, p. 62. He died A.D. 549 (*A.U.* 548).

[4] *AA. SS. Hib.*, p. 610 ff. *AA. SS. Boll.*, Oct. xii, p. 276. *V.S.H.* i, p. 3–33. *B.N.E.* i, 3–10. *Martyr. Oeng.*, March 16th, p. 82, 98. *Martyr. Gorm.*, p. 56. Mag Arnaide is referred to in the *Life* (*V.S.H.*, p. 21, 32) as a *civitas*, and seems to have been a place of considerable size, though ignored in the *Annals*. The foundation of Ross-meic-Treóin " magnum quidem monasterium prope flumen Berbha," is attributed to Abbán (*V.S.H.*, p. 21) ; but the *Life* adds : " in quo iacet beatissimus abbas sanctus Emenus " (St. Eimhin of Monaster-evan). O'Donovan (*A.F.M.* s.a. 1394) takes Lanigan severely to task for identifying Ross-meic-Treóin with the monastery of St. Eimhin (*Eccles. Hist.* i, p. 166 ; iii, p. 237–9) ; but the confusion goes back to Colgan (*AA. SS. Hib.*, p. 623, n. 13, p. 751, c. 3) and ultimately to the writer of the *Life*. It arose from the fact that the original *Ros-glas*, where St. Eimhin and his Munstermen settled, came to be known as *Ros-glas na Muimnech*, and later simply as Mainister Eimhin. When the name *Ros-Glas* had fallen into disuse the only *Ross upon the Barrow* known was *Ross-meic-Treóin*, and St. Eimhin came accordingly to be connected with that *civitas*.

[5] *Vita* in *Codex Salm.*, cc. 305–18. *V.S.H.* ii, p. 87–95. Irish transl. of latter text in the " Irish Rosary," xv, 1911. Another *Irish Life* was publ. by Macalister in *Z.C.P.* ii, p. 545–64. *Martyr. Oeng.*, April 7th, p. 105, 113. *Martyr. Gorm.*, p. 73. His *floruit* is to be placed about A.D. 600. Plummer *V.S.H.* i, p. lxix–lxx.

[6] *AA. SS. Hib.*, p. 191. *Martyr. Gorm.*, Oct. 2nd and 26th, p. 188, 192. In the *Life of Ciarán of Saigher*, ch. 25 (*V.S.H.* i, p. 228), he is said to have founded a " clarum monasterium " in the villa of Letracha.

[7] *A.U.* 548.

[8] *AA. SS. Hib.*, p. 304–6. *Martyr. Oeng.*, Febr. 11th, p. 60, 72. *Martyr. Gorm.*, p. 34. His episcopal rank and his obit are recorded in *A.U.* s.a. 577 (578).

[9] *Martyr. Oeng.*, Sept. 16th, p. 194 : " Laissrén mór Mena." Cf. p. 208. *Martyr. Gorm.*, p. 178. Laissrén died A.D. 600 (*A.F.M.*).

[10] *Martyr. Oeng.*, Sept. 14th, p. 194, 206. *Martyr. Gorm.*, p. 176. He died in A.D. 615. (*A.U.* 614.)

§4—Monasteries for Women.

St. Patrick speaks proudly in his "Confession" of the number of virgins among his converts who had consecrated their lives to God. Many, if not most of these, had taken this heroic step in despite of their parents and friends, whose ambitions for the girl-folk of the family were cast in the traditional mould. The case must, therefore, have been rare when the consecrated virgin could pursue her ideal of prayer and penance in her own home. Normally she had to leave her relatives and find a new habitation with others like herself on some suitable plot of land possessed by the missionaries. What services such virgins rendered to St. Patrick and his colleagues cannot be accurately estimated, but they were certainly considerable. To provide vestments for the clergy, cloths for the altars, decorative hangings for the walls, and to see to the general cleanliness and beauty of church interiors would doubtless be their chief work. They may also have done something as catechists among the children. The circumstances of their profession and sex make it likely that they were more or less permanently attached to definite churches or settlements ; but there was little question of strict enclosure, and they could be transferred without difficulty from one place to another, if the welfare of the mission so demanded.[1]

However numerous the consecrated virgins might be, and however meritorious their work, they remained in a state of complete obscurity until the end of the fifth century. At this period they advance suddenly into the limelight in the person of St. Brigid,[2] perhaps the greatest woman of whom

---

[1] See above p. 90–3. A canon attributed to St. Patrick (H. and S., *Councils* ii, Can. 9, p. 328) lays down that a consecrated virgin and a monk are not to drive from house to house in the same chariot ; nor may they indulge in protracted conversation. Such a canon would have no point in the days of the Second Order, when the two sexes were rigidly separated. It must, therefore, go back to the period of the First Order, and its attribution to St. Patrick is probably quite just.

[2] Oldest *Vita* by Cogitosus (fl. A.D. 620–80). Cf. *Mario Exposito* : On the earliest Latin life of St. Brigid of Kildare. *P.R.I.A.*, vol. xxx. Dublin, 1912. Published by Colgan, *Trias Thaum.*, p. 518–24. Also by Messingham : *Florilegium*, p. 191–202 ; and by the Bollandists *AA. SS.*, Febr. 1, p. 119–35. Irish lives in *B. Lism.*, p. 34–53 and *Three Middle Irish Homilies*, ed. Stokes, Calcutta, 1877. For other Latin Lives see *Bibl. Hag. Latina* i, nos. 1455, 1456, 1458–62, and *Supplement*, p. 61. For short stories in Irish about her see Plummer, *Miscell. Hagiog. Hib.* Brussels, 1925. Nos. 86, 87. Hymns in her praise in *Liber Hymn.* Ed. Atkinson and Bernard, i, p. 107–27. *Thes. Paleohib.* ii, p. 323–49. Most complete account of her life in O'Hanlon: *Lives of the Irish Saints*, vol. ii, February 1st. Excellent critical remarks on her Life by Cogitosus in Gougaud : *Chrét. celtiq.*, p. 93 and 218 ; and *Rev. Béné*, xxv, 1908., p. 172.

Irish history tells. Of her life, as far as it concerns us here, the following facts are gleaned from Cogitosus. She was born of noble[1] Christian parents in Ireland,[2] and trained from childhood in letters[3]; but study (if the statement that she applied herself to it be true) did not prevent her from performing ordinary farmyard duties, like the care of cows, and the making of butter.[4] When she reached maturity, her parents, " in the usual human way," wished her to marry, but she declared that nothing could shake her resolution to remain a virgin. At this, no doubt, her parents demurred, and there was a family scene, but Cogitosus mentions merely that Brigid had her way, and betook herself to " the most holy bishop of happy memory, Maccaille," who acceded to her request. Prostrate, therefore, before the altar she vowed her virginity solemnly to Almighty God, and received from the bishop's hand a white veil and a white dress.[5] The fame of her deeds in time drew about her a huge multitude of disciples, male and female, from all the Irish provinces. For these she founded " on the firm basis of faith " and in the open lands of the Liffey plain a great monastery, " head of almost all the churches of Ireland and overtopping (like a mountain peak) all the monasteries of the Irish,"[6] according to the inflated panegyric of her biographer. As Cogitosus is interested chiefly in recounting the glorious powers of St. Brigid as manifested by her miracles, he gives little that can be utilized as history, but we learn incidentally that her reputation for charity and hospitality was immense.[7] We hear also that she attended a public assembly, carried thither in a chariot drawn by two horses.[8] On another occasion she travelled in the same chariot to visit the local king[9]; and again she is found journey-

---

[1] On the father's side only, according to the common story, for her mother was a bond slave. Cf. *Vita* ascribed to Ultan. *Trias Thaum.*, p. 527.
[2] At Fochairt in Conaille Muirtheimhne (Faughart near Dundalk).
[3] *Vita*, ch. 1, op. cit., p. 522.
[4] Ib., ch. 2.
[5] Ib., ch. 3 : " pallium album et vestem candidam super ipsius venerabile caput imposuit." Maccaille was a disciple of St. Patrick, and this event took place at Mag Teloch in the lands of the Uí Néill (*B. Arm. Tír.*, 21a) ; but Maccaille's church and his last resting-place lay further south at Cruachu Bri Eile (Croghan Hill) in Uí Fáilge (*Martyr. Oeng.*, Apr. 25th, p. 118). Ussher (*Works* vi, p. 180. Cf. *Index Chron.*) gives A.D. 467 as date of Brigid's profession ; but for this there is no satisfactory proof. Colgan discusses her age in Appendix iv, ch. 8, op. cit., p. 619 f, and date of her birth in ch. 9, p. 620.
[6] Op. cit. *Prologue*, p. 520.
[7] Ib., ch. 2, 6, 8, 11, 15, 16, etc.
[8] Ib., ch. 18, p. 520.
[9] Ib., ch. 21, p. 521.

ing at nightfall " in the spacious plain of Brega."[1] We hear,
too, of an expedition in the course of which she happened
upon a group of men engaged in heathen rites, and about to
set off on some bloody foray. Moved by the sight, the saint
turned preacher, and by a homily on the consequences which
evil deeds must bring reduced the malefactors to penance.[2]
From all this it is evident that Kildare in Brigid's time was
organised much after the manner of the old missionary stations.
It approximated more closely to the houses founded for virgins
by St. Patrick than to the houses of strict monastic discipline
founded by St. Finnian of Clonard.

To the same period as St. Brigid[3] belongs the virgin
Moninne[4] of Cill Sléibe Cuilinn (Killeavy, near Newry,
Armagh).[5] She received the veil of virginity, according to
the " Life " written by Conchubrán, from St. Patrick's own
hand. Not only did the Apostle give Moninne wise instructions,
but he gathered about himself other virgins " that he might
rear them from their youth in the fear of the Lord, and that
supported by their aid he might succeed the more easily in
the good work that he had begun."[6] One of these virgins
was a young girl of good parentage and great beauty, who
had vowed her virginity to God while yet in childhood, and
had lived thereafter in prayer and study in her own home[7]
under the care of a pious priest. When in due course she joined
Moninne at Fochairt (Faughart near Dundalk), the community
numbered eight, and one of its members was a widow who
had brought with her an infant son.[8] This child afterwards

---

[1] Ib., ch. 27, p. 522.
[2] Ib., ch. 23, p. 521.
[3] Her death is recorded in *A.U.* s.a. 516.
[4] Also called Darerca. The latter, according to the scholiast on *Oengus, Martyr.*, p. 166, was her original name.
[5] *Vita* by Conchubranus, in *AA. SS. Boll.*, Jul. ii, p. 297–312. Cf. p. 241, 246, 296 ; and Colgan, *Trias. Thaum.*, p. 604 (vii). Re-edited by Mario Esposito, *Conchubrani Vita S. Monennae*, *P.R.I.A.*, vol. xxvii, p. 202–51. Dublin, 1910. Another Life in *Codex Salm.*, cc. 165–88. *Martyr. Oeng.* July 6th, p. 161, 166. *Martyr. Gorm.*, p. 130.
[6] *Vita*, ed. Esposito, p. 209.
[7] P. Grosjean suggests that such virgins living in their own homes were common in the time of St. Brigid. This impression he has received from *Lism. L.*, the *Betha Brigte* in Rawl., 512 (soon to be published in *Irish Texts*) and Colgan's *Tertia Vita* (B. L. 1455–6), to be published by him in *Anal. Boll.*
[8] Brigid is also made a member of the group ; but for this there is no evidence in her own *Life*. It is, of course, quite possible, especially as the settlement of virgins must have been near her home. References to the widow with her son, and to the young maiden living under a vow of virginity within her family recall the primitive period of which the tradition is preserved so strikingly in the *Book of Armagh*, and give the impression that Conchubrán in compiling this *Life* utilised ancient and reliable sources.

became a bishop. The friends and relations among whom Moninne was settled evidently felt it their duty to maintain close intercourse with the house of virgins, for their visits proved so distracting that Moninne decided to leave her native place and put her company under the direction of St. Ibar near Beg Ére.[1] Widows and matrons, some of whom belonged to princely families, had a place in Moninne's company.[2] If these felt any desire to wander from their cells the tendency was held in check by the bishop.[3] So closely, indeed, were the Sisters confined that a dry season found them cruelly worried for lack of fresh water. Not only had they none for domestic purposes, but they had not sufficient even to slake their thirst.[4] Greater still than this was the trouble caused by a young nun who fomented discord between the community and Bishop Ibar, telling the latter and his followers that the clergy were of absolutely no account since Moninne settled in the neighbourhood, so irresistibly did she attract the whole countryside to her monastery.[5] There were many enough ready to believe that the young lady with the bitter tongue spoke truly; so that Moninne thought it more prudent to leave Leinster and seek another home further to the north.[6] Her following at the time was said to number fifty.[7] On the way, according to the " Life," she paid a visit to St. Brigid, who had just constructed her monastery in the Liffey plain.[8] Later the company proceeded to Sliab Cuilinn, where Moninne definitely settled. The journey from Kildare to that portion of Armagh, if made completely by land, then occupied five or six days, according to the writer of the " Life," who says that he can speak from experience, for he had often travelled between these places himself.[9] Here once again her monastery became very popular with the people and soon had a reputation for wealth.[10] Near by, however, lived a nun whose tiny monastery was so poor that it subsisted chiefly on Moninne's charity.[11]

---

[1] *Vita*, l, ii, § 4. p. 219 : " Congretatis ibi simul multis Christi virginibus sub potestate episcopi vivebant."
[2] Ib.
[3] Ib. : " sorores cum sancta Monenna, quibus discurrendi non erat licentia."
[4] Ib.
[5] Ib., § 5.
[6] Ib., § 6.
[7] Ib.
[8] Ib.
[9] Ib.
[10] Ib., § 11.
[11] Ib., § 12.

Though the biographer relates that the abbess for many years never looked a male in the face, fearing lest through the eyes as windows death should enter into the soul, he admits that she was often abroad visiting the sick and redeeming captives.[1] She travelled by night rather than by day, and was ready on occasion to sup with her nuns in the home of a pious layman.[2] The rule of the monastery was severe. Prayer and vigils were incessant ; fasts were frequent ; sleep was taken on the hard ground ; and the land was tilled by their own toil, as in the days of the ancient hermits.[3] Food was at times so scarce that the community was in danger of death through star-vation.[4] Six churches at least in Ireland,[5] many in Britain (including one, Calvechif, near the River Trent),[6] and seven in Alba or Scotland,[7] are attributed to her zeal. Until cor-roboration is forthcoming from other sources, these expeditions abroad, and especially the pilgrimages to Rome,[8] must be regarded with suspicion. But the general story of her life accords so well with the circumstances which we know to have prevailed in the last quarter of the fifth and the first quarter of the sixth century that it would be folly to reject it. Moninne's monastery at Cell Sléibe survived,[9] but its importance in later times must have been very slight, to judge from the rare allusions to it in the *Annals*.

A generation or so later than St. Brigid and St. Moninne lived St. Ita.[10] She came of Déisi stock,[11] and wished from her earliest youth to consecrate her virginity to God, but she was prevented for a time from giving effect to her desire because of her father's opposition.[12] An angel, says the " Life," came finally to her aid, and when all obstacles had been removed

---

[1] Ib., § 16.
[2] Ib. : " Post nonnulla, impetrata petitone, illo precedente, sequuntur eum ad domum suam, lavatisque pedibus Xti ,virginum pio obsequio, et mensa apposita coenula ministratur. Potus autem de cervisia miscitur."
[3] Lib. iii, § 1.
[4] Ib., § 2.
[5] Ib., § 3 : " i.e., Focharde, deinde Cehllscleve, et post Cheneglas, et edifi-cavit ecclesiam unam in Surde, et alteram in Ahrmacha, necnon et Mitha et multas alias."
[6] Ib.
[7] Ib., § 8.
[8] *Lib.*, ii, § 8. *Lib.* iii. § 3.
[9] Cf. story preserved in *Cottonian MS*. Esposito, op. cit., p. 245 D.
[10] *Vita* in *AA. SS. Hib.*, p. 66–71. *AA. SS. Boll.* T. i, Jan., 1062–8. Cf. *Trias Thaum.*, p. 462, 46. *V.S.H.*, ii, p. 116–30. *Martyr. Oeng.*, Jan. 15th, p. 36, 42, 44. *Martyr. Gorm.*, p. 16.
[11] *AA. SS. Hib.*, p. 66, ch. 1.
[12] Ib., ch. 4.

she repaired to a church to make her solemn vow and receive the veil of virginity from the hands of the clergy.[1] Soon afterwards she migrated to the lands of Corcu Oche, which later became part of the kingdom of Uí Conaill Gabra in modern County Limerick. There at Cluain Credail (later known as Cell Ide—Killeedy), at the foot of Sliabh Luachra, she established a monastery and was joined by a great number of virgins from the surrounding districts.[2] She became patron of the Uí Conaill principality, and her place was enriched by that people with the utmost liberality.[3] Her teaching is summed up in the triad : " True faith in God with purity of heart ; simplicity of life with religion ; generosity with charity."[4] She was given to fasting,[5] and insisted much on the need of meditation and prayer.[6] The most remarkable feature of her monastery is that she seems to have established in it a school for small boys. Brendan of Clonfert, according to his " Life," spent five years of his early childhood under her care.[7] At the end of that period he was withdrawn by Bishop Erc and set to commence his literary studies. Many others received their youthful training in piety likewise from St. Ita,[8] and their reputation for holiness in later life was such that their first teacher was accorded the title, " Foster-Mother of the Saints of Ireland." After St. Brendan, the most famous of her pupils is St. Mochoemóg, who is said to have spent twenty years under her tuition before proceeding to Bangor for his more advanced studies.[9] But the length of this sojourn is open to serious doubt, as well because Mochoemóg survived Ita by about eighty years,[10] as also because the presence in her monastery of a student so mature in years would be open to grave objection. We find her, in fact, telling the small boy, Brendan, to " go off now and learn the rules of holy men, who have practised what they preached ; and do not study with virgins lest evil should be spoken of

---

[1] Ib., ch. 5.
[2] Ib., ch. 6.
[3] Ib., ch. 7.
[4] Ib., ch. 19.
[5] Ib., ch. 9.
[6] Ib., ch. 10 : " Sine impedimento in oratione et meditatione Sanctae Trinitatis persistis. Si quis enim ita fuerit Deus semper cum eo erit."
[7] V.S.H. i, p. 99.
[8] Ib. : " Haec enim virgo multos sanctorum Hiberniae ab infantia nutrivit."
[9] Vita S. Mochoem. V.S.H. ii, p. 167.
[10] Death of Ita, in A.U. s.a. 570 and 577. Death of Mochoemóg s.a. 656.

you by men."[1] All things considered, then, we are probably
right in concluding that Ita won a great reputation as the
religious educator of small boys, but that she sent these on to
masters of their own sex before the years of boyhood were
ended. Ita is said to have prophesied that the rule of her
monastery would pass after her death out of the hands of
women into the hands of men.[2] Whatever may be thought
of the prophecy, this in the event happened, for the monastery
at Cell Ide, when next heard of, is a monastery of men.[3]

A happier fate befell another monastery of women founded
about the same period by the virgin, Cairech Dergan[4] at
Cluain Boirenn in Uí Máine (Cloonburren, Roscommon).
Beyond a doubtful genealogy[5] and the date of her death,
A.D. 577 or 578,[6] nothing of this virgin is found in the records ;
but her monastery alone, beside that of St. Brigid of Kildare,
and that of St. Samthann (died 739), at Cluain Bonaig, in
Meath, remained a place of note through the centuries.

Two other virgins are mentioned in connection with
foundations which seem to have been monastic in their early
form. These are Lasair of Achad Beithe (Aghavea, barony
of Magherastephana, Fermanagh),[7] and Ricinn of Cell Rignige
(in Meath).[8] As Lasair is brought into connection with St.
Molaise of Daim-inis[9] (died 564 or 571), she belonged probably
to the sixth century. Ricinn is said in the Irish " Life " to
have been a sister of Finnian of Clonard,[10] but such a statement
in such a source carries no weight. If Achad Beithe and Cell
Rignige commenced as monasteries, we know not how long

---

[1] *Vita Brend. V.S.H.* i, p. 102.
[2] *AA. SS. Hib.*, p. 73. Cf. *Martyr. Oeng.*, p. 44 : " ní géba caillech tre
bithu mo chomarbus "—" no nun shall ever take my succession."
[3] *A.F.M.* s.a. 810 and 833.
[4] *Martyr. Oeng.*, Feb. 9th, p. 59, 72. *Martyr. Gorm.*, p. 32. Cf. *AA. SS. Hib.*,
p. 68 and p. 72, n. 20. O'Donovan : *Tribes and Customs*, p. 82, note q.
Story in *Archiv. für kelt. Lex.* iii, p. 308–9.
[5] *Martyr. Oeng.*, p. 70.
[6] *A.F.M.* 577. *Chron. Scot.*, 578.
[7] An Irish *Life*, late and poor in quality as well as incomplete, is edited
by L. Gwynn. *Eriu* v, p. 73–109. *Martyr. Gorm.*, Nov. 13th, p. 218. Cf.
Martyr. of Donegal, Nov. 13th. *Annal. Clon.* s.a. 1398. A Lasair " virgo
amans castitatem " is mentioned as a disciple of St. Finnian of Clonard
(*AA. SS. Hib.*, p. 305) and as founder of a church (not a monastery) at Daire
mac Aidmecain. Neither saint, however, nor church can be identified (Colgan,
op. cit., p. 399, n. 27).
[8] *AA. SS. Hib.*, p. 399, n. 25. Story of her and Cairech Dergan in *Archiv.
f. kelt. Lex.* iii, 308–9, and p. 405. A virgin Richena, settled in the Liffey
plain, is mentioned in the *Life* of Ita, *V.S.H.* ii, 124.
[9] *Life*, l.c., p. 75.
[10] *Lism. L.*, p. 79.

they continued to be so, but in later times they are found as simple churches. Notices, however, which represent what are probably ancient and genuine records, lead us to conclude that small groups of virgins, living under the care of a neighbouring bishop or abbot, were a common (perhaps an extremely common) feature of the Irish Church in the sixth century.[1]

§5—DOUBLE MONASTERIES.[2]

Zöckler : *Askese und Mönchtum.* Frankfurt-a-M., 1897.
Malnory : *Quid Luxovienses Monachi . . . ad regulam monasteriorum atque ad communem Ecclesiae profectum contulerint.* Parisiis, 1894.
Mary Bateson : *Origin and Early History of Double Monasteries.* Trans. *R.H.S.* N.S. xiii, 1899.
Loofs : *De Antiqua Britonum Scottorumque Ecclesia.* Leipzig, 1882.
Berlière : *Les monastères doubles aux* xii *et* xiii *siècles.* Brussels, 1923. (By way of introduction an excellent summary is given of the practice in the Orient and in the Occident before the twelfth century.)
Gougaud : *Les chrétientés celtiques.* Paris, 1911.
Varin : *Mémoire sur la cause de la dissidence entre l'Eglise bretonne et l'Eglise romaine.* Paris, 1858.

By a double monastery we understand a religious settlement where the houses or cells of both sexes were so close together that all could gather for Mass and Office in the same church, obey exactly the same rule, and be governed by the same superior. Taking these as the essential tests, the monasteries of men and women at Tabennisi (separated by the Nile and ignorant of common exercises)[3] and those of St. Basil and his sister Macrina at Annesi in Pontus (separated by the river Iris), cannot strictly be called double, though linked closely together by economic as well as by spiritual ties.

According to St. Basil's teaching, intercourse between such establishments should be confined to what was strictly necessary, and such intercourse as there was must be sternly regulated. The Superior of the monastery must speak to the Mother-Superior as little as possible, nor must he speak

---

[1] *V.S.H.* i, p. 39, § 15 : " Venit beatus Edus episcopus ad quasdam virgines quae erant sub cura sancti Kyarani episcopi." Cf. Ib., p. 220. *Vita S. Itae,* ib. ii, p. 125 : " cella sanctimonialium quae dicitur Doyre Cusgryd (unidentified)." For further references see following § 5.

[2] The excellent study of Dom Stephanus Hilpisch (*Die Doppelklöster. Entstehung und Organisation—Beiträge Zur Geschichte des Alten Mönchtums u. des Benediktinerordens, Heft.* 15), which has superseded all previous works on the same subject, did not reach me in time to be utilised. His conclusions, as far as Ireland is concerned, agree with those expressed in the present section.

[3] *H.L.* Ed. Butler ii, p. 96–7.

with any other Sister unless the Mother-Superior is present.[1] Conversation between the two monasteries, when it cannot be avoided, is to be conducted by representative senior religious. Not less than two, nor more than three, are to be present on either side. Solitary interviews are forbidden; and messages must be sent and received through the agency of Superiors.[2] Even during the hearing of confessions, the penitent must be kept within sight of a senior Sister.[3] Here, as elsewhere, the purposes for which both monasteries were erected in close proximity to each other were clearly stated —that spiritual direction might more easily be secured and maintained; that clergy might always be available for the administration of the Sacraments; that business and financial worries should fall solely on the sex for which nature seems to have designed them; and finally that the weaker sex should never lack suitable support, protection and guidance. Women religious in their turn could relieve the monks of services for which the normal male is supremely ill-fitted, such as the making of vestments and clothes, care of altar linen, and general attention to cleanliness and beauty within the church.

Despite prohibitions in both East[4] and West,[5] following the occasional scandals which occurred when communities differing in sex were established in close proximity to each other, double monasteries continued to be built. They are found in Italy, in Spain, and very frequently in Frankish Gaul from the seventh century to the close of the Middle Ages.[6]

One example of the kind can be quoted from Ireland. In St. Brigid's monastery at Kildare there was an establishment for each sex, the men under the bishop (later the abbot), and the women under the abbess. Each section was probably autonomous, but the rule was the same for both, and the church was used in common for Mass and other liturgical services.[7] There was a distinct entrance by a side door for each sex, and a high partition running down the body of the church which screened each off from the other's view, but the

---

[1] *Reg. brev. tract,* 108.
[2] *Reg. fus. tract.,* 33. Cf. *Reg. brev. tr.,* 220.
[3] *Reg. brev. tract.,* 110. Cf. Clarke. *St. Basil the Great,* p. 104-6.
[4] *Codex Just. Novell.* cxxiii, c. 36.
[5] Council of Agde, A.D. 506. Mansi, *Councils,* viii, c. 329.
[6] Berlière, op. cit., p. 7-9.
[7] *Vita Brig.* by Cogitosus. *Tr. Thau.,* p. 523-4.

abbess and her nuns entered the sanctuary to receive the Holy Eucharist.[1] Such, at least, was the custom when Cogitosus wrote, about the middle of the seventh century. It has been questioned whether this arrangement goes back to the days of the great virgin founder,[2] but there can be little doubt that it does, for its origin during the period of the Second Order is quite impossible to conceive. With the growth of monasticism in the strict sense, under St. Finnian and his disciples, women became objects of suspicion, and the relation between the sexes henceforth was one of rather distant cordiality.

Ciarán of Saigher, who was probably a contemporary of St. Brigid, and thus belonged to the First Order of Irish Saints, is reputed to have founded a monastery for virgins near Saigher, and to have placed it under the care of his mother.[3] In this case the precautions taken to avoid dangers did not prove absolutely effective, for a scandal is recorded.[4] Búithe of Mainistir Búithe, likewise a contemporary of St. Brigid, acted more wisely, for he placed the two monasteries widely apart, "lest the fair fame of his religious for virtue should in any way be impaired."[5] In the " Life of Tigernach of Cluain Eois " (an abbot-bishop of the *Candida Casa* tradition), it is said that his monastery contained a multitude of both sexes,[6] a statement which we are not in a position to control. Bairre of Cork, whose connections are with St. David's,[7] is said also to have had virgins governed by his sister in his settlements at Etargabáil ; but we are not told how far there was dependence or interdependence between the houses.[8] In the " Life " of Daig of Inis Cain Dega in Louth it is related that many virgins came to live under his rule.[9] Oenu, abbot of Clonmacnoise, took scandal at this, and sent messages to Daig with representations as to the impropriety of the practice. According to the writer of the " Life," the messengers were placated by numerous miracles wrought by the virgins in their

---

[1] *Tr. Thau.*, p. 523.
[2] Cf. Bateson, op. cit., p. 150. Gougaud l.c., p. 93.
[3] *V.S.H. Vita Ci. S.* § 8 : " sanctae virgines in cella in propinquo loco seorsum."
[4] l.c., §24.
[5] *V.S.H.* i, p. 90. *Vita*, § 10 : " Monialium quoque monasterium in remoto fieri a loco virorum ipse ordinavit, ne in aliquo fama castitatis laederetur."
[6] *V.S.H.* ii, p. 268. *Vita*, § 18 : " ac postmodum Cluniacense monasterium fundavit, ubi sacrorum virorum ac monialium ab antiquo Deo multitudo fideliter deservivit."
[7] *V.S.H.*, *Vita Aed.*, § 16. *Vita Moling*, § 23. *Vita Abbani*, § 32.
[8] *B.N.E.*, *Vita Bairre*, p. 15.
[9] *Codex Salm.*, c. 898.

presence, but he goes on to say that the arrangement was discontinued by St. Daig, who removed his female disciples to various monasteries of their own further to the north.[1] Instances are fairly common where a cell of virgins was placed under the care of a local bishop or abbot ; but the distance between the houses in these cases is represented as considerable, and there is question of guidance only, not of common exercises, so that the two monasteries did not form a single unit. Finally there is a seventh century example from Less Mór, where a house of nuns was established beside St. Carthach's monastery, but despite their proximity in space, there was strict separation, for half the city was fenced off and no woman was allowed to set foot inside it.[2]

It is clear from all this that though the guidance of virgins was often undertaken by abbot-bishops and abbot-priests, the principle of double monasteries had not established itself as a feature of the Irish Church in the sixth century. The same must be said of the later centuries. If double monasteries in England and Gaul are found closely associated with Irish missionaries the fact is worthy of attention, but the explanation cannot be sought in a direct transplantation of Irish customs. For the Irish Church could not give what the Irish Church did not itself possess. No double monastery in Gaul owed its origin to the personal efforts of St. Columban, though some were founded by his disciples. Among these foundations one at least, Faremoutiers, was governed by an abbess, the monastery of monks as well as that of nuns being under her jurisdiction.[3] In Northumbrian England the gifted abbess, Hilda, a disciple of Bishop Aidan, ruled at Whitby over religious of both sexes, as did also Ebba (traditionally regarded as a disciple of Fínán, Aidan's successor) at Coldingham.[4] Bede relates at some length that the experiment in the last-mentioned case did not prove very encouraging.

There is thus no reason to conclude that any double monastery except Kildare existed in sixth century Ireland, and in Kildare the government was held jointly by the abbess

---

[1] A noteworthy feature in this tale is the protest attributed to the abbot of Clonmacnois. Whether this took place or not is immaterial ; the point is that a leading representative of St. Finnian's school is given as a strong opponent of the double monastery idea. There can be no doubt that this was the Clonard tradition. The " Twelve Apostles of Ireland " seem to have given houses of female enthusiasts for the monastic ideal a wide berth.

[2] *V.S.H., Vita Carth.*, § 65.

[3] Bateson, op. cit., p. 151.

[4] Bede : *H.E.* iv, 19.

and the abbot-bishop.[1] If institutions of the kind are found in Northumbria and in Gaul closely connected with Irish missionaries it is because the latter had created a deeply spiritual environment in which such monasteries naturally arose. There is no direct line of genealogical descent from Ireland to England, or from Ireland to Gaul and from Gaul to England, and statements to the contrary, formerly frequent,[2] and even still to be met with,[3] need correction   In conclusion, it may be noted that no trace of such settlements is to be found in Scotland, Wales or Brittany, so that the double monastery is in no sense a characteristic of the Celtic Church.

§6—ALLEGED APOSTASY OF THE IRISH CHURCH IN THE SIXTH CENTURY.

Life of Gildas. Cymmrodorion edit. of Gildas.   Ed. Williams. London, 1899–1901.
Catalogus of Irish Saints.   Haddan and Stubbs, *Councils and Ecclesiastical Documents relating to Great Britain and Ireland.*   Vol. ii. Oxford, 1869–78.
Ussher : *Antiquitates, Works,* Vol. vi.
Colgan : *Acta Sanctorum Hiberniae.*
Lanigan : *Ecclesiastical History.* Vols. i and ii.
Zimmer : *Keltische Kirche.* *P.R.E.* Bd. x, 3rd. ed. 1901. pp. 204–43.
Gougaud : *Chrétientés celtiques.* Paris, 1911.
O'Rahilly : *Ireland and Wales.* London, 1924.

In the *Life of Gildas*, written by a monk of Ruys in Brittany some time in the eleventh century, it is stated that the Irish Church founded by St. Patrick collapsed in the sixth century. The people fell back into paganism, and the Church rose again only because of the giant labours of Gildas. " At that time," says the writer, " Ainmire was King of Ireland.[5]   He sent a message to the Blessed Gildas, asking him to come to him ; and promising to obey his teaching in everything if he would restore ecclesiastical discipline in his kingdom, for almost all had abandoned the Catholic faith in that island.   Gildas, the blessed soldier of Christ, listened to his call and came, fortified

---

[1] Miss Bateson, op. cit., p. 159, quotes from the *Acta SS. Belg.* iv, i, 747, a somewhat similar example from Gaul, where the monastery of St. Columba at Vienne, was ruled jointly by an abbot and an abbess, in virtue of the privilege of Pope John IV, dated A.D. 641.
[2] Cf. Malnory, op. cit., p. 131.   Loofs, op. cit., p. 81.
[3] Clarke. *St. Basil the Great,* p. 105. Berlière, op. cit., p. 8. Kuno Meyer, " *An Crínóg,*" *Sitzungsberichte der preuss. Akad. der Wiss.* xix, 1918, p. 363.
[4] Bateson, op. cit., p 168. Gougaud. op. cit., p. 93–4.
[5] A.D. 568–71.

with heavenly armour." His miracles were so resounding that the people treated him with excessive respect, so that he was forced for his soul's salvation to hide himself from their view. But some nobles discovered his place of retreat, and brought him to King Ainmire, who adjured him once more to apply himself to the restoration of the Irish Church, " for all, great and small, had absolutely lost the Catholic faith."[1] Gildas undertook the heavy task with a ready will. He traversed the whole country, re-built churches, instructed the clergy in the Catholic faith and in devotion to the Ho y Trinity, and cured those who had suffered severely from the poisonous bites of heresy. Tilled by such a master, the soil brought forth religious fruits afresh. Gildas then established many monasteries, and became a monk himself that he might offer more disciples to the Lord. His success was such that his name was held in the highest veneration in Ireland through the centuries.

The main point in this indictment[2]—Ireland's relapse in the sixth century into paganism, partial or complete—must be dismissed as a particularly silly fable.[3] For decades, at least, before Gildas visited Ireland in A.D. 566, the sap of religious life surged upwards with an energy that has hardly been equalled since. It would, however, be wrong to think that the monk of Ruys is drawing completely upon his imagination. He had before him in substance a sound tradition, perhaps distorted in its passage down the centuries, perhaps misunderstood and expressed in a very extravagant fashion

---

[1] " Quia penitus Catholicam fidem. a maximo usque ad minimum, omnes amiserant." AA. SS. Hib., p. 183.
[2] The Catalogus and some notices in the Lives of the Saints (Cf. Todd : St. Patrick, p. 107-11. Haddan and Stubbs, Councils i, 155, note a. Whitley Stokes, Lismore Lives, p. 343) are also cited in support of the charge ; but the Catalogus does not assert a relapse into paganism. It implies, on the contrary, that the Christian advance was steady and unbroken, though the great lights of the First Order were greater than the great lights of the Second Order. The Lives, even admitting their historical worth, deal with a renewal and revival of the faith, which need mean nothing more than an encouragement to new zeal in its practice. Thus the testimony given by the monk of Ruys is the only testimony worth considering.
[3] AA. SS. Hib., p. 189 : "anilis et inanis fabella." Ussher, Works vi, p. 470-1 : "tantum abest ut Gildae opera Hibernienses ad fidem fuerint conversi, ut Hibernensium potius industria ipse Gildas in fide et divinarum scientia plenius institutus fuisse videatur." (But the statement that Gildas studied in Ireland is a late legend. Loofs, op. cit., p. 66). Lanigan i, p. 488, note 169. Zimmer : op. cit., p. 224 : "Die hier zu Tage tretende Kritiklosigkeit ist bedauernswert." Gougaud, op. cit., p. 78 : "il faut donc renoncer à la faillite du christianisme dans l'île, soit au VIe, soit au VIIe siècle." O'Rahilly, op. cit., p. 51.

by himself. Going back to the fifth century, we are struck
by the fact that between the death of St. Patrick and the
rise of the great monastic founders few names of any consequence appear. There are St. Brigid at Kildare, Búithe
at Mainistir Búithe, Mochta, the priest at Louth, and probably
the four " pre-Patrician " saints, Ciarán of Saigher, Ailbe of
Emly, Ibar of Beg Ere, and Declán of Ard-Mór. If faith and
morals did not decay during this period, they can hardly
have shown vigour in their advance. Finnian and his colleagues
of the Second Order may have had much to correct in the
parts of the country converted, as well as much to achieve
in the backward pagan districts where they had to act as
missioners. But Finnian and his friends, as we hope to show
in the following chapter, were influenced by Gildas perhaps
more than by any other man, whence it may justly be claimed
for the British teacher that he rendered immense spiritual
help to the Irish Church of the sixth century. The faith was
not abandoned, and therefore could not be restored in full,
but it was weak and could be strengthened ; and this is the
work which Gildas, by exhortation and counsel, did. He may
indeed in a yet more pregnant sense, be said to have renewed
and reformed the Church in Ireland, for to him more than to
any other was due the predominantly monastic form which
it henceforth assumed. His visit in A.D. 566 was presumably
to consolidate this work, since the ideas he represented had been
supreme in Ireland for a generation before that date. This
is the substratum of historical truth which underlies the
Ruys tradition. Apostasy and heresy there was none ; progress
along new lines there was in plenty, and Gildas, though living
in Britain, had a leading part in the change.

CHAPTER IV

CURRENTS OF RELIGIOUS LIFE IN THE BRITISH CHURCH IN THE SIXTH CENTURY

Gildas : *De Excidio Britanniae. Epistolarum (vel praedicationum). Fragmenta.* Ed. Mommsen, *M.G.H. Chron. Min.* iii, 1894-8. Also by Williams for Cymmrodorion Society, London, 1899-1901. " Gildas " in *Realenzklopädie f. prot. Theol. u. Kirche,* vi (3rd ed.), p. 667 ff. In the *Celtic Review,* 1913—April, p. 241-5 ; August, p. 35 ff. 1914—April, p. 314 ff. 1915—Nov., p. 215 ff. 1916— June, p. 322 ff ; and in *Y Cymmrodor,* xxvii, p. 26 ff ; xxxi, p. 60 ff. Mr. A. Wade-Evans seeks to prove that the *De Excidio* consists really of two parts : an *Epistola Gildae,* written about A.D. 540, and a tract *De Excidio Britanniae* (sections 2–26 of present editions) written in A.D. 708. As the learned writer's arguments leave us completely unconvinced, the whole work *De Excidio* is treated in the following pages as a genuine product of Gildas's pen.
In the *Mediaeval Studies in Memory of Gertrude Schoepperle-Loomis,* Paris—New York, 1927, p. 229–64, M. Ferdinand Lot impugns the historical accuracy of *De Excidio,* especially of Part I. As an *ex parte* statement of Gildas's shortcomings, M. Lot's summary could hardly be excelled ; but the weakness of such advocacy is that it excites a desire to hear counsel for the defence. For a just estimate of Gildas as historian, preacher and man, Mr. Hugh Williams is still far in advance of all competitors.
Wasserschleben : *Die irische Kanonensammlung.* Leipzig, 1885.
Zimmer : *Nennius Vindicatus.* Berlin, 1893. Haddan and Stubbs, *Councils.* Vol. i.
Chevalier : *Essai sur la formation de la nationalité et les reveils religieux au Pays de Galles des origines à la fin du sixième siècle.* Lyon, 1923.
Loth : *Le nom de Gildas dans l'île de Bretagne. Rev. Celt.* xlvi (1929), p. 1–15. (Valuable grammatical notes on the name " Gildas ".)

§1—GENUINE CHRISTIANITY AS UNDERSTOOD BY GILDAS.

BECAUSE of the very close connection, already demonstrated, between the Irish and British Churches of the sixth century, and because of the influential position of the latter Church as teacher of the former, the theory and practice of religious life in the Britain of that period deserve to be investigated. Material for this purpose is unfortunately not abundant, but it is not entirely lacking. Gildas, for instance, both in his main work and in the surviving fragments of his writings supplies evidence early in date and important in character.

To his dreary sermon[1] on the ruin of Britain, composed probably in the decade before A.D. 550[2] there is prefixed a brief and fragmentary summary of native British history. Having sketched the relations of Britain with Rome[3] he proceeds to relate how " the island, paralysed with icy cold and in a far corner of the world remote from the sun," received from the highest arc of Heaven the cheering rays of the world's true sun, even Christ.[4] The precepts of Christianity met, however, with but a lukewarm reception from the British inhabitants of the island[5] (whatever may be said of foreign settlers and Roman officials) ; yet the new religion made headway, and continued to prosper until the nine years' persecution of the tyrant Diocletian.[6] Britain, like other provinces, had its martyrs before the rage of the imperial rulers abated.[7] When the era of violence had closed " all the soldiers of Christ with gladsome countenances, as if after a long and wintry night, rejoice in the calm and serene light of the celestial region. They rebuild the churches which had been levelled to the ground ; they construct and complete basilicas in honour of the holy martyrs, and show them forth in many places as emblems of victory ; they celebrate feast days ; they perform the sacred offices with purity of heart and tongue ; they exult, one and all, as children held firmly in the bosom of their mother, the Church." This sweet harmony continued until the outbreak of the Arian heresy.[8] Further trouble arose when the usurper, Maximus, proclaimed Emperor by his soldiers, crossed over to Gaul, taking with him the greater portion of three legions, and thus (in A.D. 383) robbing Britain " of her armed soldiery, of her military supplies, of her rulers, bad as these were, of her fine youth who followed in the footsteps of the usurper, and never returned."[9] Now

---

[1] *De Excid.* 37 : " Tam flebilis haec querulaque malorum aevi huius historia."

[2] Maglocunus, still ruling when attacked by Gildas (§ 32), died of the plague in A.D. 547 (*An. Cambriae*), but the date is uncertain. The *Annals of Ulster* record many deaths from this plague under A.D. 548 (549).

[3] §§ 4–7.

[4] § 7.

[5] § 9.

[6] § 9.

[7] § 10.

[8] § 12.

[9] § 14.

for the first time the country had no defenders, and was trampled on by the two fierce peoples from overseas, the Scots (Irish) from the north-west, the Picts from the north.[1] Owing to the incursions of these peoples and the appalling prostration which followed, Britain sent an embassy to Rome, appealing in moving terms for an armed force to avenge her. A legion was despatched in due course (c. A.D. 390) and was completely successful in clearing Britain of her unwelcome visitors. Having taken some measures for the protection of the provincials, the legion returned " in great triumph and joy." Their departure brought comfort to the watchful Picts and Scots who soon " like rapacious wolves, rabid with desperate hunger, jumped unhindered into the fold." Carried along by stout oarsmen and " by sails with a fair wind," they broke through all the borders, slew, destroyed, and trampled under foot their victims before they departed with the booty.[2] " Crouching like timid chickens under the trusted wings of the parent birds," the Britons again sent messengers to Rome with a tragic tale. Their appeal met with a favourable response and a second military expedition was fitted out. Again Britain was cleared of invaders ; one of the walls in the north was re-built and towers were constructed " on the sea-coast towards the south, where their ships were wont to anchor, because from that quarter also wild barbarian hordes were feared." The legions then bade Britain farewell " as men who never intended to return."[3] This, their final departure, took place in A.D. 407.[4] Three years later the Emperor Honorius could help the British cities only with the empty counsel to provide for their own safety.[5] As the imperialised Britons left to themselves proved incompetent and cowardly as soldiers calamities continued to pour in upon them, until in A.D. 446 the miserable remnant sent an abject letter to the Roman Consul Aetius. " The barbarians drive

---

[1] § 14 : " gentibus transmarinis vehementer saevis." The use of the word *transmarinae* implies that the attackers arrived generally by boat rather than by advance overland. Weak as is Bede's gloss (*H.E.* i, 12) that the term *Transmarinae gentes* was used, " not because they were outside Britain, but because they were remote with respect to the Britons and divided from them by two bays," it is hardly likely that *transmarinis* is to be understood literally, to the exclusion of the Albanian Picts and Scots.

[2] § 16. During one such incursion (c. A.D. 401) the boy Patrick, future Apostle of Ireland, was carried off into slavery.

[3] §§ 17–18.

[4] Williams, op. cit., p. 42, note.

[5] Ibid., p. 45 n.

us into the sea," they wailed, " the sea drives us back upon the barbarians. We are thus left nothing but a choice between grim alternatives—death by the sword or by drowning."[1] No help was then forthcoming. Control of the people passed into the-hands of cruel military leaders, and one of these with his counsellors made the desperate resolve to admit " those ferocious Saxons, of accursed name, hated by God and man " to repel the northern invaders.[2] The protectors soon turned their arms on the protected. Bishops, priests and people without distinction were destroyed by fire and sword.[3] " Some of the wretched survivors were captured on the mountains and killed in heaps. Others, overcome by hunger, came and yielded themselves to the enemy to be slaves for ever. . . Others departed to places beyond the sea, with loud lamentation . . . others, trusting their lives, always with trepidation of mind, to high, precipitous, fortified hills, and to thickly-wooded glades or to rocks in the sea, remained in their native land, but a prey to fear."[4] At this time, however, a leader appeared in the person of Ambrosius Aurelianus, in whose veins ran the blood of one of the old Roman families. Henceforth the British had their share in the victories as well as in the defeats ; until in the year of Gildas's own birth an unexpected triumph at Badon Hill brought peace to the older population. Owing to this relief " kings, authorities, private persons, priests and ecclesiastics, preserved severally their own rank."[5]

With so much history by way of preface Gildas leaves the past, and launches forth into a diatribe on his contemporaries. When the older generation had died away, he says, " and an age had succeeded ignorant of that storm, accustomed only to the peace we now enjoy, all the controlling influences of truth and justice were shattered. Not traces merely, but the very memory of these virtues disappeared. I make exception of a few (and they may well be called few !) who compare so feebly in number with the vast multitude lost daily to hell, that our venerable mother, the Church, hardly notices them as they rest in her bosom. These are the only genuine children whom she possesses. Let no man imagine that I am finding

---

[1] § 20.
[2] § 23.
[3] § 24.
[4] § 25.
[5] § 26.

fault with the splendid life of these men, who are revered by
all and are loved by God, who support like columns my weakness by their holy prayers, lest I fall into utter ruin."[1]   These
must, therefore, be regarded as excluded if "in melancholy
terms and with a frankness that mayhap is overdone," he
speaks out his mind about those whom he regards as ministers
of Satan, rather than as servants of Christ.[2]

Much, then, as he has to say about the corruption among
the clergy and of lawlessness among the laity, Gildas has to
admit that there exists in the British Church a small group
of elect souls whose beauty excites feelings of the highest
admiration.   The favoured few, in his eyes, are undoubtedly
those who had abandoned the world and its ambitions for the
peace and quiet of a monastic cell.   The virtues of these shone
with particular brightness when contrasted with the vice or
the lukewarmness of the princes and prelates.   Leaving
aside his treatment of the secular rulers we shall examine a
little more closely his denunciation of the bishops and clergy.

Monasticism, though it existed,[3] had no part whatever in
the public life of the Church which Gildas knew.   In Britain,
then, towards the middle of the sixth century, the ecclesiastical
organisation which prevailed was the episcopal and clerical
organisation common to the whole Christian world.   There
were, of course, local peculiarities[4] due to the preservation of
customs that had long been abandoned elsewhere, but the
place of these in the general picture of British Church
organisation was negligible.   Bishops, like princes, were
many in number.[5]   But Gildas cries out that quality has been
sacrificed to quantity.   His complaint against them is that
of Jeremias against the prophets and priests of the ancient
Covenant.[6]   "Woe unto the pastors that destroy and scatter
the sheep of my pastures," saith the Lord.   Therefore thus
saith the Lord God of Israel to the pastors that feed my
people :   "Ye have scattered my flock and have driven them
away, and have not visited them.   Behold I will visit upon
you the evil of your inclinations, saith the Lord.   For prophet

---

[1] § 26.
[2] § 26.
[3] §§ 28, 34.   *Letters*, p. 263 ff.
[4] Williams, op. cit., p. 151 : "a church of the same type as elsewhere,
only somewhat more antiquated."
[5] § 1 : "Habet Britannia rectores, habet speculatores. Habet inquam,
habet ; si non ultra, non citra numerum."
[6] Jer. xxiii 1-2, 11-12.

and priest are polluted, and in my house have I found their wickedness, saith the Lord. Wherefore their way shall be as a slippery place in darkness, for they shall be driven on and fall therein, for I will bring evils upon them, even the year of their visitation, saith the Lord."

Such indeed was the influence and power attaching to the office of bishop in sixth-century Britain that men were found base enough to purchase an episcopal see for money. " They buy," says the preacher, " for an earthly price an office that is properly obtained by holiness of life and rectitude of conduct."[1] Nay, more, they purchase this "counterfeit and profitless priesthood, not from apostles, nor from successors of the apostles, but from tyrants (the local kinglets) and from their father, the devil."[2] Judas is thus promoted to the chair of Peter, a fact which would be inexplicable did we not remember that the bishops who permitted this step and who consecrated their simoniacal colleague had secured their own sees by the same means.[3] Many were openly more anxious for ecclesiastical preferment than they were for the kingdom of heaven.[4] They were ready to cross the sea and traverse broad countries, yea, even to spend their whole substance, in acquiring the pomp and incomparable dignity of the episcopal office.[5] Having succeeded, they turn homewards with great state and great pride and prance about yet more haughtily than before.[6]

What is the conduct of these unworthy pastors[7] in their episcopal chairs ? As might be expected, they slaughter rather than nourish souls. Their example is a perpetual incentive to vice[8] ; they rarely offer up the holy sacrifice[9] ; they never stand among the altars with a pure heart ; they never reprove the people for their sins (but rather commit the same sins themselves) ; they despise the teachings of Christ ; they satisfy their own lusts and all their desires ; they hate

---

[1] § 67.
[2] Ib.
[3] Ib.
[4] § 66.
[5] § 67.
[6] Ib.
[7] § 68. Gildas, following St. Paul (Tit. i. 12) uses a still stronger expression, " bestiis ventris."
[8] § 66.
[9] "Raro sacrificantes." To the sacrificial character of the Mass, the highest act of Christian worship, evidence is also borne by the terms " Sacerdotes," " altaria," as well as by the British word for priest, " offeren," from the verb " offerre." Cf. Williams, op. cit., p. 163 and p. 159.

truth, and favour falsehood ; the honest poor they eye like serpents, whilst the impious rich they regard as angels ; they preach alms, but never give a farthing themselves. Towards the precepts of the saints, if they have ever heard of such things, they are listless and dull ; but they have plenty of time and attention for the scandalous talk of worldlings. They grieve at the loss, and rejoice at the gain, of a single penny. They are sluggish and dumb in affairs of the soul, but when it comes to secular business they are exceedingly attentive and well versed. In a word, they have nothing of the pastor but the name, and even that has been seized by violence, through the instrumentality of money. In faith and works they are unworthy of any ecclesiastical rank, not to speak of the highest rank.[1] More reprobate than Judas, who sold his Master for thirty pieces of silver, they would sell Him for a copper.

What have their unhappy flocks to hope for from such leaders ? " Shall you be corrected by these men who not only do not call themselves to what is good, but who, in the words of the prophet, ' weary themselves to commit iniquity ' ?[2] Shall you be illumined by eyes that greedily scan only those things which lead downwards to wickedness, that is to the gates of hell ? Surely, rather, according to the Saviour's saying, if you do not speedily escape from those ravenous Arabian wolves, as Lot escaped to the mountain, fleeing from the fiery rain of Sodom, ' blind led by the blind,' you shall fall equally into the pit of hell."[3]

Are all the bishops and priests[4] of Britain as bad as those just described ? Gildas confesses freely that they are not. Some are not positively bad at all, without, at the same time, being worthy representatives of their profession. They may be styled " the innocuous good," and it is characteristic of Gildas's mentality that he pours the vials of his wrath on these almost as relentlessly as on the really bad. They bear no infamous taint of schism, pride, or immorality, but compared with the great men of the Old Testament and of the New, compared with early Fathers like Ignatius of Antioch, Polycarp of Smyrna, and Basil of Caesarea, how can they have the presumption to stand

---

[1] § 66.
[2] Jer. ix, 5.
[3] § 68.
[4] § 69 : " episcopi vel presbyteri."

in a Christian assembly and claim to be true priests ?[1] They
have not entered on the narrow way that leads to life.[2] The
episcopal chair is for them a symbol of indolent comfort, not a
symbol of heavy obligations.   They are lazy, unworthy, in
every way imperfect, and as such come under censure in various
passages of both Testaments, as well as in the lessons read on
the days of their ordination or consecration.   " You are
unspotted and chaste, I grant you," says the preacher, in
effect ; " you have no part with the false pastors of whom I
have spoken ; but are you all you should be ?   Where is your
strength ; your energy ; your daring ; your uncompromising
zeal for the glory of God's house ?   Listen "—and passage after
passage of complaint against the feeble good is shouted into
their ears.[3]

Bishops and priests who led an evil life ceased by that very
fact to be true priests any longer.[4] He who consciously and
honestly called them by that name could not be regarded as a
really good Christian.[5] "How can they loose anything," he
argues, with the logic of the extreme rigorist, " so that it can
be loosed in Heaven, if they are shut out themselves from
Heaven because of their wickedness ? ".[6] And " the innocuous
good " are in an equally evil plight.   " Let no one of the
prelates flatter himself solely on his consciousness of a pure
body, because the souls of those over whom he rules (if any
one of them perish through his ignorance, or laziness, or
flattery) shall be asked of him as of their murderer on the Day
of Judgment.   For the death inflicted by the good is no sweeter
than the death inflicted by the bad."[7]   In a word, the
" innocuous good," in Gildas's eyes, deserve nothing but
unbounded contempt.

Why, it may be asked, does the reformer make no mention
of a synod, the normal instrument in that age for the repair
of the evils deprecated ?[8] The reason is obvious enough.
In such a synod the bishops would be the judges ; and as these
were exactly the persons against whom Gildas levelled his

[1] §§ 69-75.
[2] § 75.
[3] §§ 76-107.
[4] §§ 106, 108.
[5] § 108.
[6] § 109.
[7] § 109.
[8] Such synods were not unknown in the early British Church. Cf. Wasserschl.
Bussordnungen, 103. 104.   Haddan and Stubbs, *Councils,* 116.   *Sinodus
Aquilonis Britanniae.   Sinodus Luci Victoriae.*

accusations, the synodal reformers would be called on to reform themselves. In an assembly convoked for this purpose human nature would see to it that justice was tempered by a more than Christian mercy.

Gildas's one hope lay, therefore, in the little band of excellent men whom he speaks of in admiring terms. Among them, he admits, were bishops, prelates appointed to their sees in a canonical manner, wise and experienced pastors, true priests, skilled to dispense spiritual food to the household of the Lord.[1] These had risen above their surroundings, and, unlike their colleagues, were doing honour to the Christian name. Not for them, however, but for others who had no claim to hierarchical eminence was the highest praise of the reformer reserved. The monks, strictly so called, and they alone, were the perfect followers of Christ. Worried lest his strictures should be deemed to apply to these, he craves their pardon ; adding that he not only holds their life in esteem, but prefers it to all the wealth of the world. More than that—he pines and thirsts to participate in its merits and will reach that goal, God willing, some day before he dies.[2]   His place is still in the front-line trenches in the great battle against the evils of the age, but the time will come, he trusts, when he can withdraw to a monastery proper and there spend the evening of his days in obedience, seclusion and contemplation.[3]

Such a life Maglocunus, the reigning prince of Gwynedd and one of Gildas's victims, had embraced in early manhood. After a spell of struggle in which he had mercilessly crushed his uncle

---

[1] § 92.

[2] § 65 : " quorum vitam non solum laudo, verum etiam cunctis mundi opibus praefero, cuiusque me, si fieri possit, ante mortis diem esse aliquamdiu participem opto et sitio."

[3] For a different interpretation of Gildas's words see Williams, op. cit., p. 161, note 1.   The Welsh scholar's view is that Gildas is already a monk, bound to the practices of common life under a strict *regula*, and that the more perfect life for which he craves is that of the hermit in the wilderness.   We learn from St. Columban that Gildas had been questioned on this very point (the abandonment of the monastery for the hermitage) by St. Finnian (of Clonard) and that he sent back a most satisfactory reply ("Vennianus auctor Gildas de his interrogavit et elegantissime illi rescripsit." *M.G.H.* Epis. iii, p. 159) ; but Columban does not enlighten us as to the teaching of Gildas on the point.   The fact, however, that the form of monastic life with which St. Finnian (like all the saints of the Second Order) is associated was distinctly cenobitic, does not lead us to suppose that Gildas laid any great emphasis on the eremitical ideal.   At this period the movement was not towards the desert but *towards the strict observance of an exacting rule within the walls of a monastery*. Gildas, no doubt, would teach that the service of God in solitude was a yet more excellent way, but the evidence is insufficient to show that at the time when *De Excidio* was written the hermits existed as an organised class into whose ranks Gildas hoped to be admitted.

with fire and sword, he was moved by grace to return to the right way. " Meditating within thyself on the godly walk and rules of living of the monks, didst thou not vow thyself forever a monk ? Without any thought of unfaithfulness was it done, according to thine own avowal, in the sight of God Almighty before angels and before men ? Thou hadst broken, as we thought, the huge nets in which fat bulls of thy class are wont to become entangled, the nets of gold and silver, and the stronger net of thine own imperious will. Thyself didst thou snatch, like a dove from the raven . . . to the caves of the saints, safe retreats for thee and places of refreshment. . . . What and how many rewards of the Kingdom of Christ would await thy soul in the Day of Judgment, if Satan, that crafty wolf, had not snatched thee from the Lord's fold ? "[1] But Maglocunus had grown weary of the trying life, and in the hard words of the preacher, " had returned to his vomit like a sick dog."[2]

If the back-sliding kinglet was unmoved by this denunciation and continued to give the monastery a wide berth there is every reason to believe that the exhortations of the zealous writer were not always so barren of fruit. The monastic institute certainly made headway in Britain during the quarter of a century or so that elapsed between the appearance of *De Excidio* and its author's death. His own desire to embrace that holy state seems then to have been fulfilled.[3] Many details of his teaching, preserved in some fragmentary letters, belong probably to this period.

Curiously enough the longest fragment among these contains an attack upon monks not for the vulgar vices, but for pride. Contrasting their way of life with the imperfect world outside—the clerical world included—the more thoughtless monks had convinced themselves that they, at least, were not like the rest of men. They became self-satisfied and supercilious. In the words of Gildas " they find fault with all the brethren who do not share their notions and

---

[1] § 34.
[2] § 34.
[3] This is an obvious deduction from his later activity as a writer on monastic affairs (Cf. *Fragmenta*, pp. 256–69). There is direct evidence from his *Life*. Ed. Williams, op. cit., p. 342 : " iam monachus factus collegit monachos secum," but this has little weight. The expression " in nostro quoque ordine " (*De Excid.*, § 65), quoted by Williams in supporting his view that Gildas was a monk when the tract was written, refers to the sacrament of orders rather than to the " ordo monachorum." So, too, the reference from Ep. 22 of St. Jerome (*C.S.E.L.* ed., p. 185) quoted by Williams in the same place.

presumptions. Whilst they eat bread by measure, they glory
on that account beyond measure. They drink water, yes—
but they quaff also of the cup of hate ; they eschew sauce,
but they season their conversation with detraction ; they
practise long vigils, but they brand as infamous those who
sleep, saying as if to the feet and each of the other members,
' If thou be not head as I am, I shall count thee as nothing.'
Thus they treat others not with charity, but with contempt,
and that at the very time when they are meditating on the
great principles of the religious state. . . . They prefer
fasting to fraternal love, vigils to true justice, their own
fancy to common harmony, the cell to the church, strict
conduct to humility—man, in fine, to God. They are bent,
not on what the Gospel praises, but on what their own will
commends ; not on what the apostle teaches, but on what
pride teaches ; observing not that the stars in heaven are
unequal, that the choirs of angels are unequal. They fast
certainly, but their fasting profits them nothing, unless mayhap
they have other virtues. Wiser men, taught of God, set their
mind on charity, which is the fulfilment of the Law ; while
these devil's children say, perhaps to better men, whose angels
see the face of the Father, ' Depart from us, for ye are unclean '
(Matt. xviii. 10). To this the Lord makes answer : These
will be smoke in my wrath and fire burning continually
(Is. lxv. 5). The Lord calls the poor blessed, not the haughty
poor, not those who despise their brethren, but the meek.
Not the envious, but those who weep for their own or for
others' sins ; not those who hunger and thirst for water with
scorn of other men, but those who hunger and thirst for
righteousness ; not those who contemn others, but the
merciful ; not the proud, but the pure of heart ; not the
harsh, but the peacemakers ; not those who excite discord,
but those who support persecution for justice' sake, shall
possess the kingdom of heaven."[1]

Other fragments manifest a similar zeal for charity as
the fundamental Christian virtue. Excommunication is to
be sparingly practised : " Our Lord Jesus Christ did not
avoid the feasts of publicans, so that He might save sinners
and harlots."[2] Only " on account of well-proved cases of
great sins, and for no other reason, should we exclude brethren

---

[1] *Frag.* iii, p. 260.
[2] *Frag.* i, p. 256.

from the communion of the altar, and from our table, when the occasion demands it."[1] Abstinence from flesh without charity is profitless.[2] Abbots are not to be condemned if they possess cattle and vehicles, " things which do less injury to their owners, if it be with humility and patience, than the dragging of ploughs (in place of oxen) and the digging of the earth with spades where such work is accompanied by self-esteem and pride."[3] The broad principle governing property is so stated : " Whatever superabundance there be of worldly things to a monk must be regarded as luxury ; but what he is compelled to possess by necessity, not by choice, lest he fall into want, should not be counted against him for evil."[4] Monks who flee from monasteries possessing property, as if such were homes of iniquity, must not be received by other abbots without permission from the abbot whom they have deserted. The case would of course be different if the monk were fleeing from an abbot living in open sin.[5]   In general, however, the abbot of a stricter monastery should be slow to receive brethren from a monastery where the rule was more remiss, though the more lax abbot would be wrong in detaining a monk inclined to stricter ways.[6]

Great respect should be shown to superiors : " what things are honourable with us we surround these with greater honour " (1 Cor. xii. 23). Those, then, who are disobedient to their rulers must be counted as the heathen and the publican.   Bishops and abbots may judge their subjects, " whose blood, if they rule them not well, the Lord will require at their hands."[7] Bishops should not despise the inferior clergy, as the head should not despise the members[8] ; nor should judgment in any case be hasty, either of bishops and abbots about one another, or of subjects among themselves.[9] Bishops, too, and priests should remember that " they have in truth an awful Judge to Whom, and not to us, it appertains to judge of them in both worlds."[10]

Monasteries should not seek to add unduly to their

---

[1] *Frag.* vii, p. 266.
[2] *Frag.* ii, p. 258.
[3] *Frag.* iv, p. 262.
[4] *Frag.* iv, p. 262.
[5] Ib.
[6] *Frag.* v, p. 264.
[7] *Frag.* vi, p. 264.
[8] *Frag.* v, p. 264.
[9] *Frag.* vii, p. 266.
[10] *Frag.* v, p. 264.

possessions : " Cursed is he who moves boundaries and encroaches on his neighbour's territory."[1] Changes of ruler should not be made without proper regard for subjects' wishes.[2] Again, excessive fasting was not to be commended. " Better those who fast without great display and who do not abstain beyond measure from what God has created, but who are careful to preserve their hearts pure in the sight of God (who will decide, as they know, the issue of life) than those who refuse to eat flesh or take pleasure in worldly foods, who ride not on cars or on horseback, and because of these things regard themselves as superior to others. To these men death enters by the window of pride."[3] All finally should look to their conduct with great care and with fear for the uncertain issue of life, seeing that " we read in Scripture of an apostle lost by covetousness, and a thief, by confessing Christ, carried to Paradise."[4]

From these fragments we learn that Gildas's views on the whole question of the religious state were marked by profound wisdom and a very practical moderation.

§2—MONASTIC PRACTICE AT ST. DAVID'S.[5]

When the foundation of the monastery was complete, says the biographer, the zealous and saintly father, St. David, decreed such rigour of cenobitical purpose that every monk should toil at daily labour, and spend his life in common, working with his hands, " for he that labours not," in the words of the Apostle, " neither let him eat " (2 Thess. iii. 10). Knowing that untroubled rest was the fountain and mother of vices, he subjected the shoulders of the monks to salutary fatigues. For those whose whole time and thought are spent in leisurely repose develop a spirit of restlessness and tepidity and become grievously prone to lust.[6]

They thus devote themselves with growing fervour to bodily labours. They place the yoke on their shoulders, dig

---

[1] *Frag.* vi, p. 264.
[2] Ib.
[3] *Frag.* ii, p. 258.
[4] *Frag.* vi, p. 266.
[5] From the *Vita* by Rhygyfarch, §§ 21–32. Much as there is of legend in this *Vita*, the paragraphs here utilised seem to preserve a genuine tradition of monastic usage.
[6] § 21.

the ground unweariedly with mattocks and spades, carry
in their holy hands hoes and saws for cutting, provide with
their own industry all the necessities of the community.
Property they regard with disdain ; the gifts of the wicked
they reject ; riches they detest. Oxen are not introduced
for ploughing ; rather is each to himself and to the brethren
an ox, to himself and to the brethren riches. The work
completed, no complaint is heard ; no conversation held
beyond what is needful. Each performed the task enjoined
with prayer or with some suitable meditation.[1]

Labour in the fields once ended, they returned to the cells
of the monastery and spent the rest of the day till evening
in reading or writing or praying. As the shades of evening
gathered, the stroke of bell was heard, and each left his study,
leaving even the letter unfinished, to repair to the church
in silence. During the chanting of the psalms the voice is
in accord with the intention of the heart. Chanting ended,
they worship on bended knees until the appearance of stars
in the heavens brings the day to a close. After all the rest
had gone out, the Father remained behind to pour forth a
lonely prayer to God in secret for the welfare of the Church.[2]

At length the community assembles at table. Each relieves
and refreshes his wearied limbs by partaking of supper, not,
however, to excess, for too much, though it be of bread, only
produces movements of the flesh against the spirit. All partake
according to the varying condition of their bodies and their
age. Dishes in tempting variety are not laid before them,
nor provisions all too dainty. Their food is in fact bread and
herbs seasoned with salt, whilst their drink is a temperate
beverage. For the sick, the aged, and those wearied by a
long journey they provide some sustenance of a more appetising
kind, since it is improper to weigh out to all in equal measure.[3]

When grace has been said, and the bell sounds again for
spiritual duties, they hasten to the church and there give
themselves to watchings, prayers and genuflections for about
three hours. During this period nobody dares to yawn
unrestrainedly ; nobody dares to sneeze ; nobody dares
to spit.[4]

Next they compose their limbs for sleep. Waking at cock
crow, they apply themselves to prayer on bended knee ;

[1] § 22.   [2] § 23.
[3] § 24.   [4] § 25.

м

and then spend the whole day—from morning till night—without sleep. In like manner they act through other nights.[1]

From the eve of Saturday until the break of day at the first hour of Sunday they give themselves to watchings, prayers and genuflections; one hour excepted after matins on Saturday.[2]

They reveal their thoughts to the Father and obtain his permission, even for the requirements of nature. All things are in common. There is no question of " mine " or " thine " ; for anyone heard saying " my book " or what not would be subjected right away to a severe penance. They wear clothes of mean quality, especially skins. The Father's order was strictly obeyed. Great was the perseverance in the performance of their monastic duties; great the uprightness in all.[3]

He who should desire to embrace this manner of saintly life and should ask to enter the community had first to remain for ten days at the doors of the monastery as one rejected; having to bear also words of reproach. If his patience held out and he persevered in his determination till the tenth day, he was first received by the *senior* who had authority to act as porter. When he had toiled for a long time under this *senior*, and had overcome many repugnances of soul, the time at length came when he was thought fit to enter the society of the brethren.[4]

Superfluity was permitted in nothing, rather was voluntary poverty loved. The saintly Father would receive none of the substance which the novice had parted with in renouncing the world. Not a penny, in fact, was accepted for the use of the monastery. Having entered thus naked, as one escaping from shipwreck, he had no reason to extol or esteem himself above the other brethren, or to refuse, on grounds of wealth, his full share in the common toil. Should he, moreover, prove unsteady in his vocation, he could not make a violent claim on the monastery for what he had bestowed upon it, and thereby strain to breaking point the patience of the brethren.[5]

The Father himself, after daily fountains of tears and fragrant holocausts of ennobling prayers, radiant with a double flame of charity, consecrated with pure hands the due oblation of the Lord's Body. After matins he proceeded alone to intercourse with the angels. Immediately afterwards he

---

[1] § 26.   [2] § 27.
[3] § 28.   [4] § 29.
[5] § 30.

immersed himself in cold water, and stayed in it so long that every movement of the flesh was subdued. The rest of the long day was spent tirelessly in teaching, praying and genuflecting, in care for the brethren, in feeding a multitude of orphans, widows, needy, weak, infirm, and pilgrims. So he began ; so he continued ; so he ended. His life, in general, was similar to that of the Egyptian monks. So great finally was the reputation which the name of David won abroad that not only commoners but kings and princes of the world abandoned their principalities and begged admission, as postulants, into his monastery.[1]

Cenobitical life at St. David's was thus marked by considerable austerity. This is borne out by the epithet *Aquaticus*, " Waterman," applied to the founder in his *Life*,[2] because " rejecting wine and beer and everything that can intoxicate, he led a blessed life in God on bread and water only."[3] Giraldus Cambrensis relates that all David's successors in Menevia were content with the same fare until the time of Morgeneu (slain A.D. 999), whose violent death at the hands of the Norse pirates was regarded as a divine punishment for his laxity.[4] Other monasteries of " watermen " in Wales show that the example of David found imitators.[5] Gildas, as already seen, desired it to be clearly understood that establishments governed by good but less rigorous abbots deserved to be held in honour. He had no quarrel with the more austere, but he underlined the principle that charity is the queen of virtues, and that works of mortification are harmful rather than helpful, if performed in a pharisaic spirit.[6] This it need

---

[1] §§ 31, 32.
[2] § 2. Cf. *aquilentus*, § 42.
[3] § 2.
[4] *Giraldi Cambren. Opera.* Rolls ed. vi, 104.
[5] *Life*, ed. Wade-Evans, p. 62, note.
[6] Lloyd, *Hist. of Wales*, i, p. 155–6, implies that Gildas favoured the moderate, rather than the rigorous, form of monasticism. Wade-Evans, *Life*, p. 74 (Cf. 63, 95), imagines a serious difference on this point between Gildas and St. David. Gildas " set himself resolutely as a faithful Churchman, against the excesses of the Watermen," even against St. David himself, the head of the Watermen. This may have been a reason for his migration to Brittany to the great advantage of that country, but to the loss of Wales, " for it meant the removal of his powerful check on the worldlings and the fanatics who crowded him out." Such conclusions from the evidence before us are quite unjustified. Indeed, it is hardly too much to say that they give an utterly perverse interpretation of Gildas's attitude. For it is nowhere stated and nowhere implied that Gildas regarded the practices of the rigorist monks as " excesses." What he does find worthy of censure is the sense of superiority and the spirit of pride which may (though of course they need not) suggest such practices or arise from such practices.

hardly be added, is a commonplace of Christian ascetical teaching.

§3—The Influence of Gildas and the Influence of St. David on Irish Monasticism Briefly Compared.

The effect of G'ldas's personality on the Irish Church of his day seems to have been very considerable. His attack on the British bishops as monsters of ambition, ready to renounce the hope of salvation if only they could secure an episcopal see (and that because of the worldly emoluments and worldly honours attached to the office) could hardly have passed unnoticed on this side of the Irish Sea. When, on the other hand, he lauded the monastic life as the source of inestimable spiritual benefits, he was striking a note that had already been heard with enthusiasm by our countrymen. Admiration increased for the simple life of religious discipline within a monastery. It is significant that Finnian of Clonard, himself a bishop, keeps his higher order completely in the background, and that his leading disciples, like Ciarán and Colmcille, were not advanced to the episcopal grade at all.[1] Even in the North, where the influence of the *Candida Casa* was more pronounced than the influence of Britain, the ascetical, as distinct from the hierarchical, ideal was emphasised much more strongly than heretofore, though prominent churchmen in that part of the country continued, in the old traditional way, to receive episcopal orders. Thus many of the ecclesiastical rulers, as we shall see more fully in the following chapter, were abbots as well as bishops. Others were abbots, not bishops, and these in time were to become the predominant class. Monasteries were soon to become more important than sees, contrary, no doubt, to what Gildas (for all his dislike of the British bishops of his period) had ever intended or even foreseen. In Britain itself, including Cornwall, and in the diminutive Britain on

---

[1] It is obvious that the thought of advancement to the clerical state (above all to the episcopal state) might bring distraction and disquiet to monks. Cassian warns against this danger where speaking of women and bishops he says (*Inst.* xi, 18. *C.S.E.L.* ed., p. 203) : "neuter enim sinit eum quem semel suae familiaritati devinxerit, vel quieti cellae ulterius operam dare vel divinae theoriae per sanctarum rerum intuitum purissimus oculis inhaerere." And the *Hist. Laus.* xi, relates of Ammonius that to disqualify himself for the office of bishop he cut off an ear and threatened to cut out his tongue.

Gallic soil, the monastic institute was destined also to take firm root ; but in these lands, unlike Ireland, the place of the presbyter-abbot was to remain comparatively insignificant.

We have seen also that Gildas, staunch advocate though he was of the monastic ideal, recognised that considerable differences might exist between the monastic rulers. Some might be ruthlessly severe, some remiss, and between the extremes there was room for much variety. His counsel was that no genuinely religious rule should be condemned, that a broad toleration should characterise the conduct of abbots and monasteries towards one another. This principle was adopted in Ireland. We do not know that any Rule, even mildly deserving to be called lax, was ever introduced ; none certainly survived ; but between the strict Rules there were appreciable differences of degree ; yet all were admitted to be good, and all were respected.

Coming now to St. David we notice that the extreme rigour of his way of life was r ot imitated in the great Irish monasteries. There was indeed one exception, that of St. Fintan at Cluain Eidnech, where the monastic meal consisted of " bread of withered barley and clayey water of clay," where work was done exclusively by hand and where milk was shunned like poison ; but even here the influence does not seem to have come directly from St. David's, for cross-Channel connections are never mentioned. Fintan's Rule was held in some suspicion by neighbouring abbots, but it was finally tolerated. David's own disciples, Maedóg of Ferns, Scuithín of Sliab Mairge, and Modomnóc of Tibragny, have not left a name for extravagance in their monastic discipline. What the Irish borrowed then from St. David's was probably some special liturgical practices, some details of organisation, and perhaps a more severe general concept of the discipline that should prevail in a well-regulated monastery.

Gildas, therefore, not David, seems to have been chiefly responsible for the peculiar line of development on which the Irish Church entered about the middle of the sixth century. Monasticism, which had already begun to make its appeal to the Irish character, now advanced by leaps and bounds. Hitherto all the prominent churchmen had been bishops, rulers of small (and probably ill-defined) territories ; henceforth so much emphasis is laid on the diligent observance of a religious rule that the see bids fair to be lost to view behind the monastery. A few kept more or less aloof from the new movement, but the great majority subscribed gladly to its tenets. Bishops, accordingly, added monastic vows to their other obligations ; and many who would normally have received the episcopal order remained content with the less responsible status. So numerous indeed and so distinguished were the last-mentioned, that by the end of the sixth century they were coming to be regarded as the predominant element in the Irish Church. A more detailed review of the position from the point of view of church government will be given in the following chapter

CHAPTER V

MONASTERIES AND JURISDICTION IN SIXTH CENTURY IRELAND

Annals of Ulster (*A.U.*). Ed. Hennessy. Vol. i. Dublin, 1887.
Annals of the Four Masters (*A.F.M.*). Ed. O'Donovan. Dublin, 1848–51.
Book of Armagh (*B. Arm.*). Ed. Gwynn. Dublin, 1913.
Acta Sanctorum Hiberniae. Ed. Colgan. Louvain, 1645.
Vitae Sanctorum Hiberniae. Ed. Plummer. Oxford, 1910.
Martyrology of Oengus. Ed. Stokes for Henry Bradshaw Society.
    London, 1905.
Martyrology of Gorman. Ed. Stokes for Henry Bradshaw Society.
    London, 1895.
Haddan and Stubbs : *Councils and Ecclesiastical Documents relating
    to Great Britain and Ireland*. Oxford, 1869–78.

BISHOPS, as we have seen, were the ordinary (as far as
evidence goes, the *sole*) rulers of the Church in Ireland
from the days of St. Patrick to the third decade of the sixth
century. Some of these had clerical communities closely
connected with their sees, and these communities in time
assumed a strictly religious form, so that the bishop had to
add the fatherly care of a monastic family to his more general
obligations as administrator of a diocese. When again the
monastic institute achieved a popularity without parallel
in any age or country, the whole system of ecclesiastical
government was affected. Jurisdiction[1] was no longer confined
to bishops (not even to bishops who were likewise abbots),
but was exercised also by persons who did not possess the
higher order. The sixth century position may be set forth
briefly in the following paragraphs.

---

[1] Sacred power is divided into the hierarchy of order (the power to perform
sacred functions, and in particular to confer sacraments) and the hierarchy
of jurisdiction (the power to rule the faithful—to make and enforce ecclesiastical laws, and to adjudicate on ecclesiastical causes). The power of order is
conferred by ordination, nor can it be increased or diminished within the same
ordo. It is, therefore, equal in all priests alike and in all bishops alike. The
power of jurisdiction is conferred by legitimate mission, which consists in
appointment by the competent ecclesiastical superior to the spiritual office
of which there is question. These powers are essentially distinct : a bishop
may be a true bishop though he rule over no diocese ; whilst a priest (e.g.
a Vicar Capitular or a Bishop-Elect who has received his bulls of appointment, but has not yet been consecrated) may govern a diocese with full
authority.

§1—EPISCOPAL JURISDICTION EXERCISED INDEPENDENTLY OF MONASTERIES.

In A.D. 524[1] died Beóaid, Bishop of Ard Carna in Mág Luirg (Ardcarne, barony of Boyle, Roscommon).[2] Colgan speaks of his monastery at that place,[3] but the passage he cites mentions merely the fame of Beóaid among fellow-bishops and other clerics for hospitality, a virtue that could obviously be exercised in a bishop's home quite as much as in a religious house. There is not, in fact, any evidence that a monastery ever existed at Ard Carna ; nor would the existence of such an institution at a later date be convincing proof that its origin goes back to the early sixth century. Beóaid must, therefore, be considered an ordinary bishop of the Patrician type, with a small (probably vaguely defined)[4] see whose centre was the church at Ard Carna.

Of St. Cathub,[5] son of Fergus, nothing is known save that he was Bishop of Achad Cinn, and died in A.D. 555.[6] The *Four Masters*, in their notice of his death, refer to him as an abbot, but this is not supported by the older and more trustworthy records. Achad Cinn has been identified with Achad na Cille (Aughnakeely, barony of Kilconway, Antrim).[7] Whether this identification is accepted or not there is no reason to believe that the place was ever a monastery, or that its ruler held any office save that of bishop.

A similar remark applies to Fergus, Bishop of Dún Lethglaise (Downpatrick), who died in A.D. 584.[8] A monastery

---

[1] *A.U.* and *A.F.M.* s.a. 523.

[2] Short notice in *AA. SS. Hib.*, p. 562–3. Cf. *Martyr. Oeng.*, March 8th, p. 81, 92. *Martyr. Gorm.*, p. 50. *List of Irish Saints in Rawl*, MS. 485, f. 87.

[3] op. cit., p. 562.

[4] It was only when Christianity became well-nigh universal in any region that the need of determining the boundaries of each church was felt. Within the Empire the city, with the surrounding area which it governed, was regarded as the natural diocesan unit (Duchesne : *Origines du culte chrétien*, p. 11 ff. Bingham : *Eccles. Antiq.* Cf. supra, p. 85–6). Cities, however, had really a secondary place in Gaul, though their number in Roman times was said to reach 1,200 (Josephus : *De Bello Jud.* ii, 16, 4). What really counted was the country district with its people, to whom the city served only as a meeting-place. Cf. Mommsen : *Röm. Gesch.* v, p. 82 : "Die Gaue wie sie bei den Celten und den Germanen auftreten, sind durchgängig mehr Völkerschaften als Ortschaften : dieses sehr wesentliches Moment ist allen keltischen Gebieten eigentümlich."

[5] *Trias Thaum.*, p. 182, n. 195. *Martyr. Oeng.*, April 6th, gl., p. 112. *Mart. Gorm.*, p. 70 : "*epscop* Cathub, gl. mac Fergusa, epscop Achaid Chinn."

[6] *A.U.* 554 : "Cathub mac Fergusa, epscop Achid Cinn obiit.

[7] *Onomast. Goed.*, p. 7. Cf. *Trias Thau.*, p. 182.

[8] *A.U.* 583. Cf. Reeves, *Eccles. Antiq.*, p. 143-4.

is afterwards found on this site, but there is no evidence that its foundation goes back to the days of Fergus.

What of the many churches which St. Patrick, according to the records preserved in the *Book of Armagh*,[1] entrusted to bishops ? . Did these rulers find successors raised to the episcopal order ? In Armagh, Trim, and Sléibte, it is certain that they did[2]; of the other sites referred to many disappear from the records[3]; whilst others reappear only in the eighth or later centuries, and then as ordinary monasteries of the period.[4] St. Patrick was credited with a prophecy about Achad Fobuir that " there shall be good bishops here,"[5] and it is hardly too much to assume that when the prediction was committed to writing, the course of history had proved its substantial truth. Two of the primitive sees[6] are likewise mentioned in a sixth century connection, but ruled then by prelates who were devoted to the monastic ideal.[7] As already pointed out, however, the transition from an early Patrician community of clerics to a monastery proper was extremely easy, and as the general development of ecclesiastical life in Ireland favoured the yoke of regular observance, it is no surprise to find see and cell combined in the middle of the sixth century.

Incidental references to Erc (Bishop of Alltraige Caille in Kerry), who baptised St. Brendan of Clonfert[8]; Mac Cuirp " Bishop of Dál Modula, of Corco Airchind Droma," from whom Findbarr of Cork received his early training[9]; various disciples of Findbarr raised to the episcopal order,[10] Brandub, a Bishop of the Uí Cennselaig, who left the care of his flock, and undertook monastic obligations under St. Fintan[11]; Cronán of the province of the Munstermen who visited Iona

---

[1] Cf. supra, p. 78–9.
[2] Cf. § 3.
[3] *Eg.* Argetbor, Coilumbus, (Meath), Domhnach Mór in Mayo ; Cellola Tog, Dall Brónaig, Bile, Forgnaide and Raithen in Longford; Saeoil, Dun Sobairce, Telach Ceneóil Oingusa, (Antrim) ; Cell espuig Bróin, Cell Alaid, and Imgoe mór Cerrigi, (Mayo).
[4] Such are Baislic, Ardagh, Sláine, Domnach Maigen (*A. U.* 831—but perhaps there was nothing more than a church here at that date), Ail Finn, Cell Ausaille, Cell Cuilinn.
[5] *B. Arm.*, 26a.
[6] Ard Sratha in Tyrone and Cúil Raithin in Derry.
[7] See § 3.
[8] *V.S.H.* i, p. 98–99. Cf. *Lism. L.*, ll, 3354-5.
[9] *V.S.H.* i, p. 70 ff. Cf. *B.N.E.*, p. 12.
[10] *B.N.E.*, p. 15.
[11] *V.S.H.* ii, p. 104.

and concealed, as well as he was able, that he was a bishop[1] ;
Colmán Moccu Loigse, Colmcille's dear friend who lived at
Nua-Chongbáil in Loigis, and is referred to at death simply
as " a Leinster bishop "[2] ; the two bishops who resented
Carthach's intrusion, and who were left in peaceful possession
of the territory where they had settled,[3] suggest the conclusion that the number of bishops with churches and
diminutive sees would be found to be considerable if a fuller
record of sixth century ecclesiastical history had survived.

§2—Exercise of Jurisdiction by Bishops who were at the Same Time Abbots

Cormac, fourth successor of St. Patrick (died 497 ; *A.U.* 496),
is called abbot in two ancient documents preserved in the
Book of Leinster.[4] In the *Annals of Ulster* he is mentioned
simply as Bishop of Armagh, but there can be little doubt
that he combined the two offices in his own person. Running
down the *Book of Leinster* list,[5] in which the names of St.
Patrick's successors are given without any reference to their
place in the ecclesiastical hierarchy, we notice that Dubthach,
who succeeded Cormac, is given in *A.U.* (obit s.a. 512) as
bishop.   Then come Ailill I (*A.U.* 526), bishop : Ailill II
(*A.U.* 535), bishop ; Dubthach (*A.U.* 547), abbot ; Féidlimid
Finn (*A.U.* 577), abbot[6]; Cairlaen (*A.U.* 587), bishop ; Eochaid
(*A.U.* 597)[7], abbot ; Senach (*A.U.* 609), abbot ; MacLaisre
(*A.U.* 622), abbot.   At this point the general chronological
boundary set to the present chapter must be crossed, that
it may be shown whither the observation leads.   Tomméne
(*A.U.* 660), is given as bishop ; Segéne (*A.U.* 687), as bishop ;

---

[1] *Adam.* i, 44, p. 85.
[2] *Adam.* iii, 12, p. 212 : " Columbanus episcopus Lagenensis, carus Columbae amicus."
[3] *V.S.H.* i, p. 175.
[4] *Do comarbaib Patriic* and *Do Flaithesaib ocus Aimseraib h-Erenn iar
cretim.* Cf. Lawlor and Best, *P.R.I.A.* xxxv, p. 319, 339, 359 ; and Todd,
Life of St. Patrick, p. 180 and 184.
[5] With this list three others from MS. *Laud* 610, *Leabhar Breac* and the
Yellow Book of Lecan are in almost perfect agreement. Publ. Lawlor and
Best, op. cit., p. 317. Lists in Todd, op. cit., pp. 174, 177, 179.
[6] Between Dubthach and Féidlimid Finn all four lists place Fiachra,
whose name does not occur in *A.U.* The *Annals*, however, supply for this
omission by an enigmatical entry, s.a. 550 : " *Quies Davidis Farannani
episcopi Arda Macha et legati totius Hiberniae.*" Would this mean that David,
while ruling bishop of Armagh, made an effort (by circular letter or otherwise)
to vindicate the claim of his see to metropolitan rank in Ireland ?
[7] Bishop and abbot. *A.F.M.*

Fland Febla (*A.U.* 714), as abbot.   The two last-mentioned names are of particular interest, for they occur again in the *Book of Armagh*[1] in connection with Aed of Sléibte.   According to this account, Bishop Aed visited Segéne in Armagh and offered his race and his church at Sléibte to him as successor of St. Patrick.   Segéne, however, confirmed Aed in his position as ruler of the ancient settlement.   Aed, again, before his death, named Conchad to the succession at Sléibte, and the appointment was ratified by Fland Febla of Armagh, who accepted Conchad as *abbot*.[2]   Were our knowledge of Aed derived solely from the *Ulster Annals* we should never suspect that he was a bishop, for the annal of his death notices merely that he was an *anchorite* (*A.U.* 699).   When then we find Aed, *Bishop* of Sléibte, succeeded by Conchad, *abbot* of Sléibte, and Segéne, *Bishop* of Armagh, succeeded by Fland Febla, *abbot* of Armagh, the conclusion is extremely likely that Aed and Segéne, as bishops, were at the same time abbots, whilst Conchad and Fland Febla as abbots were at the same time bishops[3]—in other words that the episcopal and abbatial dignities in Armagh were united in the same person.   We have positive evidence that this was the case at Ferns, where in the very same year of Fland Febla's death (A.D. 714) the obit of Cilléne, *bishop and abbot* of that settlement is recorded. We must, therefore, conclude that the titles " bishop " and " abbot " are used almost indiscriminately for the rulers of Armagh during the sixth and seventh centuries, justification for this usage being that every ruler held in fact the two (almost equally distinguished) offices.   Negative support for this view is offered by the *Annals*, ·which never record the obit of a bishop during the incumbency of an abbot ; yet this must have at some time occurred, if the two existed side by side.

When, it may be asked, and why, were the two functions entrusted to separate persons ?   To answer the first question we shall continue our examination of the *Book of Leinster* list.   Suibne, who succeeded Fland Febla, is mentioned as bishop (obit in *A.U.* 729) ; also Congus, who followed him

---

[1] 36a.

[2] *B. Arm.* 36a : " Fáccab Aed aidacht la Conchad.   Luid Conchad du A t Machae contubart Fland Feblae a cheill dóo ocus gabsi cadessin abbaith."

[3] Fland's episcopal character is certain otherwise from the *Cáin Adamnáin* (ed. Meyer, p. 28) where he leads the guarantors of the " Law " as *suí epscop* " learned bishop " of Armagh.

as ruler (*A.U.* 749). Célepetair (757), Ferdáchrích (767), Cúdinaisc (790), Dubdáleithe (792), and Airechtach (793) are all qualified as abbots, as are their successors from that time forward to the reform of the twelfth century. In the days of Airechtach the offices of bishop and abbot were distinct, for it is recorded in the *Annals* (*A.U.* 793), that Airechtach, the abbot , and Affiath, the bishop, of Armagh, died on the same night. The change must, therefore, have taken place within the forty years, 750–790.

To the second question—why the divorce between the episcopal and the abbatial dignity ?—a fairly obvious answer may likewise be returned. Some of the greatest monasteries of the country, like Clonmacnois and Bangor (not to speak of Iona, Durrow and other settlements that looked to St. Colmcille as their Patriarch), had been ruled since their foundation by presbyter-abbots. As these had complete control within the monastic territory, which soon became very extensive, the monastery had perforce to secure the services of a bishop. For convenience sake and, no doubt, also to safeguard monastic independence, one of the monks was chosen for promotion to the higher order. Great monasteries had thus a line of bishops (men of sanctity and learning to whom profound reverence was paid) who were not burthened with the responsibility of rule. After two hundred years, that is to say by A.D. 750, this arrangement had become so much a matter of course, that it spread to the monasteries whose tradition of government was episcopal. In Armagh, as always at Clonmacnois, an abbot in priest's orders now held the reins of government, whilst the bishop confined himself to the ritual and sacramental side of the duties proper to his order. That a transformation so far-reaching should have taken place at Armagh may well cause amazement, for the *Book of Armagh*, compiled in the following century, shows clearly that the tradition of the metropolitan church remained strongly episcopal.[1] From the very fact that such a change was countenanced we must conclude that the abbatial mode of government was predominant outside of Armagh, in the middle of the eighth century.

As in the primatial see, so in the Patrician church at Trim,

---

[1] *B. Arm. Lib.*, Aug, 41a : " Rectori Airddhmachae in perpetuum est receptio *archiepiscopi heredis* cathedrae meae urbis . . . 42a"; "De honore *praesulis* Airdd Machae *episcopi* praesedentis cathedram pastoris perfecti."

the ecclesiastical rulers were at once abbots and bishops until about 750. Proof of this has been offered in an earlier chapter.[1] Similar conditions probably prevailed at Sléibte, though the history of this settlement cannot be traced between the death of Fiacc, its founder, in the days of St. Patrick, and the death of Aed (*A.U.* 699).[2]

Returning to the sixth century, we find that Aengus MacNisse, Bishop of Coinnire (Connor) in Antrim (obit. in *A.U.* s.a. 514), is credited also with the foundation of a monastery on that site.[3] His successor, Lugaid, who died in 537,[4] is referred to simply as a bishop ; as are also two further successors in the seventh and eighth centuries,[5] before any mention is made of an abbot.[6] It may well be doubted whether the monastery at Connor goes back to the days of MacNisse or even to the days of Lugaid, though there may have been some kind of a clerical community under the direction of these bishops. The monastery of Lann Ela, with which Connor in later times was closely connected, may have been responsible for the introduction of a strictly religious rule.[7] If the monastery did not exist in the sixth century, the see was ruled by a bishop ; if the monastery did exist it was ruled by a bishop who was at the same time an abbot.

Ard Sratha (Ardstraw, Tyrone), and Cúil Raithin, both sees said to owe their foundation to St. Patrick,[8] continued in the sixth century to be ruled by bishops, but these had then received a monastic training, probably at the *Candida Casa*.[9] They were thus abbots as well as bishops. Tigernach

---

[1] Supra, p. 99–100.
[2] Cf. supra, p. 103.
[3] Life by an anonymous author in *AA. SS. Boll.* T. i, Sept., p. 664 : " Connerense monasterium construitur, in quo usque hodie sedes episcopalis habetur." Further references in Reeves, *Antiq.*, p. 238.
[4] *A.F.M.* s.a.
[5] *A.U.* 658: "Dioma Dub, epscop Condcre dég." 725 : " S. Dochonna craibdeach, epscop Condere décc."
[6] First reference *A.U.* s.a. 773.
[7] In the Life of Colmán Elo (*V.S.H.* i, p. 259) it is related that Colmán came " ad civitatem Conneire, in provincia Ultorum, in qua iacet beatissimus episcopus Mac Cneyssi et habitavit sanctus Colmanus in illa civitate multis diebus . . . et ipse est secundus patronus eiusdem civitatis." Here there is no reference to a monastery, any more than in another reference to a " city " in the Life of Comgall, *V.S.H.* ii, 4. Fleming, *Collect.*, p. 304.
[8] Cf. supra, p. 78.
[9] Supra, p. 142. Coirpre of Cúil Raithin, who died about A.D. 560 (Reeves, *Antiq.*, p. 247), was succeeded by Conall, "episcopus Culerathin," who, c. A.D. 590 received Columcille with splendid hospitality. Coleraine was then a monastery : " sancto advenienti viro xenia populi multa in platea monasterii strata, benedicendo assignantur," (*Adam.* i, 50, p. 97 f.)

of Cluain Eois (Clones), who died in A.D. 549, belongs to the
same category[1]; as also Búithe of Mainistir Búithe (Monasterboice), Iarlaithe of Tuaim-dá-gualann (Tuam), Colmán of
Druim mór (Dromore) in Down, Senán of Inis Cathaig (Scattery
Island at the mouth of the Shannon), Fachtna of Ros Ailithir
(Rosscarbery, Cork), Bairre of Corcach (Cork), Commán of
Ros Commáin (Roscommon), Daig of Inis caín Dega (Inish-
kean, Louth), Finnian of Mag Bile,[2] with his successor,
Sinell (obit in A.U. 602); Etchen of Cluain fota Baetháin,
said to have ordained St Colmcille[3]; no doubt, too, the
successors of Ciarán, Ibar, Ailbe and Declán at Saigher,
Beg Ere, Emly and Ardmore respectively. Even Finnian of
Clonard, though renowned as an *abbot*, had received the
episcopal character,[4] as had Senach, who succeeded him
(died 588 : A.U. 587), and possibly Diarmuid (died 614 :
A.U. 613), commemorated briefly as third abbot. Aed, son
of Breac,[5] if his settlement at Cill-Air was really a monastery,
combined the two titles, but it is more likely that Cill-Air
was not a house of regular discipline, and that Aed should
be classed rather in the previous paragraph among the non-
monastic bishops.

Did each of these ecclesiastics exercise jurisdiction over his
monastery, over lands acquired by the monastery, and over the
sept or septs that looked to the monastery as the chief church of
their territory? Certainly. Did the head of the monastery
rule thus as bishop or as abbot? There is no evidence that
the question was ever discussed. If the distinction was made,
the tradition coming down from St. Patrick's time would
doubtless have been respected, and the head of the monastery
rule the surrounding territory as bishop. But the fashion
now was, thanks chiefly to Gildas, to Finnian and to his
disciples, to emphasise the spiritual excellence of the episcopal
office by demanding of those who held it a life of stern
renunciation under a rigorous rule.[6]

---

[1] Supra, p. 132.
[2] Supra, p. 131–2, 125.
[3] Supra, p. 133.
[4] Supra, p. 121.
[5] Supra, p. 125–6.
[6] Supra, p. 165–6.

§3—EXERCISE OF JURISDICTION BY ABBOTS WHO WERE NOT
BISHOPS.

According to the author of the *Catalogue*,[1] priests surpassed
bishops, both in number and in importance, in the Irish Church
of the sixth century. Priests, therefore, and not bishops,
give to this epoch its special character. Chief among these
presbyters were undoubtedly Ciarán of Clonmacnois,[2] Colmcille,[3] Brendan of Birr, Brendan of Clonfert, and Cainnech of
Achad Bó (all disciples of St. Finnian of Clonard),[4] with
Comgall of Bangor[5] and Coemgen of Glenn dá Locha.[6] To
these we may add five others of St. Finnian's followers :
Colmán of Tír-dá-glas, Ruadán of Lothra, Molaisse of Daiminis,
Mobí of Glas Noíden, and Senell of Cluaininis. A further
search for distinguished priests reveals Colmán of Lann Elo,
Molua of Cluain Ferta Molua, Fintan of Cluain Eidnech,
Fínán Cam of Cenn étig, Abbán of Mag Arnaide, Sinchell of
Cell Achaid, Molaisse of Inis Muiredaig, Nathí of Achad
Conaire ; probably also Colmán of Cluain Uama, Odrán of
Leitrioch Odráin, Laisrén of Menadroichid, and Caemán Brecc
of Ros ech, though the order which these possessed has not
been recorded. Ailbe, a priest in the Patrician church of
Senchua in Tir Aiello[7] (Shancoe, Sligo), died in A.D. 545[8] ;
Coemán of Enach Truim in Leix[9] (Annatruim, at foot of
Slieve Bloom), brother of St. Coemgen of Glenn dá Locha,
died five years later[10] ; Barrind of Druim Cuilinn in Fir Ceall
(Drumcullen, barony of Eglish, Offaly),[11] died towards the end of
the century.[12] Mention must also be made of Findchan, priest
and monk, who ruled a settlement on the island of Tiree, near
Iona, and who incurred the anger of Colmcille by having a
converted kinglet ordained priest without a proper period of
probation.[13] Adamnan, too, tells us something of Cormac

---

[1] H. and S., *Councils*, ii, 292.
[2] Supra, p. 119–20.
[3] Supra, p. 120–2.
[4] Supra, p. 122–3.
[5] Supra, p. 124.
[6] Supra, p. 130.
[7] Cf. *B. Arm.* 29a, 36b ; and *Trias Thau,*, p. 134.
[8] *A.F.M.* s.a.
[9] *AA. SS. Hib.*, p. 192. *Martyr. Oeng.*, Nov. 3rd, p. 236, 240 ; *Caeman
Enaig Thruim i Laigis*, p. 244.
[10] Ussher, *Works* vi, *Index chron.* s.a. 550.
[11] *AA. SS. Hib.*, p. 193. *Martyr. Oeng.*, May 21st, p. 125, 34.
[12] Ussher, l.c., s.a. 591.
[13] *Adam.* i, ch. 36, p. 68-70.

Ua Liatháin, a monastic founder whose long voyages in quest
of a hermitage in the ocean waste won him fame among contemporaries.[1] Finally there are the successors to Ciarán of
Clonmacnois, Oenu (obit *A.U.* 569 Cf. 576), Mac Nisse (*A.U.*
584), Ailither (*A.U.* 598), Tolua fota (*A.U.* 613) ; to Comgall of
Bangor, Beogna (*A.U.* 605), Sillán (*A. U.* 609), Fintan (*A.U.*
612) ; and to Colmcille, Baithéne (died A.D. 600)[2], Laisrén
(*A.U.* 604) and Fergno (*A.U.* 622).

Thus far all the priests mentioned, with the possible exception
of Ailbe of Senchua, held official position as heads of monasteries. A few others, doubtless, achieved distinction (for the
records that have survived are not complete), but definite
statements can obviously not be made about the life and work
of these.

Comparing the list of monastic rulers who were bishops
with the list of monastic rulers who were priests, we find that
there is no great difference in numbers between the two.
Again the two lists combined give a total hardly exceeding
fifty. How, then, can the author of the *Catalogus* claim that
" in this Order there were few bishops and many presbyters,
in number 300 " ? Are our records so imperfect that a
fraction only—one-sixth or one-fifth—of the eminent sixth
century ecclesiastics are commemorated whilst the names of
the great majority are lost to fame ? There is no likelihood
whatever of this. With regard to the *Catalogus*, it may be
pointed out in the first place that the round figure of 300 need
not be taken too seriously, any more than the round figure
350, " all bishops, famous and holy, and full of the Holy
Ghost," of whom the first Order was said to be composed.
In the second place, it may be recalled that beside the parent
or the principal abbatial house, there were often subordinate
houses (not to speak of isolated churches or *cellae*) governed
by priests. Thus Colmcille himself, after his departure to
Iona, had two monasteries (Derry and Durrow), and probably
many other churches under his care, and the rulers of these,
though but semi-independent, would be included by the
author among the prominent presbyters. The *Life* of Abbán,

---

[1] *Adam.* ii, ch. 42, p. 166–70. Cf. iii, 17, p. 219. A gloss in *Martyr. Gorm.*,
June 21st, styles this Cormac " abbot of Durrow and bishop and anchorite,"
but this testimony to his prelacy is very doubtful. He may, however, have
been abbot of Durrow and responsible to Colmcille for the construction of
that monastery.

[2] *Adam.* Table, p. 342–3.

a relatively obscure saint, mentions ten settlements, in addition to smaller churches and his chief monastery at Mag Arnaide, that looked to Abbán as their founder. Three of these were in Connacht,[1] one in Corcu Duibne (in modern Kerry), a fourth in Muscraige Mitine (modern Cork), two others in Muscraige Breógain (in barony of Clanwilliam, Tipperary), yet another in Mag Feimin (near Cashel), two in Meath,[2] and one in Leinster.[3] In a single case only, that of Cluain Aird Mobeccóc (Kilpeacon, Tipperary), is it mentioned to whose care the settlement was confided. Beccán or Mebeccóc, thus singled out for notice, is spoken of as a most holy and devoted man[4]; indeed, the author of Abbán's *Life* takes it upon himself to say that a better religious than Beccán never breathed, nor a better monastery than that which Beccán ruled over at Cluain árd.[5] We need not believe that all the foundations attributed to Abbán really belonged to the sixth century, but that which Beccán governed seems genuine, and there may have been one or two others, each ruled by a priest of merit. A similar argument applies to Abbán's celebrated contemporaries, though this side of their activity is not recorded in such detail.

There was thus a large number of second rate establishments, subordinate to the greater houses, and the rulers of these must be counted with the rulers of the distinguished monasteries before the total number of presbyters becomes considerable. Taking these together, and remembering that the abbot-bishops, more devoted now to the sanctification of their own lives than to government, dwelt largely within their cells, we can easily understand that priests, more than bishops, caught the writer's eye and were set down by him, in a general survey, as characteristic of the epoch. To give point to the contrast between the two periods, the earlier when bishops were everywhere in the foreground, and the later, when they had ceased to assert themselves, the author of the *Catalogus* draws the line of distinction between the two orders much too heavily. All things considered, our knowledge of the sixth century from sources other than the *Catalogus* is

---

[1] *Life, V.S.H.* i, § 22.
[2] Ib., § 32.
[3] Ib., § 27.
[4] Ib., § 22.
[5] Ib.: "sed hoc audacter dicimus, quod nu·lum religiosorem eo audivimus, neque pulcriorem et regulariorem suo monasterio (locum) vidimus."

quite good. If priests were then as numerous as the author
of the *Catalogus* claims, we are justified in asking who they
were ; and if the number that can be discovered is relatively
small, we are justified in questioning the eminence of the
rest. The fact is that the difference in numbers between the
prominent priests and the prominent bishops of the sixth
century is not great. It must, however, be conceded that the
body of priests shows the more striking names, and that the
most distinguished of the bishops, St. Finnian of Clonard
himself, played an important part in bringing this about,
seeing that the disciples most subject to his influence remained
presbyters till death. In a word, bishops were well represented,
though abbots who were merely priests were better represented,
during the period assigned to the Second Order ; and this
superior representation of presbyter-abbots, coupled with the
circumstance that priests holding minor positions were likewise many, gave the period its predominantly priestly
character.

Was the ecclesiastical control exercised by the presbyter
abbots over their monastic lands and such regions as looked
to the monastery for spiritual leadership as complete as the
corresponding control exercised by the bishop-abbots over
their monasteries and territories ? The evidence goes to
show that it was. Of the Columban monastic federation
which held sway over wide districts in Ireland and Scotland,
we have positive evidence from Bede[1] and negative evidence
from Adamnan, who knows nothing of episcopal interference
at Iona or elsewhere.   For Clonmacnois, Bangor, Achad Bó
and similar monasteries the evidence is negative only, yet
such as can hardly be called in question.   The ruler in these
settlements was the abbot and continued to be the abbot,
even when the lands possessed by the monastery had grown
to be " half of Ireland."[2] Thus St. Columban, when he settles
in Burgundy, assumes as a matter of course that his monasteries, with whatever lands they received, were independent
of the local bishops[3] ; but the general principle of monastic
independence is not found formally expressed until long
afterwards.[4]

---

[1] Bede, *H.E.* iii, c. 4.
[2] Such, in the exaggerated language of the legend, was the final extent
of Ciaran's " paroecia."
[3] Krusch : *Jonas Vita Columbani.* Leipzig, 1905, p. 8.
[4] *B. Arm., L. Ang.,* 40b, 41a.

The great presbyter founders, then, of the sixth century exercised full ecclesiastical control within the lands owned by their monastery or monasteries ; probably, too, over such districts as looked to the monastery as their chief church. It is unlikely at this early date that the territory owned by any monastery was large, but the tendency to acquire was unmistakable from the beginning. In Ireland, as in so many other countries, the generosity of the faithful (later, too, their self-interest), rather than covetous desire on the part of the monks, was mainly responsible for this. But, whether small or great, the land controlled by a monastery could not survive ecclesiastically without the services of a bishop, to ordain the necessary clergy, confirm, bless the holy oils, consecrate altars and churches, and perform the other duties reserved to the episcopal order. How were these services secured ? No doubt in the early days by friendly invitation to a neighbouring bishop, with a small see of his own centred in a church or monastery. There was, however, another solution, the consecration of one of the monks as bishop, it being understood that his powers should be restricted to the sacred functions above mentioned. The priest-abbot retained the temporalities of the monastery, and the sole right to rule. An early example of this arrangement is provided by Clonfert, where the death of Moenu, a bishop, took place in A.D. 572, whereas St. Brendan, the abbot, did not die until A.D. 578 or 583 (*A.U.* 577 ; 582). Almost certainly there were others, but of them no record has survived.[1]

§4—THE POSITION AT KILDARE.

Cogitosus, in a florid introduction to his Life of St. Brigid, describes the foundation of her monastery at Kildare.[2] When the fame of her good works, he says, had drawn to her

---

[1] Todd, *Life*, p. 9, quotes another example, that of the bishop summoned by Findchan to ordain his royal friend, Aed Dub (*Adam.*, i, 36). "It is to be observed also that the bishop, being subject to the abbot and bound to obedience, did not dare to refuse, notwithstanding his scruples, and merely stipulated that Findchan should take upon himself the responsibility of the act." But the inference here is illegitimate. All that happened is quite as easily explained if the prelate was a bishop invited in from outside and in no way subject to Findchan. Indeed, it may be argued that the incident proves rather that the prelate was of this kind, for if he lived as a monk under Findchan there was no need to insist that the latter should take the responsibility. That, as Superior, he would do as a matter of course.

[2] *Trias Thaum.*, p. 520.

innumerable people of both sexes from all the provinces of
Ireland, who wished of their own free will to vow themselves
to religion under her direction, she erected on the Liffey plain
her monastery, which is the head of almost all the Irish
churches, and the most distinguished of Irish monasteries;
its *parochia* extends, in fact, through all Ireland, and reaches
from sea to sea. Then, he continues,[1] " wishing to provide
in a wise manner and properly in all things for the souls of her
people, and anxious about the churches of the many provinces
that had attached themselves to her, she realised that she
could not possibly do without a high priest (bishop) to consecrate churches and supply them with clergy in various
grades. She sent accordingly for a distinguished man,
adorned with all virtues, then leading a solitary life in the
desert. Going herself to meet him, she brought him back in
her company to govern the church with her in episcopal
dignity, that nothing which depends on orders should be
wanting in her churches. Thereafter the anointed head and
chief of all bishops and the most blessed chief of virgins, in
pleasant mutual agreement and with the directing aid of all
the virtues, erected her principal church. At the same time,
through the merits of both, her see, episcopal at once and
virginal, spread like a fruitful vine, rich in growing branches,
and took root in the whole island. In Ireland, therefore, the
archbishop of the Irish bishops, and the abbess whom all the
abbesses of the Irish revere, hold a pre-eminent position in a
prosperous line and in perpetuity." Such is the rhetorical
account given by Cogitosus, writing about a century and a
quarter after St. Brigid's death.[2]

Chivalry, we fear, has more than its due place in this

---

[1] Ib. : " prudenti dispensatione de animabus eorum regulariter in omnibus
procurans et de ecclesiis multarum provinciarum sibi adhaerentibus sollici-
tans et secum revolvens quod sine summo sacerdote, qui ecclesias consecraret
et ecclesiasticos in eis gradus subrogaret, esse non posset, illustrem virum
et solitarium, omnibus moribus ornatum, per quem Deus virtutes operatus
est plurimas, convocans eum de eremo et de sua vita solitaria et sibi obviam
pergens ut ecclesiam in episcopali dignitate cum ea gubernaret atque ut
nihil de ordine sacerdotali in suis deesset ecclesiis accersivit. Et postea sic
unctum caput et principale omnium episcoporum et beatissima puellarum
principalis faelici comitatu inter se et gubernaculis omnium virtutum et
suam erexit principalem ecclesiam ; et amborum meritis sua cathedra episcopalis et puellaris, acsi vitis fructifera diffusa, undique ramis crescentibus,
in tota Hibernensi insula inolevit. Quam semper Archiepiscopus Hibernensium episcoporum et abbatissa quam omnes abbatissae Scotorum vene-
rantur faelici successione et ritu perpetuo dominantur."
[2] This event is chronicled in *A.U.* under the years 523, 524, 525 (i.e. 524,
525, 526).

description, and the place accorded to Kildare, if the author's rhetorical phrases are to be taken at their face value, must inevitably excite ridicule. Yet the substantial truth of the record, in so far as it depicts the relations that existed between bishop and abbess, can hardly be called in doubt. Let us see how the position arose. St. Brigid settled at Kildare late in the fifth century, when the conversion of the country was still in progress and the organisation of the Church as yet far from perfect. With a genius that was obviously quite exceptional she gathered numerous disciples about her, and won the esteem of the neighbouring peoples, in whose affairs she took a deep and extremely practical interest. After some years she found herself the most prominent religious personality in the Liffey plain. Being a woman, she could not provide the people with the ministrations proper to the clergy, so she entered into an arrangement with a bishop who would make good that deficiency. Cogitosus regards the two as in some peculiar way sharing rule and dignity : Conlaed was prevailed upon " to govern the church with her," and the see was at once "episcopal and virginal." Succeeding bishops and abbesses, too, ruled harmoniously together, each in his or her own sphere, over a *paroecia* that in the course of years had grown to remarkable dimensions.

The arrangement mentioned has few parallels in the history of the Church ; but some analogous instances have arisen, one indeed such as puts the power exercised by the lady-abbess of Kildare completely in the shade. The abbess " by the grace of God " of Las Huelgas, near Burgos, in Castile, had no bishop to share and restrict the privileges and emoluments of her position. " Lady and mistress of sixty-four villages, she conferred benefices, took action when necessary against preachers, punished seculars, received official documents directly from the Holy See, decided matrimonial and civil cases, visited pious institutions, examined candidates for the legal profession, approved confessors, gave faculties for preaching, presided at synods ; and annually, like St. Bernard at the mother house of Citeaux, sat at the head of the congregation of Abbesses from Perales, Gradefes, Carrizo, Fuencaliente, Torquemada, San Andrés de Arroyo, Tulebras, Vileña, Villamayor de los Montes, Otero, Aviá, San Ciprián, and other monasteries, which since the end of the twelfth century were subject to her rule. In Las Huelgas were interred Alfonso VIII of Castile, Princess Leonora of England, Sancho VII, Alfonso VII, Princess Berenguela, Enrique I, and some thirty other princes. There Alfonso XI and Enrique of Trastamara were crowned; Ferdinand the Saint and Edward of England received the rank of knighthood; royal marriages and state ceremonies of all kinds were numbered by the thousand."[1] And it was only when the nineteenth century was far advanced that these privileges were withdrawn by the ruling Pope !

In later days it was believed that negotiations had taken place between St. Patrick and the abbess, and that the unusual prominence enjoyed by Kildare was arranged to their mutual satisfaction, for the *Book of Armagh* relates that " between St. Patrick and St. Brigid, the columns on which all Ireland rested, a cordial friendship existed, such that they were one in heart and soul. Many miracles did Christ the Lord work through the instrumentality of each. St. Patrick, therefore, said to the Christian virgin, ' My good Brigid, your see in your own province will be left completely under your sway ; outside your province, however, to the east and to the west, it will be under my rule.' "[2] Armagh, then, had given its sanction (with reserves as to territory) to the special place enjoyed by St. Brigid and her successors. In practice the arrangement seems to have functioned perfectly, for we never hear of trouble at Kildare save such as was caused by interference from hostile secular forces.[3]

---

[1] Lampérez y Romea : *Hist. de la Arquitectura cristiana en la edad media.* T. ii, p. 429. More detailed description in *El Real Monasterio de las Huelgas*, por Dr. Amancio Rodríguez. T. i, p. 280, 315 ff. T. ii, p. 332 ff.

[2] *B. Arm., Lib. Ang.* 42, 43a : " Inter sanctum Patricium Hibernensium Brigitamque columpnas amicitia caritatis inerat tanta ut unum cor consiliumque haberent unum. Christus per illum illamque virtutes multas peregit. Vir ergo sanctus Christianae virgini ait : O mea Brigita paruchia tua in provincia tua apud reputabitur monarchiam tuam. In parte autem orientali et occidentali dominatu in mea erit."

[3] Dr. Todd (*Life*, p. 13), interpreting the text of Cogitosus, states : "It is equally clear that she had her bishop under her own jurisdiction. She engaged him to govern the church *with her*." But the conclusion here is surely faulty—*with her* and *under her* not being synonymous terms. Dr. Healy concludes more correctly from the text (*Ireland's Ancient Schools and Scholars*, p. 113) : " It is obvious from these words that Brigid herself selected St. Conlaeth or Conlaedh, to rule her churches and monasteries, but in accordance with her suggestions and advice. She, of course, conferred no jurisdiction on St. Conlaeth, but she selected the person to whom the Church gave this jurisdiction. Her biographer does not say that Conlaeth was subject to Brigid, but that Brigid chose him to govern the Church along with herself, ut ecclesiam in episcopali dignitate cum ea gubernaret." If anyone will argue from the high position enjoyed traditionally by the Abbess at Kildare (described in the *Book of Armagh*, l.c., as a *monarchia*) that the words of Cogitosus had better be interpreted of joint rule so that each act of jurisdiction,

One strange consequence of St. Brigid's unique position in the Irish Church was the growth of an absurd story to the effect that she had received the episcopal order. " Thereafter the orders were read out over her, and it came to pass that Bishop Mel conferred on Brigid the episcopal order, although it was only the order of repentance that she desired for herself. And it is then that Mae Caille lifted up a veil over Brigid's head *ut ferunt periti* ; and hence Brigid's successor is always entitled to have episcopal orders and the honour due to a bishop."[1] But in other versions,[2] Bishop Mel is said to have been irresponsible when he made this mistake, as he had become inebriated with the grace of God,[3] or at least was powerless to prevent the divine decree that this dignity should be conferred on Brigid, alone among women.[4] The story was occasioned by the exceptional honour paid, as a matter of traditional usage, to St. Brigid's successor at Kildare, an honour that in some respects could be compared with the special honour shown to bishops in the hierarchy of the Church. Brigid, as a woman, was incapable of receiving the sacrament of order.[5] If in Christian antiquity and in the early Middle Ages, deaconesses were common, and these were " ordained " with ecclesiastical rites[6] they were never regarded as belonging to the ministry of order.[7] They looked after the sick, the aged and orphans, especially those of their own sex. They prepared women neophytes for baptism,

---

to be valid, had to proceed from St. Brigid and St. Conlaed, as a single effect from a double cause, he is met by the difficulty that not a single act of joint jurisdiction can be cited from the history of Kildare. If such jurisdiction existed it would not necessarily be an abuse ; women, according to the teaching of Catholic theologians, being capable, probably, of receiving *extraordinary* jurisdiction. Cf. Albertus Magnus : In 4 Sent, D. 19a, Art. 7. Vives edit. Paris, 1894. T. xxix, p. 808. Dom. Soto : *Quartum Sent. Comment. Medina del Campo*, 1581. T. i, dist. 20, q. 1, art. 4, p. 880a–882a. A. Tamburini : *De Iure Abbatissarum.* Rome, 1683. Disp. xxxii, quaest. i–v ,xii, p. 358–64, 367–8. Ballerini-Palmieri : *Opus theol. Morale*, vol. iv, 1891. Tract. ix, ch. ii, p. 369, vol. vii, 1893. Tract. xi, ch. i, p.14–15. In modern ecclesiastical discipline (*Codex Iuris Canonici*, Can. 118) the exercise ot spiritual jurisdiction is confined to clerics ; but the question of the Pope's power to delegate jurisdiction in extraordinary cases is left untouched by this canon.

[1] *Lib. Hymn.* p. 40.
[2] Rawl. B.512 fo. 32b. Cf. Tertia Vita, Ch. 28;
[3] Cf. Acts ii, 13–15.
[4] *Lism. L.* p. 40
[5] *St. Thomas, Suppl.*, q. 39, a. l.   Wernz., *Jus. Decr.* ii, n. 80.   Cf. *Codex Iur. Can.* c., 968.
[6] Chardon : *Histoire des Sacraments* Migne : *Theol. Cursus Compl.* T. 20, col. 876, ss.
[7] Bingham : *Antiquities of the Christ. Church* i, ch. 22, p. 101.

and in an age when this sacrament was conferred commonly by immersion, helped them to and from the sacred waters. They watched, again,[1] at the church doors through which women entered, and saw that these received places, according to their condition, in the congregation, and conducted themselves becomingly during the ceremonies. As corresponding duties with regard to men devolved on the deacons, it is easy to understand how these women were everywhere called deaconesses; but, unlike the deacons, they were excluded from service at the altar. Finally, no semblance of an order corresponding to that of priest or bishop was ever conceded to the female sex.

§5—CONCLUSION.

From the development that actually took place we may judge of the extent to which St. Patrick was handicapped in fixing the site of episcopal sees by the lack of populous urban centres. Many indeed of the settlements in which he had established bishops seem to have lost all prominence in the sixth century. The selection of such-and-such a site must often have been merely experimental—one of those provisional arrangements which provide pioneers with a first solid foothold and prepare the way for a more permanent scheme of organization.

It must likewise be remembered that the fifth century is noted in our history as a period of great political disturbance, and that the regions most affected were exactly those in which St. Patrick was particularly active, the Midlands and Connacht. Niall of the Nine Hostages, his brothers, sons, grandsons and great-grandsons (one of the ablest family groups of which Irish history tells) were the cause of this disquiet. Moved by ambition, Niall and his brothers attacked and conquered the old territory of the Fir Domnonn in Northern Connacht, which thereupon became Tír Fiachrach, "Fiachra's Land," Fiachra being a brother of Niall. Another branch of Fiachra's sept conquered the kingdom of Aidne, east of Galway Bay. Brión, another brother of Niall, obtained a territory near Tuam, and a further territory called Umall, around Clew

---

[1] Bingham, op. cit., p. 102–103.

Bay. From a third brother of Niall, Ailill, is named Tír
Ailello, " Aillill's Land," represented by the Barony of
Tirerrill in modern Sligo. Three sons of Niall (Conall, Enda
and Eoghan) conquered and divided among themselves the
region now known as the county of Donegal. Another son,
Cairbre, or his immediate descendants, obtained what is
now the Barony of Carbury in Sligo, as well as lands round
Granard in Longford, and the Barony of Carbury in Kildare.
Loiguire, son of Niall, the High-King in St. Patrick's day,
secured lands beside Loch Erne, as well as in Westmeath
and in Brega. Two further sons of Niall, Máine and Fiachu,
likewise obtained territory in Westmeath, whilst Ardgal,
a grandson of Niall, was provided for in Brega. The descendants
of Niall settled in the North became known as the Northern
Uí Néill, whilst those settled in the Midlands (Meath,
Westmeath, Longford, Offaly and Kildare) became known
as the Southern Uí Néill. The latter branch kept up a long
struggle with the Leinster men, whose lands they had occupied,
and fifteen battles, at intervals varying from three to twelve
years, are mentioned in the *Annals* between A.D. 452 and 517,
when the deciding encounter at Druim Derge ended in favour
of the Uí Néill. Again Loiguire's predecessor as High-King,
Nathí, was a son of Fiachra, Niall's brother, and Loiguire's
successor, Ailill Molt, was a son of Nathí, but this ruler was
defeated and slain by a combined army of the Uí Néill, north
and south, in A.D. 483, and the High-Kingship for more than
five hundred years after that date was held uninterruptedly
by direct descendants of Niall.[1] Shifting boundaries and
much uncertainty must have been a marked feature of this
age of general political unrest ; nor is it unlikely that the claim
of the Leinstermen to their lost northern territory (with
its capital at Tara), a claim supported so often and so
vigorously by arms, was a contributing motive in St. Patrick's
decision to fix his primatial chair, not in the central Midlands,
but in the peaceful, if less accessible, North-East.

Places then that commended themselves to St. Patrick
and his missioners lost their significance as ecclesiastical
sites within a century. The formation of some new sees can
be traced back to the transitional period, those, for instance,
of Ibar at Beg Ére, Aongus Mac Nissi at Connor, Conlaed
at Kildare and Ailbe at Emly. How far a higher authority

---

[1] MacNeill, *Phases*, p. 180–92.

(the see of Armagh or a synod) participated in the foundation
of these we cannot tell. Three, at least, of the four sees just
mentioned were closely connected with monasteries from
the beginning; and the movement towards monasticism
had found favour even at Armagh, probably, too, in the
successful Patrician settlements at Sletty, Trim and Slaine.
Early in the sixth century Búithe was bishop and abbot
in the monastery that still bears his name. A little later
Finnian was bishop and abbot in Cluain Iraird. At Ard Sratha
and Cúil Rathain the Patrician bishops had found successors
who combined the two callings, having received a monastic
training at the *Candida Casa*. Near by at Cluain Eóis was
a colleague trained in the same monastery, and now, too,
a bishop. In the North-East at Druim Mór and Mag Bile,
in the East at Inis Cain Dega, in the West at Ros Commáin
and Tuam; in the South at Corcach, Ros Ailithir and Inis
Cathaig, in Ossory (probably) at Saigher and in the Déisi
(probably) at Árd Mór, were rulers who combined the two
offices. During the sixth century the custom of attaching
sees to monasteries had thus become extremely common.

There can be no doubt that the emphasis was laid on the
abbatial, rather than on the episcopal, character of the ruler,
even in the monasteries just mentioned, since extreme
enthusiasm for the monastic ideal is the outstanding feature
of the age. Here the influence from Britain makes itself very
strongly felt.[1] Gildas insisted on a high standard of personal
virtue, to be achieved through asceticism, as the prime purpose
of life. There is reason to believe that in St. Finnian of Clonard
he found a whole-hearted supporter of his views. Finnian,
too, regarded the deepening of religious life as the great need
of the day. As a means to this end nothing better could be
devised than the monastic institute, whose adoption he
therefore championed. His disciples became in due course,
the founders of great monasteries. Their example was followed
by others like Comgall of Bangor, Colmán of Lann Elo, Molua
of Cluain Ferta Molua, Fintan of Cluain Eidnech and Coemgen
of Glenn-dá-locha. Some twenty-six important monasteries
ruled by priests, not bishops, belong to the sixth, or to the

---

[1] Ireland's practical isolation from the Continent, following the Germanic
invasion of Britain and Gaul, must also be taken into account. Established
models on the Continent were thus lost to view during the period of her
ecclesiastical development.

first quarter of the seventh century.[1] Armagh and Mag Bile alone ranked with the greatest of these, and by A.D. 600 even Armagh must have found it an uphill task to maintain its position against Clonmacnois, Kildare and the Columban federation with its three peaks at Durrow, Derry and Iona. The sixth century thus shows the ecclesiastical government of the country shared in parts that were roughly equal by abbots who were bishops and abbots who were priests. In monasteries ruled by presbyters a bishop in the role of a venerated domestic official must early have become a feature. so that the supply of bishops in the Church was adequate and even abundant. In a few instances (probably many fewer than the reality) the older Patrician order appears in the person of a bishop without monastic ties ; whilst in one monastery, Mungret, the first ruler was not even a priest. Pockets of paganism were still to be met with, for the conversion of the country was not complete before the middle of the seventh century.[2] Districts can hardly have been as strictly defined as the Continental dioceses of the period, and probably increased or diminished freely, according to the fortunes of the monastery which was regarded as their religious centre. For all such districts, as for the Patrician sees of the fifth century, the ordinary term is *parochia*, a word which in the ecclesiastical language of St. Patrick's day had but one meaning " diocese," though in the next century it came to be used also of districts entrusted to priests or deacons.[3] In the many cases where a *parochia* in Ireland was ruled by a priest, and where its chief church belonged to a monastic community, it ceased thereby to be a diocese, administered according to the common law of the Church. From the canonical standpoint this is the most important feature, by far, of the national Canon Law, and it surprises us to find that its existence aroused no controversy, whilst

---

[1] These are Clonmacnois, Derry, Durrow, Clonfert, Birr, Achad Bó, Tir-dá-glas, Lothra, Daiminis, Glas Noiden, Cluaininis, Bangor, Lann Elo, Cluain Ferta Molua, Cluain Eidnech, Cenn-étig, Mag Arnaide, Cell Achaid, Glenn dá locha, Cluain Uama, Leitrioch Odráin, Menadroichid, Ross-ech, Enach Truim, Druim Chuilinn. Mungairit's first ruler, Nessan, had deacon's orders only.

[2] In the days of Féichin of Fore (died A.D. 665 or 668 : *A.U.* 664, 667) the island of Omey (Imaid Féichin), off the Galway coast, was still absolutely pagan. *V.S.H.* ii, p. 79-80. *Rev. Celt.* xii, p. 328.

[3] *Statuta Ecclesiae Antiqua.* P.L. lvi, col. 882 : " diacones et presbyteri in parochia constituti." Second Council of Vaison, A.D. 529. Can. 1 and 2. Hefele-Leclercq : *Hist. des Conciles.* T. ii, p. 1111-2.

comparatively petty issues, like the Easter reckoning and the tonsure, afforded material for prolonged discussion.

Armagh's claim to special pre-eminence as the mother-church of the nation was not questioned, but like the High-Kingship in a country where the practical independence of the local political units was a fundamental constitutional principle, the exercise of primatial authority must have been extremely difficult. During the period of the First Order, the Apostle's successors enjoyed what was really metropolitan jurisdiction, for, as " they had one head, Christ, so they had one chief, Patrick," and his successors, since the Order lasted for sixty years, at least, after Patrick's death. Under the Second Order the exercise of this jurisdiction lapsed. " They had one head, Our Lord," says the writer of the *Catalogus*, indicating by the omission of an earthly head that authoritative interference on the part of Armagh was not sought for, nor perhaps suffered. The strictly monastic character which that see had then assumed was undoubtedly responsible in great part for the change of status, since Armagh as a monastery (prescinding from its earlier historic position) was by no means the most distinguished monastery in the country. A metropolitan see, in the canonical sense, thus ceased to exist in Ireland. Such a see had not been established in Christian Britain before the Anglo-Saxon invasion, nor did it exist in the Celtic Church of Britain until the sees of Wales were made subject to Canterbury after the Norman conquest. As in Celtic Britain, so in Ireland, ecclesiastical problems were settled by synods. There are good grounds for the belief that these were held regularly in connection with the state assemblies. Thus the only sixth century synod of which we have notice was convened at Tailtiu,[1] where the great gather-

---

[1] *Adam.* iii ch. 3, p. 193-4. The casual mention of this synod by Adamnan, " A quodam Synodo," suggests that such gatherings were then held as a matter of course. It is probable that the " seniores " or ecclesiastical leaders came from all parts of the country. Brendan of Birr is the only name mentioned, and it is significant of conditions in sixth century Ireland that he, though without the episcopal order, could play a leading part in the assembly. Adamnan ignores all *acta* of this synod save the excommunication of Colm-cille. White, Ussher (*Works* vi, p. 468) and Colgan (*Trias Thau.*, p. 450) suppose that the cause of this excommunication was the part taken by Colmcille in the Battle of Cúl Dremne (A.D. 561) and the circumstances as described by Adamnan lend weight to their view. Dermait, son of Cerball, led the defeated army at Cúl Dremne. At the Tailtiu celebrations he would be president, and nothing is more natural than that he should use his great influence to get the abbot-supporter of the northern Uí Néill condemned. Dermait and his lawyer friends no doubt constructed a very plausible case

ing of the nation, under the presidency of the High-King, was wont to take place every three years. One great advantage of this arrangement was that the decisions of the synod could be announced to the multitude, and if approved by popular vote, become part of the national civil law.[1] For this there are parallels in general ecclesiastical history, the most striking, without doubt, being that of the early Oecumenical Councils, whose decrees, when confirmed by the Emperor, acquired a new status and a worldly sanction as imperial laws.[2]

Almost all jurisdiction in sixth century Ireland was exercised, therefore, from the monasteries. About half the leading abbot-rulers were bishops, about half priests, and the more illustrious names were to be found among the latter. In this way the essential connection between the episcopal

---

against the saint of Tir Chonaill. The Fathers of the synod were impressed ; but when Colmcille himself appeared and explained what had really happened, the indictment shrank into some petty charges and the excommunication was at once revoked. This is the sense which Adamnan's words convey. Tradition, which couples Colmcille's name with the Cúl Dremne battle may thus be quite correct, whilst, however, pandering to the popular love for the sensational by confusing the charge with the crime. The *Annals of Ulster* (*A.U.* 560) relate simply that the battle of Cúl Dremne was won by Colmcille's prayers, and the fact may well be that he gave moral support to his kinsmen of the North, convinced (on grounds that judges none too favourable considered worthy of respect) that the cause they represented against the High-King was just. No other incident mentioned in his *Life* is of a kind which would merit the extreme penalty of excommunication. We may take it then that he was really arraigned before a synod for active participation in the battle of Cúl Dremne, and that a hasty verdict was pronounced against him, but that the Fathers when informed of the true circumstances, annulled that verdict and exonerated Colmcille from serious guilt.

In the seventh century discussions about the Easter reckoning, a synod was held at the Mag Ailbe, where Carmán, the place of assembly for Leinster, seems to have been situated. The synod was probably part of the general celebrations, and the Fathers who comprised it were probably drawn from the local states, for the antagonists on this occasion were Laisrén of Leighlinn, and Munnu of Taghmon.

The " fraechmag " or heath of Mag Léna, near Tullamore, where another paschal synod was held (*Ep. Cummiani*, Ussher, *Works*, iv, p. 442) may again be the place where the " Aonach Cholmáin " of the Fir Ceall was celebrated.

In the great Leinster gathering at Carmán the first day (" Assembly of the Saints ") was devoted exclusively to ecclesiastical matters (Green : *Hist. of Irish State to* 1014, p. 279).

Synods, local and national, were of common occurrence in the Church during the sixth century. In Merovingian Gaul, for instance, no less than thirty synods were held between that convened at Orleans by Chlodovech (A.D. 511) and the synod of Paris in A.D. 614. Hauck : *Kirchengeschichte Deutschlands* i, 144.

[1] MacNeill : *Phases*, p. 320. Cf. A. S. Green : *History of the Irish State to* 1014, p. 280–1.

[2] Hefele-Leclercq : *Histoire des Conciles* i, p. 1–124. *Dict. de Theol. Cath.* iii, 636–76. Kneller : *Papsttum u. Konzil im ersten Jahrtausend. Zeit. f. Kath. Theol.*, 1903–4. Gelzer : *Die Konzilien als Reichsparlamente* (*Ausgew. kleine Schriften*), 1907, p. 142–55.

order and ecclesiastical government bade fair to be lost to view.　As regards the power of order, the Irish bishop differed in nothing at any period from bishops elsewhere in Christendom.　In personal dignity he ranked superior to any presbyter-abbot, but the monastic concept of his office was that he should be a saint rather than a ruler.　In course of time the temporalities, and with them effective government, tended to fall more and more into the hands of the presbyter-abbots.

SECTION III

IRISH MONASTIC LIFE c. A.D. 560-660

CHAPTER I

WITHIN THE MONASTERY

The Rule of St. Columban. Ed. Seebass : *Regula Monachorum Sancti Columbani Abbatis. Zeit. f. Kirchengeschichte,* xv, p. 366–86. Nine of its ten chapters deal with the leading principles of the religious life.

The Regula Coenobialis of St. Columban. Ed. Seebass : *Regula Coenobialis S. Columbani Abbatis. Zeit. f. K.* xvii, p. 215–34. This is really a penal code, but we can deduce from the defects selected for punishment the practices that were of precept in the Columban monasteries. Seebass (*Uber die sog. Regula Coenobialis Columbani u. die mit dem Poenitential Columbas verbundenen kleineren Zustäze Z.K.G.* xviii, p. 59–71. Cf. *über Columbas von Luxeuil Klosterregel u. Bussbuch.* Dresden, 1883, p. 43 ff.) distinguishes two recensions (*Reg.* I and *Reg.* II). *Regula* I, Chapters 1–9, belongs to the original Columban rule. *Regula* II, the younger recension, incorporates *Regula* I, but interpolates and appends additional matter. The first large addition in *Regula* II may be traced back to the original Columban Rule. The second large addition seems to be taken from an old Irish Penitential still represented by a Bobbio MS. now in the Ambrosian Library, Milan (Seebass : *Zeits. f. Kirchenrecht* vi, p. 26 f.). The *Regula Monachorum* and the *Regula Coenobialis* were united originally to form the Columban Rule. After the Saint's death the parts were separated, the first becoming independent as *Regula Monachorum,* whilst the second, expanded from material found in Columban monasteries and in some way covered by the founder's authority, became *Regula Coenobialis.* Cf. however, *Vita Columbani,* Ed. Krusch, *M.G.H. SS. RR. Merovin.* iv, p. 15–6. Parts of certain Columban authorship, the *manu propria,* as it were of the Saint, are distinguished in references by the letters *MP. ;* additions by the letters *MNP.*

The Penitential of Columban. Ed. Seebass : *Das Poenitentiale Columbani. Z.K.G.* xiv, p. 430–48. (Cf. Ib. xviii, p. 59–71.) Seebass concludes that the Penitential in its present form results from a union of two Penitentials (A and B,) that were originally independent of each other. The second of these (B), chapters 1–23, was written certainly by St. Columban. The first (A) is probably the main portion of another Penitential written by the same pen. The same may be said of chapters 26–30 of Penitential B. Penitential A was written for monks only. Seebass suggests (with probability) that its provisions go back ultimately to Clonard, where Finnian drew up the first book of this kind. Hauck : *Kirchengeschichte Deutschlands* i, p. 276 n., while agreeing in general with Seebass, thinks that chapters 9–12 of A, and chapters 26–30 of B, are fragments of old monastic rules. Into the merits of the controversy it is unnecessary to enter, for all admit that the Penitential is Irish in every part, and represents the teaching of the Irish monastic fathers in the sixth century.

Ordo Sancti Columbani Abbatis de vita et actione monachorum (three instructions and a tract on the eight principal vices) recognised by Seebass as genuine works of St. Columban, and published in *Z.K.G.* xiv, p. 78 ff.

The Life of St. Columban by Jonas. Ed. Krusch : *Vita Columbani. M.G.H. SS. RR. Merov.* iv. This illustrates and supplements the preceding documents.

The Penitential of St. Finnian, Poenitentiale Vinniani. Wasserschleben : *Bussordnungen der abendl. Kirche*, p. 108 ff. Most of the provisions of the Penitential are repeated in the Penitential of St. Columban (Cf. Watkins, *A History of Penance* ii, p. 590 ff.)

Adamnan's Life of St. Columba of Iona. Ed. Reeves. Dublin, 1857. Various details of monastic discipline are mentioned incidentally in the course of the narrative.

Vitae Sanctorum Hiberniae, vols. i and ii. Ed. Plummer. Oxford, 1910. As the matter of these lives is heterogeneous, caution has to be used in utilizing of them for the early period. This is true to a yet greater extent for the Irish lives—*Bethada Naem nErenn*, Ed. Plummer, Oxford, 1922 ; and *Lismore Lives*. Ed. Stokes, Oxford, 1890.

Monastic *Regulae* in Irish. Five deserve mention, those namely which profess to have been drawn up by Ailbe of Emly, Ciarán, Columcille and Comgall (in the sixth century) and Mochuta of Raithen and Lismore /(seventh century). *The Rule of Ailbe* has been published by Joseph O'Neill in *Eriu* ii, p. 97 ff. (Cf. *Z.C.P.* v, p. 434 ff.) ; that of Ciarán by Strachan in *Eriu* iii, p. 227–8 ; that of Comgall by Strachan in *Eriu* i, p. 191 ff. ;. that of Columcille by Meyer in *Z.C.P.* iii, p. 28–30 ; and that of Mochuta by " Mac Eclaise " (Fr. T. de Róiste) in *I.E.R.*, xxvii (1910), p. 495 ff., and Meyer in *Archiv. f. kelt. Lexikographie*, Bd. iii, H.3.. All these Rules are written in old Irish (all but that of Columcille in verse), and the date of the most ancient can hardly be much earlier than A.D. 800, so that they cannot be ascribed in their present form to the saints whose names they bear. The only question is whether they represent in any way the teaching of the early founders. There is no particular difficulty in admitting that they do. With the exception of the Rule attributed to Ailbe, which contains short references to monastic officials, hints as to the arrangements of the Divine Office, the use of food and minor matters of discipline, the Rules say nothing about the interior life of the monastery. They confine themselves rather to the virtues— charity, chastity, poverty, humility, industry, modesty, prayer, silence, gentleness, obedience—whose exercise was the monk's primary duty.

St. Columban's *Regula Monachorum* is essentially of the same kind ; and the conclusion seems justified that a *Rule*, according to Irish ideas, was designed to regulate the interior life only. Great emphasis was therefore laid on fundamental principles. Exterior life was governed by custom, fixed, it may well be, in many cases within the lifetime of the founders. Breaches of monastic custom, no less than moral transgressions, were visited with appropriate punishment. The apportioning, once for all, of the penalty to the fault, gave rise to our earliest Penitential, which is ascribed (probably with justice) to St. Finnian of Clonard himself. When laymen came to the monasteries for the "Medicamenta Paenitentiae," the satisfaction to be enacted for their delinquencies was similarly systematized, and the Penitentials, in consequence, made wider in their scope. St. Columban's *Regula Coenobialis*, for instance, seems to have been designed originally as a Penitential for his monks ; whilst the so-called *Penitential*, a work of the same kind drawn up after he had come to Gaul, seems to have been a more general treatise (based on Irish models) for the erring clergy and laity who there came under his influence, rather than for his own erring subjects.

To return to the five Rules first mentioned. Those of Ailbe, Ciarán, Comgall and Mochuta, where they recommend the commonplace monastic virtues, not details of monastic practice, may represent the teaching of the Saints named. The form in which the Rules are now found is due to writers of the late eighth or early ninth century in the four monasteries—Emly, Clonmacnois, Bangor and Lismore. Early catch-phrases in prose may have served as a basis for the poetry, just as in the *Laws* the traditional prose teaching is often neatly expressed in a later well-turned couplet.

The Rule of Columcille was destined probably for those who lived in the *disert* of Iona, or on a neighbouring island. The eremitical life was sought after in St. Colmcille's day and became fashionable in the century after his death.

For the other Rules attributed to Irish saints and for the later Rules of Maelruain and Cormac Mac Cuileannáin, as well as Continental Rules in Latin, written wholly or partially under Irish influence, see Dom L. Gougaud in *Rev. Bénéd.* T. xxv (1908), p. 167 ff. Different from all these is the so-called Rule of Echtgus Ua Cúanáin for the community of Ros Cré (published by Van Hamel in *Rev. Celt.* T. xxxvii, p. 344-9). This is in reality a treatise on the Holy Eucharist in classic verse ; and except that it may have been written in the first place for a religious community has nothing whatever to do with monasteries.

§1—Fundamental Concept of Monasticism as a " Militia Christi."

FOR the monk, as for all men, the purpose of existence was to secure eventual entry into everlasting life. The means to that end, according to Christ's own teaching, were loyal observance of the two great commandments, love of God and love of the neighbour.[1] All legislation for the

---

[1] Matt. xxii, 37, 39.

monastic state must presuppose, if it does not directly express, this truth.[1] But human nature, weakened by the Fall, is blind to its eternal interests and tends passionately towards pleasures forbidden by the Divine Law. Hence the need for struggle, especially on the part of those who devote themselves entirely to God's service. Life, then, for the monk is a perpetual warfare. He must fight against himself, lest he succumb to sensual cravings. He must fight against the world, which is interested only in earthly goods, earthly pleasures, earthly honours, and which fixes the standard of its values accordingly. He must fight against the Devil, who fears and mistrusts the monastic profession, and pursues its representatives with peculiar venom and hatred.[2]

It is not, then, sufficient that the monk should be a servant of Christ,[3] though he must be this in the fullest sense before he can think of advancing in perfection.[4] If worthy of his calling he must go further, gird on the armour of faith and descend as an athlete into the arena, there to meet the cruel attacks of savage foes.[5] He must, in fine, remain perpetually under arms, for hostile aggression never ceases, and may thus regard himself as a soldier in the Master's army. Monasticism as a " Militia Christi " and the monk as a " miles Christi " became in consequence one of the commonest concepts in monastic literature.[6] From this it passes into Irish tradition,

---

[1] It is expressed by St. Columban, *Reg. Mon. Introd.*, p. 374 : following St. Basil *Interrog.* i, *Rufin. Transl.*, PL. ciii, c. 488. Cf. *Columban Instr.* ii, p. 79. " Quid in mundo optimum est ? Auctori eius placere." Cass. *Conl.* i, 6, p. 12–3.

[2] Cass. *Conl.* viii, 16, p. 232. An Egyptian monk hears in a temple a number of devils rendering an account of their activities to Beelzebub. One had started a war, various rebellions and bloody encounters within a period of thirty days. He was whipped for his dilatory ways. Another had raised storms and caused many ships to sink, with heavy loss of life. He, too, was whipped. Similarly a third, who had caused many disputes and murders. But when a fourth announced that after forty years of labour he had brought a monk to sin against chastity, Beelzebub jumped from his throne, embraced the speaker, placed a crown upon his head, and lauded him for his brilliant achievement. Cf. *V.S.H.* ii, p. 167.

[3] Ath. *Vita Ant.* P.L. lxxiii, c. 150 : " Christi servus sum." Ib., 149 : " Christi famulus sum." *Cass. Conl.* xxiv. 26. Cf. the Welsh mauddwy (*servus Dei*). A corresponding Irish *mog Dé* is not found, but the phrase *mog saethair ocus fognama do Christ* (a slave to Christ in work and service) occurs in *Lism. L.*, p. 18.

[4] *St. Jer. Ep.*, 14, 6. *C.S.E.L.* liv, p. 53 : " Perfectus Christi servus nihil habet praeter Christum, aut si habet perfectus non est."

[5] *Lausiac Hist.* ii, p. 49 : " τοῖς ἀθληταῖς τοῦ χριστοῦ " *Cass. Inst.* v, 18 : " Athleta Christi." Ib. 19 : " Athletae Christi." Cf. *Conl.* vii, 20.

[6] Ath. *V. Ant.* P.L. lxxiii, c. 130. *Orsiesii :* " De inst. mon." P.L. ciii, c. 466. *Alb.*, p. 111. *Cass. Conl.*, i, 1 ; iv, 12 ; xxiv, 26 ; xvi, 1 ; vii, 5 ; vii, 23 ; viii, 18, etc. *Vita Mart.* 4, 14 : " Christi ergo miles sum." Cf. St. Jerome's : " quid facis in paterna domo, delicate miles ? " *Ep.* 14, 2. *C.S.E.L.*, p. 46.

where it is likewise of everyday occurrence. Jonas, for instance, speaks of Columban as a " splendid soldier,"[1] when relating that Saint's resistance to feminine blandishments. Colmcille left Ireland for Iona with twelve " fellow soldiers,"[2] and the monks who heard him disclose the secret of an erring heart at Treóit (Trevet, Co. Meath), on the Boyne, are designated by the same term.[3] Various edifying persons among the monastic brethren, Oisséne,[4] Mailodrán,[5] Findchan,[6] Lugbe[7], Diormit,[8] Ernéne,[9] and Lugaid,[10] appear also as soldiers of the spirit in Adamnan's pages.[11]

Such men would have suffered torture and death gladly at the hands of Christ's enemies, but opportunities for this were not forthcoming in Ireland until the Norse incursions began at the end of the eighth century. But if martyrdom in the strict sense by the spilling of blood was impossible, martyrdom improperly so-called, or a life of exceptional renunciation, was all the more eagerly sought after. A homily in archaic old Irish, dating probably from the last quarter of the seventh century, summarises the teaching of the Irish fathers on this subject. " Now there are three kinds of martyrdom," says the ancient record, " which are accounted as a cross to a man, to wit, white martyrdom, green[12] martyrdom and red martyrdom. White martyrdom consists in a man's abandoning everything he loves for God's sake, though he suffer fasting or labour thereat. Green martyrdom consists in this, that by means of fasting and labour he frees himself from his evil desires ; or suffers toil in penance and repentance. Red martyrdom consists in the endurance of a cross or death for Christ's sake, as happened to the Apostles in the persecution of the wicked and in teaching

---

[1] *Vita Col.*, ch. 3, p. 155 : " egregius miles."

[2] *Adam.* iii, 4, p. 196 : " commilitones."

[3] Ib. 1, 40, p. 77 : " Christique commilitones."

[4] Ib., 1, 2.

[5] Ib. i, 22 : " Christi miles."

[6] Ib. i, 36.

[7] Ib. i, 43.

[8] Ib. iii, 7.

[9] Ib. iii, 23.

[10] Ib. iii, 23.

[11] The term occurs in *A.U.*, s.a. 728 : " Christi Miles," but the corresponding annal in *Ann. Tig.*, s.a. 729, has the Irish equivalent " ridire Crist." Cf. *V.S.H.* i, p. 5 : " Dei miles, et non miles huius seculi."

[12] *Glas* as a term for colour is somewhat ambiguous, as it comprises various tints between iron grey, sky blue and green. In clothes it stands for the colour derived from the dye *glaisín*, " woad."

the law of God."[1]   Three martyr practices mentioned
specifically as precious in God's eyes are chastity in youth,
restraint where there is abundance of good things, and the
refusal of gifts whose acceptance would be prejudicial to the
frank discussion of sinful ways [2]   The monks of Munnu, or
Fintan of Teach Munnu, a stern ruler who died in A.D. 635,
are referred to as martyrs in a Litany preserved in the *Book
of Leinster*.[3]   St. Columban speaks in his Rule of the " felicity
of martyrdom " in a context which shows clearly that by
martyrdom is to be understood penance and mortification,
or the green martyrdom of the homily.[4]   Peculiar to Irish
monasticism is the division of non-bloody martyrdom into
" white " and " green," " white " representing the first great
step in renunciation of the world, and " green " the practice
of exceptional austerity within the life of religion.   Amid the
Irish monks, too, the general idea of monastic life, as a
martyrdom improperly so called, was very popular, much
more so than among the monks of any other land,[5] but the
idea itself is not of Irish origin.   It is found in the Life of
St. Anthony by St. Athanasius, who speaks of the great
hermit as a martyr in love if not in deed.[6]   St. Athanasius
goes on again to relate how St. Anthony, after a vain endeavour
to give up his life for Christ, returned to his old monastery
where by faith and strict service he merited a daily martyrdom,
wearing himself out with yet more trying fasts and vigils,
dressing in hair-cloth, neglecting the bath, and treating his
body otherwise with incredible harshness.[7]   Yet clearer is
the statement of Sulpicius Severus that though the circumstances of his age did not allow St. Martin to meet a violent
end in hatred of the faith, he nevertheless did not lack the
glory of martyrdom, for in intensity of desire he had reached
that honour.   Pains, punishments and torture unto blood

---

[1] *Thes. Paleoh.* ii, 246-7.
[2] Ib.
[3] *LL.* 373, b. 47 : " trí l. fír martir fo mám Munnu meic Tulchain" the
thrice fifty true martyrs under the yoke of Munnu, son of Tulchan. Cf.
V.S.H. Introd., p. lxxxiv, n. 4 and p. cxix.
[4] *Z.K.G.* xv, p. 385 : " hanc martirii felicitatem."
[5] Dom Gougaud :   "Les conceptions du martyre chez les irlandais."
Rev. Bénéd. T. 24, 1907, p. 360 ff.
[6] *V. Ant.*, PL. lxxiii, c. 147 : " et amore quidem iam martyr erat." Cf.
Methodius of Philippi. PG. xviii, c. 128-9.
[7] Ib. : " Ad pristinum monasterium regressus quotidianum fidei ac con-
scientiae martyrium merebatur, acrioribus se ieiuniis vigiliisque conficiens
vestimento cilicino intrinsecus, desuper pellicio utebatur, nunquam corpus
lavans," etc.

were not inflicted upon him, but he found substitutes of his own choosing. Immense, indeed, were the pangs of earthly sorrows—hunger, watching, nakedness, fasts, insults, opposition from the jealous, persecution from the evil disposed, care for those in sickness and danger—which he voluntarily endured for the sake of an eternal crown.[1] That the Irish drew directly from one or other of these sources is not impossible, but it is more likely that the borrowing was indirect through Lérins and Britain, for the concept is quite a common *motif* in the sermons of St. Cæsarius of Arles, whose ascetical training was received in the island monastery. The supply of martyrs, according to St. Cæsarius, had not ceased with the era of persecutions. Peace, too, finds them represented, not indeed such as perish by fire or sword, but such as by heroic contempt of the body render it harmless for evil.[2] " For it may be said without disrespect for those who laid down their lives during the persecutions that to afflict the flesh, overcome lust, resist avarice, and triumph over the world is to go far on the way to martyrdom.'' In one sense the simple Christian, just in the sight of God and his neighbour, may be called a martyr, but strictly speaking the title is deserved only by him who lives a mortified life in religion.[4] There is no reason to doubt that this was the teaching of Lérins in the days of Faustus of Riez no less than in the days of St. Cæsarius. The links with Ireland would then be these : some monastic traveller to Britain, like the " antistes et abbas " mentioned by Sidonius Apollinaris ; Ynys Pyr, where Cadoc received his training ; Llangarvan which that saint later founded ; and Clonard, whose close relationship with Llangarvan points to Cadoc as the teacher of St. Finnian.

---

[1] Similar thoughts are expressed in the pseudo-Cyprian tract " De duplici martyrio." Ed. Hartel iii, 3, c. 17 and 35.

[2] Caes. P.L. xxxix, c. 2301 : " Nemo dicat, fratres carissimi, quod temporibus nostris martyris certamina esse non possint ; habet enim pax martyres suos." Ib. 2159 : " Non martyrii sola effusio sanguinis consummat, nec sola dat palmam exustio illa flammarum. Pervenitur non solum occasu, sed etiam contemptu carnis ad coronam."

[3] Ib. : " Absque iniuria sanctorum in persecutionibus defunctorum dicere liceat carnem afflixisse, libidinem superasse, avaritiae restitisse, de mundo triumphasse, pars magna martyrii est."

[4] P.L. lxvii, c. 1084. Ib. c. 1162. Arnold. *Caes. von Arel.*, p. 17, note 25.

§ 2—The Monastic Novitiate.

(*a*)—*Aspirants to the Monastic State.*

Though the essential equality of all men must have been taught by the Irish monks, as it was taught by the ascetics since the first days of retirement to the desert,[1] yet recruiting for Irish monasteries seems to have been confined almost wholly to the upper and the middle classes. Colmcille, for instance, was of the noblest family in the land[2] ; Aed, son of Brecc, was a scion of the Southern Uí Néill[3] ; Abbán was of noble race[4] ; similarly Búithe,[5] Ciarán of Saigher,[6] Colmán Elo,[7] Colmán of Tír-dá-glas,[8] Declán of Ardmore,[9] Enda of Aran,[10] Maedóc of Ferns,[11] Munnu of Taghmon,[12] Ruadán of Lothra,[13] Tigernach of Cluain Eois,[14] and Berach of Cluain Coirpthe[15] ; Ciarán of Clonmacnois was the son of a chariot maker[16] ; Bairre of Cork, the son of an iron-worker[17] ; Mochoemóg, the son of an artist in wood and stone[18] ; the status of these workers in early Ireland being that of a well-to-do professional man to-day. Cainnech's father was a poet[19] ; Comgall's father a free citizen of Dál n-Araide, for he is mentioned as a soldier in the army of that territory[20] ; Carthach's father, a man of standing in his own district.[21] In

---

[1] Athan. *Vita Ant.* P.L. lxxiii, c. 162 : " licet tamen diversa sit dignitas, attamen eadem nascendi moriendique conditio est."

[2] Supra, p.

[3] *V.S.H.* i, 34 : " de nobiliori Hiberniae genere."

[4] Ib., p. 4 : " de claro genere."

[5] Ib., p. 87 : " generosis ortus parentibus."

[6] Ib., p. 217.

[7] Ib., p. 258.

[8] *Codex Salm.,* c. 445.

[9] *V.S.H.* ii, p. 32.

[10] Ib., p. 60.

[11] Ib., p. 140.

[12] Ib., p. 226.

[13] Ib., p. 262.

[14] Ib., p. 240.

[15] Ib. i, p. 76.

[16] Ib., p. 200 : " artifex curuum, et ipse erat dives."

[17] Ib., p. 65 : " faber ferrarius ducis Ráith Luin."

[18] Ib. ii, p. 164 : " honorificus artifex in lignis et lapidibus."

[19] Ib. i, p. 152.

[20] Ib. ii, p. 3.

[21] Ib. i, p. 171.

no case is it mentioned that the monk was of low degree, a noteworthy omission, for the circumstance of unusually modest birth is not one which the biographers of the day would be likely to overlook. In this respect, then, Ireland differed from Egypt, where the monks were drawn mainly from the middle and lower classes.[1] The Irish differed likewise from the Egyptian monks in the place which they conceded to intellectual pursuits, provision for a liberal education, according to the standards of the time, being a normal feature of the Irish monasteries.

A vocation, according to Cassian,[2] may spring from three sources—directly from God, by a special inspiration ; indirectly from man, through the influence of good advice or good example ; indirectly again from the force of untoward circumstances, where the loss of property or loved ones or a general dissatisfaction with what life can give results in a settled conviction that the world is a fraud and that its pleasures are contemptible. In Ireland, as elsewhere, the great majority of vocations were due undoubtedly to the second of these causes. St. Patrick extolled the monastic life ; the *Candida Casa* in Northern Britain and Llangarvan in Southern Britain showed how it could be practised. St. Finnian of Clonard was won over to a strict form of monasticism by the example of the British brethren, and in his turn attracted disciples to himself ; and so the process went on until the land was filled with monks. But vocations due to the other causes are likewise reported. Thus Mochua of Timahoe, who had spent thirty years as a soldier, was said to owe his higher call to divine inspiration.[3] A yet more famous ex-warrior (athlaech), who abandoned the world[4] in mature life, was St. Enda of Aran.[5]

Two remarkable instances of the same kind are recorded by Adamnan. The first of these relates to a certain Connachtman named Librán who had made up his mind to become a religious and join the community at Iona. On his arrival

---

[1] MacKean : *Christ. Monas. in Egypt,* p. 125.

[2] *Cass. Conl.* iii, 4. *C.S.E.L.* xiii, p. 69-71. Cassian's teaching on this point is repeated by the writer of Colmcille's life in *Lism. L.,* p. 20, l, 697 ff. : " ó thrí moduibh immorro tochuirther na daine co h-aithnius ⁊ co muinnterus in Coimded. Isé in cétna modh, etc."

[3] *V.S.H.* ii, p. 184.

[4] Cf. *Lism. L.,* p. 111, l. 3721-2 : " iar bhfácbáil in tsaeguil do ilibh dhibh."

[5] *Martyr. Oeng.,* April 5th, note. *H.B.S.* ed. p. 112.

in the island he was given temporary quarters in the guest-house. St. Colmcille, then the ruling Abbot, had a private interview with him there a day or two later, and questioned him about his native district, his family, and his purpose in coming to Iona. It transpired that the man's life had been far from edifying, that indeed his chief idea in coming so far from home was to do penance for his sins.[1] Colmcille here-upon informed him that before any steps could be taken to place him among the monks the quality of his repentance must be tested. In this monastery, continued the Saint, orders are constantly given which make the severest demands on flesh and blood. How should you care to have to face these? To which the fervent candidate replied: "What ever you say I will do, no matter how hard or how humiliating it may be." Having heard his confession, the Saint decided that seven years must be spent in penance in the neighbouring island of Tiree before the question of religious life could be again considered. A further difficulty arose because of an oath of perpetual service by which the penitent had bound himself to a friend who had paid the *eric* due from him for man-slaughter, and had thus saved him from imminent death. Librán confessed that after a few days spent in this benefactor's service he had found the life too galling to his pride and had incontinently taken his departure, the oath and his duty of gratitude notwithstanding. The Saint replied that this problem had better be left unsolved until the seven years of penance had been completed. When the day of release from Tiree at last arrived, Colmcille supplied the Connachtman with a beautiful sword, sufficient in value to repay his former benefactor for the money spent in obtaining his release. Armed with this present, and encouraged by the blessing of the Saint, Librán made his way back to his native province, where events took a much more favourable course than he could ever have anticipated. In the first place the wife of his benefactor was a lady of piety, and having learned that Librán had just passed seven years in penance on Tiree and had received the sword as a gift from Colmcille, she prevailed upon her husband not to accept it. The blessing of that holy man, the good lady added, is more profitable to us than his money. Librán was thus absolved from all obligations on the score of his former captivity. His family, however,

---

[1] Adam. ii, 39, p. 157 : ad delenda in peregrinatione peccamina.

insisted that he should undertake the care of his father and mother, both then in old age. But the father died a week later, and a younger brother offered to provide for his mother's needs, so that Librán could start again for Derry and Iona. Soon afterwards he was allowed to join the monastic family. He survived his master, and died finally after a short illness at Durrow, whither he had been sent from Tiree on monastic business.[1]

In the second instance the ending is unfortunately much less happy. A certain presbyter named Findchán, head of a monastery at Árd Cain in Tiree, induced the King of the Pictish state called Dál n-Araide to abandon his throne and become a monk on the island. Now this king, Aed Dub, had a vile name for sanguinary exploits.[2] Among his many victims was the High King, Diarmuid, son of Cerball, whom he had assassinated. With complete disregard for Irish penitential discipline, which imposed a long period of penance upon homicides,[3] Findchan not only reconciled the converted worldling to the Church, but had him ordained priest after a negligible period of trial. Aed persevered but a short time in his vocation. He returned to the North-East, won by force the sovereignty of the Ulaid, and in due course died a violent death.[4]

Amid other remarkable vocations must be mentioned that of an elderly and distinguished citizen, who left a noble and well-beloved wife, twelve sons, seven daughters, and many clients behind in the world to wonder at his resolution. Where the elderly convert from a worldly life managed to persevere he was often in his later days excessively scrupulous in the observance of the rule. Perhaps the best illustration of this attitude is afforded in the life of St. Crónán of Roscrea. It happened that St. Mochoemóg and a number of his disciples paid Crónán a visit. The monastery at Roscrea was poor, but thanks to a timely miracle worked by St. Crónán, a substantial supper could be laid before the guests and the

---

[1] *Adam.* ii, 39, p. 157–63.
[2] *Adam.* i, 36, p. 67 : " valde sanguinarius homo et multorum trucidator."
[3] *Paenit. Colum. Z.K.G.* xiv, p. 444 : Exile and three years on bread and water. The culprit may then return, but must render service to the near relatives of the person slain. Wassersch. *I.K.,* p. 96, *Hibernensis synodus :* " seven years' penance in a monastery of strict rule." Ib. *Patricius (Syn.* i *Patricii,* c. 14) : one year of penance.
[4] *Adam.* i, 36, p. 66–71. Cf. Jonas *Vita Col.* 28, p. 217, where Columban urges the King Theudebert to exchange the throne for the cloister. Theudebert refuses, and was later slain " impie."

community. The meal was evidently appreciated by the gathering of one hundred and twenty monks, for it dragged on well into the night. At last one of the brethren, old in years but young in religion, became so incensed at the course things were taking that he cried out in a loud voice : " I'm beginning to think there will be no matins in this place to-night ! " Crónán met the complaint with a gentle rebuke. " Brother," he said, " in the person of a guest it is Christ Who is received ; we ought surely to rejoice and make merry at the coming of Christ." But the hint did not fail of its effect, for the supper was soon afterwards brought to a close.[1]

Maedóc of Ferns must have been mildly amazed when a " scurrilis scholasticus " or professional satirist[2] from Munster presented himself at the monastery door and asked for admission among the brethren. But the new novice[3] kept his tongue under restraint, and in time won such respect that he succeeded Maedóc as bishop.[4] Successors to two other great saints, if we may believe their biographers, found their way to the monasteries over which they were one day to rule along yet more unusual routes. Thus the story goes that a group of raiders from Fir Tulach in Westmeath passed through Clonard on their march towards the prey. A youth amongst them, whose courage or whose strength had already begun to ebb, got left behind in the limekiln of Finnian's monastery. The abbot, hearing of this, put a scissors up his sleeve and came out to interview the youth. What happened in the kiln and afterwards is related very briefly by the biographer : " The abbot tonsured that man in the ecclesiastical fashion and he studied with Finnian, who conferred orders upon him, and he is Bishop Senach, the first heir who took (the bishopric) after Finnian."[5] St. Ciarán of Clonmacnois found a successor

---

[1] *V.S.H.* ii, p. 28.

[2] Evidently a *ferchdinte* or *rindile*. Cf. *Laws* v, 202. The influence of artists of this type was curtailed but by no means destroyed by the Convention of Druim Ceatt, where " the men of Ireland were on the point of banishing the poets by reason of their multitude and their sharpness and their complaining, and for their evil works. And moreover, they had made satires against Aed, King of Ireland." *Amra Colm. Introd. Liber Hym. H.B.S.* ed. i, p. 162–3. Cf. Keating, *Forus Feasa* ii, p. 78 ff.

[3] " Novitius " as a *terminus technicus* is not found in early Irish monastic literature ; neither is it found in Caesarius of Arles (himself a pupil of Lérins) nor in Cassian, though he uses the word now and then to translate νεόφυτος (Cf. *Inst.* iv, 30, p. 70 : *Conl.* xx, 5, p. 555.) The Benedictine rule introduced the term in its technical sense : " frater novitius ; cella novitiorum." (ch. lviii.).

[4] *V.S.H.* ii, p. 154.

[5] *Lism. L.*, p. 78, 1, 2629 ff.

in much the same fashion. One day when he was staying on Inis Aingin (Hare Island) in Loch Ree, he heard the voice of a man calling from the mainland. " Go, brothers," he said, " and bring hither a future candidate for the abbatial office." The brethren rowed across, but returned at once to protest that the owner of the voice was a mere youth, who spent his time rambling in the woods. He had never been to school, and was quite unlettered. " Return in all haste," answered Ciarán, " for the Lord has revealed to me that the owner of that voice will be your abbot when I am gone." So the brethren brought the youth to Ciarán, who tonsured him. He developed into a diligent student and pious monk, and after Ciarán's early death became the second Abbot of Clonmacnois. For the untutored youth was no other than Oenu moccu Loigse.[1]

Colmán of Lann Elo was yet more penetrating in his discernment of a hidden vocation. He heard one day the shouts of a soldier band celebrating their victory over a vanquished foe. When the soldiers came along to where he stood he stopped them and said : " Let each of you speak in turn, for there is a sheep from Christ's flock among you, and I want to find out which of you it is." This must have been news indeed to the sturdy swordsmen, but at any rate they obeyed, and Colmán said to one of their number, who was still a youth : " My son, you have been called to God's service." After a bitter struggle, the youth was allowed by his master to join the Saint's company. He lived to a good old age, became an exceedingly holy man and was credited with miraculous powers.[2] In this and the preceding cases the details need not be taken too seriously, but the stories show that the monastic noviceships had sometimes to work on very unpromising material.[3]

Not all of those who embraced religious life in Ireland or Iona came from the home country. Thus the first to die in St. Colmcille's famous monastery was a native of Britain, whose soul the holy founder saw as it was borne aloft by angels to its throne in heaven.[4] In the same community (and this, be it remembered, before Augustine set foot in

---

[1] *V.S.H.* i, p. 210. Cf. ib., p. 102 : the remarkable vocation of Colmán, son of Lenin, founder of Cloyne.
[2] Ib., p. 261–2.
[3] Cf. *Adam.* i, 3, p. 25.
[4] *Adam.* iii, 6, p. 203.

Canterbury), there were at least two Saxons, one of whom was
the baker.[1] Of the four brethren placed by St. Columban at
the four corners of the corn field to keep off the rain while the
crop was reaped, one likewise belonged to the British race[2];
nor was he without colleagues of his own nation,[3] who had
probably received their religious training at Bangor. A
Briton is mentioned also in the following of Fintan of Tech
Munnu (Taghmon), but he lived in a cell apart, almost as a
hermit.[4] The supply of candidates from Britain was maintained. They were celebrated in Irish monastic tradition for
their short tempers,[5] which must have been very short indeed to
attract attention in a land where the average native temper
was short enough! Not until the seventh century, when
missionary work among the Angles and Saxons was far
advanced, did the influx of these to Ireland become considerable. " The great plague " (of A.D. 664), says Bede, " was as
bad in Ireland as it was in England. In the former country
at that time were many Angles of the noble and the middle
classes who had left their native island in the days of Finan
and Colman, the bishops, and gone to Ireland for purposes
either of study or of asceticism. Some of these soon took
upon themselves monastic obligations, which they observed
with all faithfulness."[6] At the same period princesses and
others of the Saxons are found in the Columban monastery
of Faremoutiers in Merovingian Gaul,[7] established by
Eusthasius, the great abbot's first successor at Luxeuil,
and ruled over by the saintly Burgundofara.[8]

But the great majority of monks in the Irish monasteries
from the days of St. Finnian onwards were natives of the soil
who had followed the higher call while still in early youth.
That their numbers reached a remarkable figure was due in
no small degree to the traditional prominence accorded to
intellectual pursuits in the Gaelic scheme of civilisation.
Before the advent of Christianity the professions of druid
and poet claimed no mean percentage of the free men of the
nation. Parents and kinsfolk decided what members of the

---

[1] *Adam.* iii, 10, p. 208. Ib., 22, p. 227.
[2] Jonas *V, Col.* 13, p. 174.
[3] Ib., 20, p. 196.
[4] *V.S.H.* ii, p. 237.
[5] *V.S.H.* i, p. 264: " secundum irascibilem Brittonum naturam."
[6] Bede : *H.E.* ii, 7, Plummer's ed. p. 192.
[7] Ib., 8. Cf. *Jonas, Vita Col.* ii, 17, p. 268.
[8] Jonas, *Vita Col.* ii, 7, p. 243; ii, 11, p. 257.

family should be set aside for these careers, and the training began in childhood. After the conversion of the country to the Christian faith, druidism died a natural death, and boys who in the pagan days would have spent their youth in druidic studies were placed now under Christian teachers. The "pueri Patricii," boys entrusted to St. Patrick's care and destined for the clerical state, are mentioned incidentally more than once in the *Book of Armagh*.[1] No doubt there were defections among these,[2] but many persevered to carry on St. Patrick's work and to lead the Church in Ireland after his death. Foirtchernn, afterwards bishop of Trim, was trained from boyhood by Lommán, St. Patrick's disciple and colleague.[3] Finnian of Clonard, in his turn, was taught from boyhood by Foirtchernn,[4] from whom (it is reasonable to surmise) he received his special interest in the British Church, for Foirtchernn's mother and grandmother were both of British race.[5] Búithe of Monasterboice, whose childhood belongs to the fifth century and to a date probably earlier than Finnian's, left no account of his first teacher, at least none that has survived, for the biographer is forced to assert that the ferule was wielded in Búithe's case by angels.[6] Colmcille was fostered[7] by the pious priest, Cruithnecán, before he passed on to St. Finnian's monastery at Clonard. The youthful Columban, too, was placed under the care of some holy cleric before he left Leinster for Senell's school, and finally for Bangor.[8] Similarly with the other sixth century saints whose lives are best known to us, Abbán, who was sent to study under Ibar of Beg Ere at the age of twelve[9]; Ciarán of Clonmacnois, who was taught in boyhood by a deacon named Diarmait[10]; Coemgen of Glendalough, who was handed over

---

[1] *B. Arm.*, 10a, 29a. Cf. 8b, 24a, 24b, 454a, 454b, 30b.
[2] Thus Conall, son of Enda, son of Amolngid of Tir Amolngid (Tirawley) in Mayo, when still a small boy, was baptized by St. Patrick and placed under the care of Cethiacus, Patrick's disciple. But when Cethiacus died Conall returned to the lay state. *B. Arm.*, 20a, 20b.
[3] *B. Arm.*, 31b.
[4] *Lism. L.*, p. 75, l. 2524.
[5] *B. Arm.*, 31b.
[6] *V.S.H.* i, p. 88.
[7] *Adam.* iii, 2, p. 191: "eiusdem beati pueri nutritor." Colmcille was thus set aside and trained from boyhood for an ecclesiastical career, just as his brothers were expected to follow a worldly career, and trained by their foster-parents accordingly.
[8] Jonas *V, Col.* i, 3, p. 155. Jonas does not say that the teacher was a cleric, but the course of studies followed shows that he was.
[9] *V.S.H.* i, p. 7.
[10] Ib., p. 201.

to three holy seniors " that he might be brought up to Christ
in their cell "[1]; Colmán Elo, entrusted by his parents to a
holy senior named Colmán[2]; Comgall, who received the
rudiments of learning from "a certain cleric "[3]; Berach,
reared from babyhood by " a holy man "[4]; Barri or Findbarr,
offered by his parents to God in the persons of three anchorites[5];
Fintan of Cluain Eidnech, whose youthful years were spent in
profitable study under the priest who had baptized him[6];
Munnu, who received an ecclesiastical training from a holy
priest named Grellán, before he went to Bangor[7]; Molua,
who frequented a cell inhabited by seven " brethren and
priests." Brendan of Clonfert, Mochoemóg and others spent
their years of childhood under the maternal care of St. Ita,[8]
who as a religious instructor of the young seems to have had
no equal in her generation. A similar office in respect of
Tigernach of Cluain Eois was attributed to St. Brigid.[9]
Finally it is noted as a remarkable feature in the life of Aed,
son of Brecc, that he had no master, religious or otherwise,
until his adolescence,[10] the reason being that he was intended
by his family for the secular, not for the ecclesiastical, state.
When he reached maturity he disobeyed his parents and
entered a monastery in Munster.

The more general sixth century practice was thus that the
future monk should make his early studies and his first steps
along the way of perfection under the guidance of some pious
cleric and enter the monastery proper only when his boyhood
was coming to an end. But there were exceptions, even in
that century. We hear, for instance, of two little boys studying in the monastery of Inis Cathaig in Senán's day. One of
Senán's disciples took them both one day by boat to a rock
to cut seaweed. The disciple returned to Inis Cathaig, but
when the time came to go back for the boys he found that
the sea had carried off his boat, " and there was no other
boat on the island to succour the boys. So the boys were
drowned on the rock. Then on the morrow their bodies

---

[1] Ib., p. 235.
[2] Ib., p. 258.
[3] Ib. ii, p. 3.
[4] Ib. i, p. 76.
[5] Ib., p. 66-7.
[6] Ib. ii, p. 96.
[7] Ib., p. 226-7.
[8] *V.S.H.* i, p. 99; ii, p. 167.
[9] Ib. ii, p. 264.
[10] Ib. i, 34-5.

were borne (in by the tide) till they lay on the strand of the island." And these, says the *Life*, were the first dead to be buried in Inis Cathaig.[1] In Cainnech's monastery, too, there were three boys so small that they are called "infantes." These persevered in their vocation, but not in the home of their early training, for they gave allegiance later to St. Molua.[2] The prince of Fotharta (Barony of Forth, Wexford) also placed two of his sons in training for the religious life, one under a local anchorite, the other under St. Munnu of Taghmon. One day he started off with his retinue to visit the two boys, and found that the treatment they were receiving differed to an astonishing degree. The anchorite, in fact, handled the boy under his charge as a prince, and won encomiums therefor from the royal party, whereas Munnu had his fosterling dressed in servile garb and driving a cart with some other monks, to the great scandal of the courtiers.[3] Further references show that the presence of young students was taken as a matter of course in the monasteries.[4] St. Columban legislated for them in his Rule,[5] an evident proof, even if no other were forthcoming,[6] that their presence was a normal feature in the settlements that owed obedience to him. The placing thus of young children in monasteries with the intention that they should ultimately don the monastic habit was more common in Ireland than elsewhere, owing to the Irish system of fosterage, which resulted in the complete separation of sons and daughters from their parents during the long years that intervened between babyhood and maturity.[7] But there is nothing peculiarly Irish about the custom, which is found in many countries of both East and West since the beginning of monasticism. Patermutius, for

---

[1] *Lism. L.* p. 70, ll. 2330 ff.
[2] *V.S.H.* ii, p. 221.
[3] *V.S.H.* ii, p. 233–4.
[4] *Adam.* i, 3, p. 25–6. *V.S.H.* i, p. 212, 266; ii, 7, 12, etc.
[5] *Reg. Coen.* viii. *Z.K.G.* xvii, p. 225: "iuvenculi quibus imponitur terminus."
[6] Jonas *Vita Col.* i, 125, p. 291–2 : Agibodus began life at Bobbio "pueritia" under St. Columban. i, 26, p. 209 : Columban vows the infant Burgundofara to the Lord. In the Columban Convent founded by Burgundofara later *infantulae* are mentioned. *Vita Col.* ii, 16, p. 267.
[7] According to the Cáin Irráith "Law of fosterage fees" (*Laws*, vol. i, p. 147, ff) fosterage seems to have been the rule in families *otd fear midbuith co rig*, "from the *fear midbuith* (the well-to-do younger son with stock but without land in his own right) to the King." Included were the *ocaire*, *bóaire* (men rich in sheep or cows and owners of land), the *aire itir-dd-airig*, and the four real aristocrats, the *aire désa. aire túse, aire árd* and *aire forgaill*. Corresponding rights were enjoyed by the poets and artisans. Fosterage ended regularly for the boy at 17, for the girl at 14.

example, when he renounced the world and went to join a
coenobium in the Thebaid, brought with him his eight year
old boy, who was reared thenceforward in the monastery.[1]
St. Basil has no fault to find with this practice. "Since
the Lord says 'Suffer the little children to come unto me'
(Mark x. 14), and the Apostle praises him who from babyhood
has learned sacred letters (2 Tim. iii. 15) and elsewhere enjoins
the bringing up of children in the nurture and admonition of
the Lord, we judge every time, even that of early youth, to
be fitting for the reception of novices. Those who have lost
their parents we accept without more ado ; and become
fathers of orphans after the example of the zealous Job
(Job xxix, 12). Such, however, as are under their parents'
control when they are brought by them in person we receive
in the presence of a number of witnesses so as to give no
grounds for accusation to those who seek them but rather
to stop every unjust mouth that utters blasphemy against
us. . . . It is expedient that they be not numbered and
enrolled with the body of the brethren immediately, lest in
case of failure reproaches should fall on the life of godliness.
They should be trained in all righteousness as common children
of the brotherhood."[2] Sulpicius Severus, in his account of the
Egyptian monks, tells of two boys, one fifteen years old, the
other twelve, sent by the Abbot with a supply of bread to a
certain hermit. On their way back the boys met a serpent
which they succeeded in charming and placing in the empty
basket. Arrived at the monastery they showed their prize
with ill-concealed pride to the community. The monks
admired their courage, but the Abbot, looking at the incident
from a higher angle, and noting with sorrow that the boys
attributed their prowess to themselves and not to God, decided
that their humility must be safeguarded, and applied the
abbatial slipper.[3] The same writer informs us that when a
young girl in Gaul was cured suddenly of a serious disease
by a letter from St. Martin laid upon her breast, the maiden's
father was so moved that he at once offered his daughter to
God and vowed her to a life of perpetual virginity. "So he
took the little girl to St. Martin and offered her to him, nor
would he allow anybody else but St. Martin to place the veil

---

[1] Cass. *Inst.* iv, 27, p. 66.
[2] *Reg. fus. tract.* 15. P.L. cii, p. 498. Clarke : *Ascet. Works of St. B.*, p. 175–6.
[3] Sulp. Sev. *Dialog.* i, 10, p. 161.

of virginity upon her head.[1] " Salonius, the son of St. Eucherius, was but ten years old when he first came to Lérins[2] ; Veranius, his brother, was hardly much older ; and there is no reason to think that the two lacked companions of their own age in their religious studies.[3]

No doubt the commoner sixth century practice of placing the future ecclesiastic under the care of a cleric or hermit was more in keeping with the Irish concept of fosterage, for tradition favoured an intimate personal connection (hardly to be secured in a large institution) between the natural parent and the foster parent. As time went on, however, and monasteries multiplied, it became more usual to settle the children intended for the religious life in these. A canon in the seventh century collection designates (with an appeal to St. Jerome) the monk, the boy pupil, and the penitent as the persons regularly attached to every ecclesiastical establishment.[4]

Where the youthful novice had been reared away from home since childhood the break with family and relations would rarely cause him excessive grief, yet there often were attachments which it was none too easy to sever. An old Irish Penitential speaks ruefully of " the sorrow of separation from friends according to the flesh because of the loss of their human affection," [5] and though the language in this case is of the ninth century the experience belongs to every age. Occasions arose when the parting was particularly bitter. Abbán had a hard struggle with his parents before they agreed to let him follow his vocation, but at last he won them over to his wish and started religious life with their good-will and benediction.[6] Columban was yet more unhappily circumstanced, for his mother failed to reconcile herself to his loss. Her opposition was so violent that she threw herself on the door-

---

[1] Sulp. Sev. *Vita M*. 19, p. 128. Cf. *Lism. L*., p. 34, ll. 2812–3.
[2] Tillemont, *Mém*. xv, p. 122.
[3] Cf. *Regula Caesar. Arel*. P.L. lxvii, c. 1097 ff.
[4] Wasserschl. *I.K. Lib*., xlii, c. 15, p. 166. The principle " *Monachum aut paterna devotio aut propria professio facit* " (Council of Toledo, A.D. 633, Can. 49, Hefele-Leclercq, *Councils*, iii, 1, p. 273) was acknowledged down through the Middle Ages. For a fuller discussion of the question of *Oblati* see Seidl : " Die Gottverlobung von Kindern in Mönchs—und Nonnen-klöstern, 1872." I. Herwegen : " Studien u. Mitteilungen O.S.B." 1912. S. 543 ff. Deroux : " Les origines de l'oblature bénédictine," Ligugé, 1927 (Les éditions de la revue Mabillon i.)
[5] *Eriu* vii, ch. vi, p. 170 : " brón scartha frisna cáirde colnaidi ar gnái a ndoenachta."
[6] *V.S.H*. i, p. 4.

step before him to prevent his departure. But the son had inherited a share of the parent's determined character, and springing over her prostrate body he went forth to his destiny.[1] He might, though he knew it not, have claimed high authority for the harsh logic of his reasoning and the rude strength of his act. " The enemy is brandishing the sword above my head," says St. Jerome, " and is ready to strike me down ; what care I then for my mother's tears ? "[2] " In this matter," he says again, " the proof of filial affection is to proceed with cruelty."[3] Columban, to do him justice, was convinced that with a character such as his there was no hope of escaping contagion in the wicked world of his day. If he wished, therefore, to gain eternal life—and as a man of sense how could he wish otherwise ?—he was obliged to take refuge in the religious state.[4] Many years later in Gaul the delicately nurtured maiden, Burgundofara, whom Columban had blessed and consecrated to God in her infancy, showed equal determination in securing the welfare of her soul. When all other means to escape marriage had failed, she ran away from her father's house and betook herself to the basilica of St. Peter in Meaux. Her indignant father gave orders that she should be slain when discovered. When the soldiers found out her hiding place in the church, and announced what they had been commanded to do, her answer was : " If you think I fear death you can put my resolution to the test on this very pavement. In such a cause I should be delighted to die for Him Who died for me."[5] Matters were finally arranged between father and daughter, and the latter was allowed to give her heart, as she so ardently desired, to the Heavenly Spouse.

Where the future monk had lived in a monastery since childhood, and had decided, after he had reached the years of discretion, to continue to live under rule, there was nothing more natural than that he should abide among those who had hitherto been his teachers.[6] If, on the other hand, as happened

---

[1] Jonas : Vita Col. i, 3, p. 157.

[2] St. Jerome Ep., 14, C.S.E.L., liv, p. 48 : " gladium tenet hostis ut me perimat et ego de matris lacrimis cogitabo ? "

[3] Ib., p. 47 : " licet sparso crine et scissis vestibus ubera, quibus nutrierat, mater ostendat, licet in limine pater iaceat, per calcatum perge patrem, siccis oculis ad vexillum crucis vola ! Pietatis genus est in hac re esse crudelem."

[4] Jonas : Vita Col. i, 3, p. 155–6.

[5] Jonas : Vita Col. ii, 7, p. 242–3.

[6] Exceptions, however, might occur. Cf. V.S.H. ii, p. 221, above quoted, where boys trained in Achad Bó became monks under St. Molua.

more generally in the sixth century, his youthful years had been spent under the care of some isolated cleric or hermit, and the resolve to renounce the world and enter a monastery[1] was not come to until he had reached a certain maturity,[2] he could select the place of his future residence with greater freedom. Monastic tradition recommended that the monastery chosen should be situated far from family and friends,[3] though it was admitted that theory and practice were not always in harmony among the cenobites of Egypt. Where monks lived near their families, however, or near their old homes, the assumption was that natural ties of every kind were completely forgotten. An Abbot named Apollo was cited in illustration of the state of mind which the ascetical teachers considered it necessary to achieve. Apollo, it appears, was disturbed at some unseemly hour of the night by a brother living in the world who came to complain that his ox had got stuck in the mire of some distant marsh, and that his own efforts to release the animal had proved unavailing. As there was no response from inside the cell the clamour from outside grew every moment more querulous and more loud. Finally the Abbot Apollo put out his head and asked : " But why did you not ask our younger brother for help, for you had to pass by him on your way to me ? " To which the afflicted owner of the stricken ox replied : " Surely, Apollo, you rave, for he died fifteen years ago." " Know you not," answered Apollo, " that I died twenty years ago ? This cell is my sepulchre. In anything that concerns the present life you will get no help from me. When my father died I did not relax my mortification for a moment to bury him ; much less shall I relax it to release your ox from the mud. Go in peace !"[4] Apollo, a formidable man of God, might have discovered in St. Columban a satisfactory disciple, but he certainly would have found few others among the Irish ascetics of the sixth century.

---

[1] The Irish expression for this was " to take the habit of the clerical state." Cf. *Adam.* i, 36, p. 66 : sub clericatus habitu ii, 39 : sumpto clericatus habitu. *A.U.* s.a. 704 : post clericatum. *A.F.M.* 703 : iar ndul dó fa cuing clércechta ; but in Gaelic usually " do ghabháil chléircheachta." As a small minority only of the monks were clerics properly so-called, the term seems to have originated in the pre-monastic period, when to renounce the world meant really to become a cleric by receiving Holy Orders.

[2] Coinciding with the end of fosterage at seventeen, but it might be a couple of years earlier. Cf. Wassersch. *I.K.* lxvii, 16, where a choice of state is to be made when the age of puberty has been reached.

[3] Evag. *Rer. mon. rat.*, 5-7. *P.G.* xv, c. 1255-9. " Fly from thy native soil."

[4] Cass. *Conl.* xxiv, 11, p. 685-6.

A remedy against distracting affection for home and kin
was sought by many of these in flight. The pious woman,
from whom Columban asked advice about his future, had
herself put the principle into practice. " Fifteen years have
elapsed," she said, " since I left my home and came to this
place of pilgrimage. I chose Christ then as my leader, and I
have never since looked back. Were it not, indeed, for the
feebleness of my sex I would have crossed the sea and found
a more suitable place of pilgrimage in some foreign land."[1]
A modified form of this doctrine must have been common in
that age, if we may judge from the action of the monastic
founders. Thus, Enda, though a native of Meath,[2] made
his settlement in the western ocean, some hours sail from
" Ireland."[3] Bairre, a native of Connacht, settled in Cork ;
Brendan came from Kerry to Clonfert ; Cainnech and Abbán
from Ulster to Ossory and Wexford ; Fínán from Corcu
Duibne in Kerry to the Meath border ; Ita from Waterford
to West Limerick ; Maedóc from Connacht to Ferns ;
Mochoemóg and Mochua from Connacht to Eile and Leix,
respectively ; Molua from Limerick to Upper Ossory ; Munnu
from the far north-west to Wexford, and Ruadán from Ossory
to Lothra near Loch Derg.[4] Aed, son of Brecc, on the other
hand, settled in his home territory, as did Colmán Elo, Comgall,
Cronán of Roscrea, Fintan of Cluain Eidnech and Tigernach
of Cluain Eois. Ciarán of Clonmacnois, who was born of Meath
parents in Connacht, founded his famous monastery on the
Meath side of the Shannon ; but the Connachtmen regarded
the settlement as very largely their own, whilst the Southern
Uí Néill, in whose lands it was situated, treated the monastery
with particular favour. Colmcille, as is well known,
established his first community at Doire in the lands of his
own powerful family, but he discovered to his cost, if the
legend of Cúl Dremne can be trusted, that this was a dangerous
arrangement. Whether the claim to copyright story is
true or false there can be no doubt that his later migration
to Iona was prompted in part by the experience that the
proximity of relatives was bad for his soul's health. In this
connection a tale narrated of St. Munnu is of interest.[5] He

---

[1] Jonas : *Vita Col.* i, 3, p. 156.
[2] Zimmer, *Kelt. Beitr.* ii, p. 200 ff.
[3] Cf. *V.S.H.* i, p. 208.
[4] *V.S.H.* passim.
[5] *V.S.H.* ii, p. 229–30.

was staying at *Tech Telli*, near Durrow, when messengers arrived from the North to say that his mother was most anxious to see him. Munnu replied that he would betake himself to Louth to meet her. In due course, the mother arrived with her two married daughters, one unmarried daughter, and some other members of the family. The interview, it is to be hoped, was pleasant, but before it ended Munnu gave his relatives this warning, " Take care," he said, " never to come to me again, for if you do I will leave Ireland altogether and travel to regions beyond the sea." Distrust of one's native district,[1] or indeed of any place where worldly influences were likely to prove disquieting, was thus widespread in the sixth century.

Just then, as Columban left his home and friends in Leinster and journeyed first to Senell and then to Comgall at Bangor in the Ards of Ulster, so the young man who took his vocation seriously would be likely to seek admittance to a monastery far distant from the place of his birth.[2] If for one reason or another this could not be done, steps would at least be taken to ensure that he was not unduly disturbed by relatives. According to the Columban rule the monk might not be seen, nor spoken to, nor written to, nor heard from, without leave of the Abbot,[3] and we may be sure that this would rarely be granted. Jonas, the biographer of St. Columban, and a monk at Bobbio, never saw his parents for nine years, though they had often begged the Abbot to let him visit them. When permission to go was at last conceded, a priest and deacon were appointed to be his companions, but the feeling of strangeness, even under the parental roof, was so overwhelming that Jonas refused to tarry beyond a single night.[4] In such a matter something would depend upon personal character, but the typical Irish monk would hardly differ much from his North Italian colleague. And behind them both, at this period, were two centuries and more of monastic tradition.[5]

Where the future religious was placed in a monastery in tender years, he would, of course, grow up a monkish child,

---

[1] Cf. *Eriu* vii, p. 176, note : " Miscais in chenntuir, serc in altair "— " hatred of one's native district, love of the strange place," is here given as an axiom of monastic teaching.

[2] Columban was not the only Leinster man in Bangor, for Jonas says (*Vita Col.* i, 17, p.134) that another Columban of the same race had accompanied him from the monastery.

[3] *Reg. Coen. Z.K.G.* xv, p. 233, *MNP.*

[4] Jonas : *Vita Col.* ii, 5, p. 237–8.

[5] Cf. Cass., *Conl.* xxi, c. 9, *Inst.* iv, c. 27 ; v, c. 32 ; St. Jer. *Ep.* 14, c. 13. *Vita Paulae*, c. 6. Evagrius, *cap. prac.*, n. 95. (*P.G.* xl, c. 1249.)

a monkish boy, a monkish youth, and when the time came
for him to revise his parents' act, and vote definitely for or
against the form of life that they had marked out for him,
he would find it comparatively easy to confirm their choice.
When this had been done there would be question of little
more than fixing the date of his formal profession, for his
training as a monk had already been received. The *conversus*,
on the other hand, who had spent a large portion of his life
in worldly (and probably none too edifying) pursuits might
be called upon to give proof of his conversion by long years
of penitential exercises before permission was accorded him
to begin his training for the monastic life.[1] As the *oblatus* was
an uncommon type in the sixth century, and the *conversus*
an uncommon type at all times, we may concentrate our
attention on the class from which the majority of aspirants
to the monastic state were drawn.

In essentials, it need hardly be said, the training would
be the same for all, but there would be accidental differences
in the case of the *oblatus* and the *conversus*, due to the abnormal
circumstances under which these had commenced their
monastic life.

(b)—Course of Training within the Monastery.

The youth of fifteen, sixteen or seventeen years,[2] who
had been taught letters[3] and the rudiments of the religious
life by some pious cleric or hermit whose cell lay near his
home, and who had decided finally (on the advice of this
first master)[1] to follow the divine call and to seek entrance
into a monastery that lay far from his native district, would be
lodged, on arrival, in the guest-house.[5] In due course he would

---

[1] Cf. *Adam.* ii, 39, p. 157.

[2] The year recognised as marking the end of fosterage (seventeen) would
normally be awaited, but just as fosterage was often ended by the marriage
of the fosterling before seventeen (*Laws* ii, p. 168), so the pious youth might
embrace religious life before that age. Cf. Wassersch., *I.K.*, lxvi, 16, p. 239.

[3] It was an axiom in the Irish system that the study of religion and the
study of letters should go hand in hand. *Adam. Praef.* ii, p. 9 : " qui et a
puero Christiano deditus tirocinio et sapientiae studiis." Ib. i, 2, p. 20.
Jonas : *V. Col.* i, 3, p. 155 : " liberalium litterarum doctrinis et grammati-
corum studiis . . . dare coepit laborem," *V.S H.*, i, p. 7, etc., etc.

[4] In the case of those who founded monasteries the fact that they had
obtained permission from their religious teachers to do so is stressed. The
rule in the *Lives* is that the special capacity of the disciple should be proved
by miracles. *V.S.H.* i, p. 208, 259 ; ii, p. 16, etc. Cf. i, p. 102 : " obtenta
magistri sui licentia." Ib., p. 239 : " accepta licentia et benedictione beati
senioris."

[5] *Adam.* ii, 139, p. 157.

be visited by the Abbot and questioned about his person and his purpose.[1] If the answers were satisfactory, the aspirant would be admitted without more ado. Ireland differed in this from Egypt, where the candidate had to give proof of his constancy[2] by remaining ten days outside the door and begging, on his knees, permission to enter from every monk who passed.[3] Such a regulation would, of course, be superfluous where the aspirant was commonly a youth who had been reared from his earliest years in virtue. In Egypt and elsewhere,[4] however, the candidate's past might often be a matter of speculation, and it was a very natural precaution to ask him to submit to some rigid preliminary test.

Once accepted by the Abbot, the young man would leave the guest-house for the monastery proper, where he dressed in the monastic habit,[5] the outward symbol of his new state, and receive the tonsure, if this had not been conferred in his younger years.[6] If already weaned from temporal ambitions the last-mentioned rite would be easy enough to bear ; otherwise it was likely to cause no little mental anguish, for flowing locks were highly prized by the freemen of the race,[7] the shaved head being a mark of slavery.[8] The great change from the outward darkness of the world to the light and happiness of religion might be further emphasised by the adoption of a new name,[9] a feature constantly met with at Lérins.[10] In

---

[1] Ib.

[2] Cass., *Inst.* iv, 3, p. 50 : "experimentum constantiae suae."

[3] Ib.

[4] *Reg. Pach.* xlix, Albers, 29 : "experimentum dabit, ne forte aliquid fecerit, et turbatus ad horam timore discesserit." St. Benedict (*Reg.*, ed. Butler, c. lvii) requires four or five days of trial before the applicant is allowed into the *cella hospitum*. There he is kept some further days before he is admitted into the *cella novitiorum*. St. Isidore (*Reg. Mon.*, c. 4. P.L. lxxxi) requires that three months be spent in the service of the guests before the noviceship proper is entered.

[5] *Adam.* i, 36, p. 66 ; ii, p. 39, 156. Cf. supra, p. 213 n. 1. Also *V.S.H.* ii, 83 : "secularem habitum deseruit." Ib. p. 62 : "habitum monachi et tonsuram suscepit." Jonas : *Vita Col.* ii,, 7, p. 242–243.

[6] *Lism. L.*, p. 7, l. 213," berrad manaig." *V.S.H.* ii, p. 62, supra, note 5. Jonas : *V. Col.* ii, 9, p. 251. Bede : *H.E.* iii, 27, p. 189 : "questio non minima." *Lism. L.*, p. 78, l. 263.

[7] Cf. *V.S.H.* i, p. 254 : "comam pulcherrimam habebat, quam valde diligens nutriebat omni cura." Ib., p. 214, note 4.

[8] Cf. *Ériu* ii, p. 22. *Silva Gad.* i, 83 ; Keating, *Forus Feasa*, ed. Dinneen ii, p. 224.

[9] *V.S.H.* i, p. 68 ; *B.N.E.* i, p. 12 : "Loán to Findbarr." Stokes (*Lism. L.*, p. 300-1) prints from *LL.*, p. 354, c. 4, a list of 18 other saints who thus changed their names. A new and complete edition of this list is promised by P. Grosjean in *Irish Texts*.

[10] Faustus of Riez : "et nomen et habitum mutavimus," constantly in sermons.

the early days of the sixth century, before the monasteries
were well established, the novice might also be asked to build
his own cell,[1] but in this work he would probably have an
abundance of zealous helpers.[2] Those who mistook the
monastery for a place of moderate comfort or ease would
very soon be disillusioned, and we are not surprised to hear,
in one case at least, of a disappointed young man who took
to his heels under cover of darkness after a stay of ten
days.[3]

A special official charged with the care of novices is never
mentioned ; nor need this cause any surprise, for what the
novice had to learn could be mastered to a great degree by
imitation. If he wanted to become a monk he had but to do
as monks did. One of the elderly brethren or *seniores* would,
no doubt, be set over the newcomer, to give him needful
instruction and see that he was earnest in the practice of
virtue, but no elaborate system can be discovered even in
the most populous monasteries—no system, for instance,
like that ascribed to the Pachomian congregation by Cassian
and Palladius. According to these the novice served for a
year the *senior* who administered the guest-house. At the
end of that period, if he proved suitable, he was passed on
to a *senior* placed by the Abbot in complete control of ten
iuniores. Only after three years of probation was the novice
allowed to join the community.[4] The arrangement in Ireland
was more simple, though the training was not less strict, for
on these first years depended the success or failure of the
normal candidate's vocation to the monastic life.

Between the *senior* and the youthful novice the relation
would be chiefly that of spiritual father and spiritual child.
By word and example, the older would teach the younger
that the purpose in becoming a monk was " to cleave to God
and Him alone here on earth."[5] And as God had redeemed
the world through the merits of His Son Who " having loved
His own who were in the world, loved them to the end "

---

[1] *Lism. L.*, p. 25, l. 848.
[2] As in the Thebaid, where Or and his companions helped to build cells
for newcomers—one cutting wood, another carrying the bricks, another
spreading the mud, etc. *Hist. Mon.*, ch. 2.
[3] *V.S.H.* ii, p. 100.
[4] Cass., *Inst.* iv, 7, p. 52. Pallad., *H.L.* 32.
[5] *Reg. Coen.*, xv, p. 234. *MNP.* : " Uni adhaerere Deo hac in tellure."

(John xiii. 1), intimate union with Christ[1] and love of His Cross[2] should be the primary object of the novice's labours. He must reproduce the likeness of Christ within himself.[3] Nature, of course, has no enthusiasm for this high aim and stands in the way of its achievement, so that no progress can be recorded until nature is trampled under foot. The great advantage of a monastic rule was that it did this systematically. Thus the soul in time would be purged of worldly attachments and become really Christ-like. It would then be able to penetrate into the mysterious depths of God's revealed word and devote itself exclusively to divine contemplation. This theory of the religious life, formulated splendidly by Cassian,[4] was accepted in Ireland.[5] It led directly to the hermitage, for the monk, once the process of purification was complete, had little further need for cenobitical exercises and might consider himself impeded by the society of his

---

[1] Cf. Jonas : V. Col. 27, p. 212 : "Columban's courtier companions seek provisions without success from their friends in Mainz. Then Columban says : 'Sinite me inquit paululum ad meum abire amicum. Progressus ille ad ecclesiam pergit," with the most satisfactory results. The principle finds excellent expression in St. Athanasius, V. Ant. P.L. lxxiii, ch. 13, col. 134 : "omnibus suadens nihil amori Christi anteponendum esse." Also in St. Jerome Ep., 22, c. 39, p. 205-6 : "Love of Christ is the driving force behind the monk and virgin." Cf. likewise the Instructions of St. Basil, all modelled on the example, teaching, life and renunciation of Christ.

[2] Jonas : V. Col. ii, 13, p. 263 : "quae crucifixae mundo, Christo, non sibi vivunt." Ib., p. 281 : " post rerum amissionem nudus tollendo crucem ac sibimetipsi abnegando secutus est Christum." St. Jerm. Ep. iii, 14. C.S.E.L. liv, p. 15.

[3] Sermon iv of St. Columban, Z.K.G. xiv, p. 89 : "ne forte nobis tyrannicas introducamus imagines, Christus in nobis pingat suam imaginem."

[4] Cass. Conl. xiv, 1, p. 398-9 : "(Disciplina nostrae religionis) cuius quidem deplex scientia—prima est πρακτική, id est 'actualis,' quae emendatione morum et vitiorum purgatione perficitur ; altera θεωρετική quae in contemplatione divinarum rerum et sacratissimorum sensuum cognitione consistit." Cf. Ib., Conl. ix, 2, p. 250-1 : "Omnis monachi finis cordisque perfectio ad iugem atque indisruptam orationis perseverantiam tendit et quantum humanae fragilitati conceditur ad immobilem tranquillitatem mentis ac perpetuam nititur puritatem ob quam omnem, tam laborem corporis, quam contritionem spiritus, indefesse quaerimus et iugiter exercemus." Cf. Rothenhäusler : "Beiträge zur Gesch. des alten Mönchtums. Heft," 3, p. 52-71. St. Basil : Reg. fus. tract. clvii.

[5] Col. Reg. Mon., ch. iv, p. 376-7 : "ideo ergo nuditas et facultatum contemptus prima perfectio est monachorum ; secunda vero purgatio vitiorum ; tertia perfectissima Dei continuata dilectio ac divinorum iugis amor." Even the terms are adopted into Irish. Cf. Thes. Paleoh. i., p. 572. Wb. 12a23 : "Mad inaeclis tra in choss ishé óis achtáil et ind laám ishé óis achtáil as máa alailiu.—In the Church the foot is those who are in the Purgative Way, and the hand is those in the Purgative Way who are more than others." Ib. 12a24 : "óis teóair (gl. oculus)—those who are in the Contemplative Way." Cf. Ib. 12a31 : "vir teoricae vitae." Ib. 12a32 : "viro achtuali.—Those in the Contemplative Way are compared with the more noble members of the body, like the eye ; those in the Purgative Way with the less noble members, like the foot." 1 Cor. xii, 23-4. Lism. L., p. 30 ; "tri l. ri teóir ocus lx. ri achtáil."

brethren. But the line between cenobites and anchorites was not too rigidly drawn. In the first place, given the frailty of human nature, the work of purgation might occupy the greater part of a lifetime. In the second place, owing to the same cause, uninterrupted contemplation might tax the body beyond its strength and compel the anchorites to return once more to the varied life of the monastery. If, then, the author of the *Catalogue* designates the *ordo sanctus* or Third Order of Irish Saints (A.D. 598–664) as anchorites " who dwelt in desert places, and lived on herbs and water and by alms, for the idea of possessing anything of their own was repugnant to them,"[1] we must understand this to mean that the tendency to retire to a solitary life was more marked in the seventh century than earlier. The tendency was present from the beginning and was followed out in practice during longer or shorter periods by the saints of the First[2] and Second Orders.[3] On the other hand the leaders of the Irish Church who belong to the Third Order were not exclusively hermits, established in the desert since their youth and without monastic or other connections. Amongst them is Ultan of Ard Breccáin, a bishop, noted in Irish history for his literary and antiquarian interests, for he was the teacher of Tírechán, St. Patrick's biographer, and had placed at that writer's disposal a valuable manuscript account of the Apostle's doings.[4] Amongst them, again, was the priest Féichín, founder of a famous monastery at Fobar, and celebrated as an abbot and preacher, not as an anchorite, though he did on occasion retire for prayer to a secluded oratory on a hill-top.[5] Remarkable also is the fact that of the eighty prominent ecclesiastics, whose death is recorded in the *Annals of Ulster* within the century A.D.

---

[1] H. and S., *Councils* ii, p. 293.
[2] *B. Arm. Tir.* 26b : " et exiit Patricius ad cacumine montis super Crochan et mansit ibi xl diebus et xl noctibus." Ib. 22b : " Asicus retired to the North et fuit vii annis in insula quae vocatur Rochuil retro montem lapidum." *Tr. Thau.*, p. 520 : " Conlaeth was brought from solitude to become bishop of Kildare."
[3] *Adam.* ii, 26, p. 138 : " (Columcille) paulo longius solus, orationis intuitu, separatus a fratribus, silvam ingressus densam," etc. Cf. iii, 8, p. 205. Jonas : *V. Col.* i, 17, p. 185 : " (Columban) cum in eremo vel ieiunio vel oratione vacans deambularet," etc. Ib. p. 181 : " solitudinis amator." *V.S.H.* i, p. 165 : " (Cainnech) recessit a fratribus in aliqua silva, et occulte latebat," etc., etc. Cf. Theodoret *Hist. Relig.*, P.G. lxxxii, c. 1310-14. St Julian Sabbas, an abbot in Mesopotamia, used to leave his monks for eight and ten days at a time. Cass., *Conl.* xiv, 9, p. 544.
[4] *B. Arm. Tir.*, 17b : " ex ore vel libro Ultani episcopi, cuius ipse alumnus vel discipulus fuit."
[5] *V.S.H.* ii, 83.

600–700, only two are stated to have been anchorites.[1] In the other seventy-eight cases the title bishop or abbot is used without qualification. Documents belonging to the period do not differ from the *Annals* in this respect.[2] The conclusion is that bishops and priests retired more frequently than formerly to the wood or mountain for a season of solitary prayer, but that the sharp distinction drawn by the writer of the *Catalogue* between the Second and Third Orders is unjustified.

But the young novice just entering on his new life would waste few thoughts on the desert and its attractions. All his attention, at the moment, was fixed on the practical problem of purifying the heart of its disorderly affections.[3] He had divested himself of whatever goods he possessed before he put on the monastic habit,[4] but property was an external and therefore a minor obstacle only on the way to perfection. The real bonds that bound the soul to earth—the cravings within itself for worldly pleasures and worldly honours—must now be severed. As chief means to this end ascetical tradition, since the days of St. Anthony, had recognized prayer (public and private), study of God's word, fasts and manual work.[5] The virtues which he must cultivate, above

---

[1] *A.U.* 609: Aedán, Anchorite of Bangor. 699: Aed of Sléibte.

[2] From Bede, *H.E.* ii, c. 2, p. 83, we learn that the British bishops who met Augustine in Canterbury in conference at Augustine's Oak consulted a pious anchorite as to their line of conduct. Anchorites were thus held in honour in the British church before the end of the sixth century. Again, the Paschal Letter of Cumméne to Segéne, Abbot of Iona (A.D. 634), was addressed also to Becán the hermit (Ussher, *Works* iv, p. 432). For further instances of hermits in Ireland at this period Cf. *Adam.* i, 49, p. 95 ; iii, 49, p. 237 (Fergne, after many years as a monk, spent twelve years in solitude). Cf. Bede, *H.E.* v, 9 and 12. On the other hand the letter of Laurentius, Archbishop of Canterbury (605–19), to the Irish clergy (Bede, *H.E.* ii, 4, p. 37–8) is addressed to bishops and abbots only. Similarly, the letter of Pope-Elect John IV, A.D. 640, is addressed to bishops, priests and doctors. Again, in the long list of clergy who were guarantors for the *Cáin Adamnáin* (Ed. Meyer, p. 28–30), A.D. 697, the title anchorite is never given. See below, p. 256 ff.

[3] Cass., *Conl.* i 4, p. 10 : " puritas cordis."

[4] Cass., *Inst. V.* 3, p. 50. Jonas, *V. Col.* ii, 23,p. 231.

[5] Athan, *Vita. Ant.*, ch. 21, P.L. lxxiii, col. 146 ; " erant igitur in monte monasteria tanquam tabernacula, plena divinis choris psallentium, legentium, orantium ; tantumque ieiunandi et vigilarum ardorem cunctorum mentis sermo eius efflaverat ut," etc. Cf. Ib. col. 141. St. Jer *Ep.*, 39, 5, p. 304 : " nunc vero cum sciam toto renuntiasse te mundo et abiectis calcatisque deliciis orationi, ieiuniis, lectioni vacare cotidie," etc. Cass., *Inst.* iii, 2, p. 34 : " work and prayer never cease in monasteries." Cf. *Conl.* xviii, 2, p. 508. Jonas, *V. Col.* i, 4, p. 159: " Ibi (in Bangor) solis orationibus et ieiuniis vacare coepit et iugum Christi . . . super se ferre." It was, of course, clearly understood that these were but a means to an end, " non perfectio, sel perfectionis instrumenta." Cass., *Conl.* i, 7, p. 14.

all by imitation of the older brethren, are enumerated by
St. Jerome in a passage so apt that it was incorporated by
St. Columban in his Rule. " Let the monk," says the great
Doctor of the Church, " live under the authority of one
paternal ruler and in company with many brethren so that
from one he may learn humility, from another patience,
let one teach him silence, another gentleness of manner. He
must not do what he wants to do ; he must eat what is placed
before him ; he must have nothing but what he has received ;
he must perform the task assigned to him, and show submission
to one whom he does not like. He should be tired out before
he goes to rest and be half-asleep while still on his feet, and
be compelled to get up before his need for sleep has been
satisfied. When he is insulted he must listen without a word.
He must fear his superior as a lord, but love him as a father,
and must believe that whatever he orders is for his good.
The judgment of anybody placed over him he must never
criticize, for it is his duty to obey and to do what he is told,
according to the words of Moses, ' Hear, O Israel,' " etc.[1]
" Observe, admire, obey," may thus be given as the noviceship watchwords.[2] Diligence and industry would be rewarded
by a daily increase in prudence and spiritual wisdom, as
well as in grace and virtue.[3] It was taken as a first principle,
as all documents of this period show, that the aim should
be heroic, not high merely[4] and that it should be reached
some day by everybody. The ideal must not remain an ideal ;
it must be realized. In Irish monasticism there was no place
for mediocrity. Here lies its great strength and its great
weakness as an institution that strove to extend and perpetuate
itself in an indifferent and ease-loving world.

Almost cruel, then, was the earnestness with which the
novice applied himself to the work of subjugating his passions.
If wars could not be avoided they could at least be won.[5]

---

[1] St. Jer. *Ep.* 25, *ad Rusticum monachum*, ch. 14. *Col. Reg. Mon.*, ch. x.
Z.K.G. xv, p. 386. Cf. *Verba Seniorum* P.L. lxxiii, col. 769.

[2] Cass., *Conl.* xiv, 9, p. 408 : " hic est enim primus actualis ingressus ut
omnium seniorum instituta atque sententias intento corde et quasi muto
ore suscipias ac diligenter in pectore tuo condens ad perficienda ea potius
quam ad docenda festines." Cf. *Conl.* xviii, 2, p. 508.

[3] Cf. *Adam.* i, 3, p. 25 : " bonisque moribus et animae virtutibus paulatim
de die in diem crescet ; sapientia quoque et prudentia magis ac magis in
eo ab hac die adaugebitur."

[4] As St. Jerome had demanded, *Ep.* 58, 11, p. 540 : " Nihil in te mediocre
contentus sum : totum summum, totum perfectum desidero."

[5] St. Jer. *Ep.*, 52, s., p. 417 : " sed quod adulescentia multa corporis bella
sustineat et inter incentiva vitiorum et carnis titillationes quasi ignis in
lignis viridioribus suffocetur, et suum non possit explicare fulgorem."

The eight principal vices,[1] enumerated first by Evagrius Ponticus[2] and recognised as their foremost enemies by the monks everywhere, were attacked with ruthless vigour.[3] Offences falling under these heads and any other sins of which he might have been guilty were confessed by the novice to a priest at the beginning of his novitiate.[4] Afterwards, too, during his whole life as a novice and as a monk a confession of all faults, the petty as well as the grave, in thought[5] as well as in act, was demanded at regular intervals.[6] In Ireland at all times the *anamchara* or spiritual guide who heard such confessions was probably a priest, empowered to give his penitent sacramental absolution, though confession to a distinguished *senior* who was not a priest might be practised on occasion as an ascetical exercise. In monasteries for women confession of the latter type to the abbess, for purposes of guidance, might be recommended or even exacted.[7] This institution, too, had behind it the whole weight of monastic tradition, for it is found in the desert since the days of St. Anthony.[8] Cassian gives an excellent account of the purpose for which the custom was introduced. " True discretion," he says, quoting what the Abbot Moses said, or might have said, " is impossible without true humility. And the first proof of humility is to submit to the judgment of the elders

---

[1] Gluttony (γαστριμαρία) ; Lust (πορνεία) ; Covetousness (φιλαργυρία) ; Sorrow (λύπη) ; Anger (ὀργή) ; Spiritual Disgust (ἀκηδία) ; Vanity (κενοδοχία) ; Pride (ὑπερηφανία).

[2] *Z.K.G.* xviii, p. 602.

[3] Cass., *Conl.* v, 1, p. 121 ; v, 25, p. 145. An Irish tract on these from *Rawl. B.* 512 is published in *Z.C.P.* iii, p. 24, ff. Cf. Comgall's Rule, *Eriu* i 191 ff. Stanza 10 : " na h-ocht n-airig dualchae, oircte anmain cech duine."

[4] Cf. *Adam.* ii, 20, p. 157.

[5] *Reg. Coen.* xv, p. 232 *MNP. Paenit. Col.*, p. 441a. Cass., *Conl.* 1, 17, p. 26.

[6] Jonas : *V. Col.* ii, 3, p. 235 ; ii, 17, p. 269. *Reg. Coen.*, ch. 1 : confession twice a day. *V.S.H.* i, p. 72 ; ii, p. 106, 147, 216 : " Peccavi vere hodie quia confessionem alicui seniori non feci de iis quae ego egi hodie." 217 : " Sicut enim pavimentum scopha cotidie tergitur ita anima cotidiana confessione." *Martyr. Oeng.*, p. 94 : "tabair do choibsena, for Mochuta." Ib., p. 94, 120–2 is the adage that a soul without a confessor (anamchara) is a body without a head. Introd. to Ultan's hymn (*Thes. Paleo.* ii, p. 324) : " rochuinnig (Brenainn) cuicce (Brigit) co tartrad a coibsena cinnas roboi grád Dé aicce. Atrubart Brigit fri Brenainn ' tabair, a chlérig, do chobais *prius* . . .' Brenainn asked Brigit to manifest her conscience, as to how the love of God was with her. Brigit said to Brenainn : " Make manifest thou thy conscience first . . ." References in the later ecclesiastical literature are likewise very common. Cf. *Rule of Ailbe*, Stanza 10. *Rule of Mochuta* (whole section— Do Anamcharaid sonn). " The Monastery of Tallaght," ed, Gwynn and Purton, *P.R.I.A.*, vol. xxix, Sect. 2, 23, 44, 54, etc. *Leabhar Breac*, 261a.

[7] Jonas : *V. Col.* ii, 13, p. 263 : "quod mane per confessionem humilem matri patefecit." Ib., p. 269 : "celataque vitia, matri per confessionem prodit." Ib., p. 272 : confession three times a day customary in monastery.

[8] Athan, *V. Ant.* P.L. lxxiii, col. 151. Cf. *Conl.* ii, 11, 13, p. 49, 57.

(*seniores*) not only what we propose to do, but even what we think, so that by agreement with their decisions in everything we may know what is right and what is wrong. In this way the young man will be taught to keep on the straight path and will be preserved from Satan's tricks and snares. For deception is impossible in the case of him who directs his life, not according to his own judgment, but according to that of his elders. Clever as the enemy is he will gain no advantage over one who is ignorant of false shame, who divulges each thought that arises in his heart to his elders, and is guided by their mature judgment in his every act. The bad thought shrivels up the moment it is made public, and even before the *senior* has had time to pronounce his wise verdict the horrid serpent (dragged by confession into the light from his gloomy underground cave) scurries off as best he can and with a lively sense of confusion. In fact his suggestions have the upper hand only as long as they are hidden in the heart."[1] As an illustration of this doctrine, Cassian cites the story of the Abbot Serapion, who, as a boy in the desert, had to wait with fast unbroken day by day until 3.0 p.m. By that hour his appetite had grown so powerful that it was whetted rather than satisfied by the unsubstantial hermit meal. Serapion accordingly used to await his opportunity and slip unnoticed a loaf of bread into the breast-fold of his dress. Later, while the master prayed, the hungry disciple enjoyed a modest collation. But one day some hermit guests arrived and the conversation after dinner turned on the vice of gluttony. Alas for Serapion! The purloined loaf became like a hot coal upon his breast as the master's language grew more and more eloquent. At last he could bear the pain no longer, so he threw himself on his knees before the astonished company, produced the loaf—and wept! From that day forward his boyish appetite caused him no further difficulty.[2]

The novice's discretion, that most precious of gifts,[3] was, therefore, to be manifested primarily by the alacrity with which he renounced his own will and allowed himself to be guided by his spiritual superiors.[4] Thus he was taught first

---

[1] Cass., *Conl.* ii, 10, p. 48–9.　　　　[2] Ib. ii, p. 49–50.

[3] Cass., *Conl.* i, 23, p. 35 : " quae inter cunctas virtutes arcem et primatum tenet."

[4] Ib. ii, 11, p. 51 : " ut seniorum vestigia subsequentes neque agere quicquam novi neque discernere nostro iudicio praesumamus . . . nullo namque alio vitio tam praecipitem diabolus monachum pertrahit ad mortem quam cum eum neglectis consiliis seniorum suo iudicio persuaserit definitionique confidere."

of all to conquer his own inclinations. Were he desirous to perform any particular act then he would be called upon to do exactly the opposite.[1] The gossip, according to St. Columban's Rule, is to be condemned to silence, the excessively active to restraint and quiet, the gluttonous to fasting, the sleepy-head to long vigils, the proud to the punishment cell, and the fugitive under vow is to be compelled by force to return.[2] No fault was so minute that it escaped attention,[3] but grave transgressions were distinguished carefully from venial[4]; and the system of manifestation and guidance ensured that a predominant vice would be made the object of special attack.[5] On the positive side, too, the life of earlier saints was held up for imitation ; the life of St. Martin, perhaps, above all others, at this period[6] ; and later of St. Brigid. The former, according to his biographer, was never angry, never worried, never sad, never frivolous, never gloomy of countenance. Christ was always on his lips, piety in his heart, peace and mercy in his actions.[7] He was pale and thin and had a lowly opinion of his own person, qualities that well befitted a monk.[8] " What gravity and dignity in his words and in his ordinary conversation, how much to the point and how effective was his speech, how quickly and easily he explained the meaning of Holy Writ."[9] St. Brigid was celebrated not merely for her burning love of God,[10] a love so intense that she could fix her mind upon nothing

---

[1] Cass. *Inst.* iv, 8, p. 52–3 : " suas vincere voluntates. Quae animo eius (sint) contraria."

[2] *Reg. Coen.* xv, p. 233, *MNP.*

[3] Ib. *passim* and *Paenit. Col.*, p. 446 : " de minutis monachorum agendum est sanctionibus."

[4] *Paenit. Col.*, p. 441, 4.

[5] As counselled by Cass., *Conl.* v, 14, p. 137 : " ut adversus illud (the principal vice) adripiat principale examen." The brethren were bound to draw attention to one another's faults. If the matter were shameful, it was to be manifested first to the culprit alone. *Reg. Coen.* xv, 231–2. *MNP.*

[6] *Adam.* iii, 12, p. 211. St. Martin was among the great saints commemorated during Mass in Iona. Jonas, *V. Col.* i, 22, p. 301. St. Columban, passing through Tours, spends a whole night in prayer at St. Martin's tomb. Cf. *V.S.H.* ii, p. 60, 136, etc. Cf. Reeves, op. cit., p. 325–6.

[7] *Vita Mart.*, 27, p. 136–7.

[8] *Verb. Seniorum*, P.L. lxxiii, col. 771 : " pallor enim et macies cum humilitate decus est monachi."

[9] *Vita M.*, 25, p. 135.

[10] *Lism. L.*, p. 29, l.976, ff. One day, walking in the Curragh and admiring the beautiful fields rich with clover blossoms, she said to herself that if these fields were hers she would offer them all to the Lord of the Elements. St. Colmcille, at Swords, heard her secret thought and cried out : " God is as pleased as if she did in fact own the fields and make this offering to Him."

else,[1] but also for her great charity towards her neighbour.
" She burned with the desire to feed the poor, to banish every
hardship, to show pity to everybody in misery,"[2] and her
alms-giving was such that it was said to have drawn protests
from her nuns, " Little, in all truth, is the benefit your charity
brings to us," they complained, " you give others food and
clothes and leave us without sufficiency of either."[3] Ciarán's
charity in his youth was likewise so great that the brethren
could not endure it. " Leave us," they said, in the words of
the legend, " for we cannot suffer thee in the same place with
us." So Ciarán put his book on a wild deer's horns and went.[4]
Again, when Tuathal Moelgarb, the High-King, gave Ciarán
his royal raiment the Saint of Clonmacnois bestowed it at
once upon the poor.[5]

The liberation of captives (in an age when wars and
captives were many) was likewise a work of mercy which
the monk was expected to have very much at heart. St.
Martin had set the good example.[6] St. Patrick speaks with
admiration of the Gallo-Romans, who redeemed Christian
captives at enormous cost from the heathen Franks and the
other invading tribes.[7] Faustus of Riez, for long a distinguished
Abbot at Lérins, was famous for his kindness to the same
sufferers, as well as to travellers and to all who needed
particular attention because of the difficulties in which they
were placed.[8] St. Brigid, as a matter of course, included
this amongst her good works. " Once," says the story, " she
went into the lands of Fir Rois (in South Monaghan) to release
a captive who was in the district   Said Brigid : ' Will'st thou
free the captive for my sake ? ' The King replied : ' Though
thou should'st give me the whole realm of Breg I would not

---

[1] *Thes. P.*, ii, p. 324. St. Brendan confessed that from the day he gave
himself to piety he had never gone over seven ridges without his mind on
God. St. Brigid then confesses " by the Son of the Virgin (that) from the day
she took to piety she had never for a moment taken her mind off God."
[2] *Lism. L.*, p. 50, l. 1690 : " ba hé a sainnt : sásad bocht, dichur gacha
documla, airchisecht gacha truaigh." Cf. p. 38, l.1252, etc.
[3] Ib., p. 48, l.1601–2.
[4] *Lism. L.*, p. 129, ll.4332–4.
[5] Ib.,p. 127, l.4270–4. This is obviously based on the celebrated deed
attributed to St. Martin, the cutting of his tunic in two, that he might give
half to the beggar. *Sulp. Sev. Dial.* i, p. 181. For further instances of Ciarán's
generosity see *V.S.H.* i, p. 202, 207, 208, 209, 229.
[6] Sulp. Sev. *Dial.* ii, p. 212 : " A man whose family St. Martin had cured
sent him an offering of 100 pounds in silver—sed priusquam pondus illud
limen adtingeret redimendis id captivis continuo deputavit."
[7] *Conf.*, § 14, p. 257.
[8] Goyau : *Hist. rel. de la nation française.* T. vi, p. 62.

give thee this prisoner.' "[1] But Brigid did succeed in releasing the unhappy man. Colmcille took a warm interest in the Ossory prince, Scandlán Mór, and promised him release whether the High King, Aed, son of Ainmire, his captor, willed it or no.[2] A remarkable scene in the life of St Columban tells how the Saint of Luxeuil arrived at Besançon, and, hearing that the gaol in that town was full of condemned men awaiting death, went off to preach to them. The sermon over, Columban asks if they would do penance and be good henceforward provided they were let free. When the expected answer was given Columban ordered his attendant, Domoel, to sever their chains. Then he washed their fee, according to the sacred Gospel precedent, and ordered them to go off to the church and weep for their crimes. News was soon brought to the horrified prison governor that the cells were empty and that his guests had gone for devotional exercises into the town. The hue and cry was raised, but when the governor and his soldiers met Columban and his monks matters were satisfactorily arranged and the prisoners were not dragged back to captivity.[3] Less striking instances of the same kind occur very frequently in the lives of other Irish saints.[4]

Not only during the early years of formation but even during after-life nobody might leave the monastic enclosure without permission.[5] Such, of course, would rarely, if ever, be conceded to the novice. For the trained brethren it was more easy to obtain, as is obvious from the fact that monks are constantly to be found on journeys. When thus engaged they would travel, if possible, in companies and take precautions for their reputation and their virtue.[6] But excursions abroad were of necessity uncommon and the monks, as a rule, had to live the long years of life in one another's company.

---

[1] *Lism. L.*, p. 45, l.1520–6.

[2] *Adam.* i, 11, p. 38–9. Ib. ii, 39, p. 159, it is stated that the girdle of a captive was unloosed in token of his liberation. For the collection of money to redeem captives there was a certain amount of canonical legislation. Wassersch, *I.K.* xlii, 25, 26, p. 169.

[3] Jonas, *Vita Col.* i, 19, p. 192–3.

[4] Plummer *V.S.H. Introd.*, p. cxxxix.

[5] *Reg. Coen.* viii, p. 225, *MP.* : To go *extra sepem monasterii* without permission was punished.

[6] *Reg. Coen.* xiii, p. 230, *MP.* : "si quis monachus in una domo cum muliere dormierit duos dies in pane et aqua." Cf. Ib., p. 232, *MNP. Catalogue*, H. and S. *Councils*, p. 292. Plummer, *V.S.H. Introd.*, p. cxxi. *Regula Isaiae*, ch. i, PL. ciii, c. 429. Cass., *Conl.* vii, 26, p. 205 : the very figure of a woman was regarded as detestable.

Everything in consequence depended on the spirit of religion and fraternal charity that prevailed amongst them. That their love for one another was a constant theme in the mouth of Colmcille is clear from his last instructions. " These, dearest children, are my dying words to you, love each the other with a genuine love and live together in peace. If you do this, according to the example given you by the holy fathers God, Who comforts the good, will aid you ; and I, when I abide with Him, will make intercession for you. Not only then will He provide you with a sufficiency of earthly goods, but He will bestow on you likewise His eternal rewards, prepared for those who do His will."[1] St. Columban has a special instruction, still preserved, on this subject and interesting as an example of the addresses delivered by him to his monks Having dwelt on the two great commandments of the Law (Matt xxii. 37 ; 1 John ii. 19), and pointed out with St John that charity to be genuine must be shown by deeds (John iii 1), he goes on to contend that the true follower of Christ must take heed of the words " My peace I leave you my peace I give you " (John xiv. 27). " But what doth it avail to know that peace is good if peace is not maintained ? Things of the h ghest value are often fragile and things that are precious require to be protected with greater care. Now you may well call that fragile which is crushed by a passing word and is utterly destroyed by a tiny injury to a brother. . . Those who would observe fraternal charity must, therefore, guard against saying whatever occurs to their minds and giving expression to the lightest thought, seeing that we shall have to render an account for our idle words as well as for those that are positively harmful. We must try then not to talk much but to restrict ourselves to what is absolutely needed, for there is nothing sweeter to human nature than to discuss other people's business and to settle other people's affairs, to talk irresponsibly and give a bad time to the absent. Those who cannot say ' God has given me an eloquent tongue that I may assist the weary with my words ' (Isaias i, 4) should keep silence. If they will speak let them at least say something that makes for concord. No matter how wise a man is, if he says much, he says much that were better left unsaid. When anybody speaks falsely or dilates on another's faults or wishes another ill, he slays himself with his own weapon ; and what

---

[1] Adam. iii, 23, p. 234.

more could our worst enemy wish than this? ' Avoid
detraction,' says Holy Writ, ' lest you be plucked up by the
roots ' (Prov. xx. 13). Look at the fruits of labour that is not
to God's glory—what was planted with difficulty and only
after long and intense effort is dragged up by one word of
detraction. The building raised by patient toil is levelled
by one sentence. Each should, therefore, see to it that he
is not plucked up by the root through detraction springing
from hate ; for nobody dwells on the faults of him whom he
loves. Detraction in fact is the first-born babe of hate, and
as the progeny of such a sire is rightly obliterated. Alas !
my dearly beloved, for the house in which these faults are
not shunned. ' For if,' as the Apostle says (Gal. v 15), ' you
envy one another and bite one another (by detraction, I mean),
take care that you are not consumed by one another.' If
he who does not love lives in death what shall I say of him
who is guilty of detraction ? His unhappy state is described
better by tears than by words. For if there is one thing on
which God insists in Holy Scripture it is love ; and yet how
rarely do we find anybody who fulfils the divine command !
What excuse have we to offer ? Shall we say, ' it is too much
of a bother ; it is altogether too hard ? ' But love surely
is not wearisome ; rather is it sweet and healthy and helpful
to the heart. If in a word the heart were not sick with vices,
love (and the knowledge that it is pleasing to God) would
be its most wholesome sustenance. For nothing pleases God
better than spiritual love, chiefly because it is the sum of
His Commandments, according to the saying of the Apostle
(Rom. xiii. 8), ' he who loves his neighbour fulfils the law.'
He again who has fulfilled the law by cultivating this spiritual
love has eternal life, as St. John says, ' Brethren we know
that we have passed from death to life, because we love the
brethren. For he who loves not is in death. If there is anyone
who hates he is a murderer, and you know that the murderer
has not eternal life within him ' (1 John iii. 13–5). We must
do nothing therefore save love or hope for nothing save
punishment for ' charity is the fulfilment of the law ' (Rom.
xiii. 10). May Our Lord and Saviour Jesus Christ bestow
that grace abundantly upon us, He who deigned to give

Himself to us as the author of our peace and the God of love. To Him be glory for ever and ever. Amen."[1]

Elsewhere, too, St. Columban treats detraction as a most serious fault.[2] He who listened to the detractor without signifying disapproval was regarded as equally guilty.[3] Great care must be taken that no vengeful or envious feelings be harboured against a brother.[4] Should contention arise between any two they should compose their differences at once. Should one be ready to forgive and forget, whilst the other insists on laying the matter before the superior, the former, though the guilty party in the first instance, was to be punished only with the recitation of psalms ; whilst the latter, though the aggrieved person in the first instance was to repent for a day of his unforgiving spirit on a diet of bread and water.[5] If the feeling roused was such that one remained obstinate in contradicting the other, the delinquent was to be excommunicated temporarily from the society of the brethren.[6] If a brother was openly at fault any brother present might reprove him,[7] lest another fault of the same kind be committed. The brother so addressed had to ask pardon at once.[8] He was not allowed to tender an excuse,[9] still less to answer " you are another ! " and call the corrector's attention to some fault which he, too, might remedy.[10] In Bangor, indeed, the monk, irrespective of guilt, had to receive

---

[1] *Instr.* iv : " De dilectione spirituali." *Z.K.G.* xiv, p. 87–92. Cf. St. Aug. *Ep.*, 211 ; *C.S.E.L.* lvii, p. 369 : " non autem carnalis sed spiritualis inter vos debet esse dilectio," and Ib. p. 366 : " Caritas sic intellegitur quia communia propriis, non propria communibus, anteponit," and Ib. p. 593 : " primum propter quod estis in unum congregatæ, ut unanimes habitetis in domo, et sit vobis cor unum et anima una in Deum." St. Martin is praised for his peace-loving spirit, *Vita M.*, 26, p. 136 : " vir beatus, in quo dolus non fuit, neminem iudicans, neminem damnans, nulli malum pro malo reddens."

[2] *Reg. Coen.* vii, p. 224 *MP.*

[3] Ib.

[4] Ib. xiv, p. 231. *MP.* Cf. St. Aug. *Ep.*, 211. *C.S.E.L.* lvii, p. 368 : " quaecumque vel convicio vel maledicto vel etiam criminis objectu alteram laeserit meminerit satisfactione curare quantocius quod fecit ; et illa, quae laesa est, dimittere. Si autem invicem se laeserunt, invicem sibi debita relaxare debebunt."

[5] Ib. xii, p. 230, *MP.*

[6] Ib. vi, p. 223 *MP.* Cf. St. Aug. ut supra, p. 369 : " melior est enim, quae quamvis ira saepe temptatur, tamen impetrare festinat, ut sibi dimittat quam quae tardius irascitur et ad veniam petendam difficilius inclinatur."

[7] *Reg. Coen.* vi, p. 223, *MP.*

[8] *Reg. Coen.* viii, p. 225 *MP.*.

[9] Ib. iv, 223 ; v, 223 *MP.* : " consilium contra consilium."

[10] Ib. vi, p. 224, *MP.* : " castigans castigantem se."

rebuke on bended knee.[1] Murmuring was looked upon with especial disfavour, owing to the evil effect it was calculated to have on the whole community.[2] Conversation that might disturb the serenity of the soul was of course discountenanced.[3] Modesty and respect should characterize the brethren in their relations with one another ; and if harshness was to be avoided,[4] so too was an excessive softness that might lead to unspeakable disorders.[5] The manifestation of another's serious faults to the superior seems to have been common,[6] and a visitor might be sent round to see how all were conducting themselves.[7] Though fervour might lead to extravagance and thus defeat its own end the brethren were not to interfere with one another in such matters by usurping the functions of " soul friend."[8] Truth was insisted on so strongly that unintentional error in assertion was punished by St. Columban.[9] Even politic silence was unknown to the patriarch of Luxeuil,

---

[1] *V.S.H.* ii, 11, p. 23 : "Mos erat in monasteriis sancti Comgalli ut si quis alium increparet, quamvis ille esset culpabilis aut inculpabilis statim qui increpabatur genua humiliter flecteret."

[2] *Reg. Coen.* xiii, p. 225, *MNP.*

[3] *Reg. Coen.* xi, p. 229, *MP.* : " Bilinguis (qui) conturbet corda fratrum, e.g. by telling of a past sin or of a sin committed in the world."

[4] *V.S.H.* ii, p. 98 : " cave ne alii per rigorem tuum scandalizentur, quia testa fragilior alia testa est." Ib., p. 20 : " Comgall was afflicted with several diseases before his death, and some of the brethren said that these were inflicted by God—propter duritiam et asperitatem regulae eius." But the *Antiphonary of Bangor* shows that the Rule was loved. The notice, however, that it was exceptionally severe is credible, for Comgall was a disciple of Fintan of Cluain Eidnech, whose Rule was admittedly trying. This must be remembered in judging Columban's Rule : the Saint of Luxeuil came from Bangor and represents almost certainly the stricter side of the strict Irish tradition.

[5] *Reg. Coen.* viii, p. 229 : "ne quis alterius teneat manum." Cf. Cass., *Inst.* ii, 15, p. 30 : " Summa namque observantia custoditur ne quisquam cum alio ac praecipue iuniores vel ad punctum temporis pariter substitisse aut uspiam recessisse vel manus suas invicem tenuisse deprehendantur." The punishment for this was very severe. The regulation doubtless goes back to the earliest times. Cf. *Reg. Pachomii,* Albers 55. Modesty in washing is inculcated, *Paenit. Col. Z.K.G.* xiv, p. 447–8.

[6] *Reg. Coen.* vii, p. 224, *MP.* xv, 231, *MNP.* Cf. *Ériu* vii, p. 158, § 21. St. Augustine lays down the principle, *Ep.* 21, p. 365 : "cum dilectione hominum et odio vitiorum."

[7] *Lism. L.,* p. 79, l.2646. Finnian sends his boy Sennach to see what each monk was doing. In *Vita Flannani (Anal. Boll.* xlvi, p. 125) the cellarer sends a messenger to see how the novice Flannan was working in the mill. In Egypt cells were visited systematically during the night, and ears were cocked against the doors to discover what the occupants were doing. St. Jerome *Ep.* 22, 35, p. 199.

[8] *Reg. Coen.* xv, p. 233, *MNP.*

[9] *Reg. Coen.* xiii, p. 230 *MP.* Caesarius of Arles held this vice in particular odium. *Reg. Mon.,* c. 5 : " mentiri qui inventus fuerit disciplinam legitimam accipiat." The discipline in question consisted of forty stripes save one. Only in one other case (coming late to prayer) did Caesarius resort to corporal punishment. Arnold : *Caesarius von A.,* p. 99.

who smashed to pieces before the astonished courtiers' eyes
gifts sent by the immoral king[1] Theuderich ; who refused
to bless the same king's children, on the ground that they
were of illegitimate birth[2] ; and who proclaimed at Tours,
in presence of a faithful subject of Theuderich, the reason
for his expulsion from Burgundy : " because that dog of a
Theuderich drove me away from my brethren."[3]   But Irish
Kings, for better or for worse, were less violently exhorted
by their subject saints than were Columban's Merovingians.

That he might advance the more easily in humility, the
most difficult to acquire of the Christian virtues,[4] the young
novice would be set to perform various menial offices.   For
these a technical term was developed taken from the British
language.[5]   The washing of the feet (outside the monastery,
no doubt, the exclusive duty of slaves), was regarded as the
type of this lowly service.[6]   A chance reference shows us that
the water used was heated.[7]   In general the monk should
consider everyone better than himself,[8] and should be on his
guard lest any or all of his good practices prove an occasion
for vainglory.[9]   Gildas, as we have seen, speaks with contempt
of those " who eat bread by measure, and boast of the fact
beyond measure."[10]   How thoroughly even a great man could
efface himself in a monastery is illustrated by the history of
St. Caesarius of Arles.   Caesarius spent nine years at Lérins,
yet of these nine years we know but three incidents : he was

[1] Jonas : Vita Col. i, 19, p. 189.
[2] Ib., p. 188.
[3] Ib. 22, p. 202 : " Canis me Theudericus meis a fratribus abegit."
[4] Instr. Col. i, Z.K.G. xiv, p. 79 : " Superbiam, primum vitium, primo
ante omnia vende, et eme inde feliciter humilitatem, qua sis Christo similis,
dicenti : discite a me quia mitis sum et humilis corde."—(Matt. xi, 29.)
But a certain esprit de corps is permitted by St. Jerome : Ep. xvii, 16, p. 163 :
"'disce in hac parte superbiam sanctam ; scito te illis esse meliorem." Cf.
Cassian's long disquisition, Inst. iv, 39, p. 75 ff.
 [5] Umaldóit : Welsh ufylldod, old Cornish h:veldot, Breton vueldet, from
Latin humilitat-em (Pedersen : Vergl. Gramm. ii, p. 42).   For examples of
use cf. Lism. L., p. 35, l.1177 : " the bondmaid did umulóit and service
for them," ll. 1342, 1436, 1531, 2564, 4045, 5255, also Rev. Celt. ii, p. 388 :
" Oenmog trá nammá ised robui oc Martain ⁊ ba h-é Martain dognid umalóit
doside im ghait a iallacrand de ⁊ im nige a chos ⁊ im chumaid bid fris ciarbo
tigerna hé.   Martin had one slave only, and it was Martin who used to render
umalóit to him, taking off his sandals, and washing his feet and sitting down
to food with him, though he (Martin) was the master."   Cf. Vita Mart., 25,
p. 135.
 [6] Lism. L. p. 48, l.1623.
 [7] V.S.H. i, p. 213.
 [8] Reg. Cocn. v. p. 223, MP. : " alter alterum existimans superiorem sibi."
 [9] St. Jer. Ep., 22, 27, p. 132–3 : " ne gloriam fugiendo quaeras." Cf. Sulp.
Sev. Dial. i, 20, p. 172–3.
[10] Wassersch, I.K. lxvi, 9, p. 237–8.

appointed cellarius, found unsuitable and dismissed from office ; his health gave way and he was advised in consequence to leave the island and go to Arles to recuperate.[1] The monk, indeed, might appropriate to himself the ideal expressed by St. Jerome in another connection, to be first in the excellence of his service, last in the extent to which that service was acknowledged.[2]

During the time allowed for converse with the brethren it was assumed that the topics discussed should belong predominantly to the spiritual order. Human nature found considerable difficulty in this. Cassian speaks with admiration of a saintly old man who always went to sleep when the conversation turned on worldly things, but woke up promptly when a spiritual subject was introduced. For many of the brethren, he admits with sorrow, the charisma took the opposite form : they were all ears while the conversation was worldly, but went to sleep promptly the moment spiritual conversation commenced.[3] It was, however, inevitable, especially during the period of formation, that the matters discussed should deal chiefly with the monastic profession. Columban, in the Instructions that have survived from his pen, gives us an idea of the thoughts with which the minds of the monks were filled. " Remember, man, what thou art, and what one day thou shalt be. For what thou art, thou art but for an instant ; whilst what thou shalt be, thou shalt be for ever. Win now in the fleeting moment of time what thou shalt possess for eternity. The rewards to come are indeed such that they should induce you to triumph over the hardships of the godly life. Follow realities, not the pleasant likeness in the pool, not the alluring riches of the dream. Sell your vices and buy eternal life."[4] How again can we fly the world to which we ought to die, if the world is within us in the shape of evil desire ? By conquering ourselves, by dying to vice before we die in body. During life fear death and the eternal fire which lies beyond death ; which indeed you cannot see, but you believe in Him Who does see it and Who tells no falsehood, Our Lord Jesus Christ,

---

[1] Arnold, *Caes. von Arel*, p. 47. No wonder, then, that of St. Patrick's life at Lérins, three generations earlier, so little is known.
[2] St. Jer. *Ep.*, 60, 10, p. 560 : " inter presbyteros et coaequales primus in opere, extremus in ordine."
[3] Cass., *Inst.* v, 29–31, p. 103–5.
[4] *Instr. Col.* i, *Z.K.G.* xiv, p. 78–9.

to Whom be honour and glory for ever.[1] Elsewhere, too, the brevity and uncertainty of life, the worthlessness of worldly treasures, the greatness of eternal rewards, are placed before the monk.[2] When a girl tempted St. Ciarán he is made to resist by dwelling on the same theme : life hastens to its end ; the day of judgment is at hand ; and then——.[3] Such likewise was the burthen of the preacher's message.[4] And the notion of conflict is strongly marked, good angels on one side, Satan and his minions on the other.[5] Ordinary prudence then suggested that the monk, who took salvation seriously, should consider the adversaiy's ways and know how to act so that Satan should be completely discomfited.

To invoke the divine aid against these evil powers the sign of the cross was in constant use. St. Columban during his meditations in the woods near Luxeuil put that holy sign on his forehead frequently as a form of armour.[6] His monks did the same whenever they left the monastery.[7] Columban's successor at Luxeuil, the Abbot Athala, had a cross erected outside his cell, so that when going out or returning he could lay his hand upon it before putting the sign of salvation upon his brow.[8] A torch when lighted by a junior monk had to be handed to a senior to be thus blessed[9]; and spoons when used at table had to be treated similarly by the brethren.[10] In Iona the same custom prevailed ; for it is recorded that St. Colmcille was displeased when the holy sign was not placed on a milk vessel.[11] The " signum salutare "[12] might be placed on tools[13] and used for various pious purposes.[14] When his uncle Ernan died suddenly on

---

[1] Ib. *Instr.* ii, p. 79–86.
[2] *Reg. Coen.* xv, p. 234, *MNP.* Cf. *Vita Ant.* P.L. lxxiii, 15, col. 135.
[3] *Lism. L.*, p. 1211, ll. 4171–3.
[4] *Lism. L.*, p. 115, l.3882.
[5] *Adam.* iii, 13, p. 214 : " (sancti angeli) contra adversarias belligerant potestates, animam alicuius hospitis . . . eripere conantes." *V.S.H.* i, p. 255 : a fight with demons for soul. Cf. Cass., *Conl.* viii, 16, 17, p. 231–4. *Vita Mart.* vi, p. 116 : Satan meets St. Martin and warns him that wherever he goes the speaker will be at his side. *Vita Ant.* P.L. lxxiii, 37, col. 155 : a fight between angels and demons for soul.
[6] Jonas : *Vita Col.* i, 8, p. 166 : " crebro frontem signo crucis armans." Cf. i, 21, p. 200.
[7] Jonas : *V. Col.* ii, 9, p. 250. *Reg. Coen.* i, c. iii, p. 221, *MP.*
[8] Jonas : *V. C.* ii, 6, p. 238.
[9] *Reg. Coen.* ii, p. 220.
[10] Ib. i, p. 220. Jonas : *V. Col.* ii, 9, 249–50; also Ib. ii, 2, p. 233 ; Ib. 19, p. 274.
[11] *Adam.* ii, 16, p. 126.
[12] Ib. i, 45, p. 88.
[13] Ib. ii, 16, p. 125.
[14] Ib. ii, 29, p. 143.

the way from the harbour to the monastery, a cross was raised on the spot where life failed him and another on the spot where Colmcille stood awaiting his approach.[1] Another cross, fixed securely in a large millstone, was erected in the place where the old white horse wept for the Saint's approaching end just before his death.[2] Caesarius of Arles shows that the practice of signing oneself with the sign of the cross was very common in Gaul.[3] St Patrick made the sign of the cross upon himself a hundred times during the day and night, and never passed a cross upon the wayside without alighting from his chariot and spending a while beside it in prayer.[4] St. Jerome says that it could not be made too frequently.[5] The hermits in the Egyptian desert were wont to make the holy sign over their food and drink, before they took their repast, and one of them is credited with the statement that " where the cross passes the evil in anything is powerless."[6] As might be expected, the custom reaches still further back into Christian antiquity.[7]

Another habit which the young novice would strive at once to acquire was that of asking or receiving a blessing from the abbot or a lower superior before starting on a journey or engaging in any important work ; also when entering or leaving any house within the monastic enclosure.[8] A boy returning from the byre at Iona with the new milk on his back asks St. Colmcille to bless, as always, his burden.[9] Cailtan, one of the monks, called in haste from a neighbouring island,

---

[1] Ib. ii, 33, p. 147 ; ii, 35, p. 151. In the *Laws* the maker of any implement must put his blessing on it when it is ready for use (*Laws* i, 132, 5). In reward for this blessing he receives a tenth of the implement's value in food and drink (dúilchinne in its special sense : *Laws* v, 198–9). The refusal to impart such a blessing was punished (*Laws* vi, 3, s.v. *abarta*. D'Arbois de Jubainville : *Études sur le droit celt*, ii, 75, 118. Thurneysen : *Cóic Conara Fugill. Abhand. der preuss. Akad. Phil. Hist. Klasse Jahrg.*, 1925, No. 7, p. 77, s.v. *dúilchinne*).

[2] *Adam.* iii, 23, p. 231. For instances in lives of other Irish saints cf. *Lism. L.* p. 59–67, l. 2231 (Senan made the sign of the Cross of Christ against the monster). Ib. l. 2688 (Finnian made the sign of the cross on Ruadán's famous tree and its fluid was forthwith changed to water), *V.S.H.* i, p. 253 ; ii. 14, 63, 232. *B.N.E.*, p. 17, etc.

[3] P.L. xxxix, col. 1820, 2237, 2238, etc.

[4] *B. Arm.*, 14a. Cf. ib. 5a, 14b, 25b, 28b, 29a.

[5] *St. Jer. Ep.* 22, 37, p. 202 : " ad omnem actum, ad omnem incessum, manus pingat crucem." Cf. *Vita Mart.*, 12, p. 122, 22, p. 131. *Rev. Celt.* ii, p. 394.

[6] Palladius, *H.L.* 2. Ath. *Vita Ant.*, P.L. lxxiii, c. 132, 150, 161; Cass., *Conl.* viii, 18, p. 234.

[7] Tertullian : *De Corona*, 3.

[8] *Reg. Coen.* iii, p. 221. Jonas, *V. Col.* ii, 9, p. 250.

[9] *Adam.* ii, 16, p. 125.

receives Colmcille's benediction before he retires to the guest-
house, where very soon he dies.[1] Berach sailing away to
Tiree in the early morning comes first to the abbot's cell
that he might receive his blessing ; and Baithéne follows
suit later in the same day.[2] Still more would such a blessing
be sought when the voyage was to be from Iona to Ireland[3] ;
or into the ocean waste in quest of a real hermitage.[4]

Prayer, study and manual work occupied the young monk's
waking hours.[5] The first of these would naturally take place
in the early morning ; and again at the fixed periods during
the day. Arrangements for study and manual work would
differ in the various monasteries. But these are points which
we shall have to consider more in detail in some of the
following paragraphs.

§ 3—PROFESSION AS A MONK.

(a)—Was there a fixed period of Probation ?

So meagre is the evidence on this point that it is difficult
to come to any definite conclusion. That there was a period
of probation goes without saying, for candidates could not
be accepted before they had given proof that they were fitted
for the career which they wished to embrace. In Ireland,
as we have seen, most of the candidates for monastic life
were such as had been trained in virtue since babyhood by
some cleric or hermit. Others were reared within the
monasteries. For youths of these classes, desirous of per-
severing in the manner of living marked out for them by parents
or relatives, the question of formation would cause little
difficulty. The conversi, on the other hand, recently won
from worldliness, would need to prepare themselves by the
study and practice of asceticism for the holy and mortified
life led by the monastic brethren. In the first case progress
in spirit would have come imperceptibly with the years of
growth, and the chief consideration would be maturity.
In the second case maturity was present as a matter of course,
and the chief consideration would be progress in spirit.
There is evidence that the age regarded as meet for the

---

[1] Ib. i, 31, p. 60.　　　　　　[2] Ib. i, 19, p. 489.
[3] Ib. i, 2, p. 22.　　　　　　 [4] Ib. i, 20, p. 49.
[5] V.S.H ii, p. 223 : " Vacate semper orationibus mane ; postea lectionibus ;
deinde operamini (sic ipse [Molua] dividebat diem in tres partes) usque ad
vesperam."

profession of the normal novice was twenty years. A canon ascribed to St. Patrick,[1] and probably not later than the sixth century,[2] says that monks should bind themselves to the perfect life " in perfect age "—in other words, from twenty onwards. This would be a very wise regulation indeed, but we cannot be sure that it was generally observed. Elderly aspirants might, on occasion, be exempted from probation altogether, as we see in the case of St. Colmcille. Two guests, it appears, arrived in Iona on a certain Sunday, and when asked for what purpose they had come, replied that they wished to spend a year as pilgrims on the island. Colmcille answered that this could not be allowed unless they joined the ranks of the brethren ; to which his guests replied that the idea never had occurred to them before, but that coming from such lips they believed it to be an inspiration from God. They were, therefore, quite ready to do as the Saint had suggested. Whereupon, to the amazement of all present, Colmcille led them at once to the Church and permitted them to make their profession as monks. Later the Saint explained to his community that the two newly-professed brethren were not long for this world, that, in fact, both would die within a month.

It is thus probable that the period of formation in every instance was left very much to the sound judgment of the abbot, but that the young were not allowed to bind themselves definitely to the monastery until they had reached early manhood. Such, too, was the custom at Lérins.[3] St. Caesarius of Arles, trained in that celebrated isle, departed from its custom when he decreed in his Rule for nuns that new-comers should be tested for a year before they were admitted to a place among the sisters.[4] He did not wish, however, that

---

[1] H. and S., Councils, ii, p. 335 : " De Proposito Monachorum : Monachi sunt qui solitarii sine terrenis opibus habitant sub potestate episcopi vel abbatis . . . Ad vitam perfectam in aetate perfecta (hoc est a viginti annis) debet unusquisque constringi, non adtestando sed voto perficiendo ut est illud : Unusquisque sicut proposuit suo cordefaciat (2 Cor. ix, 7) et ' Ut vota mea reddam in conspectu Domini' (Ps.cxv, 18)," etc.

[2] Note the prominence given to the bishop as monastic superior (sub potestate episcopi vel abbatis) and the fact that the texts of Scripture quoted belong to Old Latin version. For the text of Scripture common in early Ireland see Gwynn, Book of Armagh, Introd., p. cxxxvi ff. For the text used in the British Church see Williams ed. of the De Ercidio of Gildas, p. 88–98.

[3] Cf. Löning : Gesch. des deutsch. K.R. ii, 395.

[4] Reg. Mon., c. 3, P.L. lxvii, col. 1107 : " Ei ergo quae Deo inspirante convertitur non licebit statim habitum religionis assumere . . . sed uni ex senioribus tradita annum integrum in eo quo venit habitu perseveret."

this rule should be adhered to rigidly, for the superior was empowered to allow the novice to profession before the year ended if her conduct gave promise of a holy life.[1] Later in his " Recapitulations " of the Rule, Caesarius lets the one year noviceship drop, merely demanding that the novice should be kept in the " Salutatorium " " as long as it seemed just and reasonable to the abbess."[2] When making the regulation for a fixed noviceship of one year, Caesarius (like his contemporary St. Benedict)[3] had stood under the influence of Cassian.[4] St. Basil teaches that those admitted in boyhood must be trained in all good until " reason is added and the power of discrimination." " At this point," he says, " we must allow the profession of virginity, since it is now valid and takes place with the person's own consent and judgment, reason being fully developed."[5] At Tabennisi, in the founder's time, monks seem to have been received after a preliminary examination. Later (when Palladius was in Upper Egypt, from A.D. 406–12) a noviceship had been developed: " However, the man who has come to remain with them they do not allow to enter into the sanctuary for three years. But after three years' probation and performance of the more toilsome labours he then enters."[6]

When superiors judged that the proper time had come the novice made formal profession of his intention to live as a monk under obedience for the remainder of his days.[7] This was not a mere promise, but a vow,[8] made in the oratory on

---

[1] L.c. : " De ipso tamen habitu mutando vel lecto in schola habendo sit in potestate prioris ; et quomodo personam vel compunctionem viderit, ita vel celerius vel tardius studeat temperare."

[2] Ib., col. 118 : " quantam abbatissae iustum et rationabile visum fuerit."

[3] *S. Ben. Reg.*, ed. Butler, ch. lviii.

[4] *Inst.* iv, 6–7, p. 51–2. In the life of St. Berach, who made his early studies at Glen dá locha, it is said (*V.S.H.* i, p. 77) : " Anno siquidem probationis in novitiatu elapso professionem ex more iuxta ordinis observantiam complevit," but the statement is not confirmed by other sources, and must be treated as suspect. If genuine it would show the influence of Cassian in Glendalough.

[5] *Reg. fus. tract,* xv. τότε καὶ τὴν ὁμολογίαν, τῆς παρθενίας προσίεσθαι δεῖ ὡς ἤδη βεβαίαν καὶ ἀπὸ γνώμης οἰκείας καὶ κρίσεως γινομένην.

[6] *H.L.* 32. Cf. Cass., *Inst.* iv, 6–7, p. 51–2.

[7] *V.S.H.* ii, p. 22 : " monachicam professionem apud eum fecerunt." Ib. p. 74 : " ut et ipse professionem monachi ibi faceret."

[8] *Canon xvii Patr.*, H. and S., *Councils* ii, p. 335 : " non adtestando sed voto perficiendo." *Adam.* ii, 39, p. 162 : " Votum monachicum devotus vovit." *Paenit Columb.*, p. 444 B : " Quia post votum suum peccavit et votum summ irritum fecit postquam se domino consecravit." Cf. Ib. : " si autem gradum aut votum iii annis."

bended knee with the abbot and brethren as witnes es.[1]
The solemn asseveration would probably be "in the name of
the Most High God," as in more ordinary oaths.[2] It is extremely
likely that there was a fixed formula, at least for each monastery
or group of monasteries, but no trace of such a formula has
been discovered.

What the arrangements regarding profession were at
Lérins is a matter of speculation, but it is not improbable
that they were in general agreement with those which we
find in Ireland.[3] Profession under vow is enjoined by St
Basil. Having been prepared for by careful instruction, it
should take place in the presence of witnesses and if possible
before the bishop of the diocese.[4] The professed monk was
bound by Church law, public opinion and his own conscience
so that if he departed from his obligations[5] he was to be
treated as guilty of sacrilege, having stolen what belonged
to God.[6] Nuns were in a still more intimate sense brides of
Christ, and their guilt was accordingly greater if they returned
to the world. Marriage for them was equivalent to adultery.[7]
Nor was St. Basil the first to ordain that his monks should
bind themselves before God to perform the duties of their
state. Bgoul and Schenute of Atripe had set the example
a short time after the death of Pachomius, whose rule they
modified in this as in other respects.[8] In Tabennisi and its
associate monasteries " profession " meant nothing more

---

[1] *Adam.* i, 32, p. 61 : "eodem horae momento oratorium cum sancto
ingressi, devote, flexis genibus, votum monachiale voverunt." Gildas, *De
Excidio*, ch. 36 : "*post monachi votum inritum*," shows that the British monk
of the early sixth century was bound by vow.
[2] *Adam.* i, 43, p. 84 : "per nomen excelsi Dei."
[3] Löning : *Gesch. des d. K.R.* ii, p. 400 holds that a vow was unknown at
Lérins : "Ein feierliches Gelübde hatten die Mönche nicht abzulegen," but
this is to lay too much weight on the argument *ex silentio*, and to neglect
the development which almost certainly took place after the days of Honoratus. It must be said, however, that monastic profession under vow was not
universal when Lérins was founded. Palladius, writing about A.D. 420, and
purposing to give a faithful account of contemporary monasticism, praises
Lausus for his good sense in avoiding oaths and vows, and thus saving himself
from the danger of perjury (*H.L. Prolog.*, 9). The practice seems then not
to have been generally prevalent when Palladius wrote. For a full discussion
see Clarke : *St. Basil the Great*, pp. 107–9.
[4] *Reg. fus., tract* 15 : "Μάρτυρας δὲ τῆς γνώμης τοὺς προεστῶτας τῶν
ἐκκλησιῶν, παραλαμβάνειν, ὥστε δι'αὐτῶν καὶ τὸν ἁγιασμον τοῦ σώματος ὥσπερ τι
ἀνάθημα τῷ θεῷ καθιεροῦσθαι, καὶ βεβαίωσιν εἶναι τοῦ γινομένου διὰ τῆς μαρτυρίας
[5] Ib., 14 : τὴν ὁμολογίαν ἀθετήσαντα.
[6] Ib. : "ὁ γὰρ ἀναθεὶς ἑαυτὸν τῷ θεῷ, εἶτα πρὸς ἄλλον βίον ἀποπήδησας, ἱερόσυλος
γέγονεν, αὐτὸς ἑαυτὸν διακλέψας καὶ ἀφελόμενος τοῦ θεοῦ τὸ ἀνάθημα.
[7] Clarke, l.c., p. 109.
[8] Leipoldt : *Schenute von Atripe*, p. 109.

than the concession of the monastic dress.[1] He who " changed his clothes " or " put on the monk's habit " by this very act " made profession "[2] of his new state.

What were the Irish monk's obligations in virtue of his compact with Almighty God ?[3] In general he was bound to lead a life of mortification,[4] or self-denial, the ἀπόταξις of the Greeks and the "abrenunciatio " of his Latin brethren.[5] This included the practice of the various virtues spoken of in the previous section, but above all the practice of the three fundamental virtues, poverty, chastity and obedience, which in the later middle ages were made the object of special vows. So important were these virtues in the life of the monk at all times that they must be treated of in separate paragraphs.

(b)—Poverty.

That the monk should possess no property was taken as an axiom since the beginning of monasticism.[6] Gildas, as we have seen,[7] states the principle in the following words :— " Whatever superabundance of worldly goods a monk possesses must be regarded as luxury and riches ; but that which he is compelled to possess by necessity, not by choice, must not be counted against him for evil."[8] St. Columban teaches substantially the same doctrine in a chapter of his Rule : " Covetousness," he says, " must be shunned by monks, to whom the world is crucified for Christ's sake as they are to the world (Gal. vi. 19). It is wrong for them not only to have what they do not need, but also to wish for such things. What counts for something in monks is not their income but

---

[1] *H.L.* 38 (9), *Nilus Ep.* xcvi, P.G. lxxix, c. 243. *AA. SS.* T. ii, Jan., p. 673. Cf. Rothenhäusler : *Die Anfänge der klösterlichen Profess. Ben. Mon.*, 1922, p. 27.

[2] Ib. ἐπαγγέλεσθαι, profiteri.

[3] ὁμολογία πρὸς θεόν . Cf. Rothenhäusler, op. cit., p. 21. For the connection of this " pact " with the vow of Christian ascetics in pre-monastic times cf. Wilpert : *Die gottgeweihten Jungfrauen in den ersten Jahrhunderten der Kirche,* Freiburg, 1892. Koch. : *Virgines Christi,* Leipzig, 1907. Martinez : *L'ascétisme chrétien pendant les trois premiers siècles de l'Eglise,* Paris, 1913. Rietzenstein : *Historia Monachorum und Historia Lausiaca,* Göttingen, 1916.

[4] *Col. Reg. Mon.,* 9 : " Maxima pars regulae monachorum mortificatio est."

[5] Rothenhäusler, l.c.

[6] Can. xvii attrib. to St. Patr. H. and S. ii, p. 335 : " Monachi sunt qui solitarii sine terrenis opibus habitant. Quo voto vivitur si superabundantia n omnibus devitetur in vita," etc.

[7] Supra, p. 159.

[8] Gildas, ed. Williams, *Frag.* iv. Cf. Wassersch. *I.K.* xxxix, 5, p. 150 ; and *Ériu* vii, p. 156, 10 : excommunication of cleric or nun for not giving superfluous goods of church to poor.

their good disposition. Having left all things and followed Christ Our Lord with the cross of daily fear they look for a treasure in heaven. As they will have abundance in the world to come, they ought to be satisfied in this world with the minimum that suffices to stave off extreme want, for they know that covetousness proved to be a leprosy to monks, who imitated the sons of the prophets, that it brought the betrayal of Christ and ruin on one of the disciples, that it brought death to some who were not above suspicion in their following of the Apostles." The lack of goods and contempt of riches are thus the first steps in perfection for the monk.[1] " Few things are necessary, one alone suffices, according to the Lord's Word " (Luke x, 41).[2] But spiritual wisdom is needed to understand what are those few things which the Lord spoke of to Martha.[3] No one, to begin with, should possess anything of his own, call anything his own or in any way treat anything as his own, under penalty of separation from the brethren and the performance of a heavy penance.[4] If a monk received on loan for his private use a book or other article of the monastery's property, he was to bring it back the same day.[5] Should he be responsible for damage done to the common property of the community he was to compensate for the loss caused by additional labour, or, if this was impossible, make satisfaction by penance.[6] It was wrong for the monk then to have anything that he could call his own or to use anything beyond what was strictly necessary to supply very frugal needs. This personal poverty he was to show also in his dress and his outward demeanour.[7]

But if the individual monk could not possess poverty of his own what of the monks as a corporate body ? Was the

---

[1] Col. *Reg. Mon.*, ch. iv, p. 376–7.
[2] *Reg. Mon.* iv, p. 377 : " Paucis nobis opus est, iuxta verbum domini, aut etiam uno." This is an old Latin, not the Vulgate, reading of the text. Cf. Williams, *Christ. in Early Brit.*, p. 379, n. 4.
[3] Ib.
[4] Jonas, *V. Col.* i, 5, p. 162 : "Communia omnibus omnia erant : si quispiam proprium aliquid usurpare temptasset ceterorum consortio segregatus poenitentiae ultione vindicabatur." Cf. *Reg. Coen.* ii, p. 225, *MP.* : " non dicere suum proprium aliquid." Ib. xv, p. 232, *MNP.* : " meum vel tuum dixisse, sex plagis." Ib. : anything possessed which brethren in general did not possess—deprivation and 100 stripes.
[5] *Reg. Coen.* viii, p. 225, *MNP.*
[6] *Reg. Coen.* xv, p. 232 *MNP.*
[7] *Martyr. Oeng. H.B.* ed. Note on June 7th : An apparition of Christ in fine dress is scouted as a clumsy deception by St. Moling. This incident is taken from Sulp. Sev., *Vita Mart.*, 24, p. 164 : The devil, dressed in purple and gems, appears to St. Martin, but is immediately detected.

monastery, like the monk, obliged to practise poverty ? In
the sixth century, as far as our evidence goes, the choice was
seldom offered, for the original endowments were on a modest
scale. The fact, however, remains that there was an endowment, capable, too, of increase, so that the monastery might
grow into a great and well-equipped establishment. Thus
the possession of property by the monastery was in principle
accepted By arrangement with its secular lords, the small
island of Iona (about three square miles in extent) passed
into the ownership of Colmcille and his followers. The soil,
though poor, proved capable in parts of cultivation ; whilst
other patches offered pasturage for cattle. Stock, appliances
and buildings could therefore be introduced. There were
cows, cattle, milk-pails, an old horse and a cart, a barn to
hold, a kiln to dry and a mill to grind the grain. In the small
harbour of the island were various boats, some of which
were used for journeys to Ireland.[1] In a word the monastery
possessed considerable property before Colmcille died in
A.D. 597, thirty-four years after his first settlement in the
island. We must not forget, however, the years of grinding
poverty through which the monks lived before the soil was
brought under cultivation ; nor must we imagine that
prosperity, and even affluence, came to them within one
generation. On the last day of Colmcille's life upon earth,
he visited, we are told, the monastery barn, and finding two
heaps of grain remaining over from the previous autumn,
he returned thanks to God and said :—" I congratulate
from the heart my dear monks, because this year, too, though
I should be compelled to leave them, they will have sufficient
for their needs."[2] We may conclude from these circumstances
—Colmcille's solicitude about the corn-supply just before
his death and his relief when the prospect for the coming
year gave no cause for uneasiness—that the problem of finding
food for the brethren was still very serious. Such property
as the monastery then possessed was therefore barely sufficient
to provide the monks with a modest sustenance. From this
story it may likewise be gathered that the monks in Iona
did not look forward to receiving help from their brethren

---

[1] *Adam.* iii, 23, p. 231, etc. Cf. Reeves, Ib., p. 361-3. If all these were
allowed at Iona they would, of course, be allowed in other Irish monasteries.
Even the *cella* of a virgin might have its *iumenta loci*, *V.S.H.*, p. 19. The
horse, cart and milk vessels occur again, *V.S.H.* ii, p. 26 (Roscrea).
[2] *Adam.* iii, 23, p. 230.

in Derry or Durrow. The reason probably was that the endowments of these monasteries in the sixth century were likewise of no significance.

Of Columban's foundations in Burgundy the same must be said. The great saint of Bangor had received a grant of " desert " land from Theudebert, King of Austrasia.[1] For a while the poverty of the brethren was extreme, the bark of trees and herbs being their only food.[2] Yet such was the fervour prevailing in their midst that when one of their number fell sick and was unable any longer to dine off bark and herbs, all the others made a fast of three days and offered up special prayers that God might come to the sick brother's aid.[3] Their request was heard. On another occasion a neighbouring abbot of British race brought them some car-loads of food.[4] When Columban and his monks became better known, many youths came to join them, so that two new monasteries, Luxeuil and Fontaines, had to be con-structed.[5] At this stage the total number of monks under Columban's care must have reached two hundred.[6] Fishing and chance spoils from the forest being utterly insufficient for their support, Columban led the way in clearing the local woods and preparing the ground for tillage. The skill of the Irish brethren as woodmen and their zeal as agriculturists were calculated to win the admiration of the Burgundians.[7] When Columban was driven from these monasteries after a sojourn of twenty years their prosperity was evidently assured, for there is no further mention of famine or great poverty.

At home the monks were probably saved from the severe trials which beset St. Colmcille and St. Columban in Iona and Annegray, but there is evidence that in the sixth century their position was far from assured. Colmán of Lann Elo, for instance, found himself on a certain feast of the Epiphany with no food for his community. But he was strong in faith, according to the story, and calling the cellarer he ordered him " to give sufficient to his brothers on that most holy

---

[1] Jonas, *V. Col.* i, 6, p.163
[2] Ib. 7, p. 164.
[3] Ib.
[4] Ib., p. 165.
[5] Ib., 10, p. 169–70 ; Ib., 11, p. 171 ; 15, p. 177.
[6] Ib., 17, p. 183 : Fontaines housed sixty or more monks ; nor is it likely that the number was smaller in the other two monasteries.
[7] Ib. i, 15, p. 178.

feast day." To which the astonished official replied that he would give them sufficient water from the local well, but nothing more. Before the day was past, however, a gift of various comestibles was brought to the monastery.[1] On another occasion the same Colmán found himself in one of his small churches without any food to eat. This time help was secured by one of the brethren who paid a visit to his native district and came back with a large alms.[2] It is related of St. Crónán that his community at Roscrea had to fast on an Easter Sunday, because they had nothing whatever to eat, but help was on the way to them from St. Crónán's relatives, who arrived on the following morning and presented the monks with as much food as supplied their wants until Pentecost.[3] When St. Fintan on a certain day visited his monks working in the fields, they all gathered round him and asked him as a great favour to let them have a meal. The request was not meant to be taken seriously, for the brethren knew that there was nothing in the house save the wild herbs which was their usual repast. But just at that moment visitors from South Leinster arrived with chariots and carts carrying various foods for presentation to the abbot, who was thus enabled to give his monks an excellent dinner.[4] All things considered there is reason to believe that about A.D. 600 many of the Irish monasteries were very poor and that none was really wealthy.

A notable feature of poverty as interpreted by the Irish monks is that the use of chariots seems to cause no scruples. Following the example of St. Patrick,[5] and St. Brigid,[6] the founder of Iona is found travelling in such a vehicle.[7] Crónán of Roscrea, whose penury we have just mentioned, was able to travel in a chariot, driven by a charioteer.[8] Later accounts regard the use of chariots by monks as a matter of daily occurrence.[9] The inference is that chariots were employed

---

[1] *V.S.H.* i, p. 259.
[2] Ib., p. 262.
[3] Ib. ii, p. 25. .
[4] Ib., p. 99.
[5] *B. Arm.*, 14a, 18a, 27b, 36a, 37a, etc.
[6] *Tr. Thau.*, p. 520.
[7] *Adam.* ii, 43, p. 171–2. At an earlier period, however, the use of *vehicula* had given offence, but Gildas had sided against the complainants. *Frag.* iv, p. 262. Wassersch., xxxix, 7, p. 150.
[8] *V.S.H•* ii, p. 28.
[9] *Lism. L.*, p. 129 (chariot given to Ciarán), p. 104 (for Iarlaithe of Tuam), p. 90 (in which Finnchua of Brí Gobann travels at a furious rate, not even waiting for his clerics). *B.N.E.*, p. 12 (Brendan of Birr).

not merely by kings[1] and by the comparatively well-to-do,[2] but also by the poor, so that their use by those who made profession of poverty caused neither surprise nor scandal. Riding on horseback, on the other hand, was the privilege of the aristocrat, and thus was not practised by the monks. Aidan, the gentle apostle of Northumbria, unless compelled by necessity, resolutely refused to utilise such a mode of conveyance, and made all his journeys on foot.[3]

If the monasteries, probably without exception, were poor in the sixth century, many of them became rich in the course of their later history. Given peace and freedom from economic disturbances, this development was almost inevitable. In the first place, by a curious irony of fate, the monks were indefatigable workers and were thus creating, to an ever-increasing extent, the wealth which they had solemnly renounced. In the second place the generosity of the faithful was considerable, and the monastery, being a permanent and well-organised institution, lost nothing which it had once received, so that its possessions in land, stock and appliances grew from generation to generation. Some of the founders, like St. David in Wales,[4] had sought to guard against increase in wealth by excluding animals from their lands and forcing the monks to dig and carry for themselves, but this policy was held in general disfavour. Carthach of Lismore, for instance, when he settled originally at Rathan, refused to let his monks use ploughs. " But kings, princes and leading men bestowed lands and oxen, gold, silver and other gifts upon his monastery ; whilst the interference of holy men put a stop to his scheme of having all tillage done by the spade alone."[5] Few abbots would be strong enough to compel the distribution of all produce (beyond that absolutely needed for the monks' sustenance) to the poor. In this manner a certain amount was kept over by way of addition to the working capital. With land and appliances in plenty, able management, cheap, steady, devoted and skilful labour,

---

[1] *Adam.* i, 7, p. 33. (Eochu Laib, King of the Picts, escaped from a battle *currui insidens.*)

[2] *Lism. L.,* p. 120 (parents of Ciarán of Clonmacnois.)

[3] Bede, *H.E.,* iii, 5. " non equorum dorso sed pedum incessu vectus." Cf. story Ib. iii, 15.

[4] *Life,* ed. Wade-Evans, § 22.

[5] *V.S.H.* i, p. 178, Cf. Ib. i, p. 98. Fintan's monks " manibus suis laborantes heremitarum more terram sarculo arabant. Et respuentes omnia animalia nec unam vaccam habebant." In this case, as in that of St. Carthach, in the following century, neighbouring abbots interfered.

it is no wonder that the monasteries in time became rich institutions.[1] As in all other countries where a similar development took place, the monks very soon paid a high price for prosperity. Rival claims to property marred the good relations which should have existed between men who had abandoned everything for Christ's love ; secular princes took a natural, if baneful, interest in monastic territories which were really minor principalities ; and marauders, pagan and otherwise, treated the monastery as a profitable object of attack. But these evils belong to a period much later than that which we are now studying.

Neither in the theory nor in the practice of poverty did the Irish monks differ appreciably from the monks of other lands. As early as the beginning of cenobitism the principle was accepted that the monastery might possess property for the sustenance of the brethren, though these individually might not own anything, even the most necessary article of dress. Indeed the Pachomian monks at Tabennisi were rich to a degree hardly equalled again until the later Middle Ages.[2] In answer to the question whether it "is lawful to have private property in the brotherhood," St. Basil replied that "this is contrary to the testimony in the Acts (iv. 32) concerning them that believed. So he that says anything is his private property has made himself an alien to the Church of God and to the love of the Lord Who taught us both by word and deed to lay down our life for our friends, to say nothing of external possessions."[3] In his own case St. Basil gave his patrimony to the poor, but part of his property was placed at the disposal of the brethren,[4] and he contemplates the possibility of other monks doing likewise.[5] In general

---

[1] Macalister, *Lives of Ciaran*, p. 26, 130 (Clonmacnois). *Martyr. Oeng.,* p. 88 (Saigher). *Lism. L.*, p. 26 (Colmcille's congregation would be richest in Ireland). The most striking proof of monastic wealth is, of course, the record of raids from A.D. 795 onwards. Plunder was always a motive, if not always the sole or the chief motive, in these raids.

[2] Cf. *Vita Pach.*, 81–5. Shortly after the death of Pachomius a dispute between the superior of one of the houses and the procurator-general about money matters threatened to bring the whole congregation to an untimely end.

[3] *Reg. brev. tract.* lxxxv.

[4] Bas., *Ep.* xxxvii.

[5] *Reg. brev. tract.* cccviii. Clarke : *Basil the Great*, p. 31–3 (cf. p. 45), concludes that Basil himself retained the ownership and use of some of his property ; and that his monks might likewise share money. But all the passages he quotes are consistent with absolute renunciation, and should certainly be interpreted in that sense. Cassian (*Inst.* vii, 19, p. 143) relates

the saint was anxious that distracting interference from the outside world should be excluded from the cloister, and he did not object to the monastery having money provided it could be held without infringing this principle.[1] Even the hermit in the desert might own a cow to turn his pumping machine and a pet lion to keep him company.[2] St. Martin was more strict than others on this point, for not only did he refuse favours from the great,[3] but when a brother asked that some little part of a gift might be kept to help the monastery in its extreme need he replied, " Let the Church feed and clothe us, and let us not appear to retain anything for our own use."[4] From his conduct, perhaps, the exceptionally strict views represented by St. David, St. Fintan and St. Carthach were derived. St. Augustine, writing for nuns, insists that those who bring money with them to the monastery should allow it to go into the common fund, and that no difference is to be observed between those who had been rich in the world and those who had been poor.[5] Poverty of spirit is to be cultivated diligently by all.[6] St. Jerome tells the terrible story of the monk in the Nitrian desert whose possession of one hundred *solidi* was discovered after his death. The question arose as to what should be done with this money, and the leading Fathers of the neighbourhood, in council assembled, decided that it should be buried with the owner.[7] Clerics, according to the same writer, should be careful not to seek after wealth[8] ; but he had no objection to the fitting up of monasteries with everything needful. Cassian forbids the monk to bestow anything on the community which he joins.[9] At Lérins, likewise, the property of those who entered

---

that Basil said of a certain senator, who reserved portion of his income on embracing religious life : " he has ceased to be a senator, without becoming a monk." Clarke rejects this as "a late tradition," but the rejection is altogether arbitrary.

[1] Clarke, op. cit., p. 83.
[2] Sulp. Sev. *Dial.* i, 13, p. 164–5.
[3] Ib. ii, 5, p. 187 : " postremo abeunti multa munera obtulit (Valentinianus Imperator) quae vir beatus, ut semper paupertatis suae custos, cuncta reiecit.
[4] Ib. iii, 14, p. 212.
[5] *Ep.* 211. *C.S.E.L.* lvii, p. 360.
[6] Ib., p. 362 : " Illae se aestiment ditiores quae fuerint in sustentanda parcitate fortiores." Cf. p. 361 : " quid prodest dispergere dando pauperibus et pauperem fieri si anima misera superbior efficiatur contemnendo quam fuerat possidendo ? "
[7] St. Jer. *Ep.* xxii, 33, p. 195–6.
[8] *Ep.* lii, 5, p. 422 : " obsecro itaque te . . . ne officium clericatus genus antiquae militiae putes, id est, ne lucra saeculi in .Christi quaeras militia."
[9] *Inst.* iv, 4, p. 50 : " ne usibus quidem coenobii profuturas suscipere ab eo pecunias adquiescunt." Cf. lb. iv, 13, p. 55. *Conl.* i, 10, p. 17.

was given to the poor and did not accrue to the monastery.
The brethren, by hard work and by utilizing the favourable
position of the island for fishing, secured enough for their
support and often had something over for the poor.[1]   Gifts
of money were also distributed by them to the poverty-
stricken in various towns of Southern Gaul.[2]   Later the
monastery fell into laxity, grew rich, and was in due course
plundered by the Saracens and Spaniards.[3]   Isidore of Sevilla,
in the seventh century, took elaborate precautions to ensure
that the strictest idea of personal poverty should prevail
amongst his monks,[4] but neither he nor any other monastic
father or writer up to that period took measures to prevent
the monastery (as distinct from the individual monks) from
becoming wealthy.

(c)—Chastity.

The human heart must love, as writers on the spiritual life
always recognise.[5]   Those who follow the higher call bind
themselves to bestow their love on Christ Our Lord, to the
exclusion of all less worthy objects.[6]   This chaste love must
dominate the mind as well as the body.   Therefore, as St.
Columban expressly teaches, " the chastity of the monk is
judged by his thoughts."[7]   And again he asks, " Of what
value is it to be a virgin in body if one is not a virgin also in
spirit ?   For God is a spirit, and dwells in the mind and spirit
which He sees to be immaculate."[8]   As the mind was withdrawn from things of the flesh by meditation on the Scriptures
and general care for the heavenly kingdom, so the body was
withdrawn by fasting and prayer and particularly by fleeing
from meetings with the other sex.[9]   In this particular the

---

[1] Arnold, *Caes. von A.*, p. 44.   The rule of poverty is stated by Faustus
Ep. viii " Ruiricio filio."   *C.S.E.L.* xxi, p. 210 : "primum revera bonum
est ut Christi famulus Christi pauperis vias ex toto pauper studeret incedere.'
[2] Hil. *Sermo de V. S. Honorati.* P.L. l. c. 1261.
[3] Arnold, l.c.
[4] *Reg. Mon.*, ch. 19, P.L. lxxxiii, cc. 870, 881.
[5] Cf. St. Jer. *Ep.* 22, 17, p. 166 : " difficile est humanam animam non
amare, et necesse est ut in quoscumque mens nostra trahatur affectu."
[6] Ib. 25, p. 180 : " zelotypus est Jesus ; non vult ab aliis videri faciem
tuam."
[7] *Reg. Mon.* iv, p. 377 : "castitas vero monachi in cogitationibus iudicatur."
The thought is St. Jerome's, *Ep.* 22, 5, p. 150 : "Perit ergo et mente virginitas." Cf. Ib., p. 203 : "etiam si corpore virgo est, an spiritu virgo sit,
nescio."
[8] *Reg. Mon.* iv, p. 378.
[9] Cass., *Col.* v. 4, p. 124.

Irish monks were uncompromising [1] unlike the missionary clergy who had established the faith within the country.[2] The remedy may seem to us very violent, but we must remember that Ireland was just emerging from paganism, and that sexual immorality was exceedingly common.[3] Virtue might be subjected to cruel tests.[4] Modesty and great caution in unavoidable dealings with women were therefore counselled.[5] St. Brendan of Clonfert is praised for unchivalrous conduct towards a young princess when he was ten years old. He was sitting, according to the tale, in Bishop Erc's chariot, quietly reading his psalms when the little lady jumped in and asked him to play with her. Brendan stoutly refused. The lively little maiden persisted, so Brendan took the reins, " and flogged her severely until she was crying and screaming," and ran to her father and mother with complaints about the wickedly angelic boy.[6] Such was the vigilance exercised by the abbess in the Columban monastery at Faremoutiers that one of the young nuns died without having learned that there was any difference between the sexes.[7] Failure, again, in this virtue was regarded as spiritual " ruin " *par excellence*.[8]

Some curious and often disedifying tales are told of the successful tests to which Irish monks exposed their virtue,[9] but stories of this kind need not be taken too seriously. The

---

[1] *Catalogue*, H. and S. ii, 292 : " mulierum consortia ac administrationes fugiebant atque a monasteriis suis eas excludebant." In Irish the principle was expressed " mná do móringabáil," " complete avoidance of women." *Hib. Min.*, p. 41. Illustrations of this attitude are very numerous. Cf. Plummer *V.S.H.* i., p. cxxxi, n. 5. *Reg. Coen.* xv, p. 232 *MNP. Lism. L.*, p. 103. Even the cleric who was married before his ordination and who had intercourse with his wife after that event was regarded as guilty of adultery. *Paenit. Col.*, p. 444B.

[2] *Catalogue* l.c. : " mulierum administrationem et consortia non respuebant."

[3] This is clear from the sagas and from all the early literature. For legalised immoral connections see the *Cáin Lánamna* tract in the *Senchus Mór. Ancient Laws*, vol. ii, pp. 342–408.

[4] *V.S.H.* i, 235–6, 254–5.

[5] *Paenit. Col.*, p. 447–8 B. *Lism. L.*, p. 50 (Brigid) p. 23 (Ciarán), etc.

[6] *Lism. L.*, p. 102.

[7] Jonas, *V. Col.* ii, 13. p. 262.

[8] Jonas, *V. Col.* i, 3, p. 157 : " Perge, o iuvenis, perge evade *ruinam* per quam multos conperis corruisse, declina viam quae inferi ducit ad valvas." *Paen. Col.*, p. 443 B. : " *ruina* maxima " (Child born to cleric. Seven years' penance on bread and water in a foreign land ordered as penance.) Cass., *Conl.* viii, 6, p. 232 : " *ruina* fornicationis." Cf. vi, 9, p. 162 : " *ruina* maiore." Cf. v, 12, p. 135 : " incidere in fornicationis ardorem, unde reparari aut non valeat aut vix valeat post *ruinam*." St. Jerome *Ep.*, 22, 5, p. 150 : " cum omnia Deus possit, suscitare virginem non potest post *ruinam*." Cf. ib. 13, p. 160. *Ep.* 49, 16, p. 378. Athan. *Vita Ant.*, P.L. lxxiii, c. 129 : " ille (diabolus) lubricum adolescentiae iter et ad *ruinam* facile proponebat." Cf. *Verba Sen.*, ib., c. 45 ; c. 746 : " cecidit in *ruinam* peccati cum ea (puella)."

[9] Cf. *Martyr. Oeng.*, *H.B.S.* ed., p. 41.

exceptional honour in which virginity was held by them is, of course, common to all monasticism, and finds support from St. Patrick,[1] Cassian,[2] St. Augustine,[3] St. Martin,[4] St. Jerome,[5] St. Athanasius,[6] and earlier writers back to the Apostle of the Gentiles.[7]

(d)—Obedience.

It is significant that the first chapter in St. Columban's Rule for Monks deals with obedience, for without this virtue cenobitical life is impossible to conceive.[8] St. Columban's teaching may be given at some length. " At the first word of the superior (senior)," he says, " all must rise and go to do what they are commanded, for obedience is shown to God, according to the words of Our Lord Jesus Christ, ' he that hears you hears Me ' (Luke x. 16)." If anybody therefore hears the word of command and does not rise at once to obey he is to be judged guilty of disobedience. He who questions the command commits a further crime, for not only is he disobedient, but he incites others to be refractory and thus is to be regarded as bringing destruction to many. If anyone again murmurs he, too, is to be considered disobedient, because he does not obey with his whole heart. What he does is, therefore, to be rejected, until it is clear that he is doing things with a good will. Unto what point is obedience to be shown? Unto death,[9] for the

---

[1] B. Arm., 48a, 467, 469.

[2] Conl. xxii, 5–6, p. 619–26.

[3] Ep. 211. C.S.E.L. lvii, p. 363, 364, etc.

[4] Dial. ii, 10, p. 192 : " Virginity is like a beautiful field carpeted with flowers."

[5] Ep. 22, passim. P. 175, he suggests that Tertullian, Cyprian, Pope Damascus and St. Ambrose should be read on the same subject. As the perfect example of virginity the Blessed Virgin is frequently lauded (ib., p. 168 : " Mihi virginitas in Maria dedicatur et Christo." Ep. 49, p. 386 : " Christus virgo, mater virginis nostri virgo perpétua, mater et virgo." Ep. 22, p. 169, 173, 203, 209. Ep. 52, p. 420. Ep. 39, p. 307, etc.). St. Jerome is quoted in praise of virginity in Wassersch. I.K. xlv, ch. ii, p. 180.

[6] Athan. Ep. ad Amun. P.G. xxvi, c. 1173 : " He who marries will bring forth fruit thirtyfold, but he who embraces the holy and unearthly way will bring forth fruit a hundredfold."

[7] 1 Cor. vii, 32–4.

[8] Hence Cassian's comment, Inst. iv, 30, p. 68 : " obedientiae bonum, quea inter ceteras virtutes primatum tenet." Cf. St. Jer. Ep. 22, 35, p. 197. Sulp. Sev. Dial. ii, 17, p. 170.

[9] Reg. Mon. i, p. 374 : " obedientia autem usque ad quem modum definitur ? Usque ad mortem certe praecepta est quia Christus usque ad mortem obedivit Patri pro nobis." Question and reply are evidently taken from St. Basil. Transl. by Ruf., P.L. ciii. Inter. lxv, c. 517–8 : " Usque ad quem modum obedire oportet eum qui placendi Deo implere regulam cupit ? Apostolus ostendit proponens nobis obedientiam Domini Qui factus est obediens usque ad mortem, mortem autem crucis." Cf. Inter. cxxxi, c. 535. Cass., Inst., v, 40, p. 112–3.

precept obviously goes that far, since Christ for our sakes
obeyed the Eternal Father unto death. This He tells us Himself
through His apostle, who writes (Phil. ii 5–8) : " Let this
mind be in you which was also in Christ Jesus, who being
in the form of God thought it not robbery to be equal to God ;
but He emptied Himself, taking the form of a slave, and in
appearance being found as man He humbled Himself, becoming
obedient unto death, even unto the death of the cross."
Nothing, therefore, no matter how hard and exacting, is
to be refused by the obedient who are Christ's true disciples,
but all is to be done speedily, with devotion and gladness.
If our obedience is otherwise it will not be acceptable to the
Lord, who says " he who does not take his cross and follow
Me is not worthy of Me " (Luke xiv. 27). He says again of
the worthy disciple. " Where I am there will My servant be
also " (John xvii. 24 ; xii. 26).[1] As an example of a " hard
and exacting " command, we have Columban's order to various
sick brothers to rise from their beds and take their place on
the threshing-floor, where heavy harvest work was in progress.[2]
Some thought the order too unreasonable and refused to
abide by it ; others dragged themselves to the place of toil.[3]
Then, says Jonas, by a happy disposition of Divine Providence,
those who risked their lives to obey were cured, whilst those
who stayed timidly in their beds were punished with a long
illness. When they finally did get well, they had to perform
a penance for their act of disobedience.[4] Various faults against
this virtue are provided for in Columban's penitential
discipline.[5] The obedience of a thieving crow, which brought

---

[1] *Reg. Mon.* i, p. 374–5. In all this Rule the influence of St. Basil is apparent.
Interr. lxix, c. 518 : " inobedientiae reus est." *Col.* : " inobedientiae reus
est." Ib. : " Multorum malorum causa efficitur tam sibi quam etiam ceteris,
quia aditum contradictionis pluribus aperit." *Col.* : " sed etiam *contradictionis aditum aliis aperiens* multorum destructor aestimandus est." Ib. lxxxi,
c. 519 : " alienus sit a fratrum unitate *qui murmurat et opus eius abiiciatur.*"
Col. : " Si quis vero *murmuraverit,* idcirco *opus eius abiiciatur donec . . .*"
Ib. lxv, c. 517–8 : *Texts.* " Qui factus est obediens usque ad mortem, mortem
autem crucis," and " Hoc sentite in vobis quod et in Christ Jesu," quoted.
Both also in *Col.* Much of the chapter on " Mortification " (ch. ix, p. 384–6)
likewise deals with mortification of the will by obedience.
[2] Jonas, *V. Col.* i, 12, p. 172–3.
[3] Jonas, *V. Col.* i, 12, p. 172 : " surrexerunt ergo quorum conscientiam
obedientiae ignis urebat, ad aream que venientes," etc.
[4] Ib. : " impleverunt mensuram penitentiae de suscepto inobedientiae
tempore."
[5] *Reg. Coen* viii. p. 224 *MP.* : " quod libet a senioribus impositum." Ib. x.
p. 228 *MP. (Inobediens. Nonfaciam.*—Murmuring. Excuses.) Ib. xi, p. 229,
MP. (No work to be undertaken without leave.) Ib. xiv, p. 230 *MP.* (No
contumacious replies.) Ib. xv, p. 232 *MNP.* (Where direct order or matter

back, when ordered, a glove that it had pilfered, is recorded with admiration by Columban's biographer.[1] Compared with this example, that of the cellarer who was called away just as he was about to fill his jug with beer and " glowing with the fire of obedience " hurried off at once, leaving the cock turned on, is, perhaps, unworthy of special notice.[2]

At Iona the precept of obedience was no less strictly enforced. Colmcille praises one of his monks for having journeyed in great haste in answer to his call. " Cailtan," he said, " you have done well in thus obediently hastening to my side. Rest now a little. My purpose in inviting you to me, beloved friend, was that you might end the course of life here with me in true obedience, for before this week has come to a close you will pass in peace to the Lord."[3] In the same way the brethren were ready, at a moment's notice, to set forth on long and hazardous voyages,[4] or to perform a service for the monastery.[5] They worked abroad at the local superior's desire, during the roughest weather.[6] When Cormac Ua Liatháin on one occasion sought a hermitage in the ocean, Colmcille declared that his search would be in vain, for the simple reason that Cormac had with him in his boat a certain monk whose abbot had not given him permission for the voyage.[7] Transgressions of the abbot's command were punished in Iona as at Luxeuil,[8] though Colmcille was no doubt a less stern ruler than his great namesake from Bangor.

Elsewhere in Ireland, too, the prevailing ideas about obedience were those which we have just described. In Colmán of Lann Elo's monastery, one of the brothers was so noted for this virtue that he was nicknamed " the obedient." It

---

of general discipline not carried out, excommunication and deprivation of food until the morrow.) Ib. viii, p. 225, MNP. (Even where order unreasonable to be fulfilled " ut obedientia custodiatur "). Ib. xv, p. 233, MNP (Murmuring.).

[1] Jonas, V. Col. i, 15, p. 179 : " ut non solum hominum honoribus sed etiam avium obedientia clarescant (famuli Dei)."

[2] Jonas, V. Col. 16, p. 180.

[3] Adam. i, 31, p. 60 : " bene fecisti ad me obedienter festinando."

[4] Adam. i, 18 : " qui hominis Dei obsecutus iussioni navigationem parat festinus." Cf. ii, 4, p. 109 ; ii, 5, p. 111 ; ii, 38, p. 155.

[5] Ib. ii, 3, p. 106.

[6] Ib. i, 29, p. 57 : " Quadam brumali et valde frigida die " Colmcille began to weep for the treatment the brothers were receiving at Durrow.

[7] Ib. i, 6, p. 30.

[8] Ib. iii, 16, p. 218 : " collectis fratribus, cum quadam non mediocri obiurgatione inquirit quis de illis esset transgressionis obnoxius." Ib. iii, 21, p. 226. (One of the brethren disobeys a formal order not to visit the abbot's cell, Colmcille reproves him sharply, and prophesies that he will lose his vocation and fall into sin, but that he will die in penitence.)

happened that he got sick and died while Colmán was absent, but his body retained the good disposition of its late tenant, for when Colmán, on his return, ordered "the obedient brother" to rise, the obedient brother at once did so.[1] Another brother in St. Comgall's community was distinguished likewise for his obedience. One day as they were crossing the strand while the tide was out, a member of the community reproved this youth for some defect. The obedient brother, according to custom, prostrated himself on the ground in token of submission. He who had given the reproof neglected, by some oversight, to ask him to rise and the company passed on. When they got back to Comgall the obedient brother was missed. Messengers sent back in haste to search for him found him still lying on the sand and in imminent danger of death from the incoming tide.[2] Thus he was putting into practice Columban's precept and ready to die rather than violate a rule. In another case it is related that a monk on whose body an iron band was fastened by a superior, with the result that the flesh putrified, took no means to free himself from his torments. When the abbot asked why he had taken this course he replied, "Because the body in question is not mine."[3] Again it is related that one day monks from St. Carthach's community were working beside a stream when a monk in charge suddenly called out "Colmán, get into the water," and immediately twelve Colmáns, without a moment's delay to take off clothes, jumped into the river.[4] Stock examples also occur, like that of the monk who was ordered to drown his little son ,and who started off without a word to do so,[5] and that of the brother who left the letter o half-finished and set off at the call of obedience to his new duty.[6] Imaginative writers found more original illustrations. The river Shannon, for instance, was granted leave to carry a basket from Clonmacnois to Inis Cathaig, and fulfilled its task with credit, notwithstanding the rapids at Doonass and other obstacles.[7] Ciarán, too, jumped up so quickly at the

. [1] V.S.H. i, p. 265. [2] Ib. ii, p. 12.
[3] V.S.H. i, p. 189: "quia non est meum istud corpus."
[4] V.S.H. i, p. 189.
[5] V.S.H. i, p. 159: "Frater Tulchanus plus amat filium suum quam Deum." Hence the order to drown the son. But St. Cainnech saved the son and was so incensed at the "crudele imperium" that he could hardly be appeased. Cf. Cass., Inst. iv, 27, p. 67, for a similar order.
[6] V.S.H. i, p. 153: "pro festinatione obedientiae inplendae dimidiam partem scribens litterae O, alteram partem semiplenam reliquit imperfectam."
[7] Lism. L. p. 72.

sound of the bell that the wild deer whose horns were his book-
stand grew frightened, and sped away with his book [1]   All
these incidents have little value as history, but they show
clearly the spirit of submission to authority that was expected
to reign among the monks.

Obedience was, therefore, strictly inculcated in Ireland,
but not more strictly than in other countries where the
monastic ideal was welcomed.   Cassian, who expounds so
ably the best traditions of the Egyptian ascetics, emphasizes
the care with which the young were formed in the practice
of this virtue.   Self-will had to be completely abandoned.[2]
Neglect in this particular might lead to a bad end, even after
fifty years of a holy life.[3]   On this account the tests were
severe.[4]   Some were extraordinary, as when the abbot John
ordered his disciple to get into a furnace,[5] and again to carry
water on his shoulders two miles each day to water a dry
stick.[6]   The disciple, of course, escaped from the furnace,
and his devotion to the stick was rewarded when, in the
third year, it broke into blossom.   More wonderful was the
case of the disciple sent to fetch a lioness to his senior's cell.
In a short time he appeared at the door of the hut with the
lioness by his side.   When the *senior* Paul came out and saw how
the simple obedience of his disciple had been blessed, he feared
for his humility, and therefore contented himself with the
dry remark : " Birds of a feather flock together.   You have no
brains ; neither has she.   You are well met.   Let her go."[7]
Instances are quoted which are worse than silly, like that of
the *senior* who sent his disciple at times to steal from the
brethren, and found that the young man, unlike the disciple
just mentioned, had plenty of brains for that kind of work.[8]
St. Basil lays down forcibly that the sphere of obedience is
limited by the divine law.[9]   If he who commands shows

---

[1] Ib., p. 123.
[2] *Conl.* xxiv, 23, p. 699. Sulp. Sev. *Dial.* i, 10, p. 161–2 : " quibus summum
ius est, abbatis imperio vivere, nihil suo arbitrio agere, per omnia ad nutum
illius potestatemque pendere."
[3] Ib. ii, 5, p. 44 : " Hero, after fifty years in the desert, failed to persevere
quia suis definitionibus regi quam consiliis vel conlationibus fratrum
maluit oboedire."
[4] Cass., *Inst.* iv, 24 ff, p. 63. *Conl.* iv, 10, 20, etc., p. 104, 116, etc.
[5] Sulp. Sev. *Dial.* i, 18, p. 170 ff. Cass., *Inst.* iv, 24 ff.
[6] Ib.
[7] *Verb. Sen.* P.L. lxxiii, 27, c. 755–6.
[8] *Apoph. Patrum* , P.G. lxv, c. 419.
[9] *Reg. brev. tract.* cxiv. Cf. Ruf. *Interr.* xiii, c. 505–6.

disregard for this, the disciple is bound to disobey. "There is," he says, "no small difference in the orders given, for some are contrary to the commandment of the Lord, or perhaps destroy and corrupt it by an admixture of what is forbidden ; others help the commandment of the Lord ; others again, if not obviously fulfilling it, yet contribute towards this end. . . . So that if we are given an order which fulfils the commandment of the Lord, or contributes to its fulfilment, we must receive it eagerly and carefully as the will of God. But when we receive an order from any one that is contrary to the commandment of the Lord, or destroys or corrupts it, then it is time to say, ' We must obey God rather than men ' (Acts v. 29). . . . He who hinders the doing of the Lord's command or persuades us to do what is forbidden by Him, be he ever so close a relation, or exceedingly illustrious, ought to be shunned and abominated by every-one who loves the Lord." Given that the commands are legitimate, we must obey one another as servants obey their masters,[1] never seeking to select for ourselves what we shall do,[2] and never gainsaying, "for there are no limits to obedience except death."[3] This teaching goes back to Tabennisi, where the government was very mild, yet where murmuring (in reality the negation of obedience) was so serious an offence that the brother guilty of it was segregated from the community and sent to the infirmary as a sick man.[4] The reason for thus insisting on obedience, as said at the beginning, is obvious : without obedience there can be no peace and concord, no security,[5] and without these there can be no monastery. How hard the practice was we learn from the prevalence of Sarabaites and other wandering monks who were utterly unable to renounce their own wills, who competed with one another in fasting, and spent their time sighing, visiting ladies, and sneering at the clergy.[6]

---

[1] *Reg. brev. tract.*, cxv.
[2] Ib. cxvii.
[3] Ib. clii.
[4] *Reg. Pach.* clxiv. Albers 35 : "eum habebunt ut unum de aegrotantibus, et ponetur in loco infirmorum, ibique alitur otiosus donec redeat ad veritatem." Cf. iii, xi, xxiii, xxx, lviii, etc.
[5] Cass., *Conl.* xxiv, 26, p. 709-10.
[6] Cass., *Conl.* xviii, 7, p. 513. Ib. viii, p. 516 : "one, two or three in cell without an abbot—Ut absoluti a seniorum iugo exercendi voluntates suas ac procedendi vel quo placuerit evagandi agendive quod libitum fuerit habeant libertatem." Cf. St. Jer. *Ep.* xxii, 34, p. 201.

(e)—The Position as Regards Stability.

It need hardly be said that the monastic vow was of a final character, so that he who thus bound himself was obliged to live as a monk for the remainder of his days. Of what use was it to begin well if there was no perseverance in good?[1] Apart from extraordinary circumstances, which in any age might justify a young religious in returning to the world,[2] loss of vocation was regarded as a calamity and a crime.[3] He who had brought such a fate upon himself remained, of course, within the pale of God's mercy,[4] but he was likely to have grounds for anxiety when he came to leave this world.

A different question was whether the monk was bound to spend his whole life in the same congregation or monastery. With the very strict ideas of the Irish monks about obedience, it is obvious that the last word on such matters would rest with the superiors. Genuine difficulty might, however, arise in the case where a fervent monk wished to pass from a monastery of less strict to a monastery of more strict observance. Gildas had supplied the solution for this problem about the middle of the sixth century. An abbot, he ruled, of a more lax monastery must never retain a monk who wished to join a community where the manner of life was more severe. On the other hand, the abbot of the strict community should not receive such a monk, unless the abbot whom he had just left had given leave for his departure.[5] The only case in which the fervent monk and the abbot of a strict monastery might take the law into their own hands

---

[1] St. Col. *Ep.* iv, ad *Attal. M.G.H. Ep.*, vol. iii, p. 168 : "in fine enim iudicium consistit et in exitu laus canitur." St. Jer. *Ep.* 54, 6, p. 472 : "non quaeruntur in Christianis initia sed finis." *Ep.* 71, 2, p. 3 : " coepisse multorum est, ad calcem pervenisse paucorum."

[2] Wassersch., *I.K.* xlii, 14, p. 165 : " *Sinodus Narbonensis :* A suo monasterio sola pietate patimur transire filium, cum iuxta Evangelii praeceptum parentibus oportet subministrare necessitatem ; post obitum vero eorum, nisi ad suum transeat monasterium a nobis alienus habeatur." This principle is so evident that it probably goes back to the earliest times. To inculcate stability in general St. Augustine is quoted : " Filiole, ubi summa didicisti permanere illic debes, nec desertoris nomine vagus voceris."

[3] Gildas of Maglocunus, *De Excid.*, § 34. *Paenit. Col. Z.K.G.* xiv, p. 441 A : *Discedere* classed with murder, fornication, theft, etc. *V.S.H.* ii, p. 102 : " Heu, heu, heu, iste homo vitam hic nobiscum suam non consummabit. Deinde ille infelix . . . deseruit locum et habitum suum ad saeculum tendens, et in saeculo male vivens turpiter in peccatis periit." Ib. p. 154 : " et quicunque suus monachus negaverit eum et fugitivus fuerit ab eo non sit secum in caelo." Ib., p. 150 : " filius mortis."

[4] *Adam.* iii, 21, p. 226. The young monk who lost his vocation would do penance before his death.

[5] *Frag.* v p. 164. Wassersch. xxxix, 9, p. 151 ; 6, p. 150.

was when the abbot of the laxer monastery was openly living in sin,[1] or when discipline had totally collapsed. In the latter case the monk might act on the principle, " When the ship goes down let him who can do so swim."[2] As long as the abbot retained his reputation as the ruler of a virtuous house his right to exact obedience could not be gainsaid ; and the monk who left him on his own responsibility and wandered about among the people was to be excommunicated as a fugitive, and driven back to his monastery.[3] Even nuns who had found the burden of monastic discipline more than they could bear and had fled or attempted to flee, might be treated in the same way.[4]

What, however, of the monk who might desire to abandon his community for contemplative life in the desert ? If his retirement was designed to be but for a short period there would, of course, be little objection, for this was a common practice among the great saints of the First and Second Orders[5] ; but what if his absence was designed to endure for an indefinite period or for life ?

This problem does not seem to have arisen in the Pachomian monasteries, but it certainly was present to St. Basil, who discussed it at some length. In reply to the query whether those " who go out from the brotherhood and desire to lead a solitary life (or to follow the same ideal of piety in company with a few others) should be cut off "[6] he replies ambiguously : " The Lord often said, ' The Son doeth nothing of Himself ' (John v. 19), and again, ' I am come down from heaven not to do my own will, but the will of the Father that sent me ' (John vi, 38) ; and the Apostle testifies : ' The flesh lusteth against the Spirit and the Spirit against the flesh ; and these are contrary the one to the other, that we may not do the things that we would ' (Gal. v. 17). Therefore, whatever is chosen to please one's will is alien to the character of godly men."[7] Elsewhere the distinguished Cappadocian emphasises the superiority of the common life.[8] " To begin with, no one

---

[1] *Frag.* iv, p. 162. Wassersch. 1, c. 7, p. 150 ; 12, p. 151. This is why it is expressly stated in *Adam.* i, 6, p. 30, that the superior of the monk who had left without leave was a *religiosus abbas.*
[2] Wassersch. op. cit., xxxix, 7, 151 : " nave fracta qui potest natare natet."
[3] Ib. 8 and 11, p. 151.
[4] Jon. *V. Col.* ii, 19, p. 273.
[5] Supra p. 220.
[6] ἀφορίζειν.
[7] *Reg. brev. tract.*, lxxiv.
[8] *Reg. fus tract.*, vii.

of us is self-sufficient, even as regards bodily needs . . . But apart from this the fashion of the love of Christ does not allow us to look each at his own good. For ' love,' we read, ' seeketh not its own ' (1 Cor. xiii. 5). Now the solitary life has one aim, the service of the needs of the individual. But this is plainly in conflict with the law of love, which the apostle fulfilled when he sought not his own advantage, but that of the many, that they might be saved. Secondly in such separation the man will not even recognize his faults readily, not having anyone to reprove him and to set him right with kindness and compassion. A spiritual guide is difficult to find in solitude, unless one has already formed a link with him in community life. Furthermore, living together has other benefits, not easily enumerated." St. Basil, then, seems to desire that the monk should always remain in the society of his brethren, though he is not prepared to hold that the monk who thinks otherwise and retires with permission to solitude is acting wrongly.[1] Later the Eastern Church came to regard cenobitism as a preparatory stage for the higher anachoretical life.[2] St. Jerome[3] and Evagrius,[4] both of whom had experiences of communities as well as of the desert, had their doubts about the wisdom of this step ; but we learn from Cassian that, among the Egyptian Fathers,[5] such scruples were disregarded. A frank discussion of the whole question is put in the mouth of an ancient named John, who had lived for thirty years in a monastery, then for twenty years in a hermitage, and had finally returned to end his days as a cenobite.[6] When asked why he had come back to the " junior schools,"[7] he replied that he was unable for eremitical discipline and unworthy of the high perfection which such a life implied.[8] Whilst in the desert his soul was so filled with heavenly thoughts and with the contemplation of spiritual truths that he often forgot completely about food, and could not tell at eventide whether he had broken

---

[1] Cf. Clarke, St. Bas. the G., p. 109–12. The Ascetical Works of St. Basil, p. 258, n. 1.
[2] Clarke, l.c.
[3] Ep. xxii, 34. p. 201 ; cxxv, 9.
[4] Evag. Cap. pract. 5, P.G. xl, c. 1223.
[5] The Orientals never hesitated to regard the eremitical ideal as superior. Cf. Theodoret. Hist. Rel., P.G. lxxxii, c. 1293 ff, 1305 ff, etc.
[6] Cass., Conl. xix, 3, p. 536.
[7] Ib. 2, p. 536 : "ad iuniorum scolas."
[8] Ib. : "ille velut inparem se anachoreticae disciplinae et summitate tantae perfectionis indignum . . . dicebat."

his fast during the day or not.[1] So happy was this manner
of life that it could be compared only with the blessedness of the
angels.[2]   But newcomers invaded his solitude and the
distractions in time became so serious that he decided to live
as a good cenobite rather than as a bad anchorite, making
up by obedience for what he was losing by his return to a
lower form of life.[3]   He admitted that, generally speaking,
the anchorite could not absolutely ignore material things,
because he had to manage his little affairs and provide for
his daily needs ; but, on the other hand, the cenobite could
not secure the delights of pure contemplation.[4]   He knew a
few exceptions to this rule, like the Abbots Moses and
Paphnutius, Macarius the Egyptian and Macarius the
Alexandrian.[5] Nothing could be more foolish than to retire
to solitude before bad habits had been purged and virtues
acquired by a formal course of training in a monastery.[6]
Other references show that the superiority of the eremitical
life was in Egypt almost an axiom.[7]

Thus it was, too, at Lérins, though the Gauls, much more

---

[1] Ib. 4, p. 537 : " et ita divinis meditationibus ac spiritualibus theoriis
animus replebatur ut saepe ad vesperam cibum me percepisse nescirem."
[2] Ib. 5, p. 538. " et illam conversationem angelicae beatitudini compa-
randam . . . sectatus sum."
[3] Ib. : " elegi huius disciplinae utcunque implere propositum quam in
illa tam sublimi professione carnalium necessitatum provisione torpere,
ut . . . id quod mihi de illa theoretica sublimitate subtrahitur hac obedientiae
subjectione pensetur."
[4] Ib. 9, p. 543 : " et ideo in utraque professione per omnia consummatum
invenire difficile est, quia nec anachoreta ἀκτημοσύνην, id est, contemptum
ac privationem materialium rerum, nec coenobiota theoreticam ad integrum
potest adsequi puritatem."
[5] Ib.
[6] Ib. 10, p. 544 : " quod vel maxime his evenire consuevit qui non perfecte
in coenobiis instituti, nec excoctis prioribus vitiis ad solitariam se vitam
immaturo desiderio transtulerunt. Cf. 11, p. 545 : " qui ipsas quodammodo
scolas et exercitationis hujus palaestram in qua ad plenum erudiri ac perfici
principia nostra debuerant intempestive intermissa coenobii congregatione
dereliquimus " 13, p. 547 : " nam in solitudine esse non possunt nisi quos
prius coenobiorum medicina sanaverit."
[7] Cass., Conl. xviii, 16 p. 531 : "de primis coenobii scolis ad secundum
anachoreseos gradum tendere." Ib. xviii, 11, p. 513 : " de laudabili coenobiorum palaestra ad excelsa fastigia anachoreticae tendere disciplinae."
Cf. p. 503, Ib. xviii, 6, p. 511 : " qui . . . desiderio sublimioris profectus
contemplationisque divinae solitudinis secreta sectati sunt." Ib. Conl. iii,
1, p. 68 : " (Paphnutius) sublimioris profectus ardore succensus heremi
festinavit penetrare secreta ut Domino, cui inter fratrum turbas positus
sitiebat inseparabiliter inhaerere, nullo deinceps humano consortio retrahente
facilius uniretur." Ib. Inst. v, 26, p. 108 : " alium quoque ordinem qui
excellentior habetur id est, anachoreticarum . . . videre properavimus."
Cf. Sulp. Sev. Dial. i, 10, p. 161 ; 11, p. 163 ; St. Jer. Ep. 22, 24, p. 178 ;
36, p. 200. For some excellent remarks on Martha and Mary see Verb. Sen.,
P.L. lxxiii, § 55, c. 768.

active than contemplative by nature,[1] found life in solitude altogether more trying than did the Egyptians. The monastery at Lérins stood in the north side of the island. Hermits, probably in goodly number, were to be found in the remaining portions of the isle, as also on the neighbouring Lero. To these, rather than to the monks within the monastery, the highest honour was paid.[2] Cassian was here a respected teacher,[3] and we may be sure that his doctrine on the inter-relation between the eremitical and the cenobitical way of life was approved and put into practice.

There can be no doubt that the Irish monks, too, regarded the solitary as more perfect than the cenobite. Hence the general tendency to the desert, which towards the end of the sixth century was so prominent a feature of religious life that it marked for some the beginning of a new era.[4] Much earlier in the development of monasticism in Ireland the same tendency had manifested itself so strongly that domestic discipline was endangered. Burning with desire for the more perfect life of unbroken union with God, monks were ready to treat obedience lightly and set out for the desert, even when their abbots opposed their wishes.[5] Finnian of Clonard had written to Gildas asking what should be done in such cases.[6] We do not know the terms of the Welsh saint's reply, but we are hardly likely to be wrong in concluding that he dwelt on the dangers of solitude, except for those who were far advanced in perfection, and that he urged the necessity of obedience. Further trouble is not recorded until the beginning of the seventh century, when Columban wrote to

---

[1] C. Jullian, *Rev. Hist.* xvi, p. 241.

[2] Arnold, *Caes. v. A. P.*, 521. Cf. Faustus *Ep.* viii " Ruricio filio." *C.S.E.L.* I, p. 210 : " Nam in medio saeculi institutionem eremiticam proferre quanta magnanimitas tanta est difficultas."

[3] *Conlationes* xi–xvii of Cassian were dedicated by the author to Hono-ratus, the celebrated founder of Lérins, " ingenti fratrum coenobio praesidens congregationem suam," and Eucherius, one of Lérins' most brilliant pupils, who lived as a solitary on Lero, and became Bishop of Lyons after A.D. 427. His was the " insulana angelicae congregationis militia " to which Faustus of Riez refers, *Ep.* viii, *C.S.E.L.* xxi, I, p. 210.

[4] *Catal.* H. and S., *Councils* ii, p. 293 : " Tertius ordo sanctorum qui in locis desertis habitabant et oleribus et aqua et eleemosynis (fidelium) vivebant." Cf. Ussher, *Works*, iv, p. 478. Broadly speaking, the classification is correct, but it needs to be modified somewhat. Cf. supra, p. 220-1.

[5] Col. *Ep.* iii, *ad Greg. Papam. M.G.H. Ep.* iii, p. 159 : " (monachi) qui pro Dei intuitu, et vitae perfectioris desiderio accensi, contra vota venientes primae conversionis loca relinquunt et, invitis abbatibus, aut laxantur aut ad deserta fugiunt."

[6] Ib. : " Vennianus auctor Gildam de his interrogavit et elegantissime ille respondit."

St. Gregory intimating that the danger was then increasing,[1] and asking for the great Pope's views.[2] Many monks, it seems, longed for the hermitage so intensely that they had to be let go ; or, if permission was withheld, they fled. Once again we are ignorant of the terms of St. Gregory's reply, if he did reply. As this was the period of the Third Order in Ireland, we may assume that abbots were more generous than heretofore in allowing their subjects to devote themselves to contemplation ; whilst insisting that a long and careful cenobitical training should be a necessary qualification for any such effort.[3] The anchorite would probably retain the closest connection with his own monastery[4] and return to it if he left the desert, so that the principle of stability would not be grievously affected.

Difficulty might again arise in consequence of the high esteem in which pilgrimage was held. The principle of retirement, withdrawal from one's native heath, from friends, relations and old associations, was, as we have seen, accepted more or less universally since the beginning of monasticism.[5] Such a sacrifice had not only negative value as a method of escape from inevitable distractions, but also positive value as a painful ascetical exercise. This was recognised by St. Patrick in express terms. " Whence came to me," he says, " that gift so great, so salutary, the knowledge and love of God so intense that I might part with fatherland and relations ? "[6] St. Patrick had parted in the fullest sense

---

[1] Ib. : "sed tamen discedendi studio semper maior metus accrescit."

[2] Ib. : " quid faciendum de monachis illis," etc.

[3] This is the very definition of " anchorite " in a quotation from *Isidore* adopted into the Irish collection of canons. Wassersch. xxxix, 3, p. 148.: " Tertium genus est anachoretarum, qui *iam coenobiali conversatione perfecti* semetipsos includunt in cellulis, procul a conspectu hominum remotis, nemini ad se praebentes accessum, *sed in sola contemplatione theorica viventes* perseverant." Cf. *Adam*. iii, 23, p. 237 : " Qui videlicet Virgnous, *post multos in subjectione inter fratres irreprehensibiliter expletos annos* anos duodecim *in loco anachoretarum* in Muirbulcmar, vitam ducens anachoreticam, Christi victor miles explevit." Ib. i, 49, p. 96 : " Finanus, qui vitam multis anachoreticam annis iuxta Roberetj monasterium campi irreprehensibiliter ducebat."

[4] Bede iv, 26, p. 271 : " St. Cuthbert entered as a monk at Lindisfarne, but *crescentibus meritis religiosae intentionis* ad anachoreticae quoque contemplationis secreta pervenit," on the island of Farne. He became bishop of Lindisfarne in A.D. 684, and asked to be buried in Farne " ubi non parvo tempore pro Domino militaret." (ib. 'p, 275). Oidilwald (Ethelwald) succeeded him as an anchorite on the island (ib. v, 1, p. 281). Aed of Sléibte was not merely an anchorite (*A.U.* 699) but also bishop and abbot. In later times monk-anchorites and bishop-anchorites are frequently mentioned.

[5] Supra. p. 213 ff.

[6] *Conf.*, 36, p. 246 : " Unde mihi postmodum donum tam magnum, tam salubre, Deum agnoscere vel deligere, sed ut patriam et parentes amitterem ? "

with country and friends. St. Martin had done likewise, for he was a native of Pannonia, not of Gaul. The Irish character is especially sensitive to the torment of exile[1] : all the greater reason then why this pain should be experienced. Examples from Britain were not lacking.[2] If the doctrine was sound, why hesitation or half-heartedness in putting it into practice ?[3] The question then was whether a monk under obedience might not be justified in ignoring his abbot upon this point, and setting out, if he thought fit, for some distant land. All the greater was the temptation to act independently when it was considered that pilgrimage would not merely bring advantage to the exile's own soul but to the souls of those whom he would convert from paganism or from tepidity, for in the Irish mind pilgrimage and missionary zeal were very closely connected.[4]

---

[1] Cf. Plummer, V.S.H., p. cxxiii : " The Lives also illustrate that home-sickness, so characteristic in all ages of the Irish exile, which it sometimes required a miracle to cure."

[2] Faustus of Riez was a Briton. Riocatus, also a fifth century Briton, made two pilgrimages to Lérins. (Sid. Apoll. Ep., M.G.H. viii, p. 157.) In the sixth century Samson's one message was " Tu frater, peregrinus esse debes." (Williams, Christ., p. 376.) One of Columban's first helpers in Burgundy was a British abbot—Carantoc—settled near Annegray. (Jonas, V.Col. i, 17, p. 165.)

[3] The ascetical value attached to pilgrimage is quite sufficient to explain Colmcille's expedition to Iona. Adamnan's record (Praef. ii, p. 9) that he left of his own free will alone has historical worth. More romantic accounts, however plausible, remain always within the sphere of what Reeves well calls "legendary speculation." Other Irish saints who were his contemporaries and friends were active missionaries like himself among the Scottish peoples, but their permanent residences were in Ireland. (Adam. i, 49, p. 93 ; iii, 17, p. 220.) The intimacy between Comgall and Colmcille is interesting because of Columban's mission to Gaul. Comgall saw how abundantly Colmcille's exile had been blessed, and was willing that the same experiment should be made in another field. Columban himself seems to have been responsible for the suggestion and was chosen to command the expedition. The event proved that a more capable leader could hardly have been found. Exile as a penalty for the worst crimes was also well known in the sixth century. Cf. Paenit. Col. B., p. 443 : " si quis clericus homicidium fecerit . . . X annis exul paeniteat." Ib., p. 444 : " Layman for same crime III annis inermis exul in pane et aqua paeniteat." Ib., p. 445 : " Perjury under threat of death —III annis inermis exul paeniteat." The principle, too, survived. Cf. Ériu vii, p. 148 : " ailittire fo mám apad echtraind " as penance for the constant pilfering of food.

[4] The reason for this may be the fact that the Irish monasteries supplied the territories surrounding them with spiritual ministrations. At any rate Colmcille, though he left Ireland "pro Christo peregrinari volens " (Adam. Praef. ii, p. 9), was hardly settled in Iona when he began to pay attention to the spiritual wants of the local peoples. Like St. Martin (Sulp. Sev. Dial. ii, 4, p. 185), he would be " constantly asking himself with groans why such a multitude should know nothing of Our Lord and Saviour." Columban was likewise a pilgrim (Jonas, V. Col. i, 4, p. 159 : " coepit peregrinationem desiderare." Cf. ib. 3, p. 156 : " ut mare transacto, potioris peregrinationis locum petissem." Ib. 20, p. 195.). But no sooner had he arrived in Gaul than he was anxious to engage in missionary work (ib., p. 60) : " Placet tandem arva Gallica planta terere et mores hominum ferventi aestu sciscitare ut, si salus ibi serenda sit, quantisper commorare ; si obduratas caligine

Such evidence, however, as we possess shows clearly that
the monastery might not be abandoned, even for this high
purpose, without leave of the superior.] Some monks from
St. Fintan's monastery of Cluain Eidnech, "glowing with
an excessive desire for pilgrimage and unwilling to live in
their own country," left without Fintan's consent. They
journeyed first to Bangor and then to Britain. One, at least,
of their number had troubles of conscience and returned, but
Fintan was only mildly displeased, for he was confident that
the monks had acted in good faith.[1] In St. Berach's monastery
there was a certain brother who, without waiting to ask his
superior for leave, made a vow to go on pilgrimage to Rome.
Berach liked his zeal, but he was not ready to let him go, so
he prayed that God might free the brother from his resolution.
His prayer was granted. The brother had a dream in which
he thought he made a tour to Rome under the care of an
excellent guide. He awoke quite satisfied, and said no more
about his vow.[2] Superiors themselves were warned in other
ways against indiscreet pilgrimages. Thus Coemgen was
shown that his wish to journey abroad was evil in the shape
of good and was suggested by a demon.[3] The holy bishop
Lugaid, who determined in his youth to abandon Ireland
and be a pilgrim in some foreign land, was dissuaded from
his purpose by an angel.[4] Converted in this wise he was able
himself to divert St. Comgall from a similar course.[5] In
general, then, the principle seems to be that subjects must
not set out on pilgrimage without leave from their superiors;
nor superiors without advice and reflection.

§4—THE MONASTIC FAMILY.

(a)—The Abbot.

At the head of the community or brotherhood stood the
superior, called in Ireland from the earliest times abb (from

---

arrogantiae mentes repperiant, ad vicinas nationes pertransire." Similarly,
when Theudebert offered him a foundation within his kingdom, one of the
attractions was " proximasque ad praedicandum nationes undique haberi "
(i, 27, p. 22) : Columban thought of evangelising the Veneti, but was warned
off by an angel (ib., p. 216–7). He disliked Bregenz, but promised to stay
there a while, " ob fidem in gentibus serendam " (ib., p. 213). When Eusthasius visited him at Bobbio he was ordered to evangelize the Warasqui of
lower Burgundy (ib. ii, 8, p. 243). We hear, on the other hand, of a Frankish
brother named Autiernus who pressed for leave to go to Ireland " peregri-
nandi causa " (ib. i, 11, p. 170).

[1] V.S.H. ii, p. 100–1.
[2] V.S.H. i, p. 85–6.   [3] Ib. i, p. 250.
[4] Ib. i, p. 240.   [5] V.S.H. ii, p. 7.

abbas, " father,")[1] or its Latin equivalent Pater,[2] though the more general term senior is also met with.[3] At an early period, too, the title princeps became common.[4] Not one of these terms is in origin peculiar to Ireland.[5]

In the great sixth century monasteries the founders were, very naturally, the first abbots. These had shown their

[1] Col. Ep. iii ad Greg. Papam. M.G.H. Ep. iii, p. 159 (Cf. Gildas, Frag. vii, p. 266). Reg. Coen. x, p. 229 MP. viii, p. 225, MNP. ix, p. 227, MNP. Adam. i, p 16 ; i, 2, p. 21 monachorum Abbas. A.U. 547 onwards. V.S.H. and B.N.E., passim. Wassersch. I.K. xxxvii, 29, p. 138, etc.
[2] Reg. Coen. viii, p. 225, MP. : " pater monasterii." Adam. Praef. ii, p. 4 : " monasteriorum pater et fundator." Jonas, V. Col. i, 4, p. 158 : " Commogellus egregius inter suos monachorum pater." Ib. ii, 12 : " (Burgundofara) mater monasterii." Ib., 15, p. 265.
[3] Adam. i, 37, p. 72 : " scitis quod noster senior Columba de nobis anxie cogitet."
[4] A.U. 682, B. Arm. 6a ; 22a ; 32b : " principes et episcopi." Wassersch. I.K. xxxvii, 13, p. 134. Ib. 27, p. 138, etc.
[5] Verb. Sen. P.L. lxxiii, col. 753 : " pater monasterii." Ib., col. 756-7 : St. Jer. Ep. xxii, 35, p. 199 : " patri omnium." In St. Jerome's translation of the Pachomian rule the terms are " pater monasterii," or " princeps monasterii" for the Abbot ; " praepositus," for the superior of a house within the monastery (Albers, p. 10, 13, 14, 22, etc.). Similarly, in St. Jerome's translation of the doctrine of Oresius (op. cit., p. 96, 97, 98). Princeps occurs elsewhere, too, in St. Jerome's writings (cf. Ep. 23, 2, p. 212 : " ut monasterii princeps, mater virginum fieret." Ep. 58, 5, p. 534 : " nos autem habemus propositi nostri principes Paulos, Antonios," etc.). He speaks also of a praepositus and, in one passage (Ep 66, 4, p. 651) of an $\mathring{\alpha}\rho\chi\iota\sigma\tau\rho\alpha\tau\eta\gamma\acute{o}s$ monachorum. Cassian denotes the superior generally by praepositus (Conl. xviii, 7, p. 514 : " se coenobiorum praepositis subdiderunt." Inst. v, 27. p. 103 : " cum senex Joannes magno coenobio ac multitudini fratrum praepositus advenisset ") ; and this was the term used by St. Augustine when writing his famous letter to nuns (Ep. ccxi, p. 369 : " praepositae tamquam matri obediatur). Abbas, for Cassian (Conl. ii, 13, p. 54 : " Abbas Apollo seniorum probatissimus "), as for the Orientals (St. Nilus, Ep. P.G. lxxix, 99, 223, etc. Apoph. 16, P.G. lxv, col. 335), denotes a monk distinguished for age or virtue, but not necessarily a superior. In the Latin translation of the early Oriental rule of Serapion, Paphnutius and the two Macarii, the ruler is simply Pater or Senior qui praeest (P.L. xiii, col. 436 : " volumus ergo unum praeesse seniorem super omnes fratres." Col. 437 : " is qui praeest Pater, " etc.). St. Basil refers constantly to, the superior as $\mathring{o}$ $\pi\rho o\epsilon\sigma\tau\acute{\omega}s$ (Reg. fus. tract., 27, 30, 32, etc.), but also as $\mathring{o}$ $\mathring{\epsilon}\Phi\epsilon\sigma\tau\acute{\omega}s$ (ib. 24), $\mathring{o}$ $\pi\rho o\iota\sigma\tau\acute{\alpha}\mu\epsilon\nu os$. (ib. 43), $\mathring{o}$ $\pi\rho o\kappa\alpha\theta\iota\sigma\tau\acute{\omega}\nu$ (ib. 44), $\mathring{o}$ $\pi\rho o\acute{\epsilon}\chi\omega\nu$ (ib. 49), and by periphrases such as $\mathring{o}$ $\kappa o\iota\nu\grave{\eta}\nu$ $\Phi\rho o\nu\tau\acute{\iota}\delta\alpha$ $\pi\epsilon\pi\iota\sigma\tau\epsilon\upsilon\mu\acute{\epsilon}\nu os$ (ib. 25). Rufinus, as a rule, translates it : " qui praeest " (Inter. 15, col. 506 ; Inter. 80, col. 521, etc.). Other Eastern terms for Abbot were $\mathring{\alpha}\rho\chi\iota\mu\alpha\nu\delta\rho\acute{\iota}\tau\eta s$ (H.L. 26, 18, 52, 5, etc. Epiph. Adv. Haeres. P.G. xvi, 156. Theod. Ep. P.G. lxxxiii, 1206, 1226, etc. Verb. Sen. P.L. lxxiii, c. 963) and $\mathring{\eta}\gamma o\acute{\upsilon}\mu\epsilon\nu os$ (H.L. 53, 2, St. Nilus Ep. i, cc. 98, 230. Apoph. i, cc. 187, etc.). In the early period these terms were synonymous, but from the sixth century onwards the former came to signify the ruler of several monasteries ; the latter, the ruler of a subordinate house.

The native Irish word for a superior would be airchennech (from arcenn—Mid. Welsh, arbennic. Cf. Pedersen Vergl. Gramm. ii, 5, 30). It occurs in the sense of " head " in Wb. 28 b 14 (Thes. Pal. i, p. 681), nip sí bes airchennech— " let it not be her (the woman) who is head (of the household.)" Cf. Lism. L., p. 124 : " ingen airchinnig in muilinn ' the daughter of the headman of the mill '." In ecclesiastical usage, however, airchinnech does not become common until the ninth century, when it denotes, not the abbot, but the extern (generally lay) manager of the church property.

capacity for such high responsibility by exceptional zeal and devotion during the period of their spiritual training. Among the privileges of the abbot was probably that of selecting his own successor. Even in the fifth century the second head of the Patrician church of Trim resigned his charge after a short incumbency and put a pilgrim, Cathlaid, in his stead.[1] Ciarán of Clonmacnois is said to have prophesied to the astonished brethren who his successor would be, and it is not unlikely that he left his prophecy fulfilled before departing prematurely to a better world.[2] Colmcille certainly named the second Abbot of Iona.[3] Columban acted likewise when driven from Luxeuil by the vicious Merovingian king.[4] Enda of Aran placed a superior and a vice-superior over each of his ten monasteries and decreed that when the former died the latter should succeed him.[5] Fintan of Cluain Eidnech, when dying, appointed another Fintan of noble birth and saintly manners as his successor.[6] The principle seems to have been retained in theory, however much the liberty of the abbot's choice may have been restricted in fact, for a canon of the Irish collection ordains that opposition is not to be offered to the abbot in the appointing of his successor ; yet that this step should not be taken until the clergy and people of the monastic diocese had been called together and had given their consent to the choice.[7] Fintan is represented as having taken this precaution in the case already referred to.[8] In the Columban monastery of Rebais, however, the new Abbot was elected by the brethren, and only after his predecessor's death,[9] but when this condition was accepted in A.D. 636 the affairs of the community were regulated by a mixed Columban and Benedictine rule.[10]

---

[1] *B. Arm.*, 32a.   [2] *V.S.H.* i, p. 210.
[3] *Adam.* i, 2, p. 19. Cf. iii, 23, p. 233.
[4] *M.G.H. Ep.* iii, p. 166 :   Athala was to rule the monastery, or if he preferred to follow Columban into exile, then Waldelenus.
[5] *V.S.H.* ii, p. 68.
[6] *V.S.H.* ii, p. 106 : "genere et moribus nobilis."
[7] Wassersch. *I.K.* xxxvii, 18, p. 135 : "qui contradixerit decreto principis in herede (Irish *comorba*) ordinando non est Christianus sed hereticus." Ib. 20, p. 136 : "Synodus Hibernensis dicit : "Definimus omnem principem non ordinandum nisi vocatis clericis et parochia in unum consentientibus." Cf. 21.
[8] *V.S.H.* ii, p. 105 : "cum licentia et benedictione fratrum et sanctorum qui convenerant ad ipsum visitandum." Cf. Ib. i, 9.
[9] Wassersch. p. xlv. Privilege of Bishop Burgundofaro of Meaux to Rebais : "et quum abbas eiusdem monasterii de saeculo fuerit evocatus quem unanimiter omnis congregatio illa monachorum elegerint, sibi seniorem instituant."
[10] Ib., p. xlvi.

Was the election open to all monks of the monastery or was it necessary that the new Abbot should be of the founder's kin ? Reeves has shown that the first four successors of St. Colmcille were of the race of Conall Gulban ; the genealogy of the sixth Abbot (Suibne, A.D. 652-7), is doubtful ; the seventh, eighth and ninth were again of the Cinél Conaill ; whilst the tenth (Conamail, A.D. 704-10), was of the race of Colla Uais, and was therefore one of the Airgialla. He concludes from this that succession to the abbacy was limited deliberately to the race of Conall, so that " clanship " existed, even in the community of Iona. " The surrender," he adds, " of the old Easter and Tonsure, in 716, broke down family prescription, and henceforward the abbacy became an open appointment."[1] A logical connection between these events cannot, however, be demonstrated. The election of Conamail precedes the settlement of the dispute ; nor is there any reason to believe that the acceptance of the new date led to so important a change in the constitution of the monastery.

It may, indeed, be questioned whether the restriction of the succession to the race of Conall was at any time a matter of deliberate choice. The families of the Cinél Conaill were numerous enough to provide Iona with the great majority of its monks,[2] and it is not improbable that they did so. When the time to appoint a new abbot came, there would then be few others to select from. Derry, in the same way, may have been peopled chiefly from the Cinél n-Eogain, and Durrow chiefly from the Southern Uí Néill.

That there was a tendency in Ireland to make such restrictions is willingly conceded. The case of Trim (already referred to more than once), with its ecclesiastical and secular succession side by side, suggests that the government of that Church was not decided for reasons of merit alone.[3] In the Book of Armagh we have the case of Feth Fio.[4] Elsewhere it is stated that the successor of Carthach of Lismore was always of the Ciarraige.[5] The office of vice-superior at Derry and

---

[1] Adam., p. 342.

[2] Such names, however, as Oissene moccu Neth Corb (the royal line of Leinster), Mailodran moccu Rin (of the Cuirenrige, in the Boyne Valley) and Silnan Moccu Sogin (a people settled in Galway and elsewhere in Ireland), show that the monks did not come exclusively from Tír Chonaill. Cf. MacNeill, Early Irish Population Groups, P.R.I.A. xxix, pp. 61, 83, 100.

[3] B. Arm., 32b.

[4] Ib., 33.

[5] V.S.H. i, 188 : " ille monachus de gente Chiaraige erat, de qua gente successores sunt semper sancti Carthagi."

all the higher offices at Drumcliff were reserved for the Cinél Conaill.[1] We know finally from the civil law that a time came when the principle was regarded as universally valid.[2]

Nor was a similar practice unknown in other countries. Apart from Armenia, where the primacy was transmitted in a direct line for generations,[3] we have examples in Gaul, where the retention of ecclesiastical offices in one family was common in the fifth century. When Gregory of Tours (died 594) wrote his " History of the Franks," all the bishops of that city, save five, were taken from his family. Nearly all the bishops of Gaul in the fifth century were related to one another.[4] Even Caesarius of Arles. great saint though he was, and trained in a monastery, did not cut himself off completely from family connections. His sister was an abbess ; his nephew remained beside him as a kind of secretary ; his niece again was an abbess, and others among his relatives held ecclesiastical positions of distinction.[5]

What was the position in this respect in the greatest of Irish monasteries, Clonmacnois ? Turning to the *Annals* we find that St. Ciarán's successor, Oenu moccu Loígse (died 570 or 577), came from Loígis Rete, somewhere near Maryborough.[6] His successor, MacNisse (died 585), came from the seaboard of County Down.[7] Ailither (died 599) was of the Muscraige, and was therefore a Munsterman, for the six divisions of Muscraige territory lay in Cork and Tipperary.[8] His successor, Tolua Fota (died 614), was of the Corcu Moga, a people settled in the Barony of Killian,. County Galway.[9] After him came Colmán moccu Barddene (died 628) of the sept called Dál mBarddene, originally of Ulster, but settled in historic times in County Cork, somewhere in the neighbourhood of Kinsale.[10] Next in order comes Crónán Moccu

---

[1] *Lism. L.*, p. 308.
[2] *Ancient Laws* iii, 72 ff.
[3] Duchesne : *Early Hist. of the Christ. Church.* Eng. Transl. London, 1924, vol. iii, p. 371.
[4] Cf. Hauck : *K.G.D.* i, p. 127 ; Löning : *Gesch. des deutsch. Kirchenrechts* ii, p. 233, f.
[5] Arnold : *C. von A.*, p. 14.
[6] *A.U.* 569. Cf. *Chron. Scot.*, *A. Clon.*, *A.F.M.*, *A. Tig.*, *Rev. Celt.* xvii
[7] *Chron. S.* : d'Ultaib dó. Cf. *A. Clon.*, *A.U.* s.a. 584.
[8] *A. U.* 598. *Chron. S.* : " do Muscraige a chenel." *A. Tig.* O'Don. *Book of R.*, p. 42 n.
[9] *A.U.* 613. *A. Tig.* : " do Corco Mogha." *Chron. S.*, *A.F.M.*, *Onom. Goed.* s.v.
[10] *A.U.* 628. *A. Clon. A.F.M. A. Tig.* : " do Dháil Bardani Ulad." But Cf. MacNeill, *P.R.I.A.* xxix, sect. C., no. 4, p. 96.

Loegde (died 637) of the Corcu Loegde or Dáirine, now represented by the diocese of Ross, in Cork.[1] He was succeeded by Aedlug, son of Samann (died 652), sprung from the Gailenga of *Gailenga in Chorainn*, in Sligo or Mayo.[2] After him came Baetán Moccu Cormaic (died 664), of the Conmaicne Mara, Connemara, on the Galway seaboard.[3] During the great pestilence of 665, two abbots died. The first of these, Colmán Cas, who ruled but three days, was of the Corcu Moga, in East Galway, already mentioned[4]; the second, Cumméne, was of the Greccraige of Loch Techet, whose ancient territory comprised the barony of Coolavin, portions of the neighbouring baronies of Leney and Corran, and a part of Northern Roscommon.[5] Colmán, whose death is the next to be recorded (678), was of Mag Airtig, in Northern Roscommon, near Loch Techet (Loch Gara).[6] Crónán Becc (died 694) was of the Cuailnge in Louth.[7] Osséne (died 706) was of the Calraige Tethba, settled in Westmeath and Longford, but the reference to Fremiunn shows that he came from Frewen Hill, west of Loch n-Uair (Owel), in the former county.[8] His next two successors were once more Connachtmen.[9]

Two points of considerable interest emerge from this record. The first is that the abbots of Clonmacnois for two centuries were sprung, like the founder, St. Ciarán,[10] from a tributary

---

[1] *A.U.* 636. *A.Clon. Chron. S. A.F.M. A. Tig.*, p. 184. MacNeill, op. cit., p. 40, 44 n. 46, 83. Cf. the tract " Indarba Mochuda a rRaithin," *B.N.E.* i, p. 305. This Crónán comes with Diarmait the king to expel Mochuda, and the latter reproaches him for his act, saying : " you are making a laughing stock of us both, for henceforth it will be a proverb in these parts, ' A Munsterman has expelled a Munsterman '."

[2] *A.U.* 651. *Chron. S. A. Tig.*, p. 192. *Onom. Goed.*, s.v.

[3] *A.U.* 663. *Chron. S.* : " do Conmaicne Mara a chenél." *Onom. Goed.* s.v.

[4] *A.U.* 664. *Chron. S.* 661.

[5] *A.U.* 664. *Chron. S. Onom. Goed.* s.v.

[6] *Chron. S.* 679. *A. Tig.*, p. 208. *Onom. Goed.* s.v. For exact position of Airtech see map facing title page in O'Don. *Tribes and Cust. of Hy Many*, Dublin, 1843.

[7] *A.U.* 693. *A. Tig.*, p. 213. *Onom. Goed.* s.v.

[8] *A.U.* 705. *Chron. S.* : " Fremuinn do Calraige Teptha dó." *A. Tig.*, p. 220.

[9] *A.U.* 712, 723. Failbe becc of Gailenga in Choraind (*A. Tig.*, p. 223) and Cuinles (do Sogain Connacht dó. *A. Tig.*, p. 231—Uí Máine in Galway, *Onom. Goed.* s.v.).

[10] Macalister, *Latin and Irish Lives*, p. 104 ff. The argument (p. 106) that Ciarán was not of gentle parents because he was not put out to fosterage, does not take sufficient account of the status of craftsmen. A chariot-wright had the status of a bóaire (MacNeill : Law of Franchise, *P.R.I.A.* xxxvi, Sect. C., No. 16, 1923, p. 280), and " the accurate wright of oaken houses " was equal in franchise to an aire déso (ib. p. 279). There was thus no reason why Ciarán should not have been fostered had his parents wished to entrust him to other hands. Cf. supra, p. 119.

sept, and probably all were descendants of the aboriginal pre-Celtic peoples.[1] As with the abbots, so with the rest of the community. The second is that Clonmacnois drew its monks from regions as far apart as Down and Kinsale, Connemara and Louth, and that the office of abbot was open to all without restriction. What, then, of the great Uí Néill families of the south, whose favour to Clonmacnois, recognised in the tradition of the monastery, was undoubtedly responsible for much of its distinction ? Did members of these families, when they wished to become monks, choose some other monastery ? It must be concluded that they did, for the failure of even one amongst them to rise to the highest position in Conmacnois would otherwise be inexplicable. The suggestion lies near that the Uí Néill of the south entered the monastery of Durrow, belonging to the federation of their kinsman, Colmcille, but the special regard in which Clonmacnois was held by the kings and princes of their sept, and which goes back to the days of Colmcille himself,[2] is then all the more remarkable. Incidentally the religious and moral powers latent in the older peoples appear in a very favourable light, for Clonmacnois had hardly an equal among the monasteries of the country.

In the other important settlements the family connections of the abbots cannot be determined clearly. References, however, to Senach, the second abbot of Cluain Iraird, whose first visit to that monastery was as a member of a raiding party from Fir Tulach[3] (Fartullagh, barony of Westmeath), and to Crónán, the Munsterman, who was the first to succeed Maedóc of Ferns,[4] himself a Connachtman, do not lead us to believe that such connections were essential in the sixth or the early seventh century. It must also be remembered that even later, when the preferential rights of certain

---

[1] The third abbot, MacNissi, was of the *Ulaid*, but of the petty state on the Down seaboard called by that name, rather than of the over-kingdom called *Ulaid*, which embraced the kingdoms of Dál n-Araide and Dál Riata, as well as the petty kingdom of *Ulaid*. The rulers, at least, of this state do not seem to have been Celts, for their genealogy is traced to Dedu, son of Sen. Thus they are of the *Clanna Dedad* or *Érainn*, one of the most prominent pre-Celtic peoples. Cf. MacNeill : *Early Irish Population Groups*, P.R.I.A. xxix, C., 4, p. 96–7. *Celtic Ireland*, p. 13. 91 ff.

[2] *Adam.* i, 3, p. 24 : " Colmcille, during a sojourn in Ireland, visited Clonmacnois, where he was received with the greatest honour by Ailither (the fourth abbot, died 599) and the brethren."

[3] *Lism. L.*, p. 78. Cf. *Cod. Salm. col.*, 198–9.

[4] *V.S.H.* ii, p. 154.

families were fully recognised, the condition was invariably added that the families concerned should have candidates suited—religiously and otherwise—for the office.[1] If not, there was to be no question of their appointment, though steps might be taken to secure that the family preserved its interest in the endowment. As might be expected, this arrangement led to the gravest abuses.

To assist the abbot in the various small tasks of the day, to carry his orders to the brethren and to help him generally in the more mechanical part of his duties, one of the monks was placed at his disposal as a kind of private secretary. In the Latin texts this official is called simply *minister* or servant. In the *Life of Colmcille* frequent reference is made to his loyal *minister* Diarmait, whose devotion to his saintly master was unbounded, and who was treated in return as the most intimate of friends.[2] Columban, too, had his private attendant at Luxeuil, first a fellow-countryman named Domoel, and later a Frankish brother named Chagnoald.[3] When Columban retired to solitude in the desert these were allowed to visit him with news of the more important happenings and requests for instructions where difficulties had to be met.[4] A brother sick unto death is found at Luxeuil enjoying the same privileges.[5] Columban had brought the custom with him from Bangor, where his master, Comgall, was served in the same way.[6] Moling, too, had a private attendant, who visited him at fixed intervals in his cell by the Barrow.[7] Even St. Ita had a youthful nun to render her personal service.[8] In later times the principle was accepted as a normal feature of the monastic institute.[9] The practice goes back to Gaul, where Sulpicius Severus had a boy to attend

---

[1] *B. Arm.*, 33. *Laws*, iii, 72 ff.

[2] *Adam.* ii, 30, p. 144 : "Diormitius, sancti pius minister." Cf. i, p. 33; 12, p. 40 ; 24, p. 54 ; 29, p. 57 ; 30. p. 58 ; 34, p. 64 ; iii, 11, p. 209 ; 23, p. 230 ; etc.

[3] Jonas, *V. Col.* i, 9, p. 168 : "puerulus quidam nomine Domoalis " i, 1, 28, p. 218 : "contentus tantum unius ministri Chagnoaldi famulatu." Cf. Ib. 17, p. 185.

[4] Jonas, *V. Col.* i, 9, p. 168 : " (Domoalis), qui cum certas opportunitates monasterii evenissent solus patri renuntiaret, ac fratribus observanda referret."

[5] Ib. 17 p. 184.

[6] *V.S.H.* ii p. 9 : "Frater qui erat sancti Comgalli minister, Crimthann nomine."

[7] Ib. p. 191, 200.

[8] Ib. p. 123.

[9] Wassersch. *I.K.* xxxvii, 14, p. 135 : "de eo, quod debet princeps habere ministrum."

him in his cell,[1] and finally to Egypt, where abbots and solitaries were commonly assisted by select disciples.[2]

(b)—Seniores.

Round the abbot stood the *seniores*,[3] or elder brethren (in Irish *sruthi*, sometimes *senóri*),[4] men who had grown old in the practice of virtue. These were, in a sense, the aristocrats of the monastery. Offices of authority were filled regularly from their ranks, so that the word *senior* in Irish usage suggests superiority and connotes the duty of obedience.[5] In a general way they had the direction and correction of the junior monks, an offender among whom might be called before them for examination and punishment.[6] On their judgment it would largely depend whether the novice was allowed to enter the community or was dismissed as unsuitable.[7] At Clonmacnois the seniors had a house reserved to themselves,[8] but we cannot tell when this privilege was conceded. Something similar is found at Lérins, for the "holy elders" of that island, the "senate" of the community,[9] lived apart from the rest in cells.[10] The term *senior* in the sense which it bears in Ireland is common to the whole monastic literature of the West, as may be seen from the works of Cassian, where it appears almost on every page.[11]

Where the abbot governed more than one monastery, he appointed a local superior to rule over each of the subordinate foundations. In the Iona and Luxeuil federations these

---

[1] *Ep.* ii *C.S.E.L.* i, p. 143 : "puer familiaris."
[2] *H.L.* 74 : "Macarius of Egypt had always two disciples near at hand." Ib. 73 : "Anthony attended by two disciples for last fifteen years of his life." Cf. *Verb. Sen.*, P.L. lxxiii, *Col.* 751, 754, 768, 777, 779, 782, 788.
[3] *Adam.* ii, 5, p. 111. Ib. 44, p. 175. Ib. iii, 9, p. 208 : "paucis quibusdam se circumstantibus senioribus."
[4] *B.N.E.* i, p. 21, etc. (sruithi). *Cormac's Rule*, 11 ; *Ériu* i, p. 64 (senóir). *Rule of Ailbe*, 22. *Ériu*, iii, p. 100 ; 35, p. 104. *Rule of Comgall*, 13. *Ériu* i, 13, p. 196. *Rule of Mochuta*, *I.E.R.* xxvii, 1910. *Do Monorugad Manaice*, 16 (oirmitiu na senóra). *Lism. L.*, p. 135 : "discire fri senóir." Ib., p. 308 : "cendus a sruithi." Ib., p. 7. *Ériu* vii, p. 164, 168.
[5] *V.S.H.* i, 15, 22, 23, 24, 39, 41, 67, 68, 100, etc. Col. *Ep.* i. *M.G.H. Ep.* iii. Wassersch. i, xxiii, ch. i, 2, 3, p. 75. *Adam.* ii, 4, p. 111.
[6] *Reg. Coen.* xii, p. 230, *MP.* Ib. v., p. 223, *MP.*
[7] *Adam.* i, 3, p. 25 : "puer familiaris et necdum senioribus placens."
[8] *Lism. L.*, p. 131.
[9] Eucherius *De Laude eremi.* P.L. l. c. 711.
[10] Sid. Apoll. *Ep.* ix, 3 : "de senatu Lirinensium cellulanorum."
[11] Cass., *Conl.* i, 20, 22 ; ii, 2, 10, 11, 15, 24 ; iv, 20 ; vii, 23, etc. *Inst.* ii, 3, 16 ; iii, 4 ; iv, 7, 23, etc. Cf. *Verba Sen.* P.L. lxxiii, c. 740, 742, 747, 750, etc.

establishments were fully equipped monasteries[1]; elsewhere. they were rarely more than *cellae*, churches cared for by a couple of the brethren.[2] The subordinate superior in each of the Columban groups was called a *praepositus*,[3] but in Irish documents he is called an *abbot*, in recognition of the importance of his house. The brother placed temporarily in charge of a group engaged at some special work is also styled a *praepositus*.[4] This concentration of power over many monasteries in the hands of one abbot is found at Tabennisi, at the very beginning of organized monasticism.[5] It was forbidden by the First Frankish Council at Orleans in A.D. 511,[6] and by other Frankish Councils of the sixth century,[7] but we must remember that this was a regional ordinance which had no effect outside the Frankish kingdom.

(c)—Monastic Officials.

Where the community was large it was inevitable that the more important aspects of its life should be attended to by permanent officials. Little is known about these during the course of the sixth century. In A.D. 697, however, the lines of development are clearly indicated, and the vice-abbot, cellarer and guest-master appear as the leading officers of the monastery.[8]

Most remarkable among these is the vice-abbot (*secnab*),

---

[1] Derry, Durrow, Kells, Drumcliff, etc. Annegray, Fontaines.

[2] *V.S.H.* ii, p. 7 : " et inde plurimas cellas et multa monasteria, non solum in regione Ultorum, sed per alias provincias Hiberniae construxit (Comgallus)." If this notice is true the " multa monasteria " soon became " cellae," for Bangor is the only monastery of St. Comgall of which the *Annals* preserve any record. Cf. ib., p. 231 : " ibi (in regione Ua Cinnselaig) erat cella, in qua erant monachi sancti Comgalli." Ib. i, 23 . " cell Ailbe ; cell Abbain ;" i, 37, 70 : " et ibi cellam quae dicitur Achad Durbcon edificavit. Cella Cluana," etc.

[3] Jonas, *V. Col.* i, 10, p. 170 : " dedit gubernatores praepositos de quorum religione nihil dubitabatur." Cf. *M.G.H.. Ep.* iii, p. 166. *Adam.* i, 31, p. 60 : " ad monachum nomine Cailtanum qui eodem tempore praepositus erat in cella " ; . . . i, 45, p. 86–7 : " vir venerandus Ernanum presbyterum senem suum avunculum ad praeposituram illius monasterii transmisit, quod in Hinba insula ante plures fundaverat annos." Ib. i, 41, p. 78. Cf. *V.S.H.* i, 187 : " ille iam monachus praepositus loci illius erat."

[4] Jonas, *V. Col.* ii, 24, p. 292 : *praepositus* master of works, with thirty brethren under his care. *Reg. Coen.* vii, p. 224, *MP.* ; viii, p. 224, *MP.* : " the aggrieved monk may appeal from his *praepositus* to *noster senior aut ceteri fratres* and finally to the *pater monasterii*." Cf. ib. ix, 227, *MNP. V.S.H.* ii, p. 288 : " a *praepositus* in charge of reapers."

[5] *Vita Pach.*, 9–74.

[6] Levison : *Hist. Zeitschr.* Bd. 109, 1912.

[7] Hauck : *K.G.D.*, p. 267, n. 1.

[8] *Cáin Adamnáin*, § 54. *A.U.* 696. Cf. *Ériu* i, p. 45.

in Latin *secundus abbas*,[1] but often *prior*,[2] who seems to have
been originally the *oeconomus* or administrator of the monastery's material resources.[3] So high were the responsibilities
attaching to this office that he who held it came to command
an authority second only to that of the abbot.[4] On him, more
than on any other, the daily lives of the monks depended.
Even at Luxeuil the *oeconomus* has a pre-eminence we would
hardly expect to find under so strong a ruler as St. Columban,[5]
and in Ireland the position became daily more important as
the lands of the community increased. Though placed thus
next to the abbot in power, there is no proof that the *secnab*
succeeded as a matter of course when the abbot died.[6] For a
second-in-command of this kind we find an example in the
great Pachomian monastery of Tabennisi. Palladius relates
that among its 1,300 members was the noble Aphthonius,
who became his intimate friend, " and is now second[7] in the
monastery. Him they send to Alexandria since nothing can
make him stumble, in order to sell their produce and buy
necessaries "[8] an interesting statement in view of the development in Ireland. In Tabennisi, however, the activity of the
second-in-command in the material affairs of the monastery
was accidental; in Ireland it seems to have been the rule.
St. Basil likewise decrees that a vice-abbot should be appointed
when the abbot is absent or when through bodily infirmity
or some other cause he is unable to undertake the care of the

---

[1] *V.S.H.* i, p. 96 : "qui secundus sancti Boecii abbas ei successit ibi."
Cf. Ib. ii, p. 68.
[2] *V.S.H.* i, p. 159 : "Prior in charge of monks who were drawing wood
from forest." Ib., p. 209 : "the elder brother was *abbas* and, the junior
prior." Ib., p. 266 : "vocavit ad se *priorem*." Ib. ii, p. 167 : "prior monasterii venit ad eos." *Praepositus* is sometimes used in the same sense. Cf.
V.S.H. x, p. 30 : "*praepositus* sui monasterii et procurator omnium rerum
intus et foris." Ib. ii, p. 202 : "*economus* monasterii sancti Comgalli. Quaere
equum a *praeposito*," etc.
[3] Cf. References in Plummer. *V.S.H.* i, p. cxvii, n. 8 and cxviii, n. 2.
[4] Ib., n. 1.
[5] *Reg. Coen.* xii, p. 230 *MP.* : "a leave asked of the oeconomus is not to
be asked again of abbot, without mentioning fact that former had refused."
Cf. Ib. viii, p. 225 *MNP.* ix, p. 227 *MNP.* Did the oeconomus here, too,
become the *secundus ?* Cf. Ib., p. 225 *MNP.* : "abbas vel secundus." The
equonimus Iae of *A.U.* 781 is called *prioir* in *A.F.M.* 777.
[6] In later centuries the right of succession was recognised. Plummer,
op. cit., p. xcvii, draws a distinction in this respect between the *secnab* and
the *tanaise* (abbaid), but the grounds for such a distinction are not clear.
Plummer seems to think that the abbot's *tanaise* was appointed in imitation
of the secular ruler's *tanaise*, but it is much more likely that the historical
process was the reverse.
[7] *H.L.* xxxii, p. 94 : τὸ νῦν δευτερεύων ἐν τῷ μοναστηρίῳ. Cf. *Reg. Pach.*,
Albers 66, 100, 101. Ib., p. 97. *Apoph. P.* P.G. lxv, c. 147–50.
[8] *H.L.*, l.c.

brethren ; but the distinguished Cappadocian does not recommend that the office should be permanent, still less that it should be confided to the chief steward of the monastic property. Outside of Ireland the oeconomus remained in fact an honoured, but at the same time a subordinate, official.[1]

The cellarer (*cellóir*, or *coic*) had under his charge not only the kitchen, but the supplies upon which the kitchen depended.[2] He had, therefore, to be a man in whom the fullest reliance could be placed. Over-generosity on his part might lead to unbecoming ease and laxity, whilst an all too rigorous régime might lead to murmuring, discouragement and discontent.[3] Even Caesarius of Arles proved a failure when appointed to fill this office at Lérins, and had to be superseded by another.[4] Hence much might be said in justification of a statement made in one of the later rules that the discipline of the community depends on the cellarer.[5]

In the same way the guest-master (*fertigis*),[6] was placed in a position of responsibility, as he was in constant touch with visitors who carried about them the atmosphere of the world. The brother chosen for this post would therefore be a man of great tact and virtue.

Minor officials such as the baker,[7] mason, blacksmith,[8] carpenter, miller,[9] tanner,[10] gardener,[11] porter,[12] the brother who looked after the refectory,[13] or managed the cattle,[14] or cared for the monastic cemetery,[15] are also mentioned on occasion. In duties for which no particular skill was required

[1] Cass., *Inst.* iv, 6, p. 51 ; 20, p. 60–1 ; v, 40, p. 112 ; x, 20, p. 189, etc. Cf. *H.L.* 10.
[2] In the *Lives cellarius* alternates with *cocus, dispensator, minister coquinae, dispensator, cocus, custos cellarii*. Plummer *V.S.H.* i, p. 118, n. 4, Cf. *Adam.* i, 17, p. 46 (pincerna-cellarius). Jonas : *V. Col.* i, 16, p. 179 ; ii, 11, p. 258. *Lism. L.*, p. 60, 70, 87, etc.
[3] Cf. Hildemar : *Vita et Reg. S.P. Bened.* Ratisbonae, 1880, p. 373.
[4] *Vita Caes.* i, 6, P.L. lxvii, c. 1003–4.
[5] *Rule of Ailbe*, 32 : " amal biis int acnamad, bid samlaid int ord—as the food is, so will the order be."
[6] In *Lives* also *airchindech tige oiged*, and in Latin *magister hospitum, magister hospitalis, vir cui cura hospitum et pauperum erat, minister hospitum, mansorius*. Plummer, op. cit., p. cxviii, n. 6.
[7] *Adam.* iii, 10, p. 208–9. *V.S.H.* i, p. 241.
[8] Ib. ii, p. 15. Ib. p. 237.
[9] Ib. i, p. 186. Cf. Reeves, *Adam.*, p. 362.
[10] Ib. i, p. 245, 254.
[11] *Adam.* i, 18, p. 47. *V.S.H.* i, 92.
[12] Jonas, *V. Col.* i, 22, p. 204. *Poenit. B.* p. 448. *V.S.H.* i, p. 160.
[13] Ib. ii, p. 88.
[14] Ib. i, p. 77, 79.
[15] Ib. i, p. 131.

there would be frequent changes, the monks being appointed in turn to perform the various tasks.[1]

(d)—Ordination of Monks.

Monks, like the solitaries and the early ascetics, were originally laymen and normally remained such until the end of their days.[2] Clerics of every grade were regarded by them as belonging to a distinct and absolutely superior class within the Church.[3] If the first fathers and the monastic founders could have had their way, there would therefore be no clerics among their disciples or subjects.[4] But the force of circumstances made a regulation of this kind impossible, for the sacraments had to be administered and Mass attended even in the desert, where there were no churches and no local clergy to provide the necessary services. Both cenobites and hermits had thus to supply themselves with priests.[5] This honour was accorded only to the elderly brethren of tried virtue,[6] and was oftentimes stoutly resisted as dangerous to the humility and to the general spiritual well-being of the person selected.[7] The opposition was naturally much greater when a bishop sought to ordain a monk for the service of his episcopal church, since this meant that the monk would have to leave his monastery, and modify—sometimes to an alarming extent—his manner of life. For this reason, too, the typical monk was gravely disturbed at the suggestion of his elevation to an episcopal

---

[1] V.S.H. i, p. 238. Lism. L., p. 35. Plummer, V.S.H., p. cxiv, n. 7.

[2] Such were Anthony, Pachomius and the immense majority of their disciples.

[3] Athan. Vita Ant. P.L. lxxiii, c. 156: "omnes clericos, usque ad ulti mum gradum ante se orare compellens (Antonius)." Cf. St. Jerome Ep. 14, 7, p. 55: "absit ut quicquam de his sinistrum loquar qui apostolico gradui succedentes Christi Corpus sacro ore perficiunt . . . qui sponsam domini sobria castitate conservant. Sed alia monachi causa est, alia clericorum."

[4] Cass., Inst. xi, 18, p. 203: "women and bishops equally to be avoided." Sulp. Sev. Dial. i, 5, p. 157: "priest in desert of Cyrene conceals his order as if it were something to be ashamed of."

[5] Cass., Conl. iv, 1, p. 97; ii, x, p. 287; xviii 1, p. 506; xv, p. 524, etc. H.L 7: "in Nitria there were 8 priests to serve the Church. Whilst the senior lived no other said Mass, preached or settled cases of conscience." Cf. ib. 18, 33, etc. Peregr. Silv., p. 37, 9; 58, Nilus: Orat. in Albianum. P.G. lxxix, c. 707. Greg. Nyss. Vita S. Macrinae, P.G. xlvi, c. 974.

[6] H.L. 17: "Macarius of Egypt 'counted worthy of the priesthood.'" Cf. ib. 20: "Moses, the converted robber." 46: "Rufinus of Aquileia, a man so excellent that he 'was afterwards judged worthy of the priesthood.'" 47: "Chronius, who acted as priest to 200 brethren," etc. Cass., Conl. xxi, 1, p. 574 (diaconate), etc.

[7] Vita Mart., 5, p. 115. St. Martin thought himself unworthy to be made deacon and was made exorcist only. Cf. Verba Sen., P.L. lxxiii, c. 752; 800. St. Jerome Ep. 51, 1, p. 397. For dangers to which priest exposed see Sulp. Sev. Dial. i, 21, p. 173-4; iii, 15, p. 213-4.

see.   Now and then men noted for their virtue went to absurd
lengths in their determination to avoid this honour.[1]

In Ireland, as we have seen, the great sixth century founders,
with one exception,[2] were themselves either bishops or priests,
and their successors for centuries had at least the sacerdotal
order. Every monastery of any size had likewise one or more
priests among the subject monks. Those selected for the
dignity were probably the most venerable among the
seniores, and therefore but a small proportion of the monastic
brethren.[3]   To be liturgically independent the monastery
needed also, and no doubt generally possessed, a bishop,
deacons, subdeacons and representatives of the minor
ecclesiastical orders.[4] Whether the faithful or some of the
faithful were served by a clergy distinct from these is a question
to which we shall return later.

(e)—Relations between Superiors and Subjects.

Between the abbot and his monks, as between the monks
among themselves, an exquisite spirit of charity was wont to
prevail. So much was this the case that the latinised word
for monastery (monasterium) became the ordinary Irish word
for family (muinter), secular no less than religious.[5] Colmcille's
tender care for the brethren under his government is celebrated
by Adamnan. He addressed them often in endearing terms

---

[1] *H.L* 11. Ammonius, when pressed to become a bishop, cut off his left
ear. When the Bishop of Alexandria said he could consecrate him, despite
the mutilation, " he swore to them ' If you use force to me, I'll cut off my
tongue,' so then they left him and went their way " ; but this attitude was
not universal, and there were many monks who became bishops. (Theod.
Hist. Relig. P.G. lxxxii, c. 1298, 1314, etc. Cass., *Conl.* xi, p. 314–5.)

[2] St. Nessan of Mungret, who was a deacon only. Cf. supra p. 132. The
combination *abbas et presbyter* is very old. Cf. Cass., *Conl.* xx, 1, p. 554 :
" vidimus abbatem Pinufium, qui cum esset inmanis coenobii presbyter."
Ib. ii, 5, p. 45.

[3] It is remarkable that the supply of priests in Ireland does not seem
to have been abundant. In the seventh century it was a rule of penitential
discipline, that the priest who fell after ordination should go into exile.
" But the Irish think it more fitting *because of the fewness of priests*, that such
an offender should be received back by imposition of hands, and perform
works of ministry in penance till death." (Wassers. *I.K.* xi, 3, p. 30.) The
Riaguil Pátraicc, composed probably in the eighth century, allows a single
priest to have the care of three or four churches where the number of priests
is few. (*Riag. Pat.* 13, *Ériu* i, p. 220.) St. Bernard, writing the Life of St.
Malachy in the twelfth century, mentions again with sorrow that the number
of priests in the north-east of Ireland was few. This is difficult to understand,
unless we assume that the great majority of monks did not become priests.

[4] All the ecclesiastical orders—those of bishop, priest, deacon, sub-deacon,
acolyte, exorcist, lector and ostiarius—are mentioned in the Irish Canons
(Wasserschl. *I.K.* viii, 1, 2, p. 26 ; ix, p. 26).

[5] *Montar* and *munter* are also old forms, going back to *monater* and *moniter*
for monasterium (monisterium). Thurneysen, *Handbuch,* i, p. 517. Cf. Bergin,
Stories from Keating's Hist. of Ireland, 2nd ed., 1925, p. xxx.

as " little children."[1] He wept when he saw in spirit the local superior in Durrow treating his poor monks harshly and he rejoiced when such treatment came to a sudden end.[2] When a monk engaged in the construction of the " great house " of the last-mentioned monastery lost his balance and fell, Colmcille prayed successfully that an angel might be sent to his aid.[3] On more than one occasion he left his chief monastery in Iona and journeyed back to Ireland to bring gladness and consolation to the brethren.[4] In monks, too, who were not his own he could take the kindliest interest.[5] He was always bright and genial, " filled with the joy of the Holy Ghost,"[6] and the announcement of his approaching death brought sadness to himself and tears in abundance to the good brothers' eyes.[7] In the same way St. Columban, despite the sternness of his character, inspired love, rather than fear.[8] Life was serious within his monasteries, but it must have been exceedingly happy, for the brethren at Luxeuil were filled with dismay when the King ordered his expulsion from their midst.[9] His exhortations to mutual love and charity had, therefore, not been in vain.[10] Eusthasius, trained under his direction, ruled in his stead " with paternal affection."[11] Athala, formed in the same school, was beloved by everybody.[12] Other references show that the typical Irish abbot was in the best sense of the word a father to his community.[13] He treated his subjects with confidence and

---

[1] *Adam.* ii, 28, p. 142 ; iii, 19, p. 225 ; 23, p. 234, 240. Anthony addressed his disciples in the same way (PL. lxxiii, c. 163, 166). Cf. i John ii, 1, 12, 13.
[2] *Adam.* i, 39, p. 58.
[3] *Adam.* iii, 15, p. 216-7.
[4] Ib. i, 14, p. 42 ; 38, p. 74 ; 40, p. 76 ; ii, 36, p. 152 ; 43, p. 171. Connection was otherwise maintained through legates, i, 18, p. 47 ; ii, 38, p. 155.
[5] Ib. ii, 42, p. 171 : " nostri commembres (Cormac, grandson of Lethan, and his company)."
[6] *Adam. Praef.* ii, p. 9.
[7] Ib. iii, 22, p. 228.
[8] Goyau : *Hist. relig. de la France*, p. 99 : " Columban, tel quel, inspirait plus d'attrait que de terreur."
[9] Jonas, *V. Col.* i, 20 : " Columban led away ' universis fratribus velut funus subsequentibus, nam mœror omnium corda reflexerat '."
[10] Cf. supra, p. 228-30.
[11] Jonas, op. cit, ii, 7, p. 241.
[12] Ib. ii, 4, p. 236 : " vir gratus omnibus," etc., etc.
[13] *V.S.H.* ii, p. 99 : a beautiful scene, where the monks working in the fields crowd around Fintan and take him by the hands. Yet Fintan was the most strict of abbots. Everywhere in the *Lives* the relations existing between monks and abbots are depicted as intimate and cordial. Zealous superiors might at times be so intent on the proper performance of tasks that they momentarily forgot the duty of charity. Cf. Cass., *Conl.* xix, 1, p. 534-5. A brother who brought dish in late was given a resounding stroke in the cheek by the Abbot Paul, *qui inter turbas ministrantium fratrum sollicite discurrebat.*

consideration, and received in return the highest proofs of respect and a ready obedience.[1] The monks at times might have held unfavourable views about particular acts of administration and might have expressed themselves (at least in private) with a virile frankness which left no ambiguity as to their meaning,[2] but speaking generally there can be no doubt that they were exultantly happy in their vocation. The best proof of this is perhaps the extraordinary number of noble souls who bound themselves by the monastic vow, generation after generation, for centuries.[3] In a word the monastic institute was nowhere so much in favour as in Ireland; nowhere, it is almost safe to conclude, was the monastic family happier.[4]

(f)—Penal Discipline.

What, then, of the severe penitential discipline, which weighed with particular heaviness on the monks, and threatened to make their lives intolerable? In the Frankish kingdom it aroused bitter opposition.[5] Among modern writers it has no defenders.[6] Let us examine the position in its broader aspects, see how it arose and seek to visualise it as it was visualised by the Irish churchmen of the period.

St. Columban in his *Poenitential* and his *Regula Coenobialis* lays down the principles which govern the infliction of punishment in monasteries. Just, he says, as doctors handle their patients differently according to the nature of the disease, so spiritual physicians seek to cure by their science

---

[1] *Adam.* ii, 42, p. 170 : The brethren stood while Colmcille addressed them. To rise before anyone in an assembly was a mark of respect. Cf. *Adam.* iii, 3, p. 193. *V.S.H.* i, p. 248. *Lism. L.*, p. 57, 94 ; also Sulp. Sever. *Dial.* ii, 5, p. 187. Augustine's failure to show this mark of respect to the British bishops led to unhappy consequences. Bede, *H.E.* ii, 2, p. 83. In the same way the abbot went about surrounded by monks or clerics. So much was this the case that it was an axiom " soli seniori discurrere dedecus est." (*V.S.H.* i, p. 177).

[2] *Reg. Coen.* x, p. 228, *MP.* Ib. xv, p. 233 *MP* (Legislation against murmuring). Wass. *I.K.* xxxvii, 5, p. 133.

[3] Cf. Plummer, *V.S.H.* i, p. cxi, note 4.

[4] Instances such as that recorded by Palladius (*H.L.* 29) do not occur in Ireland. Palladius describes a monastery of 300 nuns constantly fighting with one another. Dorotheus, a holy man, used to sit at a high window, "continually reminding them to keep the peace."

[5] Jonas, *V. Col.* ii, 9, p. 248–50.

[6] Cf. Malnory : *Quid Luxov. Monachi* . . . p. 38 : " The monks in time learned minus verberibus quam correptionibus credere." Hauck : *K.G.D.* i, p. 270- 1, n. 5. Hilpisch : *Gesch. des benedik. Mönchtums*, Freiburg, 1929, p. 78 : " für uns eine barbarische Ordnung." Arnold : *Caesarius von Arelate*, p. 100 : " die Barbarei der Regel des h. Columban, bei deren Lektüre der Leser die Hiebe förmlich hageln sieht ! "

the varied ailments of the soul. Wounds, fevers, defects, pains, general delicacy and weakness are met by the spiritual doctors with the treatment which promises the best results.[1] Some of the cures suggested were handed down to him from the earlier Irish Fathers ; others he had himself invented,[2] for he wished that no ailment prejudicial to the soul's health should be allowed to develop unchecked. Even the smallest defects dare not be overlooked for " he who neglects small things shall fall by little and little " (Eccl. xix. 11).[3] Columban's attitude in all this is perfectly logical ; the object of religious life is to bring the soul to the practice of unbroken contemplation ; this cannot be done without purging the soul of its defects ; which again implies the use of spiritual medicine, unpleasant to the taste and at times physically painful. Both the Poenitential and the Domestic Rule do no more than specify diseases small and great, and the remedies prescribed for their cure.

The various illnesses from which the soul may suffer are enumerated by Columban in a detail that appears to us quite unnecessary. Let us take the first three small sections of his *Regula Coenobialis*, designed exclusively for the monastic brethren. In these we hear of sins of omission, like the neglect of grace at table, or the failure to say " Amen " when grace ended, or the neglect to invoke a blessing on the spoon before use. Similarly a brother might light a lantern and forget or neglect to offer it to a senior that it might be blessed, or he might forget to bow after each psalm during public prayer in the church, or he might neglect to ask a blessing when leaving the house in which he was, or he might pass the cross erected near the door without signing himself with the holy sign, or he might begin or end his work without pausing to repeat a short prayer. On the positive side he might call something his own, or talk in a raised voice, or harm the table by negligent use of his knife, or spill something, while acting as cook or server. If what he had spilt was beer he was obliged to have water only at meals until the quantity spared was equal to the quantity wasted. In all cases where immediate confession followed the fault, the penalty was

---

[1] *Poenit. B.* p. 442-3 : " Corporum medici : spiritales medici."
[2] Ib., p. 443 : " pauca iuxta seniorum traditiones, et iuxta nostram ex parte intellegentiam."
[3] *Reg. Coen.* i, p. 220, *MP.*

reduced by half.[1] Loud talk, excuses, contradiction, public fault-finding, insubordination in any form, visits without leave outside the monastery or to the kitchen or to the cells of the brethren within the monastery, intrigue in favour of blood relations, were punished more severely. The highest penalties were reserved for detraction against the abbot,[2] and for grossly negligent treatment of the chrismal in which the Blessed Sacrament was carried on the monk's person.[3] These transgressions were classed with the major crimes like homicide, fornication, perjury, serious scandal, theft. Where the cleric of any grade had been married before he entered the clerical state and returned to his wife after ordination, his offence was regarded as adultery, and he had to do penance accordingly.[4]

Penalties vary from the recitation of a few psalms to twelve years on bread and water. The lowest total of psalms prescribed is three ; the number then rises to four, six, twelve, fifteen, twenty-four and thirty. Strokes, inflicted on the hand with a thong or scourge,[5] begin at six and rise to ten, twelve, twenty-four, fifty and a hundred, but it is expressly prescribed that more than twenty-five should never be given together.[6] A " superpositio " of silence, which seems to mean the cutting off of half the ordinary time allowed for conversation,[7] was equal to fifty strokes. The highest number of " superpositiones " imposed was three. Fasting on bread and water (the bread being limited to one *paxmatium* or small loaf) for minor offences like off-hand criticism lasted a single day ; for graver offences two days, three days, seven days,

---

[1] *Reg. Coen.* i-iii, p. 220–2.
[2] Ib. x, p. 229.
[3] Ib. xv, p. 231.
[4] *Poenit. B.*, p. 444.
[5] The Irish word for this was *abann.* Cf. *Fiach aibne,* " the duty of strap," the customary duty of flagellation. Gwynn, *Mon. of Tallaght,* § 30, *Rule of Tall.*, p. 8, 10, 14, 24, etc. *Ériu* vii, p. 158. *Mon. of Tall.,* § 43 : "imbert aibne—plying of scourge. Ib., § 37 : "cét mbuilli fort láim de abaind— a hundred strokes of a scourge on your hand." *Rule of Tall.,* p. 14, 25 : " ní buailti fiach aibne orra,—no flagellation was inflicted on them." This shows that flagellation was not self-inflicted. All through the early Middle Ages monastic castigation was administered in public, by the hand of another person. Cf. Gougaud : *Devotional and Ascetic Practices in the Middle Ages,* p. 179.
[6] *Reg. Coen.* x, p. 226.
[7] Ib. iv, ss. *Superpositio silentii* is not defined, but *superpositio* (ieiunii) is explained in *Mon. of Tall.,* § 69, as a half-ration and a half-fast, and the analogy seems to hold good. Cf. Cass., *Conl.* i, 21, p. 33 : "intellexit se circumventum . . . ut lassitudinem non necessariam, immo etiam spiritui nocituram, corpori *superponeret* (of a fast)."

ten days, fifteen days, twenty days, forty days, one hundred and twenty days, a year, two years, three years, five years, seven years, ten years, twelve years. Capital crimes, like homicide and perjury, carried with them (in addition to fasting) the penalty of exile.[1] Where a punishment extending over ten years is mentioned, it is stated that the first three only are to be on bread and water. The food may then be improved, but must not include flesh-meat or wine. Precautions against the repetition of the offence are also to be taken.[2] Those who were condemned to the performance of longer penances were not allowed to wash their hair oftener than once a fortnight, except they were engaged in dirty work, when they might enjoy this pleasure once a week, on Sundays. Where, however, the brother in question had long locks, constantly getting longer, the superior might allow him to wash more frequently.[3] With this notice we may compare a passage in St. Augustine, who prescribes that, except in cases of sickness, bathing in a monastery should not take place oftener than once a month.[4] He who refused to take his punishment, and contended proudly that he was in the right, was " removed from the liberty of Holy Church, and placed in a cell apart to do penance, until his good will became manifest "[5]; in other words, he was excommunicated. If he remained obstinate in contradiction he was expelled.[6]

Comparing the Irish penal code, expounded perfectly by St. Columban,[7] with the disciplinary measures common to monasteries throughout the Christian world, we perceive no difference in principle. St. Basil's teaching on this point is such that it might have been written by St. Columban. " Let the superior," says the great Cappadocian, " employ

---

[1] *Poenit. B.*, p. 443 : " si quis clericus homicidium fecerit . . . X annis exul paeniteat." Ib., p. 445 : " si quis laicus periuraverit . . . mortis timore . . . III annis inermis exul paeniteat in pane et aqua et duobus adhuc abstineat se a vino et carnibus."

[2] Ib. p. 443 : " si quis fornicaverit sicut Sodomitae fecerunt X annis paeniteat, III primus cum mane et aqua, VII vero aliis abstineat se a vino et carne, et non maneat cum alio in aeternum.

[3] *Reg. Coen.* ix, p. 226.

[4] *Ep.* 211, *C.S.E.L.* lvii, p. 367 : " lavacrum etiam corporum ususque balnearum non sit assiduus, sed eo, quo solet, temporis intervallo tribuatur, hoc est, semel in mense."

[5] *Reg. Coen.* vi, p. 223, *MP.* Cf. ib. xv, p. 233 *MNP.*

[6] *Poenit.*, p. 442, A. Cf. Jonas, *V. Col.* ii, 9, p. 248.

[7] *Poenit.*, p. 443 B : " Seniorum traditiones." Seebass : *Z.K.G.* xviii p. 66–7. *Codex Sang.* Cf. Greith : *Gesch. der altirischen Kirche*, p. 295 : " (Columbanus) traditionum scoticarum tenacissimus consectator." *Ériu* vii, p. 158 : stripes to the number of 700 are prescribed in this Irish Poenitential.

corrective methods after the example of doctors, not being
angry with the sick, but fighting the disease. Let him attack
the illness, and, by whatever severe treatment is necessary,
cure the soul. He will cure vainglory by prescribing exercises
of humility; idle speech by silence; excessive sleep by
watchings with prayer; sloth by work; gluttony by deprivation of food; murmuring by excommunication."[1] Again
he says, "the recipients must not accept their penalties as
a mark of a hatred, nor consider tyrannical the care which
he bestows out of compassion to save the soul. For it is dis-
graceful that those who are sick in body should allow doctors
to operate, cauterize, vex with bitter drugs, and call them
benefactors, whilst at the same time calling physicians of
the soul, who work for their salvation, by different epithets."[2]
The disposition then of a monk who receives punishment
should be " such as befits a son who is sick and at death's
door and receives treatment at the hands of him who is at
once his father and his doctor. Though the method of treatment
be bitter and painful, he must be fully convinced of both
the love and the experience of him who inflicts the punishment,
and must desire to be healed."[3] What of the sick man who
refuses to be cured? " The Superior must correct him sharply
before all the brethren and apply methods of healing by every
method of exhortation, but if after much admonition he is
still insolent, and shows no improvement in his conduct,
he becomes, so to speak, his own destroyer, and must be cut
away (with many tears and lamentations, but nevertheless
firmly) from the body, after the practice of doctors."[4] St.
Basil decides that " the time and measure of punishments
must be left to the discretion of superiors, who will have regard
to the age of the culprits, their state of soul, and the nature
of their sin."[5]

Was bodily chastisement excluded from the category of
punishments? Such a regulation would be contrary to the
general practice both of the East and of the West. In the
desert of Nitria there was a palm-tree with its whip for the
solitaries who transgressed.[6] The Rule of Pachomius orders
that forty strokes save one should be inflicted upon him who

---

[1] *Reg. fus. tract.*, li.
[2] *Reg. fus. tract.* lii.
[3] Ib. clviii.
[4] Ib. xxviii.
[5] *Reg. fus. tract.* cvi.
[6] *H.L.* vii.

led a brother into vicious ways.[1] Other Oriental rules order the use of the rod in case of serious crime,[2] or in case of obstinacy.[3] Cassian recounts that a number of the gravest faults—loud disputes, open contempt for superiors, arrogance in contradiction, going out of the monastery at will, intimacy with women, anger, brawling, undertaking work independently of superiors, love of money, private possession of superfluous goods, additional and secret meals—were punished either by the whip or by expulsion.[4] Even the mild St. Caesarius of Arles prescribes thirty-nine lashes for lying and for coming late to prayer.[5] St. Isidore of Sevilla likewise distinguishes between venial and grave offences, and orders that the latter should be purged by a long period of excommunication and by stripes.[6] St. Benedict had no hesitation in ordering the castigation of the body where words of admonition had proved unavailing.[7] Finally the civil laws of the Middle Ages recognised cases in which this form of punishment was inflicted not merely on slaves, but on freemen ; whilst episcopal tribunals and synods ordered chastisement with rods to be inflicted on children, monks, clerks in minor orders, and at times even on clergy of a higher grade.[8]

All that is peculiar about Irish discipline is that corporal punishment was inflicted for the mildest faults. This is not surprising when we consider the intensely penitential nature of Irish monasticism. " Red Martyrdom " or actual death for Christ's love being out of the question through lack of opportunity, the monk had to content himself with " white martyrdom " or a life of extreme mortification.[9] Where voluntary sufferings were eagerly sought after, a few stripes

---

[1] *Reg. Pach.*, Albers, 84.

[2] *Tertia Patrum Reg. ad Mon.* P.L. ciii, c. 446 : " aut triginta diebus a communione separetur, aut virgis caesus emendetur."

[3] Ib., *Reg. Macarii*, xxvii, c. 450 : " si quis sane non emendatur doctrina, virgis purgetur."

[4] *Inst.* iv, 16, p. 58 : " vel plagis emendantur vel expulsione purgantur."

[5] *Reg. ad. Mon.*, P.L. lxvii, c. 1100 : " ad omne opus Dei nullus tardius veniat. Si tardius veniat statim de ferula in manus accipiat." Cf. chap. v : " legitima disciplina."

[6] *Reg. ad Mon.*, ch. xvii, 3 : " Haec et his similia iuxta arbitrium Patris diuturna excommunicatione purganda sunt, et flagellis emendanda, ut qui gravius peccasse noscuntur acriori severitate coerceantur." Cf. Aly : *Die Regula Mon. Isidors von Sevilla*, Marburg, 1909, p. 12.

[7] *Reg.*, ch. ii : " improbos autem et duros ac superbos, vel inobedientes, verberum vel corporis castigatio in ipso initio peccati coerceat." Cf. ch. xxviii and xxx.

[8] Gougaud : *Devot. and Ascetical Practices*, p. 180–2. Löning : *G. des deutsch. K.R.* i, 351.

[9] Supra, p. 197–8.

inflicted by order of superiors for neglect in observing the rule
would not be considered burdensome. To proud and sensitive
natures they may, perhaps, have been much less trying than
words of public reproof or exclusion from ordinary recreation
or excommunication from the society of the brethren. At
any rate, these inflictions—introduced from outside, for
corporal punishment was nowhere prescribed in Irish civil
law[1]—became an integral part of the Irish monastic system,
and were borne without a murmur as long as that system
endured. On the Continent they were received with little
enthusiasm and were soon rejected, as were other measures
of the same kind like fasts and vigils,[2] a fact which proves
merely that the Continental concept of monastic life was
less penitential than the Irish. Wherever in Ireland the old
Adam tried to worm his way back to his old haunts he was
met with the stick. It is often stated nowadays that the old
Adam was treated with too little consideration, that Irish
monasticism was marked by a spirit of excessive rigour which
was bound to be its undoing. This is a point on which it is
difficult to pronounce judgment. Sympathy with the old Adam
is, of course, quite foreign to the tradition of Christian
asceticism, and may at once be ruled out of court. To strike
the golden mean between rigour and laxity is the perennial
problem of monasticism as it is of the whole religious life.
Where the rule is too easy, reform after reform becomes
necessary to stave off death ; where the rule is too severe
there are no monks or there are reactions that destroy much
of the rule's efficacy. The Irish system of monasticism certainly
did not maintain itself on the Continent. At home, however,
it survived for just six centuries. Were the Irish monks
extravagant in their love for Christ ? The question is ridiculous,
for in love of the Word Incarnate excess is impossible. Were
they extravagant in their struggle against the weaknesses of
the flesh, and in their use of the means—prayer and penance
—to overcome these weaknesses ? If there are any who
believe that they were, we must ask them to explain at what
point inflexible determination in such a cause ceases to be a
virtue ; and again to explain at what point heroic devotion
ends and the ludicrous or absurd commences. Monasticism in

---

[1] For the knowledge that corporal punishment is never mentioned in the
Laws, I am indebted to Professor Thurneysen.
[2] Jonas, V. Col. ii, 1, p. 231. Levison : Hist. Zeitschr. Bd. 109, 1912,
p. 1–22. Zimmer : Preuss. Jahrbücher, lvii, p. 36.

general recognised the need of a penal code,[1] which might include corporal punishment among its penalties.   That the Irish system was ready to inflict corporal punishment liberally is a strong proof of its earnestness and the heroism of its standards. Transgressions were possibly so rare that the code was largely a dead letter. Certain it is that the penal provisions of Irish monasticism were not felt to be unbecoming, still less to be a hindrance to its advancement. Religious life, for all its severity, developed tranquilly in Ireland, and continued for centuries to be embraced and lauded by multitudes.

§ 5—Buildings.

Where the site for a monastery had been accepted as suitable[2] and had been sanctified by a triduum or more of fasting and prayer,[3] the founder and his monks proceeded to put it into shape for monastic use.   If the place had hitherto been inhabited, as happened when a prince or other rich man surrendered his home entirely to the saint,[4] a long spell of tedious preliminary work could be omitted.   Otherwise the founder marked out the boundaries of his settlement, which normally took the form of a *less* or *rath*, an enclosure that afforded privacy and a certain amount of protection, without being a fortification (*dún*) or a "high place" (*dind*).   The country possessed professional rath-builders,[5] but it is unlikely that the early monks would have the desire or the means to employ these. They would, therefore, set to work themselves, first at the fosse and ditch with which the buildings would be surrounded,[6] then at the edifices within. St. Patrick, according

---

[1] In addition to the cases quoted see Cass., *Inst.* ii, 16, p. 30 ; iii, 7, p. 41. *H.L.* 33, St. Aug. *Ep.* 211, p. 365. *Verb. Sen.* P.L. lxxiii, c. 787.

[2] Jonas, *V. Col.* i, 10, p. 170 : "alium experimento locum quaerit quem aquarum inriguitas adornabat."

[3] *V.S.H.* ii, p. 170 : "triduano ieiunio . . . ipsum locum Deo consecravit in primis." Cf. Bede *H.E.* iii, 24 : "Studens autem vir Domini (Cedd) acceptum monasterii locum primo precibus ac ieiuniis a pristina flagitiorum sorde purgare et sic in eo monasterii fundamenta iacere postulavit " etc. Dicebat enim hanc esse consuetudinem eorum a quibus normam disciplinae regularis didicerat ut accepta nuper loca ad faciendum monasterium vel ecclesiam prius orationibus ac ieiuniis Domino consecrent . . ." *Lism. L.*, p. 67 : " Iar coisecrad dóib na h-indsi." *B.N.E.* i p. 16.

[4] *B. Arm.* 32a. *V.S.H.* i, p. 44, 176, 184. Ib. ii, 170, 216. *Silva Gad.* i, 38. *Rev. Celt.* v, 442. Cf. Plummer *V.S.H.* i, xcviii.

[5] Plummer, l.c.

[6] *Adam.* ii, 45, p. 143 : "*vallum* egressus monasterii (Iona)." Ib. i, 3, p. 26 : "intra eiusdem coenobii septa (Clonmacnois)." Jonas, *V. Col.* ii, 5, p. 237 : " septa monasterii densat (Bobbio)." Ib. ii, 10, p. 253 : "infra septam inrumpentes (Remiremont)."

to the writer of the *Tripartite Life*, made all his ecclesiastical
settlements on a uniform scale, allowing a diameter of 140 ft.
or a circumference of about one hundred and fifty yards.[1]
On Árdoileán, an island off the Galway coast, the wall round
the ruins was nearly oblong, and measured 38 yards in length
by 23 yards in breadth.[2] On Inis Muiredhaigh it was smaller
in extent and pear-shaped rather than circular.[3] In Glendaloch
the figure formed by the outer ditch was very irregular, owing
to the nature of the ground over which it passed.[4] Similarly
at Clonmacnois, where the length was very considerable
because of the size of the monastery.[5] At Durrow the rampart
seems to have been circular.[6] The *civitas* on the island of
Farne was surrounded by an almost circular wall made of
rough stone and sods.[7] In the only Irish monastery that has
been thoroughly investigated, that of Noendrum, there were
three concentric walls, not quite circular in form, but these
are probably of pre-Christian origin.[8] At Dundesert, County
Antrim, was a large, almost circular fosse, described to Reeves
during an examination made on the spot in 1845. Sixty years
before the trench " was about the breadth of a moderate
road ; and the earth which had been cleared out of it was
banked up inside as a ditch, carrying up the slope to about the
height of sixteen or twenty feet from the bottom. The whole
face of the slope was covered with large stones, embedded in
the earth. Concentric with this enclosure, and at about the
interval of seven yards, was another fosse, having a rampart
on the inner side, similarly constructed, and on the area
enclosed by this stood the church, east and west, 90 feet long
and 30 wide. The ruined walls were about 6 feet high and 5
thick. The burial ground was principally at the east end of
the building, and the whole space outside the walls was covered
with loose stones. The two entrances were of about the same
breadth as the fosse, and were paved with large flat stones,
but they had no remains of a gateway."[9] In Árdoileán the

---

[1] *V. Trip.* i, p. 237.
[2] Lawlor : *Book of Mulling*. Edinburgh, 1897, p. 176.
[3] Dunraven : *Notes on Irish Archit.* i, p. 44. Lawlor, l.c.
[4] Lawlor, l.c.
[5] Ib.
[6] *Adam.* iii, 15, p. 215 : " de monasterii culmine rotundi in Roboreti
Campo." Cf. Lawlor, op. cit., p. 181.
[7] Bede, *Vita Cuth.* xvii : " Est autem aedificium situ paene rotundum ;
and constructed impolitis prorsus lapidibus et cespite."
[8] H.C. Lawlor : *The Monastery of St. Mochaoi of Nendrum*. Belfast, 1925.
p. 95 ff.
[9] *Eccles. Antiq.*, p. 182.

vallum had four openings, and a cross stood at the entrance to each, on the outer side.[1] On the top of the ditch stood, in all probability, a hedge or palisade. In the Irish settlements abroad the enclosure may have been surrounded by nothing more than this, for it seems to have been penetrated easily.[2] In Ireland, too, the rampart seems to have availed little against the ill-disposed, who could break into the monastery by force when they willed.

Within the enclosure the church occupied a place so important that the word might be used as synonymous with monastery.[3] It was usually a large building (hence the descriptive terms, *magna domus*,[4] tech mór,[5] recles),[6] and was known generally by a name (eclais, tempul, domnach, basilica), adopted from Western ecclesiastical literature.[7] Owing to its constant use as a house of prayer it was often called "oratorium."[8] It was regularly made of wood, "of smoothed planks, closely and strongly fastened together,"[9] more particularly of oak (which gave good service in the

---

[1] Lawlor : *Book of Mulling.*, p. 176.

[2] Jonas, *V. Col.* ii, 10, p. 253 : Wolves broke through the protecting wall at Remiremont. Cf. ib. 5, p. 237 : "septa monasterii densat," and ib. 25, p. 294 : "septa vineae ex abbatis imperium densabant atque muniebant. Evenit ut secure arborem succiderint et de ramorum coniectura septa densarent."

[3] *Adam.* i, 5, p. 29 : "Sanctus Columba in sua commanens matrice ecclesia."

[4] Ib. iii, 15, p. 217 : "de summo culmine magnae domus."

[5] *Lism. L.*, p. 47. *V. Trip.* i, 237, etc.

[6] *Lism. L.*, p. 17, 70, 80, etc.

[7] On the different names for "church" in the Occident, cf. Kretschmer, *Zeitschr. f. vergleich. Sprachforschung auf dem Gebiete der indogerm. Sprachen.* Bd. xxxix, n. 4. Ecclesia (ὁ τῆς ἐκκλησίας οἶκος) was constantly in use since about A.D. 300. From it came the Irish *eclais*. Welsh *eglwys ;* Κυριακόν was not adopted into Latin, but was favoured by the Teutonic peoples, in whose languages it appears as *Kirche, church*, etc. Its Latin equivalent, *dominicum*, applied especially to pompous Constantinian edifices, though used also of a modest monastic church (*Reg. Pach.*, Albers, p. 26 : "Maneant (fratres) in dominico"), gives the Irish *domnach*. *Basilica*, borrowed from the civil vocabulary in the fourth century, was in use as long as the basilica type of architecture was common. It appears in Irish as *baislec*, and gives its name to a parish in Roscommon and a townland in Kerry (Baisliocán). Cf. Welsh Bassaleg in Glamorganshire. O'Mulconry, *Gloss. Archiv. für. celt.*, Lexic. i, No. 182, p. 242, defines it as "house of the heavenly King" (βασιλεύς). Latin *templum* passed into Celtic, becoming in Old Irish *tempul*, in Mid. Welsh *temhyl*, in late Cornish *tempel*. Domus gave the Italian *duomo*, German *Dom*. In Irish it appears in the compounds *doimliag*—"stone church"—and *erdam*—"antechamber," "sacristy." Cf. Pedersen, *Vergl. Gram.* i, p. 340.

[8] *Adam.* i, 8, p. 34, uses *ecclesia* and *oratorium* indifferently. Cf. ii, 36, p. 153. In the *V. Trip.* i, 237, the oratory is a tiny building 7 feet long, whereas the church proper (great house) is 27 ft. long.

[9] St. Bernard : *Life of St. Malachy*, ed. Lawlor, p. 32. Oratory at Bangor, "an Irish work, not devoid of beauty," made thus. Cf. Macalister, *Archaeology of Ireland*, p. 246. *Otia Merseiana*, ii, p. 79 : "when will these ten hundred planks be a structure of compact beauty ?"

humid Irish climate), and was therefore referred to often as
" dairtech " (oakhouse).[1] A less enduring building would be
made of poles and rods, woven together into a kind of wicker-
work and covered over with coats of clay.[2] The roof to such
buildings would consist of straw or reeds.[3] Now and then
stone churches were built,[4] generally in places where stone
was plentiful, whilst wood was scarce and could be procured
only with difficulty. Stone as building material was, in fact,
unfashionable and unpopular.[5] St. Patrick's " standard "
church was only 27 feet in length,[6] and there is reason to
think that even the most sumptuous of wooden churches
would not be great in size. On the other hand, a smaller
church was often raised beside the greater, and more were
added, seemingly without much need. As the monks performed their duties of public prayer together and also assisted
at a common Mass, the church in every monastery must have
been large enough to hold the entire community. When not
in use it might be kept locked, but this practice was certainly
not universal.[7] If it served likewise as a kind of parish church
for the surrounding laity, it would need to be exceptionally
large, but it seems more likely that these during their devotions
did not seek the shelter of a roof, being content to congregate
round the small church or oratory where the Holy Sacrifice
was being offered.[8] Dedications were not usual, but they

---

[1] Meyer, Contributions, p. 580. Pedersen, Vergl. Gram. i, p. 340. For an
interesting account of preparations to build a church see V.S.H. ii, p.194.
Moling, wishing to construct a church in honour of God in his monastery,
secured the services of an ingeniosus artifex. Wood was cut in a local glade
and floated down the Barrow to the site. Cf. also ib., p. 159. Adam. ii, 45,
p. 177. Jonas, V. Col. ii, p. 222. Lism. L., p. 76.

[2] Plummer, V.S.H. i, p. xcix, n. 2. " The Welsh word for to build, ' adeiladu,'
lit. to weave, implies this mode of construction." Cf. Lism. L., p. 47.

[3] Bede, H.E. iii, 25 : " Finán, coming from Iona, ' ecclesiam . . . non de
lapide sed de robore secto, totam composuit atque harundine texit.' "

[4] V.S.H. ii, p. 187. St. Ciannán was the first to build a church of stone
(daimliag) which gave its name to the place on which it stood (Duleek).
Cf. Macalister : Arch. of Irel., p. 246 ff.

[5] St. Bernard : Life of St. M., p. 109-110.   [6] V. Trip. i, p. 237.

[7] Adam. ii, 36, p. 153 :   When St. Colmcille arrived in Tír-dá-glas and
repaired to the church the keys could not be found.   The church at Luxeuil
was to be locked at night (Reg. Coen. xiii, p. 236 MP.), but it was open in
the day time (Jonas, V. Col. i, 17, p. 184 ; 20, p. 194).

[8] A gathering under the open sky at Clonmacnois is mentioned in a peculiar
tale publ. in Anecdota from Irish MSS, iii, p. 8-9. Cf. Ériu iv, p. 12, and
Gougaud, Rev. Celt. xli, p. 354-8. Also Wassersch. I.K. xliv, c. 3, p. 175 :
" Terminus sancti loci habeat signa (crosses) circa se." C. 4 : " the locus
sanctus was not to exceed in size the space covered by the outside court
of the tent and temple of Solomon." C. 5 and Note (e) : " The locus sanctus
was divided into three parts—(i) the most sacred (interior of the church?)
where clerics alone might enter ; (ii) where the well-conducted laity of both
sexes might enter ; (iii) where homicides and others might enter."

were not unknown.[1]   Sanctuaries are sometimes mentioned,
the term for such (nemed) being a borrowing from the Gaelic
tongue and having strong pagan connections.[2] By the side
of the church stood the sacristy,[3] and near by was a space
enclosed and consecrated as a cemetery, where the unbaptized
and those who had died in open sin were denied a last resting-
place.[4] Burial among the holy dead of a monastic cemetery
was regarded as a great privilege by the laity, and was constantly granted.   Clonmacnois had a pre-eminence all its
own as a graveyard for royalty;[5] but Iona, too, was
distinguished in this respect, as were Glendaloch and
Ferns.[6]

Next to the church the only buildings of much importance
were the refectory (praindtech)[7] and the guest-house (tech
n-oiged).[8] These would be constructed in a manner similar to
the church, but less elaborately. In some monasteries the
guest-house seems to have been placed apart from the main
buildings.[9] With the refectory went the kitchen (cuicenn *or*
cuchtair),[10] where the modest meals of the brethren were
prepared. Nearby, too, was often a pool or washing place

---

[1] At Glendalough one church was dedicated to the Holy Trinity ; another
to Our Lady. St. Columban restored the ancient basilica of St. Peter at
Bobbio (Jonas, *V. Col.* 30, p. 221). The basilica built by the Irish missionaries
at Lindisfarne, shortly after Aidan's death, was likewise dedicated to the
Prince of the Apostles (Bede, *H.E.* iii, 17). The possibility of other dedications
is suggested by Lawlor : *Book of Mull.*, p. 173. In the convent built by
St. Caesarius for his nuns at Arles, the nave was dedicated to the Blessed
Virgin, the two aisles to St. John and St. Martin (Arnold, *Caes. v. Arel.*, p. 415),
an interesting example of a triple dedication.
[2] *Lism. L.*, p. 307. Cf. Holder : *Altcelt. Sprachschatz*, p. 711 : "nemeton
' a sacred grove,'" etc. Old Irish *nemed*, gl. sacellum.
[3] *Adam.* iii, 20, p. 224 : "in quadam exedra ; exedriolae separatum con-
clave." Cf. Bede, *H.E.* iii, 17. Petrie : *Round Towers*, p. 432 ff. Lawlor :
St. Mochaoi, Key to Plan, 3.
[4] *V.S.H.* ii, p. 173. Cf. Plummer, ib. i, p. cx, n. 3 ; xciii, n. 3.
[5] *Ériu*, ii, p. 163 : The Graves of the Kings of Clonmacnoise, ed. Best.
O'Donovan : *Tribes and Cust. of Hy Many*, p. 80.
[6] *Adam.*, p. 418. Plummer *V.S.H.* i, c. x, n. 7.
[7] *Adam.* ii, 13, p. 121 : "Cum post nonam coepisset horam in refectorio
eulogiam frangere " (*St. Cainnech at Achad Bò*). Jonas, *V. Col.* i, 16, p. 179 :
" minister refecturi (refectorii)." *V.S.H.* ii, p. 99 : "ignis de cacumine refectorii fortissime exarsit.'[1] Ib., p. 179. *Ériu* i, p. 145 ; vii, p. 156.
[8] *Adam.* ii, 3, p. 106 : " sanctus suos misit monachos ut de alicuius plebeii
agello virgarum fasciculos ad hospitium afferret construendum." Ib. i, 4,
p. 27 : " preparate ocius hospitium." Ib. ii, 39, p. 157 : " in hospitio."
V.S.H. i, p. 161. Ib., p. 175 ; ii, p. 26 : " pernoctare in hospitio eius."
Ib., p. 230.
[9] *Cod. Salm.*, c. 459 : " castellum hospitum" at Clonmacnois. How far
this goes back we cannot tell. *A.U.* (cf. *A.F.M., A. Clon.*) mention a *lis oiged*
at Armagh, s.a. 1003, 1015, etc.
[10] *Lism. L.*, p. 70, 131.

(lind prainntige), where the monks could perform their ablutions before entering to take their food.[1]

Within the enclosure were the *cellae*, or habitations of the monks, detached huts made probably of wattle and thatch, and sometimes round in shape.[2] The abbot at Iona had a hut of his own, a custom that may have been general throughout Ireland.[3] The brethren, however, seem to have been housed in twos, threes, fours, sevens or even greater numbers, according to the size of the hut.[4] Separate cells might be allowed as a special privilege to aged religious in their declining years.[5] It must be noted, too, that a small or subsidiary settlement, managed by a few brethren, was called a *cella*. This might have a church and refectory of its own,[6] yet the word *cell* was applied originally not to the church, but to the habitation of those who ministered in it.[7] There might even be *cells* where there were no churches, for it is related of St. Mochua that he founded 120 *cellae*, whereas the number of churches credited

---

[1] *Lism. L.*, p. 61.

[2] The hut sites revealed at Nendrum, and belonging probably to the workshops, are circular, or nearly so (Lawlor : *St. Mochaoi*, p. 107). Cf. also surviving huts, such as those on Sceilg Michíl, but all the huts are square or rectangular inside, a fact which seems to indicate that those who constructed them were accustomed to live in square or rectangular buildings. The school at Nendrum was rectangular ; and there were other square or rectangular buildings (Ib., p. 107–9). One of the remaining two clocháin on Árdoileán is round outside but square within. *R.S.A.I. Guide to N.W. and S. Islands.* Ed. Westropp. 1905, p. 47. Cf. p. 142.

[3] *Adam.* i, 35, p. 65 ; iii, 22, p. 227 : " eius tuguriolum ad ianuam stabant quod in eminentiore loco erat fabricatum " For tuguriolum cf. Sulp. Sev., *Dial.* i, 4, p. 156. *V.S.H.* ii, p. 191 : Moling had a cell of his own near the monastery. Ib. ii, 58 : Declan was carried to his own tugurium to die. Ib., p. 144 : Maedóc of Ferns, "legens quodam die foris in cellula sua."

[4] *Reg. Coen.* xv, p. 233, *MNP.* : " cellae suae cohabitator." Cf. Ib. viii, p. 225, *MP.* Visits to fratres in cells not allowed without leave. *V.S.H.* i, p. 260 : Cell founded by Colmán Elo given in charge to four brethren. Ib., p. 208 : " septem fratres et presbyteri in una cella." Ib., p. 228 : " novem iuvenes religiosi erant in cella seorsum." Ib. p. 15 : " sancti filii qui longe a sancto Comgallo in sua cella habitabant." Ib. i, p. 214 : " quidam in domo sanctorum seniorum qui habebant cellulam seorsum in monasterio sancti Ciarani." Cf. ib. ii, p. 38.

[5] *V.S.H.* i, p. 182 : " ut aliquod solatium in senectute haberent."

[6] Ib. ii, p. 179. Cf. *Adam.* i, 17, p. 46 : Colgu returned to Ireland and became " primarius alicuius ecclesiae per multos annos." This *ecclesia* still bears his name, *Cell Colgan*, and from it the parish of Kilcolgan, in the diocese of Kilmacduagh, is called. Colgu had here a small community, for his *pincerna* (probably=cellarius) is mentioned.

[7] The native equivalent for *cella* is *both* (cf. *B.N.E.*, p. 13, *Lism. L.*, p. 26, Meyer, *Contr.*, ib., p. 342), but the Latin word was borrowed at an early date (cell. Gen. cille. Dat. cill). It may be remarked that the personal name *Cellach* is not derived from *cell*, but from *cend-loch*, " black-head," and that the name is pre-Christian in origin. Cf. MacNeill : *Ogham Inscriptions*, *P.R.I.A.* xxvii, c. 15, p. 347. *Cormac's Glossary*, Nr. 803.

to him is only thirty.[1] Such *cellae*, in many cases, became the nucleus of later parishes, just as happened in France with the *oratoria* erected at cross-roads or on the *villae* of large landowners or due to the initiative of hermits.[2] The *cells*, too, became popular as burial places for the laity.[3]

The number of huts within the monastic enclosure would depend, of course, on the number of monks subject to the rule. There is a tendency in the literature to reckon these by thousands. We may note, however, that St. Columban had three monasteries to house about two hundred monks ;[4] that the federation of his namesake at Iona embraced many monasteries and churches ;[5] and that the *cellae* attached to other settlements like Bangor were often very numerous.[6] "A gathering of the neighbouring monks," who came to Abbán to learn about their future, totalled one hundred and forty.[7] Monastic life was certainly exceedingly popular ; settlements, great and small, covered the face of the land,[8] even in the sixth century ; but it is not likely that any one of these ever contained a community that could justly be termed enormous. Huge numbers in Clonmacnois or Bangor would presuppose a scheme of organization altogether more elaborate than that which we can discover to have existed anywhere in Ireland.[9]

Special cells (or at least special facilities within their own cells) must have been provided for the monastic artists, who copied and bound books,[10] as well as for those who helped

---

[1] *V.S.H.* ii, p. 188.

[2] Goyau : *Hist. relig. de la Fr.*, p. 54.

[3] *Martyr. Oeng.*, p. 26 : " Ind locáin rogabtha dessib ocus trírib, it ruama co ndálaib, co cétaib, co mílib.—The monastic sites that were occupied by twos and by threes are (now) cemeteries, with concourses of hundreds and thousands."

[4] Jonas, *V. Col.* i, 17, p. 183 : Fontaines had 60 working brothers.

[5] Reeves, *Adam.*, p. 286 ff.

[6] Cf. Plummer, *V.S.H.*, p. cxi, n. 4.

[7] *B.N.E.*, p. 10.

[8] Plummer, *V.S.H.*, p. cxi, n. 4 : " The larger monasteries were continually throwing off new swarms, an ecclesiastical ver sacrum, which settled at a greater or less distance from the parent hive."

[9] Bede relates (*H.E.* ii, 2) that at Bangor, in Wales, the monks were divided into seven groups of three hundred or more, each group ruled (as a more or less independent unit) by its own praepositus. The Pachomian monks were divided into houses, as far as possible according to their work ; houses were grouped into tribes ; tribes into monasteries ; monasteries into twenty-four sections, which together formed the Pachomian congregation. (*Reg. Praef. H.*, 2, 6 ; *Reg.* 16 ; *H.L.* 82). A system something like this would be necessary where the monks were reckoned by thousands.

[10] *Adam. Praef.* ii, p. 9 ; i, 23, p. 53 ; iii, 23, p. 233. Binding is mentioned in Jonas, *V. Col.* ii, p. 5, p. 237 : " libros ligaminibus firmat." Transcription further in *Cod. Salm.*, cc. 439, 878, 894, 900. *Book of Mulling*, p. 11.

them in the more material side of this work, by making wax
tablets[1] and styles,[2] pens,[3] ink horns,[4] vellum and the satchels
in which books were carried.[5] Missals were needed for Mass ;
psalters and other liturgical books for the celebration of the
canonical hours. The schools had likewise to be supplied
with text-books and reading matter. Altars had to be
furnished with chalice,[6] paten,[7] cruets[8] and vestments,[9] and
the church had to be decorated.[10] The Celtic art coming down
from pagan times was not rejected, but was preserved and
perfected by the monks.[11] Crosses, again, were in constant
demand.[12] Implements were needed for house use and for
agriculture ; vehicles and boats for transport or for travel.
Bells had to be made to call the community to the various
duties.[13] The brethren had finally to be clothed and fed and
nursed back to health in case they fell sick. Numerous
offices and workshops had therefore to be provided, either
within the enclosure or as near to it as possible. No wonder,
then, that in externals the great monasteries bore some
resemblance to the Continental cities, a resemblance that
increased when lay people attached themselves as dependants

[1] *Adam.* i, 35, p. 66 : "tabula (cerata)." *V.S.H.* ii, p 143 : "ceraculum."
Ib., p. 157, *Cod. Salm.*, c. 405. *Lism. L.*, p. 110 : "clár ciartha ⁊ scribtha."
Ib. : "in tabhuill ciartha." *B. Arm.*, 35 : "poolire." *Lism. L.*, p. 29 :
"polaire." G. Coffey, *Guide to Celtic Antiquities of Christian Period*, p. 99.
[2] *Adam.*, p. 205. n, .a *V.S.H.* i, p. 160 : "graffium istud."
[3] *Adam.* ii, 29, p. 143 : "cum calamo." *V.S.H.* ii, p. 135 : "pennam
qua librum scribere posset minime habebat."
[4] *Adam.* i, 25, p. 54 : "atramenti corniculum." The native word for
atramentum was *dub* (*Lism. L.*, p. 31). *Corniculum* was translated literally
adhaircín. (Ib.)
[5] *Adam.* ii, 8, p. 115 : "libros in pelliceo reconditos sacculo habebat."
Lism. L., p. 82 : "cona theigh liubhar (tíach., Lat., *Theca* Gk., θήκη)."
[6] This seems to have been made of soft metal. Cf. *Reg. Coen.* iv, p. 222
MP. : "qui pertunderit dentibus calicem salutaris." It was sometimes
made of glass. Cf. *V.S.H.* i, p. 117 : "altaria erant de crystallo, et eorum
vascula similiter, scilicit patenae et calices et urceoli at cetera vasa." Ib., p. 53.
Lism. L., p. 9, 25 : "isin cailech, " ; p. 49 : "annsa chailiuch oifrinn."
[7] *B. Arm.*, 16b, 25a. The ordinary word for paten became *tesc*, from Latin
discus. Cf. *Thes. Paleoh.* ii, p. 415. Square patens are mentioned, *V. Trip.*,
p. 313.
[8] *Adam.* ii, p. 104. *V.S.H.* i, p. 117.
[9] Cogitosus, *V. Brig. Trias Th.*, p. 522. *V.S.H.* ii, p. 123 : "missalia
indumenta." *Lism. L.*, p. 9 : "a cocaill oifrind."
[10] *Tr. Thau.*, p. 523-4. Gold, silver, precious stones, pictures and tapestry
were used to decorate the church at Kildare.
[11] Macalister, *Archaeol. of Irel.*, p. 266 ff.
[12] Cf. supra, p. 234. and *Lism. L.*, p. 29 : "ba bés dosom crosa ⁊ pólaire
⁊ tiagha leabur ⁊ aidhme eclusdai arcena (do dénum)."
[13] *Adam.* i, 8, p. 34 : "'cloccam pulsa' cuius sonitu fratres incitati ad
ecclesiam . . . ocius currunt." Ib ii, 42, p. 170. *Reg. Coen.* ix, p. 227, *MNP.*
Ib. p., 230 *MP.* : "sonitus orationum." *Lism. L.*, p. 27. 144, etc. On the
mportance of bells as sacred objects on which oaths were taken see Plummer,
V.S.H. i, p. cv, n. 9.

or technical workers to the religious communities and set up
their own houses beside the monastic church and enclosure.
As far as we can see, this movement began in the sixth, and
was consolidated in the seventh century.

In the matter of buildings the Irish monasteries followed
the lines marked out by the monastic fathers in other
countries. At Tabennisi, for instance, and the associate
settlements of the Pachomian group, each monastery was
surrounded by a wall,[1] and within the enclosure were the
church, the refectory, the kitchen, the place for books, and
various other repositories and workshops.[2] The community
was divided into houses, with twenty-two to forty in each.[3]
Every brother had his own cell, and there was a common
meeting-room.[4] Near the door of the monastery was the
guest-house, where women were admitted, but in a place
carefully separated from the other sex.[5] All this might have
been written of Clonmacnois, save that perhaps the guest-
house on the Shannon banks would not have been available for
ladies. Round the Irish monastery the wall was made, in a
special way, of earth, and the enclosure thus protected was
called a rath ; the church, too, the refectory and the habitation
of the brethren were small in size. Each country, very naturally, adopted its own style of building, but the general principle
of simplicity was everywhere maintained.[6] Nothing in the
shape of decoration was desired or even permitted except in the
church, where austerity was sometimes discarded in favour of
artistic beauty.[7] Though single or double cells were the ideal
of the monastic fathers,[8] these cells could not be provided for
large numbers within the narrow confines of a rath. Hence the

---

[1] *Reg.* 84. *Alb.* 60 : "neque extra murum monasterii procedendi habeat
facultatem."

[2] *Reg. Praef.* 1, 3, 28, etc. *H.L.* 32. *Doctr. Ors.*, 26. *Vita Pach.*, ch. 19.

[3] *Ep. Ammon.*, 4, 11. *Reg. Praef.*, 2.

[4] *Reg.* 112, 114. *Alb.* 63–65. *Reg.* 23. *Alb.* 13, etc.

[5] *Vita*, p. 19. *Reg.* 50, 51. *Alb.* 30, 31.

[6] Cass., *Conl.* ix, 6, p. 256–7, tells an amusing story of a monk with architectural notions, building a sumptuous cell for himself in the desert.

[7] *Tr. Thau.*, p. 523–4. It is told, however, of Pachomius that he had
scruples about permitting a departure from the severest simplicity in the
building of a church. Once, when he had ordered the construction of an
elegant edifice and seen it completed, he was troubled with the thought
that his motive had been vanity. In punishment for this, and as a warning
to his disciples, he had ropes attached to the pillars and the whole building
thrown out of plumb (*Vita*, p. 7). Cf. Sulp. Sev. *Dial.* i, 5, p. 157 : "(ecclesia)
erat autum vilibus texta virgultis non multum ambitiosior quam nostri
hospitis tabernaculum, in quo nonnisi incurvus non poterat consistere."

[8] Cass., *Inst.* ii, 12, p. 28 : "unusquisque ad suam recurrens cellulam
quam aut solus aut cum alio tantum inhabitare permittitur."

need for greater buildings. In the hermitage, however, whither the anchorites retired, single cells were necessarily the rule. These were often windowless and cramped,[1] and regularly round in form, a type of construction not unknown in the Nitrian desert.[2]

§ 6—External Relations.

(a)—The Monasteries and the Church.

Monasticism was a movement of laymen, and the greatest of its early fathers, Anthony and Pachomius, never received any orders, but its connection with the ecclesiastical authorities was nevertheless of the most intimate kind. It could not, indeed, have been otherwise, for the monks, as devoted children of the Church, were bound to show obedience to its superiors, whilst again they were dependent on the clergy for the means of grace through the Sacraments. There were, it is true, hermits who professed to regard the Sacraments as unnecessary, but the story of their fate carried with it a solemn warning. Valens, for instance, " a Palestinian by race, but Corinthian in his character—for St. Paul attributed the vice of presumption to the Corinthians "—reached such a pitch of arrogance that he was deceived by demons. In fact, " he was so puffed up that he despised the Communion of the Mysteries " (Holy Communion). Finally he " became so mad that he entered into the Church, and before the assembled brethren said, " I have no need of Communion ; I have seen Christ to-day ! " Then the fathers bound him and put him in irons for a year, and so cured him, destroying his pride by their prayers and indifference and calmer mode of life, as it is said ' Diseases are cured by their opposites.' "[3] Another, " an Alexandrian by race, an excellent young man, of good natural ability and pure in his life," after many toils was likewise overcome by pride. He insulted one of the most respected of the fathers, saying, " those who obey your teaching are dupes, for one should not pay heed to any teachers save Christ." " He even abused Scripture to serve the purpose of his folly, and would say, ' The Saviour Himself said : 'Call

---

[1] Cf. *H.L.* 18, 10.
[2] *H.L.* 8, 5: " Ammon made for himself two round cells (δύο θολούς κελλίων). A θόλος was a rounded and vaulted chamber.
[3] *H.L.*, 25.

no man teacher upon earth ' (Matt. xxiii. 9). His mind
became so darkened that he, too, was put in irons, since he
was unwilling even to attend the mysteries (Holy Mass)."
Finally he abandoned his cell altogether and went back to
Alexandria, where he was a well-known figure in the theatres,
the circuses and the taverns. His life of sin brought him a
terrible disease, and he died repentant.[1] A third " became
a stranger to the teaching of holy men and intercourse with
them, and the constant communion of the mysteries (Holy
Communion), and diverged so sadly from the straight way
that he declared these things were nothing." In punishment
for his pride he was said to have fallen into gluttony and
drunkenness.[2] An absence of five weeks from the holy
mysteries was regarded by Macarius as negligence grave
enough to bring down penalties upon ordinary lay-people.[3]
Weekly reception of the Holy Eucharist was commended by
Cassian as a wise rule. Those who abstained longer, from a
sense of their own unworthiness, were condemned by that
great writer as guilty of a two-fold error ; in the first place,
they misconceived the nature of the Eucharist, which is not
a reward for goodness, but a means to goodness and purity
of soul ; in the next place, they were guilty of presumption,
for they taught that the Blessed Eucharist should be received
only by the stainless, and thus by approaching to the Holy
Table implicitly proclaimed their own worth.[4] Healthy
monasticism, therefore, accepted as an axiom the need for
frequent reception of the Holy Eucharist. Priests had in
consequence to be provided, an event that could not take
place without the consent and co-operation of the Church.

As a matter of fact, the first monks and the ecclesiastical
authorities were on the very friendliest terms. Anthony
" observed the laws of the Church most rigidly and was
anxious that all the clergy should be honoured above himself.
For he was not ashamed to bow his head to bishops and
priests ; and if even a deacon came to him for help he dis-
coursed with him on what was profitable, but gave place to

[1] Ib. 26.
[2] *H.L.* 27.
[3] Ib. 17.
[4] *Conl.* xxiii, 21, p. 670–1 : " nec tamen ex eo debemus nos a dominica
communione suspendere, quia nos agnoscimus peccatores, sed ad eam magis
ac magis est propter animae medicinam ac purificationem spiritus avide
festinandum, verumtamen ea humilitate mentis ac fide, ut indignos nos
perceptione tantae gratiae iudicantes remedia potius nostris vulneribus
expetamus."

him in prayer, not being ashamed to learn himself.[1] When
dying he left his only treasures, his two sheepskin cloaks, to
the bishops Athanasius and Serapion.[2] Pachomius had
likewise the greatest esteem for St. Athanasius, whose pastoral
letters were read in his monasteries as in all the other monasteries of Egypt.[3] In A.D. 330 the renowned Patriarch of
Alexandria visited Tabennisi, and was met by Pachomius
and his monks, who came out with singing and thanksgiving to
conduct him to the monastery.[4] Over twenty years later,
when persecuted bitterly by the Arians, he found a refuge in
their midst.[5] In an interval of peace he made a visitation in
detail of the Pachomian monasteries, and gave an enthusiastic
description of what he had seen.[6] Through his advocacy,
monasticism became popular in Rome and the West.[7]

Towards the end of the fourth century, Theophilus,
Patriarch of Alexandria, experienced difficulties with the
Egyptian monks, but this arose from the ignorance of the
monks in matters of dogma.[8] Theophilus was well affected
towards the monastic institute and raised many of those who
embraced it to the priesthood, and even to the government
of dioceses.[9] St. Basil, St. Gregory Nazianzen, St. John
Chrysostom, St. Eusebius of Vercelli, St. Martin and St.
Augustine were firm believers in the advantages of combining
the two modes of life. Owing, however, to the commanding
position which Christianity had by this time come to enjoy
within the Empire the office of priest, and still more that of
bishop, was surrounded with riches and honour, and might
easily be a source of danger to weak souls. Hence the warning
given by Cassian that the monks should keep the idea of these
dignities far from their thoughts and flee from bishops anxious
to raise them to such heights of grandeur, as they would flee
from the other sex.[10] The celebrated John of Lycopolis showed,
perhaps, more prudence when he counselled " neither to flee
from nor to seek ecclesiastical orders, but to endeavour with

---

[1] *Vita Ant.*, 67. [2] Ib., 91.

[3] Cass., *Conl.* x, 2, p. 286 : " after the feast of the Epiphany letters were
sent by the Patriarch, ' quibus et initium Quadragensimae et dies Paschae
non solum per civitates omnes sed etiam per universa monasteria desig-
netur '." Instruction in matters of faith was also sent. Cf. ib.

[4] *Vita Pach.*, 20.

[5] Greg. Naz. *Or.* xxi, 19.

[6] *Vita Pach.*, 92.

[7] Supra, p. 51, 53.

[8] Cass., *Conl.* x, 2, p. 286. Soz. *H.E.* viii, 11 f

[9] Pall. *Dial. de vita S. J. Chrys.*, P.G. xlvii, c. 59-60.

[10] *Inst.* xi, 18, p. 203.

all diligence to lead a holy life, and leave the rest to God's Providence."[1]

According to the theory expounded by Cassian the monk would have little part, save by prayer, in the collective life of the Church. An isolation so marked, in the face of ecclesiastical authorities who expected the monasteries to take a modest share in the pastoral care of souls, was hardly consistent with complete loyalty. Lérins found a solution by supplying from among its monks many excellent bishops for the churches of Southern Gaul. These retained their ascetical principles, whilst, however, ceasing generally to be monks in any true sense. Thus we find St. Hilary of Arles tramping barefoot from Council to Council and finally on to Rome. He showed great interest in the economics of his diocese, and invented, among other devices, a machine for extracting salt.[2]

The very important question of episcopal control over monastic foundations was settled for the East by the Council of Chalcedon in A.D. 451. By the fourth canon of this Council the bishop was empowered to forbid, if he thought fit, the establishment of any monastery in his diocese, and to watch over those already established with unremitting care.[3] On him then rested the final responsibility for the good behaviour of the monks; and monastic autonomy in the East ceased to have any real meaning. The monks, it must be said, had brought these restrictions upon themselves by their noisy, perfervid and often wrong-headed interference in the Origenistic and Christological struggles which for so long troubled the Orient. In the West this portion of the canon of Chalcedon never found acceptance.[4] Disputes just about the period of the Council between Faustus, Abbot of Lérins, and Theodore, Bishop of Fréjus (in whose diocese Lérins lay), were settled by the Third Council of Arles about A.D. 455. Here it was determined that the Abbot of Lérins alone was to have complete control over the *laica multitudo* (the monastic community not in ecclesiastical orders), and over the monastic property. The obligations undertaken by the monks were religious, but not canonical in character, so that violations were not visited by the Church with her sanctions. If the Bishop of Fréjus wished to ordain any of the brethren, he had

---

[1] Rufin. *H.M.,* P.L. xxi, c. 397.
[2] Goyau, *Hist. Relig. de la F.,* p. 57. Duchesne, *Hist. of Early Church* ii, p. 408.
[3] Hefele–Leclercq, *Hist. des Conc.* ii, 2, p. 779.
[4] Löning, *Gesch. d. deutsch. Kirchenrechts* i, p. 357.

to obtain permission from the abbot before so doing. If, on
the other hand, he was asked by the abbot to ordain one of
the community, he was bound to comply ; as also to administer
confirmation when necessary, and to bless the holy oils for
use in the monastic church. Except in the cases mentioned
he seems to have had no right to visit the monastery.[1] At the
Council of Agde, held in A.D. 506, under the presidency of St.
Caesarius of Arles (himself trained at Lérins) the same spirit
of confidence in the monks governs the legislation. Bishops
are not to ordain any monk without leave from his abbot ;
and they are not to interfere in the affairs of a monastery
except where the monks strive to avoid the abbot's control,
or in like cases of scandalous disorder. A Frankish Council,
held at Orléans in A.D. 511, decreed, after the manner of
Chalcedon, that abbots must remain under the power of the
bishops, and be corrected by these if they offend against the
rule. Once a year they will be cited to meet the bishop and
must appear before him in the place where he will appoint.
They must have no property beyond what the bishop deems
good to supply for their use ; and they must take no decision
of importance without his knowledge and consent. In a word,
the independent development of a monastic establishment
was made entirely impossible. A Burgundian Council,
held at Epaon in A.D. 517, under the direction of Avitus of
Vienne, decreed that no monastery should be founded without
leave of the local bishop ; and that no abbot should govern
more than one monastery.[2] The spirit of Lérins finally
prevailed,[3] though its success was long doubtful and was
not made secure until championed by the powerful voice of
St. Columban.

Sixth-century Britain, as described by Gildas, shows a
hierarchy of exceptionally imperfect bishops[4] confronted

---

[1] Löning, op. cit. ii, p. 382.
[2] Arnold, *Caes. von Arel.*, p. 236–8.
[3] This is clear from the first formula in the collection made by the monk
Marculf (A.D. 653). Cf. Arnold, op. cit., p. 416, n. 1376.
[4] Britain was, of course, not the only country where the worldly advantages
of the episcopal office whetted the appetite of the ambitious. In Chalon,
about A.D. 470, there were three candidates for the see. One exploited his
high birth ; the second won adherents by means of splendid banquets ; the
third concluded a treaty with the electors by which they were to benefit
from the goods of the Church. Through the influence of the neighbouring
bishops this unseemly struggle was brought to an end. Apoll. Sid. *Ep.* iv,
25, ed. Lütjohann, p. 76, f. Cf. Löning, op. cit. i, p. 117 : " In the Frankish
kingdom of the eighth century there were men who would stop at no crime
to become possessed of a bishopric." (Hauck, *K.G.D.* i, p. 401.)

by a group of dissatisfied ascetics. Irish monastic tradition implies that these won the upper hand and by A.D. 600 were so powerful that they gave the British Church a new and more ascetical form. In Ireland itself, as we have seen, the ordinary hierarchy established by St. Patrick became transformed in the sixth century into a monastic hierarchy. Jurisdiction was held by bishop–abbots and priest–abbots who ruled their *paroeciae*[1] from monasteries. There were bishops without monastic vows[2] (as there were other clerics without monastic vows),[3] but these did not constitute *the hierarchy of the country*, a body superior to the monks and ultimately responsible for the ecclesiastical government of the nation. To the question then, what were the relations between the monks and the ecclesiastical authorities in sixth-century Ireland, the answer is that the monks themselves were the ecclesiastical authorities. Non-monastic bishops and bishoprics were of small, almost negligible, importance. Did the Irish, we may ask, not know the general system of Church government, and did they not feel their own system, so much at variance with it, to be an anomaly ? They must have known the ordinary system of Church government, for St. Patrick had established it amongst them and they might likewise have seen it at work in Britain in the first half of the sixth century or even later. That their own system developed into something different from it was certainly an accident due in part, no doubt, to the diatribes of Gildas and the ascetical suspicion, shared by St. Finnian, that the worldly position, wealth and power then attaching to the episcopal order were calculated to prove an obstacle to perfection.[4] That monasteries founded by priests should

---

[1] Commonly in the *Book of Armagh* and in such expressions as "ut ipsi (na Dési) in parochia episcopatus eius essent, quae est magna et clara." (*V.S.H.* ii, p. 48) ; "sedes episcopalis cum sua parochia" (ib., p. 193). Cf.: "ipse (Carthach) enim episcopatum regionis Chiarraige accepit" (ib. i, p. 175). *Paroecia* or *parochia* seems almost equivalent to our modern "diocese." It is true that the parochiae were often extremely small, that they were scattered in a way unknown abroad, and were administered often by bishops who owed obedience to presbyter-abbots. These are peculiarities of native Canon Law. They were not questioned by the Holy See, and thus were not felt to be inconsistent with Catholic unity.

[2] Supra, p. 168 ff.

[3] Cf. *Adam.* i, 38, p. 74–5, the cleric here mentioned was a "homo dives et honoratus in plebe." He was anything but a monk, and died a sad death.

[4] It is interesting to observe that the complaint of St. Columban to St. Gregory the Great about the Burgundian bishops is largely that of Gildas against the British bishops of his day. Bishoprics in Gaul, looked at from the worldly standpoint, were worth having, and were paid for by the ambitious. Where a bishop had acquired his see by simony there was little good to be hoped for from him. (*M.G.H. Ep.* iii, p. 158. Cf. supra, p. 153.) Here

grow so large and powerful under their priest-successors was foreseen by nobody. Had these successors become bishops whilst remaining abbots, the ecclesiastical government of Ireland would not have differed seriously from that common elsewhere in the Church. This step could not, however, be taken without a departure from the precedent set by the venerable founders, so the abbots had to extricate themselves from their responsibilities as best they could with the aid of friendly bishops or of one of their own monks raised to the higher dignity. But it was realised that the situation was abnormal, as we see from the Northumberland mission, where the Iona fathers sent a bishop to take complete control. His two successors were likewise bishops, and all the ecclesiastical rulers appointed by the three were .bishops.[1] At home in Ireland a partial remedy was also found ; for though the temporalities of the various sees (and with them prestige and wealth) passed regularly into the hands of abbots, territorial jurisdiction in spiritual matters seems to have been retained in a large degree by bishops. As the evidence for this belongs mainly to the eighth and following centuries, it cannot be discussed at the present stage.[2]

---

is the final reason for the desire that the bishop should be a monk, whose life would do credit to his high order. Hence, again, St. Columban's determination to keep free from the local bishops. A very definite step in this direction was taken by Bertulf, his second successor at Bobbio, who resisted the claims of the Bishop of Tortona to place the monastery under his jurisdiction. Bertulf travelled to Rome, where Pope Honorius (June 11th, A.D. 628): "praebuit optatum munus ; privilegia Sedis Apostolicae largitus est, quatenus nullus episcoporum in praefato coenobio quolibet iure dominare conaretur." (Jonas, V. Col. ii, 23, p. 283.) The charter thus granted became a model, and was preserved as such (No. 77) in the Liber Diurnus of the Papal Curia: "Privilegium monasterii, in alia provincia instituti." (Cf. Th. Sickel : Prolegomena zum Liber Diurnus, ii, Sitzungsberichte der Wiener Akad. Phil.-hist., Kl. cxvii, p. 41 ff.)

[1] Bede, H.E. iii, 21 : it may be noted that Diuma, Ceollach and Trumheri were consecrated by Finan bishops of a populus (the Mid-Angles), not of a city. Trumhere was also a near relative of the King. Ib. 24, p. 180. Cf. iii, 22 : Cedd was made bishop " in gentem Orientalium Saxonum." iii, 27, p. 189, etc.

[2] The line of argument may, however, be indicated : (a) There is the evidence from the Irish Collection of Canons (ed. Wasserschleben, Leipzig, 1885), a collection described by Bradshaw (Early Collection of Canons, p. 6) as " an attempt, and there seems good ground for looking upon it as a first attempt, to form a digest of all available authorities, from Holy Scripture, from the decisions of Councils, native and foreign, and from Church writers, native and foreign, arranged methodically under sixty-five several titles ; though the method has not been carried out so fully as to produce an arrangement of the titles themselves in any but the most accidental sequence." It is agreed that the collection originated in Ireland, at the end of the seventh or in the first years of the eighth century (Bury, Life of St. Patrick, p. 235). Now the first chapter, divided into twenty chapters, deals with bishops, and gives the ordinary legislation of the Church in their regard. Chapter 22

Purely monastic bishops, or such as were raised to the higher order because of great personal piety, learning and zeal, are also met with frequently in the sixth and following centuries. Such was Gobbán, one of the three " obedient disciples " whom Carthach left behind him in Inis Pich (Spike Island, Cobh Harbour).[1] Such perhaps were the three bishops whom Mochua brought " to consecrate his churchyard and his church and to divide the land among his tenants."[2] No less than five bishops are mentioned among the followers of Senán of Inis Cathaig.[3] Seven bishops are said to have

---

especially ordains that no bishop is to seize the diocese (*paruchia*) of another, or leave his own unless urged to do so by a multitude of colleagues. If the bishop is present at a court of justice he is to decide the case, for it is unlawful for lay people to decide such questions while a bishop, scribe or saint is in attendance (ib. xxi, 28, p, 72). The bishop consecrates the monastic sanctuary lands in the presence of King and people (ib. xliv, 3, p. 175). The church or diocese (*paruchia*) of a monastery is not to be divided (ib. xlii, 21, p. 168). Bishops are attached to great churches only (ib., 22). (*b*) The position assigned to the bishop in the national civil law (*Senchus Mór*, i, 40, 54, 78, etc.). His standing is that of the king of a *tuath* (petty state), whilst the presbyter-abbot has no such privilege. In the *Crith Gablach*, written about A.D. 700, each king is associated with *one bishop*, who has the most prominent seat in the Court, next to the King and Queen. (*c*) In the *Liber de Abusionibus Saeculi* the tenth abuse is an *episcopus negligens*, i.e., a bishop who disregards his duties as a pastor. This tract is of Irish origin and older than A.D. 700 (Cf. Hellmann : *Pseudo-Cyprianus—de xii abusivis saeculi. Texte u. Unters. zur Gesch. der altchristl. Literatur*, xxxiv, 1, 1909, p. 10 ff.) ; it is possibly older than A.D. 600 (Bury, *Life*, p. 379). (*d*) Above all the *Riaguil Pátraicc* (ed. O'Keeffe, *Ériu* i, p. 216 ff.), which was probably part of the original *Cáin Pátraicc*, a piece of legislation that may be dated about A.D. 735. According to the *Riaguil* every *tuath* (petty state) is to have its chief bishop to ordain the clergy, consecrate its churches, direct its princes and leading men in matters spiritual, bless and sanctify its children after baptism. He must likewise look after the clergy, see that they perform their duties, help them to secure their rights in the State and in the Church. Finally he must see that the oratory and the graveyard are kept clean, and that the altar is properly supplied with sacred vessels and the like. The same tract speaks of clergy who do not seem to be under any monastic obligations. Cf. Wassersch. *I.K.* ii, 19, p. 18, where priests were expected to have property of their own, which they could not have if they were monks. (*e*) The old *Irish Penitential* (ed. Gwynn, *Ériu* vii, p. 140 ff., speaks likewise of a *tuath* bishop, evidently with powers of jurisdiction (p. 142, § 10). Certain cases are left to his decision (e.g., p. 166, § 2). The *clérech tuathe* is mentioned, a cleric who does not seem to have been a monk (p. 170, § 17) ; whilst priests and deacons *cen erchoiliud doer-mancha* " who have not taken vows as *doer-manaig* " are also referred to. (*e*) Odd notices, not easily dated, such as that in the *Life of St. Fintan* (*V.S.H.* ii, p. 104). According to this record a holy bishop named Brandub, a man learned, kind and humble, came to Fintan for the purpose of entering his community. The holy abbot rejoiced to see the Lord Bishop and asked " For what purpose do you come to us, holy pastor ? " The bishop replied : " Excellent father, I wish to spend the remainder of my days in your celebrated monastery. Hitherto I placed the yoke on others ; now I want to spend the little that remains to me of my life under the yoke of another." The terms in this case indicate jurisdiction.

[1] *V.S.H.* i, p. 184.
[2] *Lism. L.*, p. 142.
[3] Ib., p. 65, 66, 74.

come from Cualu to visit St. Brigid near Kildare.[1] Strangely enough a charter dated A.D. 775 from Honau on the Upper Rhine, a monastery inhabited by Irish pilgrims, is signed first by the abbot Beatus, and then by seven bishops bearing Irish names.[2] An old Irish litany commemorates as many as 141 heptads of such prelates.[3] Palladius has a curious reference to seven holy bishops who visited the ascetic Nathanael in the Nitrian desert,[4] but there is no proof that these lacked flocks and dioceses. In Irish records the number of such bishops is sometimes ridiculously exaggerated.[5]

Matters of general monastic as of general ecclesiastical importance were settled by synods, just as happened in contemporary Gaul, and in every other land where civil commotion or secular tyranny did not hinder the free development of the Church.[6] What part Armagh played in these gatherings we cannot tell, but we may conclude from our knowledge of the first synod whose list of signatories has been preserved that its pre-eminence, if not its authority, was recognised.[7] Documentary evidence of the attitude of the Irish monastic fathers towards the Holy See is afforded for the first time by the letters of St. Columban to Pope St. Gregory the Great, and two of his successors.[8] In these the Irish writer acknowledges clearly (more clearly, in fact, than any contemporary writer within the Christian world) the primacy of the Roman Pontiff.[9] He boasts that Ireland has remained steadfast in the Catholic faith as received from the successors of the Apostles ; and that no heretic or Jew

---

[1] Ib., p. 49.

[2] *M.G.H. Dipl.* i, p. 106. Cf. Hauck, *K.G.D.* i, p. 305.

[3] Publ. from *LL.* and three other MSS. by Plummer. *Irish Litanies.* *H.B.S.* ed., vol lxii. London, 1923. p. 32–8.

[4] *H.L.* 16, 3.

[5] *Lism. L.*, p. 30 : Colmcille went to Iona with 20 bishops, 40 priests, and 30 deacons and 50 students ! Cf. p. 123 : Finnian's 12 disciples become 12 bishops.

[6] Supra, p. 188.

[7] The *Cáin Adomnáin*, "Adamnan's Law," was passed by an assembly held at Birr in A.D. 697. Fland Febla, *sui-escop*, "learned bishop" of Armagh, heads the list of 40 ecclesiastical signatories, representing the chief churches of the country.

[8] *M.G.H. Ep.* iii, p. 156, 164, 170 ff.

[9] Loofs : *de Antiqua Brit. Scotorumque Ecclesia.* Leipzig, 1882, p. 95 : " Claris enim verbis, clarioribus quam ullus aequalium eius principatum illum episcopo Romano tribuit." Again, p. 97 : " proferant (Warren, etc.), si possunt, scriptorem eiusdem aetatis, vel civem ipsius urbis Romae, qui similibus verbis loquatur de potestate Papae. Luce clarius est Columbam episcopo sedis Romanae, utpote quae insignis esset traditione a Petro et Paulo profecta, quoad traditionem illam sequeretur, concessisse summam in universa ecclesia docendi et iudicandi potestatem "

or schismatic has ever been found upon the island.[1]   A
generation later, when the Irish Church became agitated by
the paschal controversy, the synod held at Mag Lena, following
the ancient Patrician canon that difficult cases were to be
referred to the Apostolic See, sent representatives to Rome
" as children to their mother."[2]   In the letter from which
this record is derived, the writer Cummian quotes with
approval[3] the saying of St. Jerome, " If anyone is attached
to the see of St. Peter, he is mine."[4]   Those who clung to their
antiquated Paschal table (preferring their own astronomical
learning to that of their wiser countrymen and that of the
Catholic world) were equally convinced of the prerogatives
of the Roman See, as their spokesman frankly admitted
at the Whitby Conference.[5]   Great as was the heat engendered
during the course of these discussions, not a word of hostile
criticism can be discovered against the Holy See as such.
If the Irish conservatives had championed a really sound
cause they might have seen the reckoning accepted by Rome
itself and by all Christendom, but their arguments in favour
of the old computation were less convincing than those of
the opposing savants in favour of the new. Within a generation
after Whitby the controversy was dead in Ireland ; though
it lived on at Iona for yet a little while. At no time, as far as
our evidence goes, were the dissenting group of churchmen
excommunicated by the others (still less by the Holy See)
for their obstinate attachment to the earlier cycle, so that
no part of the Irish Church was ever excluded from Catholic
unity. The fact, again, that missioners straight from Rome,
and those reared under their tutelage, found nothing to complain of in the Irish Church but some trivial peculiarities in

---

[1] *M.G.H. Ep.* iii, p. 171 : " Nos enim sanctorum Petri et Pauli et omnium
discipulorum divinum canonem spiritu sancto scribentium discipuli sumus,
toti Iberi, ultimi habitatores mundi, nihil extra evangelicam et apostolicam
doctrinam recipientes : nullus haereticus, nullus iudaeus, nullus scismaticus
fuit ; sed fides catholica, sicut a vobis primum, sanctorum videlicet apostolorum successoribus, tradita est. inconcussa tenetur."

[2] Wassersch. xx, 5, p. 61 : "si quae difficiles questiones in hac insula
oriantur, ad sedem apostolicam referentur " (Cf. Bury, *Life*, ch. viii, 4, and
Appendix, p. 369 ff.) Cummian *Ep. ad Segéne.* Ussher, *Syll. Works* iv, p. 442 :
" deinde visum est senioribus nostris, iuxta mandatum . . . ut si causae
fuerint maiores, *iuxta decretum synodicum*, ad caput urbium sint referendae ;
misimus quos novimus sapientes et humiles esse *velut natos ad matrem* "

[3] Ib., p. 437.

[4] *Ep.* xvi, 2, p. 69. Cf. xv, 2, p. 64. The Holy See is Noah's Ark in the
deluge of the world. He who is outside it must perish.

[5] Bede, *H.E.* iii, 25 : Colman accepts fully the implications of Matt. xvi,
18. Cf. Jonas, ii, 7, p. 242 : " beati Petri apostolorum principis." Cf. Columban *M.G.H. Ep.* iii, p. 170-7.

discipline,[1] shows that Columban's statement about the purity
of Irish faith was no idle boast. In the hagiographical literature
the connection with Rome is constantly dwelt upon, a visit
thither and respectful treatment at the hands of the ruling
Pope ranking high among the claims of any saint to renown.[2]
To regard this feature as a late development, due to the
triumph of the " Roman party " in the Paschal controversy,
is to be unhistorical on many counts. In the first place the
desire to visit Rome, and sorrow that so high a purpose cannot
be fulfilled, is expressed by St. Columban,[3] and there is no
reason why the sentiment should be confined to him, nor
why it should have been strange to the fathers of Irish
monasticism. In the second place there was no " Roman
party " and no " anti-Roman party," for both sides in the
discussion about Easter recognised the primacy of Rome,
though one was more consistent than the other in drawing
conclusions from this recognition. Union with Rome was
everywhere the sole guarantee of Catholicity.[4] Finally the
attitude of the Occident towards the Holy See as such all
through the early and the late Middle Ages was one of unfailing
reverence. The few like Marsilius of Padua in the fourteenth
century, and Wickliff and Hus in the fifteenth, who questioned
its spiritual authority, were regarded as unprincipled politicians
or fanatics. Hostility came only with the Reformation. To
read it back into documents or events of the earlier centuries
is simply to misinterpret their meaning. It is true that the
Holy See interfered little with the actual government of the
Church in Ireland during the early monastic period ; but the
same holds good of Gaul and Germany, and, indeed (to a
considerable degree) of all countries, until the twelfth century,
when a policy of greater centralisation was adopted. Similarly
the language used by St. Columban in addressing the Pope
may sound frank to modern ears ; it was unusual and not
altogether in good taste, even when written.[5] Certain

---

[1] Loofs, op. cit., p. 86 : " Levissima et brevi composita ea quae de levi-
oribus rebus inter Anglos et Scotos orta est controversia."
[2] Cf. Plummer V.S.H. i, p. cxxiii, n. 7.
[3] Ep. i, M.G.H. Ep. iii, p. 159 : " (Gregorium), non Roman, desiderans,
salva sanctorum reverentia cinerum."
[4] Cf. Arnold : Caes. von Arel., p. 230 : In Gaul no regard was had for the
Orient ; but care was taken to be in perfect agreement with Rome. Catholicity
was thus guaranteed.
[5] An excellent English translation of St. Columban's letter to Pope Boniface IV will be found in Hay : Chain of Error in Scottish History. London,
1927, p. 210 ff.

expressions, too, may not do full justice to the position of the Pope as universal teacher ; but there is scarcely one of these which any Catholic might not have used down to the solemn definition of the whole question by the Vatican Council in A.D. 1870.

Resuming, it may be said that the disciplinary differences to which objection was taken were, at no time, such as excluded the Irish Church of the Second and Third Orders, or any part of it, from Catholic unity. These differences, troublesome though petty, were fairly soon eliminated. Rome took little part in the government of the Irish Church during this period, but the same holds true of Gaul and Germany. Recognition of the primacy of the Holy See was expressed, if anything, more clearly in Ireland than elsewhere.

The horror of heretics, to which St. Columban more than once gave utterance,[1] is illustrated by the conduct of his monks towards the Arian Langobards. A priest of Bobbio, sent by his abbot to Ticino, met the Langobard king and his suite upon the way. " Ha ! " cried the king, " this is one of these Columban monks who refuse to return our salutation when we greet them ! " As soon as the priest drew near, the king laughingly bade him good-day. The monk replied with some strong words about the falsity of Arianism. The king, enraged, consulted his attendants and arranged to have the monk waylaid and beaten to death on his journey home. The programme was carried out according to plan, but the priest recovered.[2] Impatience with heresy goes back to the desert, for it is given as a characteristic of St. Anthony.[3]

(b)—*The Monasteries and the Civil Power.*

Cordial relations between the monks and the secular princes seem to have been the rule. In fact, princes of more modest status or well-to-do aristocrats appear generally as the landowners to whose generosity the monastery owed its existence. Colmcille was favoured by his own powerful kin, the Cinél

---

[1] Ib., p. 212, 221, etc.
[2] Jonas, ii, 24, p. 286–7. Cf. 25, p. 289 : A Bobbio monk, regardless of death, sets fire to a pagan *fanum ;* and Wassersch. *I.K.* xl, 4, p. 154.
[3] Athan. *V. Ant.*, P.L. lxxiii, c. 157 : " nunquam Manichaeis aut aliis haereticis saltem amicibilia verba largitus est, nisi tantum ea quae eos possent ab iniquitatis errore revocare ; denuntians talium amicitias atque sermones perditionem esse animae."

Conaill,[1] the community at Clonmacnois by the no less powerful Southern Uí Néill,[2] but whether this connection, goes back to the founder's day is very uncertain. Enda was said to have received the island of Aran as a gift from Oingus Mac Natfróich, King of Munster,[3] but no close connection was maintained between Enda's successors and the Cashel Kings. Bairre received the field on which the monastery of Cork was erected from an ordinary layman who had come to seek his cow in that place.[4] A cella erected by the same saint at Ráith Airthir (Oristown, Meath), was on a site granted by the local chieftain.[5] The King of Ossory gave Cainnech many gifts of land for his churches and cities.[6] For some of the great monasteries, such as Bangor and Glendaloch, no account has been preserved of the manner in which the founder came to occupy the territory.

Did the monasteries through their leading monks exert any considerable influence upon civil polity? That they exercised an important indirect influence is sufficiently obvious, seeing that they were the great preachers, teachers and spiritual directors of the country. In their churches the faithful were instructed and the sacraments were administered ; in their scriptoria a pious literature was produced that in time became popular far beyond the monastic boundaries. But a strong direct influence can also be traced. The legend of the revision of the Senchus Mór, by a commission consisting of three kings, three clerics and three poets,[7] is interesting in this respect, showing, as it does, the accepted view that the civil law should have the approval of the Church. Colmcille certainly played some part in public affairs. In A.D. 574 Aedán, cousin of Conall, and the new ruler of the Irish kingdom in Scotland, came to Iona and was there solemnly anointed by Colmcille,[8] who was doubtless moved to take this unusual

---

[1] Lism. L., p. 26. The statement that he was granted the site for Derry by his own people, " the race of Conall Gulban, son of Niall." (A.F.M. s.a. 535) is to be preferred to the more precise record that Aed, son of Ainmire, was the donor. Cf. Adam. ii, p. 30, p. 160, n. (r). Dairmag (Durrow) was offered to him by the prince of Tethba. Cf. op. cit., p. 23, n. (b).

[2] For the legend of foundation by St. Ciarán and Diarmait Mac Cerbaill, soon to be High-King, cf. Lism. L., p. 130. Macalister : Latin and I. Lives, p. 91, 101–2, 150–2.

[3] V.S.H. ii, p. 66.

[4] Ib. i, p. 70.

[5] Ib., p. 69.

[6] Ib., p. 166.

[7] Sanas Cormaic, s.v. nós. Laws iii, p. 30, 32. Introd. to Senchus, p. 4 ff V. Trip., p. 562.

[8] Adam. iii, 5, p. 197–201.

step by Old Testament analogies. The practice later spread all over Christian Europe. At the very beginning of his reign, Aedán was threatened with war by the High-King, Aed, son of Ainmire. In A.D. 575 he accompanied Colmcille to Druim Ceatt, in the present County Derry, where a convention was held presided over by the Irish monarch. Colmcille's part in this important council of state seems to have been of the highest consequence.[1]

Three questions were laid before the assembly for settlement. The first referred to the captivity of Scannlán, Prince of Ossory, who was held as a hostage by Aed Mac Ainmerech, but who was entitled to release at a fixed time, according to an agreement of which Colmcille was guarantor. Colmcille demanded that he should now be set free, and the assembly agreed to his request. When Scannlán became King of Ossory he ordered that a tribute should be paid to Durrow in perpetuity as a reward for Colmcille's kind act.

The second question referred to the status of the King of Dál Riata, whose kingdom was divided into two parts, one in Ireland whence his ancestors had migrated, the other across the sea in Alba, where Aedán now lived. What was the relation of the Irish Dál Riata to the High-King ? A distinguished brehon, Colmán, was asked to consider the problem in all its aspects and to propose a solution. He recommended that Dál Riata in Ireland should render to the Irish king tribute in time of peace as well as land forces in time of war ; but was to serve Aedán and his successors in Alba with its sea-forces (then, no doubt, considerable, for Dál Riata was essentially a maritime state). Colmcille recommended that the kings in Alba should make it a cardinal point of their policy never to make war on the King of Ireland, and prophesied that their kingdom would speedily disintegrate if the contrary befell.[2]

A third and yet more complicated question to be decided was the treatment to be meted out to the troublesome body of learned men then known as poets. For " the men of Ireland were on the point of banishing the poets by reason of the multitude and the sharpness of their tongues and their complaining and for their evil words. Moreover, they had made satires against Aed, King of Ireland." Colmcille

---

[1] *Adam.* i, 49, p. 91 : " Condictum regum in Dorso Cette." Preface to *Amra Colmcille, Lib. Hymn.* i, p. 162. *Keating's History*, iii, p. 78.
[2] MacNeill : *Phases*, p. 198. Cf. Reeves : *Adam.*, p. 92, n. (c).

opposed a measure so illiberal as the total extinction of these representatives of the nation's traditional learning. He recommended that their order should be reorganized ; that their number and their privileges should be curtailed ; in a word, that their position should be maintained, but in a manner less burdensome to the nation.

Colmcille's family connection with powerful kings made it, perhaps, inevitable that his advice should be sought in matters of state. What, then, of the other saints whose origin could not compare with his in nobility ? As already pointed out, it is quite probable that the ecclesiastical leaders attended regularly at the assemblies,[1] and there is every reason to believe that their word in these carried great weight. References occur to the interference of individual ecclesiastics in ordinary secular politics.[2] Some of these accounts are untrustworthy ;[3] others more or less credible. The casual manner in which such incidents are mentioned shows at least that ecclesiastical interest in affairs of state was considered quite natural at the time when the records were written. Interference, real or imaginary, led on occasion to tragic results.[4]

A significant sidelight on the attitude of the Irish monastic leaders towards kings and princes is afforded by St. Columban during the twenty-five years of his activity abroad. He was not long in Gaul when the fame of his doings reached King Gunthram of Burgundy, who asked him to appear at his court.[5] Columban soon arrived, and made a deep impression on the king and his followers by his life and learning. The king begged that he should remain within his territory, promising to provide liberally for all his needs. Columban replied that his quest was not wealth ; that his only desire was to preach

---

[1] Supra, p. 188–9.
[2] *V.S.H.* ii, p. 46 : " The selection of a prince to rule the Dési is left to Declan.—Tunc ille iuvenis a sanctis Dei benedictus est et ab omnibus ordinatus est dux." Ib. i, p. 252 : Saint Coemgen and St. Mochonne decide that the time has come for a young prince to take his father's place as ruler.
[3] Notorious in this respect is the *Life of Finnchua of Brí-Gobann,* who is represented as fighting fiercely for his brother, *through affection* (*Lism. L.,* p. 95). Once he led the Munstermen against the Clanna Néill. The Munstermen took flight and wished to flee. Finnchua threatened them. " But," said the Munstermen truly, " the Uí Néill are thrice our number." " Never mind," said Finnchua, " let each of you slay two, then the numbers will be equal ; and when they are equal let each of you slay his adversary ! " (p. 97.) This *Life* is utterly unhistorical, wrong in its genealogies, its chronology and its topography—in a word, a malevolent caricature.
[4] *Silva Gad.* i, p. 49–57.
[5] Jonas, *V. Col.* i, 6, p. 163, and Krusch, ib., n. 3.

the Gospel after the example of Him Who said " He who will come after Me, let him deny himself, take up his cross and follow Me " (Luc. ix. 28). To which Gunthram answered that if a desert was all Columban wanted he could have one within his dominions : an offer that was accepted, for Columban decided to settle with his brethren in a vast solitude of the Vosges around a ruined fort called Annegray.[1]

In A.D. 592 Gunthram died, and Burgundy became united under one sceptre with Austrasia. Childebert II, the new king, ruled but three years. He was succeeded in Burgundy by his son Theuderich, aged eight, and in Austrasia by his son Theudebert, aged ten. As both were still children the reins of government remained in the hands of their grandmother, the celebrated Brunhilde.[2] In Neustria, at the same time, the effective ruler was Fredegunde, mother of the boy-King, Chlotar II. Between the two queens there raged a deadly feud of long standing that ended only with the death of Fredegunde in A.D. 597. A rebellion in Austrasia in A.D. 599 compelled Brunhilde to leave Metz and take refuge in Burgundy with her younger grandson Theuderich, whose capital was Orléans. Under the direction of Brunhilde the young Theuderich declared war on Chlotar II and deprived him of all but a fraction of his territory. Brunhilde next urged him to take the field against his brother, but the Burgundian army refused at the last moment to engage in such a struggle.[3]

During the course of these unhappy events the Irish pilgrim had remained silent in his desert. When, however, the boy-king, Theuderich, succumbed to the failing of his race and at a precocious age became the father of illegitimate children, Columban's anger was aroused.[4] Theuderich was a constant visitor to Luxeuil, situated within his kingdom, and already winning fame far and wide throughout Gaul. Columban reproached him for his evil life, and received from him a promise that he would dismiss his concubines and enter lawful wedlock.[5] But the promise remained unfulfilled. One day when Columban happened to visit the Court near Autun, Brunhilde had the hardihood to bring the illegitimate children into his presence. Columban asked sharply what she meant.

---

[1] Ib., p. 163.
[2] Jonas, *V. Col.* i, 18, p. 186. Cf. Mühlbacher, *Deutsche Geschichte*, p. 27.
[3] *Fredeg. Chronicon.* iv, 2, 7. (*M.G.H. Script. R. Mer.* ii.)
[4] Jonas, ib., p. 187.
[5] Jonas, ib., p. 187.

"They are the king's children," she replied; "strengthen them with your blessing." "Never," cried Columban, in an outburst of righteous indignation; "they are the offspring of brothels, and will never hold a sceptre in their hands." Brunhilde, in a terrible rage, ordered the children to be removed. A mandate was sent to the monastery that no monk should leave its boundaries; and the neighbours were forbidden to render it the least assistance.[1] Columban again visited the Court to protest against such treatment. The king had meanwhile repented, and when he heard that Columban was at the gate he commanded that a sumptuous banquet should be prepared for him. Columban's astonishment knew no bounds when this was laid before him, and he was told that it had been got ready by the king's directions. "The Most High rejects the gifts of 'the impious" (Eccles. xxxiv, 23), he said, and seizing the cups and dishes he smashed them to fragments; the wine and other liquids he poured upon the ground.[2]

Moved by this vehemence, Theuderich again promised amendment and again failed to extricate himself from the meshes in which he was held. Hearing of his renewed lapses, Columban sent him a letter couched in the strongest terms and threatened to excommunicate him if improvement was long deferred [3]

Brunhilde's anger ran high when she read this letter. She stirred up the king, the courtiers and the time-serving bishops of the kingdom to take action against Columban. The king himself paid a hostile visit to Luxeuil, asking why it differed in certain practices (its peculiarly Irish customs) from the other churches of the realm, and why it kept a portion of its buildings closed from the view of fellow-Christians. St. Columban, "who was of a bold and spirited nature,"[4] replied that it was not his custom to throw open the cells of God's servants to lay people; that he had suitable places prepared where all such would be received as guests.[5] The king

---

[1] Ib. i, 19, p. 188.
[2] Jonas, ib., p. 189.
[3] Ib.: "litteras ad eum verberibus plenas direxit, comminaturque excommunicationem, si emendare dilatando non vellit."
[4] Ib., p. 190 : "ut erat audax atque animo vigens."
[5] Ib., p. 190 : "respondit, se consuetudinem non habere, ut saecularium hominum et religione alienis famulorum Dei habitationes pandant introitum ; se et opportuna aptaque loca ad hoc habere parata, quo omnium hospitum adventus suscipiatur."

answered that if Columban profited by royal generosity he must permit every part of the monastery to be open to visit. Columban replied that if the bestowal of gifts was to be construed as giving rights to violate monastic discipline, gifts of any kind côuld not be accepted. " If," he said, " you have come here to destroy the monastery of God's priests and to weaken the rule, it will not be long until your kingdom falls to pieces and your descendants are engulfed in ruin." The king had already entered the refectory, but lacked courage to proceed further. He left hurriedly, saying that Columban's evident wish to receive a martyr's crown at his hands would not be gratified. He would have him, however, expelled from the kingdom and sent back the way he came. Columban replied that he would never leave the monastery where he had settled unless driven forth by force.[1]

Theuderich gave effect to his threat, and had Columban, with his Irish followers, removed to Nantes, where a trading ship was to carry them home to Ireland.[2]

Meanwhile war had broken out between the brothers Theuderich and Theudebert, and the former was compelled to hand over Alsace to the latter.[3] Columban, after experiences which it is unnecessary to recount, found himself free at Nantes, with the possibility of continuing his pilgrimage and undertaking new plans for the spiritual improvement of people with whom he might come into contact. We soon find him at Soissons at the Court of Clothar II of Neustria.[4] The king urged him to settle in his dominions, but the offer was unacceptable, though he consented that one of his able disciples should stay behind and found a monastery after the pattern of Luxeuil.[5] With his accustomed courage, Columban called Clothar's attention to the abuses that prevailed at his court, and had the satisfaction to see that his admonitions were heeded.[6]

From Soissons he proceeded to Metz, where he was well received by King Theudebert, who likewise bade him stay

---

[1] Ib., p. 191 : " se dicit de coenobii septa non egressurum nisi violenter abstrahatur."

[2] Ib., p. 191 ; 20–24, p. 194–206.

[3] *Fredegar. Chron.* iv, 37. Jonas, *V. Col.* i, 24, p. 207.

[4] Jonas, ib.

[5] Ib. i, 21, p. 199.

[6] Ib., 24, p. 207 : " castigatusque ab eo ob quibusdam erroribus, quos vix aula regia caret, spondit se Chlotarius iuxta eius imperium omnia emendaturum."

within his kingdom and apply himself to the conversion of the Alemanni and other heathen tribes who dwelt beyond the Rhone. Columban agreed to devote himself for a while to this work and the eastern shore of the Lake of Constance was selected as the place of his activity.[1] He sailed down the Moselle to Coblenz, and then rowed up the Rhine past Mainz, Worms and Speyer to the territory of the Alemanni.[2]

Having learned toward the end of two years of missionary labours in these regions that the brothers Theuderich and Theudebert were again about to engage in war, he hastened to the latter and begged of him to look to the welfare of his soul. " Abandon the world while you still have the opportunity," he advised " and join the brethren in a cloister, or the time may come when you will have to take this step on your own despite."[3] Theudebert laughed at the suggestion. A Merovingian king become a monk ! Who ever heard of such an idea ? In the sequel, war broke out between the rival brothers. Theuderich won two battles at Toul and Zülpich. Theudebert was taken prisoner and brought in chains to Chalons. By order of Brunhilde he was placed in a monastery, but was soon handed over to the headsman for execution.[4]

As the lands along the Lake of Constance had now fallen into Theuderich's power, Columban thought it better to seek a more favourable field for his missionary labours. He considered first the claims of the Wends, a Slavic tribe settled further to the East, but he learned in a vision that this was not the divine plan, and so turned his face towards Italy. We soon find him at the Court of the Langobard King Agilulf in Milan.[5] This monarch, though an Arian, had allowed his son Adalwald to be baptized a Catholic, and he now received Columban with honour and permitted him to settle wherever he willed within his dominions. Columban first tarried for a while at Milan, to combat the Arian heretics, enemies of the Catholic faith. Against these he wrote a tract " full of

---

[1] Ib., 27, p. 2–11.
[2] Ib., p. 212–3.
[3] Ib., 28, p. 217 : " ad Theudebertum accedit, eumque suadet ut coeptae arrogantiae supercilium deponeret, seque clericum faceret . . . nec simul cum damna presentis regni aeternae pateretur vitae dispendia." The exchange of throne for cloister was already known in Ireland. Cf. *Adam.* i, 36, p. 67 ; and ib., note 9, for similar instances.
[4] Ib. p. 218–19 : " furens Theudebertum fieri clericum rogavit ; at non post multos dies impie nimis post clericatum perimi iussit."
[5] Ib. 30, p. 220.

learning ";[1] whilst he penned also a letter to the Pope, urging him to greater watchfulness and to greater activity against the heretics of northern Italy. Wishing, finally, to return to the well-beloved monastic surroundings he moved on towards the Trebia and the Apennines, where, at a place called Bobbio, he found a site suitable to his purpose. Very soon there arose around the half-ruined Bobbio basilica the monastery of SS. Peter and Paul. Shortly afterwards, on November 23rd, 615, Columban died, and found in his new Italian foundation a last resting-place.[2]

Looking back upon his history, we notice that he was intimately connected with five kings. His aim in Gaul was not merely to do good to his own soul by living a mortified life in exile, but also to do good to the souls of others by offering them abundant spiritual help. He took it as a matter of course that the King—even the heretic Langobard King—should co-operate in this work. Hence his repeated appearances at various Courts. He took no active part in political changes, though he was not averse to these when they promised to prove advantageous to religion.[3] The severity with which he castigated royal vice recalls Old Testament parallels. In a word, Columban was anxious that the monastery and the civil power should live on intimate terms. The civil power should give the monastery protection and if necessary modest material support. The monastery, in return, should provide the state with a power-house of spiritual energy ; it should look particularly to the civil ruler himself and keep him upon the path of virtue, for good laws, justly enforced, were the people's best safeguard, and such government could certainly not be expected where the ruler himself was neither just nor moral.

Monastic leaders at home seem to have been actuated by exactly the same principles as Columban. They were not concerned with civil policy as such, but they were concerned with the development of the country along Christian lines.

---

[1] Ib., p. 221 : " actum est, dum ille penes Mediolanium urbem moraretur et haereseorum fraudes, id est Arrianae perfidiae, scripturarum cauterio discerpi ac desecari vellet, contra quos etiam libellum florenti scientia edidit."

[2] Ib., p. 223.

[3] He prophesied the coming success of Chlotar II over all his rivals (Jonas, i, 20, p. 198. Cf. ib. 29, p. 219, 222), and showed more sympathy with this king than with any other. Chlotar later tried to prevail upon Columban to return from Bobbio to Luxeuil. Columban refused, but begged the King to show favour to that monastery. Though a suppliant, however, he was no sycophant, for " litteras castigationum effamine plenas regi dirigit."

They thus had to interest themselves in legislation and, as a consequence, in those responsible for legislation—the princes and the peoples in their assemblies. Their influence with these was great, yet not sufficient to secure the abandonment in practice of some ancient customs that could not be reconciled with the Christian code of morality. The laws governing marriage are the chief case in point.[1] A canon attributed to St. Patrick ordains that clerics are to be tried in ecclesiastical courts.[2] Many small endowments of land were free from civil tribute,[3] but extensive estates bore corresponding civil duties;[4] otherwise the whole economy of the nation would have been thrown out of balance. Grants of land brought with them, too, in many cases, restrictions as to the appointment of superiors, and in time the introduction of a new body of lay managers of monastic property. Beyond this there is no evidence of any attempt on the part of the State to rob the ecclesiastical leaders of their independence or to reduce them to a position of subservience. In this respect the Irish Church was much better situated than its older sister in Merovingian (and even in Carolingian) Gaul.[5] St. Martin,

---

[1] Cf. *Laws*, ii, p. 342–408. The *Cáin Lánamna*, "law of social relationships," here published, contains the substance of Irish civil law governing the marriage contract. Nearly all its features are pre-Christian ; some, in fact, primitive. Many clauses may be mere legal theory ; but the preservation of the Law and the diligence with which it was commented upon imply that it was no dead letter. As it permits frequent divorce and the having of two wives simultaneously, under certain conditions, it must have held its place despite the efforts of the Church leaders to oust it, and introduce in its stead the Canonical regulations regarding marriage. Cf. Wasserschl. xxv, 6, p. 78 ; xlvi, 30–2, p. 193 for the Canon Law ; Cf. *Adam.* ii, 41, p. 165–6 ; *Lism. L.*, p. 90, and *V.S.H.* i, p. 250 for contrary practice.

[2] Wasserschl, xxi, 26, p. 72.

[3] *B. Arm.*, 22b, 25b, 41a, 41b, : "ecclesia libera." Wassersch, *I.K.* xxix, 6; p. 101 : "Si ecclesia sit Catholica et ab omni censu libera." *Lism. L.*, p. 143.

[4] Senán (*Lism. L.*, p. 63) refuses to acknowledge the right of Lugaid Cíchech, King of Rathlin, to tribute from his island, on the ground that subordination to an earthly king was unbecoming. Such an attitude might lead to no trouble where the monastic property was small as at Inis Cathaig, but it obviously could not be defended where the monastery had large possessions. Even the warlike Finnchua of Bri-Gobann agrees to the rent fixed by the King, and promises to render it. (Ib., p. 88.) The Irish collection of Canons recognises both classes of churches, those free and those liable. Cf. supra, note 3, and ib. : "si ecclesia fuerit sub censu regali." Ib. xlii, 28, p. 170 : "si ecclesia sub censu regis deguerit et mundialibus quibusdam funibus constricta sit." Cf. also ib. xxv, 10, p. 78 : tribute one of the things which are Caesar's.

[5] The Frankish Council of Orléans, in A.D. 511, met by *order* of the King, Chlodovech, who himself drew up the list of matters to be discussed. The decrees of the Council were submitted to him for confirmation. No layman within his kingdom might become a cleric without permission from him or from one of his judges. For the King's support in land and money the Church had thus to pay a high price (*M.G.H. Conc.* i, p. 2, 4.). After the death of Chlodovech, royal power and state domination over the Church became still greater. Hauck. *K.G.D.* i, p. 146-167.

in the latter country, had set an example which later church-men were too weak to follow.[1]

Mutual esteem and good-will between the ecclesiastical and civil authorities was, as has been said, the rule. One point only in the early period seems to have caused real difficulty. This was the claim to ecclesiastical sanctuary, jealously enforced by the monastic leaders and often violated by the kings and princes. The legends of Colmcille's battles mention sanctuary as a question at issue.[2] Similarly the remarkable legend of the cursing of Tara, said to have been perpetrated by "the twelve apostles of Ireland" during the reign of Diarmait mac Cerbaill as High-King.[3] The prominence of a monastic founder might be estimated by this test.[4] In the Law of Adamnan, passed in A.D. 697, the right of ecclesiastical sanctuary is guaranteed and protected under heavy penalties.[5]

(c)—The Monasteries and the People.

In the first half of the sixth century (and in places to a much later date) the Irish monk might be called upon to undertake missionary work within his own country.[6] As the monastic institute extended and the great majority of bishops and priests were such as had bound themselves to the observance of a religious rule, the cure of souls devolved likewise, to a great degree, upon the monasteries.[7] A lively interest in religion seems to have characterized the people ; but the beauty and purity of Christian worship did not lead at once to the abolition of popular pagan practices. The origin of these was lost in the mists of antiquity ; but their place in the traditions of the race was almost unassailable, and their eradication in consequence a task of the most formidable

---

[1] Sulp. Sev. *V. Mart.* 20, p. 129 and *Dial.* ii, 6, p. 187–8.
[2] Two of the three battles are said to have been caused by the slaying of offenders who had placed themselves under Colmcille's protection. Reeves, *Adam.*, p. 247–55.
[3] *Silva Gad.* i, p. 72 ff. Cf. *Book of Rights*, p. 53. MacNeill, *Phases*, p. 234 f.
[4] Thus, it was claimed for Finnchua of Brí Gobann by the caricaturist who wrote his life that his protection lasted a year, a quarter, and a month beyond that of any other saint. (*Lism. L.*, p. 90) : " uair comairce mis ꝁ raithi ꝁ bliadne aicesein sech gach noebh aile."
[5] *Cáin. Adom.*, § 36 : " full díre for slaying, burning or theft within the *faithche* : half díre for these crimes in the sanctuary land outside the *faithche.*"
[6] Cf. *V.S.H.* iii, p. 132 : " (*Molaisse of Daiminis*) multas pertransiens regiones, vi verbi ad fidem Christi populosam multitudinem convertit, ac miraculis confortavit." Cf. i, p. 54, etc.
[7] Ib. i, p. 90 : " de illo monasterio . . . multi viri sancti creverunt. atque pastores perfecti effecti sunt animarum."

kind.[1] When again the new establishments came to possess lands, tenants had to be secured for their cultivation, and a class of lay clients settled around the parent church or its dependent cells. The monks were naturally bound, in a special way, to undertake the spiritual care of these. So intimate, indeed, was the union between the monastic principality and its lay clients that the latter are called, like the community, *manaig*, and in many records are distinguished only with difficulty from the religious family.[2] The form of tenure by which their lands were held varied, just as in the case of secular lordships. Though the relation was not exactly one of legal contract,[3] each side had accepted rights and duties. " The social connection which exists between the church and its tenants, is instruction in the faith, and mass and the offering of requiem for the soul from the church to its tenants ; and the receiving of every son to instruction ; and of every tenant to right repentance. Tithes and first fruits and alms are due to the church from the tenants ; and full honour-price in time of health, but a third of the honour-price at the time of death. The church has the right of pronouncing judgment upon its tenants ; of bearing witness and giving proof that will be accepted as final against them ; and this in the case of both *saer*-stock and *daer*-stock tenants, and on every other member of the *tuath*, even though he is a *saer*-stock tenant on ecclesiastical land, except there is another church equal in dignity that lays claim to him."[4] Where such a tenant had become, for any reason, destitute, he was supported by the church.[5] This also applied to the last survivor of a vanished kin "without relatives, without land, without cattle."[6]

We may take it as probable that the growth in monastic property, which put the monks on the way to become wealthy

---

[1] Cf. Rhys., *Celtic Heathendom* (The Hibbert Lectures for 1886), Edinburgh, 1888. Wood-Martin, *Traces of the Elder Faiths of Ireland*, 1902. In the Irish hagiographical literature (cf. Stokes, *Lism. L.*, p. cix ; Plummer, *V.S.H.* i., p. cxxix–clxxxviii) various superstitious survivals are mentioned, including belief in fairies and leprachauns, belief in magic, the sacrifice of a human being to ensure the safety of a building, lucky days, going *deiscl*, or righthandwise, to bring good fortune , *tuaithbel*, or lefthandwise, to bring ill fortune, the cult of trees and wells (cf. Rhys, op. cit., p. 105. Caesarius of Arles was troubled with similar survivals in what had been the territory of the Aedui. P.L. xxxix, c. 2239, 2271, etc. Cf. Sulp. Sev. *Vita Mart.* 13, p. 122. H. Gaidoz, *Encyclopédie des sciences religieuses*, v, p. 440 f., an l Bertrand, *La Religion des Gaulois*, 1897. Goyau, *Hist. rel. de la France*, p. 97), belief in sorcery, charms and dreams.
[2] *Laws, Gloss.* vol. vi, s.v. *manach* and *manchuine*.
[3] *Laws* ii, p. 354 : *tabuirt* here is distinguished from *cor*—a strict legal contract
[4] *Laws* ii, p. 344.   [5] Ib., p. 354.
[6] Ib. : "gin fine, gin tír, gin inille."

corporations, belongs to the seventh century. At this time, too, the rights just mentioned (to tithes, first fruits and alms) were claimed and apparently recognized by the tenants.[1] A problem which caused much discussion among the Fathers was whether gifts should be accepted from notorious sinners. In practice, if not in theory, Columban had answered this question with a vehement negative, for he scattered the viands and broke the cups and dishes when a banquet was prepared for him by the evil-living Burgundian king.[2] At home, however, the attitude adopted by the monastic rulers was more conciliatory. Following the example of St. Martin[3] they were willing to accept the gifts for distribution among the poor ; but unwilling to receive them for the support of the monastery.[4]

At an early date, the right of women to leave a portion of their personal property by will to the church or monastery where they worshipped is attested in a synodal decree.[5] To a later period must be assigned the notices of traditional taxes paid to certain monasteries. That of Mochua, for instance, claimed the right to a cow from every king and nobleman, a raiment from every *ollam*, a pig from every house in the north, a screapal[6] from every household.[7] Bangor, it is said,

---

[1] Wassersch, *I.K.* xxv, 9, p. 78 (quoting St. Jerome, *Comm. in Matt.* xxii, 21) : " Quae sunt illa, quae Dei sunt ? Decimae, primitiae, oblatio, timor." Cf. St. Jer. *Ep.* 64, 2, p. 590 (in the Old Testament) : " primitiae ciborum et omnium frugum atque pomorum offeruntur antistiti, ut habens victum atque vestitum absque ullo impedimento securus et liber serviat Domino." Cf. *Lism. L.*, p. 56. *Laws* i, 50.

[2] Supra, p. 310.

[3] Sulp. Sev. *Dial.* iii, 14 : " mox ad eum Lycontius divina expertus beneficia convolavit, nuntians simul et agens gratias, domum suam omni periculo liberatam, centum etiam argenti libras obtulit, quas vir beatus nec respuit nec recepit, sed priusquam pondus illud monasterii limen adtingeret redimendis id captivis continuo deputavit. Et cum eo suggeretur a fratribus, ut aliquid ex eo in sumptum monasterii reservaret, omnibus in angusto esse victum, multis deesse vestitum : nos, inquit, ecclesia pascat et vestiat, dum nihil nostris usibus quaesisse videamur."

[4] Wasserschl. *I.K.* ii, 24, p. 19 : " de eo quod dona iniquorum a sacerdote recipienda sint, ut tamen pauperibus erogentur et captivis." Cf., however, *V.S.H.* ii, p. 184 : " quam (villam) sanctus Mochua cum omnibus suis rebus incendi iussit ne de peccatoris ellemosinis vel possessionibus famulus Christi portionem aliquam haberet." The discussion went on into the eighth century. Cf. *Monastery of Tall.*, p. 128, § 4.

[5] Wasserschl. *I.K.* xli, 10, p. 161.

[6] Some notion of the Irish system of currency may be gleaned from the following list. The unit of value was the milch cow—*bó* (also *unga ;* a word that never represents a coin). The *bó* = 24 *miaich* (sacks of corn or malt) or 24 *screpaill.* The *screpall* = 3 *pingine.* A *bó-inlaeg* (in calf heifer) = 16 screpaill. A *samasc* (three-year-old heifer not yet in calf) = 12 screpaill A *colpthach* (two-year-old heifer) = 8 screpaill. The *dairt* (yearling heifer) and *dairtid* (yearling bull) varied in value.

[7] *Lism. L.*, p. 142.

received 140 milch cows yearly from the King of Ulaid.[1] Finnchua's biographer revels in the enumeration of such tributes.[2] As a result of similar gifts and payments, added to the fruits of the monks' hard work, the monasteries became wealthy[3] and thus were among the principal objects of pillage when the Norse invasions began.

Monks, like slaves, pilgrims, and, in general, those who lived in absolute dependence upon others, were not allowed to become guarantors for the fulfilment of legal obligations.[4] In the matter of law, again, the monasteries were privileged and protected in various ways.[5]

The principle, strongly insisted on, that Christ Himself was received in the person of a stranger, made the monks extremely anxious to treat guests with the greatest consideration.[6] A commodious site was therefore chosen for the hospice, and special lands were on occasion set aside for its better maintenance.[7] Cronan of Ros Cré moved his monastery to a more convenient position, because the original establishment was inaccessible for travellers.[8] Columban had a hospice attached to Luxeuil where even a king might find suitable shelter.[9] A guest at Bangor is found voyaging with Comgall's monks in what is now Belfast Lough.[10] When Cainnech of Achad Bó arrived at Iona he was met by Colmcille and the brethren and received "honourably and hospitably."[11] Similar treatment was accorded to all visitors from Ireland.[12] It extended indeed far beyond the expected limits, as the following story will show. One day when Colmcille was living at Iona he hailed a passing brother and said, " Three days hence you are to proceed to the western part of this island and wait there

---

[1] *Lism. L.*, p. 86.
[2] Ib., p. 89–97.
[3] *Lism. L.*, p. 132 : Colmcille's supposed prophecy that Saigher was to be wealthy doubtless expresses the later fact. Cf. ib., p. 121.
[4] Wassersch. *I.K.* xxxiv, 3, p. 122.
[5] Ib. xxi, 3, p. 73 ; xxx, 5, p. 104 ; xlii, 22, 29, 30, 31, p. 168–171.
[6] *V.S.H.* i, p. 118 : "ducentes secum cum reverentia hospites, in quibus Christum credebant se hospitio collocare." Ib. ii, p. 28 : " Frater, in hospite recipitur Christus ; ideo debemus in adventu Christi gaudere et epulari." Ib., p. 223 : "hospites semper pro Christo recipite." Ib., p. 193.
[7] Ib., p. 216 : " domum hospitum hic facite, et meliores de agris vestris in usum eius tradite."
[8] Ib., p. 27 : "in locum desertum ubi non possunt hospites et pauperes me facile invenire, non ero."
[9] Jonas, *V. Col.* i, 19, p. 190. Cf. *Reg. Coen.* viii, p. 225, *MNP.*
[10] *Adam.* iii, 13, p. 214.
[11] Ib. i, 11, p. 28 : "cui Sanctus cum fratribus obviam venit et ab eo honorifice et hospitaliter susceptus est."
[12] Cf. Ib. i, 31 and 32, p. 61.

upon the shore. There you will be visited by a crane, carried by the force of the winds from the north of Ireland. It will arrive after the hour of noon, spent and weary and almost at the end of its strength and will fall beside you on the coast. Take it up kindly ; bring it to the nearest house and there minister to it as a guest for three days and three nights. Its strength will then be completely regained ; it will be unwilling to tarry with us any longer, but will fly back to the sweet land of Ireland, whence it came." So, in fact, it happened.[1] We hear again of guests at Clonard, Clonmacnois and Cork[2] ; but the fact was so commonplace that it rarely deserved special mention.[3] Where notice was given of the coming of a distinguished visitor, abbot and brethren alike went out to meet him.[4]

As most guests arrived bespattered and hungry, their first bodily needs were water in which to wash, and food. Before anything else, however, they would repair to the church to thank God for their safety.[5] Warm water for a foot-bath was then fetched, and this office was performed (after the manner of Christ washing the feet of His Apostles at the Last Supper) by the abbot or by one of the monks.[6] If the day of arrival were an ordinary fast day the fast was relaxed, and the brethren were permitted to share in the better food offered to the guest[7] ; so that the community as a whole took an

---

[1] lb i, 48, p. 90–1.

[2] *Lism. L.*, p. 122, 128. *B.N.E.* i, p. 18 : " ticfat aidhedha uaisle sunn aniu ⁊ frithalid iat im biadh ⁊ im fotraccadh, ' noble guests will come here (to Cork) to-day, and minister to them with food and bathing '."

[3] Most references are incidental. Cf. Wasserschl. *I.K.* xliv, 8, p. 177 : " in termino loci sancti in quo laici hospitantur."

[4] *Adam.* i, 3, p. 24 ; i, 4, p. 28 ; i, 30, p. 59 : " eamus proselyto obviam." i, 45. p. 87.

[5] *Adam.* i, 3, p. 24 : " hymnisque et laudibus resonantes, honorifice ad ecclesiam perducunt (Colmcille)." Ib. ii, 36, p. 152 ; ii, 42, p. 168 (Cormac) : " oratorium cum omnium admiratione et gratiarum ingreditur actione." *V.S.H.* i, p. 116,

[6] *Adam.* i, 4, p 27 : " aquam ad lavandos hospitum pedes exhaurite." *Lism. L.*, p. 132. *B.N.E*, i, p. 18. *V.S.H.* i, p. 72 : preparate iam in adventu illorum hospitum balneum et cibum. Solvantur calciamenta de pedibus vestris, ut laventur aqua, et postea balneate." Ib. i, p. 116 : " post haec abbas cum suis monachis coeperunt lavare pedes hospitum, cantantes, ' Mandatum novum do vobis ' " etc. Ib. i, p. 209. Ib. ii, p. 14, Ib., p. 223, Cf. Bede, *H.E.* ii, 28, Sulp. Sev. *V. Mart.* 25, p. 135 : " Aquam manibus nostris ipse (Martinus) obtulit ; ad vesperam autem pedes ipse nobis abluit, nec reniti aut contraire constantia fuit."

[7] *Adam.* i, 26, p. 54–5 : " Crastina quarta feria ieiunare proponimus, sed tamen, superveniente quodam molesto hospite, consuetudinarium solvetur ieiunium." *V.S.H.* ii, p. 197 : " et ieiunabat quotidie nisi in dominicis et summis festivis, usque ad occasum solis, nisi hospites et peregrini advenirent." Ib., p. 249 and n. 7.

intimate human interest in the advent of visitors. Particular care would probably be taken of the poets, who, like the modern press, could do endless injury to those who did not meet with their approval. Against the shafts of their satire there was hardly any defence. Generosity being a national virtue, the mere suggestion of niggardliness was a matter about which saints as well as sinners were extremely touchy.[1]

If, however, the dread of poetic satire gave an added keenness to monastic hospitality in Ireland, it was not responsible for the introduction of the custom, or for the common forms which it took. These, in fact, are found in the monasteries of all countries. Faustus of Riez, one-time Abbot of Lérins, was noted for his kindness to travellers.[2] St. Martin washed the feet of his guests and refused to listen to any protestations of unworthiness on their part.[3] Cassian proves by an amusing example that guests were constantly passing to and fro in Egypt.[4] He states that the law of fasting was abrogated in their honour, except on Wednesday and Friday[5]; and he asserts that this relaxation, though based on a perfect motive,[6] was not without its inconveniences.[7] St. Basil teaches that the Christian must practise hospitality towards the brethren quietly and frugally,[8] and gives many practical hints as to the manner in which this is to be done without prejudice to discipline in his monasteries.[9] Visitors were excellently received at Nitria, though they were not allowed to spend more than a week in idleness.[10] The writer of the *Historia. Monachorum* describes the reception of himself and his party by the monks when they appeared in these parts. The monks espied them when they were already a long distance off, and vied with one another in showing them welcome. Some brought water ; others food. Others again washed their feet

---

[1] .Plummer, *V S.H.* i, p. cii–iii and cxiii. *Adam.* i, 42, p 79–80. *Lism. L.,* p. 90–1.

[2] Goyau, *Hist. relig. de la Fr.,* p. 62.

[3] Supra, p. 319. n. 6.

[4] *Inst. V.* 25, p. 102 : One of the seniors presses Cassian to take more food, and when he politely declines, the senior comments :" ego iam sexies diversis advenientibus fratribus mensam posui hortansque singulos cum omnibus cibum sumpsi et adhuc esurio ; et tu primitus nunc reficiens iam te dicis non posse ! "

[5] Ib. 24, p, 102.

[6] Ib. : " ieiunium, licet utile sit et necessarium, tamen voluntarii muneris est oblatio ; opus autem caritatis impleri exigit praecepti necessitas."

[7] *Conl.* xix, 6, p. 540–1.

[8] *Morals* xxxviii. *Ascet. Works,* p. 111.

[9] *Reg. fus. tract.* xxxii-xlv. *Reg brev tract* cccxiii.

[10] *H.L.,* 7.

and their garments.[1] Elsewhere he tells us of the treatment received by visitors in the monastery governed by the Abbot Apollo near Hermopolis. On the arrival of expected visitors the monks went out to meet them, singing psalms, for such was the custom among the brethren ; and having bowed down their faces to the ground, they kissed them. Then all proceeded, some in front and others behind, singing psalms until they reached Apollo. He also bowed to the earth, kissed the visitors, led them to the guest-house, and, after prayer, washed their feet and invited them to rest.[2]

Pachomius had also *exinodochia* or guesthouses for visitors of both sexes, and the care with which these were governed shows that they were constantly occupied.[3] Finally birds, beasts, lions and even hyenas and serpents excited the kindly interest of the monks and on occasion benefited from their food supplies.[4]

Attached to various monasteries were penitents, some, no doubt, publicly excommunicated,[5] who had come to expiate their crimes under monastic supervision before absolution and their re-admission to the community of the faithful. Provision for these was made by St. Finnian of Clonard himself,[6] and their presence in a monastery or in its neighbourhood is a normal feature of sixth century monasticism. The length of their penance depended on the offences of which they had been guilty. At Iona there were at least two settlements for penitents, one on the island of Tiree and the other on the island of Hinba.[7] At Luxeuil the *medicamenta paenitentiae* were as eagerly sought as the means for restoring bodily health in a modern hospital.[8] A certain Church in Ireland was called *Cell na nDér* " the Church of the tears," because, through the founder's merits, tears of penitence were

---

[1] *H.M.* 23.
[2] *H.M.* 8.
[3] *Reg. Pach.* 50–51. *Alb.* 30–31. *Vita Pach.* 21. Cf. *AA. SS.* T. iii, Maii, p. 305–7. *Amél.* xvii, p. 58–9.
[4] *H.L.* 16, 18, 23. *H.M.* 6. Cass. *Conl.* xvi, 2, p. 440–1. Sulp. Sev. *Dial.* i, 13–16, p. 164–9.
[5] Excommunication was practised by the Irish saints. *Adam.* ii, 24, p. 136 : " cum alios ecclesiarum persecutores excommunicare coepisset." Columban's threat, Jonas, *V. Col.* i, 19, p. 189. Cf. *V.S.H.* ii, p. 172. *Codex Salm.*, c. 874. Wassersch. *I.K.*, ch. xl, p. 153, ff.
[6] His tariff of penances was seemingly the first of its kind. Cf. supra, p. 193–5.
[7] *Adam.* i, 21, p. 50 ; i, 30, p. 59 ; ii, 39, p. 157.
[8] Jonas, *V. Col.* 1, 5, p. 161 ; 10, p. 170 : " undique ad penitentiae medicamenta plebes concurrere " ii, 1, p. 232 ; 8, p. 245 ; 15, p. 265 : " post digna paenitentiae medicamenta " ; 19, p. 273 ; 25, p. 290

granted to those who prayed in it.[1] Women, as well as men, seem to have undergone courses of penance ; for St. Jerome is cited to this effect.[2] His hard words about lady penitents are also quoted. " Some of them," he says, " are unwilling to live in full retirement and under obedience ; but vicious, garrulous, tale-bearing, troublesome, they ramble (from cell to cell), and of course bring no advantage to the others."[3] Whether Irish women penitents deserved such a castigation we cannot tell. The institution of penitents living in the closest connection with monasteries continued, and is found flourishing vigorously in the eighth century.[4]

All who were in distress were sure of kindness and consideration at the hands of the Irish monks. Even in days when the resources of the monasteries were very meagre everything possible was done to relieve the poor. We have already seen something of the extent to which monastic almsgiving was carried.[5] The aristocratic Colmcille was conspicuous for this as for other virtues. When he discovered a thief about to steal his seals, he reminded him of God's prohibition against such deeds and told him to come to the monastery whenever he was in need. Then he ordered wethers to be killed and given to the unfortunate man, lest he should sail back empty-handed. Later he ordered the local superior on Tiree to send him a fat ox and six measures of grain. These presents the poor thief did not live to see, for he had died before they reached him, and in fact they were consumed at his funeral.[6] Elsewhere it is related that he stopped for the night in the house of a poor man named Nessan. Before his departure he blessed all that his host possessed and prophesied his future prosperity.[7] Again he helped a miserable poor father of a family who had no means of supporting his wife and children.[8] Professional beggars who went around with a wallet from door to door were not, however, held in much esteem.[9]

---

[1] *V.S.H.* i, p. 18.
[2] Wassersch. *I.K.* xlv, 12, p. 183 : " sicut in viris duo genera sunt, sancti et paenitentes, ita in mulieribus virgines et penitentes sunt."
[3] Ib. 15, p. 184.
[4] Cf. *Mon. of Tall.*, §§ 11, 74. *Rule of Tall.*, 37 : " the *aos peannaide* ' penitents ' at Clonfert are attached to the monastery, for they recite the psalms, etc., with the monks." Cf. ib. 51–54.
[5] Supra, p. 225 ff.
[6] *Adam.* i, 41, p. 78–9. To the example of *Xenia* given by Reeves (p. 97) add Athan. *Vita Ant.* P.L. lxxiii, c. 150 : " quasi *Xenia* de monte portans."
[7] *Adam.* ii, 21, p. 130–1.
[8] Ib. 37, p. 153–4.
[9] Ib. 20, p. 131.

Like the other Irish saints Colmcille was sympathetic and helpful towards the sick.[1] He does not seem to have come into contact with lepers, but the disease must have made its appearance in Ireland as in Gaul[2] during the sixth century. All through the Middle Ages it was the most common, as it was the most terrible, of afflictions. Its cure is thus one of the most frequent miracles ascribed to the saints.[3]

Very naturally, too, the lot of slaves, especially slave girls, appealed to the heart of the monastic fathers, and many were liberated through their means. Mochua was celebrated in this respect.[4] The condition of the slave-girl seems to have been pitiable.[5] We are thus not surprised to hear that Colmcille, in one instance, prays for punishment on a Pictish druid, who refused to liberate a captive Irish maiden bound to his service as a slave. The druid fell sick and sent for Colmcille for aid ; but this was rendered only after the promise had been given to set the maiden free.[6] It need hardly be added that these acts of charity were in accordance with monastic practice everywhere.[7]

(d)—Interrelations between the different Monasteries.

Glancing through the life of St. Colmcille, the best-known (thanks to his biographer) of the sixth century saints, we are struck by the very friendly relations which existed between him and his contemporaries. St. Comgall, founder of Bangor, was one of his particular friends. Adamnan recounts a meeting between the two " on a quiet summer's day " near Dún Ceithirn in Northern Derry.[8] Comgall visited him, possibly many times, at Iona.[9] When some of Comgall's monks, with a guest whom they were carrying, were drowned in Belfast Lough, Colmcille, warned at Iona by a heavenly voice, called

---

[1] Ib. 40, p. 163.
[2] Help for lepers is enjoined by the 4th Council of Orléans (549), c. 21, and the 10th Council of Lyons (583), c. 6. Hefele-Leclercq, *Hist. des Conciles* iii, p. 207.
[3] For a formidable list of such cures and for other valuable information see Plummer, *V.S.H.* i, p. cx, n. 9 and Addenda.
[4] *Lism. L.*, p. 145. Cf. Jonas, *V. Col.* ii, 10, p. 154.
[5] For the hardships inflicted on slave girls cf. *Cáin Adamnáin*, § 2, where the treatment supposed to have been meted out to all women seems to be that really meted out to the *cumal*.
[6] *Adam.* ii, 33, p. 146–7.
[7] Cf. Sulp. Sev. *Dial.* ii, 7, p. 188. Cass. *Conl.* xiv, 4, p. 401 ; xv, 5, p. 431 ; xxiv, 3, p. 677–8. *Inst.* x, 22, p. 192 *H.L.* 10, 14, 32. *Vita Pach.*, 4, *H.M.* 8, 20.
[8] *Adam.* i, 49, p. 92.
[9] Cf. ib. iii, 17, p. 220.

the brethren suddenly into the church and bade them pray
for the souls of the deceased.[1] Keeping this intimacy in mind,
the later legend which describes the two as going to war
over the ownership of a Derry church[2] must be said to lack
all credibility. That, however, the local states to which both
belonged might settle their differences by force of arms, was
a possibility which the two friends recognized, and which,
no doubt, they heartily regretted.[3]

On a certain journey to Iona, Comgall was accompanied
by no less than three of the sixth century monastic founders,
Cainnech of Achad Bó, Brendan of Clonfert and Cormac
Ua Liatháin,[4] whose establishment is a matter of speculation.
The first-mentioned of these was a native of County Derry,
but his principal church was in Ossory. Adamnan relates
that one day when Colmcille and a number of the brethren
were on the open sea and in great danger of being submerged,
the brethren cried out to the abbot that he should implore
God to bring them safe to land. Colmcille replied, " To-day
the duty of praying for your safety is not mine, but Cainnech's."
Wonderful to relate, Cainnech in Achad Bó was moved at
that moment by an interior voice and hurrying from the
refectory, where he had just commenced his daily meal, he
ran to the oratory, losing in his haste a sandal off one foot.
When the brethren expressed their astonishment he exclaimed,
" Surely this is no time to eat, whilst Columba's boat is in
danger on the sea ! " His prayer for the safety of Colmcille
and his companions was heard.[5] A pretty story is told of
Cainnech's staff, which he had left inadvertently behind
him when leaving Iona, but which caught up with him on his
way back to Ireland.[6] Brendan of Birr was also a friend of
Colmcille's and took his part with effect at a synod where his
conduct was under discussion.[7] Colmán moccu Loígse, a
Leinster bishop and founder of Nua-congbáil in Loígis, was
likewise " a dear friend of Colmcille,"[8] and the latter had

---

[1] Ib. iii, 13, p. 213 f.
[2] Cf. Reeves, op. cit., p. 253–4.
[3] Ib. i, 49, p. 93 : " nam mei cognationales amici et tui secundum carnem
cognati, hoc est Nellis nepotes et Cruthini populi, in hac vicina munitione
Cethirni belligerantes committent bellum."
[4] Ib. iii, 17, p. 220.
[5] Ib. ii, 13, p. 120–1.
[6] Ib. ii, 14, p. 123.
[7] Ib. iii, 3, p. 193.
[8] Ib. iii, 12, p. 212 : " carus Columbae amicus."

Mass offered for the repose of his soul on the day of his death.[1]
So, too, Colmán moccu Salnai, founder of Lann Elo, whom
we find about to set out on a journey to Iona.[2] During a long
visit to Durrow, Colmcille decided to pay a call at Clonmacnois.
When news of his approach arrived, the brethren about the
monastery and in the adjacent fields, led by their abbot,
Ailither (ruled A.D. 585-99), issued forth to meet the blessed
Columba as if he were an angel of the Lord. When they
reached him all prostrated themselves upon the ground,
then rose and kissed him reverently. A procession was next
formed, and with hymns and canticles Colmcille was led to
the church.[3] So great was the enthusiasm of the brethren
at Clonmacnois that it was thought better to construct a
rude sedan chair carried by four men and place Colmcille
upon it lest he should suffer any inconvenience from the
multitude that surrounded him.[4]

Hardly less remarkable was the welcome afforded Colmcille
by Conall, Bishop of Coleraine. Offerings of various kinds
were made by the surrounding people who gathered in numbers
on the monastery green. Here the presents were blessed and
accepted by the Saint, who profited by the occasion to address
his benefactors, and bring some of them to a better way of
life.[5]

On another occasion Colmcille is found visiting the brethren
at Tír-dá-glas, whose founder, Colmán, son of Crimthann,
had been his fellow-student at Clonard. Here, too, his
reception was of the friendliest nature.[6]

The same spirit runs through the whole of the early monastic
literature. When Finnian of Mag Bile visited Comgall, that
great Saint and his brethren rejoiced to receive a guest of
such distinction.[7] Abbán pays a call on Berchan, and is
received by him with honour.[8] When he wishes to visit
Brendan of Clonfert an angel announces his approach, and
Brendan comes forth to receive him with great joy.[9] Ailbe
of Emly accompanied Enda to the King of Cashel to request
that the island of Aran might be given in gift for monastic

[1] Ib.
[2] Ib. i, 5, p. 29.
[3] Ib. i, 3, p. 23-4.
[4] Ib.
[5] Ib. i, 50, p. 98.
[6] Ib. ii, 36, p. 152.
[7] V.S.H. ii, p. 13.
[8] Ib. i, p. 25.
[9] Ib. p. 29.

purposes.[1] Comgall received Cainnech with delight and asked
him to preach to the brethren when Sunday came.[2] Ciarán
of Clonmacnois sent a monastic habit as a present to Senán
of Inis Cathaig.[3] The instances in fact are almost innumerable
where the rulers or brethren of one monastery were welcomed
by those of another.[4] The welcome, as already stated, had a
material side in the good food or modest banquet offered
after the customary services had been rendered. So common
was this feature that it was burlesqued by the imaginative
writer of St. Findchua's life. When this abbot was informed
that Ronán the Fair, a holy elder of Fir Breg, was on the
way to visit him with some companions, he is reported to have
exclaimed : " Let a vessel of ale, enough to intoxicate fifty,
and food enough for a hundred be given them, and if they deem
that insufficient, add more ! "[5] When Colmcille was feted
at Clonmacnois, according to a later tale, the wine was
particularly good.[6]

Special relations of intimacy between two or more
monasteries are a feature of the hagiographical literature,
and must go back to the seventh century, if not, as often
asserted, to the days of the founders. The word for this in
Latin is *fraternitas*, " brotherhood," in Irish *oentu* " union "
or *cotach* " covenant."[7] According to this arrangement,
monks in the one monastery shared in the prayers and merits
of the other ; and each helped the other whenever the rights
of either were endangered.[8] Relations of this kind existed
between Clonard and Llangarvan,[9] between Clonmacnois
and Saigher,[10] between Clonmacnois and Glendaloch,[11] between

---

[1] Ib., p. 56.
[2] Ib., p. 157.
[3] Ib., p. 212.
[4] Cf. Ib. i, p. 29, 43, 44, 57, 61, 96, 161, 168, 177, 180, 194, 230, 248 ; ii,
11, 14, 93, 101, 147, 152, 175, etc.
[5] *Lism. L.*, p. 88.
[6] Ib., p. 131 : a big feast was prepared for Colmcille and his community,
and it was commonly said that at no subsequent feast was the wine as good
as it was on that night. But the assertion was questioned by some of the
experienced brethren.
[7] Cf. *V.S.H.* i, p. 25 : " Tunc sanctus Berchanus et sanctus Abbanus
firmissimam fraternitatem inter se et suos monachos venturos usque ad
finem mundi fecerunt. Eandem etiam fraternitatem alia vice cum sancto
Brendano et sancto Moling et sancto Flannano et sancto Munnu et cum
aliis multis firmaverunt." *Lism. L.*, p. 86 : " 7 dogniat a n-aenta 7 a cotech
annsin a triur .i. Ailbhe 7 Comgall 7 Finnchua."
[8] *Cod. Salm.*, c. 934.
[9] *Cambro. B. Saints*, p. 78–9.
[10] *Lism. L.*, p. 132.
[11] Ib., p. 133.

Connor and Lann Elo,[1] and between a very large number of other monasteries.[2]

In A.D. 636 occurs the first mention of serious differences between monks. Some time earlier the Munster Saint, Carthach or Mochuda, had settled at Rathan, within easy distance of Clonmacnois, Durrow, Lann Elo, Clonard and numerous minor foundations. The older monasteries objected to a new establishment in a district already so well provided for, and they asked the Uí Néill rulers to prevail upon Carthach to return to his own province A heroic tale still extant gives a piquant description of the event.[3] Historically the incident is of importance, for it shows that by the date mentioned the leading monasteries had begun to acquire possessions in places distant from the parent church. Had the property of Clonard, Clonmacnois, Durrow and Lann Elo lain around these monasteries, had it been small in area, and had there been no desire to add to it, the settlement of another community at Rathan would have caused no anxiety. Thus the desire for property is already a source of discord between the Irish monks. As the monastic property grew, disputes about land became common, and in later centuries led to disedifying cares and scenes and at times to bloodshed.[4] In the early period, while the possessions of all were still meagre, there was no such temptation to discord, and a spirit of cordial good fellowship between all monks characterized Irish monasticism as it had characterized monasticism in general since the days of Pachomius.[5]

§ 7—PRAYER AND DEVOTIONS.

(a)—Private Prayer.

That the Irish monks cultivated the spirit of prayer goes without saying ; for were they not by profession enthusiastic followers of Him who was accustomed to pass so much of His time in " the prayer of God " ? (Luke vi. 12), Again the chief

---

[1] *V.S.H.* i, p. 259.

[2] A long list of examples is collected by Plummer, *V.S.H.* i, p. xci, n. 4. Cf. *Lism. L.* pp 60, 61–2, 75, 124, 127, 13, etc. The *eclais oentad* of the Irish Penitential (*Eriu* vii p. 156, § 10) seems to be an isolated independent church thus connected with a monastery.

[3] Indarba Mochuda a rRaithin, publ. in *B.N.E.* i, p. 300 ff. Cf. *A.U.* s.a. 635.

[4] Cf. *Lism. L.*, p. 133, 139. Wasserschl. *I.K.* xxxii, 24, p. 117 ; xlii, 8, p. 163–4. *V. Trip.*, p. 78. *A.U.*, s.a., 759, 763, 806.

[5] *Reg. Pach.*, 51. *Alb.*, 31. *Vita Pach.*, 28, 77, 87. *H.L.*, 7, 18. *Ep. Ammon. Prolog.*

negative purpose of monastic life was the systematic extirpa-
tion of vice, between which purpose and prayer there is an
exceedingly close connection. Purity of heart and the practice
of the other virtues assist prayer ; whilst prayer in its turn
obtains grace and leads to that abiding union of the soul
with God which is Christian perfection. The vices and
disorders of the flesh were, therefore, mortified that the soul
might not be fettered in its effort of ascent towards God.
Purified from passions and free from thoughts and worries
likely to prove distracting, the heart is capable of intimate
and unbroken converse with the Lord, which is the aim of
every work.[1]

In the early period (at least until the works of Pope St.
Gregory the Great became known in Ireland)[2] the great
teacher in matters appertaining to prayer was certainly
Cassian. Utilizing in arbitrary fashion a text of St. Paul
(1 Tim. ii, 1) the Gallic writer proceeds to elaborate a whole
science of prayer.[3] He begins by dividing this into four kinds :—
(1) Supplication, the imploring of God to pardon our sins.
This form of prayer belongs especially to beginners in the
spiritual life, who have not yet triumphed over their passions.
They ask God to blot out the past and grant them complete
triumph over their weaknesses. (2) Prayer, " by which we
offer or promise something to God." Examples of this are
the promise to renounce all worldly interests and to serve
God with the whole strength of the mind ; to be perfectly
chaste, imperturbably patient, to pluck the roots of anger
and sadness from the heart. (3) Intercession, or petition in
fervour of spirit, whether for those dear to us or for the peace
of the world. (4) Thanksgiving, by which the mind, conscious
of past or present favours, or of the future bliss prepared
for it, gives thanks to God in transports of unutterable love.
The soul in this state, like Mary at the feet of Christ (Luke x
38 ff.), contemplates God continually and the things of God,
and utters frequently glowing or " fiery " prayers which
cannot be grasped or expressed by the mouth of man.[4]

---

[1] *Conl.* ix, 2, p. 250.
[2] Columban *Ep.* iii. *Ep. Cum. ad Segéne* (Ussher, *Works*, iv., p. 439)
(circa A.D. 634) : " Ad Gregorii Papae, urbis Romae episcopi (a nobis in
commune suscepti, et oris aurei appellatione donati) verba me converti,
qui etsi post omnes scripsit, tamen est merito omnibus praeferendus."
[3] *Conl.* ix, p. 260.
[4] Ib. 15, p. 262 : " ferventissimas saepissime novimus preces *ignitasque*
prodire." Ib. p. 263 : " ad illam *ignitam* et quae ore hominum nec compre-
hendi nec exprimi potest orationem ferventissimo corde raptantur."

Christ Our Lord, according to Cassian, taught by word and example these four forms of prayer.[1] They are all useful and needful for monks, who may employ now one, now another of them just as it suits their moods. Yet ordinarily the four kinds of prayer correspond to different stages of progress in the spiritual life, and the monk should try to pass systematically from the lower to the higher, for the sublimer kind is not easily reached except through the regular course.[2]

Later writers retain Cassian's division, as the basis of the science of prayer, but the second and third forms (both proper to those who have already progressed in their quest of virtue) are combined, and three stages only are distinguished, called the Purgative, the Illuminative, and the Unitive ways. Sometimes, however, the prayer of the Illuminative way, inspired by love of God and the neighbour, and concerned with the acquiring of virtues and intercession for others, is called the " Prayer of Affections and Acts " ; thoughts of God's goodness and love and of the joys of heaven lead to richer unitive prayer accompanied with ineffable joy (the " Prayer of Aspirations ") ; which in turn leads to a yet higher state in which the soul contemplates God in transports of love ("Acquired or Active Contemplation ").[3]

Finally, according to Cassian, speaking of the higher forms of union with God, " the mind will come to that incorruptible prayer which is not engaged in looking on any image and is not articulate by the utterance of any voice or words ; but with the intentness of the mind aglow, it is produced by an ineffable transport of the heart, by some insatiable keenness of spirit ; and the mind, being placed beyond all senses and visible matter, pours it forth to God with unutterable groans and sighs."[4] This is contemplation in its highest form, or, in modern terms, " mystical prayer."[5]

While this period of exaltation lasts the mind is sometimes completely absorbed or lost in ecstasy. Though all the impressions of sense are transcended and language fails, the

---

[1] Ib. 17, p. 264.
[2] Ib. 15, 16, p. 263–4. Cf. Pourrat, *Christ. Spir.*, p. 126–9. Butler, *Bened. Mon.*, p. 63–7.
[3] Butler, op. cit., p. 67.
[4] *Conl.* x, ii, p. 305–6.
[5] Pourrat, op. cit., p. 127, f. Butler, op. cit., p. 79 and p. 75, where he points out that the use of " mysticism " in this sense is quite modern. The first great mystic among the monks is Macarius the Egyptian, whose system has been studied by Stoffels, *Die mystische Theologie Makarius des Aegypters u. die ältesten Ansätze Christlicher Mystik.* Bonn, 1908.

powers of mind and soul are operating at high tension, so that the state is the reverse of quietistic. Cassian makes no mention of the more striking outward phenomena such as trance and rapture ; nor of visions or revelations. He makes it clear that the condition was not deliberately sought for, still less produced by dubious processes, but that it happened quite simply, often on the most trivial of occasions.[1]

In the Irish documents, no instruction is found on the method of private prayer, and it was obviously taken for granted that everyone knew how to do this instinctively. Given silence and quiet, good-will and purity of soul, the rest followed naturally once the monk had placed himself in the presence of God. The stages of progress marked out by Cassian should be reached in due course.

Following the Saviour's command "to watch and pray always" (Luke xxi. 36), a sentiment re-echoed by St. Paul (1 Thes. v. 17), St. Columban lays down that after the exercises of public prayer everyone should pray in his own cell.[2] The monk requested a prayer when entering a house ; also when leaving to serve ; the mode of petition being an inclination towards the senior in charge, lest the law of silence should be violated.[3] If, however, he met a senior monk whilst walking he requested a prayer on bended knee.[4] The intercessory power of another's prayers was regarded as very high.[5] Before work the monk stopped for a moment to pray ; after work he stopped a moment to pray.[6] It was stated as a self-evident principle that "no exercise should receive greater attention and diligence than prayer" for "there is nothing as useful and as conducive to salvation as to knock at the Creator's door with a multitude of prayers and eager requests."[7]

---

[1] Butler, op. cit., p. 81–2.

[2] Reg. Mon. vii, p. 379 : "quibus absolutis unusquique in cubiculo suo orare debet." Cf. St. Jer. Ep. 22, 25, p. 178 : "semper te cubiculi tui secreta custodiunt, semper tecum sponsus ludat intrinsecus. Oras : loqueris ad sponsum. Legis : ille tibi loquitur," Sulp. Sev. Vita M. 26, p. 136 : "interiorem vitam illius . . . et animum semper caelo intentum nulla unquam explicabit oratio . . . ita Martinus dum aliud agere videretur semper orabat."

[3] Reg. Coen. xiv, p. 231 MP. Ib. ix, p. 227 MNP. Cf. St. Jer. Ep. 22, p. 201-2 : "egredientes hospitium armet oratio ; regredientibus de platea oratio occurrat antequam sessio ; nec prius corpusculum requiescat, quam anima pascatur."

[4] Ib.

[5] Jonas, V. Col. ii, 15, p. 256.

[6] Reg. Coen. iii, p. 221 MP.

[7] Jonas, V. Col. ii, 19, p. 251 (Eusthasius, before a synod in Gaul) : "nihil enim plus desudare debemus quam orationi incumbere. Nihil enim tam utile tamque salutare quam Creatorem multiplicatione precum et adsiduitate orationum pulsare."

Everyone in fact, should go as far in this good work as his particular fervour suggested and his particular capacity, mental and physical, permitted.[1]

In general, the prayer of the monks would be of a very simple and spontaneous kind, confined mainly to operations of the heart and will.[2] On occasions, however, it might take a more elaborate form, when the faculties of imagination and intellect would also be brought into play. St. Columban suggests that the intellect should have an important part in the development of the monk's spiritual character. " What," he asks, " is best in this world ? To do the will of its Maker. What is His will ? That we should do what He has ordered, that is, that we should live in righteousness and seek devotedly what is eternal. How do we arrive at this ? By study. We must, therefore, study devotedly and righteously. What is our best help in maintaining this study ? The intellect, which probes everything, and, finding none of the world's goods in which it can permanently rest, is converted by reason to the one good which is eternal."[3] We find him again at Annegray putting this doctrine into practice, for he is alone in a secluded glade with a book on his shoulder " and discoursing with himself about the sacred writings."[4] During the periods of retirement for prayer which the Irish monks so often allowed themselves[5] it is extremely likely that " meditation " of this kind was common ; all the more so because the allegorical treatment of Holy Writ in search of hidden or " spiritual " meanings is essentially an intellectual process.

A very large proportion of the Irish monks progressed so far in prayer that they were capable of unbroken con-

---

[1] *Reg. Mon.* vii, p. 380.

[2] Well-known prayers like the *Pater Noster* and the *Apostles' Creed* were probably repeated frequently. Cf. Jonas, *V. Col.* ii, 15, p. 266 : " dominicam orationem symbolumque dicere." Cass. *Conl.* ix, 13, ss., p. 265 ff.

[3] *Instr.* ii : " Qualiter monachus Deo placere debet." *Z.K.G.* xiv, p. 79–80·

[4] Jonas, *V. Col.* i, 8, p. 166 : " et librum humero ferens de scripturis sacris secum disputaret." Cf. St. Jer. *Ep.* 4, 2, p. 22 : " nosti hoc esse christianae animae pabulum, si in lege Domini meditetur die ac nocte."

[5] Supra, p. 260 f. Private prayer during the night should also be taken into account. Cf. *Adam.* iii, 20, p. 224 : " quadam hiemali nocte, supra memoratus Virgnous (Fergno Brit) in Dei amore fervens, ecclesiam orationis studio aliis quiescentibus solus intrat ibidemque in quadam exedra devotus orabat." It was common to stand at prayer (ib. 21, p. 225), sometimes with arms extended (ib. 16, p. 218). At other times all are found prostrate before the altar. (Ib. 13, p. 214 : " cito ante altarium surgens, inter fratres pariter in oratione prostratos.") Cf. Cass., *Conl.* xxi, 26, p. 601 : " et ita cunctorum motuum suorum primitias protensione manuum, incurvatione genuum et totius corporis prostratione persolvunt."

templation. The evidence for this is the growth of the anachoretical habit. When vices had been purged and the soul by constant effort had reached a state of great intimacy with God, there was no longer (according to Irish teaching) a compelling reason for continuing the ordinary petty exercises of the *coenobium*. The soul thus favoured might accordingly retire, for a longer or shorter spell, to solitude, there to live unfettered in union with its Creator. Anachoretical life, as we know from the *Catalogus*, became a marked feature of Irish monasticism from about A.D. 600 onwards.

Just as contemplation was looked upon as the normal result of a spiritual life of self-conquest and prayer, so it was expected that some among the contemplatives would reach mystical heights in their union with God. Amongst those upon whom this wonderful grace was conferred was St. Colmcille. On one occasion, according to his biographer, the grace of the Holy Spirit came upon him, so that he remained in his cell for three days without movement, neither eating nor drinking. Through the crevices of the door light oozed during the night hours.[1] In periods of special fervour he retired to the west of the island, giving strict orders that nobody should seek him out. A curious monk who disobeyed his instructions and hid on a certain hill-top to watch Colmcille's movements saw the holy angels " citizens of the heavenly Kingdom " descending to speak with him ; but when these discovered that they were being observed by prying human eyes, they departed incontinently for heaven.[2] The hill where this happened was afterwards called " The Hill of the Angels."[3] On another night while he was in " an ecstasy of mind," an angel descended bearing a glass book with a list of kings.[4] Again he saw the soul of a good smith " rather devoted to almsgiving " and distinguished for his general spiritual excellence, carried to eternal glory.[5] Many were the other mysterious phenomena which his attendant Diormit might have revealed had he not had good reasons for keeping silent.[6] Similar events were not unknown in the Columban monasteries in Gaul. Thus Athala, second abbot of Bobbio, was vouchsafed a vision of heaven before his death.[7] A young nun of Faremoutiers had a similar experience.[8]

[1] *Adam.* iii, 18, p. 222–3.   [2] *Adam.* iii, 16, p. 217–8.
[3] Ib. ii, 44, p. 175.   [4] Ib. iii, 5, p. 197.
[5] Ib. 9, p. 207.   [6] Ib. 7, p. 205.
[7] Jonas, *V. Col.* ii, 5, p. 239.   [8] Ib. 15, p. 264.

Another nun of the same monastery who had received special external marks of divine favour, grew disobedient, self-confident, contemptuous of others, and finally died an imperfect death.[1]

At home in Ireland, examples of unusual supernatural benefits are likewise constantly recorded. Féichin of Fobar is rapt in ecstasy ;[2] Laisrén before death receives a visit from the Blessed Virgin, St. Peter and St. Paul[3]; Ailbe had a place beside the sea, where the marvels of the divinity were revealed to him.[4] Visions of angels were so frequent that they almost appear commonplace.[5] The vision of St. Fursa was famous not only in Ireland but in western Europe during the lifetime of the Saint.[6] Whatever be the truth of many of these stories they show at least the conviction that those who had been raised to the higher forms of prayer should receive at times striking external rewards for their intimacy with God.

(b)—Public Prayer.

Those who had devoted their lives to God, should, according to St. Jerome, spend their nights like the treehopper, passing untiringly from one exercise of devotion to another.[7] Among these exercises were the night vigil, and the morning psalms and prayer, which with the day " offices " at the third, sixth and ninth hours, and at nightfall made up the traditional Christian system of public prayer.[8] St. Augustine speaks

---

[1] Ib. 16, p. 267–8.

[2] *V.S.H.* ii, p. 79 : " cum in quandam mentis extasim vir Dei raperetur."

[3] Ib., p. 140.

[4] Ib. i, p. 63 : " habebat sedem iuxta mare, in qua orabat ad Deum et Dei mirabilia cernebat."

[5] *V.S.H.* i, p. 24, 28, 50 ; ii, 5 : " angelica visione qua quotidie fruebatur," 224, 235, etc. *Lism. L.*, p. 77, 122, etc. Cf. St. Jer. *Ep.* 22, 7, p. 154 : " et ut mihi ipse testis est Dominus, post caelo oculos inhaerentes nonnunquam videbar mihi interesse agminibus angelorum et laetus gaudensque cantabam." Sulp. Sev. *Vita M.* 21, p. 130 : " constat etiam angelos ab eo plerumque visos ita ut conserto apud eum invicem sermone loquerentur." Ib. *Dial.* iii, 11, p. 208 ; 13, p. 211.

[6] Bede, *H.E.* iii, 19. Cf. *Z.C.P.* ix, p. 168 ff. For other visions cf. *Lism. L.*, p. 127, 128, 302, 319–20. *Fís Adamnáin* in Stokes : *Three Months in the Forests of France*, 1895, p. 265–79. *Rev. Celt.* xxx, p. 349–83. Cf ib. xii, p. 420 ff. *Otia Merseiana*, i, p. 113–9.

[7] *Ep.* 22, 17, p. 166–7 : " esto cicada noctium. Lava per singulas noctes lectum tuum," etc.

[8] Ib. 37, p. 201 : " quamquam apostolus semper nos orare iubeat, et sanctis etiam ipse somnus oratio sit, tamen divisas orandi horas habere debemus ut si forte aliquo fuerimus opere detenti ipsum nos ad officium tempus admoneat. Horam *tertiam, sextam, nonam, diluculum quoque ac vesperam*, nemo qui nesciat." Ib. : " noctibus bis terque surgendum, revolvenda de scripturis quae memoriter tenemus."

of collective prayer in church at the fixed hours, but there is no need for him to specify what these are, as they were known to all.[1] Up to this period, however, and indeed during the fifth and sixth centuries to the time of Pope St. Gregory the Great, there was no stable and uniform method of arranging the canonical hours.[2] Cassian found to his disappointment that the different customs in Egypt and the Orient were almost as numerous as the monasteries and cells.[3] He recalls the ancient custom in the monasteries of Egypt and the Thebaid, but to seek its re-introduction would be obviously a forlorn hope. Cassian explains that in Egypt the public offices were originally but two (one at vespers, the other during the night). Day hours were celebrated in Palestine and Mesopotamia; whilst at the time of writing seven had come to be regarded as the usual number of canonical hours in the West.[4]

According to the *Catalogus* the saints of the First Order, St. Patrick's helpers and their successors for two generations, had but one system of celebrating the hours.[5] When the Saints of the Second Order came into intimate connection with the British Church in the person of Cadoc and others, towards the middle of the sixth century, they adopted a new mass liturgy, doubtless also a new arrangement of the hours.[6] By the end of the century there were various systems in vogue,[7] but variety was not felt to endanger in any way

---

[1] *Ep.* 211. *C.S.E.L.* lvii, p. 361 : " orationibus instate horis et temporibus constitutis."

[2] Bäumer, *Gesch. des Breviers*, 1895, p. 143.

[3] *Inst.* ii, 2, p. 18 : " totque propemodum typos ac regulas vidimus usurpatas quot etiam monasteria cellasque conspeximus."

[4] *Inst.* ii, 4, p. 20. Ib. iii, 2, 3, p. 34. Ib. iii, 4, p. 39 : " qui typus. liceat ex occasione videatur inventus . . . tamen illum numerum, quem designat beatus David, quamquam spiritalem quoque habeat intellectum secundum litteram manifestissime supplet : Septies in die laudem dixi tibi " (Ps. cxviii, 164). The seven hours are Matins, Lauds, Prime, Terce, Sext, None and Vespers. Cf. Bäumer, op. cit., p. 146. Butler, *Ben. Mon.*, p. 59, n. 2.

[5] H. and S., *Councils*, ii, p. 292.

[6] Ib.

[7] *Reg. Mon.* vii, p. 378 : " de cursu psalmorum et orationum modo canonico quaedam sunt distinguenda, *quia varie a diversis de eo traditum est.*" *Catal.* H. and S. *Councils* ii, 292 : " diversas missas celebrabant et diversas regulas." *Regula* here seems to correspond with *celebratio* in previous part. *Missa*, too, seems to have the narrow sense of *mass*, though in *Adam.* ii, 5, p. 112 ; iii, 2, p. 191 ; iii, 23, p. 233, *missa* is used of the divine office. Cf. Cass., *Inst.* ii, 7, p. 23 : " ad celeritatem missae quantocius properantes—' hurrying as quickly as possible to the end of the divine office '." Ib. iii, 5, p. 40 : " *missa canonica celebrata usque ad lucem . . . vigilias extendunt.*" Ib. 8, p. 42 : " post vigiliarum *missam.*" Cabrol, *Dic. d'Archéol.* ii, c. 2354. Bäumer, *Gesch. des Brev.*, p. 2. It may be noted that the word for *mass* is not derived from *missa* in any of the Celtic languages.

the unity of the faith [1] As time went on the Irish systems, whatever their differences in detail, must have conformed to a general plan, for in the eighth century we find the *Cursus Scottorum* treated of as a uniform whole and compared with five other important *Cursus* of the Catholic world.[2]

St. Columban uses *cursus* and *synaxis* almost indifferently as a name for all the canonical hours together. The last-mentioned word was made popular by Cassian, who employed it in his writings times without number.[3] Ordo psallendi,[4] officium psallendi[5] and simply *horae* (*canonicae*[6] or *regulares*[7]), are also found, as well as *missa* and *celebratio*.[8] *Opus Dei*, a name made popular by St. Benedict, occurs, but does not necessarily suppose Benedictine influence, for the words were used in this sense at Lérins, and were adopted by St. Caesarius of Arles.[9] *Horae* and *celebratio* must have become the most popular terms, for it is to them that the Irish words for the divine office as a whole, *trátha* and *celebrad*, correspond.

There is no proof that the number of the hours celebrated was everywhere the same in Ireland.[10] Prime was known in

[1] *Reg. Mon.* vii, p. 380 : "sunt autem quidam Catholici—whose mode of celebrating the hours differs from that which he prescribes."
[2] *Ratio Decursus* (by an anonymous writer judged to be of the eighth century), publ. by J. Wickham Legg in *Miscellanea Ceriani*, Milan, 1910, p. 151 ff. Cf. H. and S., *Councils* i, p. 138–40. *Cursus Scottorum* in *Trip. L.* i, p. cxx. *Antiphon. of Bangor*, ed. Warren ii, p. xxv–vi. Moran, *Essays on the Origin, etc. of the Irish Church*, p. 243–6.
[3] *Inst.* ii, 10, p. 25 : "cum igitur praedictas sollemnitates quas illi 'synaxis' vocant, celebraturi conveniunt." Ib. ii, p. 27 ; 17, p. 31. *Conl.* viii, 16, p. 232 ; ix, 34, p. 282 ; 36, p. 284 ; x, 10, p. 299 ; xiii, 1, p. 362 ; xv, 1, p. 426 ; xvii, 3, p. 467, etc.
[4] *Reg. Coen.* xv, p. 232 *MNP.*
[5] Jonas, *V. Col.* ii, 23, p. 284 : "expleto psallendi officio."
[6] In the late *Ordo* of Kilros, p. l-lix, c. 565.
[7] *Cod. Salm.*, c. 903.
[8] Supra, p. 334, n. 7.
[9] *V.S.H.* i, p. 114 : "coeperunt fratres opus Dei peragere." Ib. ii, p. 155. Bäumer, *Gesch. des Brev.*, p. 2. *Ordo Psalmod. Lirinensis.* Caes. *Reg. ad. Virg.*, c. 10. *AA. Sanct. Boll.* T.I., Jan. (1645 ed., Antwerp), p. 753.
[10] Cass. (*Inst.* iii, 4, p. 38-9) says that Prime was introduced first into Bethlehem to prevent the monks from sleeping too long after the night office, and passed thence to other monasteries. Cf., however, St. Basil, *Reg. fus. tract.* 37, where he distinguishes prayer at dawn (seemingly Prime) from prayer at midnight and prayer before dawn. Reeves, *Adam.*, p. 346, finds mention of Prime in iii, 11, p. 209 : "mane primo suum advocat saepe memoratum ministratorem," but there is no reference to a canonical hour in this passage. Perhaps Reeves was misled by the verbal resemblance to Cass., *Inst.* iii, 3, p. 38 : "ita enim et ille primo mane conduxisse describitur, quod tempus designat matutinam nostram solemnitatem ; dein tertia, inde sexta," etc., where the canonical hour is really meant. It was known in Ireland in the seventh century, as is clear from the *Antiph. of Bangor*-hora secunda (passim) and Jonas, *V. Col.* ii, p. 284. Cf. *Mon. Tall.*, p. 145, 25 : "ó anteirt dia luaoin co matin dia cetaoni, 'from Prime on Monday to Matins on Wed.'." *Thes.* i, 3 (Palatine MS. of eighth or ninth century : "antert, tert," etc. No direct reference to Prime is found in the *V.S.H.*

the seventh century; Compline[1] hardly so early. St. Brendan in the paradise of Birds is said to have found a system of five hours (vespers, vigils, terce, sext and none) that harmonizes exactly with the number quoted by St. Jerome.[2] The oldest arrangement mentioned in the native language (Teirt; medón lái; nóin; espartu; midnocht; iarmérge—terce, sext, none, vespers, nocturns, matins)[3] agrees with the arrangement recorded in the life of St. Melania the Younger, written about A.D. 451.[4] As the double night office is testified to by St. Columban,[5] we may take it as all but certain that the sixfold division of prayer was that which commonly prevailed in the sixth century. When Prime was added the number was raised to seven.[6]

Why were these hours, rather than others, selected as the proper times for public prayer? The reasons given are of the mystical order. Thus terce recalled the sending of Christ to Pilate and the descent of the Holy Ghost upon the Apostles; sext the hour of Adam's sin and of the Crucifixion; none the death of Christ on the Cross and the angelic visit to the centurion Cornelius; vespers the hour of sacrifice in the Old Law; nocturns the creation of the elements; matins the denial of Peter, and Christ's sufferings in the house of Caiphas.[7]

For purposes of comparison the arrangement of the ecclesiastical year and of the different hours as described by Cassian may be given in some detail.[8] In Egypt the Feast of the Epiphany was not yet separated from the Feast of Christmas, and the mysteries of both were celebrated on the former day. On that Feast, too, a letter was despatched from the Patriarch of Alexandria to all the churches of Egypt

---

[1] *V.S.H.* i, p. 118: "omnes cum magna maturitate ad completorium properabant." *Deired lái* and *diu(d) lai* occur in *Mon. Tall.*, § 30, p. 138, but there is no indication that they are to be understood as the canonical hour of Compline. Neither is it mentioned in the Céle Dé *Ordo* of Kilros, representing eighth century practice; so that its introduction seems to date at the earliest from the ninth century. *Fadg*, which appears to mean Compline, occurs in the later *Rule of Tall.* § 97, p. 56. Cf. Gwynn, *Introd.* i, xxiv–v), and in the list of hours given in the *Lebor Brecc*. (Publ. by Best in *Miscell. pres. to Kuno Meyer*, Halle, 1912, p. 142 ff.)

[2] Supra, p. 333, n. 8.

[3] Publ. by Best in *Ériu*, iii, p. 116.

[4] Rampolla: *Santa Melania Giuniore.* Nota xlii. p. 262. *Analecta Boll.* viii, p. 49 ff.

[5] *Reg. Mon.* vii, p. 379: "ad medium noctis; ad matutinum."

[6] *Thes. Pal.* i, 3.

[7] *Ériu*, iii, p. 116. *Antiphon. of Ban.*, n. 19, 20, 23, 25, 28, 29. *Miscellany*, p. 307 ff. Cf. Cass., *Inst.* iii, 3, p. 35–7.

[8] Cass., *Inst.* iii, 1–12, p. 33–45. Cf. Cabrol, art. "Cassian," in *Dict. d'Archéol.*, c. 2350 ff.

announcing the date of Easter and the beginning of Lent.
After the Feast of the Resurrection came a period of fifty days
(quinquagesima) set aside for rejoicing ; a period in which
every day was treated liturgically as a Sunday. A remarkable
feature in the Egyptian system was the importance given to
Saturday. All through the year this day was honoured, almost
as if it were Sunday ; not, of course, because of any sympathy
with Jewish customs, but because two days repose were
thought necessary after the hardships of the preceding five.[1]

The night office (nocturnae solemnitates) was considered
the most important. On the vigils of Saturday and Sunday
it was celebrated with particular solemnity On these nights,
as on the ordinary week nights, it was divided into three parts,
for it lasted several hours, and therefore could not be carried
through successfully without a fair amount of variety. The
first part, on the solemn vigils of Saturday and Sunday, consisted of three " antiphons " (probably psalms chanted by
two choirs). All stood during these. Then the monks seated
themselves[2] while one of their number chanted three further
psalms ; but all intervened at short intervals with a versicle
repeated aloud. Finally three lessons from Holy Scripture
were read. On the other days the night vigils consisted of
twelve psalms (the " canonical number," believed to have
been revealed by an angel[3]) and two lessons only were read,
one from the Old, one from the New Testament. Every psalm
was sung slowly and with great gravity, and at the end of
each a " collect " or improvised prayer was said, to resume,
as it were, the petitions or thanksgivings just expressed.[4]
To avoid distractions, long psalms were broken into two or
three parts, according to their length, and prayers were
intercalated at the pauses, " for it was thought better to chant
ten verses with proper attention than a whole psalm with
confusion of mind."[5] Similarly the young monk who tried
to gain time by rushing through a psalm, was soon brought
to a standstill, for at a sign from the senior who presided,
all rose to pray as if the psalm had ended ; but when the

---

[1] *Inst.* iii, 9, p. 43–4.
[2] The reason for this is given *Inst.* ii, 12, p. 27 : owing to fasts and work,
the brethren would be physically unable to stand during the whole psalmody.
Hence they sit—cuncti sedilibus humillimis insidentes.   Cf. *Inst.* iii, 8,
p. 43 : "humi vel sedilibus humillimis insidentes."
[3] *Conl.* ii, 12, p. 27: "hunc sane canonicum duodenarium psalmorum
numerum." *Inst.* ii, p. 20–2.
[4] *Inst.* ii, 7, p. 23.
[5] *Inst.* ii, 11, p. 26.

prayer was over the hurrying brother had to recommence at the point where he was interrupted. If he hurried again his headlong career was interfered with in exactly the same way. Thus nothing whatever was gained by unseemly haste.[1]

Vespers were recited in the same way as vigils. They took place at the eleventh hour (five or six o'clock in the evening), by candle light, whence the office was known as *lucernalis*, or *lucernaris hora*.[2]

In the monasteries of Gaul there was a morning office (*matutina sollemnitas*), separated by a short interval only from the vigils or night office.[3] After this came, in Bethlehem and in many parts of the West, the office of Prime; in the East, outside of Egypt, and generally in the West, the other offices of terce, sext and none.[4]

Psalms, as has been seen, formed the principal part of the canonical hours. The doxology " Gloria Patri et Filio et Spiritui Sancto " was chanted in Egypt after the "antiphons"; in Gaul and elsewhere after the psalms.[5] In Egypt, however, there were pauses for prayer at the end of each psalm or portion of psalm. All then stood to pray; next prostrated themselves on the ground for a moment; then rose and with extended arms continued their prayer.[6] The prostration on the ground tended to be prolonged for the very human purpose of getting a slight rest;[7] but the risk of sleep made this most undesirable. While the abbot or a priest recited the prayer all listened in profound silence. Otherwise, too, the rule of reverence during prayer was rigidly enforced. He who caused a disturbance by coughing, yawning, sighing, groaning or similar weakness was severely punished.[8] Late-comers were likewise penalised. At the night vigils he who had not arrived before the second psalm was ended, had to stay at the door and beg pardon of the others as they came forth; for the day offices, the margin of safety was still narrower, since ingress was forbidden after the completion of the first psalm.[9]

---

[1] Ib., p. 26–7.
[2] *Inst.* iii, 3, p. 38.
[3] Ib. 4, p. 38.
[4] Ib., p. 38–9. Cf. iii, 2, p. 34.
[5] *Inst.* ii, 8, p. 24.
[6] Ib. ii, 7, p. 23.
[7] Ib.: "non tam orationis quam refectionis obtentu."
[8] Ib. ii, 10, p. 25–6. Cf. Ib. 5, p. 22. *Aug. Ep.* 211, p. 361: " psalmis et hymnis cum oratis Deum, hoc versetur in corde quod profertur in voce."
[9] *Inst.* iii, 7, p. 41.

Ordinarily the psalm was recited or chanted by one monk standing in the centre, whilst the others listened with great attention, and at the proper place responded with a versicle.[1] Though twelve was the " canonical " number with angelic connections, certain solitaries chanted fifty, sixty, or more psalms during the night office.[2] The psalms seem to have been recited according to their order in the psalter, but at the morning office, later called lauds, and at prime, psalms were chosen for the ideas which they expressed.[3] *Alleluia* was not used as a response to a psalm unless it stood in the title.[4]

All lessons were read from Holy Writ. On Saturdays and Sundays the two lessons were taken from the New Testament ; one from the Gospels, the second from St. Paul or from the Acts of the Apostles.[5]

Meals were considered in a sense part of the divine office, and were therefore preceded and followed by the recitation of psalms.[6]

St. Columban divided the night office into three parts, the first *ad initium noctis*, the second *ad medium noctis*, the third *ad matutinam*.[7] As Vespers (to judge from the *Bangor Antiphonary*) preceded these the number of hours seems to have been greater than at Iona.[8] Columban, like Cassian, distinguishes between " the most reverent nights, viz., Saturday and Sunday,"[9] and the ordinary nights of the week. Like Cassian, too, he knows " the canonical number of twelve psalms," and prescribes that number for vespers, nightfall and the midnight office.[10] He knows that there are Catholics who never go beyond this number, but employ it at the four

---

[1] *Inst.* ii, 5, p. 22.
[2] Ib.
[3] Ib. iii, 6, 7, 8, p. 41–3.
[4] Ib. ii, 11, p. 27.
[5] Ib. ii, 6, p. 23.
[6] Ib. iii, 12, p. 45 : " (refectio) quam et praecedere consuetudinarii psalmi solent et subsequi." *H.L.*, 22.
[7] *Reg. Mon.* vii, p. 379. Methodius of Olympus (martyred A.D. 311), *Sympos.* v, 2 (P.G. xviii, c. 100) and Cass., *Inst.* iii, 8, p. 42, reckon vespers as the first night office. Bäumer, op. cit., p. 58. Batiffol, *Histoire du Bréviaire Romain*, Paris, 1893, p. 4.
[8] *Adam.* iii, 23, p. 233 : " ad vespertinalem Dominicae noctis missam ingreditur ecclesiam." Ib. 1, 37, p. 73 : " vespertinales Dei laudes." Ib. 23, p. 234 : " media nocte pulsata personante clocca . . . ad ecclesiam pergit." Ib., p. 239 : " hymnis matutinalibus terminatis," but these seem to have followed at once on the midnight office. Cf. Faremoutiers, Jonas, *V. Col.* ii, 21, p. 276 : " ruente ergo diei crepusculo cum matutinas laudes Domino cecinissent."
[9] *Reg. Mon.* vii, p. 300.
[10] Ib. : " canonicus duodenarius psalmorum numerus." *Reg. Coen.* iii, as in Cass., *Conl.* ii, 12, p. 27, for vespers and nocturns.

night offices, vespers, midnight, cockcrow and dawn ; trebling, however, the twelve at the last-mentioned office on the nights preceding Saturday and Sunday.[1] This seems to him to be an imperfect arrangement, for it imposes too light a task upon the monks during the long winter nights, and too heavy a task during the short summer nights, since the intervals between the frequent calls leave no time for rest.[2] He lays down, then, as his guiding principles that the length of the chief night office should vary according to the length of the night, and that special attention should be paid to the most holy nights preceding Saturday and Sunday.[3] Following certain of the Irish Fathers, he prescribes, therefore, that at the principal office (ad matutinam) twenty-four psalms should be recited on the ordinary summer nights, thirty-six on the ordinary winter nights.[4] On the nights preceding Saturday and Sunday, on the other hand, there were to be twenty-five " antiphons," that is to say, twenty-five psalms sung by two choirs, joined with fifty psalms recited " in directum," so that on the two nights aforesaid, the whole psalter was recited at the early morning office.[5] This arrangement was to be observed from the first of November to the twenty-fifth of March. From the latter date onwards three psalms were dropped weekly until, by the twenty-fourth of June, only thirty-six psalms remained. After the last-mentioned date three psalms were added weekly until the total of 75 was again reached.[6] According to the tradition handed down by the seniores, the day-hours should consist of three psalms and end with a series of six prayers in the form of versicles.[7] The prayers were to be made in the following order : 1, For our

---

[1] *Reg. Mon.* vii, p. 380.

[2] Ib. : " qui cursus sicut in hieme parvus esse videtur, ita in aestate satis onerosus et gravis invenitur dum crebris in noctis brevitate expeditionibus non tam lassitudinem facit quam fatigationem." Cf. Cass., *Inst.* iii, 8, p. 42 : " idcirco seniores hiemali tempore quo noctes sunt longiores usque ad quartum gallorum cantum per monasteria moderantur." Can 18 of *Councils of Tours* (A.D. 567) prescribes a similar increase or decrease in number of psalms recited (Mabillon, *Disquisitio de cursu Gallicano.* P.L. xxii, c. 405.)

[3] *Reg. Mon.* vii, p. 380 : " noctibus vero reverentissimis, dominicis scilicet vel sabbatis."

[4] Ib. p. 379 : " quotidiani hiemalis xxxvi psalmi cursus, xxiv autem per totum ver et aestatem."

[5] Ib. : " in quibus xxv canunt antifonas psalmorum eiusdem numeri duplicis, qui semper tertio loco duobus succedunt psallitis." On this difficult passage see Dom. G. Morin, " Explication d'un passage de la règle de saint Colomban relatif à l'office des moines celtiques." *Rev. Bénéd.* T. xii, p. 203.

[6] Ib., p. 378–9.

[7] Ib., p. 379 : " per diurnas terni psalmi horas . . . statuti sunt a senioribus nostris cum versiculorum augmento."

sins. 2, For the whole Christian people. 3, For priests and clergy. 4, For those who bestow alms. 5, For peace among kings. 6, For enemies.[1]

In Bangor likewise the night office was divided into sections, *ad initium noctis, ad medium noctis, ad matutinam*.[2] To these three celebrations were added the day offices of prime (ad secundam), terce, sext, none and vespers.[3] Collects were appended to certain Canticles, Hymns and Psalms.[4] The chief canticles in use were the " Canticum Moysi " (Exod. xv. 1–19),[5] "the Song of Moses " (Deut. xxxii. 1–43)[6] the " Benedicite omnia opera Domini Domino " (Dan. iii. 26, 57–88)[7] the " Benedictus " (Luke i. 68–80).[8] The " Gloria in Excelsis Deo " was chanted at vespers and at the morning office[9]; the " Te Deum " on Sundays.[10] Eight " collects " are appointed to be said after the " Canticle of Moses," seven others after the " Benedicite " and another seven after the three final psalms of the psalter, which were recited at the morning office.[11] The collects to be said after the various hours are very numerous.[12] Lessons from the Gospel are mentioned[13]; and there is evidence that the Pax, Creed and Pater Noster had their place in the divine office.[14] Saturday ranked with Sunday (no doubt, too, with the natalicia martyrum,[15] if not with the feast days of the other saints)[16] as a day of special solemnity.[17] Though particular psalms for various occasions are referred to, the indications are

[1] Ib., p. 379.

[2] *Antip. of Bang.* (ed. Warren, London, 1895). In the legend of Lough Neagh it is asserted that " Comgall despatched Beoan, son of Innle, to have speech of Gregory [the Great in Rome] and to bring back canonical order and rule " (MacNeill, *Béaloideas* ii, p. 118–9) but a special connection between the liturgy of Bangor and that of Rome cannot be demonstrated.

[3] Ib., p. 19–20. The list of hours is : 1, ad Secundam ; 2, ad Tertiam ; 3 ad Sextam ; 4, ad Nonam ; 5, ad Vespertinam ; 6, ad initium noctis ; 7, ad Nocturnam ; 8, ad Matutinam.

[4] Ib., p. 24. [5] Ib., p. 1.

[6] Ib., p.8. [7] Ib., p. 8.

[8] Ib., p. 7. [9] Ib., p. 31.

[9] Ib , p. 10 From the form of the Canticle of Moses—*Audite, caeli quae loquor*—ib., p. 35, it is clear that it was recited by chanters, whilst the rest of the community repeated only a refrain. Cf. *Adam.* iii, 12, p. 211 : " ad cantores."

[11] Cf. *V.S.H.* i, p. 125 : " usque ad vigilias matutinales, et tunc inceperunt psaimum, ' Laudate Dominum de caelis,' usque in finem (i.e. psalms 148, 149, 150)."

[12] Ib., p. 19–21, 23 ff. [13] Ib., p. 25–6.

[14] Warren, op. cit., p. 61–2.

[15] Ib., p. 12 : " hymnus in natali Martyrum, vel sabbato ad matutinam."

[16] Cf. *Adam.* ii, 45, p. 101, 182 ; iii, 11, p. 40 : " natalis beati Brendeni dies."

[17] *Antip. Bang.*, p. 12. Cf. Warren, op. cit., p. xxiii–iv.

nowhere such as permit the complete reconstruction of the morning office or of any other hour.[1]

Hymns are quoted in honour of Christ, the Apostles, St. Patrick, St. Comgall. St. Camelach, three also for the midnight office, for the morning office on Sunday, and for the morning office on Saturday, or on a martyr's anniversary.[2] A hymn was likewise sung while the priests of the community were receiving Holy Communion,[3] another accompanied the blessing of wax. Few as are these hymns, that for the midnight office " Mediae noctis tempus est "[4] is of great interest, for it is found at Luxeuil[5] and in the Rule of St. Caesarius for his nuns at Arles.[6] Caesarius again, as he expressly declares, took his arrangement of the psalmody almost entirely from Lérins.[7] Another of the Lérins hymns, ascribed to St. Ambrose, is found in the Franciscan *Liber Hymnorum*.[8] Strangely enough when the ninth century is reached, Continental manuscript hymnaries are discovered to belong to two classes, of which one, non-Irish, is derived from the Lérins tradition, whilst the second, Irish in character, shows no connection with Lérins. It is this later Irish collection which found favour at Rome and which is even still well represented in the Roman Breviary.[9]

---

[1] But cf. *Church Quarterly Review*, xxxvii, Jan., 1894, p. 351 ff, and *I.E.R.* xvi, June, 1895, p. 635 ff.

[2] *Antip. Bang.*, p. 3–19.

[3] This is the " Sancti venite, Christi corpus sumite " ascribed to St. Sechnall. (*V. Trip.*, p. 394 ff.) It is the oldest Eucharistic hymn in existence.

[4] Ib., p. 11. This hymn is closely connected with the dogma of the Trinity. Cf. the opening and the closing stanzas :—

" 1. Mediae noctis tempus est　　　　" 13. Dignos nos fac, Rex hagie
　　Prophetica vox admonet　　　　　　　Futuri regni gloriae
　　Dicamus laudes ut Deo　　　　　　　Aeternis ut mereamur
　　Patri semper ac Filio.　　　　　　　Te laudibus concinere.

2　Sancto quoque Spiritui　　　　　14. Gloria Patri ingenito
　　Perfecta enim Trinitas　　　　　　　Gloria Unigenito
　　Uniusque substantiae　　　　　　　Simul cum Sancto Spiritu
　　Laudanda nobis semper est."　　　　In sempiterna saecula."

[5] Seebass, *Ueber Columba von Luxeuils Klosterregeln*, p. 25 ff.

[6] *AA. SS. Boll.* T. i, Jan. (Antwerp ed., 1643). *Recapitulatio*, p. 735.

[7] Ib., § xi, n. 66 : " ordinem etiam quomodo psallere debeatis ex maxima parte secundum regulam monasterii Lyrinensis in hoc libello indicavimus inserendum."

[8] *Lib. Hym.*, H.B.S. ed., London, 1897. It is entitled *Hymnus Vespertinus*, and its authorship is attributed to St. Ambrose.

[9] Cf. C. Blume, *Der Cursus S. Benedicti Nursini u. die liturgischen Hymnen des*, 8–9 *Jahrhunderts*, Leipzig, 1908, p. 134 ff. and *Rev. Bénéd.* xxv. p 367 ff. In A—the independent series connected with the Lérins tradition—the hymns for the small hours are :—

　　　　Post matutinis laudibus (Prime).
　　　　Certum tenentes ordinem (Terce).
　　　　Dicamus laudes Domino (Sext).
　　　　Perfectum trinum numerum (None).

When the brethren were engaged far from the church, reaping, fishing or journeying, the task of the moment was interrupted when the time came to say one of the canonical hours.[1] As in Egypt, so also in Ireland, grace before and after meals was regarded as a minor office of public prayer.[2]

Punctuality at the divine office was insisted on. Colmcille was noted for his zeal in this respect, and was in the church almost before the bell had ceased to sound.[3] Failure to hear the bell was not accepted as an excuse by St. Columban.[4] The abbot or his representatives, surrounded by the dignitaries of the monastery, took their places in the middle of the oratory, whilst the brethren gathered on the right and on the left.[5] Standing was the usual posture,[6] but on solemn feast days the brethren were allowed to sit during part at least of the ceremonies.[7] The psalms were to be sung clearly without cough or stutter.[8] A fine voice, such as that possessed by Colmcille, was much appreciated.[9] Silence and reverence were expected to reign during the celebration ; and woe to the brother who slept or tittered, or, above all, broke into laughter, no matter how funnily the chanter or reader stumbled in note or lesson.[10] After every psalm, the brethren bowed[11] (towards the altar) and at the end of the psalms, when the collects were being said, they threw themselves on their knees. Having recited " Deus in adiutorium meum intende, Domine ad adiuvandum me festina " three times in silence

---

In B, on the other hand, the Irish series, the corresponding hymns are :—
    Iam lucis orto sidere (Prime).
    Nunc sancte nobis Spiritus (Terce).
    Rector potens, verax Deus (Sext).
    Rerum Deus, tenax vigor (None).
It is to be regretted that the *Book of Hymns for every day of the week*, written by St. Colmcille, has not survived (*Adam.* ii, 9, p. 116).

[1] *V.S.H.* ii, p. 155. Ib., p. 227 *Acallam na Senórach*, ed. Stokes, *Irische Texte*, iv, 1, p. 82.
[2] *Reg. Coen.* xii, p. 230 *MP* ; xiv, 23 *MP.* Jonas, *V. Col.* i, 27, p. 215. *V.S.H.* i, p. 206. Cf. Pall. *H.L.*, 22 : Anthony sang a psalm twelve times and repeated twelve prayers before he sat down to his frugal meal.
[3] *Adam.* iii, 23, p. 234.
[4] *Reg. Coen.* xii, p. 230 *MP.*
[5] Ib. ix, p. 227 *MNP.*
[6] *Adam.* i, 37, p. 73 : " nec in auribus eorum qui secum in ecclesia *stabant* " (at the psalmody).
[7] *Reg. Coen.* ix, p. 227 *MNP.* : " in magnis autem solempnitatibus quando audiunt sonum sedere in cotidiano praecepto pene mediante iubentur sedere."
[8] *Reg. Coen.* iv, p. 224 *MP.* Cf. Ib. xv. p. 233 *MNP.*
[9] *Adam.* i, 37, p. 73 : Colmcille's voice could be heard a thousand yards off ; yet melodious.
[10] *Reg. Coen.* xii, p. 230 *MP.* ; xiv, p. 231 *MP* ; iv, p. 222 *MP.*
[11] *Reg. Coen.* ii, p. 221 *MP.* : " humiliatio in ecclesia post finem cuius-cumque psalmi."

all rose together. On Sundays and during Paschal tide the brethren were not asked to go on their knees, but were allowed to bow instead.[1]

When we compare the Irish arrangement, adopted by St. Columban, with that described by Cassian the generic resemblance is at once apparent. Saturday as a day of liturgical importance is prominent in both systems. Similarly the fifty days of rejoicing after Easter, the *nocturnae solemnitates* (the chief office within the twenty-four hours), and the general reverence with which these exercises of public prayer were accompanied. On the other hand the Irish system is much more developed than that which was known in Egypt. It contains, six, seven or eight periods of formal prayer instead of the two periods recognised by the Egyptians; and the early morning office has expanded to a point known indeed among the Egyptians, but not held in particular favour. If, then, the system in vogue in Ireland made its way westwards from the regions of the Nile it is likely to have undergone many changes upon the way.

Such, in effect, was the tradition preserved within Ireland itself. According to the eighth century writer, already referred to as the author of a tract on the six principal arrangements of the hours,[2] the *cursus Scottorum* or Irish arrangement owed its origin to St. Mark. That Evangelist, the writer asserts, preached the Gospel not only in Egypt, but also in Italy. St. Gregory Nazianzen and the eastern monks, Basil, Anthony, Paul, Macarius, John and Malchus adopted his system. Cassian introduced it into Gaul. It was accepted at Lérins by St. Honoratus, St. Caesarius of Arles, Saint Germanus, Porcarius and Lupus. St. Germanus and St. Lupus taught St. Patrick, who brought the *cursus* to Britain and Ireland. Thus it became the *cursus Scottorum*, and was re-introduced to the Continent at the end of the sixth century, by St. Columban and Wandilochus (Waldelenus?).[3] The role ascribed to St. Mark is here imaginary, and the personal references to the other saints do not admit of proof, but the four links—Egypt, Lérins, Britain and Ireland—hold well

---

[1] *Reg. Coen.* ix, p. 228 *MP.* : " in commune autem omnes fratres omnibus diebus ac noctibus tempore orationum in fine omnium psalmorum genua in oratione . . . flectere debent, sub silentio dicentes *Deus,*" etc. (Ps. lxix, 2.) Cf. Cass., *Conl.* x, 10, 297 ff, for prominent place given to this prayer in Egypt. According to the Rule of Ailbe, stanza 20, it was to be recited after every psalm : *Deus in auditorium i forcuinn cech sailm.*

[2] Supra, p. 386, n. 6.　　　　　　　[3] Jonas, *V. Col.* i 14, p. 174.

together, and the chain thus formed is substantially sound. Egyptian customs, in other words, made their way to Lérins and Southern Gaul, whence they passed, through the good offices of St. Patrick and various other Britons of the fifth and sixth century, to Ireland. It is natural to expect that they were modified upon the way and again when they reached their new home in the far west. Great, however, as are the differences, the Egyptian outline in the Irish system is unmistakable.

Perhaps because they were less capable of contemplation than the Easterns, the Irish monks showed an exceptional zeal in reciting psalms and other vocal prayers. This trait remained with them through the centuries. Remarkable later is the devotion to the long psalm 118, apparently because of its unusual length. Genuflections and prostrations in phenomenal number during prayer are likewise a mark of later Irish asceticism.[1]

(c)—The Mass.

Mass, the great central act of Christian worship, was celebrated on Sundays and feast days.[2] Chief among these festivals was Easter Day.[3] Christmas is also mentioned,[4] and the anniversary of various saints such as St. Martin of Tours,[5] Saints Peter and Paul,[6] and the monastic founder

---

[1] The spirit dominates all the Irish Rules. Cf. Rule of Ailbe, *Ériu* iii, p. 97 f, stanza 17: " Cét sléchtain dó fri biet tossuch laithi ria chestaib' Trí cóicait diliu toscaib. co cét sléchtain cach fescair. ' He is to make a hundred genuflections when reciting the *Beati* (Ps. 118),' at the beginning of day, before questions (are discussed or studied) ; (he is to recite) the three fifties (i.e. the whole psalter), dearer than (other) works, with a hundred genuflections at each vespers'." The same is taught in an interpolated stanza in the Rule of Comgall. *Ériu* i, p. 191 ff, stanza 3a: " Cét sléchtain dó fri biat, matin fescar . . A hundred genuflections at the *Beati*, morning and evening." . . . Cf. *Mon. of Tallaght*, §§ 1, 5, 28, 30, 47, 70 and 31, 33, 34. Palladius (*H.L.* 26) mentions a monk who recited by heart 15 psalms, then the long psalm (*Beati*) and other prayers while on a journey. Cf., ib. 48 for psalm-singing in a standing position all through the night ; and Cass., *Inst.* ii, p. 18, for condemnation of excess.

[2] *Reg. Coen.* ix, p. 228 *MNP.* : " in omni dominica et solempnitate . . . Et quamdiu *offeratur* non multum discurratur." Jonas, *V. Col.* ii, 16, p. 226–7. *Adam.* i, 40, p. 66–7 ; 44, p. 86 ; iii, 17, p. 222.

[3] Ib. ii, 39, p. 158 : " ut in Paschali solemnitate ad altarium accedas et Eucharistiam sumas." Ib. iii, 23, p. 228. *V.S.H.* ii, p. 212–3. *Lism. L.*, p. 107 : St. Brendan and his crew spend Easter day and two nights on whale's back. Cf. p. 48.

[4] *Adam.* ii, 9, p. 117. *V.S.H.* i, p. 226 : " mass on Christmas morning." *V.S.H.* i, 145. St. Ita regrets the absence of St. Brendan, her disciple, and says : " O si videam oculis meis sanctum Brandanum . . . et sumam de manibus eius corpus Domini mei Jesu Christi *hac instanti nocte nativitatis eiusdem Domini mei*."

[5] Jonas, *V. Col.* ii, 13, p. 263 : " Sacrata sollemnitas beati antestitis Martini transitus."

[6] Ib. ii, 23, p. 283 : " vigilia passionis beatorum Petri et Pauli apostolorum."

to whom the establishment owed its existence.[1] The fifty
days after Lent ranked more or less as Sundays[2] and the
relief from the hardships of the year was then such that
brethren might picture paradise to themselves as a perpetual
Eastertide.[3] A special Mass might also be offered when the
death of a friend was announced.[4]

In the mass, the Body and Blood of Christ[5] become present
in a mysterious and adorable manner[6] by the ministry of
the priest,[7] and Christ, the stainless victim,[8] is offered to
God as a true sacrifice[9] for the living and the dead.[10] The

---

[1] *Adam.* ii, 45, p. 181 : " tui (S. Colmcille) natalis missarum sollemnia."
[2] *Adam.* ii, 9, p. 117 : " usque ad Paschalium consummationem dierum "
(Whitsuntide). Ib. iii, 23, p. 229 : " laetitiae festivitas." Cf. Cass., *Conl.* xxi,
20, p. 594–5.
[3] *Lism. L.*, p. 115 : " tochaithiumh na mórcásc."
[4] *Adam.* iii, 11, p. 210. Ib. 12, p. 211–2.
[5] *Adam.* i, 44, p. 85 : " Christi corpus ex more conficere." Jonas, *V. Col.* ii,-
16, p. 266–7 : " cum quadam ex his iam corpus Domini accepisset ac sanguinem libasset, et sacro choro inserta cum comparibus caneret : ' Hoc
sacrum corpus Domini et Salvatoris sanguinem sumite vobis in vitam peren-
nem '." *Antiph. Bang.*, p. 31 (112) contains the same words, adding *Alleluia*.
Again the formula *V.S.H.* i, p. 125, is almost exactly the same. *V.S.H.* ii:
20 : " ut acciperet de manu eius corpus et sanguinem Christi." Ib., p. 223 :
" communionem corporis et sanguinis Christi accepit ab eo." Ib., p. 122
193.
[6] *Adam.* i, 40, p. 77 : " sacra Eucharistiae mysteria." Ib. iii, 12, p. 211 :
" sacra oportet Eucharistiae celebrare mysteria."
[7] *Adam.* i, 44, p. 86 : " a Sancto iussus Christi corpus ex more conficere."
Ib. i, 40, p. 76 : " quendam audiens presbyterum sacra Eucharistiae mysteria
conficientem." Ib. iii, 11, p. 210 : " sacra Eucharistiae ministeria."
[8] *V.S.H.* i, p. 125 : " immolabant Agnum immaculatum Deo omni-
potenti."
[9] *Adam.* i, 40, p. 77 : " sacrae oblationis mysteria." Ib. iii, 17, p. 222;
" sacram oblationem." *Reg. Coen.* iv, p. 222 : " sacerdos offerens " ; ix,
p. 227 *MNP.* : " oblationem dominicam." *V.S.H.* ii, p. 193 : " in oblationem
corporis et sanguinis Christi." Ib., p. 172 : " Ipse Deo modo sacrificium
offert." Cf. Wasserschl. ii, 9, p. 141. H. and S., *Councils* ii, p. 329–30.
Canons attrib. to St. Patrick, etc., can. 24, 27, 28, 30. Sulp. Sev. *Dial.* iii,
10, p. 208 : " testatur . . . vidisse se Martini manum *sacrificium offerentis*
vestitam quodammodo nobilissimis gemmis." Caes. of Arles, P.L. xxix,
c. 2276 : " quando munera *offeruntur* et corpus vel sanguis Domini consecra-
tur." Jonas, *V. Joannis*, p. 334 : " ut hostias Deo absque populari tumulta
offeret. (From *offerenda* came the Irish *oifrend*, ' Mass,' Welsh *offeren*, Cornish
oferen, Breton *oferenn*. Pedersen. *Vergl. Gram.* i, p. 211. Cf. p. 225 and ii,
p. 21. Stokes, *Lism. L.*, p. lxxxvii and xiii : " aifrinntar leis ' He says
Mass ')." *Reg. Coen.* iv, p. 222 : " ordinem ad sacrificium qui non custodierit
(*MP*) ad offerendum (*MNP.*). Ib. xii, p. 230. Wasserschl. *I.K.* ii, 8, p. 14 :
" De causis quibus immolavit Christus primus in novo testamento sacerdos."
Ib. 9 : " De modis quibus nunc ecclesia immolat." *V.S.H.* i, p. 53 : " invenit
sacerdotem stantem ante altare et volentem offerre sacrificium." Ib. ii,
67, 172, 17 (from *sacrificium* came the Irish *sacarbaic*, Holy Eucharist,
Middle Welsh *segyrffyc*. Peder. *Verg. Gram.* i, p. 221. Cf. Stokes, *Lism. L.*,
p. lxxxviii.) *Sacrificium* in this sense occurs frequently. Cf. *V.S.H.* i, p. 226 ;
ii, p. 20 : " Monachi S. Comgalli aliquibus diebus ante obitum suum volebant
quotidie sacrificium divinum ei dare." Ib., p. 125, 223, 267, etc.
[10] Wasserschl. *I.K.* ii, 9, p. 14–5 : " Nunc ecclesia multis modis offert
Domino, primo pro seipsa . . . tertio pro animabus defunctorum."

altar on which such sacred mysteries took place was naturally treated with profound respect.[1] Preparation for the solemn ceremonies might be made the day before.[2] Deacons would then bring wine and water in cruets,[3] and particles of bread, some to be consecrated, others to be blessed,[4] on the following day. Mass was celebrated at an early hour,[5] but might be postponed to midday on a great feast-day.[6] When several priests were present, one was selected for the office, and he might invite another to break the consecrated bread with him.[7] A bishop, however, broke the consecrated bread alone, in token of his superior order[8]; nor might any priest celebrate in his presence, without his express permission.[9]

Ablutions were performed by the celebrant before Mass.[10] Then he vested[11] and entered the church, assisted at least by a deacon.[12] Availing ourselves of the Stowe Missal, which seems to go back in substance to the first half of the seventh century,[13] we can follow the great sacrificial act through its various stages.

Before the celebrant's entry came the confession of sins ;

---

[1] *Reg. Coen.* xiii, p. 230 *MP* : The altar at Luxeuil was consecrated by an Irish bishop, Aed. *Colum. Ep.* iv. *M.G.H. Ep.* iii, p. 167. Cf. P.L. xxix, c. 2166, 2168 : " in qua benedictus vel unctus est lapis, in quo nobis divina sacrificia consecrantur." Cf. *Laws* i, p. 232, 234.

[2] *Reg. Coen.* ix, p. 227 *MNP.* : " si quis voluerit in die sabbati praeparet oblationem dominici."

[3] *Adam.* ii, 1, p. 104 : " ad fontem sumpto pergit urceo, ut ad sacra Eucharistiae ministeria aquam, quasi diaconus, hauriret." This turned into wine. Ib. i, 44.

[4] *Reg. Coen.* iv, p. 222. *MP.* : " eulogias (panes qui in ecclesia a sacerdote benedicuntur olimque distribuebantur iis qui . . . diebus festis et dominicis non sumebant eucharistiam. Seebass. l.c., from *Menard.* P.L. ciii, c. 1223) : immundus accipiens xii percussionibus."

[5] *V.S.H.* ii, p. 172 : " modo sacrificium offert, et postea tertiam cantabit horam." *Adam.* iii, 11, 12, p. 210–11. Warren, *Liturgy and Rit. of the Celtic Church,* p. 142.

[6] *Adam.* ii, 45, p. 181–2 : " hora sexta."

[7] Ib. i, 44, p. 86 : "ut simul quasi duo presbyteri Dominicum panem frangerent."

[8] Ib., p. 85–6.

[9] *V.S.H.* i, p. 53, n. 7. Cf. *Cod. Salm.,* c. 245 ; and Rees, *Cambro. Br. S.,* p. 120.

[10] *Adam.* ii, 45, p. 181 : " manuum et pedum peracta lavatione." But the washing here may be accidental, as the brethren had just returned from a voyage.

[11] Vestments are referred to, *V.S.H.* ii, p. 123. *Trias Th.,* p. 522.

[12] *Reg. Coen.* iv, 222 *MNP. Adam.* ii, 1, p. 104 : " ipse quippe illis in diebus erat in diaconatus gradu administrans." Wasserschl. *I.K.,* l, iii. *De diacono,* p. 20–22. Cf. Cass., *Conl.* iv, 1, p. 98 : " semper abbate Paphnutio spiritales hostias offerente hic (Daniel presbyter) velut diaconus . . . permansit."

[13] Wordsworth, *The Mystery of Grace,* London, 1901, p. 92. Quoted by Dom Gougaud, *Celtiques* (liturgies). *Dict. d'Archéol. Chrét.* T. ii, 2975. For a full discussion of the Missal's age see the same writer l.c. cols. 2974–5 ; for its contents cols., 3006–14. The short account here given is summarised from Dom Gougaud.

then the litany of the Saints, recited probably in a kneeling position before the altar ; next two prayers. At this stage wine and water were poured into the chalice and the celebrant took his place at the altar. After the introductory prayer came the " Gloria in excelsis," followed by two fixed prayers and diverse others that varied according to the celebration. The number of these seems to have been unusually large. Next comes the Epistle, followed by versicles that possibly represent a gradual, then by a short and two longer prayers. At this point the chalice was half-uncovered ; which seems to signify that one of the two cloths placed upon it was removed. The formula " Dirigatur, Domine, etc.," was chanted three times ; similarly the words " Veni, Domine, sanctificator omnipotens et benedic hoc sacrificium praeparatum tibi." After the Gospel there was a short prayer, followed by the *Credo* and the offertory, when the chalice was wholly uncovered. Between the offertory and the preface came the memento for the dead, when the names of the dear ones entered on the diptychs were pronounced. A prayer *post-Sanctus* followed the *Sanctus*. Then came the " Canon of Pope Gelasius " comprising the *Te igitur, Memento etiam, Domine, Communicantes* (with variations for Christmas, Epiphany, Easter, the Ascension, Pentecost), *Hanc igitur, Quam oblationem, Qui pridie.* The words from *Accepit Jesus panem* to the end of the consecration were called the *periculosa oratio.* Here the priest bowed three times in token of repentance ; the people prostrated themselves and lay in profound silence. Not a sound was to disturb the celebrant during the solemn moments of consecration. At the *Nobis quoque peccatoribus,* St. Patrick figures among the Saints expressly named. The breaking of the Sacred Species took place before the *Pater Noster.* If the celebrant were a bishop he broke alone ; if a priest he was aided by a fellow priest. There followed an expression of belief in the great mystery : " We believe, O Lord, we believe that in this breaking of Thy Body and this pouring forth of Thy Blood we were redeemed ; and we trust, strengthened as we are by the reception of this sacrament, that what we now possess in hope we shall enjoy in truth and enduringly when we reach the heavenly kingdom." Next comes the *Pater Noster,* and in due course the *Pax, Communion* of celebrant, priests and people, an *Agnus Dei,* Eucharistic antiphons, Post-Communion prayers and the announcement that the rite has ended: *Missa acta est. In pace.*

An examination of the different elements in the Stowe Missal shows that its affinities are with the Church in Gaul, but that it has been influenced by the liturgies of Spain, Milan, and (above all) Rome.[1] From other liturgical documents that have survived we know that there was much diversity of rite in the celebration of Mass in Ireland.[2] This, as the author of the *Catalogue* assures us, goes back to the sixth century, to the Saints of the Second Order, and was due in part to the intimacy of Irish Churchmen with the Britons.[3]

Preaching commonly accompanied the celebration of Mass. St. Columban lays down that all monks should be present at the sermon, except the door-keeper and the cook, and these are to make an effort to attend when the signal is given. The sermon, it would seem, took place at the end of the Gospel.[4] No doubt the laity, too, were expected to attend. As in Gaul,[5] so in Ireland, it was extremely difficult to prevail upon the people to abandon servile work on Sundays.[6] To counteract this negligence, Churchmen came to lay down rules for the observance of Sunday that remind us forcibly of the Sabbath laws elaborated by the Jewish Rabbis.[7] Coming to Mass and sermon was no small test of the people's devotion, for the ceremonies must have lasted at least two hours.[8] Standing, as we have seen, was the usual posture, except at the consecration, when those present prostrated

---

[1] Gougaud, op. cit., c. 3014.

[2] Ib., c. 2971–6.

[3] H. and S., *Councils*, ii, p. 292–3.

[4] *Paenit. B.*, p. 448 : " ante praedicationem die dominica toti, exceptis certis necessitatibus, simul sint conglobati, ut nullus desit numero praeceptum audientium excepto coco ac portario, qui et ipsi, si possint, satis agant ut adsint, quando tonitruum evangelii auditur."

[5] P.L. xxxix, c. 2240 : Caesarius of Arles complains that some of his flock abstain from work on Thursday in honour of Jupiter, but are not ashamed to work on Sunday. No one was to speak or eat with such as persisted in this evil course. They were also to be punished with stripes, " that at least they might fear pain of body when they have no thought for the salvation of their souls."

[6] *V.S.H.* i, p. 43, 263. *Cod. Salm.*, c. 282. *V. Trip.*, p. 192, 222. *Silva Gad.* i, 53.

[7] *V.S.H.* ii, 15, etc. The *Cáin Domnaig*—" Law of Sunday " (cen tairmthecht ind itir—not to transgress it in any way), passed seemingly in the ninth century, became one of the four major laws of Ireland (*Martyr. Oeng.*, p. 40. *Thes. Pal.* ii, p. 306) Publ. O'Keeffe, *Ériu*, ii, p. 192 ff. It forbids strongly all work on Sunday. Cf. p. 194 : " nach dam agus nach mug agus nach cumal forsatabarthar saebmám isin Domnuch cíit a súile uli déra fola fri Dia, uair ro-saer Dia dóib al-lá sin, ' Every ox and bondman and female slave on whom a wrongful burden is laid on Sunday, the eyes of all of them shed tears of blood towards God, for God has freed that day for them all.' "

[8] In Gaul they lasted one and a half or two hours, P.L. xxxix, c. 2279 : " unius aut duarum horarum spatio patientiam praebeamus . . ." and the Irish ceremonies were hardly shorter.

themselves. We do not know whether the people, as in Gaul, brought rugs and couches to sit upon during the sermon[1]; or whether, like the Gauls, they clapped, waved handkerchiefs and shouted themselves to hoarseness when the preacher was particularly eloquent.[2] The atmosphere of severe asceticism surrounding Irish monasteries was certainly such that enthusiasm dangerous to the preacher's humility was not likely to be tolerated.

From references already made to hymns and chanting we know that music flourished in the liturgical offices. Great saints might disapprove of this as a " voluptuous delight,"[3] but the prevailing opinion was otherwise.

(d)—Holy Communion.

According to ancient monastic practice, Holy Communion was received every Sunday;[4] often, too, on Saturday, where Mass was celebrated on that day.[5] Those presumptuous enough to imagine that their souls could survive for long without this divine food were likely to find melancholy proof that their view was utterly mistaken.[6] Christ's Body and Blood were to be received with fear and reverence, but also with faith and love;[7] and on every day of the week, where a custom to this effect prevailed.[8] General sinfulness, as distinct

---

[1] Permission to do this was given by St. Caesarius to the sickly ; but was extended to themselves by numbers of the healthy, op. cit., c. 2319.

[2] The same custom prevailed in the Orient. Sidonius Apollinaris describes how he shouted himself hoarse at the sermons of Faustus of Riez (*Ep.* ix, ed. Lütjohann, p. 152.)

[3] Caes. of Arles. *Hom.* 12, P.L. xxxix, c. 2220 : "voluptuosa delectatio aurium." Yet Caesarius did an immense amount to foster Church music in Gaul. The Irish saints were hardly more consistent. Cf. *Lism. L.* xiii–v : Brendan of Clonfert, on principle, never listened to the music of the world. Ib., p. 118. Becc mac Dé prophesied the birth of St. Ciarán. "There," he said, "O son of the wright, in thy nice chasuble, with thy choirs, thy melodies, thy chariots, thy songs."

[4] *H.L.*, 59 Cass., *Conl.* xxiii, 21, p. 671 : "multo melius est ut *singulis* ea (sacrosancta mysteria) *dominicis* ob remedium nostrarum aegritudinum praesumamus." Ib. vii, 28, p. 207–8.

[5] *H.L.*, 32 Cass. *Conl.* xviii, 15, p. 525.

[6] *H.L.*, 17, 25, 27, St. Basil, *Morals*, xxi.

[7] St. Basil, *Morals*. xxi, lxxx, 22. *Reg. Brev. Tract.* clxxii. Cass. *Inst.* i, 19, p. 14. *Conl.* xxii, 5, p. 619–21.

[8] St. Jer. *Ep. ad Lucinum* lxxi, 6 (*C.S.E.L.*, 55, p. 687) : " De eucharistia (quod quaeris) an accipienda cotidie quod Romana ecclesia et Hispaniae observare perhibentur . . . ego illud breviter te admonendum puto : traditiones ecclesiasticas, praesertim quae fidei non officiunt, ita observandas ut a maioribus traditae sunt ; nec aliarum consuetudinem aliarum contrario more subverti . . eucharistiam quoque absque condemnatione nostri semper accipere . : . sed unaquaeque provincia abundet in sensu suo et praecepta maiorum leges apostolicas arbitretur." (Representatives of the Old Easter computation might have quoted this passage with effect during the paschal controversy.)

from actual sin not yet wiped away by penance, and the commission of an involuntary fault, even of a serious kind, were not regarded as sufficient grounds for abstaining from Holy Communion on the appointed day.[1]

In Ireland, too, Holy Communion was received regularly on Sundays and on feast days[2]—in other words, on the days when Mass was celebrated. Serious transgressions of the Rule might be punished by exclusion from the Holy Table.[3] On the other hand, nobody was obliged to receive Holy Communion during Mass.[4] Those who were privileged to approach were[5] expected at Luxeuil to make three prostrations on their way to the altar.[6] They received usually under both species ; but newcomers, because of their inexperience, and the very awkward of all ages, were not permitted to partake of the chalice.[7] While the priests of the community were receiving Holy Communion a Eucharistic hymn was chanted at Bangor.[8] There and elsewhere[9] the words, " Receive this Sacred Body of the Lord and the Blood of the Saviour unto life everlasting," were sung after the reception of the Blessed Sacrament. Perhaps the finest encomium ever paid to St. Brigid is the statement of her biographer that " she was a consecrated casket for keeping Christ's Body and His Blood."[10]

It goes without saying that the greatest reverence was

Cass. *Conl.* xiv, 8, p. 406 : St. Basil (*Ep.* 93, P.G. xxxii, c. 485–6) recommends the practice of daily communion. He made it a rule himself to receive four times a week and oftener if a festival day occurred. Cf. *H.M.* 8. St. Aug, *Ep.* 54 (*C.S.E.L.* xxxiv, p. 162) : " peccata si tanta non sunt, ut excommunicandus quisquam homo iudicetur, non se debet a quotidiana medicina Dominici corporis separare." Caes. Arel. P.L. xxxix, c. 1801.

[1] *Conl.* xxiii, 21, p. 670 : " nec tamen debemus nos a dominica communione suspendere, quia nos agnoscimus peccatores, sed ad eam magis ac magis est propter animae medicinam ac purificationem spiritus avide festinandum." Ib. xxii, 5, p. 260. Cf. Bas. *Reg. fus. tract.*, 309.

[2] *Adam.* i, 44, p. 85, iii, 12, p. 211 ; iii, 17, p. 221 : " die dominica ex more." Jonas, *V. Col.* ii, 16, p. 266–7.

[3] Jonas, *V. Col.* ii, 13, p. 263 : " et quoadusque paenitentiae interdictae normam implesset, se a corpore Domini privaret."

[4] *Reg. Coen.* ix, p. 227 *MNP.* : " quando offertur oblatio nemo cogatur coactus accipere sacrificium praeter necessitatem."

[5] Jonas, *V. Col.* ii, 13, p. 263 : " cumque illa sacri corporis privatione interdictu audisset . . . flere coepit. Pervigilans ergo ea nocte . . . ne tanti damni incurreret causam ut a corpore Christi sua culpa segregaretur . . ."

[6] *Reg. Coen.* ix, p. 227 *MNP.*

[7] Ib. : " et novi quia indocti, et quicumque fuerint tales ad calicem non accedant." Ib. iv, p. 222 *MP.* : " qui pertunderit dentibus calicem salutaris, vi percussionibus," Jonas, *V. Col.* ii, 16, p. 267.

[8] Supra, p. 342, n. 3 and n. 5.

[9] Luxeuil (Jonas, *V. Col.* ii, 16, p. 267). Clonfert ? (*V.S.H.* i, p. 125).

[10] *Lism. L.*, p. 50 : " ba comra choisecartha coiméta chuirp Críst ocus a fhola."

paid to the Holy Eucharist. The most important element in preparation was undoubtedly cleanliness of heart, secured chiefly through confession. " Especial diligence in the making of confessions (above all as regards disturbances of soul) is to be shown before Mass, lest anybody should approach the altar unworthily, that is to say, with an unclean heart. For it is better to wait until the heart is quite healthy, free from scandal and envy, than to proceed insolently to the judgment of the tribunal. For the altar is Christ's tribunal, and His Body and Blood which lie upon it judge those who approach unworthily. Not only then are capital sins and sins of the flesh to be avoided before Communion, but also sins of thought and diseases that spring from sickliness of soul before the union of true peace and the joining fast of eternal salvation."[1] Again, the Blessed Sacrament was reserved in small vessels called *chrismals*, which the monks carried with them when going to work in the fields or on voyages.[2] He who let such a chrismal drop, though no harm befell it, was punished with twelve stripes.[3] To lose it might entail penance for a whole year.[4] If the Sacred Species became corrupt they were to be burned and the ashes buried near the altar.[5] If they fell into water, this was to be drunk at once and the Holy Eucharist consumed.[6] Every form of negligence brought its appropriate penalty.[7] Reservation somewhat of this kind was not unknown to monastic history, for St. Basil relates that anchorites who lived far away from Church or a priest were accustomed to keep the Holy Eucharist in their cells ;[8] but this was certainly a very unusual practice. The Irish custom shows, at any rate, the desire for frequent Communion,

---

[1] *Col. Paenit. B.* (26 to end), p. 448. Cf. Jonas, *V. Col.* ii, 19, p. 274 ; " mater urget ut per confessionem pandantur vitia et sacri Corporis communione roborentur." The need of purity for soul before Communion unduly stressed, gave rise later to doubts about the daily reception of the Sacrament. Cf. Hauck, *K.G.D.* i, p. 187 : " Bedenken gegen den täglichen Abendmahlsempfang der Laien findet man erst in der Karolingerzeit " (*In den Eligius von Noyon zugeschriebenen Predigten*, s. Hom. 8 : " et illud a multis quaeritur, si quotidie quilibet fidelis debeat corpus et sanguinem Christi accipere, an se aliquibus diebus a tanto sacramento subtrahere.)

[2] *Reg. Coen.* iv, p. 222 *MNP. V.S.H.* ii, p. 11 : " cum sanctus Comgallus esset solus in agro foris operans posuit chrismale suum super vestimentum suum." Ib., p. 173. *Cod. Salm.*, c. 286. *Ducange* s.v.

[3] *Reg. Coen.* viii, p. 226 *MP.*

[4] Ib. x, p. 231 *MP.*

[5] Ib.

[6] Ib.

[7] *Paenit. A.* p. 442 ; *B.* p. 444.

[8] *Ep.* 93. P.G, xxxii c. 486

recommended, as already noted, by St. Basil, St. Augustine and St. Jerome.

A regular feature in the lives of the Saints is the administration of Holy Communion, under this aspect called *viaticum*, to the dying.[1] It was regarded as fitting that this last kindly act should be rendered by one of the dying Saint's particular friends.

(e)—Penance.

Confession, as an ascetical practice, is met with very frequently, especially in Luxeuil and the other monasteries that followed the Columban Rule. As the purpose of such confession was chiefly to secure guidance of the best quality, it might be made to an experienced abbess by the nuns subject to her authority.[2] A clumsy brother confesses to St. Columban that he had broken a plough-share and knocked off his thumb![3] The practice goes back ultimately to Egypt, where it is found almost in excess, for the Egyptians were inclined to see faults where in reality there were none. Conversely the Syrians and the Greeks were inclined to boast of virtues which they did not possess and conceal the vices which they did.[4] In the Columban Rule confession of faults was made regularly twice a day, first before dinner and again at some suitable hour before bedtime.[5] Elsewhere the principle

---

[1] *B. Arm. Muir.* 15 B. : " adpropinquante autem hora obitus sui sacrificium (Irish *sacarbaic*=the Holy Eucharist) ab episcopo Tassach, sicut illi Victor angelus dixit, ad viaticum beatae vitae acciperat." Jonas, *V. Col.* i, 17, p. 184 : Finding his namesake and countryman Columban dying *St. Columban at Luxeuil* : " corpus Christi abeunti de hac vita viaticum praebet." Ib. 10, p. 257 : " viaticoque sumpto animam caelo reddidit." Ib. 25, p. 291 : " tantum viaticum capere et valedicere fratribus regressus." *V.S.H.* i, p. 73 : " accepto aeterno viatico corporis et sanguinis Christi . . . suum spiritum felicissimuum Deo emisit." Ib., p. 137 : " accepto salutis viatico." Ib. ii, p. 20 ; p. 105 : " accepto divino viatico " ; Ib. p. 223.
[2] Jonas, *V. Col.* ii, 13, p. 263 : " delictum—quod mane per confessionem humilem matri patefecit." Ib. 17, p. 269 ; 19, p. 272 : in Faremoutiers confession was made *three* times a day, not *twice*, as in Luxeuil, Donatus having added an extra confession to those prescribed by St. Columban. Ib., p. 272–3 : " in hanc ergo labem mentes supradictarum puellarum diaboli iacula dimerserant, ut nulla confessio vera ab ore prodiret, seu quae in saeculo commiserant seu quae cotidiana fragilitas adtrahebat vel in cogitatione vel in sermone vel in opere ne vera confessio per paenitentiae medicamenta rursus reddiret sospitati." Ib., p. 279.
[3] Ib. ii, 3, p. 234–5. Cf. *Adam.* ii, 38, p. 156.
[4] *Verb. Sen.* P.L. lxxiii, c. 781.
[5] *Reg. Coen.* i, p. 220 *MP*. : " ante mensam sive ante lectorum introitum sive quandocumque fuerit facile."

is laid down that as a floor is swept every day once or oftener
with a broom, so the soul should be cleansed once or oftener
every day by Confession."

More important than this ascetical exercise was, of course,
the sacrament of penance, with its four constituent elements :
contrition, confession, satisfaction, and absolution. Sins
were distinguished as capital or venial according to their
gravity.[2] In the nature of the case, capital sins occurred
most commonly among the laity, and it was thus these who
benefited chiefly by the penitential discipline in the monasteries. Both at Iona and at Luxeuil they are found present
in numbers.[3] Given true contrition, there was no stain, no
matter how disfiguring, that could not be wiped out of the
soul.[4] Had not St. Martin exclaimed, when Satan argued
the impossibility of recovery for those who had once fallen :
" If you yourself, miserable creature, would stop campaigning
against mankind, and repent of your deeds even in this hour,
when the Day of Judgment is at hand, trusting in the Lord
Jesus Christ, I would promise you mercy."[5]

He who committed a serious sin was obliged to confess it
(often on his knees and publicly), to promise amendment,
and fulfil the works of satisfaction imposed.[6] The principle,
long fixed in the tradition of the Church, is stated well by
Pope St. Gregory the Great, and adopted from him into the
Irish Canons. " Punishment will be measured according to

---

[1] V.S.H. ii, p. 217. Cf. Jonas, V. Col. ii, 17, p. 269 : "nec omnino per-
confessionem pectoris sui aream purgare studuit." Cf. Cass. Conl. ii, 11,
p. 52. Inst. ii, 13, p. 28 ; iv, 9, p. 53. Verb. Sen. P.L. lxxiii, c. 798.
[2] Paenit. B., p. 443. Reg. Coen. i, p. 220 MNP.
[3] Adam. i, 20, p. 50 ; 17, p. 46 ; 28, p. 56 ; 30, p. 58 ; 50, p. 99 ; ii, 39,
p. 158, etc. Jonas, V. Col. i, 10, p. 170 : " beatus Columbanus cernens undique
ad penitentiae medicamenta plebes concurrere." Cf. Ib. i, 5, p. 261 ; ii, 1,
p. 232 ; 8, p. 245 : "multosque eorum ad paenitentiae medicamenta per-
traxit ; " 15, p. 265 ; 25, p. 290. V.S.H. ii, p. 233 : "quidam agens paenitentiam in civitate Sancti Munnu." Also, supra, p. 320.
[4] Adam. i, 30, p. 59. Jonas, V. Col. ii, 10, p. 254 : " nullum enim Dominus
perire desiderat, sed semper quamvis gravibus delictis obrutum per paenitentiae fomenta redire expectat." Cf. the beautiful words of St. Augustine :
" De laude paenitentiae," in Wasserschl. I.K. xlvii, 1, p. 196 ; and Ep. 211,
p. 359 : "ne habeatis paenitentiam Judae traditoris sed potius lacrimas
Petri pastoris."
[5] V. Mart. 22, p. 131.
[6] Adam. i, 30, p. 59 : " Sancto obvius occurrit, cum fletu et lamento,
ante pedes eius ingeniculans, flexis genibus, amarissime ingemuit, et coram
omnibus qui ibidem inerant, peccantias confitetur suas. Sanctus tum . . .
ad eum ait : surge, fili, et consolare ; dimissa sunt tua quae commisisti
peccamina ; quia sicut scriptum est ' Cor contritum et humiliatum Deus
non spernit '." The penitent was then sent to the penitential station in
Mag Luinge.

the gravity of the sin, for just as the doctor cannot cure the sick man unless he has examined him thoroughly with his hands or eyes, so the wise man cannot cure the sins of sinners without confession ; for with the heart we believe unto justice, but with the mouth confession is made unto salvation."[1] Hence the need for a fixed confessor, so strongly insisted on that the saying, " a person without a confessor is like a body without a head," became proverbial.[2] Confession was especially necessary before Mass, " lest anyone should approach unworthily to the altar "[3] ; also before death, so that when Brandub, King of Leinster, was assassinated, it is noted as particularly regrettable that he died without confession and viaticum.[4] Where the sins were heinous a long period of public penance might be imposed before absolution.[5] Mag Luinge in Tiree and the island of Hinba were public penitential stations in connection with Iona.[6] For terrible crimes like incest, exile till death in a foreign land might be demanded as part of the penitent's satisfaction.[7] Monks and clerics who fell, especially into sins against chastity, were treated with great severity.[8] An imposition of hands seems to have accompanied the admission of the sinner to the state of

---

[1] Wasserschl. *I.K.* xlvii, 17b, p. 202 (n. 1). But the system of graded penance goes back to St. Basil and earlier. It was in common use in the provinces of Asia Minor in the fourth century. Cf. Watkins, *A History of Penance*, London, 1920. *I.*, p. 319 ff. The Irish Penitentials do ' not differ in principle from such documents as the letters of St. Cyprian to Antonianus or the canonical epistles of St. Basil. They tend to be more elaborate and detailed than such ancient documents '. Ib. ii, p. 757. J. T. MacNeill (*The Celtic Penitentials and their Influence on Continental Christianity*, Paris, 1923) stresses unduly " the survival of paganism in Goidelic Christianity," and exaggerates in consequence the differences between the Irish and the more ancient form of penitential discipline.

[2] *Martyr. Oeng.*, p. 64, 180–2. Cf. *V.S.H.* i, 73 ; ii, p. 106 : " quomodo in patria mea vivam et tibi confitear peccata mea ? " Ib., p. 148, 219. Cf. St. Jer. *Ep.* 41, p. 314 : " (Sabelliani) rigidi sunt, non quo et ipsi peiora non peccent, sed quod hoc inter nos et illos sit, quod illi erubescunt confiteri peccata quasi iusti ; nos dum paenitentiam agimus, facilius veniam promeremur."

[3] *Paenit. B.* (26 to end), p. 448.

[4] *V.S.H.* ii, p. 157.

[5] Supra, p. 281.

[6] *Adam.* i, 30, p. 50–1 ; 30, p. 58 ; ii, 39, p. 158 ; iii, 8, p. 206.

[7] *Adam.* i, 22, p. 52 : " Tunc deinde miser in litore flexis genibus leges paenitentiae expleturum se promisit iuxta Sancti indicationem. Cui Sanctus ait : Si duodecim annos inter Brittones cum fletu et lacrymis paenitentiam egeris nec ad Scotiam usque ad mortem reversus fueris forsan Deus peccato ignoscat tuo." *V.S.H.* i, p. 253 : exile punishment for murder. Cf. supra, p. 281.

[8] *Paenit. A.* p. 441 ; *B.* p. 443. Wasserschl. *I.K.* xxix, 14, p. 152 : the monk who became a father was to spend his life in tearful lamentations.

penitence.[1] Symptomatic of the hard life they had to lead were the prohibition against frequent washing of the hair,[2] and the order that they should pray kneeling, whilst others prayed standing, on festivals and days of relaxation.[3] Fasting was likewise a feature of the penitential state, and we hear of " the penitent old man without blood or flesh, but thin, miserable leather upon his hard, bare bones."[4] When the period of penance had expired they returned to him who had imposed it, were absolved and admitted as ordinary members of the faithful to the Holy Table.[5]

Compared with the system of public penance found elsewhere in the West, the Irish system must be termed mild ; for penitents were allowed to perform their various exercises in the comparative privacy of a monastery or a penitential station. Their penances had no place in the public liturgy. Reconciliation again took place without much ado, and probably often through the ministry of priests who had received general permission for the purpose from their religious superior. To grasp the full extent of these differences we must keep before our eyes the practice in other countries. " Public penance," says Sozomen, speaking of the fifth century, " was carefully maintained in the churches of the West and especially in that of the Romans. There the place of those who are in penance is conspicuous : they stand with downcast eyes and with the bearing of mourners. When the Divine Liturgy is concluded, not partaking of those things which are lawful to the initiated, with wailing and lamentation they cast themselves prostrate on the ground. So also the whole congregation of the church with loud crying is suffused with tears. After this the bishop first arises and raises the prostrate ones ; and having prayed in a fitting manner on behalf of the sinners doing penance, he dismisses them. Meanwhile in private each spends as much time as the bishop has appointed in voluntary self-affliction, or in fastings, or without ablutions, or in abstinence from food, or in such

---

[1] This seems to be the meaning of St. Brigid's wish. (*Martyr. Oeng.*, p. 66. *Thes. Pal.* ii, p. 330) that the *grád aithrige*—" order of penance " should be bestowed upon her. For the five grades of penance found in the early Church see Watkins, op. cit., i, p. 239.

[2] *Reg. Coen.* ix, p. 226 *MP.*

[3] Ib.

[4] *Lism. L.*, p. 113.

[5] *Adam.* ii, 39, p. 158 : " Post septenorum expletionem annorum diebus ad me huc quadragesimalibus venies, ut in Paschali solemnitate ad altare accedas et Eucharistiam sumas."

other modes of penance as have been assigned. On the
appointed day, having discharged his penalty like some debt,
he is absolved from his offence and takes part in the assembly
with the people."[1] The Irish system, though undoubtedly
a sufficient hardship for those who submitted to it, certainly
did not equal this in severity.

Private penance, or the absolution and reconciliation of
sinners by the bishop or his priests without obliging them to
join the ranks of the "penitents," was always practised in
the Church.[2] It belonged, as might be expected, particularly
to death-beds. The Irish Fathers, from Finnian of Clonard
onwards, allowed it very commonly also in time of health.
Combined with the comparatively mild form of public penance
already mentioned, it proved to be a great attraction in the
Irish monasteries, and it was not in Burgundy only that
"the people flocked from all sides to the medicaments of
penance." The penitential books were enlarged and multiplied to meet this need. That the Irish system was in no way
out of harmony with Catholic tradition is shown by its complete
adoption in Canterbury under Archbishop Theodore (appointed
A.D. 668). Far from insisting on the severe Continental
system, the new archbishop accepted that employed by the
Irish missionaries. He went even further, for in the *Penitential* which he inspired, and which still bears his name, he
gave the Irish system a much more orderly arrangement than
it had till then reached. Though not without considerable
opposition, the Irish system finally prevailed throughout the
Western Church.[3]

(f)—Cult of Saints and Veneration of Relics.

In the hymn ascribed to St. Patrick[4] "the prayers of
Patriarchs "[5] are included among the elements of strength
through which the Apostle arises. The prayers of St. Colmcille
were invoked during his lifetime and still more frequently
after his death.[6] When in danger of shipwreck at sea St.

---

[1] Sozomen, *Hist. Eccles.* vii, 16. In Watkins, op. cit. i, p. 424.
[2] Historical conspectus in Galtier, *De Paenitentia*, Paris, 1923, p. 198 ff.
Cf. Watkins, op. cit. i, p. 352 ff.
[3] Watkins, op. cit., ii, p. 756 f, 761 f, 769 f.
[4] *Foid fiada. Liber Hymn.*, p. 133 ff. *Thes. Pal.* ii, p. 354 ff.
[5] I n-ernaigthib h-uasalathrach.
[6] *Adam.* ii, 5, p. 112,; 13, p. 120 ; 39, p. 161 ; 40, p. 163. Ib. i, 1, p., 13 :
princes defeated in battle ; others won thrones by virtue of his prayers,
ii, 45, p. 180.

Colmcille himself implored the assistance of St. Cainnech of Achad Bó.[1] Colmcille, when dying, promised to intercede for the brethren in Heaven.[2] His clothes and books were placed on occasion on the altar when a special favour was sought for.[3] To the hymn of Secundinus in praise of St. Patrick there is added in the *Antiphonary of Bangor* the antiphon " May Patrick the bishop pray for us all, that the sins of which we have been guilty may forthwith be remitted."[4] St. Comgall is also invoked that by his merits and prayers the community might be preserved in peace.[5] Elsewhere the martyrs of the Church and the fourteen deceased abbots of Bangor are invoked.[6] At the beginning of the Ordinary of the Mass in the Stowe Missal there is a litany in which the Blessed Virgin, St. Peter, St. Paul and the other apostles and evangelists are asked to come to the aid of all present.[7] St. Martin was held in especial esteem by the Irish monks as well in the early period[8] as in the later period when the scribe of the *Book of Armagh* wrote in Greek characters : " Through the prayers of Martin, I pray the Sovereign Lord to grant me the divine gifts of wisdom."[9]

St. Patrick seems to have possessed relics of Saints Peter and Paul, Stephen and Lawrence, and to have left them at

---

[1] Ib. ii, 13, p. 120–2.
[2] Ib. iii, 23, p. 234 : " et ego, cum ipso manens, pro vobis interpellabo."
[3] Ib. ii, 45, p. 176 : " beati viri vestimenta et libros, inito consilio, super altare, cum psalmis et ieiunatione, et eius nomine invocatione, posuimus."
[4] Ed. Warren, p. 16 :—
Patritius episcopus
Oret pro nobis omnibus
Ut deleantur protinus
Peccata quae commisimus.
[5] Ib., p. 19 : " per merita et orationes S. Comgilli abbatis nostri omnes nos Domine in tua pace custodi."
[6] Ib., p. 12, 28. *Thes. Pal.* ii, p. 232 :
Horum sanctorum merita
Abbatum fidelissima
Erga Comgillum congrua
Invocamus altissima
Uti possimus omnia
Nostra delere crimina
Per Jesum Christum aeterna
Regnantem in saecula.
[7] Ed. Warner, p. 3. Warren, *Liturgy and Ritual of the Celtic Church,* p. 226.
[8] *Adam.* iii, 12, p. 212 : " cum illa consueta decantaretur deprecatio in qua sancti Martini commemoraretur nomen." Jonas, *V. Col.* i, 22, p. 201. *Stowe Missal,* Warner, p. 6. 14, Warren, op. cit., p. 238. Cf. Sulp. Sev. *Dial.* ii, 8, p. 190 : and *Ep.* ii, p. 145 : " spes tamen superest illa sola, illa postrema, ut quod per nos obtinere non possumus, saltem pro nobis orante Martino mereamur."
[9] *B. Arm.,* p. 438.

Armagh, where they were afterwards counted among the city's chief treasures.[1] When the deputation sent by the Synod of Mag Léne to Rome about A.D. 630, returned from that city they brought with them relics of martyrs, which were highly prized for the miraculous cures with which they became associated.[2] Even desert places in which relics were buried deserved high honour, for they were visited by God and by angels.[3] St. Columban, in his letter to Pope Sabinian, asks that Pontiff to be mindful of him in his holy prayers near the ashes of the Saints[4]; in the letter to Pope Boniface IV, he concludes : " For the rest, O Holy Father and brethren, pray for me, a most wretched sinner, and for my fellow pilgrims near the holy places and the ashes of the Saints ; and particularly near Peter and Paul "[5] Relics are also mentioned in the Stowe Missal.[6] Besides the bodily remains of saints various articles connected with them were treasured ; among these were bells and staffs, books, portions of clothing, a stone pillow, tools and other articles.[7] These were often used as title-deeds to certain rights by the representatives of the Saints.[8] Oaths were also constantly taken upon them, it being understood that violation meant outrage to the Saint, and a call for condign punishment.[9] Where relics were so highly valued it is little wonder that relic-mongering was sometimes attempted, and that so-called pious thefts were not always looked upon as morally reprehensible.[10]

---

[1] *B. Arm. Tir.* 17a : " et portavit ab illo partem de reliquiis Petri et Pauli, Laurentii et Stephani ; quae sunt in Machi." Cf. Ib. 29b. *Lib. Ang.* 41b: " de speciali reverentia Airdd Machae . . . Nihilominus venerari debet honore summorum martyrum Petri et Pauli, Stephani, Laurentii et ceterorum."

[2] Ussher, *Works,* iv, p. 443 : " et nos in reliquiis sanctorum martyrum et scripturis quas attulerunt probavimus inesse virtutem Dei."

[3] Wasserschl. *I.K.* l, 1, 2, p. 208. Cf. Ib. xliii, 5, p. 172 ; xliv, 9, p. 177.

[4] *M.G.H. Ep.* iii, p. 165 : " Vale, dulcissime in Christo Papa, memor nostri in sanctis orationibus, iuxta sanctorum cineres."

[5] Ib. p. 177 : " De cetero, sancte Papa et fratres, orate pro me vilissimo peccatore et meis comperegrinis, iuxta loca sancta et sanctorum cineres, et praecipue iuxta Petrum et Paulum."

[6] Warner, p. 9. Warren, op. cit., p. 233 : " quorum hic reliquias specialiter colimus."

[7] Plummer, *V.S.H. Introd.,* p. cxxviii.

[8] Ib.

[9] Ib. p. cxxix. In *Cáin Adomnáin* 34, the *fethalta* or emblems of a church are mentioned. According to *Rawl. B.* 512, fol. 44b (cf. Windisch, *Worterb. s. v.*), the five chief emblems of every church are its staff, capsule of relics, cross, bell and book of Gospels : " cúic primfethail cecha ecalsa .i. bachall agus meinister agus cros agus cloc agus catur."

[10] Plummer, l.c.

§ 8—Work

(a)—Manual.

Manual labour was looked upon by the peoples of antiquity
as degrading, and was performed very largely by slaves.
When the supply of slaves decreased and their place on the
land was taken by *coloni* or *quasi-coloni* the status of work
was but very little enhanced.[1] This was a point of view
which the Church could obviously not accept. Was not Christ
Our Lord Himself " the carpenter's son," and were not the
Apostles, for the most part, poor, simple labourers ? Work,
then, was not merely necessary, but honourable. The monks
from the beginning applied themselves to it with the greatest
assiduity. When certain mystical spirits among them thought
that this was inconsistent with Holy Writ, which taught,
after all, that Mary had chosen the better part, they were
dealt with summarily. A monk of violently contemplative
convictions, so the story goes, arrived one day in Sinai, and
finding the brethren working he expostulated, " Why," said
he, " labour for the food that perisheth ? " The abbot Sylvan
made no reply, but led the monk to his cell. When the hour
of none arrived nobody thought of fetching the contemplative
to the refectory. After some time the pangs of hunger won
the upper hand, and the monk went out to look for the
abbot. " What ? " said he, " is there no meal to-day ? Why
did you not call me ? " " Spiritual men," replied the abbot
sweetly, " have no need of the food that perisheth. We, poor
people, being through and through material, are compelled
to eat. That is why we work. You have chosen the better
part. All day long you contemplate and read the Holy
Scriptures. You are above taking interest in such earthly
subjects as food." This was more by much than the contemplative had bargained for and there was nothing to do
but to confess his mistake and implore the abbot's pardon.
" So you realize," commented Sylvan " that Mary cannot
do without Martha. If there were no Martha, Mary would
have been unable to contemplate and, therefore, unable to
merit praise from the Saviour."[2]

---

[1] Pauly—Wissowa, *Realenzyklop. der klass. Altertumswissenschaft.* Article
colonatus, etc. Dill, *Roman Society in the last Century of the Western Empire,*
London, 1898. Levasseur, *Histoire de l'industrie et des classes ouvrières en
France au moyen âge.* T. 1. Paris, 1900. Boissonade, *Le Travail dans
l'Europe chrétienne au moyen âge.* Paris, 1921.

[2] *Verb. Sen.* P.L. lxxiii, c. 768.

Union of work and prayer was habitual among the Egyptian monks, who in cases went so far as to weave mats during the night psalmody.[1] They appealed to the words of St. Paul that the brethren should eat bread earned by their labour in silence.[2] "When the Lord," says St. Basil, "forbade us to work for the meat that perisheth He taught us to work for the meat that abideth unto eternal life . . . This again the Lord showed in another place when He said ' My food is to do the will of Him who sent Me ' (John iv. 30). But if it is God's will that we should nourish the hungry, give drink to the thirsty, clothe the naked and so forth, it is very necessary that we should imitate the apostle who said, ' I showed you all things, how that so labouring you should support the weak ' (Acts xx. 35). Since then we have these precepts delivered us from the Lord through the Gospel and the Apostle, to be anxious or to work for one's own sake is clearly forbidden. But, according to the Lord's command-ment, we should be anxious and work eagerly on account of our neighbour's need."[3] This was the practice of the solitaries who wished to produce not merely sufficient to supply their own wants, but sufficient also for the needs of hospitality and for abundant almsgiving.[4]

Valuable as was work from the point of view of charity towards the brethren, it was equally valuable from the point of view of the worker's spiritual advancement, for it was a splendid ascetical exercise. Its good results in this respect gave rise to the Egyptian adage that " the monk who works is tempted by one devil only ; the lazy monk by a thousand devils."[5] Cassian discusses the subject at length in the tenth book of his *Institutes* in chapters whose titles indicate sufficiently the nature of their contents : (VIII) That he cannot but be disturbed who does not want to be satisfied with the work of his hands. (IX) Not only the apostle, but also his companions worked with their hands. (X) The apostle did this to give us good example. (XI) He taught the same in words. (XII) His saying " If anyone will not work neither

---

[1] *Reg. Pach.* 5, P.L. xxvi, c. 69. *Alb.*, p. 16.

[2] 2 *Thess.* iii, 6–12.

[3] *Reg. brev. tract.* ccvii. Cf. ib. cxix, cxxi. *Reg. fus. tract.* xvi, lxi.

[4] Ath. *V. Ant.* 3, 4, P.G. xxvi, c. 843 ff. Epiphanius *Expos. fidei* P.G. xlii, c. 830. St. John Chrys. *De Sacerdotio* vi, 6, P.G. xlviii, c. 682. *Hom. in Matt.*, 8, P.G. xlvii, c. 88. Theodoret, *Hist. Relig.* xxx. *Vita Pach.* 4. H.L. 10 14, 32. H.M. 8, 20. St. Jer. *Ep.* 130. C.S.E.L. lvi, p. 193.

[5] *Inst.* x, 23, p. 192.

let him eat " (2 Thess. iii, 10). (XIII) His saying " We have heard that some are disturbed among you " (2 Thess. iii. 11). (XIV) Manual work cuts off many vices. (XV) But kindness is also to be shown towards the negligent and the lazy. (XVIII) How the words should be understood, " It is more blessed to give than to receive " (Acts xx. 35).[1]

Work, whether agriculture or some form of craftmanship, was thus for the monks a universal law ; but care was taken that it should not be carried to excess, with consequences fatal to recollection and prayer.[2] Two other points called for serious attention in the great monasteries where work was highly organised—the disposal of produce or of the money received for produce ; and the prevention of growth in wealth which naturally tended to accumulate where wants were few and where activity was intense and well-ordered.

Speaking of the sale of products, St. Basil says that " we must try to secure both that the products of our work are not disposed of at a distance, and that we do not court publicity for the sake of selling. For it is more fitting to remain in one place and more beneficial for mutual edification and the accurate observance of daily life ; so that we prefer to reduce the price somewhat, rather than go beyond our borders for the sake of trifling gain. Where, however, experience has shown this to be impossible, we must select localities and cities inhabited by religiously minded people, so that our journey be not unfruitful ; and a number of the brethren, each bearing the products of his own work, must go together to the gatherings called ' Fairs.' " They are to travel together, " and accomplish the way with psalms and prayers and mutual edification." They are also to lodge together and to keep close to one another during the actual process of sale.[3] The arrangement at Tabennisi was more or less the same.[4] Here the growth in wealth soon led to a threatened schism.[5]

Among the Irish monks manual labour[6] likewise held an important place ; for the principle is clearly stated that " the monk is fed and clothed by the labour of his hands."[7]

---

[1] Ib., p. 181–6.
[2] Cass., *Conl.* xviii, 7, p. 514–5.
[3] *Reg. fus. tract.* xxxix.
[4] *Vita* 73, in *AA. SS. Boll.* T. iii Maii. *Arabic Life. Annales*, p. 510, 642.
[5] Ladeuze, *Le cénobitisme pakhomien*, p. 227 f.
[6] *Adam.* ii, 28, p. 142 : "opus materiale."
[7] *V.S.H.* i, p. 131 : "monachus enim labore manuum suarum nutritur et vestitur."

The different tasks were assigned by a special officer, who was changed from time to time.[1] Work began in the early morning,[2] when the brethren betook themselves, each to his allotted duty. First of all came the claims of agriculture in its various branches, ploughing,[3] sowing,[4] reaping,[5] winnowing,[6] transport back to the barn.[7] The cows, too, had to be milked,[8] the mill[9] and the kiln[10] attended to. The cook[11] and the baker,[12] and, no doubt, the carpenter[13] and the smith, were constantly occupied, whilst chariots or boats (according to the situation of the monastery) might require to be got ready for a journey.[14] Small tasks, like serving in the refectory, were performed in turn by the brethren.[15] Enda is found digging with his own hand great ditches round his monastery.[16] At Durrow, again, the abbot and the brethren are found building a house in the depth of winter and suffering keenly from the cold.[17] The making of roads, too, could prove a very toilsome labour.[18] Iona possessed a horse and cart,[19] yet the brethren are discovered carrying loads on their backs home to the monastery from the corn field.[20] Some abbots

---

[1] *Adam.* i, 37, p. 72 : " (Baithenus) iisdem in diebus inter eos operum dispensator."

[2] *Adam.* iii, 12, p. 211 : " dum fratres mane ad diversa monasterii opera prepararent." But cf. ib., p. 223 : " vacate semper orationibus mane ; postea lectionibus ; deinde operamini usque ad vesperam."

[3] *Adam.* ii, 44, p. 175. Jonas, *V. Col.* ii, 3, p. 235 : brother ploughing ' quasi miliario uno ' from the monastery. *V.S.H.* i, p. 36 : " perge ad arandum nobis his diebus." Ib., p. 59, 179, 203 ; ii, p. 152. *Lism. L.*, pp. 32, etc.

[4] *Adam.* ii, 44, p. 175. *Cod. Salm.*, c. 228. *V.S.H.* ii, 157, 158.

[5] *Adam.* i, 37, p. 71 : " post messionis opera." Jonas, *V. Col.* i, p. 173 : " venerunt omnes falceque . . . secant segetem." Ib., p. 174 : " messores." Threshing is referred to ib. 12, p. 172 : " ut messem in area virga cedant." *V.S.H.* i, 27 : " plures messores," p. 158, 188, 238 ; ii, 92, 155 : " Sanctus Moedhog cum centum quinquaginta fratribus in messe," etc. *Cod. Salm.*, c. 226.

[6] *Adam.* i, 28, p. 56 ; iii, 23, p. 230.

[7] Ib. i, 37, p. 72. Jonas, *V. Col.* i, 17, p. 182 : Barn filled miraculously with wheat.

[8] *Adam.* i, 16, p. 125 : " post vaccarum reversus mulsionem." iii, 23, p. 231.

[9] Reeves, *Adam.*, p. 362. Jonas, *V. Col.* ii, 2, p. 233 ; 25, p. 290-1.

[10] *Adam.* i, 45, p. 88 : " ante ianuam canabae."

[11] *V.S.H.* ii, 15, 99 ; i, p. 238.

[12] *Adam.* iii, 10, p. 208.

[13] Ib. ii, 45, p. 176-7. *V.S.H.* ii, p. 194-5. Cf. Jonas, *V. Col.* i, 15 p. 178. i, 30, p. 222 ; ii, 25, p. 194.

[14] *V.S.H.* ii, p. 155. *Adam.* i, 18, p. 47 ; ii, 3, p. 106 ; 5, p. 111.

[15] *V.S.H.* i, p. 238. *Cod. Salm.*, c. 272.

[16] *V.S.H.* ii, p. 62.

[17] *Adam.* i, 29, p. 58.

[18] *Vita Flann. Anal. Boll.* xlvi, p. 131.

[19] *Adam.* ii, 28, p. 142.

[20] Ib. i, 37, p. 72.

forbade the use of oxen or ploughs in the fields altogether.[1] Comgall of Bangor made life so hard for his subjects that the terrible combination of diseases from which he suffered before death was regarded by not a few as a punishment here on earth for his excessive rigour.[2] Fishing,[3] brewing,[4] and bee-keeping[5] might keep one or more of the brethren busy on occasion. Before hedges and walls became common in the seventh century,[6] kine, calves, sheep, pigs and goats had to be kept from straying, a task that fell as a rule to the boys about the monastery. Nobody was to undertake work according to his own desires,[7] or to apply himself to any work, no matter how necessary, without orders.[8] Negligence and unpunctuality were punished[9]; and the studious were warned that their love for books was not to lead them to any depreciation of more material work.[10] This had a place even in a great abbot's day, for Adamnan assures us that Colmcille never let an hour pass that he did not devote to prayer or study or writing or manual work. Nobody was thus exempt from this exercise.[11]

---

[1] So St. Fintan, *V.S.H.* ii, p. 98.

[2] *V.S.H.* ii, p. 20.

[3] Jonas, *V. Col.* i, 11, p 171–2. *V.S.H.* ii, p. 7, n. 6. Cf. Sulp. Sev. *Dial.* iii, 10.

[4] *V.S.H.* ii, p. 29. Ib., p. 220–1.

[5] Ib. i, p. 97. Further reference in Plummer, *V.S.H. Introd.*, p. xcvii.

[6] *LU.*, 128a (ed. Best and Bergin, p. 320) : " ní bíd clad na hairbi na caissle im thír in nHére isind aimsir anall co tánic rémis mac nAeda Sláni acht maigi réidi. ' There used to be neither ditch nor fence nor stone walls round land in Ireland then, down to the time of the sons of Aed Sláine, but unbroken plains '." *V.S.H.* i, p. 152, no. 13. Ib., p. 172, 201–2, etc. Plummer's conclusions (op. cit., p. xcv–vii) on " the prevalence of pastoral as compared with agricultural pursuits," are not borne out by the *Laws*. Any typical passage in these (e.g. *Laws* ii, 356, 358—Lánamnas contincuir) shows that ploughing and tillage have a most important place beside cattle-rearing in the life of the ordinary household. Agricultural, as distinct from pastoral, pursuits were, however, favoured by the great increase in population during the sixth century (which led to the enclosing of lands in the seventh—*LU.* 128a) and by the fact that corn (rather than butter, milk and meat) was the staple article of diet for the monks. The later *Lismore Lives* show the two branches of agriculture fairly evenly balanced, but the gain seems to be slightly on the side of tillage. (Cf. Stokes, *Lism. L.*, p. xcviii.)

[7] *Reg. Coen.* xv, p. 232, *MNP*.

[8] Ib.

[9] Ib., p. 233, *MNP*; x, p. 229, *MP*.

[10] Ib., p. 233, *MNP*.

[11] *Adam. Praef.* ii, p. 9 : " nullum etiam unius horae intervallum transire poterat quo non aut orationi aut lectioni vel scriptioni vel etiam alicui *operationi* incumberet." Cf. Molua's excellent advice to his disciples, *V.S.H.* ii, p. 223 : " mei carissimi fratres, bene colite terram et bene laborate, ut habeatis sufficientiam cibi et potus et vestitus. Ubi enim sufficientia fuerit apud servos Dei, ibi stabilitas erit ; et ubi stabilitas in servicio fuerit, ibi religio erit. Finis autem religionis vita aeterna erit." Even nuns had to work in the garden, Jonas, *V. Col.* ii, 17, p. 178. Of a king it is said : " He gave himself to manual labour like any monk." *Martyr. Oeng.*, March 11th, p. 93.

(b)—Intellectual.

The intellectual training of the Irish monk about the beginning of the seventh century was derived from the union of two distinct cultures—one Celtic and native to the soil ; the other Christian and Latin, introduced in the fifth century by St. Patrick and his missionaries. To understand the development of letters in monastic Ireland, the origin and character of the two cultures must be briefly sketched.

(α) *Native Intellectual Culture.*

According to Julius Cæsar, there were two classes of definite account and dignity among the Celts of Gaul. The first class consisted of druids, the second of knights. " The former are concerned with divine worship, the due performance of sacrifices, public and private, and the interpretation of ritual questions. A great number of young men gather around them for instruction, and hold them in high honour. In fact it is they who decide in almost all disputes, public and private ; and if any crime has been committed or murder done, or there is any dispute about succession or boundaries, they also decide it, determining rewards and penalties. If any person or people does not abide by their decision they ban such from sacrifice ; which is their heaviest penalty. Those that are so banned are reckoned as impious and criminal ; all men move out of their path and shun their approach and conversation, and no justice is done if they seek it, no distinction falls to their share."[1] Again he says : " The druids usually hold aloof from war, and do not pay war-taxes with the rest. They are excused from military service and freed from all liabilities. Tempted by these great rewards, many young men come to them of their own accord to receive their training ; others are sent by parents and relatives. Report says that in the schools of the druids they learn by heart a great number of verses, and therefore some people remain twenty years under training. And they do not think it proper to commit these utterances to writing, although in almost all other matters and in their public and private accounts

---

[1] *De Bello Gallico*, vi, 13. These and the following passages will be found in English in Kendrick : *The Druids*, London, 1927, p. 77 ff. (Originals, p. 212 ff.) Cf. also Black, *Druids and Druidism. A List of References*. New York Public Library, 1920. Rice Holmes, *Cæsar's Conquest of Gaul*, Oxford, 1911. Jullian, *Histoire de la Gaul*, Paris, 1924 (5th ed.), vols. i, ii, iii, vi. MacCulloch, *The Religion of the Ancient Celts*, Edinburgh, 1911. *Cambridge Med. Hist.* ii, xv, p. 460 ff ; 472 ff.

they make use of Greek letters. I believe that they have adopted the practice for two reasons—that they do not wish the rule to become common property, nor those who learn the rule to rely on writing and so neglect the cultivation of the memory. For in fact it usually does happen that the assistance of writing tends to relax the diligence of the student and the action of the memory. The cardinal doctrine which they seek to teach is that souls do not die, but after death pass from one to another ; and this belief, since the fear of death is thereby cast aside, they hold to be the greatest incentive to valour. Besides this they have many discussions as touching the stars and their movement, the size of the universe and of the earth, the order of nature, the strength and the powers of the immortal gods, and hand down their lore to young men."[1]

From these passages it is clear that the druids assisted at sacrifices,[2] acted as judges in civil, criminal and inter-state cases, were philosophers and students of nature. They were, in fact, a learned body, organised as a corporation, with privileges so great that membership of it was regarded as highly desirable. They had schools, and were skilled in letters, but propagated their doctrines by word of mouth only, not thinking it fitting to commit them to writing.

Remarkable in Cæsar's narrative is the account that the functions of philosopher, judge and instructors of the young are combined in the same person. Strabo, writing soon afterwards, suggests the conclusion that Cæsar classes various intellectual professions under the common title of druidism. " Among all the Gallic peoples, generally speaking," writes Strabo, " there are three groups of men who are held in exceptional honour : the Bards, the Vates, and the Druids (βάρδοι τε καὶ οὐάτεις καὶ δρυίδαι). The Bards are singers and poets ; the Vates diviners and natural philosophers ; while the Druids, in addition to natural philosophy, study also moral philosophy. The druids are considered the most just of men, and on this account they are entrusted with the

---

[1] *De Bello Gallico*, vi, 14.
[2] Cf. Diod. Siculus, v. 31 : " It is a custom of the Gauls that no one performs a sacrifice without the assistance of a philosopher, for they say that offerings to the gods ought to be made only through the mediation of these men, who are learned in the divine nature and, so to speak, familiar with it ; and it is through their agency that the blessings of the gods should properly be sought." Strabo, *Geograph.* iv, 4 : " But they would not sacrifice without the druids."

decision, not only of private disputes, but of public disputes
as well. In former times they even arbitrated cases of war
and made the opponents stop when they were drawn up for
battle. Murder cases, in particular, were turned over to
them for decision."[1] Ammianus Marcellinus, writing in the
fourth century of the Christian era, supports this testimony,
for he says : " In these regions, as the people gradually
became civilized, attention to the gentler arts became more
common, a study introduced by the Bards and the Euhages
and the Druids. It was the custom of the Bards to celebrate
the brave deeds of their famous men in epic verse accompanied
by the sweet strains of the lyre. The Euhages strove to
explain the high mysteries of nature. Between them came
the Druids, men of great talent, members of the intimate
fellowship of the Pythagorean faith. They were elevated by
searching into secret and sublime things, and with grand
contempt for the mortal lot, they professed the immortality
of the soul."[2] This again is very like the account given by
Diodorus Siculus, who notes that the Bards " applaud some,
while they vituperate others." He calls the Druids
" philosophers and theologians," and speaks of divination
as a common practice.[3]

Other authors recount the suppression of the Druids by
the Roman power in Gaul. When Pliny wrote his *Natural
History*, about A.D. 77, the druids had degenerated into
magicians,[4] and hardly a vestige of their judicial, educational
or political influence remained.

In Ireland, unlike Gaul, Celtic civilization was not disturbed
by foreign conquest. The three classes mentioned by Strabo
must have existed, for their names are found in Old Irish
and have passed down to the modern language. For Strabo's
δρυίδαι we have *drúid* (Nom. Sing. drui, Modern draoi) ;
for his οὐάτεις we have *fáthi* (Nom. Sing. *fáith*) ; for his
βάρδοι we have *báird* (Nom. Sing. *bárd*). The druids, being
" philosophers and theologians," with a traditional theory of
life hostile to Christianity, were naturally the missioners'
chief enemies, and are represented as such in the early accounts
of St. Patrick's activities. With the triumph of Christianity
they lost their age-old position, and became ordinary sooth-

---

[1] Strabo, *Geographica*, iv, 4.
[2] Ammianus Marc. xv, 9.
[3] *Histories* v, 31.
[4] *Nat. Hist.* xvi, 249 : " ita suos appellant *magos*."

sayers. As these again were discredited because of their superstitious practices, the ancient name druid fell into dis-. repute, so that it came to be represented in Latin by exactly the same word (magi) as that used by Pliny of the fallen order in Gaul. Their legal lore was, however, preserved as an independent tradition, and those who specialised in it were called *brithemuin* (Nom. Sing. *brithem* from *breth*, " To give judgment.") *Fáthi*, though sometimes used in its original sense[1] in close connection with *drúid*, comes to be restricted in meaning to the prophets of the Old Testament. The duties finally of Strabo's βάρδοι are shared in Ireland by bards and by a second and superior class of poets called *filid* (Nom. Sing. *fili*), who not merely composed verse, but preserved the old epic literature of the nation, were skilled in topography and genealogy, and at times, like the οὐάτεις of Strabo, ventured into the dangerous regions of oracle and prophecy.[2] The bards, on the contrary, were mere minstrels without learning.[3]

Through the instrumentality of these classes, who seem to have been strong in numbers and well endowed, a body of literature and a rude form of scholarship were transmitted from generation to generation. The Ulster cycle, Ireland's most important contribution to the world's literature, describes events that belong to the period about the beginning of the Christian era. Irish heroes figuring in the stories are equipped and conduct themselves in the same manner as the Gauls described by the Greek traveller, Poseidonius ; and several articles of their dress and armour correspond exactly to La Tène Continental types of that age. Similarly the Fenian, or second great cycle of Irish literature, describes conditions that belong probably to the third century of the Christian era. As in Gaul before the conquest, the tradition of oral teaching was universal. Even after the introduction of a written literature this feature of the native schools was not abandoned, for a qualifying test in the order of poets was

---

[1] Cf. *LU*. (ed. Best and Bergin), p. 7 : "a fháthe ind ríg." Ib., p. 143 : "a Feidelm banfáith co acci in sluag ? "

[2] *Cormac's Gloss*. No. 756 : Cormac represents the *fili* as sole possessor of three methods of divination—the *imbas forosnai, teinm lóida* and *dichetal di chennaib cndime*. The first two of these were forbidden by St. Patrick, but the third was allowed because it was based on mere knowledge and did not include the offering of sacrifice to the powers of evil.

[3] Cf. Zimmer, *Die keltischen Literaturen I. B.* (*Kultur der Gegenwart*, i, xi, 1, p. 46 ff.) Quiggin, " Celtic Literature," in *Encycl. Britann.*, 11th ed., p. 625 ff. De Blacam, *Gaelic Literature Surveyed*, p. 127.

the number of stories known by heart. Thus the *oblaire* or lowest grade of *fili* knew seven stories ; the *taman*, ten ; the *drisac*, twenty ; the *fochlocon*, thirty ; the *macfuirmid*, forty ; the *doss*, fifty ; the *cana*, sixty ; the *clú*, eighty ; the *ánruth*, one hundred and seventy-five ; and the *ollam*, or poet of the highest degree, three hundred and fifty. The *ollam* was allowed twenty-four attendants, the train of a provincial king, and the number seems to have been still greater before the sixth century, when the pretensions of the poets led to a threat of their extinction.

In the sixth century, then, the *poets* in Ireland are a great and powerful body.' They are rich, socially of high status, organised for instruction and entertainment, and the learning they represent is an inheritance from the Celtic past, absolutely distinct from that of the Greek and Roman world.

(β) *Latin Culture* (¹),

Wherever the Roman went he brought his language with him ; and with Latin came Roman civilisation. Aquitaine in Gaul, where the character of the people was somewhat effeminate, passed at an early period under Roman domination. But the work of systematic Romanization had its centre rather at Lyons. Thence the new language was propagated through the Gauls. By the fifth century the victory of Latin was complete. It was the language of culture, of government, of society ; the language of the camp ; the language of communication between masters and their cosmopolitan households of slaves. Finally, it was the official language of the Church and of the schools. From Gaul it passed to Britain, which, according to Tacitus, was superior to Gaul in its natural capacity for education.[2] Every town

---

[1] Norden, *Die antike Kunstprosa vom vi Jahrhundert vor Ch. bis in die Zeit der Renaissance*. Leipzig—Berlin, 1915–8. Roger, *L'enseignement des lettres classiques d'Ausone à Alcuin*, Paris, 1905. Sandys, *History of Classical Scholarship*, Cambridge, 1906–8. Freeman, *Historical Essays*, Ser. i and ii, London, 1871, 1873. Dill, *Roman Society in the last Century of the Western Empire*, London, 1898. Kaufmann, *Rhetoren—u. Klosterschulen in Gallien während des 5 u. 6 Jahrhunderts* (Raumers *Historisches Taschenbuch*, 1869). Jullian, *Les premières universités françaises* (*Revue internat. de l'enseignement*, 1893). Scott Holmes, *The Christian Church in Gaul*, London, 1911. Haarhoff, *Schools of Gaul*, Oxford, 1920. De Labriolle, *Latin Christianity from Tertullian to Boethius*, Eng. transl., London, 1924.

[2] *Agric.* 21 : " Iam vero principum filios liberalibus artibus erudire, et ingenia Brittanorum studiis Gallorum anteferre."

of any consequence seems to have had its school and its rhetors or schoolmasters.

Having finished his elementary education the child was taught "grammar," the art which deals with "grammata" or letters. During this period chief emphasis was laid on the poets, like Homer and Menander, Horace, Vergil, Terence and Plautus ; and the orators, like Demosthenes and Cicero. The teacher would select a passage from one of these and read it aloud to his pupils with proper attention to punctuation, pronunciation, expression and metre. Stress was laid upon elocution, as the purpose of the teacher was to restore as far as possible the spoken word in its first impressiveness and melody. After the reading came the exposition, when the master took up the grammatical, historical, scientific, artistic or literary points, suggested by the passage, and lectured on them to his pupils. Learning by heart and writing exercises were common.

From the grammarian the boy passed into the hands of the rhetor and studied "rhetoric." Here the proximate end in view was encyclopaedic knowledge ; the ultimate end oratory. Discussion and declamation characterized the school. To persuade his audience (to do his will, whether good or evil) the youth trains himself in culture of mind and manners, and in gaining the esteem of his fellow-citizens. To know the art of speaking is to know the art of commanding. The rules of composition became more and more artificial as national and even party ideals disappeared, and oratory had to seek its inspiration in the virtues or the weaknesses of the Emperor.

Flogging was everywhere the inevitable counterpart of teaching ; but then there were lazy schoolboys like St. Augustine, who admitted that he never would have learned anything save for the rod.[1] The barbarous harshness and militarism of the Romans were not, however, sufficient to quell bustle and excitement on the school-benches or to divert the boys' attention from their " nuts," handball, bird-catching, and the rest.

Higher education in the fourth century was confined almost wholly to the nobility, who had come to look upon it as their monopoly. Some of the " curiales " and the " corporati " may have cultivated their intellect to the highest point, but

---

[1] *Conf.* i, 12 ; "non enim discerem, nisi cogerer."

many were content with mere literacy. As we go down the social scale, those who passed beyond the elementary school were probably the exceptions.

Throughout the Empire an education in "rhetoric" was the mark of a cultured gentleman, a condition of imperial appointments, the first mark of distinction between Romans and barbarians. Rhetoric invaded the Church, both as to matter and method, and, though great minds like Tertullian and St. Jerome had serious misgivings as to its character, there was no suggestion that the Church should create a new educational system. In the schools the rhetorical system was looked upon as indispensable.

A good example of the triumph of rhetoric at Lérins is St. Hilary of Arles. Honoratus, his biographer, speaks enthusiastically of his eloquence, of the copious gems of oratory which he produced, the shades and shapes of his descriptions. Contemporary savants judged that he had attained to something altogether beyond either eloquence or learning, something entirely superhuman. But he could speak with simplicity to the untutored. Lupus, again, "was trained in the schools and filled with the doctrines of the rhetors." Parallelism, repetition, chiasmus, assonance, alliteration and the other arts of the rhetorical tradition appear constantly in homilies and sermons. Thus the ideal of oratory persisted, even in the Christian pulpit.

In the Church, however, the victory of the ancient rhetorical tradition was never complete. Before congregations of simple and unlettered people the preacher had almost of necessity to descend to greater directness of style. Among the clergy the system prevalent in the schools was often adopted, but was never defended. St. Jerome attacked Hilary of Poitiers for his ornate sentences, his long periods, and his tragic manner, so completely out of harmony with his purpose as a Christian teacher. Elsewhere he proclaims that sighs, not applause, are the measure of the preacher's success[1]; and he enunciates the principle (almost unintelligible for the period) that "as far as I am concerned, all I want is to speak so that I can be understood."[2] Indeed the reaction against flowery language

---

[1] *Ep.* 52, 8, p. 428 : "dicente te in ecclesia non clamor populi sed gemitu suscitetur ; lacrimae auditorum laudes tuae sint."

[2] *Ep.* 36 (*C.S.E.L.* xxxiv, p. 281) : "sint alii diserti . . . mihi sufficit sic loqui ut intellegar, et ut de Scriptura disputans Scripturarum imiter simplicitatem."

led to the cultivation of simplicity. So far was this carried
that Sidonius Apollinaris, the most artificial of rhetorical
writers, talks ridiculously of his " countrified style " (pagana
rusticitas).[1]

On the general question of pagan education the leaders of
the Church were divided into two camps. Sulpicius Severus
condemned all literature except the Bible and the theological
writings of the Fathers. Tertullian, Arnobius and Lactantius
turned their backs upon heathen literature. For St. Jerome
the difference between pagan and Christian writers was the
difference between darkness and light. Pagan philosophy
was false and dangerous ; pagan poetry inflamed passion ;
pagan education and literature were nothing but " the clever-
ness of the sophist, the trick of the rhetor, the warped imagination of the Bard." To do justice to this attitude we must
remember on the one hand the earnestness of the Christians,
on the other hand the tenacity of paganism, entrenched from
time immemorial in the schools, where the subject matter in
both lower and upper classes was the ancient mythology, but
one step removed from religion. Again there was the open
hostility of the pagan teachers, proud of their traditions and
bitterly scornful of Christianity and Christians.

But whatever his dislike for paganism and its schools,
St. Jerome scouts the idea that Christians should not avail
themselves of them. Ignorance, he says, and holiness do not go
necessarily hand in hand. Besides, he argues, the weapon of
rhetoric is necessary against the enemies of Christ's Church.
Controversies have to be conducted with these, and it would
be well for all Christians if they were like himself—afraid of
no opponent. St. Augustine, too, contends, on the principle
of " spoiling the Egyptians," that whatever is good in pagan
education and literature should be utilized. St. Paulinus of
Nola and Prudentius adopted the same viewpoint, whilst
Sedulius in the dedication of his *Carmen Paschale* maintains
that divine truths make a better appeal if presented in pleasing
form. The pagan authors had thus to be studied.

Ultimately the Church accepted the liberal view of St.
Augustine and St. Jerome, and adopted pagan letters. St.
Jerome expounded the lyric and comic poets to young people
at Bethlehem ; whilst his monks made copies of Cicero. St.

---

[1] *Ep.* viii, 16, 3. Cf. St. Jer. *Ep.* 52, 9, p. 428: " multo melius est ex duobus
imperfectis rusticitatem sanctam habere quam eloquentiam peccatricem."

Augustine made Platonism the basis of his philosophy. Vergil was read not merely because of form, but because of the prophecy supposed to be contained in the fourth *Eclogue*. Roman law was regarded by the Church as a dim reflection of divine justice, and was transmitted by her to the barbarians ; whence it passed as a heritage to the civilized world.

By the side of the pagan schools the Church set up elementary schools for the masses, ignoring the rigid class-distinctions which prevailed within the Empire ; but, for one reason or another, progress in this respect was slow. Semi-theological schools in which religious and secular studies were simultaneously prosecuted also grew up in Gaul about the beginning of the fifth century. Greatest among these schools was Lérins. The illustrious names in the early history of this monastery are all of aristocrats who had received in youth the finest intellectual training which the rhetors could give. When won over to the monastic ideal they entered as heirs into a new inheritance, the study of the Holy Scripture. For ever since the days of the first fathers in the desert immense emphasis had been laid on the reading of Holy Writ.[1] There was no monk or solitary who did not know large portions of it by heart. Abbots who could explain its meaning and elucidate obscure passages were highly honoured.[2] St. Basil had decreed that the Scriptures alone were to be used for literary studies in his schools. " Teachers will use the language of the Scriptures, and in place of myths will tell the boys stories of wonderful deeds and educate them by maxims from the *Proverbs*."[3] A natural result of so much preoccupation with the inspired writings was that a certain science of Scripture study was elaborated.

At Lérins from the beginning the course of studies seems to have been mainly exegetical and theological. The titles of Eucherius's works are in themselves significant : *Formulae*

---

[1] *H.L.* 4 : " Didymus, blind since he was 4 years old, ' interpreted the Old and New Testament word by word, and such attention did he pay to doctrine, setting out his exposition of it subtly yet surely, that he surpassed all the ancients in knowledge." Ib. 11 : "Ammonius could repeat 6,000,000 lines ! " Ib. 18, 26, 32, 55. Bas. *Reg. brev. tract*, ccxxxv–vi : " those entrusted with leadership are to learn the Gospels by heart." St. Jer. *Ep.* 22, 17, p. 165 : " tenenti codicem somnus obrepat et cadentem faciem pagina sancta suscipiat." *Ep.* 52, 7, p. 426 : " nunquam de manibus tuis sacra lectio deponatur." St. Aug. *Ep.* 211, p. 368 : " codices certa hora singulis diebus petantur." *Verb. Sen.*, P.L. lxxiii, c. 762. Cass., *Conl.* xiv, 1, p. 398 ; 10. p, 411. *Inst.* xi, 16, p. 202, etc.

[2] *H.L.*, 47. *H.M.*, 27.

[3] *Reg. fus. tract.*, xv.

spiritualis intellegentiae, Instructionum Libri, Dialogorum Liber. In these he discusses and explains Holy Writ : " *Secundum historiam, secundum tropologiam, secundum anagogen.*"[1] " Historia " covers all that has to do with the literal interpretation of Holy Scripture ; " tropologia " leads to its deeper meaning ; whilst " anagoge " leads to the inmost recesses of sacred thought concealed beneath the commonplace words of the inspired writer. Allegory was thus put in the place of honour, and the author's speculative and imaginative gifts allowed full scope. Vincent of Lérins and Faustus of Riez show by their works the prominence which theology held in the island school. Distinctly pagan education, though not neglected, was not regarded as the thing that really mattered. St. Patrick, well versed in Holy Writ and a sound theologian, shows the main trend of the teaching. Unlike his great contemporaries he had not benefited by a rhetorical education in boyhood, and his grasp of Latin was weakened by years of captivity outside the Empire. Again, at the beginning of the sixth century, when Caesarius leaves Lérins for Arles, he needs to have his education completed by a rhetor.[2] He never, however, showed any sympathy with the declamations and applause of the rhetorical school ; and when a bishop he revolutionized Christian preaching by excluding rhetoric from his pulpit.

Disciples of Lérins carried the educational system of that monastery—the study of Holy Writ and of theology, and the study of profane letters as a necessary aid—to many parts of Gaul. By the beginning of the sixth century the problem of pagan literature was solved in this sense. Caesarius, for all his tenderness of conscience, studies pagan authors without scruple, and a generation later, Gregory of Tours (died 594) allows his students to pass through the seven arts of Martianus Capella, and to write poetry. So much of artificial rhetoric as survived was used in a living cause, and dialectic was profitably employed in the investigation of interesting and obscure questions. As against the hollowness of pagan moral teaching the Christian schools saw to it that their pupils practised what they were taught and lived according to the laws of God and the Church.

---

[1] Cf. Cass., *Conl.* xiv, 8, p. 404.
[2] Yet " grammar, rhetoric and dialectic " were at this time, as earlier, taught at Lérins. *Chron. sacr. insulae Lérin.* ii, 130. The rhetor in question, Pomerius, was an African by birth. He was a theologian as well as a rhetor, and became a priest at Arles. Cf. *Caes. von Arel.*, p. 82–3.

When St. Patrick came to Ireland he brought with him the Lérins tradition ; but the deficiency (viewed from the rhetorical standpoint) of his own education and the condition of affairs in the country did not favour the rapid propagation of the new learning. Such simple instruction as was given by him or his helpers to their converts and to the young neophytes destined for ecclesiastical orders was based probably on Holy Writ. To enable them to read this, they were given an elementary grounding in Latin.[1] When they had progressed sufficiently to be able to read the psalter and had acquired a general mastery of Catholic doctrine and practice (the *lex catholica*), they were ready to join the missionaries and assist in the work of evangelization. No evidence of any kind is forthcoming that classical learning made an appreciable advance in Ireland during the fifth century.

In Britain, however, there seems to have been a development corresponding in some degree with the development in Gaul. At the beginning of the fifth century the land was still a province of the Empire, and must have been supplied with rhetorical schools of the type common within the Empire at that period. The difficulties raised against St. Patrick in Gaul because of his *rusticitas* were re-echoed in Britain by the clergy who had been trained in these schools. To justify his mission in the eyes of these *rhetorici* is the purpose of his " Confession." During the course of the century a new direction was given to the schools in Britain owing to the influence of Lérins. Faustus of Riez, the distinguished abbot of that monastery, was himself a Briton, and he was visited, certainly by one, and probably by many prominent ecclesiastics from his own country. The result, as at Lérins, was a union of biblical with the old rhetorical studies and the shifting of emphasis from the latter to the former. Illtud's monastery at Llanilltud (Ynys Pyr=Caldey Island) is the first school of note in Britain where the Lérins system becomes discernible. A generation later the most prominent monastery in Britain is not Llanilltud, but Llangarvan, founded by St. Cadoc, who was probably a disciple of St. Illtud. St. Samson of Dol, St. Pol of Léon and Gildas are represented as Cadoc's pupils.[2] Through the half-Briton, half-Irish Churchman, Fortchernn of Trim, Finnian of Clonard was brought into contact with

---

[1] *B. Arm. Tir.*, 18a, 26a, 29b. : " abgatoria."
[2] Williams, *Christ. in Early Brit.*, p. 321, 331, 359, 360.

Cadoc, and became an enthusiastic supporter of the Lérins
monastic ideal. By means of Finnian's numerous disciples
this spread throughout the whole island. In Britain, too,
Gildas shows the influence of Lérins, for his learning is predominantly biblical, though his turgid style seems to be a
product of some degenerate rhetorical school. Gildas,
according to Irish tradition, helped to shape the Church in
Ireland in the sixth century, and there can be no doubt that
the model which he sought to impose was that of Lérins.
When Cadoc died and Llangarvan sank into insignificance
its place in Britain was taken by Menevia under St. David,
but in this monastery the ascetical interest was much greater
than the educational.

Since the clergy and monks displaced and succeeded the
druids as the " philosophers and theologians " of the nation,
it was taken for granted that they should devote themselves
to study. Thus in the lives of all the sixth-century saints
the learning of letters is mentioned as a matter of course.
Again, as already pointed out, the monks seem to have been
taken from the well-to-do classes—those, in other words, who
could afford to have their children fostered, for fosterage
then was the rough equivalent of what we would now call a
good education.

(γ) *The two cultures side by side in Ireland. Their fusion
a gradual process.*

It is certain that in the sixth century this Christian Latin
learning of the Lérins tradition predominated in the monasteries. The Holy Scriptures were the chief course of study,
and theology was not neglected ; whil-t profane literature
was read because of the mastery which it gave of the Latin
language, and its general usefulness in the understanding
of the sacred text.

At the beginning of the sixth century the native tradition
of culture was still suspect, owing to its close connection with
paganism,[1] but the gulf of separation between the two cultures
was narrowing. In the third or fourth decade of the century,
Colmcille takes lessons from a representative of the old learning.
A generation later he uses his influence in favour of the native

---

[1] The Irish language, in which native pagan culture was preserved, was
regarded as " heathen." Similarly, the German dialects, in the days
of St. Boniface. (Bon. *Ep.* 45 : "qui baptizati sunt per diversitatem et
declinationem linguarum *gentilitatis.*")

tradition at Druim Ceatt. From this it may be deduced that the majority of the *filid* were then Christian, for it is hardly likely that Colmcille would have sought to perpetuate the privileges of a pagan class. Union of the two cultures in the monastic schools probably began about A.D. 600. It came, as might be expected, by way of the native language, for, whatever the monks might write, they spoke Irish and preached in that language to the people. Then the question arose why Irish should not be written just as Latin was, for the intellectual treasures of the native language were hitherto transmitted by word of mouth only. Taking Latin as their model, the monks studied the sounds and structures of the spoken tongue, and evolved a system of orthography which made the writing of Irish as easy as the writing of Latin. When the homily preserved at Cambrai was written, probably before the end of the seventh century, the orthography of the language is definitely fixed and does not change in its essential parts for centuries. This implies a period of evolution going back to the beginning of the seventh century, if not earlier. Now, and now only, did an Irish *literature* become possible, for the Ogham script, elaborated, it would seem, from the Latin alphabet by the *filid*, was quite unsuited for literary purposes. It may be noted finally that the fusion of the two cultures placed the monasteries in a position of extreme strength and made possible the wonderful results, religious and intellectual, which they were to achieve at home and abroad during the following centuries.

Having accepted, assimilated and fostered the national culture, their influence in Ireland was immense ; having assimilated classical culture which the Church saved for Europe, they were able to return to the Continent and play no mean part in repairing the intellectual losses caused by the barbarian invasions.

(δ) *Study in the Early Monasteries.*

Elementary studies were made in the Irish monasteries only by *oblati*, and the number of these seems to have been very small in the sixth century. As a rule, the boy destined for a religious career was handed over at the age of five or seven[1] to a cleric or hermit and had made some progress in

---

[1] *V.S.H.* i, p. 99 ; ii, p. 37. He would be in fosterage up to this age. Cf. ib. : " a parentibus et nutritoribus suis concorditer."

letters before he sought admission among the monastic
brethren.[1] Columban, according to his biographer, had
studied grammar, rhetoric, geometry and Scripture before
he departed finally from his parents' home.[2] Study in
youthful years for the future monk is so much a matter of
course that it is a commonplace in the biographies. Now
and then when the master's name is unknown, the tutorial
office is ascribed to angels.[3] Those who were converted in
mature years from other professions would be expected to
make good their deficiency in learning.[4] The danger of
knowledge was well known, but the danger of ignorance was
considered to be incomparably greater.[5] To the Irish mind
an illiterate monk was a contradiction in terms.

Speaking in general, monastic studies may be divided into
three main branches—1, Study of the Latin languages, which
might lead in time to a study of the Latin authors whose
names are inseparably associated with the concept of a liberal
education ; 2, study of " the ecclesiastical rules," or theology
in its widest sense, including dogma, moral, canon law and
ritual ; 3, study of the Sacred Text, especially of its hidden
meanings, according to the method expounded by Cassian
and Eucherius.[6] The palm for the highest form of knowledge
was awarded without hesitation to the last-mentioned. He
who excelled in it received as time went on the title of " suí
littre," " Doctor of the Letter " (of Scripture), and ranked with
the " ollam " (he who had reached the highest degree in the

---

[1] Supra, p. 207–8.
[2] Jonas, V Col. i, 3, p. 156 : " ne frustrato labore, quem potissimo ingenio
desudaverat in grammaticam, rhetoricam, vel divinarum scripturarum
seriem, in saeculi inlecebris occuparet."
[3] V.S.H. i, p. 87.
[4] V.S.H. i, p. 35.
[5] Ib. ii, p. 210 : " multi enim intellectu et arte liberali decepti sunt et
inde causam habuerunt ruinae." Ib., p. 184 : " spiritus ignorantiae"—a great
evil.
[6] V.S.H. i, 35 : " litteras et scripturas." Ib. 68 : " ut disceret et legeret."
Ib. 76 : " peractis infantilibus annis litterarum studiis traditur imbuendus."
Ib. 88 : " psalmos ceterumque officium ecclesiasticum (didicit)." Ib. 100 :
" flagrans amore sacrarum scripturarum cogitavit ut sanctum episcopum
visitaret." Ib. 174 : " bene legit et bene didicit in diversis scripturis."
Ib. 259 : " misit eum . . . ad alios sanctos abbates . . . ut videret regulas et
religionem eorum et disceret scripturas ab eis." Ib. ii, 22 : " ut sanctas
legeret scripturas et disciplinam ecclesiasticam a sanctis patribus disceret."
Ib. 76 : " in sacris litteris et in bonis moribus (erudiendus)." Ib. 142 : " ad
studium liberale." Ib. 164 : " in moribus honestis scientiaque litterarum
nutrivit eum Deo." Ib. 190 : " didicit divinam scripturam ceterasque dis-
ciplinas." Ib. 226 : " legere et discere ecclesiasticos mores." Ib. 240 : " legens
diversas scripturas." Adam. ii, 1, p. 103–4.

traditional native learning) as the chief scholar of the nation.[1]

As Latin learning was propagated by books, in contradistinction to the traditional Celtic learning, which was propagated by word of mouth only, *lectio,* " reading," became the ordinary monastic word for study, and *legend* (from the Latin *legendum*),[2] became the Old Irish term for the knowledge which accrued from such reading. But *lectio* was used in the widest sense even outside of Ireland during the Middle Ages. A twelfth century definition of the word as " the attentive study of Holy Writ undertaken with all the application of which the mind is capable,"[3] renders perfectly the Irish idea of *lectio divina.* Along with this, however, went the ordinary unqualified *lectio* of writings that made no claim to be inspired.[4]

It would be difficult to overestimate the place which the Bible held in the monastic system of education. Once the boy had mastered the alphabet,[5] a psalter, whole or in part, was placed in his hands.[6] When he was able to read the psalms he committed many of them to memory.[7] This must have been of immense advantage during the singing of the canonical office, especially during the night hours, when the artificial light provided was probably very inadequate. What aids to the student in the shape of paradigms, vocabularies, grammatical treatises, were available in the sixth century we cannot tell, but they were abundant in later times. After the psalms would come other portions of the Sacred Text, like St. Matthew and the Acts of the Apostles.[8] A more advanced course, suitable to adolescence, would be the twelve minor prophets.[9] St. Columban, while still in early manhood,

---

[1] Cf. MacNeill, *Law of Status, P.R.I.A.,* xxxvi. No. 16, p. 313.

[2] Pedersen, *Vergl. Gram.* i, p. 222 ; ii, p. 29. Thurneysen, *Gram.,* p. 416.

[3] Quoted in Gorce : *La Lectio Divina,* Paris, 1925, p. iv.

[4] They are thus distinguished in Bede, *H.E.* iv, 23 ; v, 18, 20 : *Sanctae Scripturae, Divinae Scripturae* and *scripturae.* Cf. *V.S.H.* i, p. 7: " coepit statim in scripturis proficere, non solum in divinis sed ceterarum artium, sicut mos est iuvenum aliquid gustare de dulcedine et astutia disciplinarum auctorum."

[5] *V.S.H.* i, 67: " ut alphabetum legat et tondatur."

[6] Ib., p. 165, n. 2 ; p. 201 ; ii, p. 157. *Cod. Salm.,* cc. 166, 190, 446, 916.

[7] Bede, *H.E.* iii, 5 : " Aedan's disciples employed themselves—aut legendis Scripturis aut psalmis discendis."

[8] *B.N.E.,* i, p. 15.

[9] *V.S.H.* ii, p. 19 : "iuvenis quidam legens duodecim minores prophetas apud sanctum Sinellum." Cf. Jonas, *V.Col.* i, 3, p. 157 : " Quem (Columban) vir sanctus (Senell) omnium divinarum scripturarum studiis inbuit."

had made such progress that he composed in pleasing Latin
a commentary on the Psalter.[1] Just before his death in Italy
he composed a theological treatise against the Arians.[2]

From the peculiarly British way in which Latin was pronounced in Ireland, and which reflects itself in the orthography of the native language, it is clear that the Irish monks
had Britons as their chief Latin teachers. These are to be
connected with St. Finnian and St. Cadoc, rather than with
the early missionaries, whose educational influence seems to
have been restricted. From Britain, too, in all probability,
came the first supply of books. The transcription of these
was a common occupation in the Irish monasteries and was
zealously performed as early as the sixth century. Colmcille
and his successor were both accomplished scribes,[3] and they
were not the only members of the community at Iona who
practised the art.[4] Many of the other monasteries were
equally well provided for.[5] There was thus an excellent supply
of books available during the hours devoted to study.[6] They
were written with pen and ink on vellum, and the gatherings
or leaves were held together by some form of binding.[7]
Jottings not destined for preservation, on the other hand,
were made with an iron style on wax tablets, or on flat stones
like slates.[8] Young students used the same for their first
exercises in writing, efforts, alas, that were not always blessed
with the fullest success, for we hear of a youth whose scrawl

[1] Jonas, V. Col. i, 3, p. 158 : " (ut) psalmorum librum elimato sermone
exponeret." Colmcille was likewise most skilled in Holy Writ. Adam. iii,
18, p. 223 : " scripturarum quoque sacrarum obscure quaeque et difficillima
. . . mundissimi cordis oculis patebant."
[2] Ib. 30, p. 221.
[3] Adam. i, 23, p. 53 ; 25, p. 54 ; ii, 8, p. 115-6 ; 9, p. 116-7 ; 16, p. 125 ;
25, p. 143 ; 44, p. 175 ; iii, 15, p. 215 ; 23, p. 233.
[4] Ib. i, 23, p. 53.
[5] Cod. Salm., cc. 439, 894, 900. Martyr. Oeng., pp. 90, 168, 202, 244.
Wasserschl. I.K. xxi, 28, p. 72 ; xlviii, 5, p. 204. The writing of the four
Gospels took 40 days (V.S.H. i, 24), but a case is recorded where they were
transcribed in a day from an exemplar received on loan. (Ib. ii, p. 133.)
The numberless references to study and books in Lism. L. imply abundant
supplies. Cf. p. 25 (l.828) ; 28 (958) ; 29 (985) ; 47 (1567-9) ; 59 (1956-7) ;
60 (1976 ff.) ; 75 (2525) ; etc.
[6] V.S.H. ii, p. 233 ; i, p. 252 ; ii, p. 135 ; p. 144. Adam. i, 24, p. 53 ;
35, p. 65 ; 43, p. 80, etc. Jonas, V. Col. i, 30, p. 94. Reg. Coen. viii, p. 224
MP. : " ut melius lectionem discat." On the importance of study cf. Sulp.
Sev. in praise of St. Jerome, Dial. i, 19, p. 161 : " totus semper in libris est ;
non die neque nocte requiescit ; aut legit aliquid semper aut scribit."
[7] Supra, p. 291. Jonas, V. Col. i, 5, p. 237 : " (Athala) libros ligaminibus
firmat."
[8] Supra, p. 292. Specimens of school tablets in slate or stone in Lawlor,
Monastery of Nendrum, plate xii.

was so bad that none could tell whether it was caused by a human hand or by a bird's claw![1] Transcription, as an ascetical occupation, was practised, as has been noted, by St. Martin's and St. Jerome's monks, and even by the solitaries of Nitria and the disciples of St. Pachomius at Tabennisi.[2]

As the Sacred Scriptures were the chief subject of study, it follows that books of the Old and the New Testaments were the most common volumes to be transcribed. Other ecclesiastical writers were not, however, neglected, and the profane authors must have had their place. An examination of Columban's works shows reminiscences of Persius, Vergil, Horace, Sallust, Ovid, Juvenal and of the Christian poets, Juvencus, Prudentius and Ausonius.[3] Cumméne in his Paschal letter to Segéne of Iona (c. A.D 632) cites not only Holy Writ, but the decisions of various synods of the East and West, then St. Jerome, St. Augustine, St. Cyprian, St. Gregory the Great, and paschal cycles ascribed to various authors—Anatolius, Theophilus, Dionysius, Cyrillus, Morinus, Victorius and Pachomius.[4] Ailerán the Wise (died A.D. 665) in his *Interpretatio Mystica progenitorum Christi*, quotes Origen[5] and Philo, as well as St. Jerome and St. Augustine.[6] It is therefore extremely likely that patristic, ecclesiastical and profane writings were copied by the Irish scribes from the earliest days of monasticism.

The learned monks, as was becoming, devoted some of their time to teaching. Finnian's remarkable influence on the whole course of the development of the Church in Ireland must have come largely from his gifts as a pedagogue. St. Colmcille at Iona had at least one pupil receiving instruction from him.[7] Schools are mentioned in connection with various

---

[1] *V.S.H.* ii, p. 13.
[2] Supra, p. 372. *Sulp{ Sev. V. Mart.* 10, p. 120 : " ars ibi exceptis scriptoribus nulla habebatur." Cf. *Rev. Celt.* ii, p. 392. *H.L.* 13, 32.
[3] Gundlach, *M.G.H. Ep.* iii. *Ep. Col.*, notes.
[4] Ussher, *Works*, iv, pp. 432–43.
[5] To the question whether Christians should read Origen and others whose writings contain errors, St. Jerome replies (*Ep.* 62, 2, p. 593–4) : " Origenem propter eruditionem sic interdum legendum arbitror, quomodo . . . nonnullos ecclesiasticos auctores Graecos pariter et Latinos ut bona eorum eligamus vitemusque contraria."
[6] P.L. lxxx, c. 327 ff. Cf. Esposito, *P.R.I.A.* xxviii, c. 1910, p. 73. Roger, *L'enseignement des lettres classiques*, p. 258. Gougaud, *Chrét. Celt.*, p. 259.
[7] *Adam.* iii, 21, p. 226 : " vir beatus cuidam suo sapientiam discenti alumno nomine Berchan . . . denunciavit, inquiens, Caveto, fili, ne hac sequenti nocte, iuxta tuam semper consuetudinem, ad meum appropinques hospitiolum."

other monasteries.[1] The most striking evidence in this respect
is afforded by the Venerable Bede, who speaks of the English
students who frequented Ireland for study purposes in the
seventh century. These were supplied with books and
supported free of charge during their studies.[2] All accounts
agree that questions from Holy Writ were the chief subjects
discussed. Though school buildings doubtless existed,[3] we
are justified in concluding from Bede that the highest form
of instruction was of a more private and personal character
imparted by the distinguished teachers among the monks to
students who visited them in their cells.[4]

Beyond the alphabet and some chance words and phrases,
there is no evidence that Greek was studied, known or taught
in the early Irish monastic schools.[5] This, indeed, is exactly
what we should expect, for the Continental culture which
Ireland received came to it from Lérins through Britain, and
in Lérins the serious study of Greek did not exist. Long
before the foundation of the monastery, Greek in Gaul had
declined almost to vanishing point. Speaking of the appointment of a Greek rhetor in A.D. 376, the Emperors express
doubts whether anybody fit to fill the post can be found.
Ausonius, who had neglected Greek at school, afterwards
became proficient in the language, but whenever he ventures
to speak Greek in public he has to translate the simplest
words and phrases. Even in the South of Gaul, where Greek

---

[1] *Cod. Salm.*, c. 227 (Bangor) ; 891, 894 (Daiminis). *V.S.H.* ii, p. 165
(Ros ailither) : "magnum studium scholarium." Ib., p. 228. Cf. O'Curry,
Manners and Customs, p. 76–81. Joyce, *Social History of Ireland*, i, 408 ff.

[2] *H.E.* iii, 27 : "quos omnes Scotti libentissime suscipientes victum eis
quotidianum sine pretio, libros quoque ad legendum et magisterium gratu
itum praebere curabant."

[3] The remains of a large stone school-house have been discovered at
Nendrum. Lawlor, *Mon. of Nen.*, plate iii, facing p. 75.

[4] Bede, l.c. : "circumeundo per cellas magistrorum." A work entitled
Rhetorica Alerani was known in the twelfth century, but seems to have been
lost (Manitius, *Gesch. der latein. Literatur des Mittelalters*, i, p. 10). To the
old rhetorical studies we owe the statement of place, time, person (and cause)
with which so many Irish tales begin. (Cf. Sulp. Sev. *Dial.* ii, 7, p. 188 :
"Quid tu, inquit, non vides, quod solent docere grammatici, locum, tempus
et persônam.")

[5] *V.S.H.* i, 141 : "altare paratum fuit (by Gildas for St. Brendan) habens
librum (missal) graecis conscriptum litteris." It was regarded as a miracle
that Brendan could read this as if the characters were Latin. In the *Book
of Armagh* (11a) the *Pater Noster* in Latin is written in Greek letters ;
similarly an invocation of St. Martin (438a). Columban knew some Greek
words (Letter to Bon. IV, *M.G.H. Ep.* iii, p. 170). A few also are found in
Adamnan (*Praef.* ii, p. 5 ; ii, 39, p. 158 and note n) ; and in the *Antiph.
of Bangor*. Ed. Warren ii, pp. 39, 47, 48, 56, 82, 97, 100. Cf. Gougaud, *Chrét.
Celt.*, p. 247–8. Esposito, *Studies* i, p. 665 ff (the evidence in detail, p. 668–72).
MacNeill, *Phases*, p. 243–4.

culture was still a living memory, the study of Greek letters was exceptional. But a certain elementary knowledge of Greek was necessary, and therefore persisted. The " Litterae formatae," letters of commendation given to travelling priests by their bishops, were sometimes drawn up in the language of the Eastern Empire. Again, the decrees of bishops were often marked with certain Greek letters to indicate their authenticity. How low the standard of Greek studies was at Lérins is proved by the Books of Instruction written by Eucherius for his son Salonius. In these books are to be found, among the " more difficult questions," the commonest Greek words (talentum, obol, Theos, drachma, hagios, angelos, etc.), from Holy Writ, or ritual, and the exposition consists mostly in mere translations.[1] If there were Greek studies in Ireland before the last quarter of the seventh century, it would be indeed interesting to know whence they had drawn their origin.

§ 9—OTHER FEATURES

(a)—*Clothes.*

At Tabennisi each monk wore a sleeveless linen tunic reaching to the knees and secured by a girdle. Over this was a goatskin, and round the neck was a thin cape, to which was attached a hood.[2] The monk usually went barefoot, but he was provided with sandals in seasons of extreme heat or extreme cold, when infirm or when setting out on a journey. Then, too, he carried a *baculus* or staff.[3] A special linen cloak was provided for use within the cell. Garments not actually in use were in charge of the assistant-superior of the house.[4] All garments were washed at fixed periods.[5]

St. Basil lays down that the monks must dress alike, in useful garments that will serve night and day. Hair-cloth was allowed for purposes of mortification.[6] Shoes were to be chosen for their plainness, cheapness and good wearing qualities.[7] If clothes or shoes got too worn or too old, the

---

[1] Haarhoff, *Schools of Gaul*, p. 220-3.
[2] *Reg. Praef.*, 4.
[3] *Reg.* 61, 81, 101.
[4] *Reg.* 66, 70, 72.
[5] *Reg.* 67-71.
[6] *Reg. fus. tract.* xxii ; *Brev. tract.* xc.
[7] *Reg. fus. tract.* xxii.

monk was to reflect that they were better than he deserved. All articles of apparel must be obtained from the authorities,[1] and be treated with care so that they do not wear out prematurely.[2]

Adding to these paragraphs the excellent advice tendered by St. Augustine to his nuns, that they should try to please by their good conduct, not by the cut of their garments,[3] we have the main principles governing the use of dress in monasteries.[4] Here and there, differences in detail occur. In Gaul, for instance, the supply of clothing allowed was more copious than in Egypt, for the amount that sufficed along the Nile would be ridiculously inadequate in the colder northern clime. The sheepskin, too, was abandoned, since in Gaul it would cause nothing but derision.[5] But, speaking generally, the customs in this respect were the same in all lands.

In Ireland we hear of a *tunica*, or inner garment. That which St. Colmcille was wearing at his death was white in colour.[6] Over this was worn a *cuculla*,[7] or *casula*,[8] seemingly a woollen garment of coarse texture, provided with a *capa*[9] or hood. In cold weather or on journeys it might be covered by an *amphibalus* or cloak.[10] Columban, like Cassian, but unlike St. Basil, allowed a change of clothes at night.[11] Sandals were worn constantly,[12] not merely on special occasions, such as journeys, as in Egypt. A reference is found to St. Columban's gloves [13] and where that stern abbot led his

---

[1] *Reg. brev. tract.* clxviii.

[2] *Reg. brev. tract.* lxx.

[3] *Ep.* 211, p. 362–3 : " non sit notabilis habitus vester nec affectitis vestibus placere sed moribus." Cf. St. Jer. *Ep.* 52, 5, p. 424 : " (Clerici) non ornentur vestibus sed moribus." Ib. *Ep.* 22, 28, p. 186 : for a fierce attack on "social" priests. Ib. 35, p. 199 : he allows a tunic, cloak and reed mattress to all religious.

[4] Details are discussed by Cass., *Inst.* i, 1–9, p. 8–14.

[5] Cass., *Inst.* i, 10, p. 15.

[6] *Adam.* ii, 27, p. 141 : "depositis vestimentis, excepta tunica " ; ii, 44 p. 175 : "candida tunica."

[7] Ib. ii, 24, p. 136.

[8] *V.S.H.* i, p. 208 : "et dedit ei (pauperi) sanctus Ciaranus casulam suam ; ipse autem postea ibat in pallio tantum (where *pallium = tunica*)." In *Lism. L.*, p. 128 (11, 4306–10) *casal* and *cochull* are taken as synonymous.

[9] *V.S.H.* ii, p. 11 : "(cum) crismale eius super capam eius vidissent."

[10] *Adam.* i, 3, p. 25 : when Colmcille visited Clonmacnois he was wearing an *amphibalus ;* also when he went to Druim Ceatt, to attend the royal conference. (Ib. ii, 6, p. 113.)

[11] *Conl.* ix, 5, p. 255–6. *Reg. Coen.* xii, p. 230 *MP.* ; ix, p. 227, *MNP*

[12] *Adam.* ii, 13, p. 122 ; iii, 12, p. 210 : "fratres se calceantes." Jonas, *V. Col.* i, 17, p. 181. *V.S.H.* ii, p. 12. *B.N.E.* i, p. 17. Wasserschl. *I.K.* lxvi, 8, p. 237, where angelic authority is quoted for the custom.

[13] Jonas, *V. Col.* i, 15, p. 178 : "tegumenta manum quos Galli *wantos* (French *gants*) vocant."

disciples were sure to follow, so that we may take it as certain
that gloves were worn during work at Luxeuil. After the
manner of holy men of the Old Testament and the early
fathers of the desert, the Irish monks regularly carried a staff
with them on their journeys.[1]   This was used not merely
against the dogs of vice and invisible beasts, but also to work
miracles.[2]   In form they were simply sticks with a crook,
not spiral-headed like the later crozier.   Saints often
exchanged them as a mark of affection or as a seal to the
pact of confraternity.   Sometimes they were enshrined in
precious metals and given striking names.   Most famous of
all staffs was the *bachall Isa*, said to have been given to St.
Patrick by Christ Our Lord Himself, and preserved at Armagh
as one of the city's priceless heirlooms.[3]

We are not told how often garments were washed by the
Irish monks, but it is likely that this took place frequently,
for the standard of personal cleanliness was high.   Apart
from ascetical bathing in ice-cold water, practised by the
saints,[4] we hear constantly of washing, especially of the head
and feet.[5] St. Brendan on his travels is said to have discovered a land whose inhabitants implored him, " saying,[6]
' We are in an awful state in this place, owing to the fleas,
for they outnumber the grains of sand on the sea-shore ! '
Then the man of God took pity on them and prayed, saying,
' O Lord, free them from this misery, for they have given us
hospitality in Thy Name ! ' And so it was done."   With
housing conditions such as they then were, it is likely that

---

[1] Cass., *Inst.* i, 8, p. 13–4. *Conl.* xi, 3, p. 315.   *Verb. Sen.* P.L. lxxiii, c. 754,
where the *senior* threatens to use it on a certain brother. Ib., cc. 753, 778,
etc.   *V.S.H.* i, p. 166 : robber addresses St. Cainnech as " O baculate."
Hence the Breton *belek* " priest." In *Lism. L.*, p. 59 (l. 1955) it is used in
the sense of " tonsure ".

[2] Jonas, *V. Col.* ii, 2, p. 233 ; 24, p. 287. For innumerable instances from
the *Lives* see Plummer, *V.S.H. Introd.*, p. clxxvi–vii.

[3] The bachall with the bell (clocc) and relic shrine (meinistir) of the founder
were regarded as a church's chief emblems, and were used in the collection
of dues, etc. So important did these become that a penance of 40 years
was imposed on him who stole them ; whereas the penance for stealing
an altar or an ordinary shrine was only seven years. (*Ériu*, vii, § 7, p. 154.)

[4] Cf. Dom Gougaud, *Devotional and Ascetical Practices*. London, 1927,
p. 173.

[5] *Reg. Coen.* ix, p. 226, *MP.* : " penitents are not to wash their heads
more than once a week, unless there is some special reason." This implies
that washing among the ordinary brethren was very frequent. Cf. Ib., p. 227,
MNP. Paenit. B. (25 to end), p. 448. St. Augustine in the warm African
climate allowed a bath once a month only, except in time of sickness.
(*Ep.* 211, p. 367.)

[6] *V.S.H.* i, p. 140.

Irish saints would often be called upon to exercise their·
thaumaturgical powers against the same pest nearer home.

(b)—Food.

Food, according to St. Columban,[1] should be poor in quality
and taken in the evening ; not, however, to satiety, just as
drink should never be taken in such quantity as to produce
drunkenness. The purpose in taking food is to sustain the
body without doing it spiritual injury. Proper foods for this
purpose are vegetables (as well those of the shell family like
peas and beans as greens), flour mixed with water and a little
loaf of bread. Foods other than these are calculated to burden
the stomach and suffocate the soul. Those whose minds are
set upon the rewards of eternity should see nothing in food
save its usefulness in reaching this goal. Food, therefore,
should be taken in moderation, just as work is undertaken in
moderation, for real discretion consists in such maceration of
the flesh that spiritual progress is not rendered impossible.
If abstention from food, then, goes too far, it is a vice, not a
virtue, for virtue supports good. We are bound, therefore,
to fast every day, just as we are bound to take food every day,
and because of the very fact that we do eat every day, the
indulgence allowed to the body must be poor in quality and
meagre in quantity ; for we eat every day because we must
advance every day, pray every day, work every day, study
every day.

Although Columban states that food should not be taken
before evening, his meaning seems to be that it should not be
taken before the afternoon, for supplementary references
show that the ninth hour (about 3.0 p.m.) was the usual meal-
time. The consumption of food before that hour was an
offence, particularly heinous if it took place on the two weekly
fast-days, Wednesday and Friday.[2] Consideration, however
was shown towards the sick, the delicate[3] and those engaged
at hard manual work[4] or on journeys.[5] To enter the kitchen
after dinner (when the remains of the meal could still be

---

[1] The following paragraph is a paraphrase (practically a translation) of
ch. iii, *De cibo et potu* of Columban's *Reg. Mon.* (p. 375–6).
[2] *Reg. Coen.* xiii, p. 230 *MP.*
[3] Ib.
[4] Jonas, *V. Col.* i, 17, p. 183.
[5] *Reg. Coen.* ix, p. 228 *MNP.* : even penitents on a journey might eat
at the 3rd hour, and reserve something for the journey's end.

secured),[1] or to pilfer edibles before the appointed meal-time, were weaknesses visited with appropriate penalties.[2] Waste even of crumbs in the kitchen or refectory was sedulously to be avoided, and nobody might have the smallest collation outside the monastery walls without leave.

Columban implies that there is to be but one meal a day in his monasteries, so that his words about perpetual fasting are to be understood in their literal sense. The regulation was certainly modified on Sundays, feast-days and during the Paschal season, at least to the extent of allowing more and better food.[3] The arrival of guests brought with it the same privileges and the abandonment of the fast if it were an ordinary Wednesday or Friday.[4] In places of milder observance, like Iona, it is likely that there were two meals (a dinner—*prandium*—and supper—*coena*) on all days of the week save the two just mentioned.[5] In Lent, however, probably in all monasteries of Irish observance, there would be but one meal, and that at nightfall, instead of at the ninth hour.[6]

The chief article of food was certainly bread. Columban and his brethren during their first nine days in the Vosges country lived on bark and herbs[7]; and Columban afterwards, during a period of retirement in the desert, is found living on blackberries and water.[8] He was then so thin, according to his biographer, that he might easily be mistaken for a spectre.[9] At Cluain Eidnech, under St. Fintan, vegetables were the only food.[10] At Bangor, under St. Comgall, bread, vegetables and water constituted the meal. But milk and milk foods were later introduced, following, no doubt, the custom of

---

[1] *Reg. Coen.* viii, p. 225, *MP*.
[2] Jonas, *V. Col.* ii, 22, p. 279. For later regulations cf. *Ériu*, vii, p. 148.
[3] *Adam.* iii, 12, p. 211 ; i, 21, p. 50–1. *V.S.H.* ii, p. 16. Jonas, *V. Col.* i 12, p. 173.
[4] *Adam.* i, 26, p. 545   "superveniente quodam hospite consuetudinarium solvitur ieiunium." *V.S.H.* ii, p. 197. Ib. p. 249.
[5] Bede, *H.E.* iii, 5 : " Aedan and companions from Iona were accustomed ' per totum annum, excepta remissione quinquagesimae paschalis quarta et sexta sabbati ieiunium ad nonam usque horam protelare '." This implies a meal about noon on the other days.
[6] Reeves *Adam.*, p. 355, note h., quotes Ratramnus of Corbey to this effect : " Scotorum natio consuetudinem habet per monasteria . . . omni tempore praeter dominicos festosque d'es ieiunare, nec nisi vel ad nonam vel ad vesperam corpori cibum indulgere." *V.S.H.* ii, p. 197 : " (Moling) ieiunabat quotidie, nisi in dominicis et summis festivis, usque ad occasum solis." All are likely to have imitated this during the Lenten season.
[7] Jonas, *V. Col.* i, 7, p. 165. Cf. *V.S.H.* i, p. 105.
[8] Ib. 27, p. 216. Cf. 6, p. 163–4.
[9] Ib. 9, p. 167–8 : " erat cibis ita adtenuatus ut vix vivere crederes."
[10] *V.S.H.* ii, p. 99 : " olera agrestia."

monasteries where these had always been allowed.[1] At
Daiminis, under St. Senell, the wheat was not winnowed, but
straw and grain were all ground up together, mixed with water
and baked on hot stones. This arrangement was rightly
regarded as very severe.[2] At Iona the supply of arable land
and pasture land was not great, so that the brethren can have
had but little milk and little grain. They helped themselves
out, however, with oxen, sheep, seals and fish.[3] Some of the
saints objected on principle to the use of milk, butter and
flesh in the monasteries[4]; but this was unusual. None, as
far as can be discovered, objected to the use of fish where such
could be procured,[5] and few objected to the use of game, whose
tender flesh, it was argued, was not likely to excite the bodily
appetites.[6]

To the question whether intoxicating drink should be
allowed at meals or no, the Irish monastic fathers returned
no unanimous answer,[7] but public opinion on the whole seems
to have been against the teetotallers. The monk who drank
nothing but water for thirty years was regarded as a great
exception and his example was not followed with enthusiasm.[8]
Beer was used in Columban's monasteries, and the sternness

---

[1] Ib., p. 113 : "panis et olera et aqua tantum erant in illa coena. Lac
et cetera alimenta in monasterio Sancti Comgalli antea incognita erant."
[2] Ib., p. 228 : "gravissima regula."
[3] *Adam.* ii, 3, p. 106 (barley) ; 4, p. 109 (bread) ; i, 41, p. 78 (seals) ;
ii, 16, p. 125 (milk) ; ii, 19, p. 128-9 (fish) ; 25, p. 143 (cattle) ; i, 41, p. 78
(wethers). It may be noted that people in general at this period lived on
milk and milk products during the summer months, and on flesh only when
the supply of the other foods ceased. The period during which flesh was
used was called *aimser cua.*
[4] *V.S.H.* ii, 98 : No butter, milk or flesh allowed in Fintan's monastery.
It is implied that this was not the case elsewhere.
[5] Jonas, *V. Col.* ii, p. 171 (Columban). *Adam.* ii, 19, p. 128-30 (Colmcille).
V.S.H. ii, p. 15-6 (Comgall). Ib., p. 209 : Molua killed a fat calf for Maedóc.
Then he learned that Maedóc ate no flesh (showing his training at St. David's,
where flesh was not allowed). Molua saved the situation by turning the veal
into fish. Ib., p. 245 (Ruadan).
[6] Jonas, *V. Col.* ii, 25, p. 292-3. : Brethren engaged putting hedge
round the vineyard are given duck to eat.
[7] The matter was still in dispute in the eighth century. Maelruain of
Tallaght was asked by his friend Duiblitir to allow the Tallaght monks
beer on the three chief feasts, but Maelruain refused, saying : "As long as
my injunctions are obeyed in this place, the liquor that causes forgetfulness
of God shall not be drunk in this place." "Well," replied Duiblitir, "my
monks shall drink it, and they shall be in heaven along with yours." "My
monks," said Maelruain, "who shall keep my rule shall not need to be
cleansed by the fire of Doom, for they shall be clean already. Your monks,
however, may perchance have something for the fire of Doom to cleanse."
(*Mon. Tall.*, § 6, p. 129-30. Cf. *Ériu*, vii, p. 182—note by E. J. Gwynn.)
[8] *V.S.H.* ii, p. 238. Cf. *Lism. L.*, p. 80 : Ruadán of Lothra had a fine
elm tree from which flowed a beautiful beer. And "the monks of Ireland
yearned to Ruadán."

of the Saint stopped short at the decree that he who had
spilled any should drink water only until the amount spared
equalled the amount wasted.[1] Cronán of Roscrea worked a
miracle to provide his guests with beer, and the result was so
successful that they all became inebriated![2] The penalty
for this was forty days on bread and water.[3] We hear
of water turned into fine beer for a nun's supper[4]; and of a
carload of the same liquid being brought by the youthful
Maedóc to Menevia.[5] In general, however, the quality of the
beer cannot have been very wonderful, for it is equated with
whey![6] Wine was also not unknown at festivals.[7] A fountain
is mentioned which produced water and whey on fast-days,
milk on Sundays and the festivals of martyrs, beer and wine
on the greater ecclesiastical feasts.[8] This probably represents
the true gradation and the occasions on which the different
kinds of beverage were used. Milk would be carried on
journeys, because of its high food value.[9]

In all these customs the Irish monks show that they are
proceeding along the direct line of monastic tradition. Everywhere in the Orient the ninth hour was the normal mealtime.[10]
The pangs of hunger were felt as a rule terribly about midday,
with danger to the monk's vocation, so that the " noon-day
devil " was spoken of in jest as the monk's greatest enemy.[11]
On Saturday, Sunday and feast days two meals were often
allowed.[12] Bread was the staple article of diet, and the little
loaf (paxamatium—παξχμάσιον) became classic, even in
the West, where it was adopted by St. Columban.[13] Vegetables

---

[1] Jonas, *V. Col.* 16, p. 179; 17, p. 183. Ib. 16, p. 180. *Reg. Coen.* iii,
p. 221 *MP*.
[2] *V.S.H.* ii, p. 29 : " valde inebriati sunt."
[3] *Ériu*, vii, p. 146.
[4] *V.S.H.* i, p. 271.
[5] Ib., p. 146.
[6] *AA. SS. Hib.*, p. 379a : " pro potu calicem cervisiae sive de sero lactis
bibebat."
[7] *V.S.H.* i, p. 214. *Lism. L.*, p. 131 : the wine had come from the Franks
to Clonmacnois, 'and a piece of the cask remained until lately.'
[8] *Rév. Celt.* x, p. 50.
[9] *Adam.* ii, 38, p. 155. Cf. *V.S.H.* ii, p. 13 : milk allowed to sick and aged
at Bangor. On the general question of food cf. also *Lism. L.*, p. 31 (l.1055),
37 (1229), 63 (2080), 81 (2734–7), 82 (2738–9), 124 (4178 ff), 125 (4190–9).
144 (4829). Also the interesting rules laid down by Cummian, *Ériu*, vii, p. 176,
[10] Ath. *V. Ant.* lxxiii, c. 155. *Verb. Sen.* Ib. c. 768. *H.L.* 2. Cass., *Conl.* ii,
11, p. 49 : xvi, 19, p. 455 ; xix, 16, p. 552 ; xxi, 11, p. 585 ; 23, p. 598.
St. Jer. *Ep.* 22, 35, p. 197–8.
[11] Cass., *Inst.* x, p. 174 : " daemon meridianus."
[12] *Inst.* iii, 12, p. 45.
[13] *Reg. Coen.* x, p. 228 *MP*. Cf. Cass., *Inst.* iv, 14, p. 56. *Conl.* ii, 19, p. 61
etc.

and herbs were also common,[1] and oil was looked upon as a delicacy.[2] St. Martin lived on herbs, and on one occasion, having taken hemlock by mistake, was almost poisoned to death.[3] But at Easter he ate fish,[4] and his biographer has a pleasing story of the whole brotherhood betaking themselves to the riverside " because it was holiday-time," to watch a skilful fisherman among the monks plying his art.[5] A *huge* salmon is mentioned as a catch.[6]

The theory of food in its relation to virtue is discussed by Cassian, and more forcibly still by St. Jerome. According to the former, man is like the eagle. He can fly into the azure heavens beyond the eyes of men, but a time comes when he must descend to earth and eat carrion, " ventris necessitate."[7] Three kinds of gluttony are to be avoided if the monk is to make any progress in virtue :—1, Eating before the fixed hour ; 2, eating too much ; 3, eating food excessively good in quality.[8] Elsewhere the struggle against appetite is compared with the effort of a general to take a well-defended ci⁺y. His best plan is to cut off the food supplies.[9] St. Jerome says bluntly that a liberal consumption of food, and especially of wine, cannot but end in lust.[10] He recommends bread, water and herbs as the proper diet for religious.[11] On the question of intoxicating drink he is the most rabid of teetotallers.[12]

Food, according to St. Basil, must be simple, cheap and

---

[1] *Conl.* ii, 5, p. 45. *Inst.* iv, 11, p. 54, etc.

[2] *Conl.* xix, 6, p. 539–40. At first one drop was used " to ward off vanity." Later, as Cassian complains, the drops tended to multiply.

[3] *V. Mart.* 6, p. 117.

[4] Sulp. Sev. *Dial.* iii, 10, p. 207.

[5] Ib. : " processimus cuncti, utpote feriatis diebus, videre piscantem."

[6] Ib. : " *immanem* esocem diaconus extraxit."

[7] *Conl.* v, 20, p. 146.

[8] *Inst.* v, 23, p. 100. With No. 2 cf. *Ériu*, vii, p. 148 : " conadgaib inge a sechi—' till his skin gets tight '." But this canon is not directed exclusively against monks.

[9] *Verb. Sen.* P.L. lxxiii, c. 772.

[10] *Ep.* 55, 2, p. 488 : " etenim luxuria mater libidinis est, ventremque distentum cibo et vini potionibus irrigatum voluptas genitalium sequitur." In *Ep.* 31, 3, p. 251 he warns against the absurdity of celebrating the feasts of martyrs with banquets.

[11] *Ep.* 22, 9–10, p. 156–7.

[12] *Ep.* 69, 9, p. 696 : " in vino luxuria ; in luxuria voluptas ; in voluptate impudicitia est." Cf. *Ep.* 54, 9, p. 476 and 474–5 : " non Aetnaei ignes, non Vulcania tellus, non Vesevus et Olympius tantis ardoribus aestuant ut iuveniles medullae vino plenae dapibus inflammatae." *Ep.* 22, 8, p. 154 : " vinum fugiat pro veneno." Ib. : " quid oleum flammae adiicimus ? " Ib. 155 : An amusing effort to explain away St. Paul's advice to Timothy to take a little wine for his stomach's sake—a text that has always proved awkward for advocates of total abstinence.

such as is easily prepared. Bread and fish are recommended because it is with these that Our Lord fed the multitude. The monk must eat what is set before him, but if he wants more or better, owing to hard work, a journey or sickness, the authorities at discretion may provide it for him. Water is the common drink, but a little wine is allowed for the health's sake.[1]

At Tabennisi there were two meals daily, the first at midday, the second in the evening. Many came to one only of these. Others received food of a more austere quality—bread, salt and water—in their cells. Special consideration was shown for age, infirmity and hard work.[2]

St. Jerome made a fierce onslaught on the Gallic monks for the generous way in which they helped themselves to food, but Sulpicius Severus points out that it is wrong to compare East and West in these matters. " Heavy eating would indeed be gluttony in Greeks, but it is nature in the Gauls."[3] The Irish followed St. Jerome rather than Sulpicius, and agreed also with the former[4] that it was better to eat a little every day than to fast for two or three days and then indulge in a square meal.

(c)—Fasting.

Fasting, according to a canon incorporated in the Irish collection, is of three kinds :—1, Ordinary abstention from food ; 2, *stations,* or abstention on such days as Wednesday and Friday and the week-days during Lent ; 3, abstention from " wet " or appetising food.[5] When St. Columban lays down that the monk should fast every day, he does not mean that every day should be a *statio,* but rather that abstinence should be practised in the quantity and quality of the food consumed. Days of universal observance, as stated, were the Wednesday and Friday of each week outside the paschal

---

[1] *Reg. fus. tract.* xviii, xix, xxi. *Reg. brev. tract,* lxxi, cxxi-iv, cxxxxv.
[2] Supra, p. 34-5.
[2] *Dial.* i, 8, p. 160 : "libellum legi, in quo tota nostra natio monachorum ab eo vehementissime vexatur et carpitur . . . quod dixerat nos usque ad vomitum solere satiari. Ego autem ita sentio de orientalibus illum potius monachis quam de occidentalibus disputasse, nam edacitas in Graecis gula est, in Gallis natura."
[4] *Ep.* 54, 10, p. 477 : "parcus cibus et venter semper esuriens triduani ieiuniis praeferatur, et multo melius est cotidie parum quam raro satis sumere." Cf. *Verb. Sen.,* c. 766.
[5] Wasserschl. *I.K.* xii, 2, p. 34.

season, and the forty days of Lent.[1] The arrival of a guest
on an ordinary Wednesday and Friday brought with it dis-
pensation from fast.[2] On the other hand, two Lents were
added to the Lent before Easter which was observed everywhere in the Church. The first of these occupied the forty
days before Christmas, and corresponds to what was later
called Advent ; the second occupied the forty days after
Whitsuntide.[3]

This custom seems to have grown up in Ireland in the first
half of the seventh century. It is found firmly established
about A.D. 650[4] ; but no traces of it can be discovered in the
sixth century. The spirit from which it sprang goes back,
however, to the beginning of Irish monasticism. Colmcille's
devotion to fasting and watches passed the bounds of
credibility[5] ; and his zeal was transmitted to his successor[6]
and to his later followers.[7] Columban added to involuntary
fasts, of which he experienced more than one in his lifetime,[8]
many others voluntarily undertaken. Shortly after his
arrival in Annegray, one of the brethren fell sick. Columban
and his followers had neither the food nor the medicine needed
to bring him back to health, and had to content themselves
with rendering him spiritual aid. All therefore dropped their
usual repast, miserable as it was, and fasted for three days
in the hope that God would hear their prayers and put the
suffering brother on the way to recovery. Their sacrifice was
not in vain.[9] Among Columban's disciples the same spirit is
clearly discernible, and is not infrequently associated with
miraculous powers.[10]

Amid the Irish monastic fathers zeal in the exercise of
fasting was no less marked. Maedóc of Ferns fasted forty

[1] Cf. Jonas, V. Col. ii, 19, p. 274 : "praesertim quadragesimae diebus
usque adventum sanctae paschae."
[2] This is also canonical. Wasserschl. xii, 15, p. 37.
[3] Lebor Brecc 261b, 74 : "samchorgus ocus gemchorgus—'summer Lent
and winter Lent'." 9b7 : "ón corgus mór—'great Lent'." (Ordinary
Lent in spring). Cf. Ériu, vii, p. 177.
[4] H.E. iii, 27, p. 193–4 : "Egberct (died A.D. 729, aged 90) added to his
other exercises of piety 'nationibus Scottorum vel Pictorum exemplo vivendi
. . . ut semper in quadragesima non plus quam semel in die reficeret, non
aliud quam panem ac lac tenuissimum et hoc cum mensura gustaret . . .
Cuius modum continentiae etiam xl diebus ante natale Domini totidem
quoque post peracta sollemnia Pentecostes . . . semper observare curabat."
[5] Adam. Praef. ii, p. 9.
[6] Ib. iii, 8, p. 206–7.
[7] Ib. ii, 44, p. 76.
[8] Jonas, V. Col. 6–7, p. 163–5. Ib. 22, p. 204 ; 27, p. 214–5
[9] Jonas, V. Col. i, 7, p. 164.
[10] Ib. ii, 5, p. 237 ; 8, p. 245 ; 23, p. 285.

days and forty nights, neither eating nor drinking anything, after the example of Elias and Moses, and (more important still) of the Lord Himself.[1] It is interesting to note that when the three Lents became an institution fixed by custom, they were called in Irish " the Lent of Elias in the winter ; the Lent of Jesus in the spring ; the Lent of Moses in the summer."[2] When Colmán Elo put four of his monks in occupation of a certain *cella* they subsisted on so little food that three of them died. The fourth, though young, refused to depart from their way of life and likewise died a premature death.[3] St. Brendan and his followers before departing in quest of the Land of Promise armed themselves against sp'ritual enemies with a fast of forty days.[4] Moling fasted every day, except Sunday, until sunset, unless guests came to seek his hospitality.[5] Before the foundation of a new monastery a strict fast of three days was the rule.[6] Fasting was considered an excellent means of inducing Almighty God to bestow his choice favours, and expressions were used in this respect that almost transgress the limits conceded to heroic faith.[7] Fasting had also a less reputable use in secular affairs, the plaintiff being so convinced of the justice of his cause that he was willing to die of starvation if the defendant did not satisfy his claim.[8] The origins of this custom are uncertain, but it is obvious that they have nothing to do with Christianity or monasticism.

Going back further into the history of the monasteries we find that fasting was a practice to which St. Martin was much attached.[9] St. Jerome recommends fasting the whole year round, but more severely during the Lenten season, and less severely at Pentecost.[10] To be really of advantage to the

---

[1] *V.S.H.* ii, p. 153.

[2] *Martyr. Oeng.,* p. 42 : " corgus Eli isin gemrad ; corgus Isu i n-errach : corgus Moysi is t-samrad."

[3] *V.S.H.* i, p. 260.

[4] Ib., p. 107.

[5] Ib. ii, p. 197.

[6] *V.S.H.* i, 170, *B.N.E.* i, p. 17. Bede, *H.E.* iii, 24, p. 177 : " dicebat enim hanc esse consuetudinem eorum a quibus normam disciplinae regularis didicerat ut accepta nuper loca ad faciendum monasterium vel ecclesiam prius orationibus ac ieiuniis Domino consecrent."

[7] *V.S.H.* i, p. 60 ; ii, p. 68, 73–4, etc.

[8] *V.S.H.* ii, p. 17, 18, 45–6 etc. For a more detailed account of fasting in Ireland through the centuries see Dom Gougaud, *Devotional and Ascetical Practices,* Pt. 2, ch. i. *Fasting in Ireland,* pp. 147–58.

[9] Sulp. Sev. *V. Mart.* 14, p. 124. *Dial.* ii, 5, p. 186.

[10] *Ep.* 22, 35, p. 200. Cf. ib., p. 164, 165. *Ep.* 39, 3, p. 299–300. *Ep.* 41, 3, p, 313. *Ep.* 54, 7, p. 473.

soul, fasts should be " pure, chaste, simple, moderate, not superstitious."[1] If thus, they will provide excellent armour against the flesh and make satisfaction to God for offences committed against His Sovereign Majesty.[2] Cassian asserts that in apostolic times fasting was perpetual and universal, and that the fixed fast of Lent was introduced only because of the tepidity which later manifested itself among Christians.[3] He recommends that fasts should not be extended beyond five days a week,[4] notes that the custom (which we have seen to have prevailed in Ireland) of dropping all fasts between Easter and Pentecost was common in Egypt,[5] and tries to establish the wise principle that differences of sex, age, state, occupation, etc., must be taken into account in deciding how far every religious should go in the practice of this form of asceticism.[6] Extremes, he thought, were in no case to be commended.[7] St. Basil set his face against self-imposed fasts, or indeed any fasts that made the monk unable to take ordinary food.[8] At Tabennisi, Wednesday and Friday (outside of the paschal season) were the ordinary fasts, at first for superiors only, afterwards for the whole community. During Lent they were said to abstain from all kinds of cooked food.[9]

Needless to say, the desert provided examples of remarkable feats in the matter of fasting. St. Anthony took food every two or four days only[10]; Adolius in Lent every five days, otherwise every two.[11] Macarius of Alexandria spent a whole Lent on cabbage leaves[12]; Simeon the Stylite many Lents on nothing at all.[13] Even in the earliest time the period from Easter to Pentecost was regarded as sacred ; and the example of her who said, " Fasting is insufficient ; I give it an ally in the shape of toilsome watching," found many imitators.[14]

---

[1] *Ep.* 52, 12, p. 435.
[2] *Verb. Sen.* P.L. lxxiii, cc. 746, 756, 773. Cass., *Conl.* v, 4, p. 122–3.
[3] *Conl.* xxi, 30, p. 605–6.
[4] *Inst.* iii, 9, p. 44.
[5] *Inst.* ii, 18, p. 32.
[6] *Inst.* v, p. 84–5.
[7] *Conl.* ii, 19, 22, 24, pp. 61–3. Cf. *Inst.* ii, 18, p. 31–2 ; iii, 9, p. 43 ; 10 44 ; v. 5, p. 85 ; 24, p. 102 ; 26, p. 103. *Conl.* xxi, 25, p. 600 27, p. 602–3
[8] *Reg. brev. tract.* cxxix.
[9] *Vita Pach.* 19. *Reg. Praef.* 5. *H.L.* 18.
[10] Ath. *V. Ant.* 3.
[11] *H.L.* 43.
[12] Ib. 18. (14).
[13] Theod. *Hist. Rel.* P.G. lxxxii, c. 1463.
[14] *H.L.* 57.

(d)—Silence.

This virtue was considered so important by St. Columban that he devoted to its consideration a special chapter.[1] He begins by saying that the rule of silence should be diligently observed. The monk is justified in using speech only when it is necessary or useful ; and even then he must speak with great caution and weigh his words carefully. From the tenor of the chapter it is clear that what Columban has specially in mind is uncharitable, contentious garrulous, doubtful, conversation ; or anything that might savour of levity. Silence was insisted on particularly in the refectory,[2] and was imposed as a penance for the violation of other rules.[3] Even children undergoing training in the monastery were expected to observe it for a large portion of every day.[4] No account occurs of fixed periods, daily or otherwise, during which the monks were allowed to speak together, but the very fact that silence is imposed as an ordinary penance implies that conversation was an ordinary phenomenon. On feast-days, too, we find talk proceeding in the refectory.[5] On other days there was reading,[6] no doubt of homilies and spiritual treatises. Sometimes, during silence hours, the brethren communicated by signs.[7]

All this was in accordance with monastic tradition. Cassian speaks of the value of silence, especially for the young.[8] No conversation of any kind was allowed among the Egyptian monks whose life he describes.[9] Instead of indulging in idle or unkind talk they meditate on a text of Scripture or repeat a psalm quietly to themselves during the day while they are engaged at their various occupations. St. Basil says, too, that the practice of silence is beneficial for novices, " for, if they control the tongue, they will at once give sufficient proof of continence and will learn in peace, eagerly and attentively, from those that are skilled in instruction, how they must ask and answer questions, for there is a tone of voice and a

---

[1] *Reg. Mon.*, ch. ii, p. 375.
[2] *Reg. Coen.* i, p. 220 *MP.* Cf. ib. xv, p. 232 *MNP.*
[3] Ib. iv, p. 222–3 *MP.* Cf. v, p. 223 ; vi, ib. ; viii, p. 226 *MP.*
[4] Ib. viii, p. 225, *MP.* On silence cf. further ib. xv, p. 232–4 *MNP.*
[5] *V.S.H.* ii, p. 28.
[6] Ib., p. 278 : " refectorium ingressi sunt, ubi nulli loqui permissum est praeterquam soli lectori."
[7] *V.S.H.* i, p. 116–8. *Cod. Salm.*, c. 186.
[8] *Conl.* xiv, 9, p. 408–9.
[9] *Inst.* ii, 15, p. 30.

symmetry of language and an appropriateness of occasion
and vocabulary which are peculiar to religious, and can be
learned by him only who has unlearned his former habits.
Now silence induces forgetfulness of the past, and affords
leisure to learn good habits. A novice, therefore, must keep
silence (except, of course, at psalmody), unless he is constrained
either by some special need concerning the care of his own
soul, or by some unavoidable necessity springing from the
work he has in hand, or by some question that is put to him."[1]
Elsewhere he lays down the very sane principle that the value
of silence depends altogether on time and place.[2] Monastic
silence consisted, as a matter of fact, in the moderate use of
the tongue, for, without considerable restraint on that
dangerous organ, purity of heart and religious perfection
would be impossible. On the other hand, conversation on
pious subjects could be of the highest benefit. St. John
Chrysostom speaks of the Syrian monks in glowing terms.
" All," he said, " in their conversation breathes a spirit of
peace. Unlike ourselves they have nothing to say about
things that do not concern them in the appointment of so-and-
so as prefect ; the loss of high office by so-and-so ; the death
of one ; the unfortunate law-suit of another, and more silly
talk of the same kind. They speak only of the eternal truths.
To listen to them is like listening to conversation in paradise,
for they are always speaking of the things of heaven, of
Abraham's bosom, the crowns won by the saints, the choirs
of those who follow Christ. They never make the smallest
allusion to affairs of this present life. They are no more
interested in us than we are in the doings of ants. The
Heavenly King, the troubles of life, the temptations of the
devil, the doings of the saints, these are the sole subjects of
their conversation."[3]

At Tabennisi, too, the rule of silence was observed and
worldly conversation was altogether eschewed.[4] There and
elsewhere in Egypt reading in the refectory was unknown.[5]
This custom took root first in Cappadocia,[6] and spread thence
gradually to the monasteries of the Christian world.

---

[1] *Reg. fus. tract.* xiii.
[2] *Reg. brev. tract.* ccviii.
[3] *In Matt. hom.*, 69, P.G. lviii, cc. 653-4.
[4] *Reg.* 60, 68, 116. *Alb.* 37, 57.
[5] Cass., *Inst.* iv, 17, p. 58.
[6] Ib. *Aug. Ep.* 211, p. 361.

The desert, of course, had its heroes of taciturnity, as of all other ascetical exercises.[1]

(e)—Sleep.

The curtailment of sleep as a means of mortifying the flesh is found at an early period among pious people such as Origen. Not only did this great scholar banish wine from his table and restrict himself in food to necessaries, but he limited his sleeping hours to the minimum.[2] St. Anthony often spent the whole night in vigils, and when he did sleep it was on the bare ground or lying on a mat made of rushes.[3] Dorotheus, a Theban ascetic, who spent sixty years in a cave, did not allow himself even the luxury of sleeping on a mat. " God is my witness," says the author of the Lausiac History, " that I never knew him to stretch his legs or go to sleep on a rush mat, or on a bed, but he would sit up all night long and weave ropes of palm leaves to provide himself with food. I ascertained that this had been his manner of life from youth, and that he had never deliberately gone to sleep. When working or eating, however, he was often overcome by fatigue and dropped off into slumber. Once when I tried to induce him to rest a little on the mat he was annoyed and said : ' If you can persuade angels to sleep, you will also persuade the zealous man.' "[4] Macarius of Alexandria made a yet more determined effort to equal the angels by doing without sleep altogether, and reached before long the very brink of lunacy.[5] The hermits at Scete slept on mats, with a bundle of papyrus reeds for a pillow[6]; others from the neighbourhood of Alexandria confined their sleep to a couple of hours before dawn.[7] At Tabennisi the time between evening prayers and midnight was set aside for sleep, but brethren who wished to practise vigils during those hours might do so. Some availed themselves of this privilege. The rest retired to their cells, whose doors were left open. They were allowed no pillows ; but in the great heats of summer they might sleep on the roofs.[8] Seats

---

[1] *Apoph. Patr.* P.G. lxv, c. 403. Greg. Naz. *Poema ad Hell,* P.G. xxxvii, c. 1455. *H.M.* 6. Theod. *Hist. rel.* 19. P.G. lxxxii, cc. 1427–30.
[2] *Euseb. H.E.* vi, 3.
[3] Ath. *V. Ant.* 5–7, P.L. lxxiii, c. 131.
[4] *H.L.* 2.
[5] Ib. 18.
[6] Cass., *Conl.* i, 23, p. 36.
[7] Cass., *Conl.* vii, 34, p. 214.
[8] *Reg.* 126. *Vita Pach.* 67. *Reg.* 81, 87, 107. *Alb.* 48, 52.

for sleeping and beds were a later development.[1]   If the
monks awoke during the night they prayed.   St. Basil says
merely that untimely and immoderate sleep is to be avoided,[2]
and we may be sure that a fairly liberal period for rest was
conceded to his monks.   St. Martin always slept on the bare
ground covered by a quilt of hair-cloth.   When visiting a
church on one occasion a bed of straw was prepared for him
in the sacristy and a fire was lighted beneath the room to
keep the floor warm.   St. Martin, however, had no desire for
a soft bed and pitched the straw away.   It fell, unfortunately,
on a spot which the fire from beneath made hot, and during
the night it became ignited, with consequences almost fatal
to the Saint.[3]   Vigils and hard beds were likewise the rule at
Lérins.[4]

At Iona the monks had beds, each provided with a pallet
(probably of straw) and a pillow.[5]   Colmcille himself slept on
a bare stone, and his pillow was of the same material.[6]   His
vigils, in the oratory or in remote parts of the island,
during the long winter nights, are commemorated by his
biographer.[7]   Where he led, the others would, of course,
follow.[8]

The amount of time available for sleep for those who wished
to take it would depend on the number or length of the
canonical hours.   At Iona it seems clear that the monks were
free to sleep from vespers until midnight,[9] a period which
in summer cannot have been very long, though in winter it
might reach some seven hours.   In other monasteries like
Bangor, where there was an extra office "at the beginning
of the night," the time available before midnight cannot
have been considerable.   At Bangor again, as in the Columban

---

[1] *H.L.* 32.   Sozomen, *H.E.* iii, 14.   Cf. Ladeuze, *Le cénob. pakh.*, p. 264.
[2] *Reg. fust. tract.* xxxii.
[3] Sulp. Sev. *Ep.* i,   *C.S.E.L.* i, p. 140.
[4] Hilar. Arel. *Sermo de Vita S. Hon.*, P.L. l. c. 1259 :   "fortissimos quosque
et recenti adhuc conversatione praevalidos in ieiuniis vigiliisque."
[5] *Adam.* ii, 30, p. 144 :   "infirmi ad lectulum stans."   Ib. iii, 23, p. 233 :
"in lectulo residet."
[6] Ib. iii, 23, p. 233 :   "ubi pro stramine nudam habebat petram, et pro
pulvillo lapidem."
[7] Ib. iii, 16, p. 219 :   "quantae et quales, ad beatum virum in hiemalibus
plerumque noctibus insomnem, et in locis remotioribus aliis quiescentibus
orantem, angelicae fuerint frequentationes."
[8] Examples from the lives of other Irish saints are given by Reeves, l.c.,
note g.
[9] *Adam.* iii 23 p. 233 :   Colmcille retires to bed after the "vespertinalem
Dominicae noctis missam," and rises when he hears the bell sound for the
midnight office.

monasteries abroad, the interval between the midnight office and the morning office must have been short (on the mornings of Saturday and Sunday, indeed, inconsiderable), but it is not certain that sleep was allowed during this interval. It is thus impossible to decide the exact amount of sleep which was permitted in any of the monasteries, but the presumption is that the amount was never liberal and in many places was exceedingly meagre. It was taken in the cells, but there was no objection on principle to a dormitory.[1]

(f)—Austerities.

St. Columban has a long chapter " on mortification,"[2] but strangely enough it deals exclusively with internal mortification of the will by obedience. Not a word is said about the more striking external practices which we call in general " asceticism." He does, indeed, mention practices of a milder kind—the cultivation of a peaceful disposition, restraint of the tongue, the undertaking of no journey without permission —but the emphasis is obviously laid on the spirit of ready and joyful obedience, rooted in true humility. The conclusion is not that St. Columban was opposed to bodily penance even of the most severe kind, but that he wished his monks to be guided in this, as in all things else, by their superiors. If the monks had made progress sufficient to justify their aspiring to the anachoretical way of life, and if allowed to retire to the desert, they might take the law into their own hands. Whilst they were members of the monastic community their first duty was to obey.

Ascetical exercises of what may be called the natural order of course abounded in every Irish rule.[3] Fasts were many, food was poor and scarce ; work was hard and humiliating ; the time for sleep was short ; much of the night was spent in public prayer ; conversation with human kind, even with the brethren, was reduced to small dimensions. Then there were penances, including castigation with a rod or strap, for failure to fulfil obligations. St. Columban punished involuntary as well as voluntary failings, and we may be sure that he was not alone in this respect. The humble acceptance and loyal execution of superiors' commands was in itself an exercise

---

[1] Jonas, V. Col. ii, 19, p. 272 : there was a dormitory at Faremoutiers.
[2] Reg. Mon. Cf. ix, p. 384.
[3] Cf. the foregoing sections.

which might call for heroic sanctity. Relaxations, finally, like leave to talk and a slight improvement in food, were of the least exciting kind. The ordinary life of the Irish monk was thus as mortified as could well be imagined, and if it wa- at the same time a happy life the happiness was admittedly that of martyrdom.[1]

To the mortification inseparable from the monastic profession voluntary austerities of a more trying kind were added. The most common of these was the practice of praying with extended arms, a very tiring exercise, all the more esteemed because it represented the attitude of the Crucified. So general was the custom in Ireland that a special word crosfigell (from crucis vigilia) was invented to denote it.[2] From the use of figell (vigilia) we may conclude that the exercise was regarded as particularly appropriate to private prayer performed during the night hours. A cognate type of mortification consists in repeated genuflexions, either independently or at intervals between psalms or fixed prayers.[3] Ascetic immersions, or the standing naked in cold water for a considerable time, are likewise mentioned.[4] Some carried the war against the Old Adam to such lengths that they allowed animals or worms to devour their flesh.[5] Outlandish mortifications, such as that attributed to Finnchua of Brí Gobann (said to have remained suspended from iron hooks for seven years),[6] occur in the later lives. Parallels for these are found in the lives of the early hermits.[7] There is no reason to believe

---

[1] Reg. Mon. ix, p. 385 : " neque hanc martyrii felicitatem poterat conplere quis. . ." It may be noted that in the old Irish homily on martyrdom, white martyrdom (the lowest form) consists in external mortification, like renuncia tion, fasting and labour ; blue martyrdom (the second form) consists in internal mortification or triumph over the will and inclinations ; whilst red martyrdom (the highest form) is actual death by violence for Christ's sake. (Thes. Pal. ii, p. 247.)

[2] Cf. Dom Gougaud, Dev. and Ascet. Practices, p. 10–12. La prière les bras en crois (Rassegna gregoriana vii, 1908, cc. 345–6). Chrét. celt., p. 98–9. Best in Ériu, i, p. 105.

[3] Gougaud, Chrét. celt., p. 97–8.

[4] Gougaud, Dev. and Ascet. Practices, pp. 159–178.

[5] V. Trip., p. 242. Lism. L., p. 89. Martyr. Oeng., p. 42, 44. Cf. also Plummer, V.S.H. Introd., p. cxvi, n. 14.

[6] Lism. L., p. 88. Martyr. Oeng., p. 246.

[7] H.L. 11 : " Ammonius, to keep down desire, heated irons and applied them to his body." Ib. 18 : " Macarius spent six months in a marsh infested by mosquitos. He looked so hideous on his return that he was recognised by his voice only." Ib. : " Owing to the excess of his asceticism, the hairs of his beard did not even sprout." Ib.38 : " Evagrius spent a winter's night in a well." Ib. 43 : "Adolius was so thin that he was suspected of being a phantom." Ib. 48 : " Eustathius's body had become so dried up that the sun shone through his bones."

that they were ever frequent, or even that they would have met with approval from the great founders like St. Columban, who lauds discretion as a most necessary virtue in the monk, and notes that virtue lies in the centre between two opposing poles of excess.

(g)—*Sickness, Death and Burial.*

In Irish monasteries, as in all others,[1] special care was taken of the sick brethren. A pitiful account is given by Jonas of the opening days in Annegray, when one of St. Columban's followers fell sick with fever and there was no food or medicine of any kind to give him.[2] The great patriarch and the other brethren could but fast and pray, and this they did until relief came. Later a private attendant from among the monks assists a sick brother in his last illness.[3] Colmcille, too, is found more than once at a sick brother's bedside.[4] Even the sick who had no connection with the monastery were looked after with kindness by the monastic brethren.[5] This tender consideration for the sick and infirm became a feature of Irish monastic tradition.[6]

When all human efforts had failed, and the hour of death was seen to be approaching, the monk was exhorted to prepare his soul for the coming journey.[7] The very nature of his life made it unlikely that he would have anything upon his conscience to trouble him before his departure from the world, but, if he had, an opportunity of confession would be afforded him. Then followed that most solemn of death-bed ceremonies, the administration of Holy Viaticum to the dying brother.[8] The abbot himself would officiate at this duty.[9] If it were he, however, who happened to be dying, one of his friends from a neighbouring monastery might be invited to do him that service.[10] Then the dying man, if

---

[1] *H.L.* 13. *Reg. Pach. Praef.* 5, Ib. 42, 50. *Vita Pach.* 34. *Alb.* 24, 25, 30. St. Jer. *Ep.* 22, 35, p. 199. *St. Aug. Ep.* 211, p. 368. *Bas. Reg. fus. tract.* xix, lv.
[2] Jonas, *V. Col.* i, 7, p. 164.
[3] Ib. 17, p. 184.
[4] *Adam.* ii, 30, p. 144 ; iii, 6, p. 203.
[5] Especially the lepers. Cf. *V.S.H.* i, p. 193. Plummer, *Introd.,* p. cx, n. 9.
[6] *Ériu,* vii, p. 146, § 5.
[7] Jonas, *V. Col.* ii, 11, p. 258.
[8] *V.S.H.* i, 73, 199, 215, 233, 257, etc.
[9] Jonas, *V. Col.* i, 17, p. 184.
[10] *V.S.H.* i, p. 257 ; ii, 20, 58, etc.

able, gave a farewell kiss to all and intoned an antiphon for
the departing.[1]

St. Ciarán of Clonmacnois, when the hour of his decease
was approaching, " commanded that he should be carried
outside, out of the house, and, looking up into heaven, he
said : ' Hard is this way, and this needs must be.' To him
the brethren said : ' We know that nothing is difficult for
thee, father ; but we unhappy men must greatly fear this
hour.' And being carried back into the house, he raised his
hand and blessed his people and clergy ; and having received
Holy Communion, he gave up the ghost. And lo ! angels
filled the way between heaven and earth, rejoicing to meet
St. Ciarán."[2] Such holy deathbeds were a delight to the
brethren, who crowded round the bedside, singing psalms,
and aiding, as well as they could, the dying brother in his
last agony.[3]

When the final moment had come and gone there would
be no tears, for the day was, in fact, a natal day,[4] when the
brother was born to a new life and had taken his place in his
real home in heaven. Sighs might, however, be permitted as
a tribute of affection[5] to the deceased. The Office for the Dead
would begin at once,[6] but might continue for three days,
during which period the praises of God were sung in many
psalms.[7] One Mass or more would also be celebrated, and
the same would be done in neighbouring monasteries where
the dead man was known and honoured.[8] Meanwhile the
body, wrapped in linen cloths, would remain laid out in its
dead owner's cell.[9] When the moment for burial arrived it
was borne thence with psalms and prayers to the hallowed
earth of the monastic cemetery,[10] there to await the resurrection
among so many of the holy brethren.[11] Thirty days after the

---

[1] Jonas, V. Col. ii, 25, p. 291-2.
[2] V.S.H. i, p. 215. Cf. Lism. L., p. 132 (l.4450 ff) and the death of Blesilla.
St. Jer. Ep. 39, 1, p. 295.
[3] Cf. Bede, H.E., ed. Plummer i, p. 374-9.
[4] Adam. ii, 45, p. 182 ; iii, 11, p. 210.
[5] Sulp. Sev. Ep. iii, p. 150 : " si quidem fides flere prohiberet gemitum
tamen extorquebat adfectus."
[6] Jonas, V. Col. ii, 20, p. 276. Ib. 17, p. 270.
[7] Adam. iii, 23, p. 239: " ternis diebus et totidem noctibus honorabiles
rite explentur exequiae." V.S.H. ii, p. 105.
[8] Ib. iii, 11, p. 210 ; 12, p. 211.
[9] Adam. iii, 23, p. 239.
[10] Ib. Cf. Sulp. Sev. Ep. iii, C.S.E.L. i, p. 150-1.
[11] Adam. ii, 39, p. 162-3 : " in uno meorum moreris monasteriorum et cum
electis erit pars tua meis in regno monachis, cum quibus in resurrectionem
vitae de somno mortis evigilabis." Cf. Wasserschl. I.K. xviii, 3, p. 56-7.

burial a commemoration Mass was celebrated,[1] and this was probably repeated at each recurring anniversary.[2] Did the soul need purgation it would be helped by these Masses, as also by the prayers of the devout, the alms given by Christians, the fasts performed by brethren and friends.[3] Names of those who had died with a reputation for extraordinary sanctity were entered in the missal, for commemoration at Mass.[4] Thus closed the career of the monk on earth. He had known much of the hardship, but none of the fever and the fret of life. He had reached his Master and his home, where he would abide now for eternity.

---

[1] Jonas, *V. Col.* ii, 12, p. 262 : " tricesimo die, cum eius commemorationem ex more ecclesiastico facere conaremus," etc.

[2] *Adam.* ii, 45, p. 182. Cf. Cass., *Conl.* xix, 1, p. 534.

[3] Wasserschl. *I.K.* xv, 1, p. 42.

Cod. Salm., c. 460.

CHAPTER II

CONCLUSION

§ I

Unity of Irish Monastic Observance.

NUMEROUS as were the " Rules " in the Irish monasteries of the sixth century, the difference between them seems to have been confined to unimportant matters of detail. Cluain Eidnech and Bangor ranked as monasteries of especial severity; and there probably were others, for in the days of Gildas we find the problem of those who wished to pass from a mild to a stern rule or contrariwise exercising the minds of the monastic fathers. References, however, occur to the interference of neighbouring abbots when a particular custom in another establishment did not meet with their approval; and it is evident that by A.D. 600 the manner of observance in all the Irish monasteries was substantially the same. It is thus possible to speak of a general Irish observance and to consider it as a whole, abstracting from those minor variations of mere local interest which lie quite outside the main lines of development.

§ 2

How far derived from earlier sources.

Not only the fundamental principles of monasticism, but all features of the monastic institute as it was known in Ireland within the period under discussion belong in origin to a much earlier date. Progress from the purely eremitical to the semi-eremitical, and from the semi-eremitical to the cenobitical mode of life, had taken place in Egypt in the fourth century. The Tabennisiot congregation was more highly organized than that founded by St. Colmcille or St. Columban—in many respects, indeed, more highly organized than any monastic brotherhood known in the Church until the rise of Cluny. In these early settlements the three-fold division of the day into hours assigned for psalmody, reading and work was already indicated. One meal a day at the ninth hour was the rule, from which it was unusual to diverge. Tabennisi was less rigorous in matters of food, clothes and

404

sleep than the semi-eremitical colonies ; but it emphasised obedience as one of the most necessary monastic virtues. Even in Tabennisi the close association of monasticism with the desert was not altogether lost to view, for individualism was not entirely repressed. To this early period, too, belongs the introduction of monasteries for women.

From the days of Pachomius onwards the arrangement of cenobitical life remained essentially as he had left it, though with various additions and modifications, according to the character and needs of those who had adopted it. Thus Schenoudi of Atripe demanded from each monk a formal declaration in writing, and before witnesses, that he would observe the rule. He also admitted that the anachoretical way of life was superior to the cenobitical, and therefore allowed monks of approved virtue to retire to the hermitage. In the monasteries founded in Palestine by St. Jerome, Rufinus and Melania the Elder, the Pachomian foundations were taken as a model, but the copying of manuscripts seems to have been the only form of manual work, and psalmody took place at regular intervals many times during the day and night. In Syria and Mesopotamia hermits were much more common than cenobites, and the life was penitential even to extravagance. St. Basil in Cappadocia set his face against Syrian habits and adopted the Pachomian system, repressing, however, all individualism in the matter of austerity and ascetical exercises. For him cenobitism was the highest form of life. He endeavoured to bring into his monasteries a kindlier family spirit than had ever reigned in Tabennisi or in its dependencies. He was also anxious that monasteries should have schools where boys might be trained in godliness ; and that his monks should devote themselves to the service of the sick and suffering, observing thus the second great commandment of Christianity and participating in the traditional charity of the Church.

At Vercelli under St. Eusebius, and Hippo under St. Augustine, the clerical and the cenobitical states of life were united, for the clergy took upon themselves monastic obligations. Elsewhere in Italy and Africa there were monasteries of the ordinary Pachomian type. St. Martin, at Tours, combined the life of a monk with that of a missionary preacher. His settlements at Marmoutier and Ligugé were semi-eremitical rather than cenobitical in character. Owing to his exertions new life was infused into religion in Gaul, and many of the country districts, till then completely pagan, were won to the Christian faith.

Honoratus at Lérins founded his monastery frankly after Egyptian models. The framework of his system was Pachomian, but much greater stress was laid upon solitude than at Tabennisi. Cassian's theory of the spiritual life gave support to this practice. The monastery proper was thus used for purposes of purgation, and when the monk had arrived at the stage where he was capable of uninterrupted contemplation he retired to the " desert " and lived there as an anchorite. The religious and moral perfection necessary before the monk could aspire to such heights was pursued within the monastery with great zeal. Poverty, chastity, obedience, fasts, vigils, Bible-reading, were practised as in Egypt. In liturgical prayer, and especially in the possession of beautiful hymns the monks of Lérins were in advance of the Egyptians. The insular situation of the monastery was of considerable advantage to it in an age of incursions and terrible unrest. Most important of all, however, was the development of a new learning based on the old learning of the rhetorical schools, but completely different in character. Not oratory was the aim, but profound knowledge of the Holy Writ and a better understanding of the truths of faith. In the first half of the fifth century Lérins was the holy isle *par excellence* of Europe.

Here St. Patrick studied and here he acquired that excellent knowledge of the Holy Scriptures and that solid grounding in Catholic teaching which stood him in good stead when he came to Ireland. He was, therefore, no ignorant man, though he was not trained in the artificial rhetoric of the schools which in his day was almost synonymous with learning. Many of those who are called his " monks " were doubtless formed in the same monastery, among them that Assicus who was placed as bishop and abbot at Ailfind and who showed his predilection for the anachoretical way of life by running away to Donegal, where he eluded the search of his monks for seven years. Not, however, until the first quarter of the sixth century did monasticism make progress worth recording in Ireland. This time, again, the impulse came from Lérins, if indirectly through the British monasteries closely connected with the Mediterranean foundation. This connection possibly goes back to the days of St. Patrick. It is found in the second half of the fifth century when the Briton, Faustus, was abbot of Lérins. The tradition coming from Lérins appears at Llanilltud, whence it passed to Llangarvan under Cadoc and to Gildas. These two British churchmen influenced St. Finnian of Clonard, with the result that the Lérins tradition crossed for the second time to Ireland. As the land was now Christian, the monastic institute was enabled to take root, and by the end of the sixth century it was supreme throughout the country. As at Lérins so in Ireland, moral and religious perfection is the aim; the anachoretical is held in higher esteem than the cenobitical form of life; and advanced studies, exegetical and theological in character (prepared for by a wide study of Latin authors, pagan as well as Christian), are a normal feature of monastic life. The Irish system of monasticism is thus remotely Egyptian, but hails more proximately from Lérins, whence it came at first directly through St. Patrick (but in circumstances so unfavourable that it made no lasting impression), then early in the sixth century indirectly through Britain, to enter upon a triumphant course that did not cease for centuries.

§3
How far original.

The elements of Irish monasticism are all found elsewhere, if nowhere all together. Original in Ireland is the combination of elements and the emphasis laid on some rather than others, with the result that the system has an individuality very distinctly its own. Surprising in the first place is the combination of apostolical and anachoretical ideals. The monk pines for the desert, where he hopes one day to settle permanently, yet meanwhile he has intense interest in the spiritual welfare of the world. He is ready and even anxious to perform the duties ordinarily entrusted to the secular clergy (who by their profession have to mix with men), and when he travels abroad to break the dearest ties that bind him to earth he cannot refrain from missionary work. St. Martin may have been his exemplar in this respect; Lérins certainly was not. For this reason again the abbots regularly, and many of the Irish monks, received ecclesiastical orders, yet no Irish monastery bore much resemblance to the communities ruled by St. Eusebius and St. Augustine. These were houses of clergy who happened to be monks; the Irish were communities of monks who happened in part to be clergy. The essence of monasticism might seem to be retirement from the world, contemplation, peace ; yet the very life-breath of Irish monasticism seems to be apostolic work for souls.

Severe bodily austerity is a marked feature of the Irish monastic system. This is found everywhere in Egypt, though reduced in the Pachomian foundations to a measure which could be borne without difficulty. In Ireland little effort at restraint can be discovered. The quantity of food and drink is reduced to the barest minimum, and its quality is expected to be extremely unappetising. Battling with sleep was a common form of asceticism ; but the amount of un-broken slumber which could have been enjoyed by the least fervent does not seem to have been considerable, for the number and length of the night offices of prayer put prolonged rest out of the question. Regulations regarding clothes and furniture were governed by the view that it was almost im-possible to exceed in poverty. Added to these mortifications were exposure to heat and cold, labours undertaken to wear down the body, various individual exercises of asceticism voluntarily undertaken. Again the desert was the goal held out to every monk, and if he failed to reach it during life he might at least abide there temporarily once or oftener in the year. Austerities of all sorts were expected to accompany these periods of lonely contemplation—fasts, vigils, exposure, nakedness, self-inflicted penances. The preoccupation with austerities which runs through all Irish ascetical writings even of a late period shows that this was the national tradition. Thus, though the body of Irish monasticism was predominantly cenobitical, the spirit which animated it was everywhere anachoretical.

Noteworthy, too, is the apparently matter-of-fact way in which zeal for studies, the higher as well as the lower, is worked into the Irish system. Such a union of hard study and hard discipline is unique, unless it be at Lérins, where the severity of the life led by the brethren is unknown to us. Its explana-tion in Ireland is probably to be sought in the native schools of druids, fáthi, filid, bards, which preceded Christianity. The monks were felt to be the successors to the two orders first mentioned of these, and thus were expected to apply themselves not only to religion, but also to the cultivation of the intellect. When they likewise took up the study of the native language and literature, their extraordinary position in the life of the country was assured. Owing to the Celtic, as distinct from the imperial, character of Irish civilisation, many small features of monastic life in Ireland have no parallels elsewhere. In a category by itself must be placed the prominence of the abbots as ecclesiastical rulers, a development which arose partly from the popularity of the monastic institute and partly, perhaps, from an ascetical fear of the worldly advantages then commonly attached to the episcopal office in Christian lands.

§4

(d)—Comparison with Benedictine observance.[1]

As the Irish and Benedictine observances came into conflict in England and Gaul in the seventh century, and the former was eliminated by the latter, it may be well to sketch briefly the chief differences between the two. St. Benedict (died after A.D. 547, about the same time as St. Finnian of Clonard) found before him in Italy a great body of monastic traditions going back ultimately to Egypt. In early life he was completely under the influence of these. Having left Rome as a youth somewhere about A.D. 500, he lived for a while with "holy men," then suddenly withdrew to a cave at Subiaco. For three years his life was that of an anchorite. He surpassed in his love for retirement the great majority of his Egyptian exemplars, for he spent three years evidently without Mass or Communion or any part whatever in the liturgical life of the Church. His whereabouts and his holy life becoming known, he was elected abbot of a monastery at Vicovaro. For unexplained reasons his failure in this office was complete, and he returned again to Subiaco. Disciples gathered about him, and a colony of anchorites after the Egyptian model was soon formed. According to the account left by St. Gregory the Great, a local priest persecuted the colony, and Benedict felt himself constrained to move to another site. Monte Cassino was chosen as the most suitable place for this purpose. A new monastery was built, with a basilica in honour of St. Martin, an oratory in honour of St. John the Baptist, a guest-house, workshops, and a place for books. Here St. Benedict wrote his Rule and here he died. About A.D. 581 Monte Cassino was sacked by the Lombards and its

---

[1] Butler, *Benedictine Monachism*. London, 1924. Hilpisch, *Geschichte des benediktinischen Mönchtums*. Freiburg i. Br., 1929. Delatte, *Commentaire sur la règle de Saint Benoit*. Paris, 1913.

community migrated to Rome, where a new monastery was
founded beside the Lateran. Nothing is known of this.
When, however, St. Gregory the Great, before he became
Pope, established the monastery of St. Andrew on the Coelian
Hill, he came into touch with the Benedictine monks, and
probably derived much from their institute.   With the
mission of St. Augustine to Canterbury the Benedictine Rule,
or some form of it, was brought to England, and, aided
mightily by the Popes, began to make headway there and
elsewhere.

St. Benedict, when he came to draw up his Rule at Monte
Cassino, felt it wise to depart from monastic tradition as then
known in a number of important respects.   His experience
at Subiaco and at Vicovaro had taught him that however
excellent the customs derived from Egypt might be in themselves, they certainly were not suited to the characters with
whom he lived in daily contact.   The rigours of Eastern
discipline were altogether beyond what Italians of the sixth
century would tolerate.   Leaving such rigours aside, St.
Benedict set himself to compose, in his own words, " a very
little rule for beginners."   " We are going," he says in the
Prologue, " to set up a school in God's service, in which we
hope we shall establish nothing harsh, nothing burthensome."
He speaks with admiration of the eremitical life, then, as we
have seen, commonly regarded as the most perfect realization
of the religious ideal, but for this very reason he does not deal
with it further.   He legislates only for cenobites, those " who
serve as Christ's soldiers under a rule or abbot," and who are
determined to persevere in the monastery until death.   On
this point he lays great weight, much greater than any of his
predecessors among the monastic founders ;   much greater
than the Irish fathers, who did not think themselves justified
in holding back a monk who wished to transfer himself to a
monastery where the discipline was more austere.   The
monastery for St. Benedict is to be a family where all the
members persevere till death.   As a school of God's service
it is to have three main duties—self-renunciation, prayer,
work.   In keeping with this principle that there should be
" nothing harsh, nothing burthensome," these duties were
to be none too onerous.   The word " mortification " is
studiously avoided.   In the matter of diet, St. Benedict
allows each monk a pound of bread daily, two dishes of cooked
food, and a third of fruit or young vegetables, a menu that

would have shocked the Fathers of the desert and have sounded incredible to Irish ears. He allows also more than half-a-pint of wine every day. During the greater part of the year his monks enjoyed more than eight hours of unbroken sleep every night ; during the summer months five or six hours by night, and a siesta by day. Not only a blanket, but a mattress, coverlet and pillow were permitted, so that the monk could rest in comfort. New clothes are to be provided before the old ones are worn out. Clothes are to fit properly and must be warmer in winter, lighter in summer. Two cowls or cloaks, a liberal supply of shoes, socks and similar articles were also added, in contrast with the utter poverty and nakedness which was the Egyptian (and the Irish) ideal. The elements of monasticism preserved by the Saint are all traditional. Thus he draws on the writings of Cassian and St. Basil, the monastic letter of St. Augustine, the Apophthegmata or Sayings of the Fathers, the Latin translation of the Rule of Pachomius, and other early sources in the composition of his Rule. Having, however, deliberately discarded eremitical life, severe bodily austerities, individualistic spirituality and prolonged psalmody (for the chanting of the psalter at the canonical hours occupied a whole week, though recited from beginning to end by Columban's monks at the two morning offices of Saturday and Sunday), and centralized organization after the Pachomian model (adopted, too, by St. Colmcille and St. Columban), St. Benedict in his Rule is said rightly by Dom Butler to represent less a development than a revolution.

If, again, the Benedictine Rule is remarkable for its spirit, it is no less remarkable for its form. It is really the first monastic rule that can be called genuine legislation. Before his time all the documents designated " Rules " are but brief treatises on the monastic virtues, arranged without much order, with directions here and there on isolated points of conduct. St. Basil's " Rules " are replies to questions of the most varied kinds, many of them having no connection whatever with monasticism. St. Columban's " Rule for Monks " deals wholly with the fundamental virtues, and his " Domestic Rule " is a mere penal code. Monasteries at this period were, in fact, ruled by custom, not by law, and great latitude was left to the abbot, who could make his personality felt in a very effective way. St. Benedict's Rule changes all this. It is legislative in form and well ordered, a phenomenon

due, as has often been suggested, to the Saint's membership
of a race that excelled all others of the ancient world in the
making of laws. Many points hitherto governed by custom
are definitely fixed by legal enactment in St. Benedict's
Rule. This, in consequence, tends to be supreme, whilst the
personality of the abbot, himself bound on every side by its
provisions, tends to recede into the background.

If we ask why the Benedictine observance, as fixed by the
Benedictine Rule, became supreme all over Europe and ousted
the Irish and other systems from the places where they had
long been in force, the reasons seem to be chiefly three. In
the first place, the comparative mildness of the Rule made a
wide and very natural appeal. Benedictine life was hard
enough, but it could not be compared in severity to discipline,
like the Irish, that preserved the harsher Egyptian tradition.
In the second place, it was more complete, for its seventy-three
chapters covered large fields entirely neglected by the earlier
fathers. This advantage, however, should not be unduly
stressed. Before St. Benedict's time the lack of legislation
on such questions as the election of abbot caused no undue
inconvenience, and after St. Benedict's time similar matters
were arranged for centuries in Ireland by custom, not by law.
Difficulties, of course, arose, but the same or greater troubles
are found in the Benedictine monasteries, legislation notwithstanding. In the third place, is the support given by the
Holy See to the Benedictine Rule, from the reign of St. Gregory
onwards. The importance of this has often been exaggerated,
but it certainly was very considerable. If we picture to ourselves St. Columban and his monks settled in the Eternal
City, in daily touch with a Pope like the Great St. Gregory,
and perhaps entrusted with a missionary enterprise to some
distant land like England, we realize somewhat what such
support could mean. This is a question on which the last
word has not yet been said.

In conclusion, two points of interest may be noted. The
older monastic tradition, abandoned by St. Benedict, made its
influence felt again in the later centuries, when the Benedictine
Rule was supreme upon the Continent. The reforms connected with the names of St. Benedict of Aniane and the
monks of Cluny are very largely a return to the Irish system,
though the combination of learning with austerity as a normal
feature of the reformed rule is absent. Secondly, the Irish
system was sufficiently strong in organization to survive at

home for almost seven centuries. When at last it collapsed and an influx of new religious life had to be sought from abroad, it was not the Benedictine Rule but the more austere Rule of the Cistercians that appealed to the Irish churchmen. Thus the fundamental attachment of Irishmen to their old system continued. The development of these points will not here be attempted, as it belongs properly to a work dealing with the later centuries.

BIBLIOGRAPHY

Author's Note

The author would like to express his gratitude to a former pupil in University College, Dublin, Miss Máire Kelly, now a distinguished member of the staff in the Library of Trinity College, Dublin. Without her help the Bibliography could not have been compiled.

Miss Kelly would like to acknowledge the generous assistance given to her not only by the Library staff of Trinity College but also by the Librarian of the Royal Irish Academy and the Assistant Secretary of the Royal Society of Antiquaries of Ireland.

ABBREVIATIONS

Anal. Bolland.	Analecta Bollandiana
IBL	Irish Book Lover
IER	Irish Ecclesiastical Record
IHS	Irish Historical Studies
JACAS	Journal of Ardagh and Clonmacnoise Antiquarian Society
JCHAS	Journal of the Cork Historical and Archaeological Society
JCLAS	Journal of the County Louth Archaeological Society
JDCHS	Down and Connor Historical Society's Journal
JGAHS	Journal of the Galway Archaeological and Historical Society
JKAS	Journal of the Kerry Archaeological Society
JRSAI	Journal of the Royal Society of Antiquaries of Ireland
NMAJ	North Munster Antiquarian Journal
RIA Proc.	Proceedings of the Royal Irish Academy
UJA	Ulster Journal of Archaeology
ZCP	Zeitschrift für celtische Philologie

Abate, G. 'La tomba del Ven. Giovanni Duns Scoto nella chiesa di S. Francesco a Colonia'. *Miscellanea francescana* 45.

Adams, R. F. G. 'Some New Notes on Fore'. *Ríocht na Midhe* 1, no. 1 (1955): 9–13.

Aigrain, René. 'L'apport de l'Irlande à la pensée chrétienne médiévale'. In *Le miracle irlandais*. Paris: Robert Laffont, 1956. Dublin: Clonmore and Reynolds, 1959.

Alton, E. H., et al. *Evangeliorum quattuor codex Cenannensis auctoritate Collegii Sacrosanctae et Individuae Trinitatis juxta Dublin auxilioque Bibliothecae Confederationis Helveticae.* Berne: Urs Graf-Verlag, 1950–51.

Amann, E. *L'époque carolingienne.* Paris: Blond et Gay, 1937.

Ancient Monuments Advisory Council for Northern Ireland. *A Preliminary Survey of the Ancient Monuments of Northern Ireland.* HMSO, 1940.

Anderson, Alan O. 'Ninian and the Southern Picts'. *Scottish Historical Review* 27: 25–47.

Anderson, Alan O., and Anderson, Marjorie O., ed. and trans. *Adomnan's Life of Columba.* London: Nelson, 1961.

Anderson, Marjorie O. 'Columba and Other Irish Saints in Scotland'. *Historical Studies* 5: 26–36.

Andrews, John. *Ireland in Maps: An Introduction with a Catalogue of an Exhibition Mounted in the Library of Trinity by the Geographical Society of Ireland.* Dublin: Dolmen Press, 1961.

Antheunis, L. 'Some Irishmen in Belgium in Past Centuries'. *IER* 81 (1954): 196–201.

Arbman, Holger. *The Vikings.* London: Thames and Hudson, 1961.

Ardill, J. R. *The Date of St Patrick.* Dublin: Church of Ireland, 1932.

——. *St. Patrick, A.D. 180.* London: John Murray. Dublin: Hodges, Figgis, 1931.

Artmann, H. C. *Der Schlüssel des heilige Patrick: religiöse Dichtungen der Kelten.* Salzburg: Otto Müller Verlag, 1959.

Ashe, Geoffrey. *Land to the West: St Brendan's Voyage to America.* London: Collins, 1962.

Ashley, Anne. *The Church in the Isle of Man.* London: St Anthony's Press, 1958.

Attwater, D. 'Some Saints of Cornwall'. *Old Cornwall* 7, fasc. 2: 53–72. Reprinted 1968.

Aubineau, M. *Codices Chrysostomici Graeci 1: Britanniae et Hiberniae.* Paris: Centre National de la recherche scientifique, 1968.

——. 'Glanes hagiographiques dans les manuscrits grecs de Grande-Bretagne et d'Irlande'. *Anal. Bolland.* 86 (1968): 323–31.

Auchmuty, J. J. 'Ireland and the Celtic Peoples in Toynbee's *Study of History*'. *Hermathena* 70: 39–64.

Bachellery, Édouard. 'Les gloses irlandaises du manuscrit Paris Latin 10290'. *Études Celtiques* 11 (1964–65): 100–30.

Bailey, Richard N. 'The Clogher Crucifixion: A Northumbrian Parallel and Its Implications'. *JRSAI* 93 (1963): 187–88.

Báiréad, Fearghus. 'St Patrick's Itinerary through County Limerick'. *NMAJ* 4: 68–73.

Baker, E. P. 'The Cult of St Oswald in Northern Italy'. *Archaeologia* 94 (1951): 167–94.

Bannerman, John. 'The Convention of Druim Cett'. *Scottish Gaelic Studies* 11 (1966): 114–32.

——. 'Notes on the Scottish entries in the early Irish annals'. *Scottish Gaelic Studies:* 149–70.

——. 'The Dál Riata and Northern Ireland in the Sixth and Seventh Centuries'. In *Celtic Studies: Essays in Memory of Angus Matheson.* Edited by James Carney and David Greene. London: 1968.

Barclay, Vera. *Saints by Firelight.* London: Sheed and Ward, 1931.

——. *Saints of these Islands.* London: Sheed and Ward, 1931.

Bardy, Gustave. 'Saint Columban et la Papauté d'après les Épitres'. *Mélanges Colombaniens* (1951): 103–18.

Barley, M. W., and Hanson, R. P. C., eds. *Christianity in Britain, 300–700: Papers Presented to the Conference on Christianity in Roman and Sub-Roman Britain held at the University of Nottingham, 1967.* Leicester: Leicester University Press, 1968.

Barrault, A. 'L'influence de Saint Colomban et de ses disciples dans les Monastères de la Brie'. *Mélanges Colombaniens* (1951): 197–208.

Barron, Thomas J. 'Stone Head, Clannaphillip Church, Co. Cavan'. *JRSAI* (1941): 113.

Barry, John. 'The Appointment of Coarb and Erenagh'. *IER* 93: 361–65.

——. 'The Coarb and the Twelfth-Century Reform'. *IER* 88: 17–25.

——. 'The Coarb in Medieval Times'. *IER* 89: 24–35.

——. 'The Distinction between Coarb and Erenagh'. *IER* 94: 90–5.

——. 'The Duties of Coarbs and Erenaghs'. *IER* 94: 211–18.

——. 'The Erenagh in the Monastic Irish Church'. *IER* 89: 424–32.

——. 'The Lay Coarb in Medieval Times'. *IER* 91: 27–39.

——. 'The Status of Coarbs and Erenaghs'. *IER* 94: 147–53.

Barth, Medard. 'Der Kult des heiligen Kolumban im Elsass'. *Mélanges Colombaniens* (1951): 259–75.

Battelli, Guido. 'La leggenda di Santa Colomba'. *Bibliofilia* 31 (1929).

Battiscombe, C. F., ed. *The Relics of St Cuthbert.* Oxford: Printed at the University Press for the Dean and Chapter of Durham Cathedral, 1956.

Bauer, Robert. *Irland: Die Insel der Heiligen und Rebellen.* Leipzig: Wilhelm Goldmann Verlag, 1938.

Bauerreiss, Romuald. *Kirchengeschichte Bayerns.* 4 vols. St Ottilien: Eos Verlag der Erzabtei, 1949–53.

——. *Kirchengeschichte Bayerns.* 2nd rev. ed. St Ottilien: Eos Verlag der Erzabtei, 1958.

——. 'Das Kleeblatt des heiligen Patrik'. *Seanchas Ardmhacha* 2 (1961–62): 92–94.

Bayley, A. R. 'Patrick's Purgatory'. *Notes and Queries* 182: 67–68.

Bell, Maurice, ed. 'Wilfric of Haselbury, by John, Abbot of Ford'. *Somerset Record Society* 47.

Bell, William, and Emerson, N. D., eds. *The Church of Irland, AD 432–1932: Report of the Church of Ireland Conference . . . 1932.* Dublin: Church of Ireland, 1932.

Berardis, Vincenzo. *Italy and Ireland in the Middle Ages.* Dublin: Clonmore and Reynolds, 1950.

Bergamaschi, A. 'Il penitenziale di S. Colombano'. *Mélanges Colombaniens* (1951).

Best, Richard Irvine. *The Commentary on the Psalms with Glosses in Old Irish, Preserved in the Ambrosian Library, Milan*. Dublin: Royal Irish Academy, 1936.

——. 'An Irish Version of the Somniale Danielis'. In *Féil-Sgríbhinn Eóin Mhic Néill* (1940), edited by John Ryan.

——, ed. *Martyrology of Tallaght*. London: Henry Bradshaw Society, 1931.

——. 'The Yellow Book of Lecan'. *Journal of Celtic Studies* 1: 190–92.

Best, Richard Irvine, and Bergin, Osborn, eds. *Lebor na Hudre: Book of the Dun Cow*. Dublin: Royal Irish Academy, 1929.

Best, Richard Irvine, Bergin, Osborn, and O'Brien, M. A., eds. *The Book of Leinster, formerly Lebar na Núachongbála*. 5 vols. Dublin: Institute for Advanced Studies, 1954–67.

Best, Richard Irvine, and MacNeill, Eoin, introduction by. *The Annals of Inisfallen, Reproduced in Facsimile from the Original Manuscript (Rawlinson B 503) in the Bodleian Library*. Dublin: Royal Irish Academy. London: Williams and Norgate, 1933.

Bibliotheca Celtica, 1929–33. New ser., vol. 1. Aberystwyth: University of Wales, 1939.

Bieler, Ludwig. 'Anecdotum Patricianum: Fragments of a Life of Patrick from MSS Cotton Vitellius E vii and Rawlinson B 479'. In *Measgra i gCuimhne Mhichíl Uí Chléirigh*.

——. 'An Austrian Fragment of a Life of St Patrick'. *IER* 95: 176–81.

——. 'Der Bibeltext des heiligen Patrick'. *Biblica* 28 (1947): 31–35, 236–63.

——. 'The Christianisation of the Insular Celts'. *Celtica* 8: 112–25.

——. 'Christianity in Ireland during the Fifth and Sixth Centuries: A Survey and Evaluation of Sources'. *IER* 101: 162–67.

——. 'The Chronology of St Patrick'. In *Old Ireland* (1965).

——. 'Codices Patriciani Latini'. *Anal. Bolland.* 63 (1945): 242–56.

——. *Codices Patriciani Latini: A Descriptive Catalogue of Latin Manuscripts relating to St Patrick*. Dublin: Institute for Advanced Studies, 1942.

——. 'Glimpses of St Patrick's Spiritual Life'. *Doctrine and Life* (March 1961): 126–32.

——. 'Hibernian Latin'. *Studies* 43 (1954): 92 ff.

——. 'Hibernian Latin and Patristics'. *Studia Patristica* 1 (1957).

——. 'The Humanism of St Colombanus'. *Mélanges Colombaniens* (1951): 95–102.

——. 'The Hymn of Secundinus'. *RIA Proc.* 55, sect. C: 117–27.

——. 'Insular Palaeography: Present State and Problems'. *Scriptorium* 3: 267–89.

——. 'Interpretationes Patricianae'. *IER* 107: 1–13.

——. *Ireland: Harbinger of the Middle Ages*. London: Oxford University Press, 1963.

——. 'Irish Manuscripts in Medieval Germania'. *Bulletin of the Irish Committee of Historical Sciences* 77: 2–4.

——. 'Irish Manuscripts in Medieval Germania'. *IER* 87: 161–69.

——, ed. *The Irish Penitentials*. Dublin: Institute for Advanced Studies, 1963.

——. *Irland: Wegbereiter des Mittelalters*. Olten, Lausanne, Freiburg: Urs Graf-Verlag, 1961.

——. 'The Island of Scholars'. *Revue du Moyen Âge Latin* 8 (1952): 213–34.

——. 'Die lateinische Kultur Irlands im Mittelalter in der Forschung des zwanzigsten Jahrhunderts'. *Historische Zeitschrift* 2 (1965): 260–76.

——. 'Letter of Credence by Donatus Magrahe, Prior of Lough Derg, for Nylanus O Ledan, Priest and Pilgrim'. *Clogher Record* 2 (1958): 257–59.

——, ed. *Libri Epistolarum Sancti Patricii Episcopi*. Dublin: Stationery Office, 1952.

——. 'Libri Epistolarum Sancti Patricii Episcopi: Addenda'. *Analecta Hibernica* 23: 313–15.

——. 'The Life and Legend of St Patrick'. *IER* 70 (1948): 1087–91.

——. *The Life and Legend of St Patrick: Problems of Modern Scholarship*. Dublin: Clonmore and Reynolds, 1949.

——. 'Manuscript Studies in Ireland, 1949–50'. *Scriptorium* 5: 330–31.

——. 'Manuscript Studies in Ireland, 1951–52'. *Scriptorium* 7: 323–25.

——. 'Manuscripts of Irish Interests in the Libraries of Scandinavia'. *Studies* 54 (1965): 252 ff.

——. 'The Mission of Palladius'. *Traditio* 6: 1–33.

——. 'The *Notulae* in the Book of Armagh'. *Scriptorium* 8: 89–97.

——. 'Palaeography and Spiritual Tradition'. *Studies* 29 (1940): 269 ff.

——. 'Patrician Studies in the *Irish Ecclesiastical Record*'. *IER* 102: 359–66.

——. 'Patriciology: Reflections on the Present State of Patrician Studies'. *Seanchas Ardmhacha* 4 (1961–62): 9–36.

——. ' "Patrick and the Kings": Apropos a New Chronology of St Patrick'. *IER* 85: 171–89.

——. 'The Place of Saint Patrick in Latin Language and Literature'. *Vigiliae Christianae* 6, no. 2 (1952).

——. 'The Problem of "Silva Focluti" '. *IHS* 3 (1942–43): 351–64. *IHS* 4: 104–5.

——. 'Recent Research on Irish Hagiography'. *Studies* 35: 230–38, 536–44.

——. 'St Patrick a Native of Anglesey?' *Éigse* 7 (1953): 129–31.

——. 'St Patrick and Rome'. In *The Irish Augustinians in Rome, 1656–1956*, edited by J. F. Madden. Rome: St Patrick's, 1956.

——. 'St Patrick and the British Church'. In *Christianity in Britain, 300–700* (1968): 123–30.

——. 'St Patrick and the Coming of Christianity'. In *A History of Irish Catholicism*, vol. 1, fasc. 1. Dublin: Gill, 1967.

——. 'St Patrick and the Irish People'. *Review of Politics* 10 (1948): 290–309.

——. 'St Patrick's Purgatory: Contributions towards an Historical Topography'. *IER* 93: 137–44.

——. 'St Severin and St Patrick: A Parallel'. *IER* 82: 161–66.

——. 'Sidelights on the Chronology of St Patrick'. *IHS* 6: 247–60.

——. 'Studies on the Text of Muirchú 1: The Text of MS Novara 77'. *RIA Proc.* 52, sect. C: 179–220.

[Bieler] 'Studies on the Text of Muirchú 2: The Vienna Fragments and the Tradition of Muirchú's Text'. *RIA Proc.* 59, sect. C: 181–195.

———. 'The Text Tradition of Dicuil's *Liber de mensura orbis terrae*'. *RIA Proc.* 64, sect. C: 1–31.

———. 'Towards an Interpretation of the So-called "Canones Wallici" '. In *Medieval Studies Presented to Aubrey Gwynn, SJ* (1961).

———. 'Trias Thaumaturga'. In *Father John Colgan, OFM*.

———. 'Versus Sancti Columbani: A Problem Re-stated'. *IER* 76: 376–82.

———. 'Vindiciae Patricianae: Remarks on the Present State of Patrician Studies'. *IER* 79: 161–85.

———. 'Was Palladius Surnamed Patricius?' *Studies* 32: 323–26.

———, trans. *The Works of St Patrick: St Secundinus' Hymn on St Patrick*. London: Longmans, Green. Westminster (Maryland): Newman Press, 1953.

Bieler, Ludwig, and Bischoff, Bernhard. 'Fragmente zweier früh-mittelalterlicher Schulbücher aus Glendalough'. *Celtica* 3: 211–20.

Bigelmair, Andreas. 'Die Gründung der mitteldeutschen Bistümer'. In *Sankt Bonifatius:* 247–87.

———. 'Die Passio des heiligen Kilian und seiner Gefahrten'. *Würzburger Diözesangeschichtsblätter* 14/15: 1–25.

Binchy, D. A. 'Ancient Irish Law'. *Irish Jurist,* new ser. 1 (1966): 84–92.

———. 'The Background of Early Irish Literature'. *Studia Hibernica* 1: 7–18.

———. 'Bretha Crólige'. *Ériu* 12, part I (1934).

———. 'The Date of the So-called "Hymn of Patrick" '. *Ériu* 20: 234–37.

———. 'The Fair of Tailtiu and the Feast of Tara'. *Ériu* 18: 113–38.

———. *The Linguistic and Historical Value of the Irish Law Tracts.* London: Humphrey Milford, 1944.

———. 'The Old-Irish Table of Penitential Commutations'. *Ériu* 19: 47–72.

———. 'The Passing of the Old Order'. *International Congress of Celtic Studies, Proceedings.* Dublin, 1959.

———. 'Patrick and his Biographers: Ancient and Modern'. *Studia Hibernica* 2 (1962): 7–173.

———. 'St Patrick's "First Synod" '. *Studia Hibernica* 8 (1968): 49–59.

Bischoff, Bernhard. 'Das griechische Element in der abendländischen Bildung des Mittelalters'. *Byzantinische Zeitschrift* 44: 27–55.

———. *Die südostdeutschen Schreibschulen und Bibliotheken in der Karolingerzeit,* vol. 1. Leipzig: Harrassowitz, 1940.

———. *Mittelalterliche Studien: Ausgewählte Aufsätze zur Schriftkunde und Literaturgeschichte.* Stuttgart: Hiersmann, 1966–67.

———. 'Theodulf und der Ire Cadac-Andreas'. *Historisches Jahrbuch der Görresgesellschaft* 74: 92–98.

———. 'Eine verschollene Einteilung der Wissenschaften'. *Archives d'histoire doctrinale et litteraire du moyen-âge* 33 (1958): 5–20.

———. 'Wendepunkte in der Geschichte der lateinischen Exegese im Frühmittelalter'. *Sacris Erudiri* 6 (1954): 189–281.

———. 'Zur Frühgeschichte des mittelalterlichen Chirographum'. *Archivalische Zeitschrift* 50/51: 297–300.

Bischoff, Bernhard, and Hofmann, Josef. *Libri Sancti Kyliani: die würzburger Schreibschule und die Dombibliothek im VIII und IX Jahrhundert.* Würzburg: Schöningh, 1952.

Bittermann, Helen R. 'The Influence of Irish Monks on Merovingian Diocesan Organization'. *American Historical Review* 40 (1935): 232–45.

Blanke, F. *Columban und Gallus: die Urheschichte des schweizerischen Christentums.* Zürich: Fretz and Wasmuth, 1940.

——. 'Neue Beobachtungen zum Missionswerk Columbans des Jüngeren: Columban in Bregenz'. *Evangelisches Missions-Magazin* 97 (1953): 165–80.

——. 'Neue Beobachtungen zum Missionswerk Columbans des Jüngeren: In Wangen und Arbon'. *Evangelisches Missions-Magazin* 6: 172–86.

——. 'Neue Beobachtungen zum Missionswerk Columbans des Jüngeren: Von Metz bis Tuggen'. *Evangelisches Missions-Magazin* 95 (1951): 164–79.

Bliss, A. J. 'The Inscribed Slates at Smarmore (Co. Louth)'. *RIA Proc.* 64, sect. C: 33–60.

Blouet, M. le Chanoine. 'The Coffret of Mortain'. In *The Miracle of Ireland,* edited by Daniel-Rops (1959).

Bollandistes, Société des, eds. *Bibliotheca hagiographica latina antiquae et mediae aetatis.* Brussels: Société des Bollandistes, 1898–1901. New impression 1949.

Bolton, Charles A. 'Centenary of St Aidan, Irish Apostle to the Anglo-Saxons'. *IER* 76: 105–10.

——. 'The Saint on Croagh Patrick'. *IER* 70: 681–86.

——. 'St Patrick and the Easter Fire'. *IER* 69: 215–20.

——. 'St Patrick's Breastplate: An Interpretation'. *IER* 75: 226–31.

Bonser, Wilfred. *An Anglo-Saxon and Celtic Bibliography.* Oxford: Blackwell, 1957.

Booth, H. C. 'The Culdees'. *Ars Quatuor Coronatorum* 57: 23–70.

Bórd Fáilte Éireann. *National Monuments of Ireland.* Dublin, 1964.

Bourniquel, Camille. *Ireland.* Trans. by John Fisher. London: Vista, 1960.

——. *Irlande.* Paris: Editions du Seuil, 1955.

Bouyer, Louis. *The Meaning of the Monastic Life.* London: Burns and Oates, 1957.

Bowen, E. G. 'The Celtic Saints in Cardiganshire'. *Ceredigion: Journal of the Cardiganshire Antiquarian Society* (1950).

——. 'The Irish Sea in the Age of the Saints'. *Studia Celtica* 4: 56–71.

——. *Saints, Seaways and Settlements in the Celtic Lands.* Cardiff: University of Wales Press, 1969.

——. 'The Settlements of the Celtic Saints in South Wales'. *Antiquity* 19 (1945): 175–86.

——. *The Settlements of the Celtic Saints in Wales.* Cardiff: University of Wales Press, 1954.

——. 'The Travels of the Celtic Saints'. *Antiquity* 18 (1944): 16–28.

Boylan, P. *The Book of the Congress, Dublin, 1932.* Wexford: John English, 1934.

Boyle, Alexander. 'Saint Ninian: Some Outstanding Problems'. *Innes Review* 19: 57–70.

Brady, John. 'Early Christian Meath'. *Ríocht na Midhe* 1, no. 4 (1958): 5–13.

——. 'The Nunnery of Clonard'. *Ríocht na Midhe* 2, no. 2: 4–7.

——. 'The Origin and Growth of the Diocese of Meath'. *IER* 62 (1949): 1–13, 166–76.

——. 'St Patrick's Well'. *Ríocht na Midhe* 3: 218.

Breathnach, R. A. 'The Early Irish Muse'. *Studies* 46 (1957): 340 ff.

Bringmann, Rudolf. *Geschichte Irlands: Schicksalsweg eines Volkes.* Bonn: Athenäum-Verlag, 1953.

Brittain, M. F. *The Medieval Latin and Romance Lyric to AD 1300.* Cambridge: Cambridge University Press, 1937.

Brod, Walter M. 'Der St Kilians-Kalendar des Stiftes Neumünster'. In *Heiliges Franken* (1952).

Broderick, James. *A Procession of Saints.* London: Burns and Oates, 1949.

Bromwich, Rachel. 'The Character of the Early Welsh Tradition'. In *Studies in Early British History,* edited by Nora K. Chadwick.

Brooke, Christopher. *Europe in the Central Middle Ages, 962–1154.* London: Longmans, 1964.

Brooks, E. St John. 'Irish Daughter Houses of Glastonbury'. *RIA Proc.* 56, sect. C (1954): 287–95.

Brophy, E. F. 'Three Carlow Monasteries: Augha, Clonmore and St Mullins'. *Carloviana* 1, no. 16 (1967): 9–13.

Brophy, P. J. 'St Patrick's Other Island'. *IER* 75: 243–46.

Browne, Arthur C. L. *The Origin of the Grail Legend.* Cambridge (Mass.): Harvard University Press, 1943.

Brown, Stephen J. 'The High Crosses of Great Britain and Ireland'. *IER* 78: 285–88.

Bruckner, Albert. 'Einige Bemerkungen zur Erforschung des früh-mittelalterlichen Heiligenkultes in der Schweiz'. In *Studi di paleografia, diplomatica, storia e araldica in onore di Cesare Manaresi.* Milan: A. Giuffrè, 1953.

Buchanan, R. H. 'Corbelled Structures in Lecale, County Down'. *UJA* 19 (1956): 92–112.

Buchberger, M. *Lexikon für Theologie und Kirche.* Freiburg-im-Breisgau: Herder, 1960.

Bulletin des relations artistiques France-Allemagne. Numéro spécial: l'Architecture Monastique. Mayence, May 1951.

Bulloch, James B. E. *The Life of the Celtic Church.* Edinburgh: Saint Andrew Press, 1963.

Bullough, D. A. 'Columba, Adomnan and the Achievement of Iona'. *Scottish Historical Review* 43: 111–30; 44: 17–33.

Burckhardt, Titus. 'Considérations sur un évangéliaire irlandais: le Livre de Kells'. *Scriptorium* 3: 155–158.

Busch, H., and Lohse, B., eds. *Romanesque Sculpture.* London: Batsford, 1962.

Büttner, Heinrich. 'Amorbach und die Pirminlegende'. *Archiv für mittelrheinische Kirchengeschichte* 5: 102–7.

Byrne, Francis Joseph. 'Early Irish Society'. In *The Course of Irish History* (1967).

——. 'Ireland before the Norman Invasion'. *IHS* 16: 1–14.

——. 'The Ireland of St Columba'. *Historical Studies* 5: 37–58.

Cahill, E. 'The Celts and the Gaels'. *IER* 46 (1935): 239–56.

——. 'Influence of Irish on Medieval Europe'. *IER* 46 (1935): 464–76.

——. 'Irish in the Danish and Pre-Norman Period'. *IER* 47 (1936): 337–54.

——. 'Irish in the Early Middle Ages'. *IER* 46 (1935): 363–76.

Calvez, Hervé. *Les grands saints Bretons.* Grenoble: Arthaud, 1936.

Campbell, M. A., ed. *Athelwulf: De abbatibus.* Oxford: Clarendon Press, 1967.

Cappuyns, Maïeul. *Jean Scot Érigène, sa vie, son oeuvre, sa pensée.* Louvain: Abbaye du Mont César; Paris: Desclée, 1933.

Carey, F. M. 'The Scriptorium of Reims during the Archbishopric of Hincmar (845–882)'. In *Classical and Mediaeval Studies in Honor of Edward Kennard Rand,* edited by L. W. Jones. New York: The Editor, 1938.

Carney, James. 'Comments on the Present State of the Patrician Problem'. *IER* 92 (1959): 1–40.

——. 'The Deeper Level of Early Irish Literature'. *Capuchin Annual* 36: 160–71.

——, ed. *Early Irish Poetry.* Cork: Mercier Press, 1965.

——. 'The Ó Cianáin Miscellany'. *Ériu* 21: 122–47.

——. 'Old Ireland and Her Poetry'. In *Old Ireland* (1965).

——. *The Poems of Bláthmac Son of Cú Brettan together with the Irish Gospel of Thomas and a Poem on the Virgin Mary.* Dublin: Irish Texts Society, 1964.

——. *The Problem of St Patrick.* Dublin: Institute for Advanced Studies, 1961.

——. 'Sedulius Scottus'. In *Old Ireland* (1965).

——. *Studies in Irish Literature and History.* Dublin: Institute for Advanced Studies, 1955.

——. 'Two Old Irish Poems: The Irish Gospel of St Thomas, and On the Virgin Mary'. *Ériu* 18: 1–43.

Carney, James, and Green, David. eds. *Celtic Studies: Essays in Memory of Angus Mathieson, 1912–1962.* London: Routledge and Kegan Paul, 1968.

Carney, Maire, 'Inisfallen, Home of sanctity of Learning'. *Assissi* (1940).

——. 'The Works of the Sixth Day'. *Ériu* 21: 148–66.

Carpentier, Paul. *Saint Laurent O'Toole, Archevêque de Dublin (1128–1180): La Conquête anglaise en Irlande.* Paris: J. Gabalda, 1953.

Carthage, Father, OCSO. *The Story of St Carthage, otherwise Saint Mochuda.* Dublin: Browne and Nolan, 1937.

Carty, Francis. *Irish Saints in Ten Countries.* Dublin: Duffy, 1942.

——. *Two and Fifty Irish Saints.* Dublin: Duffy, 1941.

Catrin, Paul. 'L'influence colombanienne à l'abbaye de Maroeuil-en-Artois'. *Mélanges Colombaniens* (1951): 243–46.

Cayre, Fulbert. 'Irish Spirituality in Antiquity'. In *The Miracle of Ireland,* edited by Daniel-Rops (1959).

Celtic Studies, International Congress of. *Proceedings, 1959: The Impact of the Scandinavian Invasions on the Celtic-speaking Peoples.* Dublin: Institute for Advanced Studies, 1962.

Cerbelaud-Salagnac, Georges. 'The Monasteries of Ireland: Nurseries of Saints'. In *The Miracle of Ireland,* edited by Daniel-Rops (1959).

——. *Saint Patrick, Apostle of Ireland,* translated from the French by Fergus Murphy. Dublin: Clonmore and Reynolds, 1959.

Cerbelaud-Salagnac, Georges, and Cerbelaud-Salagnac, Bernadette. *Irlande île des saints.* Paris: Fayard, 1961. *Ireland Isle of Saints,* translated from the French by the Earl of Wicklow. Dublin: Clonmore and Reynolds, 1966.

Chadwick, H. M. 'The End of Roman Britain'. In *Studies in Early British History* (1954).

——. *Early Scotland.* Cambridge: Cambridge University Press, 1949.

Chadwick, Nora K. *The Age of the Saints in the Early Celtic Church.* Oxford: Oxford University Press, 1963.

——. 'Bede, St Colmán and the Irish Abbey of Mayo'. In *Celt and Saxon* (1963).

——. 'The Celtic Background of Anglo-Saxon England'. *Yorkshire Celtic Studies* 3: 13–32.

——. *Celtic Britain.* London: Thames and Hudson, 1964.

——. *The Celts.* London: Penguin, 1970.

——. 'The Colonization of Brittany from Celtic Britain'. *Proceedings of the British Academy* 51 (1965): 235–99.

——. 'Early Culture and Learning in North Wales'. In *Studies in the Early British Church* (1958).

——. 'Intellectual Life in West Wales in the Last Days of the Celtic Church'. In *Studies in the Early British Church* (1958).

——. 'The Lost Literature of Celtic Scotland'. *Scottish Gaelic Studies* 7: 115–183.

——. *Poetry and Letters in Early Christian Gaul.* London: Bowes, 1955.

——. 'St Ninian: A Preliminary Study of Sources'. *Transactions of the Dumfrieshire and Galloway Natural History and Antiquarian Society* 17 (1959).

——, ed. *Studies in Early British History.* Cambridge: Cambridge University Press, 1954.

——. 'The Vikings and the Western World'. *International Congress of Celtic Studies, Proceedings.* Dublin: 1959.

Chadwick, Nora K., et al. *Celt and Saxon: Studies in the Early British Border.* Cambridge: Cambridge University Press, 1963.

——, et al. *Studies in the Early British Church.* Cambridge: Cambridge University Press, 1958.

Chadwick, Owen. 'The Evidence of Dedication in the Early History of the Welsh Church'. In *Studies in Early British History* (1954).

——. *John Cassian: A Study in Primitive Monasticism.* Cambridge: Cambridge University Press, 1950.

——. *Western Asceticism*. London: S.C.M. Press, 1958.

Champneys, Arthur. *Irish Ecclesiastical Architecture*. London and Dublin, 1910. Reprint Shannon: Irish University Press, 1971.

Chappatte, Marcel. 'Un disciple de Colomban: Ursanne'. *Mélanges Colombaniens* (1951): 385–91.

Chauviré, Roger. *Histoire de l'Irlande*. Paris: Presses Universitaires de France, 1949.

Christiani, M. le Chanoine. 'St Patrick and the Christian Origins of Ireland'. In *The Miracle of Ireland,* edited by Daniel-Rops (1959).

Christmann, Ernst. 'St Pirminius und Pirminiuslande im Licht der Namenforschung'. *Archiv für mittelrheinische Kirchengeschichte* 5: 77–101.

Chute, Desmond. 'On St Colomban of Bobbio'. *Downside Review* 67 (1949): 170–82.

Clarke, Michael. 'The Abbey, Wicklow'. *JRSAI* 73 (1943): 1–14.

Coccio, E. M. 'La cultura irlandese precarolina'. *Studi Medievali* 8 (1967): 257–420.

Coens, Maurice. 'Les Vies de S. Cunibert de Cologne et la tradition manuscrite'. *Annal. Bolland.* 47 (1929): 338–68.

Cohausz, Alfred. 'St Kilian Mitpatron des Erzbistums Paderborn'. *Heiliges Franken* (1952).

Colgan, John, ed. *Acta Sanctorum Veteris et Majoris Scotiae seu Hiberniae Sanctorum Insulae*. Dublin: Stationery Office, 1948. (Reflex facsimile reprint of 1645 edition published at Louvain.)

Colgrave, Bertram. 'The Earliest Saints' Lives Written in England'. *Proceedings of the British Academy* 44 (1958): 35–60.

——. *Two Lives of St Cuthbert: A Life by an Anonymous Monk and Bede's Prose Life*. Cambridge: Cambridge University Press, 1940.

Colum, Padraic. *The Legend of St Columba*. London: Sheed and Ward, 1936.

Concannon, Helena. 'Jonas of Bobbio', *Studies* 39 (1950): 301 ff.

——. *The Queen of Ireland: An Historical Account of Ireland's Devotion to the Blessed Virgin*. Dublin: Gill, 1938.

——. 'Silva Focluti, Silva uluti, or Silva Virgulti?' In *Féil-Sgríbhinn Eóin Mhic Néill* (1940).

——. *The Blessed Eucharist in Irish History*. Dublin: Browne and Nolan, 1932.

——. *Saint Patrick: His Life and Mission*. Dublin: Talbot Press, 1931.

Connellan, M. J. 'Airtech's Western Boundary'. *IBL* 31: 125–6.

——. 'Loch Airill'. *JACAS* 2 (1946): 49–51.

——. 'St Brocaidh of Imliuch Brocadha'. *JGAHS* 23: 138–47.

——. 'St Muadhnat of Kill Muadhnat'. *JGAHS* 21: 56–62.

——. 'St Patrick's Two Crossings of the Shannon'. *JACAS* 12: 78–84.

——. 'St Raoilinn of Teampaill Raoileann'. *JGAHS* 20: 145–50.

——. 'Sliabh ua nAilealla and Bearnas ua nAilealla'. *JRSAI* 80: 237–41.

——. 'Three Patritian Bishops and Their Seats in Airteach'. *JGAHS* 24: 125–29.

Connolly, A. G. 'Clogher in Celtic and Anglo-Norman Ireland'. In *St Macarten's Seminary Centenary Souvenir*. Drogheda, 1940.

Conway, Colmcille. 'Colmcille: Missionary or Deportee?' *Donegal Annual* 5: 224–43.

———. 'An dá Cholmcille'. *Irisleabhar Mhuighe Nuadhat* (1963): 8–21.

Coolen, Georges. 'Saint Colomban et saint Omer'. *Mélanges Colombaniens* (1951).

Coombes, James. *A History of Timoleague and Barryroe.* Timoleague, 1969.

Cordner, W. S. 'The Cult of the Holy Well'. *UJA* 9 (1946): 24–36.

Cordoliani, A. 'Les computistes insulaires et les écrits pseudo-alexandrins'. *Bibliothèque de l'École de Chartres* 106 (1946): 1–34.

———. Review of Bieler, L.: *The Life and Legend of St Patrick,* 1949. *Bibliothèque de l'École de Chartres* 109: 112–15.

———. 'Le texte de la Bible en Irlande du Ve au IXe siècle'. *Revue Biblique* 57 (1950): 5–41.

Corish, P. J. 'St Patrick and Ireland'. *IER* 95 (1961): 223–28.

Coulton, G. G. *Scottish Abbeys and Social Life.* Cambridge: Cambridge University Press, 1933.

———. *Life in the Middle Ages.* Cambridge: Cambridge University Press, 1930.

Cousin, Patrice. 'La psalmodie chorale dans la Règle de saint Colomban'. *Mélanges Colombaniens* (1951): 179–92.

Cox, Liam F. 'Íseal Chíaráin, the Low Place of St Cíarán: Where Was It Situated?' *Journal of the Ardagh Antiquarian Society* 12: 52–65.

———. 'Parentage, birth and early years of St Cíarán'. *JACAS* 2 (1946): 52–62.

Coyle, Michael. 'Holy Wells in the Parish of Dunleer'. *Seanchas Ardmhacha* 2 (1956): 192–205.

———. 'St Brigid's Well, Dunleer'. *JCLAS* 13: 175–78.

Craig, Maurice, and the Knight of Glyn. *Ireland Observed: A Handbook to the Buildings and Antiquities.* Cork: Mercier Press, 1970.

Craster, Edmund. 'The Patrimony of St Cuthbert'. *English Historical Review* 69 (1954): 177–99.

Crawford, S. J. *Anglo-Saxon Influence on Western Christendom, 600–800.* Oxford: Oxford University Press, 1933.

Crone, G. R. *Early Maps of the British Isles, A.D. 1000–1579.* London: Royal Geographical Society, 1963.

Cross, T. P. *Motif-index of Early Irish Literature.* Bloomington: Indiana University Press, 1952.

Crozier, I., and Lowry-Corry, D. 'Some Christian Cross-slabs in Co. Donegal and Co. Antrim'. *JRSAI* 68 (1938): 219–25.

Cuenin, M. le Chanoine. 'Une fondation colombanienne: Moutier-Grandval'. *Mélanges Colombaniens* (1951): 393–404.

Culhane, R. 'The Bangor Hymn to Christ the King'. *IER* 74: 207–19.

———. 'St. Patrick and Italy'. *IER* 82: 308–17.

Curle, C. L. 'The Chronology of the Early Christian Monuments of Scotland'. *Proceedings of the Society of Antiquaries of Scotland* 74 (1939–40): 60–116.

Curtayne, Alice. 'Five Irish Saints (SS Patrick, Colmcille, Brendan, Ita, Columbanus)'. *Capuchin Annual* (1945): 269–76.

———. 'Five More Irish Saints (SS Declan, Brigid, Jarlath, Finbarr, Malachy)'. *Capuchin Annual* (1946): 381–92.

——. *Lough Derg: St Patrick's Purgatory*. London and Dublin: Burns and Oates, 1944.

——. *St Brigid of Ireland*. Dublin: Browne and Nolan, 1955.

——. 'Saints and Scholars: The Spade Work'. *IER* 70, ser. 5 (1948): 33–39.

Curti-Pasini, G. B. 'Il culto di San Colombano in San Colombano-al-Lambro'. *Mélanges Colombaniens* (1951).

Curtis, Edmund. *History of Medieval Ireland from 1086–1513*. London: Methuen, 1938.

——. 'Norse Dublin'. *Dublin Historical Record* 4: 96–108.

Daniel-Rops, Henri, ed. '"The King of Love": (Hymn of St Colomban)'. In *The Miracle of Ireland* (1959).

——. 'Le miracle irlandais'. In *Le miracle irlandais* (1956).

——, ed. *Le miracle irlandais*. Paris: Robert Laffont, 1956.

——, ed. *The Miracle of Ireland,* translated from the French by the Earl of Wicklow. Dublin: Clonmore and Reynolds; London: Burns, Oates and Washbourne, 1959.

Darlington, Reginald R. *The Vita Wulfstani of William of Malmesburg*. London: Royal Historical Society, 1928.

Davenport, A. 'Patrick's Purgatory'. *Notes and Queries* 181: 67.

Davidson, Hilda Ellis. *The Golden Age of Northumbria*. London: Longmans, 1958.

Davies, Oliver. 'Ballynascreen Church and Legends'. *UJA* 4 (1941): 57–63.

——. 'Church Architecture in Ulster'. *UJA* 6 (1943): 61–68. *UJA* 7 (1944): 53–61.

——. 'The Churches of County Cavan'. *JRSAI* 78 (1948): 73–118.

——. 'Clogher Crosses and Other Carved Stones'. *UJA* 1 (1938): 227–30.

——. 'Davy's Island Church, Lower Lough Erne'. *UJA* 1 (1938): 222–24.

——. 'Killeavy Churches'. *JCLAS* 9 (1938): 77–86.

——. 'Killinagh Church and Crom Cruaich'. *UJA* 2 (1939): 98–104.

——. 'Movilla Abbey'. *UJA* 8 (1945): 33–8.

——. 'Old Churches in County Louth'. *JCLAS* 10: 5 ff; 11: 21–7.

——. 'Old Churches in the Parish of Rossinver, Co. Leitrim'. *UJA* 9 (1946): 76–9.

——. 'A Summary of the Archaeology of Ulster'. Part I. *UJA* 11 (1948): 1–42. Part II. *UJA* 12 (1949): 43–76.

——. 'White Island Church Door'. *JRSAI* 69 (1939): 112–115.

Davies, Oliver, and Paterson, T. G. F. 'The Churches of Armagh'. *UJA* 3 (1940): 82–103.

——. 'Ecclesiastical Remains in Co. Cavan'. *UJA* 3 (1940): 154–6.

——. 'The Head of Saint Patrick at Armagh'. *UJA* 3 (1940): 68.

Davies, W. H. 'The Church in Wales'. In *Christianity in Britain, 300–700* (1968).

Davignon, Henri. 'The Irish in Belgium'. In *The Miracle of Ireland,* edited by Daniel-Rops (1959).

Dawson, Christopher. 'The Classical Tradition and the Origins of Mediaeval Culture'. *Studies* 20 (1931): 209–24.

——. 'The "Dark Ages" and Ireland'. In *Studies* 21 (1932): 259–68.

——. *La religion et la formation de la civilisation occidentale.* Paris: Payot, 1953.

Day, J. G. F., and Patton, H. E. *The Cathedrals of the Church of Ireland.* Dublin: A.P.C.K., 1932.

Deansley, Margaret. *A History of Early Mediaeval Europe from 476 to 911.* London: Methuen, 1960.

——. *A History of the Mediaeval Church, 590–1500.* London: Methuen, 1962.

——. *The Pre-Conquest Church in England.* London: Black, 1961.

——. *Sidelights on the Anglo-Saxon Church.* London: Adam and Charles Black, 1962.

Deansley, Margaret, and Grosjean, Paul. 'The Canterbury Edition of the Answers of Pope Gregory I to St Augustine'. *Journal of Ecclesiastical History* 10: 1–49.

De Blacam, Aodh. 'The Glory of Armagh: AD 444–1944'. *Irish Monthly* 72: 91–100.

——. 'The Monk who Might be King (St Colmcille)'. *Irish Monthly* 69 (1941): 409–20.

——. *Saint Patrick: Apostle of Ireland.* Milwaukee: Bruce Publishing Co., 1941.

——. *The Saints of Ireland: The Life-stories of SS Brigid and Columcille.* Milwaukee: Bruce Publishing Co., 1942.

De Búrca, Seán. 'The Patricks: A Linguistic Interpretation'. *Lochlann* 3 (1965): 278–85.

Décarreaux, Jean. *Les moines et la civilisation en occident, dès invasions à Charlemagne.* Paris: Arthaud, 1962.

——. *Monks and Civilization from the Barbarian Invasions to the Reign of Charlemagne.* Translated by Charlotte Haldane. London: Allen and Unwin, 1964.

De Croocq, Ch. *Un Saint de la Flandre Française: Saint Winoc, abbé de Wormhout, patron de Bergues (vers 640–717).* Lille, 1944.

De Doctrina Ioannis Duns Scoti: Acta Congressus Scotistici Internationalis Oxonii et Edinburghi, 1966. Vol. 4: *Scotismus decursu saeculorum.* Rome: Studia Scholastico-Scotistica, 1968.

Deery, Hugh. 'Ancient Christian Burial Places of Drumholm'. *Donegal Annual* 3: 110–13.

Delaruelle, É. 'Charlemagne et l'Église'. *Revue d'histoire de l' Église de France* 39 (1953): 165–99.

Delehaye, H. *The Legends of the Saints; With a Memoir of the Author by P. Peeters,* translated by D. Attwater. London: G. Chapman, 1962.

——. *L'Oeuvre des Bollandistes à travers trois siècles, 1615–1915.* Bruxelles: Société des Bollandistes, 1959.

Delius, Walter. *Geschichte der irischen Kirche von ihren Anfängen bis zum 12. Jahrhundert.* München: Reinhardt, 1954.

De Moreau, Édouard. 'La vita Amandi Primer et les fondations monastique de S. Amand'. *Anal. Bolland.* 67 (1949): 447–64.

Dempsey, Anthony. 'The Saint of Iona'. *Capuchin Annual*, 1939: 122–8.

De hÓir, Eamonn. 'Blúire Cillsheanchas faoi Fhairche Chill Dara'. *Dinnsheanchas* 2 (1966): 29–38.

De Paor, Liam. 'Antiques of the Viking Period from Inchbofin, Co. Westmeath'. *JRSAI* 92 (1962): 187–91.

——. 'The Limestone Crosses of Clare and Aran'. *JGAHS* 26: 53–71.

——. 'Séadchomharthaí Chuilmchille'. *Irisleabhar Mhuighe Nuadhat* (1963): 51–5.

——. 'A Survey of Sceilg Mhichíl'. *JRSAI* 85 (1955): 174–87.

——, et al. *Great Books of Ireland*. Dublin: Clonmore and Reynolds, 1967.

De Paor, Máire. 'The Relics of St Patrick'. *Seanchas Ardmhacha* 4 (1961–62): 87–91.

——. *See also* MacDermott, Máire.

De Paor, M., and De Paor, L. *Early Christian Ireland*. London: Thames and Hudson, 1958.

De Reynold, Gonzague. 'Saint Colomban, la mission irlandaise et la Suisse'. *Mélanges Colombaniens* (1951).

——. 'Saint Colomban, Saint Gall et la formation de la Suisse'. In *Le miracle irlandais* (1956).

Devoto, Giacomo. 'Criteri linguistici e criteri archeologici nella definizione del problema gallico'. *Celtica* 3: 324–31.

Díaz y Díaz, M. C. 'Isidoriana, I: Sobre el "liber de ordine creaturarum"'. In *Sacris Erudiri* 5 (1953): 147–66.

Dickson, M.-P. S. *Anselme: textes choisis*. Namur: Ed. du Soleil Levant. 1960.

Dictionnaire d'histoire et de géographie ecclésiastique. Paris: Letouzey et Ané, 1953.

Dienemann, Joachìm. *Der Kult des heiligen Kilian im 8. und 9. Jahrhundert*. Würzburg: Kommissionsverlag Ferdinand Schöningh, 1955.

Diesner, H.-T. *Jugend und Mönchtum des Fulgentius von Ruspe*. Reprint from *Helikon* 1 (1961): 677–85.

Dillon, Myles. 'Celtic Religion and Celtic Society'. In *The Celts*.

——. *Early Irish Literature*. Chicago: University of Chicago Press, 1948.

——, ed. *Early Irish Society*. Dublin: Three Candles, 1954.

——, ed. *Irish Sagas*. Cork: Mercier Press, 1959.

——. 'Laud Misc. 610'. *Celtica* 5: 64–76.

——, ed. *Lebor na Cert: The Book of Rights*. Dublin: Educational Company of Ireland, 1962.

——. 'Scél Saltrach na Rann'. *Celtica* 4: 1–43.

——. 'The Vienna Glosses on Bede'. *Celtica* 3: 340.

Dillon, Myles, and Chadwick, Nora K. *The Celtic Realms*. London: Weidenfeld and Nicolson, 1967.

Dinklage, Karl. 'Würzburg im Frühmittelalter'. *Vor- und Frühgeschichte der Stadt Würzburg, Mainfränkische Heimatkunde* 3 (1951): 63–154.

Diringer, David. *The Illuminated Book: Its History and Production*. 2nd ed. London: Faber, 1967.

Doble, Gilbert H. 'Celtic Hagiography and the Sources for the Early

History of Cornwall'. *Yorkshire Society for Celtic Studies* (1935–36): 10–17.

——. *Saint Petrock, Abbot and Confessor.* Shipston-on-Stour: King's Stone Press, 1938.

——. *Saint Senan, Bishop Abbot and Confessor.* Shipston-on-Stour: King's Stone Press, 1928.

——. *The Saints of Cornwall.* Truro, 1923–1944. Reprint, edited by Donald Attwater. Truro: Dean and Chapter, 1960.

Dodd, B. E., and Heritage, T. C. *The Early Christians in Britain.* London: Longmans, 1966.

Dodwell, C. R., and Turner, D. H. *Reichenau Reconsidered.* London, 1965.

Dold, Alban, ed. *Das irische Palimpsestsakramentar in CLM 14429 der Staatsbibliothek München.* Beuron: Beuroner Kunstverlag, 1964.

Doll, Anton. 'Das Pirminkloster Hornbach: Gründung und Verfassungsentwicklung bis Anfang des 12. Jahrhunderts'. *Archiv für mittelrheinische Kirchengeschichte* 5: 108–42.

Dolley, R. H. M. 'The Dublin Pennies in the name of Sihtric Silkbeard in the Hermitage Museum at Leningrad'. *JRSAI* 93 (1963): 1–8.

——. 'The 1843 (?) Find of Viking-age Silver Coins from Tipperary'. *JCHAS* 68: 41–7.

——. *The Hiberno-Norse Coins in the British Museum.* London: British Museum, 1966.

——. 'New Light on the 1837 Viking-age Coin-hoard from Ballitore'. *JRSAI* 92: 175–86.

——. *Viking Coins of the Danelaw and of Dublin.* London: British Museum, 1965.

Dowle, Anthony, and Finn, Patrick. *The Guide Book to the Coinage of Ireland from 995 A.D. to the Present Day.* London: Spink, 1969.

Downey, G. 'Education in the Christian Roman Empire: Christian and Pagan Theories under Constantine and His Successors'. Reprint from *Speculum* 32 (1957).

Drögereit, R. 'Bonifatius, die angelsächsische Mission und Niedersachsen'. Reprint from *Jahrbuch für niedersächsische Kirchengeschichte* 52 (1954).

Du Bois, Marguerite Marie. *Saint Columban: A Pioneer of Western Civilisation.* Translated by James O'Carroll. Dublin: Gill, 1961.

——. 'St Colomban and His Disciples'. In *The Miracle of Ireland* (1959).

——. *Saint Colomban (c.540–615): un pionnier de la civilisation occidentale.* Paris: Editions Alsatia, 1950.

——. 'St Columbanus'. In *Irish Monks in the Golden Age* (1963).

Duckett, E. S. *Alcuin, Friend of Charlemagne: His World and His Work.* New York: Macmillan, 1951.

——. *Anglo-Saxon Saints and Scholars.* New York: Macmillan, 1947.

——. *The Gateway to the Middle Ages.* New York: Macmillan, 1938

——. *Monasticism.* London: Cresset Press, 1967.

——. *The Wandering Saints.* London: Collins, 1959.

Dufrenne, Suzy. *L'Illustration des psautiers grecs du moyen âge.* Vol. I. Paris: Klincksieck, 1966.

Duft, Johannes. 'Das Gallus-Erbe in der St Galler Stiftsbibliothek'. In *Sankt Gallus Gedenkbuch* (1952).

——. 'Der heilige Gallus in der stift-st. gallischen Kunst'. In *Sankt Gallus Gedenkbuch*.

——. 'Die irischen Reklusen Findan und Eusebius'. *Montfort* 8.

——. 'Iromanie—Irophobie. Fragen um die frühmittelalterliche Irenmission exemplifiziert an St Gallen und Alemannien'. *Zeitschrift für schweizerische Kirchengeschichte* 1.

——. St Colomban dans les manuscrits liturgiques de la bibliotheque abbatiale de Saint-Gall'. *Mélanges Colombaniens* (1951).

——. 'St Columban in den St Galler Handschriften'. In *Zeitschrift für schweizerische Kirchengeschichte* 59 (1965): 285–96.

——, ed. *Sankt Gallus Gedenkbuch. Zur Erinnerung an die Dreizehnhundert-Jahr-Feier vom Tode des heiligen Gallus am 16. Oktober 1951.* St Gallen: Verlag der katholischen Administration, 1952.

Duft, Johannes, and Meyer, Peter, eds. *Die irischen Miniaturen der Stiftsbibliothek St Gallen.* Olten-Bern-Lausanne: Urs Graf-Verlag, 1953.

——. *The Irish Miniatures in the Library of St-Gall.* Olten: Urs Graf-Verlag, 1954.

Duignan, Michael. 'The Clogher Cross'. *St Macarten's Seminary Centenary Souvenir* (1940).

——. 'The Moylough (Co. Sligo) and Other Irish Belt-reliquaries'. *JGAHS* 24: 83–94.

——. 'Three Pages from Irish Gospel-books'. *JCHAS* 57 (1952): 11–17.

Duke, John A. *The Columban Church.* London: Oxford University Press, 1932.

Du Manoir de Juaye, Hubert. 'Notre Dame Reine d'Irlande. Paris, 1956'. In *Maria: études sur la Sainte Vierge,* edited by Hubert Du Manoir. Paris: Beauchesne, 1949.

Dumont, C. *Aelred de Rievaulx.* Paris: Éd. du Cerf, 1961.

Dunleavy, Gareth W. *Colum's Other Island: The Irish at Lindisfarne.* Madison: University of Wisconsin Press, 1960.

——. 'Old Ireland, Scotland and Northumbria'. In *Old Ireland* (1965).

——. 'Some Holy Heroes of Irish Monasticism and Their Relations with Scotia Minor'. *Mediaeval Studies* 19: 129–36.

Durrow, Book of. See Luce, A. A.

Easson, D. E. *Medieval Religious Houses: Scotland.* London: Longmans, Green, 1958.

Egan, Patrick K. 'The Parish of Ballinasloe'. *JRSAI* 91 (1961): 128.

Elbern, V. H. 'Die Dreifaltigkeitsminiatur im Book of Durrow. Eine Studie zur unfigürlichen Ikonographie im frühen Mittelalter'. *Wallraf-Richartz-Jahrbuch* 17 (1955): 7–42.

——, ed. *Das erste Jahrtausend: Kultur und Kunst im werdenden Abendland am Rhein und Ruhr.* Dusseldorf: Schwann, 1964.

——. 'Irische Kunst'. *Lexikon für Theologie und Kirche,* 5 (1960): 750–3.

Elderkin, G. W. *Related Religious Ideas of Delphi, Tara and Jerusalem.* Springfield (Mass.): Pond-Ekberg Co., 1961.

Ellard, Gerald. *Master Alcuin, Liturgist.* Chicago: Loyola University Press, 1956.

——. *Ordination Anointings in the Western Church before 1000 A.D.* Cambridge (Mass.), 1933.

Ellis, John Tracy. 'Saint Patrick in America'. *American Benedictine Review* 12: 415–29.

Emerson, N. D. *St Columba and His Mission.* Dublin: A.P.C.K., 1963.

Engel, Wilhelm. 'Neue Forschungen zur mittelalterlichen Kilianslegende'. In *Heiliges Franken* (1952).

——. 'Weitere Forschungen zur mittelalterlichen Kilianslegende: Landesgeschichte-Predigt-Gebet'. In *Heiliges Franken* (1952).

Engelmann, Ursmar. *Der heilige Pirmin und sein Missionsbuchlein.* Konstanz: J. Thorbecke, 1959.

English, M. 'De donderheilige Sint Donatus en zijn verering in West Vlaanderen'. Reprint from *Biekorf* 60 (1959): 65–73, 103–10, 141–50.

Esposito, Mario. *Itinerarium Symonis Semeonis ab Hybernia ad Terram Sanctam.* Dublin: Institute for Advanced Studies, 1960.

——. 'Latin Learning and Literature in Mediaeval Ireland: I–V'. *Hermathena,* 44 (1929): 225–60; 47 (1932): 253–71; 48 (1933): 221–49; 49 (1935): 120–65; 50 (1937): 139–83.

——. 'Notes on a Latin Life of St Patrick'. *Classica et Mediaevalia* 13 (1952): 59–72.

——. 'The Patrician Problem and a Possible Solution'. *IHS* 10 (1956): 131–55.

——. 'St Patrick's "Confessio" and the "Book of Armagh"'. *IHS* 9: 1–12.

Evans, Daniel Simon, ed. *Buched Dewi, gan Rhygifarch, o lawysgrif Llanstephan 27.* Cardiff: Gwasg Prifysgol Cymru 1959.

Evans, E. E. *Irish Heritage.* Dundalk: Tempest, 1945.

——. *Prehistoric and Early Christian Ireland: A Guide.* London: Batsford, 1966.

Evans, Joan. *Monastic Life at Cluny, 910–1157.* Oxford: Oxford University Press, 1931.

Even, Arzel. 'Sources médiévales pour l'étude de l'antiquité celtique'. *Ogam* 9: 45–66.

Ewig, E. 'Die ältesten Mainzer Patrozinien und die Frühgeschichte des Bistums Mainz'. Reprint from *Das erste Jahrtausend* (Düsseldorf, 1962).

——. 'Le culte de S. Martin à l'époque franque'. *Revue d'histoire de l'Église de France* 48 (1962): pp. 1–18.

——. 'Die Kathedralpatrozinien im römischen und im frankischen Gallien'. *Historisches Jahrbuch* 79 (1960): 1–61.

——. *Trier im Merowingerreich, Civitas, Stadt, Bistum.* Trier: Paulinus-Verlag, 1954.

Eyre, G. Edward, ed. *European Civilisation: Its Origin and Development.* 7 vols. London: Oxford University Press, 1934–39.

Fahy, E. M. 'Inishleena Abbey and Other Sites in the Lee Valley'. *JCHAS* 62 (1957): 65–76.

———. 'Skeam Island Church'. *JCHAS* 67 (1962): 138.

Fare, Sainte. *Sainte Fare et Faremoutiers. Treize siècles de vie monastique.* Abbaye de Faremoutiers (S.-et-M.), 1956.

Farren, Robert. *The First Exile.* London: Sheed and Ward, 1944.

Fenagh, Book of. See Hennessy, W. M.; Macalister, R. A. S.

Fenton, James. 'Monasteries on the Great Royal Highway from Tara'. *Catholic Bulletin* 19: 469–78.

Ferguson, J. *Pelagius.* Cambridge: Heffer, 1956.

Ferrari, Guy. *Early Roman Monasteries: Notes for the Histories of the Monasteries and Convents at Rome from V through the X century.* Vatican City: Ponificio Istituto di archeologia cristiana, 1957.

Festugière, A.-J. 'Le problem littéraire de l'Historia monachorum'. *Trierer theologische Zeitschrift* (1954): 355–70; (1955): 25–41.

Filip, Jan. *Celtic Civilization and Its Heritage.* Prague: Czechoslovak Academy of Sciences and Artia, 1962.

Finberg, H. P. R. *Lucerna: Studies of Some Problems in the Early History of England.* London: Macmillan, 1964.

———. 'St Patrick at Glastonbury'. *IER* 107: 345–61.

Flatrés, Pierre. *Géographie rurale de quatre contrées celtiques, Irlande, Galles, Cornwall et Man.* Rennes: Plihon, 1957.

Fleischmann, Aloys. 'Chant in the Early Irish Church'. *Iris Hibernia* [Fribourg] 1936: 40–45.

———. 'References to Chant in Early Irish MSS'. In *Féil Sgríbhinn Tórna.* Cork: Cork University Press, 1947.

Fleischmann, A., and Gleeson, Ryta. 'Music in Ancient Munster and Monastic Cork'. *JCHAS* 70: 79–98.

Flood, J. M. 'An Elizabethan Dramatist on St Patrick'. *Irish Monthly* 76: 421–426.

Flower, Robin. *Catalogue of Irish Manuscripts in the British Museum.* Revised and passed through the Press by Myles Dillon. 3 vols. London: British Museum, 1953.

———, ed. 'Epistola Lentuli'. In *Féil-Sgríbhinn Eóin Mhic Néill* (1940).

———. *Ireland and Medieval Europe.* London: Humphrey Milford, 1928.

———. 'Irish High Crosses'. *Journal of the Warburg and Courtauld Institutes* 17 (1954): 87–97.

———. *The Irish Tradition.* Oxford: Clarendon Press, 1947.

———. 'The Two Eyes of Ireland: Religion and Learning in Ireland in the Eighth and Ninth Centuries'. In *The Church of Ireland, A.D. 432–1932,* edited by W. Bell and N. D. Emerson, 1932.

———. *The Western Island.* Oxford: Clarendon Press, 1944.

Foligno, Cesare. *Latin Thought during the Middle Ages.* Oxford: Clarendon Press, 1928.

Folz, R. *Études sur le culte liturgique de Charlemagne dans les églises de l'Empire.* Paris: Les Belles Lettres, 1951.

Fontaine, J. 'Alle fonti della agiografia europea: storia e leggenda nella vita di S. Martino di Tours'. *Rivista di storia e letteratura religiosa* 2 (1966): 187–206.

———. 'Une clé littéraire de la "Vita Martini" de Sulpice Sévère: la typologie prophétique'. In *Mélanges Christine Mohrmann.* Utrecht, 1963.

[Fontaine] 'La vocation monastique selon S. Isidore de Séville'. *Théologie de la vie monastique* (Paris, 1961).

Foote, J. T., and Wilson, D. M. *The Viking Achievement*. London: Sidgwick and Jackson, 1970.

Fournée, Jean. *Enquête sur le culte populaire de Saint Martin en Normandie*. Nogent-sur-Marne: Société Parisienne d'Histoire et d'Archéologie Normandes, 1963.

Fox, Cyril. *Pattern and Purpose: A Survey of Early Celtic Art in Britain*. Cardiff: National Library of Wales, 1958.

Frank, Hieronymous. *Die Klosterbischöfe des Frankenreiches*. Münster: Aschendorff, 1932.

Fraser, John. 'The Gaelic *Notitiae* in the Book of Deer'. *Scottish Gaelic Studies* 5 (1938): 51–66.

———, et al. *Irish Texts*. Fasc. 1–4 London: Sheed and Ward, 1931–33.

Freeman, A. Martin, ed. *Annals of Connacht: Annála Connacht A.D. 1224–1544*. Dublin: Institute for Advanced Studies, 1944.

Freeman, T. W. 'Historical Geography and the Irish Historian'. *IHS* 5: 139–46.

Frend, W. H. C. 'The Christianization of Roman Britain'. In *Christianity in Britain, 300–700* (1968).

———. *Martyrdom and Persecution in the Early Church*. Oxford: Blackwell, 1965.

Frere, W. H. *Bibliotheca Musico-Liturgica*. Nashdom Abbey, 1932.

Friend, A. M. J. 'The Canon Tables of the Book of Kells'. In *Medieval Studies in Memory of A. Kingsley Porter*, vol. 2. Cambridge (Mass.): Harvard University Press, 1939.

Frolow, A. 'The Veneration of the Relic of the True Cross at the End of the 6th and the Beginning of the 7th Centuries'. In *St Vladimir's Seminary Quarterly*, 1958.

Gaffney, J. J. *Life of St Brigid*. Dublin: Browne and Nolan, 1931.

Gallico, Paul. *The Steadfast Man: A Life of St Patrick*. London: Michael Joseph, 1958.

Gamber, K. *Codices liturgici latini antiquiores*. Freiburg (Schweiz): Universitätsverlag, 1963.

———. 'Das Kassian- und Zeno-Patrozinium in Regensburg'. *Deutsche Gaue* 49 (Kautbeuren, 1957): 17–28.

Ganshof, F.-L. 'Charlemagne et son héritage'. In *Charlemagne: oeuvres, rayonnement et survivances*. Aix-la-Chapelle, 1965.

———. 'La dîme monastique du IXe à la fin du XIIe siècle'. *Cahiers de civilisation médiévale* 11 (1968): 413–20.

———. 'L'Église et le pouvoir royal dans la monarchie franque sous Pépin III et Charlemagne'. *Settimane di studio . . . sull' alto medioevo* 7. (Spoléto, 1959, 1960.): 95–141; 314–18.

Gasnault, P. 'Le tombeau de S. Martin et les invasions normandes dans l'histoire et dans la légende'. *Revue d'histoire de l'Église de France* 47 (1961): 51–66.

Gaudemèt, Jean. 'Les aspects canoniques de la règle de Saint Colomban'. In *Mélanges Colombaniens* (1951).

Gebhardt, Bruno. *Handbuch der deutschen Geschichte. Vol. 1: Frühzeit und Mittelalter.* Stuttgart: Union Deutsche Verlagsgesellschaft, 1954.

Gedenkgabe zum zwölfhundersten Todestag herausgegeben von der Stadt Fulda in Verbingdung mit den Diözesen Fulda und Mainz. (Saint Boniface.) Fulda: Parzeller, 1954.

Genicot, L. *Les lignes de faîte du moyen age.* Tournai: Casterman, 1961.

——. *La spiritualité médiévale.* Paris: A. Fayard, 1958.

Geoghegan, A. T. *The Attitude Towards Labour in Early Christianity and Ancient Culture.* Washington: Catholic University of America Press, 1945.

Geoghegan, Cathal. 'Early Christian Monuments in Ireland'. *Journal of the Academy of Christian Art* 1: 39–43.

Ghellinck, J. de. *Littérature latine au Moyen Âge.* Paris: Blond et Gay, 1939.

Gilson, Étienne. *L'esprit de la philosophie médiévale.* Paris: J. Vrin, 1932.

Gleeson, Dermot F. 'The Coarbs of Killaloe Diocese'. *JRSAI* 79 (1949): 160–69.

——. *A History of the Diocese of Killaloe.* Parts 2–4: The Middle Ages. Dublin: Gill, 1962.

——. *Roscrea: A History of the Catholic Parish of Roscrea from the Earliest Times to the Present Day.* Dublin: Three Candles, 1947.

——. 'Saint Patrick in Ormond'. *NMAJ* 8: 42–4.

Gleeson, D. F., and MacAirt, S. 'The Annals of Roscrea'. *RIA Proc.* 59, sect. C: 137–80.

Godel, Willibrord. 'Irisches Beten im frühen Mittelalter: eine liturgie- und frömmigkeitsgeschichtliche Untersuchung'. *Zeitscrift für katholische Theologie* 85 (1963): 261–321; 389–439.

Godfrey, John. *The Church in Anglo-Saxon England.* Cambridge: Cambridge University Press, 1962.

Goedheer, A. J. 'Irish and Norse Traditions about the Battle of Clontarf'. *JRSAI* 68 (1938): 1–50.

Gogan, L. S. 'The Ardagh Chalice'. *JRSAI* 37 (1932): 112.

——. 'The Home of St Patrick'. *IER* 75 (1951): 193–204.

——. 'The Martin-Patrick Relationship'. *IER* 96 (1961): 283–9.

Gómez-Moreno, M. E. 'Las miniaturas de la Biblia visigótica de San Isidoro de León'. *Archivos Leoneses* 15 (1961): 77–85.

Good, James. 'The Mariology of the Bláthmac Poems'. *IER* 104: 1–7.

——. 'The Mariology of the Early Irish Church'. *IER* 100: 73–9.

Gougaud, Louis. 'The Achievement and Influence of Irish Monks'. *Studies* 20 (1931): 195–208.

——. *Anciennes coutumes claustrales.* Ligugé: Abbaye Saint-Martin, 1930.

——. *Christianity in Celtic Lands.* London: Sheed and Ward, 1932.

——. 'Le culte de Saint Colomban'. *Revue Mabillon* 25 (1935): 169–78.

——. *Ermites et reclus. Études sur d'anciennes formes de vie religieuse.* Ligugé: Abbaye St Martin, 1928.

——. *Modern Research with Special Reference to Early Irish Ecclesiastical History.* Dublin: Hodges, Figgis, 1929.

——. 'Les plus anciennes attestations du culte de Saint Patrice'. *Ephemerides Liturgicae*, N.S. 5 (1931): 182–185.

[Gougaud] 'The Remains of Ancient Irish Monastic Libraries'. In *Féil-Sgríbhinn Eóin Mhic Néill* (1940).

———. *Les Saints irlandais hors d'Irlande.* Louvain: Bureau de la Revue d'Histoire Ecclésiastique; Oxford: Blackwell, 1936.

———. 'Les Surnuméraires de l'emigration scottique (VIe–VIIIe siècles)'. *Revue Bénédictine* 43 (1931).

Goulden, J. R. W. 'The Lost Church of Aran'. *JGAHS* 26: 35–41.

Goy, B. *Aufklärung und Volksfrömmigkeit in den Bistümern Würzburg und Bamberg.* Würzburg: F. Schöningh, 1969.

Grabar, A. N. 'Miniatures gréco-orientales. II. Un manuscrit des homélies de Saint Jean Chrysostome à la Bibliothèque Nationale d'Athènes'. In *Seminarium Kondakovianum: Recueil d'études, archéologie, histoire de l'art, études byzantines,* vol. 5. Prague: Institut Kondakkov, 1932.

Graham, Rose. *An Essay on English Monasteries.* London: Bell, 1939.

Grannell, Fergal. 'Ferns'. In *Dictionnaire d'histoire et de géographie écclésiastiques,* fasc. 94: 1121–64.

Gray, P. 'St Ernan of Cluain Deochra'. *JACAS* 2, no. 9: 27–32.

Green, Edward R. R. *Essays in Scotch-Irish History.* London: Routledge and Kegan Paul, 1969.

Greene, David, *Fingal Rónáin and Other Stories.* Dublin: Institute for Advanced Studies, 1955.

———. 'Some Linguistic Evidence Relating to the British Church'. In *Christianity in Britain, 300–700* (1968).

Greene, David, and O'Connor, Frank. *A Golden Treasury of Irish Poetry, 600–1200.* London: Macmillan, 1967.

Griffe, Elie, *La Gaule chrétienne à l'époque romaine.* Paris: Letouzey et Ané, 1964–66.

———. 'Les origines chrétiennes de la Gaule et les légendes clémentines'. *Bulletin de littérature ecclésiastique* 56 (Toulouse 1955): 3–22.

———. 'Les paroisses rurales de la Gaule'. *La Maison-Dieu,* fasc. 36 (Paris, 1953): 33–62.

———. 'La pratique religieuse en Gaule au Ve siècle: "Saeculares et sancti"'. *Bulletin de littérature ecclésiastique* 63 (1962): 241–67.

———. 'Les premiers lieux du culte chrétien en Gaule'. *Bulletin de littérature ecclésiastique* 58 (1957): 129–50.

———. 'En relisant la "Vita Martini" de Sulpice Sévère'. *Bulletin de littérature ecclésiastique* 70 (1969): 184–98.

———. 'La Vie de S. Germain d'Auxerre'. *Bulletin de littérature ecclésiastique* 66 (1965): 289–94.

Griffiths, Geraint, and Owen, Huw Parri. 'The Earliest Mention of St. David'. *Bulletin of the Board of Celtic Studies* 17, part 3 (Nov. 1957): 185–93.

Grosjean, Paul. 'The Alleged Irish Origin of St Cuthbert'. In *The Relics of Saint Cuthbert,* edited by C. F. Battiscombe (1956).

———. 'Analyse du Livre d'Armagh'. *Anal. Bolland.* 62 (1944): 33–41.

———. 'Catalogus codicum hagiographicorum latinorum bibliothecarum Edinburgensium'. *Anal. Bolland.* 47 (1929): 31–8.

———. 'Deux textes inédits sur S. Ibar'. *Anal. Bolland.* 77 (1959): 426–50.

———. 'An Early Fragment on Saint Patrick in Uí Briúin Breifne, Contained in the Life of St Benen (Benignus) of Armagh'. *Seanchas Árdmacha* 1: 31–44.

——. 'Édition et commentaire du *Catalogus Sanctorum Hiberniae secundum diversa tempora* ou *De tribus ordinibus sanctorum Hiberniae*'. *Anal. Bolland.* 73 (1955): 197–213; 289–322.

——. 'Gloria postuma S. Martini Turonensis apud Scottos et Brittannos'. *Anal. Bolland.* 55: 300–48.

——. 'Hagiographica celtica'. *Anal. Bolland.* 55 (1937): 96 ff; 284 ff.

——. 'Hibernica e schedis bollandianis'. *Anal. Bolland.* 50 (1932): 139–46.

——. 'The life of St Columba from the Edinburgh MS'. *Scottish Gaelic Studies* 2: 111–171. Supplementary note, ibid. 3: 84–85.

——. 'Le martyrologe de Tallaght'. *Anal. Bolland.* 51 (1933): 117–224.

——. 'Notes d'hagiographie celtique'. *Anal. Bolland.* 62 (1944): 63 (1945); 69 (1951); 70 (1952); 72 (1954), etc.

——. 'Notes sur les documents ancien concernant S. Patrice'. *Anal. Bolland.* 62 (1944): 42–73.

——. 'Notes sur quelques sources des Antiquitates de Jacques Ussher-Edition de la *Vita Commani*'. *Anal Bolland.* 77 (1959): 154–87.

——. 'Notulae hibernicae'. *Anal. Bolland.* 49 (1931): 98–101.

——. 'The Pedigree of Saint Caelainn'. *Journal of Celtic Studies* 1: 193–8.

——. 'La prophétie de S. Malachie sur l'Irlande'. *Anal. Bolland.* 51 (1933): 318–24.

——. 'Recherches sur les débuts de la controverse pascale chez les Celtes'. *Anal. Bolland.* 64 (1946): 200–44.

——. 'S. Caelani cum ave colloquium'. *Anal. Bolland.* 47 (1929): 39–43.

——. 'S. Comgalli vita latina: accedunt duae narrationes gadelicae'. *Anal. Bolland.* 52 (1934): 343–6.

——. 'S. Patrice d'Irlande et quelques homonymes dans les anciens martyrologes'. *Journal of Ecclesiastical History* 1 (1950): 151–71.

——. 'S. Patricius in monte Cruachan Aighle'. *Anal. Bolland.* 50 (1932): 346–57.

——. 'Quelques remarques sur Virgile le grammairien'. In *Medieval Studies Presented to Aubrey Gwynn, S.J.* (1961).

——. 'Un source insulaire d'additions à un manuscrit du martyrologe hiéronymien'. *Anal. Bolland.* 65 (1947): 139–56.

——. 'Sur quelques exégètes irlandais du VIIe siècle'. *Sacris Erudiri* 7 (1955): 67–98.

——. 'A Tale of Doomsday Colum Cille Should Have Left Untold'. *Scottish Gaelic Studies* 3: 73–83.

——. 'Trois pièces sur S. Senan'. *Anal. Bolland.* 66 (1948): 199–230.

——. 'Une vie de S. Secundinus disciple de S. Patrice'. *Anal. Bolland.* 61 (1940): 26–34.

——. 'Vie, Invention et Miracles de S. Nectan de Hartland'. *Anal. Bolland.* 71 (1953): 376–414.

——. 'Les vies de S. Finnbarr de Cork, de S. Finnbarr d'Écosse et de S. Mac Cuilinn de Lusk'. *JCHAS* 58 (1953): 47–54.

——. 'Les vies de S. Finnbarr de Cork, de S. Finnbarr d'Écosse et de S. Mac Cuilinn de Lusk. Appendice: Description du MS. E.3.8 du College de la Trinité à Dublin'. *Anal. Bolland.* 69 (1951): 324–47.

[Grosjean] 'Vies et miracles de S. Petroc'. *Anal. Bolland.* 74 (1956): 131–88.

——. 'Virgil of Salzburg'. In *Irish Monks in the Golden Age* (1963).

——. 'Virgile de Salzbourg en Irlande'. *Anal. Bolland.* 78 (1960): 92–123.

——. 'Vita S. Brendani Clonfertensis e codici Dubliniensi'. *Anal. Bolland.* 48 (1930): 99–123.

——. 'Vita S. Ciarani episcopi de Saigir ex codice hagiographico Gothano'. *Anal. Bolland.* 59 (1941): 217–71.

Grundmann, H. 'Adelsbekehrungen im Hochmittelalter: Conversi und nutriti im Kloster'. In *Adel und Kirche: Festschrift für Gerd Tellenbach* (1968).

Guest, Edith M. 'Irish Sheela-na-Gigs in 1935'. *JRSAI* 66 (1936).

Guillamont, A. 'Le dépaysement comme forme d'ascèse dans le monachisme ancien'. *Annuaire de l'École Pratique des Hautes Études, Section des sciences réligieuses* 76 (1968–69): 31–58.

Guillemain, Bernard. 'Les saints irlandais en France'. In *Le miracle irlandais,* edited by Daniel-Rops.

Gundersen, Borghild. 'Irish Contributions to Norwegian Viking-culture'. *IER* 70 (1948): 1063–7.

Guttenberg, E. von, and Wendehorst, A. *Das Bistum Bamberg. 2. Teil: Die Pfarreiorganisation.* Berlin: W. de Gruyter, 1966.

Guy, J. Cl. 'Un dialogue monastique inédit'. *Revue d'ascétique et de mystique* 33 (1957): 171–88.

——. 'Un "Entretien monastique" sur la contemplation'. *Recherche de Science religieuse* 50 (1962): 230–41.

Gwynn, Aubrey. 'The Annals of Connacht and the Abbey of Cong'. *JGAHS* 27: 1–9.

——. 'The Continuation of the Irish Tradition at Würzburg'. *Würzburger Diözesangeschichtsblätter* 14/15: 57–81.

——. 'The Cult of St Martin in Ireland'. *IER* 105 (1966): 353–64.

——. 'The Early History of St Thomas' Abbey, Dublin'. *JRSAI* 84 (1954): 1–35.

——. *A History of the Diocese of Killaloe.* Vol. 1, part 1: The Early Period. Dublin: Gill, 1962.

——. 'Ireland and France at Luxeuil'. *Studies* 39 (1950): 251 ff.

——. 'Ireland and Rome in the Eleventh Century'. *IER* 57 (1941): 213–32.

——. 'Ireland and Würzburg in the Middle Ages'. *IER* 78: 401–11.

——. 'The Irish Missal of Corpus Christi College, Oxford'. In *Studies in Church History* 1 (1964): 47–68.

——. 'The Irish Monastery of Bangor'. *Mélanges Colombaniens* (1951).

——. 'Irish Monks and the Cluniac Reform'. *Studies* 29 (1940): 409 ff.

——. 'Irland'. *Lexikon für Theologie und Kirche* 5 (1960): 745–8.

——. 'Irland und Würzburg im Mittelalter'. *Mainfränkisches Jahrbuch für Geschichte und Kunst* 4 (1952): 1–10.

——. 'Lanfranc and the Irish Church'. *IER* 57 (1941): 481–500; 58 (1941): 1–15.

——. 'New Light on St Kilian'. *IER* 88 (1957): 1–16.

——. 'The Origins of St Mary's Abbey, Dublin'. *JRSAI* 79 (1949): 110–25.

——. 'The Origins of the Diocese of Waterford'. *IER* 59 (1942): 289–96.

——. 'The Origins of the See of Dublin'. *IER* 57 (1941).

——. 'St Lawrence O'Toole as Legate in Ireland (1179–1180)'. *Anal. Bolland.* 68 (1950): 223–240.

——. 'St Patrick and Rome'. *IER* 95 (1961): 217–22.

——. 'Some Notes on the History of the Book of Kells'. *IHS* 9: 131–61.

——. *The Writings of Bishop Patrick, 1074–1084.* Dublin: Institute for Advanced Studies, 1955.

Gwynn, Aubrey, and Hadcock, R. N. *Mediaeval Religious Houses: Ireland.* London: Longmans, 1970.

Gwynn, Edward. *Book of Armagh: Patrician Documents.* Dublin: Irish Manuscripts Commission, 1937.

——. 'The Early Irish Church and Paganism'. In *The Church of Ireland, A.D. 432–1932,* edited by W. Bell and N. D. Emerson, 1932.

——, ed. *The Metrical Dindshenchas,* Part 5. Dublin: Royal Irish Academy, 1935.

——. 'Notes on the Irish Penitential'. *Ériu* 12: 245–9.

Hadcock, R. Neville. *Map of Monastic Ireland.* Rev. ed. Dublin: Ordnance Survey, 1965.

Haendler, Gert. 'Geschichte des Frühmittelalters und der Germanenmission'. In *Die Kirche in ihrer Geschichte,* Vol. 2. Göttingen: Vandenhoeck and Ruprecht, 1961.

Haliday, Charles. *The Scandinavian Kingdom of Dublin.* Dublin: Gill, 1884. Reprint Shannon: Irish University Press, 1969.

Hall, M. D. J. *English Mediaeval Pilgrimages.* London: Routledge and Kegan Paul, 1965.

Halliden, William. 'The Irish Believing in Christ'. *IER* 95 (1961): 160–6.

Hallier, Amédée. *The Monastic Theology of Aelred of Rievaulx.* Translated from the French by C. Heaney. Shannon: Irish University Press, 1969.

Hamilton, G. F. *St Patrick and His Age.* Dublin: Church of Ireland, 1932.

Hammerich, L. L. *Visiones Georgii: visiones quas in Purgatorio Sancti Patricii vidit Georgius miles de Ungaria A.D. MCCCLIII.* Copenhagen, 1931.

Hammermayer, Ludwig. 'Zur Geschichte der Schottenabtei St Jacob in Regensburg. Neue Quellen aus schottischen Archiven'. *Zeitschrift für bayerische Landesgeschichte* 22 (1959): 42–76.

Handley, J. E. 'Gaelic Culture in the West of Scotland'. In *Féilscríbhinn Tórna.*

Hannan, Thomas. *Iona and Some Satellites.* London: Chambers, 1937.

Hanson, R. P. C. *St Patrick: A British Missionary Bishop.* Nottingham: University of Nottingham, 1965.

——. *St Patrick: His Origins and Career.* Oxford: Clarendon Press, 1968.

Harbison, Peter. *Guide to the National Monuments of Ireland.* Dublin: Gill and Macmillan, 1970.

Harden, Arthur Robert. *La vie de saint Auban.* Oxford: Blackwell, 1968.

Harris, Silas M. 'The Kalendar of the Vitae Sanctorum Wallensium'. *Journal of the Historical Society of the Church in Wales* 3 (1953): 3–53.

——. 'A Llanbadarn Fawr Calendar'. *Ceredigion* 2 (1952): 18–26.

——. *Saint David in the Liturgy*. Cardiff: University of Wales Press, 1940.

Harris, Dorothy C. 'Saint Gobnet, Abbess of Ballyvourney'. *JRSAI* 68 (1938): 272–7.

Harris, Silas M. 'Our Lady of Cardigan'. In *Cymdeithas Ceredigion Llundain, Llawlyfr 1952–53*.

——. *Y Wyry Wen o Ben-Rhys*. Egmanton: The author, 1951.

Hart, M. C. R. *The Early Charters of Eastern England*. Leicester: Leicester University Press, 1966.

Hartnett, P. J. 'Holy Wells of East Muskerry, Co. Cork'. *JCHAS* 52 (1947): 5–17.

——. 'Rossinver Church and Graveyard, Co. Leitrim'. *JRSAI* 84 (1954): 180.

Hartnett, P. J., and Eogan, G. 'Feltrim Hill, Co. Dublin, a Neolithic and Early Christian Site'. *JRSAI* 94 (1964): 1–38.

Hatt, Jean Jacques. *Celts and Gallo-Romans*. Translated from the French by James Hogarth. London: Barrie and Jackson, 1970.

Hawkes, William. 'The High Cross of Moone'. *Reportorium Novum* 1: 228–36.

——. 'The High Crosses of Castledermot'. *Reportorium Novum* 1: 247–62.

Hayes, R. J. 'List of Manuscripts Relating to Ireland in the Bibliothèque Nationale, Paris'. National Library of Ireland, *Report of the Council of Trustees, 1949–50*: 9–120.

——, ed. *Manuscript Sources for the History of Irish Civilisation*. 11 vols. Boston (Mass.): G. K. Hall, 1965.

Hayes, Richard. *Old Irish Links with France*. Dublin: Gill, 1940.

Hayes-McCoy, G. A. 'Irish Dress and Irish Pictures'. *Studies* 40 (1951): 303.

Healy, John. *Stories of Ancient Kells: A Lecture*. Mullingar: Westmeath Examiner, 1938.

Hecker, Clemens. *Die Kirchenpatrozinien des Archidiakonats Aargau im Mittelalter*. Küssnacht am Rigi: V. Kreienbühe, 1946.

Heist, William W., ed. *Vitae sanctorum Hiberniae ex codice olim Salmanticensi nunc Bruxellensi*. Bruxelles: Société des Bollandistes, 1965.

Hémon, R. *Christmas Hymns in the Vannes Dialect of Breton*. Dublin: Institute for Advanced Studies, 1956.

——. *Trois poèmes en moyen-Breton* [*Le Trépas de Madame la Vierge Marie, Les Quinze Joies de Marie, La Vie de l'Homme*]. Dublin: Institute for Advanced Studies, 1962.

Hencken, H. 'Lagore Crannóg: An Irish Royal Residence of the 7th–10th Centuries, A.D.' *RIA Proc.* 53, sect. C: 1–247.

——. 'Some Early Irish Illuminated MSS'. *Gazette des Beaux-Arts* 43: 135–50.

Henderson, I. *The Picts*. London: Thames and Hudson, 1967.

Hennessy, W. M., ed. *The Annals of Lough Cé*. Dublin: Stationery Office, 1939.

Hennessy, W. M., and Kelly, D. H., eds. *The Book of Fenagh*. Dublin: Stationery Office, 1939.

Hennig, John. 'Abel's Place in the Liturgy'. *Theological Studies* 7 (1946): 126–41.

——. 'Appellations of Saints in Early Irish Martyrologies'. *Mediaeval Studies* 19 (1957): 227–33.

——. 'A Bibliographical Note on the Schottenkloster of St James, Ratisbon'. *IBL* 31 (1950): 79–81.

——. 'Cataldus Rachav: A Study in the Early History of Diocesan Supremacy in Ireland'. *Mediaeval Studies* 8 (1946): 217–44.

——. 'The Feast of the Assumption in the Early Irish Church'. *IER* 75: 97–104.

——. 'Feasts of the Blessed Virgin in the Ancient Irish Church'. *IER* 81: 161–72.

——. 'The Félire Oengusso and the Martyrologium Wandalberti'. *Mediaeval Studies* 17 (1955): 219–26.

——. 'Fortunatus in Ireland'. *UJA* 13 (1950): 93–103.

——. 'St Columbanus in the Liturgy'. *IER* 62 (1943): 306–12.

——. 'The Functions of the Martyrology of Tallaght'. *Mediaeval Studies* 26 (1964): 315–28.

——. 'Ireland's Place in the Tradition of the Martyrologium Romanum'. *IER* 108: 385–401.

——. 'Irische Einflüsse auf die frühen Kalendarien von St Gallen'. *Zeitschrift für schweizerische Kirchengeschichte* 48: 17–30.

——. 'The Irish Background of St Fursey'. *IER* 77 (1952): 18–28.

——. 'The Irish Counterparts of the Anglo-Saxon *Menologium*'. *Mediaeval Studies* 14 (1952): 98–106.

——. 'Irish Literature on the Continent'. In *Irish Art Handbook*, 1943.

——. 'Irish Monastic Activities in Eastern Europe'. *IER* 65: 394–400.

——. 'The Irish Monastic Tradition on the Continent'. *IER* 87: 186–93.

——. 'Irish Saints in the Liturgical and Artistic Tradition of Central Europe'. *IER* 61, ser. 5 (1943): 181–92.

——. 'Iroschottische Mönche'. *Lexikon für Theologie und Kirche* 5 (1960): 763–4.

——. 'The Literary Tradition of Irish Saints in the Order of the Canons Regular of the Lateran'. *Comparative Literature Studies* 19: 17–21.

——. 'The Literary Tradition of Moses in Ireland'. *Traditio* 7 (1951): 197–204.

——. 'The Liturgical Veneration of Irish Saints in Switzerland'. *Iris Hibernia* 3. no. 5 (1957): 23–32.

——. 'The "Megas Kanon" of Andrew of Crete and the "Félire" of Oengus the Culdee'. *Mediaeval Studies* 25 (1963): 280–93.

——. 'A Note on Ireland's Place in the Literary Tradition of St Brendan'. *Traditio* 8: 397–402.

——. 'A Note on the Calendar of Cashel'. *Scriptorium* 6: 101–102.

——. 'Old Ireland and Her Liturgy'. In *Old Ireland* (1965).

——. 'The Place of Irish Saints in Medieval English Calendars'. *IER* 82: 93–106.

——. 'The Place of the Fathers in Early Irish Devotional Literature'. *IER* 84: 226–34.

[Hennig] 'Sacramentaries of the Old Irish Church'. *IER* 96 (1961): 23–8.

——. 'St Albert, Patron of Cashel: A Study in the History of Diocesan Episcopacy in Ireland'. *Mediaeval Studies* 7 (1945): 21–39.

——. *Studies in Early Western Devotion to the Choirs of Saints.* Reprint from *Studia Patristica* 8, Berlin, 1966.

——. 'Studies in the Latin Texts of the Martyrology of Tallaght, of Félire Oengusso and of Félire hUí Gormáin'. *RIA Proc.* 69, sect. C, no. 4 (1970).

——. 'Studies in the Liturgy of the Early Irish Church'. *IER* 85 (1951): 318–33.

——. 'Studies in the Tradition of the Martyrologium Hieronymianum in Ireland'. *Studia Patristica* 1 (1957).

——. 'With Irish Saints along the Alps'. *Irish Rosary* 59: 470–3.

Henry, Françoise. 'The Antiquities of Caher Island, Co. Mayo'. *JRSAI* 77 (1947): 23–38.

——. 'Archaeology: The Early Christian Period'. In *A View of Ireland,* edited by J. Meenan and D. A. Webb. Dublin: British Association for the Advancement of Science, 1957.

——. *Art irlandais.* Dublin: Three Candles, 1954.

——. *L'art irlandais.* Editées à l'atelier monastique de l'Abbaye Sainte-Marie de la Pierre-qui-vire (Yonne), 1963–64. Éditions Zodiaque.

——. 'L'art irlandais et son influence sur le continent. In *Le miracle irlandais* (1956).

——. *Croix sculptées irlandaises.* Dublin: Three Candles, 1964.

——. 'A Cross at Durrow (Offaly)'. *JRSAI* 93 (1963): 83–4.

——. 'Les Crosses Pré-Romanes'. *Iris Hibernia* 3, no. 4 (1956): 35–45.

——. 'Les débuts de la miniature irlandaise'. *Gazette des Beaux-Arts,* 1950.

——. 'The Decorated Stones at Ballyvourney, Co. Cork'. *JCHAS* 57 (1952): 41–2.

——. 'Un domaine nouveau de l'histoire de l'art: l'art irlandais du VIIIe siècle et ses origines'. *Gazette des Beaux-Arts* 17: 131–44.

——. *Early Christian Irish Art.* Dublin: Cultural Relations Committee, 1963.

——. 'Early Christian Slabs and Pillar Stones in the West of Ireland'. *JRSAI* 67 (1937): 265–79.

——. 'Early Irish Monasteries, Boat-shaped Oratories and Beehive Huts'. *JCLAS* 11: 296–305.

——. 'Early Monasteries, Beehive Huts and Dry-stone Houses in the Neighbourhood of Cahirciveen and Waterville, Co. Kerry'. In *RIA Proc.* 58, sect. C: 45–166.

——. 'The Effects of the Viking Invasions on Irish Art'. *Proceedings of the International Congress of Celtic Studies, Dublin 1959.* Dublin: Institute for Advanced Studies, 1962.

——. *Irish Art during the Viking Invasions, 800–1020 A.D.* London: Methuen, 1967.

——. *Irish Art in the Early Christian Period to A.D. 800.* London: Methuen, 1965.

——. *Irish Art in the Romanesque Period, 1020–1170 A.D.* London: Methuen, 1970.

——. 'Irish Culture in the Seventh Century'. *Studies* 37 (1948): 267 ff.

——. *Irish High Crosses*. Dublin: Three Candles, 1964.

——. 'An Irish Manuscript in the British Museum (Add. 40, 618)'. *JRSAI* 77: 147–66.

——. 'Megalithic and Early Christian Remains at Lankill, Co. Mayo. *JRSAI* 82 (1952): 68–71.

——. 'New Monuments from Inishkea North, Co. Mayo'. *JRSAI* 81 (1951): 65–9.

——. 'On Some Early Christian Objects in the Ulster Museum'. *JRSAI* 95 (1965): 51–64.

——. 'Les origines de l'iconographie irlandaise'. *Revue Archéologique* 31 (1930).

——. 'Remains of the Early Christian Period in Inishkea North, Co. Mayo'. *JRSAI* 75 (1945): 127–55.

——. 'Remarks on the Decoration of Three Irish Psalters'. *RIA Proc.* 61, sect. C: 23–40.

——. *La Sculpture irlandaise pendant les douze premiers siècles de l'ère chrétienne*. Paris: Leroux, 1933.

——. 'The Seven Bishops'. *Béaloideas* 15: 257–60.

——. 'Three Engraved Slabs in the Neighbourhood of Waterville (Kerry) and the Cross on Skellig Michael'. *JRSAI* 78 (1948): 175–7.

Henry, Françoise, and Marsh-Micheli, G. L. 'A Century of Irish Illumination (1070–1170)'. *RIA Proc.* 62, sect. C: 101–64.

Henry, Françoise, and Ó Riordáin, Seán P. 'Irish Culture in the Seventh Century'. *Studies* 37 (1948): 267 ff.

Henry-Rosier, Marguérite. *Dans la barbarie Mérovingienne: St Colomban*. Paris: Éditions Spes, 1950.

Herrmann, Léon. 'Du nouveau sur Saint Patrick?' *Revue Belge de Philologie et d'Histoire* 25: 805–12.

Hertling, Ludwig. 'St Gall in Switzerland'. In *Irish Monks in the Golden Age* (1963).

Hesbert, René-Jean. 'Les compositions rhythmiques, en l'honneur de St Colomban'. *Mélanges Colombaniens* (1951).

Hickey, Elizabeth. 'North Cross at Ahenny'. *JRSAI* 85 (1955): 118–21.

Hill, R. 'Christianity and Geography in Early Northumbria'. In *Studies in Church History* 3 (1966).

Hillgarth, J. N. 'The East, Visigothic Spain and the Irish'. *Studia Patristica* 4 (1961): 442–56.

——. 'Old Ireland and Visigothic Spain'. In *Old Ireland* (1965).

——. 'Visigothic Spain and Early Christian Ireland'. *RIA Proc.* 62, sect. C: 194.

Hitchcock, F. R. Montgomery. 'The Confession and Epistola of Patrick and Their Literary Affinities in Irenaeus, Cyprian and Orientius'. *Hermathena* 47 (1932): 202–38.

——. 'The Latinity of St Patrick Compared with the Latin Translation of Irenaeus's Treatise'. *Hermathena* 54 (1939): 93–109.

——. 'Notes and Emendations on the Latin Writings of St Patrick'. *Hermathena* 51 (1938): 65–76.

Hlawitschka, Eduard. *Franken, Alemannen, Bayern und Burgunder in Oberitalien (774–962)*. Fribourg-en-Brisgau: E. Albert, 1960.

Hobson, A. R. A. *Great Libraries*. London: Weidenfeld and Nicolson, 1970.

Hodgkin, Robert Howard. *History of the Anglo-Saxons*. Oxford: Clarendon Press, 1935.

Hoebanx, J. J. *L'abbaye de Nivelles des origines au XIVe siècle*. Bruxelles: Palais des Académies, 1952.

Hofmann, Josef. 'Das älteste Kiliansoffizium'. In *Heiliges Franken* (1952).

Hofmeister, A. *Festschrift Adolf Hofmeister . . . herausgegeben von Ursula Scheil*. Halle (Saale): Niemeyer, 1955.

Hogan, James. *The Irish Manuscripts Commission*. Cork: Cork University Press, 1954.

Holenstein, Josef. 'Ancient Irish Miniatures in the Monastery-Library of St Gall'. *Iris Hibernia* [Fribourg-en-Suisse] (1950).

Holzapfel, Helmut. 'Eine Kiliansreliquie in Niederbayern' *and* 'St Kilian in Thüringen'. *Heiliges Franken* (1952).

Holzherr, G. *Regula Ferioli*. Einsiedeln: Benziger, 1961.

Hömberg, A. K. 'Studien zur Entstehung der mittelalterlichen Kirchenorganisation in Westfalen'. *Westfälische Forschungen* 6 (1953): 46–108.

L'Homme et son destin d'après les penseurs du moyen âge. Actes du Congrès de philosophie médiévale (1958). Louvain: Nauwelaerts, 1960.

Hoogterp, P. W. 'Étude sur le Latin du Codex Bobiensis (K) des Évangiles'. D. Litt. thesis, University of Gröningen, c. 1930.

Hopkin-James, Lemuel John. *The Celtic Gospels: Their Story and Their Text*. Oxford: Oxford University Press; London: Humphrey Milford, 1934.

Howell, W. S. *The Rhetoric of Alcuin and Charlemagne: A Translation*. Princeton: Princeton University Press; London: Milford, 1941.

Howells, W. W. 'The Early Christian Irish: The Skeletons at Gallen Priory'. In *RIA Proc.* 46, sect. C. (1941): 103–219.

Hughes, Kathleen. 'British Museum MS Cotton Vespasian A. XIV (Vitae Sanctorum Wallensium): Its Purpose and Provenance'. In *Studies in the Early British Church* (1958).

——. 'The Celtic Church and the Papacy'. In *The English Church and the Papacy in the Middle Ages*.

——. 'The Changing Theory and Practice of Irish Pilgrimage'. *Journal of Ecclesiastical History* 11 (1960): 143–51.

——. 'The Church and the World in Early Christian Ireland'. *IHS* 13: 99–116.

——. *The Church in Early Irish Society*. London: Methuen, 1966.

——. 'The Cult of St Finnian of Clonard from the Eighth to the Eleventh Century'. *IHS* 9: 13–27.

——. 'The Distribution of Irish Scriptoria and Centres of Learning from 730–1111'. In *Studies in the Early British Church* (1958).

——. 'The Historical Value of the Lives of St Finnian of Clonard'. *English Historical Review* 69 (1954): 353–72.

——. 'Irish Monks and Learning'. In *Monjes y los Estudios IV. Semana de Estudios Monasticos, Poblet, 1961*. Poblet, 1963.

——. 'The Offices of St Finnian of Clonard and St Cianán of Duleek'. *Anal. Bolland.* 73 (1955): 342–72.

———. 'On an Irish Litany of Pilgrim Saints Compiled c. 800'. *Anal. Bolland.* 77 (1959): 305–31.
Hughes, Michael W. 'The End of Roman Rule in Britain: A Defence of Gildas'. *Transactions of the Honourable Society of Cymmrodorion*, sessions 1946–47.
Hull, Vernam. 'Apgitir Chrábaid: The Alphabet of Piety'. *Celtica* 8: 44–89.
———. 'Cáin Domnaig'. *Ériu* 20: 151–77.
———. 'The Death of the Three Sons of Diarmait Mac Cerrbeóil'. *ZCP* 25 (1955): 91–100.
———. 'The Middle Irish Apocryphal Account of "The Seventeen Miracles at Christ's Birth"'. *Modern Philology* 43, no. 1 (1945): 25–39.
Hunt, John. 'The Cross of Muiredach, Monasterboice'. *JRSAI* 81 (1951): 44–7.
Hynes, John. 'St Caillin'. *JRSAI* 61 (1931): 39–54.

Ignesti, I. *S. Pierdamiano: scritti monastici.* Siena: Cantagalli, 1959.
Inisfallen, Annals of. See Best, R. I.; MacAirt, Seán.
Irish Catholic Historical Committee. *Papers Read at the Conference on Diocesan and Local History, Easter, 1956.* Dublin: Gill, 1956.

Jaager, W. *Bedas metrische Vita Sancti Cuthberti.* Leipzig: Mayer and Müller, 1935.
Jackson, Kenneth H. 'Angels and Britons in Northumbria and Cumbria'. In *Angels and Britons: O Donnell Lectures.* Cardiff: University of Wales Press, 1963.
———. 'The Celtic Aftermath in the Islands'. In *The Celts,* edited by J. Raftery (1964).
———. *A Celtic Miscellany: Translations from Celtic Literatures.* London: Routledge and Kegan Paul, 1951.
———. *Language and History in Early Britain: A Chronological Survey of the Brittonic Languages, First to the Twelfth Century.* Edinburgh: Edinburgh University Press; London: Oliver and Boyd, 1953.
———. *The Oldest Irish Tradition: A Window on the Iron Age.* Cambridge: Cambridge University Press, 1967.
———. 'Some Remarks on the Gaelic *Notitiae* in the Book of Deer'. *Ériu* 16: 86–98.
———. 'The Sources for the Life of Saint Kentigern'. In *Studies in the Early British Church* (1958).
———. *Studies in Early Celtic Nature Poetry.* Cambridge: Cambridge University Press, 1936.
Jackson, Robert Wyse. *The Cathedrals of the Church of Ireland.* Dublin: A.P.C.K., 1971.
———. 'Ecclesiastical Remains at Birchgrove, Roscrea'. *JRSAI* 69 (1939): 46.
Jacobsthal, Paul. *Early Celtic Art.* Oxford: Clarendon Press, 1944.
———. *Imagery in Early Celtic Art.* London: Humphrey Milford, 1942.
James, John Williams. *A Church History of Wales.* Ilfracombe (Devon): A. H. Stockwell, 1945.

[James] ed. *Rhigyfarch's Life of St David*. Cardiff: University of Wales Press, 1967.

Janssens, Hubert. 'St Willibrord and Ireland'. *IER* 77 (1952): 356–65.

Jecker, Gall. 'St Pirmins Erden- und Ortsheimat'. *Archiv für mittel-rheinische Kirchengeschichte* 5: 9–41.

——. 'Die Verehrung des heiligen Columban in der Schweiz'. *Mélanges Colombaniens* (1951).

Jennings, B., ed. *The Acta Sanctorum of John Colgan, Reproduced with Introduction*. Dublin: Stationery Office, 1948.

Johanek, Peter. *Die Frühzeit der Siegelurkunde im Bistum Würzburg*. Würzburg: F. Schöningh, 1969.

John, Eric. *Land Tenure in Early England*. Leicester: Leicester University Press, 1960.

——. *'Orbis Britanniae' and Other Studies*. Leicester: Leicester University Press, 1966.

——. 'Some Latin Charters of the Tenth Century Reformation in England'. *Revue Bénédictine* 70 (1960): 333–59.

Johnston, T. J. *The Celtic Expansion*. Dublin: A.P.C.K., 1965.

Jonas. *Vita Columbani et discipulorum eius. Testo a cura di M. Tosi Versione italiana di E. Cremona e M. Paramidani*. Presentazione di E. Franceschini et J. Leclercq. Plaisance: Emiliana Gráfica, 1965.

Jones, A. H. M. 'The Western Church in the Fifth and Sixth Centuries'. In *Christianity in Britain, 300–700* (1968).

Jones, C. W. *Saints' Lives and Chronicles in Early England*. Ithaca: Cornell University Press, 1947.

Jones, F. *The Holy Wells of Wales*. Cardiff. University of Wales Press, 1954.

Jones, Gwyn. *A History of the Vikings*. London: Oxford University Press, 1968.

——. *The Legendary History of Olaf Tryggvason*. W. P. Ker Memorial Lecture, Glasgow, 1968. Glasgow: Jackson, 1968.

Jörg, Peter Joseph. 'Die Gründung des Bistums Würzburg'. *Heiliges Franken* (1952).

Jungmann, Josef A. *The Mass of the Roman Rite: Its Origins and Development*. New York: Benziger, 1951–55. (Originally published as *Missarum Sollemnia*. Wien: Herder, 1952).

Kaftannikoff, Luba. 'Discovery of High Crosses at Kilfenora'. *NMAJ* 5: 33.

Keane, Edward. 'St Patrick's Journey through West Limerick'. In *North Munster Studies* (1967).

Kelleher, John V. 'Early Irish History and Pseudo-history'. *Studia Hibernica* 3: 113–27.

——. 'The Pre-Norman Irish Genealogies'. *IHS* 16: 138–53.

Kells, Book of. See Alton, E. H.

Kelly, Eugene T. 'Early Irish Art and Society'. *Éire-Ireland* 1, no. 3: 39–55.

Kelly, Matthew J. 'Three Monasteries of Drogheda'. *JCLAS* 10: 25–41.

Kendrick, T. D. *The Druids: A Study in Keltic Prehistory*. London: Cass, 1966.

——. 'Gallen Priory Excavations, 1934–35'. *JRSAI* 69 (1939): 1–20.

——. *A History of the Vikings*. London: Cass, 1968 (originally published 1930).

——. *Late Saxon and Viking Art*. London: Methuen, 1949.

——, et al. *Evangeliorum quattuor Codex Lindisfarnensis; Musei Britannici Codex Cottonianus Nero D. IV permissione Musei Britannici totius codicis similitudo expressa*. Oltun et Lausanna Helvetiae: Urs Graf, 1956.

Kengel, Rainer. 'Das irische Mönchtum'. In *Heiliges Franken* (1952).

Kenney, James F. 'Early Irish Church History as a Field for Research by American Students'. *Catholic Historical Review* 17 (1931).

——. 'St Patrick and the Patrick Legend'. *Thought* 8 (1933): 1–34; 213–29.

——. *The Sources for the Early History of Ireland, Ecclesiastical: An Introduction and Guide*. New York, 1929. Reprint Shannon: Irish University Press, 1968.

Keown, Patrick. 'The Shrines of Clogher'. *St Macarten's Seminary Centenary Souvenir* (1940).

Ker, Neil R. *Fragments of Medieval Manuscripts Used as Pastedowns in Oxford Bindings*. Oxford: Oxford Bibliographical Society, 1954.

——. *Medieval Manuscripts in British Libraries*. Vol. 1: London. Oxford: Clarendon Press, 1969.

Kerlouégan, François. 'Essai sur la mise en nourriture et l'éducation dans les pays celtiques, d'après le témoignage des textes hagiographiques latins'. *Études Celtiques* 12 (1968–69): 101–46.

——. 'Le Latin du *De Excidio Britanniae de Gildas*'. In *Christianity in Britain, 300–700* (1968).

Kilbride-Jones, H. E. 'Early Christian Cemetery at Kilbride, near Bray, Co. Wicklow'. *JRSAI* 69 (1939): 173–6.

Kilger, Laurenz. 'Der hl. Kolumban in Tuggen'. *Mélanges Colombaniens* (1951).

——. 'Vom Leben des heiligen Gallus'. In *Sankt Gallus Gedenkbuch* (1952).

Killanin, Michael Morris, 3rd baron, and Duignan, Michael V. *The Shell Guide to Ireland*. London: Ebury Press, 1967.

King, A. A. *Liturgies of the Past*. London: Longmans, Green, 1959.

Kinsella, Nivard. 'St Patrick as Model'. *IER* 96 (1961–62): 129–37.

——. 'St Patrick's Way to Sanctity'. *IER* 95 (1961): 146–159.

——. 'The Spirituality of St Patrick's "Confession"'. *IER* 91: 161–73.

Kirby, D. P. 'Bede's Native Sources for the *Historia Ecclesiastica*'. *Bulletin of John Rylands Library* 48, no. 2 (1966).

Kirschbaum, E. *Lexikon der christlichen Ikonographie*. Vol. 1. Freiburg-im-Breisgau: Herder, 1968.

Klauser, Renate. *Der Heinrichs- und Kunigundenkult im mittelalterlichen Bistum Bamberg*. Bamberg: Historischer Verein, 1957.

Klauser, Renate, and Meyer, Otto. *Clavis mediaevalis. Kleines Wörterbuch der Mittelalterforschung*. Wiesbaden: Harrassowitz, 1962.

Kneen, J. J. *The Place-names of the Isle of Man. Parts IV–VI*. Douglas: Yn Cheshaght Ghailckagh, 1927–1929.

Knott, Eleanor. 'A Poem of Prophecies'. *Ériu* 18: 55–84.

Knott, Eleanor, and Murphy, Gerard, *Early Irish Literature*. London: Routledge and Kegan Paul, 1966.

Knowles, David. *Great Historical Enterprises and Problems in Monastic History*. Edinburgh: Nelson, 1963.

——. *The Monastic Order in England, 943–1216*. Cambridge: Cambridge University Press, 1963.

——. *The Religious Houses of Medieval England*. London: Sheed and Ward, 1940.

Knowles, David, and Hadcock, R. Neville. *Medieval Religious Houses: England and Wales*. London: Longman's, Green, 1953.

Knowles, David, and Obolensky, Dimitri. *The Christian Centuries: Vol. II. The Middle Ages*. London: Darton, Longman and Todd, 1969.

Knowles, David, and St Joseph, J. K. S. *Monastic Sites from the Air*. Cambridge: Cambridge University Press, 1952.

Knox, R. B. 'The Decline of Early Irish Monasticism'. *Bulletin of the Irish Committee of Historical Sciences* 39 (1945).

Kobler, Arthur. 'Des heiligen Gallus Tod, Grab und Reliquien'. In *Sankt Gallus Gedenkbuch* (1952).

Koch, Margrit. *Sankt Fridolin und sein Biograph Balther: irische Heilige in der literarischen Darstellung des Mittelalters*. Zürich: Fretz und Wasmuth, 1959.

Kramer, Theodor, ed. *Heiliges Franken, Festchronik zum Jahr der Franken-apostel 1952*. Würzburg: Echter-Verlag, 1952.

Krappe, Alexander H. 'St Patrick and the Snakes'. *Traditio* 5: 323–30.

Kristeller, P. O. *Latin Manuscript Books before 1600*. 2nd ed. New York: Fordham University Press, 1960.

Krüger, Gustav. 'A Decade of Research in Early Christian Literature, 1921–1930. *Harvard Theological Review* 26 (1933).

Lageman, Adolf. *Der Festkalendar des Bistums Bamberg im Mittelalter*. Bamberg: Historisches Verein, 1967.

Lahert, Richard. *The History and Antiquities of the Parish of Dunnamaggan*. Tralee: Kerryman, 1956.

Laistner, M. L. W. *The Intellectual Heritage of the Early Middle Ages*. Edited by Chester G. Starr. Ithaca: Cornell University Press, 1957.

——. *Thought and Letters in Western Europe, A.D. 500 to 900*. 2nd ed. London: Methuen, 1957.

Lambrechts, P. *L'exaltation de la tête dans la pensée et dans l'art des Celtes*. Brugge: De Tempel, 1954.

Laporte, J. *Le Pénitentiel de S. Columban*. Tournai: Desclée, 1958.

——. 'Les sources de la biographie de Saint Colomban'. *Mélanges Colombaniens* (1951).

——. 'Saint Colomban, son âme et sa vie'. *Mélanges de science religieuse* 6 (1949): 49–56.

Laprat, R. 'Les rapports de Saint Colomban et de la Gaule Franque aux VIe et VIIe siècles'. *Mélanges Colombaniens* (1951).

Latham, R. E. *Revised Medieval Latin Word-list from British and Irish Sources*. London: Oxford University Press for British Academy, 1965.

Latreille, A., Palanque, J. R., et al. *Histoire du Catholicisme en France. Vol. 1: Des origines à la chrétienté mediévale*. Paris: Spes, 1957.

Laureilhe, M.-Th. 'Saint Martin en Ariège'. *Bulletin de la Société ariègeoise des Sciences, Lettres et Arts* 20 (1962–63): 21–64.

Lawlor, H. C. 'Degen of Kilconriola'. *UJA* 1 (1938): 32–35.

——. 'Early Irish Monasticism'. In *The Church of Ireland, A.D. 432–1932*, edited by W. Bell and N. D. Emerson, 1932.

Leask, Harold G. 'Carved Stones Discovered at Kilteel, Co. Kildare'. *JRSAI* 65 (1935): 1–8.

——. 'The Characteristic Features of Irish Architecture from Early Times to the Twelfth Century'. *NMAJ* 1 (1936): 10–21.

——. *Fore, Co. Westmeath*. Dublin: Stationery Office, 1938.

——. *Glendalough, Co. Wicklow: Official, Historical and Descriptive Guide*. Dublin: Stationery Office, 1950.

——. 'Irish Architecture and Sculpture in the Early Christian Epoch'. In *Christian Art in Ancient Ireland*, edited by J. Raftery.

——. *Irish Churches and Monastic Buildings*. vol. 2, 3 vols. Dundalk: Dundalgan Press, 1955–1960.

——. 'Killoughternane Church, Co. Carlow'. *JRSAI* 73 (1943): 98–100.

——. 'Rahan, Offaly: The Larger Church'. *JKAS* 12: 111–114.

——. 'Rathmore Church, Co. Meath'. *JRSAI* 63 (1933): 153–66.

——. 'St Canice's Cathedral, Kilkenny'. *JRSAI* 79 (1949): 1–9.

——. 'St Mochta's House, Louth'. *JCLAS* 9 (1937): 32–35.

——. 'St Patrick's Cross, Cashel, Co. Tipperary: An Enquiry into Its Original Form'. *JRSAI* 81 (1951): 14–18.

——. *St Patrick's Rock, Cashel, Co. Tipperary*. Dublin: Stationery Office, 1940.

——. 'Tullylease, Co. Cork: Its Church and Monuments'. *JCHAS* 43 (1938): 101–108.

Leask, Harold G., and Macalister, R. A. S. 'Liathmore-Mochoemóg (Leigh), Co. Tipperary. *RIA Proc.* 51, sect. C: 1–14.

Leatham, Diana. *The Story of St Brigid of Ireland*. London: Faith Press; New York: Morehouse-Gorham, 1955.

Lebor Gabala Érenn: The Book of the Taking of Ireland. See Macalister, R. A. S.

Lebor na Huidre: Book of the Dun Cow. See Best, R. I.

Le Bras, Gabriel. 'Les pénitentiels irlandais'. In *Le miracle irlandais*, edited by H. Daniel-Rops (1956).

——, ed. *Saint Germain d'Auxerre et son temps*. Communications présentées à l'occasion du 19e Congrès de l'Association bourguignonne de Sociétés Savantes réuni à Auxerre, 29 juillet–2 août 1948. Auxerre: Imprimerie L'Universelle, 1950.

Lebreton, J., and Zeiller, J. *History of the Primitive Church*. London: Burns and Oates, 1942–1947.

Lebreton, M.-M, Leclercq, J., and Talbot, C. H. *Analecta Monastica*. 3rd ser. Rome: Orbis Catholicus, 1955.

Lecan, The Book of. See Mulchrone, Kathleen.

Leclercq, Jean. *L'amour des lettres et le désir de Dieu: initiation aux auteurs monastiques du moyen âge*. Paris: Éditions du Cerf, 1957.

——. 'Aspects historiques du mystère monastique'. *Convivium* N.S. 6 (Torino 1956): 641–9.

——. *Aux sources de la spiritualité occidentale: étapes et constantes*. Paris: Éditions du Cerf, 1964.

——. *Chances de la spiritualité occidentale*. Paris: Éditions du Cerf, 1966.

——. 'L'Écriture Sainte dans l'hagiographie-monastique du haut moyen âge'. In *La Bibbia nell' alto medioevo* (Spoleto, 1963).

——. *Les études dans les monastères du Xe au XIIe siècle*. Reprint from *Los Monjes y los estudios* (Poblet, 1963).

——. *Études sur le vocabulaire monastique du moyen âge*. Rome: Herder, 1961.

——. 'La flagellazione volontaria nella tradizione spirituale dell'occidente'. Repr. from *Il Movimento dei Disciplinati nel Settimo Centenario dal suo inizio* (Perugia, 1962).

——. 'Grammaire et humour dans les textes du moyen âge'. *Annales de la Société royale d'archéol. de Bruxelles* 50 (1961): 150–6.

——. *L'idée de la royauté du Christ au moyen âge*. Paris: Éditions du Cerf, 1959.

——. 'Le monachisme du haut moyen âge (VIIIe–Xe S.)'. In *Théologie de la vie monastique* (Paris, 1961).

——. 'Monachisme et pérégrination du IXe au XIIe siècle'. *Studia Monastica* 3 (1961): 33–52.

——. 'Mönchtum und Peregrinatio îm Frühmittelalter'. *Römische Quartalschrift* 55 (1960): 212–25.

——. *Nous avons besoin de l'ordre monastique*. Clervaux: Abbaye Saint-Maurice, 1953.

——. *Otia monastica: études sur le vocabulaire de la contemplation au moyen âge*. Roma: Orbis Catholicus, 1963.

——. *Recueil d'études sur S. Bernard et ses écrits*. Vol. 1. Roma: Edizione di storia e letteratura, 1962.

——. 'Un recueil d'hagiographie Colombanienne'. *Anal. Bolland.* 73 (1955): 193–6.

——. 'S. Romuald et le monachisme missionaire'. *Revue Bénédictine* 72 (1962): 307–23.

——. 'Un traité sur la "Profession des Abbés" au XIIe siècle'. *Studia Anselmiana* 50 (1963): 177–91.

Leclercq, J., Vandenbroucke, F., and Bouyer, L. *La Spiritualité du moyen âge*. Paris: Aubier, 1961.

Leech, Roger H. 'Cogagh Gaedhel re Gallaibh and the Annals of Inisfallen'. *NMAJ* 11 (1968): 13–21.

Leeds, E. T. *Celtic Ornament in the British Isles down to A.D. 700*. Oxford: Clarendon Press, 1933.

Le Goff, J. 'Le culte de Saint Colomban en Bretagne'. In *Mélanges Colombaniens* (1951).

Lehmacher, Gustav. 'The Ancient Celtic Year'. *Journal of Celtic Studies* 1: 144–7.

——. 'Die heilige Brigitta und die keltische Göttin Brigit'. *Rheinisches Jahrbuch für Volkskunde* 4 (1953): 125–41.

Leinster, The Book of. See Best, R. I.

Lemarignier, J.-Fr. *Étude sur les privilèges d'exemption et de juridiction ecclésiastiques des abbayes normandes depuis les origines jusqu'en 1140.* Paris: Picard, 1937.

Leonard, Pádraig. 'A Reconsideration of the Dating of the Slab of St Berichtre at Tullylease, Co. Cork'. *JCHAS* 58 (1953): 12–13.

——. 'A Swiss Achievement of Interest to Ireland'. *Iris Hibernia* 3, no. 4 (1956): 67–8.

Le Roux, Françoise. *Les Druides.* Paris: Presses Universitaire de France, 1969.

Leslie, Shane. *St Patrick's Purgatory.* London: Burns, Oates and Washbourne, 1932; Dublin: Three Candles, 1961.

Lethbridge, T. C. *Herdsmen and Hermits: Celtic Wayfarers in the Northern Seas.* Cambridge: Bowes and Bowes, 1950.

Letts, Winifred M. *Saint Patrick: the Travelling Man.* London: I. Nicholson, 1932.

Levison, Wilhelm. *An Eighth-century Poem on St Ninian.* Gloucester, 1940.

Levron, J. *Les saints du pays angevin.* Grenoble: Arthaud, 1943.

Lewis, C. W. 'Agweddau ar Hanes Cynnar yr Eglwys yng Nghymru'. *Llên Cymru* 3–4 (1963): 125–171.

Lewis, Lionel S. *Glastonbury, 'The Mother of Saints': Her Saints, A.D. 37–1539.* London: Mowbray, 1927.

Lievens, R. 'De origine monasterii Viridisvallis van Pomerius'. Repr. from *Ous geestelijk* 34 (1960).

Lindisfarne, Book of. See Kendrick, T.D.

Lionárd, Pádraig. *See* Leonard, Pádraig.

Lismore, Book of. See Macalister, R. A. S.

Little, George A. *Brendan the Navigator: An Interpretation.* Dublin: Gill, 1945.

——. 'The Picture of Patrick'. *Capuchin Annual* (1942): 601–6.

Liversage, G. D. 'Excavations at Dalkey Islands, Co. Dublin, 1956–1959'. *RIA Proc.* 66, sect. C: 53–233.

Livingstone, Peadar. *The Fermanagh Story.* Enniskillen: Cumann Seanchais Chlochair, 1969.

Lloyd, John Edward. *A History of Wales from Earliest Times to the Edwardian Conquest.* London: Longmans, 1939.

Loomis, C. Grant. *White Magic: An Introduction to the Folklore of Christian Legend.* Cambridge (Mass.): Mediaeval Academy of America, 1948.

Lorchin, Aimée. 'La Vie scolaire dans les monastères d'Irlande aux Ve–VIIe siécles'. *Revue du moyen âge latin* 1 (1945): 221–36.

Los, Cornelius. *Die altirische Kirche. Urchristentum im Westen.* Stuttgart: Urachnaus, 1954.

Lot, Ferdinand. *Nennins et l'Historia Brittonum: étude critique, suivi d'une édition des diverses versions du texte.* Paris: H. Champion, 1934.

Lough Cé, Annals of. See Hennessy, W. M.

Louis, René. *Autessiodurum christianum. Les églises d'Auxerre, des origines au XIe siècle.* Paris: Clavreuil, 1952.

[Louis] *L'Église d'Auxerre et ses évêques avant saint Germain.* Auxerre: Société des fouilles archéologiques, 1951.

——. 'St Patrick's Sojourn in Auxerre and the Problem of the Insula Aralanensis'. *Seanchas Árdmhacha* 4, no. 2 (1961–62): 37–44.

Love, H. W. *Records of the Archbishops of Armagh.* Dundalk: Dundalgan Press, 1965.

Lowe, Elias Avery. *Codices Latini Antiquiores: A Palaeographical Guide to Latin MSS prior to the Ninth Century.* Oxford: Clarendon Press, 1934–63.

Löwe, H. 'Pirmin, Willibrord und Bonifatius'. In *La conversione al cristianesimo nell' Europa dell' alto medioevo* (Spoleto, 1967).

Lowry-Corry, Dorothy. 'Holywell Church, near Lough Macnean'. *JRSAI* 65 (1935): 223–30.

——. 'The Market Cross at Lisnaskea'. *JRSAI* 65 (1935): 153–6.

——. 'A Newly Discovered Statue at the Church on White Island, Co. Fermanagh'. *UJA* 22 (1959): 59–66.

——. 'Note on the History of Davys Island and Its Church, and on the Chapel of Ballymactaggart'. *UJA* 1 (1938): 224–6.

——. 'St Molaise's House at Devenish, Lough Erne'. *JRSAI* 66 (1936): 270–84.

——. 'The Sculptured Crosses of Galloon'. *JRSAI* 64 (1934): 165–76.

——. 'The Sculptured Stones at Killadeas'. *JRSAI* 65 (1935): 23–33.

——. 'Templenaffrin Church, County Fermanagh'. *UJA* 1 (1938): 25–31.

Loyer, Olivier. *Les Chrétientés celtiques.* Paris: Presses Universitaires de France, 1965.

Lübeck, Konrad. 'Eine iroschottische Missionsstation in Fulda'. *Fuldaer Studien* 2: 85–112.

Lucas, A. T. 'Irish-Norse Relations'. *Journal of the Old Wexford Society* 1 (1968): 17–19.

——. 'Irish-Norse Relations: Time for a Reappraisal?' *JCHAS* 71: 227–36.

——. 'The Plundering and Burning of Churches in Ireland, 7th to 16th Century'. In *North Munster Studies* (1967), pp. 172–229.

——. 'The Sacred Trees of Ireland'. *JCHAS* 68 (1963): 16–54.

——. 'The West Cross, Monasterboice: A Note and a Suggestion'. *JCLAS* 12: 124–5.

Luce, A. A., et al. *Evangeliorum quattuor Codex Durmachensis. Auctoritate Collegii Sacrosanctae et Individuae Trinitatis juxta Dublin totius codicis similitudinem accuratissime depicti exprimendam curavit typographeum.* Olten: Urs-Graf; New York: Duschnes, 1960.

Luddy, Ailbe J. *Life of St Malachy.* Dublin: Gill, 1930.

Luff, S. G. A. 'An Examination of St Ninian's Position as a Father of British Monasticism'. *IER* 80 (1953): 17–27.

Lyons, P. 'Double-Bullaun [stone] at Park, Parish of Rathgormuck, Co. Waterford'. *JRSAI* 78 (1948): 178.

Mac Áirt, Seán, ed. *The Annals of Inisfallen.* Dublin: Institute for Advanced Studies, 1951.

——. 'St Patrick and Armagh, a Symposium: II. The Chronology of St Patrick'. *Seanchas Árdmhacha* 2, no. 1: 4–9.

Macalister, R. A. S. 'The Ancient Inscriptions of Kells'. *JRSAI* 64 (1934): 16–21.

——. *Ancient Ireland: A Study in the Lessons of Archaeology and History.* London: Methuen, 1935.

——, ed. *Book of Fenagh: Supplementary Volume.* Dublin: Stationery Office, 1939.

——, ed. *The Book of MacCárthaigh Riabhach; or, The Book of Lismore.* Dublin: Stationery Office, 1950.

——, ed. *The Book of Uí Maine, Otherwise Called the Book of the O Kellys.* Dublin: Stationery Office, 1942.

——. *Corpus Inscriptionum Insularum Celticarum.* 2 vols. Dublin: Stationery Office, 1945, 1949.

——, ed. *Lebor Gabála Érenn: The Book of the Taking of Ireland.* 4 vols. Dublin: Educational Company of Ireland, 1938–41.

——. 'A Lost Glendalough Inscription Rediscovered'. *JRSAI* 73 (1943): 67–69.

——. *Monasterboice.* Dundalk: William Tempest, Dundalgan Press 1946.

——. 'The Origin and Nature of the Irish Books of Annals'. *Bulletin Irish Committee of Historical Sciences*, no. 12 (1941).

——. 'The Panel Representing the Traditio Evangelii on the Cross of Muiredach at Monasterboice'. *JRSAI* 62 (1932): 15–18.

——. 'The Problem of "Silva Focluti"'. *IHS* 4 (1944–45): 103–4.

——. *The Secret Languages of Ireland.* Cambridge: Cambridge University Press, 1937.

——. 'Silva Focluti'. *JRSAI* 62 (1932): 19–27.

——. 'The Sources of the Preface to the "Tigernach" Annals'. *IHS* 4 (1944–45): 1–57.

——. 'The Story of Clonmacnois'. *Proceedings and Reports of the Belfast Natural History and Philosophical Society.* 2nd ser., vol. 1, pt. 1.

MacArthur, William P. 'The Identification of Some Pestilences Recorded in the Irish Annals'. *IHS* 6: 169–89.

McBride, B. St Clair. 'Brian Boru'. *History Today* 19: 264–72.

Mac Bride, Patrick. 'St Patrick's Purgatory in Spanish Literature'. *Studies* 25 (1936): 643–53.

Mac Cana, Proinnsias. 'The Influence of the Vikings on Celtic Literature'. *Proceedings of the International Congress of Celtic Studies*, Dublin: 1959.

Mac Carthy, Charles J. F. 'The Celtic Monastery of Cork'. *JCHAS* 48 (1943): 4–8.

——. *Early Medieval Cork: An Outline Guide to Cork City and County in the 9th Century.* Cork: Tower Books, 1969.

——. 'A Lost Manuscript [Leabher Uí Cruimin]'. *JCHAS* 40 (1935): 56.

——. 'St Finbar and His Monastery'. *JCHAS* 40 (1935): 57–81; 41 (1936): 13–19, 85–91; 42 (1937): 16–24, 96–110.

——. 'Saint Finnbarr of Cork'. *JCHAS* 48 (1943): 1–4.

McCarthy, E. J. 'Portrait of St Columban'. *IER* 74: 110–115.

——. 'Portrait of St Columban'. *Mélanges Colombaniens* (1951).

[McCarthy] *Saint Columban, by the Count of Montalembert*. English edition. St Columbans (Nebraska): Society of St Columban, 1928.

McClintock, H. F. 'Irish and Highland Dress'. *Antiquity* 20.

——. 'The "Mantle of St Brigid" at Bruges'. *JRSAI* 66 (1936): 32–40.

——. *Old Irish and Highland Dress and that of the Isle of Man*. Dundalk: Dundalgan Press, 1950.

MacDermott, Máire. 'The Crosiers of St Dympna and St Mel and 10th-century Irish Metal-work'. *RIA Proc.* 58, sect. C: 167–195.

——. 'The Kells Crozier'. *Archaeologia* 96 (1955): 59–113.

——. 'An Openwork Crucifixion Plaque from Clonmacnois'. *JRSAI* 84 (1954): 36–40.

McDermott, Michael. 'Domhnach Airthir Maighe hi Críc Ua mBriúin'. *Seanchas Árdmhacha* 2, no. 2 (1957): 433–38.

——. 'St Patrick and Armagh, A Symposium: V, Professor Carney's Arguments'. *Seanchas Árdmhacha* 2, no. 1: 27–31.

MacDonagh, J. C. T., and MacIntyre, Edward. 'Bibliography of County Donegal. Parts I–II'. *Journal of the County Donegal Historical Society* 1, no. 1 (1947): 49–80; 1, no. 2 (1948): 151–64.

MacDonnacha, Frederic. 'Beathaí Chiarán Chluain Mhac Nóis: a gcoibhneas dá chéile agus a mbunús'. *Catholic Survey* 1: 219–27.

MacEoin, G. S. 'Dán ar Chogadh na Traoi [attributed to] Flann Mainistreach'. *Studia Hibernica* 1 (1961): 19–53.

——. 'The Date and Authorship of Saltair na Rann'. *ZCP* 28: 51–80.

——. 'Invocation of the Forces of Nature in the Loricae'. *Studia Hibernica* 2 (1962): 212–17.

——. 'Some Icelandic Loricae'. *Studia Hibernica* 3 (1963): 143–54.

Mac Erlean, John. 'Silva Focluti'. *Anal. Bolland.* 57 (1939): 334–63.

Mac Fhinn, Eric. 'Athchuinghe as Ailfinn'. *Galvia* 6 (1959): 15–17.

Mac Giolla Phádraig, Brian. 'The Location of Coeman, Maccoem Patraic'. *JRSAI* 73 (1943): 100–5.

McGoldrick, P. J. 'The Place of St Patrick's Captivity'. *IER* 51: 314–15.

McGreevy, C. 'Was St Cuthbert a Kells Man?' *Ríocht na Midhe* 3: 155–7.

McGurk, Patrick. 'The Irish Pocket Gospel Book'. *Sacris Erudiri* 8 (1956): 249–70.

——. *Latin Gospel Books from A.D. 400 to A.D. 800*. Bruxelles: Éditions Erasme; Amsterdam: Standard Boekh, 1961.

Mac Ivor, Dermot. 'The Boundaries of Fir Rois'. *JCLAS* 15: 144–79.

——. 'The Church of Kildemock'. *Seanchas Ardmhacha* 2, no. 2 (1957): 390–417.

——. 'The History of Fir Rois'. *JCLAS* 15: 321–48.

——. 'In Search of Saint Díomóc'. *JCLAS* 13: 225–51.

Mackay, Donald. 'New Light on the Book of Deer'. *Scottish Gaelic Studies* 5: 50.

McKeown, L. 'The Monastic Houses of Co. Down before and after the Coming of the Normans'. *JDCHS* 7: 53–64.

——. *St Patrick and Down and Connor*. Armagh: Diocesan Committee, 1961.

McKeown, M. J. 'The Shrine of St Patrick's Hand and the Shrine of St Fillan's Hand'. *JRSAI* 63 (1933): 244–7.

MacKinney, L. C. *Bishop Fulbert and Education at the School of Chartres.* Notre Dame Mediaeval Institute, 1957.

McLaughlin, Terence Patrick. *Le très ancien droit monastique de l'Occident; étude sur le développement général du monachisme.* Ligugé (Vienne): Abbaye Saint-Martin; Paris: A. Picard, 1935.

MacLennan, D. M. 'The Cathach of Colum-cille'. *Transactions of the Gaelic Society of Inverness* 35: 2–25.

MacLeod, Catríona. 'Mediaeval Wooden Figure Sculptures in Ireland'. *JRSAI* 75 (1945): 167–82, 195–203; 76 (1946): 89–100, 155–70; 77 (1947): 53–62.

MacLoughlin, James. 'Higher Education in Medieval Ireland'. *IER* 44 (1934): 56–66, 167–87, 267–81.

MacManus, F. *St Columban.* New York: Sheed and Ward, 1962.

McNally, Robert E., ed. *Old Ireland.* Dublin: Gill, 1965.

——. '*Dies Domenica:* Two Hiberno-Latin Texts'. *Mediaeval Studies* 9 (1947): 355–61.

——. 'Old Ireland: Her Scribes and Scholars'. In *Old Ireland.*

McNamara, G. 'Notes towards a Recent Bibliography of County Donegal'. *Donegal Annual* 6, no. 2: 175–184.

MacNamee, J. J. 'The Chronology of the Life of St Ciaran of Clonmacnois'. *JACAS* 2, no. 10: 3–16.

——. *History of the Diocese of Ardagh.* Dublin: Browne and Nolan, 1954.

MacNaught, J. C. 'Celtic Monasticism'. *Transactions of the Gaelic Society of Inverness* 35: 321–42.

McNeil, H. Cameron. *Saints and Sites in Mann.* London: S.P.C.K., 1928.

MacNeill, Eoin. 'Archaisms in the Ogham Inscriptions'. *RIA Proc.* 39, sect. C: 33–53.

——. 'The Beginnings of Latin Culture in Ireland'. *Studies* 20 (1931): 39–48.

——. *Early Irish Laws and Institutions.* London: Burns, Oates and Washbourne, 1935.

——. 'The Historical St Patrick'. In *Saint Patrick, A.D. 432–1932: A Fifteenth Century Memorial Book,* edited by Paul Walsh, 1932.

——. 'The Hymn of St Secundinus in Honour of St Patrick'. *IHS* 2, no. 6 (1940): 130–53.

——. 'The Language of the Picts'. *Yorkshire Celtic Studies* 2: 3–45.

——. 'The Other Patrick'. *Studies* 32 (1943): 308–14.

——. *Phases of Irish History.* Dublin: Gill, 1968. (Originally published 1919.)

——. 'Prolegomena to a Study of the Ancient Laws of Ireland with an Introduction and Notes by D. A. Binchy'. *Irish Jurist* 2 (1967): 106–15.

——. *Saint Patrick, Apostle of Ireland.* London: Sheed and Ward, 1934.

——. *Saint Patrick.* New ed., rev. Edited by John Ryan. Dublin: Clonmore and Reynolds; London: Burns and Oates, 1964.

——. 'Silva Focluti'. *RIA Proc.* 26, sect. C: 249.

——. 'The Vita Tripartita of St Patrick'. *Ériu* 11: 1–43.

McNeill, J. T., and Ganer, H. M. *Medieval Hand-books of Penance: A Translation of the Libri Poenitentiales and Selections from Related Documents.* New York: Columbia University Press, 1938.

MacNeill, Máire. *The Festival of Lughnasa*. London: Oxford University Press, 1962.

MacNeill, Patrick. 'The Identification of Foclut'. *JGAHS* 22: 164–73.

MacNiocaill, Gearóid, ed. 'Annála Geara as Proibhinse Árd Macha [BM. Add. 30512, ff. 39rb–40rb]'. *Seanchas Árdmhacha* 3, no. 2 (1959): 337–40.

——. 'Annála Uladh agus Annála Locha Cé, 1014–1220'. *Galvia* 6 (1959): 18–25.

——, ed. 'De disposicione corporis Maria⟨e⟩ et mira pulchritudine eius Epifanius e⟨pi⟩scopus'. *Éigse* 8 (1956): 70–3.

——. *Notitiae as Leabhar Cheanannais, 1033–1161*. Dublin: Cló Móráin, 1961.

——. 'Sur l'identité de S. Mainchín'. *Anal. Bolland.* 85 (1967): 59–63.

MacPhilibín, An tEaspag Liam. *See* Philbin, William J.

MacQueen, John. 'History and Miracle Stories in the Biography of Nynia'. *Innes Review* 13: 115–29.

——. 'A Lost Glasgow Life of Saint Thaney (Saint Enoch)'. *Innes Review* 6 (1955): 125–30.

——. *St Nynia*. Edinburgh: Oliver and Boyd, 1961.

McTernan, John C. *Historic Sligo*. Sligo: Yeats Country Publications, 1965.

Maestri, Annibale. 'Il culto di San Colombano abbate in Italia'. *Mélanges Colombaniens* (1951).

——. *Il culto di San Columbano in Italia*. Piacenza: Bibliotheca Storica Piacentina, 1955.

Mag Riabhaigh, S. 'In Mensura Fidei Trinitatis'. *An Sagart* 5 (1962): 3–8.

——. 'Pádraig Misnéir'. *An Sagart* 4, no. 1 (1961): 19–25.

Maguire, M. F. 'The Smith of St Patrick'. *Carloviana* 1, no. 2 (1963): 14–15.

Maher, Edward. 'St Fiacre'. *Old Kilkenny Review* 13: 48–56.

Mahr, Adolf, ed. *Christian Art in Ancient Ireland,* vol. 1. Dublin: Stationery Office, 1932.

——. 'The Early Christian Epoch'. *Christian Art in Ancient Ireland,* vol. 2.

——. 'Irish Early Christian handicrafts'. *NMAJ* 1 (1936): 57–66.

Maillier, C. *Le culte de S. Martin en pays drouais*. Dreux, 1961.

Mâle, Émile. *La fin du paganisme en Gaule et les plus anciennes basiliques chrétiennes*. Paris: Flammarion, 1950.

Malone, E. E. 'The Monk and the Martyr'. *Studia Anselmiana* 38 (1950): 201 ff.

Manceron, P. 'Notes sur les origines de la paroisse de St Columbin (Loire-Inférieure)'. *Mélanges Colombaniens* (1951).

Mansoor, M. 'Oriental Studies in Ireland from Times of St Patrick to the Rise of Islam'. *Hermathena* 62: 40–60.

Marilier, J. 'Le monastère de Moutier-Saint-Jean et ses attaches colombaniennes'. *Mélanges Colombaniens* (1951).

Marique, J. M. F. *Leaders of Iberean Christianity (50–650 A.D.)*. Boston: St Paul Editions, 1962.

Markert, Emil. 'Zur Deutung des Namens Kilian'. In *Heiliges Franken* (1952).

Marsh, Arnold. *St Patrick's Writings: A Modern Translation.* Dundalk: Dundalgan Press, 1961.

Marsh, Thomas. 'St Patrick's Terminology for Confirmation'. *IER* 93: 145–54.

Martin, Saint. *Saint Martin dans l'art et l'imagerie.* Tours: Musée des Beaux-Arts, 1961.

——. *Saint Martin et son temps. Mémorial du XVIe centenaire des débuts du monachisme en Gaule (361–1961).* Rome: Herder, 1961.

Martin, F. X. 'Bibliography of Patrician Literature'. In *St Patrick* (1964).

——. 'Gerald of Wales: Norman Reporter on Ireland'. *Studies* 58: 279 ff.

Marx, Jean. *Les littératures celtiques.* Paris: Presses Universitaires de France, 1959.

Masai, F. *Essai sur les origines de la miniature dite irlandaise.* Brussels: Éditions Érasme, 1947.

——. 'Miniature mosane ou miniature saxonne? A propos du Sacramentaire de Wibald de Stavelot (Bruxelles, B.R. 2034–35)'. *Scriptorium* 13 (1959): 22–6.

Mason, M. E. *'Active Life' and 'Contemplative Life': A Study of the Concepts from Plato to the Present.* Milwaukee: Marquette University Press, 1961.

Mason, T. H. 'The Devil as Depicted on Irish High Crosses'. *JRSAI* 72 (1942): 131–5.

——. *The Islands of Ireland.* London: Batsford, 1936.

——. 'St Brigid's Crosses'. *JRSAI* 75 (1945): 160–6.

Masseron, Alexandre. 'Saint Malachie vu par Saint Bernard'. In *Le miracle irlandais,* edited by Daniel-Rops.

Matheis, Eugen. *Pirminius festschrift. Erweiterte Neuauflage.* Hornbach, 1957.

Maxwell, Herbert. *The Place Names of Galloway.* Glasgow: Jackson, Wylie, 1930.

Mayer, M. 'Münster und Radfeld: irisch-keltische Missionsposten?' *Schlern-Schriften,* fasc. 101 (1953): 97–122.

Mayer, Theodor. 'Die Anfänge der Reichenau'. *Zeitschrift für die Geschichte des Oberrheins* 101: 305–352.

Mazal, Otto, and Unterkircher, Franz. *Katalog der abendländischen Handschriften der Österreichischen Nationalbibliothek.* Wien: Georg Prachner Verlag, 1967.

Meehan, Denis, ed. *Adamnan's 'De Locis Sanctis'.* Dublin: Institute for Advanced Studies, 1958.

Megaw, B. R. S. 'Who Was St Conchan? A Consideration of Manx Christian Origins'. *Journal of the Manx Museum* 6, no. 29 (1962–63).

Megaw, J. V. S. *Art of the European Iron Age.* London: Adams and Dart, 1971.

Meile, Josephus, 'Die Gallusstiftung als Ausgangspunkt der st gallischen Kultur'. In *Sankt Gallus Gedenkbuch.*

Mélanges Colombaniens: Actes du Congrès International de Luxeuil, 20–23 juillet, 1950. Paris: Éditions Alsatia, 1951.

Mellot, Jean. 'Les fondations colombaniennes dan le diocèse de Bourges'. *Mélanges Colombaniens* (1951).

Meroney, H. 'Irish in the Old English Charms'. *Speculum* 20: 172–82.

Merzbacher, Friedrich. 'Das Kiliansbrauchtum'. *Heiliges Franken* (1952).
——. 'Das Kilianssymbol des würzburger und mainzer Domkapitels'. *Heiliges Franken* (1952).
——. 'Zur Rechtgeschichte und Volkskunde der würzburger Kilian-sverehrung'. *Würzburger Diözesangeschichtsblätter* 14/15: 27–56.
Mescal, Daniel. *The Story of Inis Carthaigh (Scattery Island)*. Dublin: O Donoghue and Co., 1902.
Meslin, M. S. *Vincent de Lérins: le Commonitorium*. Namur: Éd. du Soleil Levant, 1959.
Mesmer, Gertrude. 'The Cult of St Patrick in the Vicinity of Dracken-stein'. *Seanchas Árdmhacha* 4, no. 2 (1961–62): 68–75.
Metz, René. 'L'action de Saint Colomban en Alsace'. *Mélanges Colombaniens* (1951).
——. 'La consécration des vierges dans l'église franque d'aprés la plus ancienne vie de Sainte Pusinne'. *Revue des science religieuses*, 1961.
Metzger, Joseph. *Das katholische Schrifttum im heutigen England*. Munich: Verlag Kösel-Pustet, 1937.
Meyer, Otto. 'Sankt Kilian im mittelalterlichen Bamberg. Eine hagio-graphisch-kulturgeschichtliche Skizze'. *Frankenbund, Bunderbriefe* 4 (1952): 2–3.
Meyer, Peter. 'Zur Ornamentik des Evangeliars von Kells'. *Graphis* 24 (1949): 335–6, 342.
Meyer, Verena. 'Columban im Nibelungenlied?' *Theologische Zeit-schrift* 8: 70–2.
Ní Mhaol-Chróin, Caitlín. *See* Mulchrone, Kathleen.
Micheli, G. L. 'Recherches sur les manuscrits irlandais décorés de Saint-Gall et de Reichenan'. *Revue Archéologique* 7, ser. 6: 188–223.
Millot, René-P. *L'épopée missionaire. Aventures et missions au services de Dieu, de S. Paul à Grégoire XV.* Paris: Fayard, 1956.
——. Irlandais au péril des flots'. In *Le miracle irlandais*, edited by Daniel-Rops (1956).
Misonne, D. 'La charte de Saint-Martin de Tours en faveur de Gérard de Brogne'. *Revue Bénédictine* 70 (1960): 540–61.
Mitchell, Gerard. 'Commutation of Penances in the Celtic Penitentials'. *IER* 40 (1932): 225–39.
——. 'The Penitential of St Columbanus and Its Importance in the History of Penance'. *Mélanges Colombaniens* (1951).
——. 'St Columbanus on Penance'. *Irish Theological Quarterly* 18: 43–54.
Mohrmann, Christine. 'How Latin Became the Language of Early Christendom'. *Studies* 40 (1951): 277 ff.
——. *The Latin of St Patrick: Four Lectures*. Dublin: Institute for Ad-vanced Studies, 1961.
Moloney, M. 'Kilcooley: Foundation and Restoration'. *JRSAI* 74 (1944): 219–23.
Momigliano, Arnoldo, ed. *The Conflict between Paganism and Christianity in the Fourth Century*. Oxford: Clarendon Press, 1963.
Monastica 1 (1960). Montserrat: Abadía.
Montalembert, Charles, Comte de. *Précis d'histoire monastique*. Edited by the Benedictines of Oosterhout. Paris: Vrin, 1934.

Mooney, Canice. 'The Archives at Simancas as a Source for Irish Ecclesiastical History'. *Proceedings of the Irish Catholic Historical Committee* (1955): 18–21.

——. 'Paenitentiarium S. Maol Ruain'. *Celtica* 2: 299–304.

——. 'Saint Cathaldus of Taranto'. In *Irish Monks in the Golden Age* (1963).

Moore, Desmond F. *Dublin*. Saol agus Cultúr in Éirinn, no. 13. Dublin: Three Candles, 1965.

Moore, W. J. *The Saxon Pilgrims to Rome and the Schola Saxonum*. Dissertation, Fribourg: Faculté des lettres, 1937.

Moreau, A. *La vie de S. Germain d'Auxerre*. Auxerre: La Liberté de Yonne, 1948.

Moreau, E. de. 'La "vita Amandi prima" et les fondations monastiques de S. Amand'. *Anal. Bolland.* 67 (1949): 447–464.

Morris, Ernest. 'Ancient Bells of Celtic Saints'. *Apollo* 28: 282–7.

Morris, Henry. 'The Holy Wells of Donegal'. *Béaloideas* 6: 143–62.

——. 'The Iconography of St Patrick'. *JDCHS* 7: 5–29.

——. 'The Muiredach Cross at Monasterboice'. *JRSAI* 64 (1934): 203–12.

——. 'St Patrick and the Politics of His Day'. *Studies* 21 (1932): 7–19.

——. 'Silva Focluti [note on]'. *JRSAI* 62 (1932): 225.

——. 'Some Ulster Ecclesiastical Bells'. *JRSAI* 61 (1931): 61–4.

——. 'Where King Laeghaire Was Killed'. *JRSAI* 68 (1938): 123–9.

——. 'Who was "Old Patrick"?' *JDCHS* 9: 5–22.

——. 'The Wood of Foclut: Silva Focluti'. *JDCHS* 8: 5–16.

Morris, J. 'Dates of the Celtic Saints'. *Journal of Theological Studies* 17 (1966): 380 ff.

Mörsdorff, K. 'Irischer Wahlmodus'. *Lexikon für Theologie und Kirche* 5 (1960): 753–4.

Mortimer, Robert Cecil. *The Origins of Private Penance in the Western Church*. Oxford: Clarendon Press, 1939.

Most, W. G. *The Syntax of the Vitae Sanctorum Hiberniae*. Washington: Catholic University of America Press, 1946.

Mould, D. D. C. Pochin. *The Celtic Saints: Our Heritage*. Dublin: Clonmore and Reynolds, 1956.

——. *Ireland of the Saints*. London: Batsford, 1953.

——. *The Irish Saints*. Dublin: Clonmore and Reynolds; London: Burns and Oates, 1964.

——. 'Naomh Colmcille'. *IER* 99: 381–91.

——. *Saint Brigid*. Dublin: Clonmore and Reynolds, 1965.

Mulcahy, C. 'The Hymn of St Secundinus in Praise of St Patrick'. *IER* 65: 145–9.

——. 'The Irish Latin Hymns: "Sancti Venite" of St Sechnall (d. cir. 447) and "Altus Prosator" of St Columba (521–597)'. *IER* 58, ser. 5 (1941): 385–405.

Mulchrone, Kathleen, ed. *Bethu Phátraic: The Tripartite Life of Patrick*. Dublin: RIA, 1939.

——, ed. *The Book of Lecan: Leabhar Mór Mhic Fhir Bhisigh Leacáin*. Dublin: Stationery Office, 1937.

[Mulchrone] ed. *Caithréim Cellaig*. Dublin: Stationery Office, 1933.
——. 'Ferdomnach and the Armagh Notulae'. *Ériu* 18: 160–3.
—— [Ní Mhaol-Chróin, Caitlín]. 'Macalla as Cluain-mhac-Nóis, A.D. 1050'. *Galvia* 1: 15–17.
——. 'The Mission of Patricius Secundus Episcopus Scottorum'. *IER* 85: 155–70.
——. 'The Old-Irish Form of Palladius'. *JGAHS* 22: 34–42.
——. 'Tirechán and the Tripartite Life'. *IER* 79: 186–93.
——. 'The Tripartite Life of Patrick: A Lost Fragment Discovered'. *JGAHS* 20.
——. 'What Are the Armagh *Notulae*?' *Ériu* 17: 140–4.
Mulchrone, Kathleen, FitzPatrick, E., and Pearson, A. I. *Catalogue of Irish Manuscripts in the Royal Irish Academy, Index II.* Dublin: R.I.A., 1958.
Mullarkey, T. 'St Marys Abbey, Devenish: An Architectural Survey'. *Clogher Record* 4: 9–15.
Müller, Iso. 'Zu den Anfängen der hagiographischen Kritik'. *Schweizer Beiträge zur allgemeinen Geschichte* 8 (1950): 108–34.
——. 'Zum geistigen Einfluss der kolumbanischen Bewegung im mittleren Europa'. *Zeitscrift für schweizerische Kirchengeschichte* 59 (1965): 265–84.
Müller-Lisowski, Käte. 'La légende de St Jean dans la tradition irlandaise et le druid Mog Ruith'. *Études Celtique* 3 (1938): 46–70.
Munding, Emmanuel. *Die Kalendarien von St Gallen aus XXI Handschriften neuntes bis elftes Jahrhundert.* Beuron: Beuroner Kunstverlag, 1948.
Mundó, P. A. 'Les anciens synodes abbatiaux et les "Regulae SS. Patrum"'. *Studia Anselmiana* 44 (1959).
Murphy, Gerard. *Early Irish Lyrics.* Oxford: Clarendon Press, 1956.
——. *Early Irish Metrics.* Dublin: R.I.A. and Hodges, Figgis, 1961.
——. 'Eleventh or Twelfth-century Doctrine Concerning the Real Presence'. In *Medieval Studies Presented to Aubrey Gwynn* (1961).
——. 'The Origin of Irish Nature Poetry'. *Studies* 20 (1931): 87–102.
——. 'St Patrick and the Civilising of Ireland'. *IER* 79: 194–204.
——. 'The Two Patricks'. *Studies* 32 (1943): 297–307.
Murphy, T. A. 'The Oldest Eucharistic Hymn'. *IER* 46 (1935): 172–6.
Murray, L. P. *Our Lady's Island in History and Legend.* Wexford: Wicklow People, 1940.
——. 'The Wood of Foclut' [Summary of article by John MacErlean in *Anal. Bolland.* 57: 3–4]. *JCLAS* 9, no. 2 (1938): 166–8.
Musurillo, H. 'History and Symbol: A Study of Form in Early Christian Literature'. *Theological Studies* 18 (1957): 357–86.
Myers, J. N. L. 'Pelagius and the End of Roman Rule in Britain'. *Journal of Roman Studies* 40 (1960): 21–36.

Nash-Williams, Victor E. *The Early Christian Monuments of Wales.* Cardiff: University of Wales Press, 1950.
Natale, A. R. *Influenze merovingiche e studi calligrafici nello scriptorium di Bobbio, Sec. VII–IX.* Milan: Bibliotheca Ambrosiana, 1950.

——. *Studi paleografici: arte e imitazione della scrittura insulare in Codici Bobbiesi*. Milan: Edizioni del Capricorno, 1950.

Nerney, D. S. 'The Blessed Eucharist in the Libri S. Patricii'. *IER* ser. 5, 58 (1941): 331–44.

——. 'A Study of St Patrick's Sources'. *IER* 71: 497–508; 72: 14–27, 97–111, 265–81.

Neu, H. 'Eine mittelalterliche Heiligenlitanei aus Malmedy'. In *Aus Mittelalter und Neuzeit. Festschrift zum 70 Geburtstag von Gerhard Kallen*. Bonn, 1957.

Neundorfer, B. 'Zur Entstehung von Wallfahrten und Wallfahrtspatrozinien im mittelalterlichen Bistum Bamberg'. *Bericht des Hist. Vereins Bamberg* 99 (1963): 1–132.

Nicholl, Donald. 'Celts, Romans and Saxons'. *Studies* 47 (1958): 298 ff.

Niermeyer, M. J. F. *Mediae Latinitatis Lexicon Minus*. Leyde: Brill, 1954.

Nolan, M. J. 'The Bell of Bangor Abbey'. *JRSAI* 63 (1933): 243–4.

Noonan, P. J. *Glendalough: Souvenir, History and Guide*. Wexford: Wicklow People, 1941.

Nordenfalk, C. 'Before the Book of Durrow'. *Acta Archaeologica* 18 (1947): 141–74.

Norman, E. R., and St Joseph, J. K. S. *The Early Development of Irish Society: The Evidence of Aerial Photography*. Cambridge: Cambridge University Press, 1969.

Nowlan, Kevin. 'The Ancient Church and Parish of Kilternan, Co. Dublin'. *Dublin Historical Record* 2: 38–40.

Nunan, Francis. *Kerry's Ancient See and Shrine, Artfert-Brendan*. Tralee: Kerryman, 1950.

Oakley, Thomas P. 'Celtic Penance: Its Sources, Affiliations and Influence'. *IER* ser. 5, 52 (1938): 147–64, 581–601.

——. 'The Penitentials as Sources for Mediaeval History'. *Speculum* 15: 210–23.

O'Boyle, James. *Life of St Malachy, Patron Saint of Down and Connor*. Belfast: P. Quinn, 1931.

Ó Briain, Félim. 'The Blessed Eucharist in Irish Liturgy and History'. In *Studia Eucharistica*. Antwerp: N.V. de Nederlandsche Bockhandel, 1946.

——. 'The Expansion of Irish Christianity to 1200: An Historicographical Survey'. *Bulletin of the Irish Committee of Historical Sciences*, no. 19 (1942).

——. 'The Feast of Our Lady's Conception in the Medieval Irish Church'. *IER* ser. 5, 70 (1948): 687–704.

——. 'The Hagiography of Leinster'. In *Féil-Sgríbhinn Eóin Mhic Néill* (1940).

——. 'Irish Hagiography: Historiography and Method'. In *Measgra i gCuimhne Mhichíl Uí Chléirigh*. Dublin: Assisi Press, 1944.

——. 'Irish Missionaries and Mediaeval Church Reform'. In *Miscellanea Historica*, edited by Alberti de Meyer. Louvain, 1946.

——. 'Miracles in the Lives of the Irish Saints'. *IER* 66 (1945): 331–42.

——. 'Saga Themes in Irish Hagiography'. In *Féilscríbhinn Tórna*.

O'Brien, M. A. 'Miscellanea Hibernica' [includes note on St Patrick's Confession]. *Études Celtique* 3 (1938): 362–73.
——. 'The Old Irish Life of St Brigid'. *IHS* 1: 121–34, 343–53.
Ó Buachalla, Liam. 'Cill na Cluaine and Kilacloyne'. *JCHAS* 44 (1939): 135.
——. 'Commentary on the Life of St Finbarr'. *JCHAS* 70 (1965): 1–6.
——. 'The Construction of the Irish Annals, 429–466'. *JCHAS* 63 (1958): 103–15.
——. 'The Ecclesiastical Families of Cloyne'. *JCHAS* 50 (1945): 83–8.
——. 'The Homeplace of St Finbarr'. *JCHAS* 68 (1963): 104–6.
——. 'Notes on the Early Irish Annals, 467–550'. *JCHAS* 64 (1959): 73–81.
O'Byrne, Cathal. 'St Patrick's Valley'. *Irish Rosary* 44: 193–9.
O'Carroll, James. 'The Chronology of Saint Columban'. *Irish Theological Quarterly* 24 (1957): 76–95.
——. 'The Luxeuil Congress in Honour of the Fourteenth Centenary of St Columban, 1950'. *IER* 75: 490–8.
——. 'Monastic Rules in Merovingian Gaul'. *Studies* 42 (1953): 407–19.
Ó Cillín, Proinsias. 'Ar Tháinic na Rómhánaigh go hÉirinn?' *Galvia* 2: 7–19.
O'Clery, Michael. *Genealogiae Regum et Sanctorum Hiberniae*. Edited by Paul Walsh. Dublin: Gill, 1918.
Ó Coindealbháin, S. 'Holy Wells'. *JCHAS* 51 (1946): 158–63.
Ó Conbhuí, C. 'The Lands of St Mary's Abbey, Dublin'. *RIA Proc.* 62, sect. C: 21–86.
O'Connell, D. J. 'Easter Cycles in the Early Irish Church'. *JRSAI* 66 (1936): 67–106.
O'Connell, Philip. 'Castle Kieran'. *Ríocht na Midhe* 1, no. 3 (1957): 17–33.
——. 'A Castlekieran Cross-slab'. *JRSAI* 87 (1957): 167–8.
——. *The Diocese of Kilmore: Its History and Antiquities*. Dublin: Browne and Nolan, 1937.
——. 'Kells—Early and Mediaeval'. *Ríocht na Midhe* 2, no. 1 (1959): 18–36; 2, no. 2 (1960): 8–22.
——. 'St Farannan of Donoughmore. *Journal of the Proceedings of the Clonmel Historical and Archaeological Society* 1, no. 4: 64–7.
——. *Schools and Scholars of Breiffne*. Dublin: Browne and Nolan, 1942.
——. 'Sources for the Life of St Mogue'. *Breifne* 1: 130–54.
Ó Corráin, Donncha. 'Studies in West Munster History: The Regnal Succession in Ciarraighe Luachra'. *JKAS* 1: 45–48.
——. 'Studies in West Munster History: Altraighe'. *JKAS* 2: 27–37; 3: 19–22.
Ó Cuilleanáin, Cormac. 'The Dublin Annals of Inisfallen [250 A.D.– 1320]'. In *Féilscríbhinn Tórna*.
Ó Cuív, Brian. 'An Early Irish Poem of Invocation to Our Lady'. *Studies* 44 (1955): 207 ff.
——. *Literary Creation and Irish Historical Tradition*. London: Oxford University Press, 1965.
——, ed. *Seven Centuries of Irish Learning, 1000–1700*. Dublin: Stationery Office, 1961.

O'Daly, Maureen. 'Three Poems Attributed to Maol Cobha'. *Ériu* 21: 103–15.

Ó Danachair, Caoimhín. 'The Holy Wells of Corkaguiney, Co. Kerry'. *JRSAI* 90 (1960): 67–78.

——. 'The Holy Wells of County Dublin'. *Reportorium Novum* 2: 68–87.

——. 'The Holy Wells of Co. Limerick'. *JRSAI* 85 (1955): 193–217.

——. 'The Holy Wells of North County Kerry'. *JRSAI* 88 (1958): 153–64.

O'Doherty, John F. 'Independence, Continuity and the Church of St Patrick'. *IER* 44 (1934): 449–65.

——. *Laurentius von Dublin und das irische Normannentum*. Maynooth: St Patrick's College, 1933.

——. 'The Place of St Patrick's Captivity'. *IER* 51: 430–1; 54: 426–30.

——. Review of *The Two Patricks* by T. F. O'Rahilly (1942). *IHS* 3 (1942–43): 323–9.

——. 'St Columbanus and the Holy See'. *IER* 42 (1933): 1–10.

Ó Doibhlinn, Éamon. 'Domhnach Mór'. *Seanchas Árdmhacha* 2, no. 1 (1956): 166–77; 2, no. 2 (1957): 418–32.

——. *Domhnach Mór*. Omagh: Clólann na Struaile, 1969.

Ó Domhnaill, M. *Beatha Gillasius Ardmachanus*. Dublin: Stationery Office, 1939.

Ó Donnchadha, Tadgh, ed. *An Leabhar Muimhneach*. Dublin: Stationery Office, 1940.

O'Donnell, Augustine. *St Patrick's Rock*. Cashel Press, 1961.

O'Donoghue, John. 'St Patrick's Day Custom'. *JCHAS* 44 (1939): 62.

O Donoghue, Noel-Dermot. 'The Spirituality of St Patrick'. *Studies* 50 (1961): 152 ff.

O Donovan, John, ed. *Three Fragments of Irish Annals Copied from Ancient Sources by Dubhaltach MacFirbisigh*. Dublin: Irish Archaeological and Celtic Society, 1860.

O Driscoll, Desmond. 'The White Island Sculptures'. *JRSAI* 72 (1942): 116–9.

O'Dwyer, B. W. 'Gaelic Monasticism and the Irish Cistercians, c. 1228'. *IER* 108: 19–28.

Ó hÉailidhe, P. 'Fassaroe and Associated Crosses'. *JRSAI* 88 (1958): 101–10.

——. 'The Rathdown Slabs'. *JRSAI* 87 (1957): 75–88.

——. 'Some Unpublished Antiquities of the Early Christian Period in the Dublin Area'. *JRSAI* 89 (1959): 205–7.

Ó hEaluighthe, D. 'St Gobnet of Ballyvourney'. *JCHAS* 57 (1952): 43–61.

Ó Faracháin, Roibeárd. 'Our greatest Exile'. *Capuchin Annual*, 1939.

Ó Fiaich, Tomás. 'Irish Peregrini on the Continent: Recent Research in Germany'. *IER* 103: 233–400.

——. 'The Monastic Life in Early Christian Ireland'. *Capuchin Annual* 36: 116–34.

——. 'Saint Colmcille in Ireland and Scotland'. In *Irish Monks in the golden age*.

——. 'St Patrick and Armagh'. *IER* 89: 153–70; 95 (1961): 229–35.

Ó Fiaich, Tomás, and Connolly, Turlough. *Irish Cultural Influence in*

Europe, 6th to 12th Century. Dublin: Cultural Relations Committee of Ireland, 1967.

O'Flanders, A. *(pseud.)*. *Van sinte Brigida (de Iersche) beschermster van stal en neerhof*. Tielt: Lannoo, 1946.

Ó Foghludha, R. 'Footprints of St Finbar'. *IER* 74: 242–50.

Ní Ógáin, Úna, and O Dwyer, Robert. *Dánta Dé, Hymns to God, Ancient and Modern*. Dublin: Three Candles, 1928.

Ó Gallachair, P. 'Coarbs and Erenaghs of Co. Donegal'. *Donegal Annual* 4: 272–81.

——. 'Columban Donegal'. *Donegal Annual* 5: 262–74.

——. 'Patrician Donegal'. *Donegal Annual* 5: 70–9.

——. 'Site of Monastery at Trillick, Co. Tyrone'. *Clogher Record* 6 (1966): 198 ff.

——. 'Where Was St Colmcille Born at Gartan?' *Donegal Annual* 5: 219–22.

O'Hare, Charles. 'The Pascal Controversy in the Celtic Churches'. *IER* 40 (1932): 337–49, 492–503; 41 (1932): 266–76, 615–29; 42 (1933): 366–77.

——. 'St Augustine and the Conversion of England'. *IER* 38 (1931): 124–41, 285–99.

O Hegarty, Maureen. 'Clara Old Church and Freneystown Castle'. *Old Kilkenny Review* 11: 55–60.

Ó h-Iceadha, G. 'Excavation of Church Site in Old Kilcullen Townland, Co. Kildare'. *JRSAI* 71 (1941): 149–51.

Ó hInnse, Séamus, ed. *Miscellaneous Irish Annals*. Dublin: Institute for Advanced Studies, 1947.

O'Kearney, Nicholas, ed. *The Prophecies of Saints Columcille, Maeltamlacht, Ultan, Senan, Bearcan and Malachy*. Dublin: Duffy, 1945.

O'Kelly, J. J. *Ireland's Spiritual Empire*. Dublin: Gill, 1952.

O'Kelly, Michael J. 'The Belt-shrine from Moylough, Sligo'. *JRSAI* 95 (1965): 149–88.

——. 'Church Island near Valencia, Co. Kerry'. *RIA Proc.* 59, sect. C: 57–136.

——. 'An Island Settlement at Beginish, Co. Kerry'. *RIA Proc.* 57, sect. C: 159–94.

——. 'St Gobnet's House, Ballyvourney, Co. Cork'. *JCHAS* 57 (1952): 18–40.

O'Kelly, Michael J., and Kavanagh, Séamus. 'An Ogam-inscribed Cross-slab from County Kerry'. *JCHAS* 59 (1954): 101–10.

Ó Laoghaire, Diarmuid. 'Early Irish Spirituality'. *Capuchin Annual* 36: 135–47.

——. 'Old Ireland and Her Spirituality'. In *Old Ireland* (1965).

Oliver, Jane. *Isle of Glory*. London: Collins, 1947.

Ó Lochlainn, Colm. *Cruach Phádraic: Ireland's Holy Mountain*. Dublin: Three Candles, 1961.

——. 'An Irish Version of the Prayers of St Nierses of Clai'. *IER* 95 (1961): 361–71.

——. 'Roadways in Ancient Ireland'. In *Féil-Sgríbhinn Eóin Mhic Néill* (1940).

——, trans. 'Lúireach Phádraic: St Patrick's Breastplate'. *Studies* 50 (1961): 1 ff.

O'Meara, John J. 'The Confession of St Patrick and the Confessions of St Augustine'. *IER* 85: 190–7.

Ó Moghráin, Pádraig. 'Naomh Bréanainn Chluain Fearta agus Ceap-Sinsear na Máilleach'. *Béaloideas* 22 (1953): 154–90.

Omon, Lucien. 'Le passage de Saint Colomban dans la Brie'. *Mélanges Colombaniens* (1951).

Ó Mórdha, Séamus. 'Tighearnach Chluain Eois'. *St Macarten's Seminary Centenary Souvenir* (1940).

Ó Murchadha, Domhnall. 'Stone Sculpture in Pre-Norman Ireland'. *Capuchin Annual* 36: 172–200.

O Murnaghan, Art. 'A Note on the Cross in Irish Archaeology'. *JCLAS* 11: 61–2.

Ó Nualláin, Gearóid. 'Pádraig Apstal Éireann'. *IER* 51 (1938): 256–67.

Oppenheim, Philip. *Das Mönchskleid im christlichen Altertum*. Freiburg i. Br.: Herder, 1931.

——. *Symbolik und religiöse Wertung des Mönchskleid im christlichen Altertum*. Münster i. W.: Aschendorff, 1932.

O'Rahilly, T. F. 'Notes on Irish Place-names'. *Hermathena* 23 (1933): 196–220.

——. Review of Ludwig Bieler, *The Life and Legend of St Patrick* (1949). *IHS* 8: 268–79.

——. *The Two Patricks: A Lecture on the History of Christianity in Fifth-century Ireland*. Dublin: Institute for Advanced Studies, 1942.

Ó Raifeartaigh, T. 'Leasú Eagarthóra Sa Litir faoi Choroticus'. *Studia Hibernica* 2 (1962): 174–81.

——. 'The Life of St Patrick: A New Approach'. *IHS* 16 (1968): 119–37.

——. 'Pádraig agus na *Seniores*'. *Seanchas Árdmhacha* 4, no. 2 (1961–62): 45–67.

——. 'The Reading *Nec a me orietur* in Paragraph 32 of Saint Patrick's Confession'. *JRSAI* 95 (1965): 189–92.

——. 'St Patrick and Armagh, A Symposium: III. Na teoiricí nua'. *Seanchas Árdmhacha* 2, no. 1: 9–21.

——. 'Saint Patrick's Twenty-eight Days' Journey'. *IHS* 16 (1968): 395–416.

——. 'Some Observations on Tense-usage in Saint Patrick's Writings'. *IER* 108: 209–13.

O'Reilly, M. 'Ardbraccan'. *Ríocht na Midhe* 1, no. 2 (1956): 15–20.

O Reilly, Patrick M. 'The *Fractio Panis* in the Stowe Missal'. *Iris Hibernia* 4, no. 1 (1958): 62–8.

Ó Ríordáin, Seán P. *Antiquities of the Irish Countryside*. Cork: Cork University Press, 1942.

——. 'The Genesis of the Celtic Cross'. In *Féilscríbhinn Tórna*.

——. 'Irish Culture in the Seventh Century'. *Studies* 37 (1948): 279 ff.

——. 'Roman Material in Ireland'. *RIA Proc.* 51, sect. C: 35–82

Ó Searcaigh, Séamus. 'Beatha agus saoghal ré Cholumcille'. *Irisleabhar Muighe Nuadhat* (1947).

——, ed. *Beatha Cholm Chille*. Dublin: Stationery Office, 1967.

O'Shaughnessy, D. F. 'St Molua's Well—Emlygrennan'. *JCHAS* 37 (1932): 90–1.

Oskamp, H. P. A. 'Notes on the History of Lebor na hUidre'. *RIA Proc.* 65, sect. C: 117–37.

Oslender, Frowin. *Initium Sancti evangelii: Initialen der frühen Buchmalerei.* Kassel: Friedrich Lometsch Verlag, 1959.

Ó Súilleabháin, Pádraig. 'Sermons on St Patrick on the Continent'. *IER* 101: 170–1.

O'Sullivan, Denis. 'The Monastic Establishments of Mediaeval Cork'. *JCHAS* 48 (1943): 9–18.

O'Sullivan, J. 'Old Ireland and Her Monasticism'. In *Old Ireland* (1965).

O'Sullivan, William. 'Notes on the Scripts and Make-up of the Book of Leinster'. *Celtica* 7.

O'Toole, Edward. *Leighlin Diocese: Its Ancient Boundaries and Divisions.* Carlow: St Mary's College, Knockbeg, 1936.

——. 'The Primitive Churches of Rathvilly, Co. Carlow'. *JKAS* 11: 59 ff.

Oulton, J. E. L. 'The Apostles' Creed and Belief Concerning the Church'. *Journal of Theological Studies* 39 (1938): 239–43.

——. *The Credal Statements of St Patrick as Contained in the Fourth Chapter of His Confession: A Study of Their Sources.* Dublin: Hodges, Figgis; London: Oxford University Press, 1940.

Oury, G. 'L'idéal monastique de la vie canoniale: le Bienheureux Hervé de Tours (†1002)'. *Revue Mabillon* 52 (1962): 1–31.

——. 'Les messes de S. Martin dans les sacramentaires gallicans, romano-francs et milanais'. *Études Grégoriennes* 5 (1962): 73–97.

Ozenda, Lucien. 'La paroisse St-Colomban-de-Lantosque (diocèse de Nice)'. *Mélanges Colombaniens* (1951).

Pächt, O., Dodwell, C. R., and Wormald, F. *The St Albans Psalter (Albani Psalter).* London: Warburg Institute, 1960.

Pancotti, Vincenzo. *La Chiesa di Santa Brigida.* Piacenza: A. Del Maino, 1928.

Paringer, Benedikt. 'Wie die Bayern Christen wurden Weltenburg und die iro-fränkische Mission'. In *Zwiebelturm* 4 (1952): 88 ff.

Parkes, George B. *The English Traveller to Italy. I. The Middle Ages (to 1525).* Rome: Edizioni di Storia e Litteratura, 1954.

Patch, H. W. *The Other World According to Descriptions in Mediaeval Literature.* Cambridge (Mass.): Harvard University Press, 1950.

Paterson, T. G. F. 'Brigid's Crosses in County Armagh'. *JCLAS* 11: 15–20.

——. 'The Cult of the Well in County Armagh'. *UJA* 11 (1948): 127–30.

Patrick, Saint. *Beatha Phádraig* (edited from RIA MS 23, no. 24). Dublin: Stationery Office, 1940.

'Paulinus'. 'Baptism and Episcopal Consecration in the Celtic Churches'. *JDCHS* 7: 65–72.

Paulsen, P. 'Koptische und irische Kunst und ihre Ausstrahlungen auf altgermanische Kulturen'. *Tribus* (1952–53).

Penco, G. 'Le figure bibliche del "Vir Dei" nell'agiografia monastica'. *Benedictina* 15 (1968): 1–13.

——. 'L'imitazione di Cristo nell'agiografia monastica'. *Collectanea Cisterciensia* 28 (1966): 17–34.

——. 'Il monachesimo in Italia'. In *Nuove Questioni di Storia Medioevale*. Milano, 1964.

——. *Storia del monachesimo in Italia dalle origini alla fine del medio ero*. Roma: Edizioni paoline, 1961.

Pender, Séamus. 'The O Clery Book of Genealogies'. *Analecta Hibernica* 18 (1951).

Pepperdene, Margaret W. 'Baptism in the Early British and Irish Churches'. *Irish Theological Quarterly* 22: 110–23.

——. 'Bede's *Historia Ecclesiastica*: A New Perspective'. *Celtica* 4: 253 ff.

Phibbs, C. B. 'The Problem of Dating Ancient Irish Buildings'. *Hermathena* 54 (1939): 54–92.

Philbin, William J. [MacPhilibín, An tEaspag Liam], trans. *Mise Pádraig: nua-aistriú gaeilge ar scríbhinní Naomh Pádraig*. Dublin: FÁS, 1961.

Pickman, Edward M. *The Mind of Latin Christendom*. Oxford: Oxford University Press, 1937.

Piel, A. *Les Moines dans l'Église: textes des Souverains Pontifes*. Paris: Éditions du Cerf, 1964.

Piggott, Stuart. *Celts, Saxons and the Early Antiquaries*. Edinburgh: Edinburgh University Press, 1967.

——. *Scotland before History*. Edinburgh: Nelson, 1958.

Pinkman, John. 'The Monastery of Gallen, Offaly'. *JACAS* 2, no. 10: 48–51.

Pirolley, E. 'Saint Colomban et Faverney'. *Mélanges Colombaniens* (1951).

Pisani, Vittore. 'La religione degli antichi Celti'. In *Storia delle religioni*. Turin: Utet, 1954.

Porter, Arthur Kingsley. *The Crosses and Culture of Ireland*. London: Humphrey Milford; Oxford University Press, 1931.

——. 'An Egyptian Legend in Ireland'. *Jahrbuch für Kunstwissenshaft* (Marburg University) (1930).

Porter, W. S. 'Early Spanish Monasticism'. *Laudate: Quarterly Review of the Benedictines of Nashdom* 10 (1932): 2–16, 66–80, 156–68.

Potter, K. R. *Willelmi Malmesbiriensis monachi Historia novella*. Edinburgh: Nelson, 1955.

Powell, Douglas. 'The Textual Integrity of St Patrick's Confession'. *Anal. Bolland.* 87 (1969): 387–409.

Power, Patrick. 'The Abbey of Molana, Co. Waterford'. *JRSAI* 62 (1932): 142–52.

——. 'Ballygarran Cill, near Waterford'. *JRSAI* 71 (1941): 63–4.

——. 'The *Cill* or *Cillín*: A Study in Irish Ecclesiology'. *IER* 73 (1950): 218–25.

——. *Crichad an Chaoilli, Being the Topography of Ancient Fermoy*. Cork: Cork University Press, 1932.

——. 'Cross-inscribed Pillar-stone, Ballygarran, near Waterford'. *JCHAS* 43 (1938): 124.

[Power] 'Early Bishops of Lismore'. *IER* 68: 42–52.

———. 'The Mass in the Early Irish Church'. *IER* ser. 5, 60 (1942): 197–206.

———. 'Our Ancient Ruined Churches'. *IER* 75: 420–9.

———. 'Some Old Churches of Decies'. *JRSAI* 68 (1938): 55–68.

———. *Waterford and Lismore*. Cork: Cork University Press, 1937.

Powell, T. G. E. *The Celts*. London: Thames and Hudson, 1958.

Pralle, Ludwig. 'Ein keltisches Missale in der Fuldaer Klosterbibliothek'. *Fuldaer Geschichtsblätter* 30: 8–21.

Preisendanz, Karl. 'Reginbert von den Reichenau. Aus Bibliothek und Skriptorium des Inselklosters'. *Neue heidelberger Jahrbücher* (1953): 1–49.

Price, Laim. 'Glencolumbkille, Co. Donegal, and Its Early Christian Cross-slabs'. *JRSAI* 71 (1941): 71–88.

———. 'Glendalough: St Kevin's Road'. In *Féil-Sgríbhinn Eóin Mhic Néill* (1940).

———. 'Place-name Study as Applied to History'. *JRSAI* 79 (1949): 26–38.

———. *The Place-names of Co. Wicklow*. 7 vols. Dublin: Institute for Advanced Studies, 1945–67.

———. 'St Broghan's Road, Clonsast'. *JRSAI* 75 (1945): 56–9.

———. 'Sculptured Cross-base at Oldcourt, near Bray, Co. Wicklow'. *JRSAI* 89 (1959): 97.

Price, Liam, and Stephens, F. E. '"Bullaun" Stones near Derrylossary Church, Co. Wicklow'. *JRSAI* 78 (1948): 179–81.

Prinz, Friedrich. 'Abriss der kirchlichen und monastischen Entwicklung des Frankenreiches'. In *Karl der Grosse*, vol. 2. Düsseldorf, 1965.

———. *Frühes Mönchtum im Frankenreich. Kultur und Geselleschraft in Gallien, den Rheinlanden und Bayern am Beispiel der monastischen Entwicklung (4. bis 8. Jahrhundert)*. Munich: R. Oldenbourg, 1965.

Proudfoot, V. B. 'Excavations at the Cathedral Hill, Downpatrick, Co. Down'. *UJA* 17 (1954): 97–102.

Q. . . . , J. C. 'The Early Monastic Associations of Spike Island and Cork Harbour'. *JCHAS* 41 (1936): 47–8.

Quadri, R. 'Aimone di Auxerre alla luce dei "Collectanea" di Heiric di Auxerre'. *Italia medioevale e umanistica* 6 (1963): 1–48.

Radford, C. A. Ralegh. 'The Early Christian Monuments of Scotland'. *Antiquity* 16 (1942): 1–18.

———. 'The Early Church in Strathclyde and Galloway'. *Mediaeval Archaeology* 11 (1967): 105 ff.

———. 'Two Reliquaries Connected with South-west Scotland'. *Transactions of the Dumfriesshire and Galloway Natural History and Antiquarian Society* 22 (1955): 115–23.

Raftery, Joseph, ed. *The Celts*. Cork: Mercier Press, 1964.

———, ed. *Christian Art in Ancient Ireland*. Vol. 2. Dublin: Stationery Office, 1941.

———. 'Ex oriente . . .' *JRSAI* 95 (1965): 193–204.

——. 'Excavation of a Reilig at Ballyknockan, Co. Wicklow'. *JRSAI* 73 (1943): 151–2.

——. 'A Travelling-man's Gear of Christian Times'. *RIA Proc.* 60, sect. C: 1–8.

Ranson, Joseph. 'St Maelruan'. *Past* 5: 161–7.

Raoul, Père. 'Saint Colomban a-t-il été supplanté par Saint François en Corse au moyen âge?' *Mélanges Colombaniens* (1951).

Rapp, Urban. 'Das Leben des heiligen Kilian in einem frühottonischen Bilderzyklus'. In *Heiliges Franken* (1952).

——. 'St Kilian und seine Gefährten in der Malerei'. *Heiliges Franken* (1952).

Réau, Louis. *Iconographie des saints.* 3 vols. Paris: Presses Universitaires, 1958–1959.

Rees, Alwyn, and Rees, Brinsley. *Celtic Heritage: Ancient Tradition in Ireland and Wales.* London: Thames and Hudson, 1961.

Reiffenstein, Ingo. 'Das althocheutsche Muspilli und die Vita des heiligen Furseus von Péronne—zwei Visionen des Frühmittelalters'. *Südostdeutsches Archiv* 1 (1958): 88–104.

Reinhard, John R. *The Survival of Geis in Mediaeval Romance.* Halle: Niemeyer, 1933.

Reinhardt, H. *Das St Galler Klosterplan.* St Gallen: Fehr, 1952.

Reuther, Hans. 'Die Darstellung der Frankenapostel in der deutschen Plastik'. In *Heiliges Franken* (1952).

Reynold, Gonzague de. 'Saint Columban: la mission irlandaise et la Suisse'. *Mélanges Colombaniens* (1951).

——. 'St Colomban, St Gall and the Formation of Switzerland'. In *The Miracle of Ireland* (1959).

Rice, David Talbot. *The Beginnings of Christian Art.* London: Hodder and Stoughton, 1957.

——, ed. *The Dark Ages: The Making of European Civilization.* London: Thames and Hudson, 1965.

Riché, Pierre. *Éducation et culture dans l'Occident barbare, VIᵉ–VIIIᵉ Siècle.* Paris: Éd. du Seuil, 1962.

Richmond, I. A. *Roman and Native in North Britain.* Edinburgh: Nelson, 1958.

Robinson, John L. 'St Brigid and Glastonbury'. *JRSAI* 73 (1943): 97–9.

Roche, Aloyius. *A Bedside Book of Irish Saints.* Dublin: Browne and Nolan, 1941.

Roe, Helen M. 'Cadaver Effigial Monuments in Ireland'. *JRSAI* 99 (1969): 1–20.

——. 'The High Crosses of Co. Armagh: A Photographic Survey'. *Seanchas Árdmhacha* 1, no. 2: 107–12.

——. 'The High Crosses of Co. Louth: A Photographic Survey'. *Seanchas Árdmhacha* 1, no. 1: 101–14; no. 2: 107–14.

——. 'The High Crosses of East Tyrone: A Photographic Survey'. *Seanchas Árdmhacha* 2, no. 1 (1956): 79–89.

——. *The High Crosses of Kells.* Meath Archaeological and Historical Society, 1959.

——. *High Crosses of West Ossory.* Kilkenny: Kilkenny Archaeological Society, 1958.

[Roe] 'An Interpretation of Certain Symbolic Sculptures of Early Christian Ireland'. *JRSAI* 75 (1945): 1–23.

——. 'The Irish High Cross: Morphology and Iconography'. *JRSAI* 95 (1965): 213–26.

——. 'The Roscrea Pillar'. In *North Munster Studies,* edited by Etienne Rynne, 1967.

——. 'A Stone Cross at Clogher, Co. Tyrone'. *JRSAI* 90 (1960): 191–206.

——. 'Two Baptismal Fonts in County Laoighis'. *JRSAI* 77 (1947): 81–3.

Ronan, Myles V. 'Cross-in-circle Stones of St Patrick's Cathedral'. *JRSAI* 71 (1941): 1–8.

——. 'Early Foundations of St Patrick, St Brigid and St Coluimchille'. *Journal of the Academy of Christian Art* i, no. 1: 36–8.

——. 'Patrician Churches—Their Form and Material'. *IER* 41 (1932): 356–69.

——. 'St Mary's Abbey, 841–1156–1539'. *An Fiolar* 1, no. 2: 53–8.

——. 'St Patrick's Staff and Christ Church'. *Dublin Historical Record* 5: 73–4.

Rousseau, O. *Monachisme et vie religieuse d'après l'ancienne tradition de l'Église.* Chevetogne: Monastère, 1957.

Rüsch, Ernst Gerhard. 'Das Charakterbild des Gallus im Wandel der Zeit'. In *Historischer Verein des Kantons.* St Gallen, 99 Neujahrsblatt (1959).

Russell, J. C. 'Arthur and the Romano-Celtic Frontier'. *Modern Philology* 48 (1951): 145–53.

Rutledge, D. 'Thoughts on a Columban Nunnery'. *IER* 83 (1955): 108–21.

Ryan, Alice M. *A Map of the Old English Monasteries and Related Ecclesiastical Foundations, A.D. 400–1066.* Ithaca: Cornell University Press, 1939.

Ryan, John. 'The Abbaical Succession at Clonmacnois'. In *Féil-Sgríbhinn Eóin Mhic Néill* (1940).

——. 'The Achievements of Our Irish Monks'. In *Irish Monks in the Golden Age.*

——. 'The Ancestry of St Laurence O'Toole'. *Reportorium Novum* 1: 64–75.

——. 'The Battle of Clontarf. *JRSAI* 68 (1938): 1–50.

——. 'The Breastplate of Saint Patrick: A Hymn'. In *The Miracle of Ireland,* edited by Daniel-Rops (1959).

——. 'Brian Borumha, King of Ireland'. In *North Munster Studies,* edited by Etienne Rynne, 1967.

——. 'The Cáin Adomnáin'. In *Studies in Early Irish Law.* Dublin: Royal Irish Academy, 1936.

——. 'The Church at the End of the Sixth Century'. *IER* 75 (1951): 17–29.

——. 'Clonmacnoise'. *JACAS* 2, part 1 (1939): 26–35.

——. 'The Constitution of the Early Irish Church'. In *Saint Patrick: A Fifteenth Century Memorial Book,* edited by Paul Walsh, 1932.

——. 'The Convention of Druim Ceat'. *JRSAI* 76 (1946): 35–55.

——. 'A Difficult Phrase in the "Confession" of St Patrick'. *IER* 52 (1938): 293–9.

——. 'Dom Louis Gougaud, O.S.B.' *Studies* 30 (1941): 451 ff.

——. 'The Early Irish Church and the Holy See'. *Studies* 49 (1960): 1 ff.

——. 'The Early Irish Church and the See of Peter'. In *Medieval Studies Presented to Aubrey Gwynn*.

——. *Early Irish Missionaries on the Continent and St Vergil of Salzburg*. Dublin: Irish Messenger Office, 1924.

——. 'Ecclesiastical Relations between Ireland and England in the Seventh and Eighth Centuries'. *JCHAS* 43 (1938): 109–12.

——. 'The Falling World'. In *Irish Monks in the Golden Age*.

——, ed. *Féil-Sgríbhinn Eóin Mhic Néill: Essays and Studies presented to Eoin MacNéill on the Occasion of his Seventieth Birthday*. Dublin: Three Candles, 1940.

——. 'The Historical Content of the Caithreim Ceallachain Chaisil'. *Bulletin of the Irish Committee of Historical Sciences*, no. 14.

——. 'Ireland and the Holy See: Carolingian Renaissance to the Gregorian Reform'. *Studies* 50 (1961): 165–74.

——. 'Irish Learning in the Seventh Century'. *JRSAI* 80 (1950): 164–71.

——. 'Irish Missionary Work in Scotland and England. In *The Miracle of Ireland*, edited by Daniel-Rops (1959).

——, ed. *Irish Monks in the Golden Age*. Dublin: Clonmore and Reynolds; London: Burns and Oates, 1963.

——. 'Iroschottische Kirche'. *Lexikon für Theologie und Kirche* 5 (1960).

——. 'The Mass in the Early Irish Church'. *Studies* 50 (1961): 371 ff.

——. 'Origins and Ideals of Irish Monasticism'. *Studies* 19 (1930): 637 ff.

——. 'Palladius and Patricius'. In *An Iodh Morainn*, 1942.

——. 'Pre-Norman Dublin'. *JRSAI* 79 (1949): 64–83.

——. 'The Sacraments of the Early Irish Church'. *Studies* 51 (1962): 508 ff.

——. 'St Columba of Derry and Iona'. *Studies* 52 (1963): 37–51.

——, ed. *St Patrick*. Dublin: Clonmore and Reynolds; London: Burns and Oates, 1964.

——, ed. *Saint Patrick*. (Thomas Davis Lectures.) Dublin: Stationery Office, 1958.

——. 'St Patrick, Apostle of Ireland'. *Studies* 49 (1960): 1–4; 50 (1961): 113–51.

——. 'St Patrick's Purgatory'. *Studies* 21 (1932): 443–60.

——. *Toirdelbach Ó Conchubhair*. Dublin: National University of Ireland, 1966.

——. 'The Two Patricks'. *IER* 60 (1942): 241–52.

Rynne, Etienne. 'The Art of Early Irish Illumination'. *Capuchin Annual* 36: 201–22.

——. 'Excavation of a Church-site at Clondalkin, Co. Dublin'. *JRSAI* 97 (1967): 29–37.

——, ed. *North Munster Studies: Essays in Commemoration of Monsignor Michael Moloney*. Limerick: Thomond Archaeological Society, 1967.

Sage, C. M. 'The Manuscripts of St Aelred'. *Catholic Historical Review* 34 (1949): 440.

Salmon, P. 'Le Lectionnaire de Luxeuil et ses attaches colombaniennes'. *Mélanges Colombaniens* (1951).

——. *Le Lectionnaire de Luxeuil.* 2 vols. Rome: Abbaye Saint-Jérôme, 1944, 1953.

——. *L'Office divin au moyen âge.* Paris: Éditions du Cerf, 1967.

Sambin, M. P. *Ricerche di storia monastica medioevale.* Padua: Antenore, 1959.

Sawyer, P. H. *The Age of the Vikings.* London: Edward Arnold, 1962.

Scantlebury, C. 'A Tale of Two Islands—Dalkey Island and Inis Pádraig'. *Dublin Historical Record* 15: 122–8.

——. 'Tallaght, Co. Dublin: Its Monastery and Its Castle'. *Dublin Historical Record* 16: 65–71.

Schaffran, Emmerich. 'Beziehungen zwischen Österreich und der irisch-angelsächsischen bildenden Kunst im frühen Mittelalter'. In *Österreich und die angelsächsische Welt,* 1961.

Schlick, J. 'Composition et chronologie des "De virtutibus S. Martini" de Grégoire de Tours'. *Studia Patristica* 7 (1966): 278–86.

Schmid, Karl. *Kloster Hirsau und seine Stifter.* Fribourg-en-Brisgau: Eberh. Albert Verlag, 1957.

Schmid, Toni. 'Le culte en Suède de Ste. Brigide l'Irlandaise'. *Anal. Bolland.* 61 (1961): 108–15.

Schmidt, Leopold. 'Patritiusverehrung im Burgenland und in den angrenzenden Gebieten von Niederösterreich und Steiermark'. *Burgenländische Heimathblätter* 24 (1962): 148–60.

Schreiber, Georg. 'Der irische Seeroman des Brandan: ein Ausblick auf die Kolumbus-Reise'. In *Festschrift Franz Dornseiff zum 65. Geburtstag.* Leipzig: VEB Bibliographisches Institut, 1953.

——. *Irland im deutschen und abendländischen Sakralraum.* Köln und Opladen: Westdeutscher Verlag K. und O., c. 1955.

——. *Irland im deutschen und abendländischen Sakralraum: zugleich ein Ausblick auf St Brandan und die zweite Kolumbusreise.* Cologne: Westdeuscher Verlag, 1956.

——. 'St Pirmin in Religionsgeschichte, Ikonographie, Volksfrommigkeit'. *Archiv für mittelrheinische Kirchengeschichte* 5: 42–76.

——. *Die Sakrallandschaft des Abendlandes mit besonderer Berüchtsichtigung von Pyrranäen, Rhein und Donau.* Düsseldorf: Schwann, 1937.

——. *Die Wochentage im Erlebnis der Ostkirche und des christichen Abendlandes.* Köln und Opladen: Westdeutscher Verlag, 1959.

Schulze, H. K. 'Heiligenverehrung und Reliquienkult im Mittelalter'. In *Festschrift für Friedrich von Zahn* 1 (1968): 294–312.

Schwarz, Wilhelm. 'Die Schriften Ermenrichs von Ellwangen'. *Zeitschrift für wurttembergische Landesgeschichte* 12: 181–9.

Selmer, Carl. 'The Beginnings of the St Brendan Legend on the Continent'. *Catholic Historical Review* 29: 169–76.

——. 'The Irish St Brendan Legend in Lower Germany and on the Baltic Coast'. *Traditio* 4 (1946): 408–15.

——. 'The Lisbon "Vita Sancti Brandani Abbatis"': A Hitherto Unknown Navigation Text and Translation from Old French into Latin'. *Traditio* 13 (1957): 313–44.

——. *Navigatio Sancti Brendani Abbatis: From Early Latin MSS*. Notre Dame: University of Notre Dame Press, 1959.

——. 'A Study of the Latin MSS of the Navigatio Sancti Brendani'. *Scriptorium* 3: 177–82.

Selzer, Alois. *St Wendelin: Leben und Verehrungeines alemannisch-fränkischen Volksheiligen*. Mödling-bei-Wein: St Gabriel Verlag, 1962.

Senger, Max. *Irland: die seltsame Insel*. Zürich: Guttenberg, 1956.

Senior, Elizabeth. 'St Manachan's Shrine'. *JACAS* 8: 80–7.

Sexton, Eric H. L. *A Descriptive and Bibliographical List of Irish Figure Sculptures of the Early Christian Period with a Critical Assessment of Their Significance*. Portland (Maine): Southworth-Anthoensen Press, 1946.

Seymour, St John D. *Irish Visions of the Other World*. London: S.P.C.K., 1930.

Shaw, Francis. 'Comments on the "editio princeps" of the Book of Durrow'. *Éigse* 10: 300–4.

——. 'Early Irish Spirituality: "One, Holy, Catholic and Apostolic"'. *Studies* 52 (1963): 180–98.

——. 'The Linguistic Argument for Two Patricks'. *Studies* 32 (1943): 315–22.

——. 'The Myth of the Second Patrick, A.D. 461–1961'. *Studies* 50 (1961): 5–27.

——. 'Post-mortem on the Second Patrick'. *Studies* 51 (1962): 237–67.

——. Review of *St Patrick: His Origins and Career*, by R. P. C. Hanson (1968). *Studies* 57 (1968): 186–91.

——. 'St Patrick, Man of God'. *Seanchas Árdmhacha* 4, no. 2 (1961–62): 1–8.

Shaw, R. C. 'Prolegomena to a Re-appraisal of Early Christianity in Man Relative to the Irish Sea Province'. *Proceedings of the Isle of Man Natural History and Antiquarian Society* 7, no. 1 (1967).

Sheed, F. J., ed. *The Irish Way, 432–1932*. London: Sheed and Ward, 1932.

Sheehy, Maurice P. 'Concerning the Origin of Early Medieval Irish Monasticism'. *Irish Theological Quarterly* 29: 136–44.

——. 'The Relics of the Apostles and Early Martyrs in the Mission of St Patrick'. *IER* 95 (1961): 372–6.

Sheldon, Gilbert. *The Transition from Roman Britain to Christian England*. London: Macmillan, 1932.

Sheldon-Williams, I. P. 'An Epitome of Irish Provenance of Eriugena's *De Divisione Naturae*'. *RIA Proc.* 58: 1–20.

——. 'A List of Works Doubtfully or Wrongly Attributed to Johannes Scotus Eriugena'. *Journal of Ecclesiastical History* 15: 76–98.

Sheldon-Williams, I. P., and Bieler, L., ed. *Johanni Scotti Eriugenae Periphyseon (De Divisione Naturae): Liber Primus*. Dublin: Institute for Advanced Studies, 1968.

Shetelig, Haakon, ed. *Viking Antiquities in Great Britain and Ireland*. Oslo: Aschehoug, 1940–54.

Silvestre, Hubert. 'Le commentaire inédit de Jean Scot Érigène au metre

IX du livre iii du *De Consolatione philosophiae* de Boèce'. *Revue
d'Histoire Ecclèsiastique* 47: 44–122.

[Silvestre] *Les manuscrits de Bede à la Bibliothèque royale de Bruxelles
Léopoldville, 1959.* Studia Universitatis 'Louvanium', Philos., 6.

——. 'La véritable épitaphe de Dungal, reclus de Saint-Denis et auteur
des "Responsa contra Claudium" ?' *Revue Bénédictine* 61: 256–9.

Simms, G. O. *The Book of Kells.* Dolmen Press, 1961.

——. 'Some Notes on the Text of the Book of Kells'. *Hermathena* 74
(1949): 9–11.

Simonetti, M. 'Sulla tradizione manoscritta delle opere originali di
Rufino'. *Sacris Erudiri* 9 (1957): 5–43.

Simpson, W. Douglas. *The Celtic Church in Scotland.* Aberdeen, 1935.

——. 'Eileach an Naoimh Reconsidered'. *Scottish Gaelic Studies* 8:
117–129.

——. *The Historical St Columba.* 3rd ed. Edinburgh: Oliver and Boyd,
1963.

——. 'More Thoughts on the Celtic Church'. *Scottish Gaelic Studies* 10:
1–15.

——. *Saint Ninian and the Origins of the Christian Church in Scotland.*
Edinburgh: Oliver and Boyd, 1940.

——. 'Some Thoughts on the Celtic Church in Scotland'. *Scottish Gaelic
Studies* 5: 169–82.

Sisam, Kenneth. *Studies in the History of Old English Literature.* Oxford:
Clarendon Press, 1953.

Sitwell, Gerard. *St Odo of Cluny.* London: Sheed and Ward, 1958.

Slover, Clark H. 'Early Literary Channels between Britain and Ireland'.
University of Texas Studies in English 6 (1926): 5–12; 7 (1927): 5–11.

Smith, M. 'Monasteries and Their Manuscripts'. *Archaeology* (Cambridge, Mass.) 13 (1960): 172–7.

Snieders, Irène. *L'influence d'hagiographie irlandaise sur les vitae des saints
irlandais de Belgique.* Louvain, 1928.

Southern, R. W. *The Life of St Anselm, Archbishop of Canterbury.* Edinburgh: Nelson, 1962.

——. 'St Anselm and Gilbert Crispin, Abbot of Westminster'. *Mediaeval
and Renaissance Studies* 3 (1954): 78–115.

——. *Saint Anselm and his Biographer: A Study of Monastic Life and
Thought, 1059–c.1130.* Cambridge: Cambridge University Press,
1963.

Sprandél, R. *Das Kloster St Gallen in der Verfassung des karolingischen
Reiches.* Freiburg im Breisgau: E. Albert, 1958.

Staerkle, Paul. 'Von den Sankt Gallus-Patrozinien'. In *Sankt Gallus
Gedenkbuch* (1952).

Stauber, J. 'Influences irlandaises dans la christianisation des Slaves
polabes et des Polonais'. *Études Slaves et Est-Européennes* 3 (1958–59):
1–23.

Stegmüller, Fr. 'Das Trinitätssymbolum des hl. Martin von Tours'. In
Festschrift für Bischof Dr. Albert Stohr (Mainz, 1960).

Steinacker, Harold. 'Die römische Kirche und die griechischen Sprach-
kenntnisse des Frümittelalters'. *Mitteilungen des Instituts für öster-
reichische Geschictsforschung* 72: 28–66.

Stéphan, J. *St Brannoc's Chapel and Well, Braunton in Devon.* Bristol, 1958.

Stephens, F. E. 'An Interlinear Design in the Book of Kells'. *JRSAI* 76 (1946): 213–4.

Stevenson, R. B. K. 'The Chronology and Relationships of Some Irish and Scottish Crosses'. *JRSAI* 86 (1956): 84–96.

——. 'The Shannon Shrine'. *JRSAI* 77 (1947): 156–7.

Stokes, Whitley, ed. *The Tripartite Life of St Patrick.* 1887. Reprint Kraus Reprints Ltd., 1965.

Strachan, L. R. M. 'Patrick's Purgatory'. *Notes and Queries* 182: 111.

Studer, B. 'Zu einer Teufelserscheinung in der "Vita Martini" des Sulpicius Severus'. In *Oikoumene* (Catania, 1964).

Sulpice, Sévère. *Vie de Saint Martin. Introduction, texte et traduction par Jacques Fontaine.* Paris: Éditions du Cerf, 1967–69.

Swartwout, R. E. *The Monastic Craftsman in Britain and Europe North of the Alps during the Middle Ages.* Cambridge: Heffer, 1932.

Szövérffy, Josef. 'The *Altus prosator* and the Discovery of America'. *IER* 100: 115–8.

——. 'Der irische "Liber hymnorum" und die Synaxarien'. *Litteraturwissenschaft Jahrbuch* 3 (1962): 335–44.

——. *Irisches Erzählgut im Abendland. Studien zur vergleichenden Volkskunde und Mittelalterforschung.* Berlin: Erich Schmidt, 1957.

——. 'Manus O'Donnell and Irish Folk Tradition'. *Éigse* 8: 108–32.

——. 'Some Notes on Legend Migration in Irish and Continental Tradition'. *Iris Hibernia* 3, no. 4 (1956): 46–63.

Tallaght, Martyrology of. See Best, R. I.

Tallon, Maura. 'An Irish Medieval Manuscript in Hereford Cathedral Chained Library'. In *Irish Book* 3: 26–9.

Taylor, A. B. 'The name "St Kilda"'. *Scottish Studies* 13: 145.

Taylor, Henry Osborn. *The Classical Heritage of the Middle Ages.* 4th ed. New York: Ungar; London: Constable, 1957.

Tempest, H. G. 'The Monastery of Inismocht'. *JCLAS* 10: 342–5.

Théologie de la monastique. Études sur la tradition patristique. Paris: Aubier, 1961 (Théologie, 49).

Thomas, A. C. 'The Evidence from North Britain'. In *Christianity in Britain 300–700* (1968).

Thomas, C. 'Ardwall Isle: The Excavations of an Early Christian Site of Irish Type'. *Transactions of the Dumfriesshire and Galloway Natural History and Antiquarian Society,* 3rd ser., 43 (1966).

——. 'An Early Christian Cemetery and Chapel on Ardwall Isle, Kircudbright'. *Mediaeval Archaeology* 11 (1967).

Thompson, A. Hamilton. *Bede: His Life, Times and Writings.* Oxford: Clarendon Press, 1935.

Thompson, E. A. 'The Conversion of the Visigoths to Catholicism'. *Nottingham Mediaeval Studies* 4 (1960): 4–35.

——. 'A Note on St Patrick in Gaul'. *Hermathena* 79 (1952): 22–9.

——. 'The Origin of Christianity in Scotland'. *Scottish Historical Review* 37 (1958): 17–22.

Thurneysen, R., Ryan, John, et al. *Studies in Early Irish Law.* Dublin: Royal Irish Academy, 1936.

Thurston, H. *Familiar Prayers, Their Origin and History, Selected and Arranged by P. Grosjean, S. J.* London: Burns and Oates, 1953.

Thurston, H., and Attwater, D., eds. *Butler's Lives of the Saints.* 4 vols. Rev. ed. London: Burns and Oates, 1956.

Tierney, James J. 'The Celtic Ethnography of Posidonius'. *RIA Proc.* 60, sect. C: 189–275.

——. 'The Celts and Classical Authors'. In *The Celts.*

——, ed. *Dicuili Liber de Mensura Orbis Terrae.* Dublin: Institute for Advanced Studies, 1967.

Tierney, Michael. 'The European Background of St Patrick's Mission'. *Studies* 21 (1932): 199–212.

Tolhurst, J. B. L. 'St Kyneburga of Gloucester' *Pax* (Prinknash) (Summer 1943): 85–7.

Tolstoy, Nikolai. 'The Origins of Irish Christianity'. *Bulletin of the Irish Committee of Historical Sciences* 93: 1–2.

——. 'Who was Coroticus?' *IER* 97: 137–47.

Tommasini, Anselmo M. *Irish Saints in Italy.* London: Sands, 1937.

Towill, E. S. 'Saint Mochaoi and Nendrum'. *UJA*, ser. 3, 27 (1964): 103–20.

Toynbee, Jocelyn M. C. 'Pagan Motifs and Practices in Christian Art and Ritual in Roman Britain'. In *Christianity in Britain, 300–700* (1968).

Trachsel, Emile. *De Colomban aux Gueux: épisodes.* Bruxelles: Imprimerie des Sciences, 1949.

Travis, James. *Miscellanea Musica Celtica.* New York: Institute of Mediaeval Music, 1968.

Trepos, Pierre. 'Les Saints bretons dan la toponymie'. *Annales de Bretagne* 61 (1954): 372–406.

Tüchle, Hermann. 'Probleme der Pirminforschung'. *Freiburger Diözesanarchiv* 72 (1952): 21–32.

Turner, D. H. 'The "Reichenau" Sacramentaries at Zürich and Oxford'. *Revue Bénédictine* 75 (1965): 240–76.

Ua Brádaigh, Tomás. 'Kilpatrick'. *Ríocht na Midhe* 2, no. 1 (1959): 37–44.

Ueding, Leo. *Geschichte der Klostergründungen der frühen Merowingerzeit.* Berlin: E. Ebering, 1935.

Uí Máine, The Book of. See Macalister, R. A. S.

Ullmann, W. 'On the Use of the Term "Romani" in the Sources of the Earlier Middle Ages'. *Studia Patristica* 2 (1957): 155–63.

Ulrich, Bischof. *Bischof Ulrich und der Augsburger Religionsfriede. Neue Quellenforschungen zum Augsburger Gedenkjahr.* Augsburg: Seitz, 1955.

Unterkircher, Franz, ed. *European Illuminated Manuscripts in the Austrian National Library.* London: Thames and Hudson, 1967.

Vaillat, Claudius. *Le culte des Sources dans la Gaule antique.* Paris: Leroux, 1932.

Vanderhoven, Hubert, Masai, François, and Corbett, P. B. *Aux Sources du monachisme bénédictin. Vol. 1: La règle du maître.* Bruxelles, 1953.

Van Der Meer, F., and Mohrmann, C. *Atlas of the Early Christian World*, translated and edited by Mary F. Hedlund and H. H. Rowley. London: Nelson, 1958.

Van Der Zenden, C. M. 'Autour d'un manuscrit latin du Purgatoire de S. Patrice de la Bibliothèque de l'Université d'Utrecht'. *Neophilologus* 10 (1925): 243–9.

——. 'Un chapitre intéressant de la Topographia Hibernica et le Tractatus de Purgatorio Sancti Patricii'. *Neophilologus* 12 (1927): 1–6.

——. *Étude sur le Purgatoire de Saint Patrice accompagnée du texte latin d'Utrecht et du texte Anglo-normand de Cambridge*. Amsterdam: H. J. Paris, 1928.

Van Dijk, S. J. P. 'The Origin of the Latin Feast of the Conception of the Blessed Virgin Mary'. *Dublin Review* (1954): 251–67; 428–42.

Vannereau, Gabriel S. *Pelerin d'Auxerre, évêque et martyr*. Cosne-sur-Loire: Éd. du Val de Loire, 1958.

Varagnac, André. 'Pérennité du message de Saint Colomban'. *Mélanges Colombaniens* (1951).

Vendryes, Joseph. 'Druidisme et christianisme dans l'Irlande du moyen âge'. *Comptes-rendus de l'Academie des Inscriptions et Belles-Lettres* (1946): 310–29.

——. 'Poème de saint Patrice sur une dent tombée'. *Études Celtiques* 3 (1938): 95–104.

——, et al. *Les Religions des Celtes, des Germains et des anciens Slaves*. Paris: Presses Universitaires de France, 1948.

'The Veneration of St Patrick in Italy and Spain'. *Seanchas Árdmhacha* 4, no. 2 (1961–62): 101–103.

Verbist, G. H. *Saint Willibrord, Apôtre des Pays-Bas et fondateur d'Echternach*. Louvain: Bibliothèque de l'Université Paris: Desclée de Brouwer, 1939.

Verne, A. *Fugitive Saint* [St Dympna]. Franworth (Bolton): Catholic Printing Co., 1961.

Vinay, G. 'Interpretazione di S. Colombano'. *Bollettino storicobibliografico subalpino* 46 (1948): 5–30.

Vogel, Cyrille. *La discipline penitentielle en Gaule, des origines à la fin du VIIe siècle*. Paris: Letouzey et Ané, 1952.

——. *Introduction aux sources de l'histoire du culte chrétien au moyen âge*. Spoleto: Centro Italiano di Studi Sull' Alto Mediaevo, 1966.

——. *Le pécheur et la pénitence dans l'Église ancienne*. Paris: Éditions du Cerf, 1966.

——. 'Le pèlerinage pénitentiel'. *Revue des sciences religieuses* 38 (1964): 113–53.

Volbach, W. F. *Early Christian Art: The Late Roman and Byzantine Empires from the Third to the Seventh Centuries*. London: Thames and Hudson, 1961.

Wade-Evans, Arthur W. 'Bonedd y Saint'. *Revue Celtique* 50 (1933).

——. *Nennius' 'History of the Britons' together with the 'Annals of the Britons' . . . etc.* London: S.P.C.K., 1938.

——. *Welsh Christian Origins*. Oxford: Alden Press, 1934.

Wainwright, M. F. T., ed. *The Problem of the Picts*. Edinburgh: Nelson, 1955.

Walker, G. S. M. 'On the Use of Greek Words in the Writings of St Columbanus of Luxeuil'. *Archivum Latinitatis Medii Aevi* 21.

——, ed. *Sancti Colombani Opera*. Dublin: Institute for Advanced Studies, 1957.

Wall, J. Charles. *The First Christians of Britain*. London: Talbot, 1929.

Wall, Thomas. 'An 18th-century Dublin Life of S. Patrick'. *Reportorium Novum* 3: 121–36.

Wallace-Hadrill, J. M. *Bede's Europe*. Jarrow-on-Tyne: St Paul's Rectory, 1962.

——. *The Fourth Book of the Chronicle of Fredegar*. Edinburgh: Nelson, 1960.

——. *The Long-haired Kings and Other Studies in Frankish History*. London: Methuen, 1962.

——. 'St Aidan in England'. In *Irish Monks in the Golden Age* (1963).

Walpole, R. N. 'The "Pèlerinage de Charlemagne"'. *Romance Philology* 8 (1955): 173–86.

Walsh, James J. *High Points of Mediaeval Culture*. Milwaukee: Bruce, 1937.

Walsh, Paul. 'Ancient Westmeath'. *Ríocht na Midhe* 1, no. 1 (1955): 20–35.

——. 'The Annals Attributed to Tigernach'. *IHS* 2, no. 6 (1940): 154–9.

——. *The Book of Fenagh*. Dublin: Browne and Nolan, 1940.

——. 'The Book of Lecan'. *IER* ser. 5, 51 (1938): 66–81.

——. 'Christian Kings of Connacht'. *JGAHS* 17: 124–43.

——. 'Dating of the Annals of Inisfallen'. *Catholic Bulletin* 29: 677–82.

——. 'The Dating of the Irish Annals'. *Bulletin of the Irish Committee of Historical Sciences* 11 (1941).

——. *The Four Masters and Their Work*. Dublin: Three Candles, 1943.

——. *Irish Men of Learning*. Dublin: Three Candles, 1947.

——. 'More Fragments of Meath History: Short Annals of Leinster'. *IBL* 24: 56–60.

——. 'Recent Studies on the Patrician Documents'. *IER* 39 (1932): 232–42.

——, ed. *Saint Patrick, A.D. 432–1932. A Fifteenth Centenary Memorial Book*. Dublin: Catholic Truth Society of Ireland, 1932.

——. 'Shrine of Colman of Lynn'. *IBL* 27: 200–1.

Walsh, T. J., and O Sullivan, Denis. 'Saint Malachy, the Gill Abbey of Cork, and the Rule of Arrouaise'. *JCHAS* 54 (1949): 41–60.

Walshaw, R. S. *Migrations to and from the British Isles: Problems and Policies*. London: Cope, 1941.

Ware, James. *De scriptoribus Hiberniae*. Libri duo. 1639. Reprint Farnborough (Hants): Gregg Press, 1966.

Warnke, Karl. *Das Buch vom Espurgatoire S. Patrice der Marie de France und seine Quelle*. Halle: Niemeyer, 1938.

Warren, W. L. 'The Interpretation of Twelfth-century Irish History'. *Historical Studies* 7: 1–19.

Warterer, J. W. 'Irish Book-satchels or Budgets'. *Mediaeval Archaeology* 12 (1968): 70–82.

Waterhouse, G. 'Another Early German Account of St Patrick's Purgatory'. *Hermathena* 48 (1933): 114–16.

Waterman, D. M. 'The Early Christian Churches and Cemetery at Derry, Co. Down'. *UJA* 30 (1967): 53–75.

——. 'An Early Christian Mortuary House at Saul, Co. Down'. *UJA* 23 (1960): 82–8.

——. 'An Early Medieval Horn from the River Erne'. *UJA* 32: 101–4.

Waters, E. G. R. *The Anglo-Norman Voyage of St Brendan, by Benedeit: A Poem of the Early Twelfth Century*. Oxford: Clarendon Press, 1928.

——. *An Old Italian Version of the Navigatio Sancti Brendani*. Oxford: Oxford University Press, 1931.

Waters, Ormonde D. 'Some Notes on Rath-Colpa'. *Ríocht na Midhe* 3: 260–2.

Watkin, Aelred. *The Great Chartulary of Glastonbury*. 2 vols. Frome: Butler and Tanner, 1947.

Watson, W. J. 'Early Irish Influences in Scotland'. *Transactions of the Gaelic Society of Inverness* 35: 178–202.

——. 'Saint Cadoc'. *Scottish Gaelic Studies* 2: 1–12.

Wattenbach, Wilhelm, and Levison, Wilhelm. *Deutschlands Geschichts-quellen im Mittelalter: Vorzeit und Karolinger. Fasc. 1: Die Vorzeit von den Anfängen bis zur Herrschaft der Karolinger*. Weimar: Böhlau, 1952.

Webster, Charles A. 'The Diocese of Ross and Its Ancient Churches'. *RIA Proc.* 40, sect. C: 255–95.

Weigel, H. 'Das Patrozinium des hl. Martin'. *Blätter für deutsche Landes-geschichte* 100 (1964): 82–106.

Weijenborg, R. 'Deux sources grecques de la "Confession de Patrice"'. *Revue d'Histoire Ecclésiastique* 62: 361–78.

Weisgerber, Leo. 'Eine Irenwelle an Maas, Mosel und Rhein in ottoni-scher Zeit?' In *Aus Geschichte und Landeskunde* (1960).

——. 'Die Spuren der irischen Mission in der Entwicklung der deut-schen Sprache'. *Rheinische Vierteljahrsblätter* 21 (1949–50): 117–32.

Wendehorst, A. *Das Bistum Würzburg, 1: Die Bischofsreihe bis 1254*. Berlin: W. de Gruyter, 1962.

——. *Killian*. Würzburg, 1969.

Went, Arthur E. J. 'Irish Monastic Fisheries'. *JCHAS* 60 (1955): 47–56.

Werckmeister, Otto Karl. 'Die Bedeutung der "Chi"—Initialseite im Book of Kells'. In *Das erste Jahrtausend: Kultur und Kunst im werdenden Abendland an Rhein und Ruhr* (1964).

——. *Irische-northumbrische Buchmalerei des 8. Jahrhunderts und monas-tische Spiritualität*. Berlin: de Gruyter, 1967.

——. 'Three Problems of Tradition in Pre-Carolingian Figure-style: From Visigothic to Insular Illumination'. *RIA Proc.* 63, sect. C: 167–89.

Wheeler, G. H. 'St Patrick's Birthplace'. *English Historical Review* 50 (1935): 109–113.

Wheeler, Henry. 'Cross Slabs at Inishkeel, Co. Donegal'. *JRSAI* 64 (1934): 262.

Wheeler, Mortimer. *Rome beyond the Imperial Frontiers*. London: Bell, 1954.

White, Newport B. The 'Dignitas Decani' of St Patrick's Cathedral, Dublin. Dublin: Stationery Office, 1957.

——, ed. Extents of Irish Monastic Possessions, 1540–1541. Dublin: Stationery Office, 1943.

——. Irish Monastic and Episcopal Deeds, A.D. 1200–1600. Dublin: Stationery Office, 1936.

White, Newport J. D. The Date of St Patrick: The Internal Evidence of His Latin Writings. Dublin, 1932.

Whitelock, D. 'The Old English Bede'. Proceedings of the British Academy 48 (1962): 57–90.

Widding, O. Alkuin i norsk-islandsk overlevering. Copenhagen: E. Munksgaard, 1960.

Widding, O., and Bekker-Nielsen, H. 'A Debate of the Body and the Soul in Old Norse Literature'. Mediaeval Studies 21 (1959): 272–89.

——. 'An Old Norse Translation of the "Transitus Mariae"'. Mediaeval Studies 23 (1961): 324–33.

Widding, O., Bekker-Nielsen, H., and Shook, L. K. 'The Lives of the Saints in Old Norse Prose'. Mediaeval Studies 25 (1963): 294–337.

Willard, R. 'The Testament of Mary: The Irish Account of the Death of the Virgin'. Recherches de Théologie ancienne et médiévale 9 (1937): 341–64.

Williams, Ifor. Lectures on Early Welsh Poetry. Dublin: Institute for Advanced Studies, 1944.

Williams, J. E. Caerwyn. 'Bucheddau'r Saint'. Bulletin of the Board of Celtic Studies 11 (1944): 149–57.

Williams, Watkin. Monastic Studies. Manchester: Manchester University Press, 1938.

Wilmart, A. Auteurs spirituels et textes dévots du Moyen âge latin. Paris: Blond et Gay, 1932.

Wilson, James. 'The Reliability of Jonas'. Mélanges Colombaniens (1951).

Wiltshire, E., and Wiltshire, R. J. 'A Cross and Cillín in Upper Lockstown, Co. Wicklow'. JRSAI 95 (1965): 249.

Winmill, Joyce M. 'Iona and Lindisfarne'. IER 80 (1953): 106.

Wolpers, Theodor. Die englische Heiligenlegende des Mittelalters. Tubingue: Niemeyer, 1964.

Wolzfeld, Alphonse, ed. Pfarrei Kaundorf: Saint Pirmin 12e Centenaire. Festschrift zum zwölfhundertjährigen Jubiläum des Ardennenheiligen St Pirmin, 753–1953. Luxemburg: Paulusdruckerei, 1953.

Wormald, Francis. The Miniatures in the Gospels of St Augustine. Cambridge: Cambridge University Press, 1954.

——. 'The Seal of St Nectan'. Journal of the Warburg Institute 2 (1938): 70–71.

Wotke, F., ed. Das Bekenntius des heiligen Patrick und sein Brief an Gefolgsleute des Coreticus. Freiburg: Herder, 1940.

——. 'Patricius, Pauly-Wissowa-Kroll'. Realenzyklopädie 18, 2.2 (1949): 2233–41.

Wulff, Winifred. 'Contra incantationes' [scribal note]. Ériu 12: 250–53.

Zagiba, Franz. 'Die irisch-schottische Mission'. Kirchenmusikalisches Jahrbuch 41 (1957): 1–3.

——. 'Die irische Slavenmission und ihre Forsetzung durch Kyrill und Method'. *Jahrbuch für Geschichte Osteuropas* 9 (1961): 1–56.

Zoepfl, Friedrich. *Das Bistum Augsburg und seine Bischöfe im Mittelalter.* Munich: Schnell and Steiner, 1955.

Zumkeller, Adolar. *Urkunden und Regesten zur Geschichte der Augustin klöster Würzburg und Münnerstadt.* 2 vols. Würzburg: F. Schöningh, 1966–67.

INDEX OF PLACES

INDEX OF PERSONS

INDEX OF SUBJECT-MATTER

A1

DATE DUE

JAN 4 79			
JUN 2 73			
DEC 1 9 '89			
NOV 1 2 '90			
GAYLORD			PRINTED IN U.S.A.